W9-CRT-743

Volume V.

The Sermons of John Donne

BLUNHAM CHURCH, IN BEDFORDSHIRE

THE
SERMONS
OF
JOHN DONNE

Edited,
with Introductions
and Critical Apparatus, by
GEORGE R. POTTER
and
EVELYN M. SIMPSON

In Ten Volumes

V.

UNIVERSITY OF CALIFORNIA PRESS
BERKELEY AND LOS ANGELES
1959

Gen'l

UNIVERSITY OF CALIFORNIA PRESS
BERKELEY AND LOS ANGELES, CALIFORNIA

❖

CAMBRIDGE UNIVERSITY PRESS
LONDON, ENGLAND

95308

DEC 2 9 1959

BX
5133
D68
V.5

Copyright, 1959, by
THE REGENTS OF THE UNIVERSITY OF CALIFORNIA
PRINTED IN THE UNITED STATES OF AMERICA
BY THE UNIVERSITY OF CALIFORNIA PRINTING DEPARTMENT
DESIGNED BY WARD RITCHIE

Table of Contents

Volume V

Contents

List of Illustrations

Volume V

The illustrations have been reproduced by permission of the National Buildings Record, London, from photographs taken by them. For their courtesy and services we here record our thanks.

THE EDITORS

Introduction

THE PROBLEM of the undated sermons is perhaps the most formidable with which an editor has to deal. Out of the 160 sermons by Donne which are extant, no fewer than 72 are undated in the Folios and Quartos. Since our edition is planned on a chronological basis, it would have been a counsel of despair to print all these in a solid block in our last four volumes. It was obviously necessary to find an approximate date for as many of these sermons as possible.[1]

In the first place we were able to assign dates to six sermons through evidence afforded by the manuscripts, which have been collated by us for the first time. Thus the sermons on *John* 5.22 and *John* 8.15 are dated "January 30, 1619" [1619/20] in three manuscripts, *D, E,* and *M,* and they are described as having been preached "one in the fore-noone, the other in the afternoone."[2] The dating of these two enabled us to date approximately two others which clearly belonged to the same series.[3] Though we could not give their exact date, they must have been preached within two or three months after January 30, 1619/20. Again, we have been able to date the marriage sermon on *Hosea* 2.19 as having been preached on May 30, 1621, through evidence supplied by *E,* which describes it as preached at the marriage of "M^ris Washington," and by *M,* which states that it was preached

---

[1] A start had been made on this problem by the present editor as long ago as 1913 in an article, "A Chronological Arrangement of Donne's Sermons," by E. M. Simpson (née Spearing), *Modern Language Review,* VIII, 468–483. This was corrected and reprinted in *A Study of the Prose Works of John Donne,* 1924, pp. 340–355, and was revised and enlarged in the second edition, 1948, pp. 339–356. George Potter worked on the dating of the Lincoln's Inn sermons in his editing of *A Sermon Preached at Lincoln's Inn,* 1946, pp. 3–7, and was able to assign the series of sermons on Psalm 38 to the year 1618 (see Vol. II of our edition, pp. 13–14).

[2] Vol. II of our edition, pp. 39–40, 440–441.

[3] These are the sermons on *Job* 19.26 and 1 *Cor.* 15.50, which we have printed as Nos. 3 and 4 in Vol. III. For a discussion of their relation to the sermons on *John* 5.22 and 8.15 see our Introduction, Vol. III, pp. 6–7.

at St. Clement Danes. The marriage register of this church gave the date, and this was confirmed by a contemporary reference in Chamberlain's *Letters*. Similarly the sermon on *Genesis* 2.18, described in the Folio merely as "Preached at a Mariage," was described in *M* as "Preached at the Mariage of Sir Francis Nethersole," and Chamberlain's *Letters* (II, 291) showed that Nethersole's marriage to Lucy Goodyer took place in February, 1619/20.[4] Thus the manuscripts have enabled us to place six sermons, undated in the Folio, in their places in Volumes II and III.

Another means of dating undated sermons is by their position with regard to a number of dated sermons. One of the clearest cases of this kind is that of the Fifth Prebend Sermon, which is undated, though the four preceding Prebend Sermons are all dated. By observing that the Second and Third were preached respectively on January 29 and November 5, 1626, and that the Fourth was preached on January 28, 1627, we deduce that the Fifth must have been preached sometime in the autumn of that year, probably in November, and we have placed it in that position in Volume VIII. Having thus decided its place by external evidence, we find that the manner and tone of the sermon make it fit perfectly into the pattern of the surrounding sermons. Similarly, the series of Christmas sermons which Donne preached as Dean runs in unbroken sequence at the beginning of *LXXX Sermons* (except for the year 1623, when Donne was suffering from his severe illness) from 1622 to 1628. The last sermon of this series is undated, and we conclude that it must belong to Christmas, 1629.[5] Again, we have assigned the Easter sermon on 1 *Thessalonians* 4.17 to the year 1622 because that is the only year of Donne's career as Dean which lacks an Easter sermon, and he was bound as Dean to preach on Easter Day unless prevented by illness.

Another method which has helped us to give an approximate though not a definite date is that of considering where the sermon was preached. Since Donne's tenure of office as Reader at Lincoln's

[4] For a discussion of the Nethersole sermon see Vol. II, pp. 42–43, and for the Washington sermon, Vol. III, pp. 19–21.

[5] Less obvious examples of this method may be found in Vol. VII, where we have assigned three undated sermons (Nos. 8, 13, and 14) to the years 1626–1627. For our reasons see Vol. VII, p. 16 for No. 8, pp. 28–32 for No. 13, and p. 32 for No. 14.

Inn lasted from October, 1616, to February 11, 1621/2, all sermons described merely as "Preached at Lincoln's Inn" must be placed between those two dates.[6] Again, as Donne was not appointed as Vicar of St. Dunstan's till March, 1624, the three undated sermons described as "Preached at St. Dunstan's" must be later than April 11, 1624, when he preached his first sermon as Vicar. Again the undated sermons described as "Preached at St. Paul's" must be later than his election as Dean in November, 1621. Therefore we have assigned all undated Lincoln's Inn sermons to Volumes II and III, and have relegated the undated St. Dunstan's sermons to Volume X.

Occasionally a sermon may be dated by a political reference, if this is sufficiently definite. Such a reference may be found in the second sermon on *Matthew* 18.7, which with its accompanying sermon must have been preached in late November, 1620.[7] And we have assigned the Candlemas sermon on *Romans* 12.20 to February 1621/2 because of its political references.[8] Generally, however, such references are too vague to do more than give us an indication that the sermon was preached within a certain period, perhaps of two or three years' duration.

We decided when planning our edition that we would divide the remaining undated sermons into two blocks: one in Volume V containing those sermons which seemed to us to have been preached before the middle of 1623,[9] and the second in Volume X containing those which we believed to have been preached after that date, or which we had no good reason to place earlier.

We feel that the time spent on this task has been worth while, because there is generally a continuity of thought between the sermons

---

[6] The two sermons which Donne preached at Lincoln's Inn as an honoured guest after he had given up his office there are carefully dated in their titles. See Vol. IV, Nos. 4 and 15.

[7] Vol. III, pp. 10–13.

[8] Vol. III, pp. 41–42.

[9] This rather arbitrary date was fixed because our original intention was that George Potter should edit the first eighty sermons, and Evelyn Simpson the second eighty, and the latter editor should start work on Vol. VI while the former was working on Vol. I (second half). Later events proved that it would have been better to have had a different line of demarcation.

which Donne preached in one particular period. This continuity was regularly interrupted each summer by the recess of two or three months which Donne spent at his country parishes, and in the autumn and winter sermons we often find a new trend of thought appearing. Or again, a longer interruption may have been provided by such an occurrence as his serious illness in the winter of 1623 or by the plague epidemic in London from June to December, 1625. A still longer interruption was provided in 1619 from April to the end of the year by his absence on the Continent with Doncaster's embassy. When he began preaching again in January, 1620, there is a marked difference in the tone and substance of his sermons. This is apparent in the newly dated sermons as well as in those which were already dated in the Folios. Often the division of our edition into volumes of approximately equal size[10] may cut across this division of periods in Donne's preaching career. Still, it is worth while to follow the development of these trends of thought, and unless the majority of the sermons are arranged in a correct sequence it would be impossible to do this. In the present volume we shall try to indicate roughly where, in our opinion, the undated sermons belong. We acknowledge, however, by placing them in this volume, that we cannot date them exactly, and that a wide field remains open for conjecture. The best hope of dating the several sermons which were preached at christenings and churchings lies in the possible discovery, in letters or documents of this period, of references to Donne's having preached on such and such an occasion.

The undated sermons fall naturally into several small groups. The first of these consists of three Whitsunday sermons. Unlike the Christmas and Easter sermons, which for the most part are arranged in the Folio according to their dates, the Whitsunday sermons are placed in an odd sequence—1627, 1628, one undated, 1629, six undated. Donne as Dean was required to preach at St. Paul's on Whitsunday, so we may assign six of these to the remaining years at St.

---

[10] For example, the first period of Donne's time at Lincoln's Inn ends with his departure abroad in April, 1619. This occurred after No. 11 in Vol. II, and there follow three sermons (Nos. 12–14) preached during the Continental tour. The second period at Lincoln's Inn begins with No. 15 of Vol. II, and this and its succeeding sermons are closely linked with the first few sermons of Vol. III.

Paul's.[11] This leaves us one sermon, which was probably preached earlier, while Donne was still Reader at Lincoln's Inn. George Potter, who had given special attention to the Lincoln's Inn sermons, felt sure that the Whitsunday sermon on *Acts* 10.44 (No. 1 in the present volume) must be assigned to this period, on account of its number of legal references and its general affinity with the Lincoln's Inn sermons. He was unable, however, to affix any specific date to it. It is unlikely to be earlier than 1618, and in 1619 Donne was with Doncaster's embassy on the Continent. It may therefore have been preached in 1618, 1620, or 1621. We should note that the vacation between the Easter and Trinity terms was very short, and that Donne was required to preach at Lincoln's Inn once (not twice a Sunday, as in full term) on Whitsunday, because it was the Sunday after the end of the Easter term.

We find some ground for assigning 1622 as a possible date for the sermon on *Romans* 8.16 in what seems to be a reference to the course of the Thirty Years' War. In 1622 Whitsunday fell on June 9. On May 11[12] news had reached London of the defeat of the Palatinate army by Tilly on May 6.

In the present sermon Donne tells his hearers that they can be "Heires of the joy, and heires of the glory of heaven; where if thou look down, and see Kings fighting for Crownes, thou canst look off as easily, as from boyes at stool-ball for points here; And from Kings triumphing after victories, as easily, as a Philosopher from a Pageant of children here."[13] This seems to be a rather rueful attempt, nearly a month after the first shock of the news, to console himself and his hearers for what must have been a very bitter pill. We know from Donne's letters to Goodyer of October 5, 1621, of September, 1622,

---

[11] That is, if we assume that Donne was well enough to preach on Whitsunday, 1630. We have no definite evidence that he was unwell; the question is discussed fully in Vol. IX, p. 31.

[12] In his letter to Carleton of that date Chamberlain wrote: "I began this letter in better hope then I am like to end, for since dinner here is a constant report of a great overthrow geven to Count Mansfeld by Don Gonsales de Cordova and Tilli, wherin they are saide to have slaine 5000 foot, 2000 horse, besides great numbers taken, and all the ordinance lost, and all the spoyle and bootie ..." (*Letters,* ed. McClure, II, 437).

[13] P. 75.

and from an undated letter which seems to belong to July, 1623,[14] how eagerly he followed the progress of the war, and with what regret he heard of the loss of town after town by the Palatinate armies. If there had been a victory for the Protestant side, Donne would not have recommended his hearers to take the news philosophically.

The third Whitsunday sermon in this group can be conjecturally assigned to 1623 because of its comparative freedom from controversial matter. Prince Charles and Buckingham were in Spain during the spring and summer of that year, and the negotiations for Charles's marriage to the Infanta were in full swing. Donne was willing enough to obey the King's instructions to abandon for the time the preaching of violent attacks on the Church of Rome. The sermon is a reasonably good one, and it opens with one of those elaborate nautical similes in which Donne delighted. This one reminds us that he had been a gentleman adventurer in the two naval expeditions of 1596 and 1597, and that he had seen for himself much of what he describes in his first paragraph:

As when a Merchant hath a faire and large, a deep and open Sea, into that Harbour to which hee is bound with his Merchandize, it were an impertinent thing for him, to sound, and search for lands, and rocks, and clifts, which threaten irreparable shipwrack; so we being bound to the heavenly City, the new Jerusalem, by the spacious and bottomelesse Sea, the blood of Christ Jesus, having that large Sea opened unto us, in the beginning of this Text, ... It may seeme an impertinent diversion, to turne into that little Creek, nay upon that desperate, and irrecoverable rock, ... But there must be Discoverers, as well as Merchants; for the security of Merchants, who by storme and tempest, or other accidents, may be cast upon those sands, and rocks, if they be not knowne, they must be knowne. So though we saile on, with a merry gale and full sailes, with the breath of the holy Ghost in the first Part, ... yet we shall not leave out the discovery of that fearfull and ruinating rock too, ...[15]

If we are right in assigning this sermon to 1623, it must have been preached only ten days later than the last sermon in Volume IV, the one preached at Lincoln's Inn at the dedication of the new chapel on Ascension Day, 1623. We think that it will be found to have several links with that sermon, and with others preached in the early part of that year.

[14] *Letters* (1651), pp. 82–84, 165–167, 211–212, 229–232.
[15] P. 77.

This sort of evidence, however, is not conclusive, so we have not attempted to fit these three sermons into the volumes of dated sermons, but have printed them here in the order in which they occur in *LXXX Sermons.*

It may seem strange that out of seven christening and churching sermons only two should have names affixed to them. The absence of names was probably due to John Donne junior, who was responsible for the publication in 1649 of *Fifty Sermons* in which all these sermons, together with the wedding sermons, first appeared. In 1649 and the years preceding and following, Donne's son was actively engaged in trying to curry favour with the Parliamentarians who were now the dominant party. The year 1649 saw the execution of Charles I, and all the nobles who had actively supported him were out of favour; some fled into exile, and their estates were confiscated. The younger Donne was anxious to obliterate traces of his father's connections with these noblemen, and to bring to the front the names of any of the powerful Parliamentarian nobles whose patronage he was seeking. By 1648 he had become chaplain to Basil, Earl of Denbigh, to whom he dedicated the 1649 Folio of the *Sermons.* A little earlier he had dedicated his edition of his father's *Biathanatos* to Philip Herbert, Earl of Pembroke and Montgomery, who had enjoyed the patronage of King Charles early in the reign, but, being disappointed of his hopes of further favours, had deserted to the Parliamentarians and had become an important figure in their councils.

When Donne's son published a collection of his father's letters as *Letters to severall Persons of Honour* in 1651, he dedicated the volume to Mistress Bridget Dunch, "whose husband was high in the esteem of his kinsman, Oliver Cromwell." She herself was the niece of Sir Thomas Lucy, to whom some of Donne's letters were addressed, and she was also a very rich woman.[16] In the forefront of the volume the younger Donne placed five letters addressed to Bridget White, who became the wife of Sir Henry Kingsmill of Sydmonton, Hampshire, and was a patroness of literary men. He had earlier sent her a copy of his father's *Biathanatos.*

---

[16] See an article by R. E. Bennett, "Donne's *Letters to severall Persons of Honour,*" *PMLA,* LVI, 120–140, esp. pp. 133–134.

I. A. Shapiro[17] and R. E. Bennett have demonstrated that John Donne junior substituted the name of Sir Thomas Lucy for that of Sir Henry Goodyer at the head of five letters in the volume. Since both Bridget Dunch and Lady Kingsmill were connected with Sir Thomas Lucy, it was important to represent the elder Donne as a valued correspondent of that gentleman.

We have no reason to think that in *Fifty Sermons* Donne's son substituted any names, but he evidently omitted the names of any noble persons who might have been displeasing to the Roundheads. We have already shown[18] that this was what he did with the titles of the marriage sermons printed as Nos. 2 and 3 of *Fifty Sermons,* where the names of Nethersole and Washington, which are given in the MSS of these sermons, have been suppressed, while the names of Lord Herbert of Cherbury (a kinsman of the Earl of Montgomery) and of Egerton are given in full in the title of Sermon 1.

Thus when we find that the only names given for the christening and churching sermons are those of Lady Doncaster (the Countess of Carlisle) and Lady Bridgewater, we are not surprised. The Countess of Carlisle survived her husband by many years and became a friend of the Parliamentarians Pym and the Earl of Holland, so she was therefore acceptable. Her brother the Earl of Northumberland, who had been Admiral of Charles's fleet, deserted to the Parliamentarians and served under them.

It is possible that among the sermons without a title one or two may have been preached at the christening of either the son or one of the daughters of Richard, Earl of Dorset, for the Earl was a kind patron of Donne, and we know from his wife's *Diary* that Donne stayed with them at Knole in 1617[19] and probably on other occasions. They had five children in all, out of whom only two daughters survived infancy. A son was born to them on February 2, 1620, but he died of the measles six months later.[20] Or Donne may have preached

---

[17] "The Text of Donne's *Letters to severall Persons," Review of English Studies,* VII, 291–301.

[18] Vol. III, pp. 20–21.

[19] See Vol. I of the present edition, pp. 129–130.

[20] Chamberlain, *Letters,* II, 288: "The earle of Dorset is a prowde man of a younge sonne his Lady brought him the second of this moneth." *Ibid.,* p. 315: "The earle of Dorsets young and only sonne died the last weeke of the measells" (letter of August 4, 1620).

at the baptism of one of the children of Edward, fourth Earl of Dorset, who succeeded his brother in 1624, and who seems to have been equally kind to Donne, whom he had known before his accession to the earldom. In 1612 he had married Mary, daughter of Sir George Curzon, and by her he had several children, some of whom died in infancy. His elder surviving son Richard was born in 1622, and there was also a younger son. He stood high in favour with King Charles, who made him Lord Chamberlain and Lord Privy Seal, and he remained consistently loyal to Charles throughout the Civil War. His two sons fought in the King's army, and the younger was killed at Chawley in 1646. He was therefore deprived of his offices by the Parliament, and John Donne junior would be anxious in 1649 to suppress all mention of his name in connection with any of the elder Donne's works.

It seems best to include the whole of this block of baptismal and churching sermons in the present volume, because it was only in this earlier part of Donne's ministry that he was likely to have had time and energy to spare for this kind of preaching. His serious illness in the winter of 1623–24 made a fairly long break in his work, and in March, 1624, he became vicar of St. Dunstan's-in-the-West. He took his work there seriously, and we have four sermons preached there in the first year of his ministry at the church; he may have preached others which he did not trouble to preserve. The long series of eight sermons on the Penitential Psalms in Volume IX of our edition can also be attributed probably to the years 1624–1625.[21] He also preached five Prebend Sermons at St. Paul's in the years 1625–1627. In the summers of 1628 and 1629 he was busy with the work of two ecclesiastical commissions.[22] Professor R. C. Bald has found by examination of documents in the Public Record Office that Donne's name constantly appears together with the names of the Bishops of London, Exeter, and others in connection with the transaction of ecclesiastical business. Donne's legal training evidently caused him to be much in demand.

---

[21] Vol. IX, p. 37.

[22] For 1628 see W. Milgate, "Donne the Lawyer," *Times Literary Supplement,* August 1, 1942, and for 1629, Gosse, *Life and Letters of John Donne,* II, 262–263.

Finally, in the autumn of 1628 he had an attack of quinsy complicated with high fever which disabled him from preaching for some time. When he resumed his duties at St. Paul's and St. Dunstan's he can have had no time to spare for christening and churching sermons. All his energy was required for his regular work, until in the summer of 1630 his fatal illness overtook him.

The four baptismal sermons (Nos. 4–7) afford no clues to when and where they were preached, and they are therefore printed here in the order in which they occur in the Folio of 1649. There are several references to the puritanical dislike of the use of the sign of the cross in baptism, but this was a long-standing objection which had been raised in the reign of Elizabeth and continued to be pressed throughout the reigns of James I and Charles I. All of them contain some good passages, but they are not very distinguished examples of Donne's art. Sermons 4, 5, and 7 are chiefly concerned with the necessity and meaning of baptism, and Sermon 6 insists on the connection between Christian baptism and the doctrine of the Trinity.

Perhaps the most interesting sermon of this group is No. 4, in which Donne takes his text from the seventh chapter of one of his favourite books, the *Revelation* of St. John the Divine. The vision recorded in this chapter had previously inspired Donne's famous sonnet "At the round earths imagin'd corners, blow Your trumpets, Angells..." It opens thus: "And after these things I saw four angels standing on the four corners of the earth, holding the four winds of the earth, that the wind should not blow on the earth, nor on the sea, nor on any tree. And I saw another angel ascending from the east, having the seal of the living God: and he cried in a loud voice to the four angels, ... saying, Hurt not the earth, neither the sea, nor the trees, till we have sealed the servants of our God in their foreheads." Donne reproduces it here:

Here you shall see the *Angell that comes from the East,* (yea, that Angel which *is the East,* from whence all beams of grace and glory arise, for so the Prophet calls *Christ Jesus* himself, (as S. *Hierome* reads that place) *Ecce vir, Oriens nomen ejus, Behold him, whose name is the East*) you shall see him come with the seal of the living God, and hold back those Angels which had power given them to hurt the Sea, and the Earth, and you shall hear him say, *Hurt not the earth, nor the sea, nor the trees, till we have sealed the servants of our God in the foreheads.* And as you shall see him forward, so you shall see him large, and bountifull in imprinting that Seal, you shall see *an hundred and forty four thousand of the Tribes of the Children of Israel,* and you shall see *a great multitude, which no man can number, of all Nations, and kindreds, and people, and tongues, stand before the Throne, and before the Lamb, and cry out, and say, Salvation commeth of our God, that sitteth upon the Throne, and of the Lamb:* and you shall see all the Angels stand round about the Throne, and about the Elders, and the four Beasts, all falling upon their faces, and worshipping God, saying, *Amen, praise, and glory, and wisdome, and thanks, and honour, and power, and might be unto our God, for evermore, Amen.* And this is good company, and good Musique.[23]

At first sight it may seem that Donne was applying this text perversely, for St. John's vision was of the Church Triumphant in heaven, and it was intended to encourage the persecuted Christians of Asia Minor, who found the might of the Roman Empire employed to crush them. It seems out of place at the baptism of a small infant in a professedly Christian society. But Donne's use of it here is one more example of his profound sense of human solidarity. The child who is to be baptized has been born into a human family, but the members of this family will fail and die. By baptism he is admitted into the fellowship of Christ's Church here on earth, and as Donne has reminded us elsewhere, the Church Militant and the Church Triumphant "are not two Churches, but this the Porch, and that the Chancell of the same Church, which are under one Head, Christ Jesus."[24] To those who believe, as Donne did, in the Communion of Saints, the child is already potentially a member of the throng seen by the Seer, and there is a constant intercourse between heaven and earth.

The first of Donne's churching sermons (No. 8) was that "preached at Essex house, at the Churching of the Lady Doncaster." The Prayer Book of 1559 provided a short and simple service entitled "The Thanksgiving of Woman after Child-Birth, Commonly Called, The Churching of Women," but for ladies of high rank this was often enlarged by the addition of a sermon. It is fairly certain that this particular sermon must have been preached in December, 1618. In November, 1617, James Hay (later Viscount Doncaster) married, as his

[23] P. 97.
[24] Vol. VII, p. 340.

second wife, the beautiful Lady Lucy Percy, the younger daughter of Henry, ninth Earl of Northumberland. The Earl, who had been a prisoner in the Tower for a number of years, had strongly opposed the marriage. His family, the Percies, had had endless border fights with the Scots, and he was proud of his position as a member of the old English aristocracy. When he heard of the proposed match, which had been encouraged by the Countess of Bedford, he ordered his daughter to remain with him in the Tower, saying "that he meant not to part with her but that she shold kepe him companie, adding withall that he was a Percie and could not indure that his daughter shold daunce any Scottish giggs."[25] However, the King strongly favoured the match, and when the wedding took place he and Prince Charles honoured the wedding supper with their presence.

The register of baptisms at St. Clement Danes Church, London, records for November 27, 1618, "Charles Hay, Sonne to the Lord Hay, Viscount Doncaster, baptised in Essex house." This was Doncaster's London house, and the child was probably baptized there instead of in the church because it was a sickly infant and near death. The burial register of St. Clement Danes has the entry for December 3, only six days later, "Charles Hay, Sonne of the Lord Hay, Viscount Doncaster." As far as we can discover, no other child was born to Lady Doncaster. The register of St. Clement Danes contains no other baptismal entry relating to her or her husband, and all later accounts speak of her as childless.

It may seem surprising that after the death of the infant a sermon should have been preached at the churching of the mother, but the service itself was a thanksgiving not for the birth of the child, but for the safe deliverance of the mother from the peril of childbirth, which in those days proved fatal to a high percentage of women. Moreover, Lady Doncaster was at this time a young woman of nineteen, and it must have seemed probable that she would have other children.[26]

Donne's sermon dwelt chiefly on the thought of purification. According to the Jewish law (*Leviticus* 12.1–8), a woman was unclean

---

[25] Chamberlain, *Letters,* II, 58.

[26] The death of the first child was very frequent. Charles the First's queen, Henrietta Maria, lost her first son within a few hours of his birth, though later she produced a large family.

for forty days after the birth of a male child, and at the end of that time she had to bring a sacrifice to the priest, who would offer it for her purification. There is no mention of this in the Prayer Book Office, but we can compare Milton's sonnet on the death of his second wife in childbirth, and his vision of her all in white:

> Mine as whom washt from spot of child-bed taint,
> Purification in the old Law did save.

The purification, however, of which Donne speaks here is one applicable to the whole congregation present. First, there is the water of baptism, and then the washing of the soul by repentance for sins committed daily. It is a tactful sermon, in which there is no particular reference to the young mother, but a consideration of Donne's text from the Canticles: "I have washed my feet, how shall I defile them?" with the answer near the close: "There are answers enough to this *Quomodo, How, how should I defile them,* if thou aske the world: but aske thy Saviour, and he shall tell thee, *That whosoever hath this water, shall never thirst more, but that water shall be in him an ever-lasting spring;* that is, he shall find meanes to keep himselfe in that cleannesse, to which he is come; and *neither things present, nor things to come shall separate him from the love of God.*"[27]

The two sermons (Nos. 9 and 10) which follow are probably the two parts, divided by Donne himself, of a single sermon, while the heading "Preached at the Churching of the Countesse of Bridgewater" has been misplaced in the Folio at the beginning of the second sermon. Donne explains early in the first sermon that the text has a threefold meaning. It is first a *commination* or threatening, secondly a *commonition* or warning, and thirdly a *consolation*. We can hardly suppose that Donne preached the first two sections, which are full of threatening and warning, at the churching of some unnamed lady, and then started a sermon for the churching of a great lady, his old friend Frances Egerton, Countess of Bridgewater, with the words, "Thus far we have proceeded in the first acceptation of these words, according to their principall, and literall sense, as they appertain'd to the *Jewes,* and their state; so they were a *Commination;* . . ."[28] To have

---

[27] P. 182.
[28] P. 198.

behaved in this way would have been an insult to both ladies, and it is clear that Donne decided, when writing out his sermons, to do as he had done with his notes of his sermon at The Hague,[29] and to expand one sermon into two. In the original sermon it is probable that the long disquisition on God's judgments on the Jews which occupies most of the first of these two sermons was compressed into a few paragraphs, as it would be very unsuitable for the churching of any lady. The second sermon, which is much more suitable, contains an express reference to the Countess: "...And in both these latter senses [*commonition* and *consolation*], the words admit a just accommodation to this present occasion, God having rais'd his honorable servant, and hand-maid here present, to a sense of the *Curse,* that lyes upon *women,* for the transgression of the first woman, which is painfull, and dangerous *Child-birth;* and given her also, a sense of the last glorious resurrection, in having rais'd her, from that Bed of weaknesse, to the ability of coming into his presence, here in his house."[30]

Since the Countess of Bridgewater bore her husband fifteen children, we have a wide choice of possible dates for this particular sermon, but it seems likely that it was preached after the birth of an heir, for most of the children were daughters. Two sons had died early, before Donne's ordination, and then came several daughters, but on June 2, 1621, Chamberlain wrote: "There was a great christning the last weeke of the earle of Bridgwaters sonne where the Prince, the Marquis Buckingham, and the old countesse of Darbie were gossips [i.e., godparents]."[31] Unfortunately the child did not live very long. On April 19, 1623, Chamberlain wrote that the Earl's "only sonne died yesterday, but there is hope left seeing his lady is with child, and redy to lie down," and two months later, on June 14, he reported that a son had been born. This must have been John,[32] who survived his father and became the second Earl of Bridgewater. A younger son, Thomas, was born a year later. It is probable that

---

[29] See Vol. II of our edition, pp. 38–39, 269.

[30] P. 198 of the present volume.

[31] Chamberlain, *Letters,* II, 379.

[32] The *Dictionary of National Biography* gives the date of his birth as 1622, but this cannot be correct, in view of Chamberlain's statement of April 19, 1623.

Donne's sermon for Lady Bridgewater's churching may have been either for the birth in 1621 or for that in 1623.

We may note here that Donne was evidently on very friendly terms with the Earl and Countess, for he sent them copies of three of his printed sermons, two of which have the inscription, "J. Bridgewater ex dono Authoris,"[33] and the Earl possessed a manuscript (which we have called the Ellesmere MS) containing eight of Donne's other sermons. Moreover in November, 1627, Donne preached the wedding sermon at the marriage of the Earl's daughter, Lady Mary Egerton, to the eldest son of Edward Herbert, afterwards Lord Herbert of Cherbury.[34]

Our next sermon (No. 11) offers several points of interest. It is the only sermon described as having been preached at the Temple Church, though of course Donne may have preached there other sermons which have not been preserved. The only contemporary reference discovered so far to Donne's preaching there is in a letter dated "Midsom' day 1615" and written "to S' Edw Herbert att Paris" by "Richard Prythergh."[35] Herbert's correspondent writes: "this day M' Donn preached att our Temple / he had to much learninge in his sermon for ignoramus." This is a topical allusion to the Cambridge play of *Ignoramus,* in which Ignoramus is a common lawyer. It had been presented before King James on March 8, 1614/15, with much applause. On May 20, 1615, Chamberlain wrote: "On Saterday last the King went again to Cambrige to see the play *Ignoramus* which hath so netled the Lawiers that they are almost out of all patience..."[36]

We cannot be sure that this sermon on *Esther* 4.16 was the very one which proved too learned for Richard Prythergh. If it were so, it would be the second earliest of Donne's sermons which we possess, for hitherto we have had only the sermon preached at Greenwich on

[33] See Vol. I, p. 13, of the present edition. The volume containing these was formerly in the library of Bridgewater House, and is now in the Huntington Library.

[34] This sermon is printed as No. 3 in Vol. VIII of our edition.

[35] Professor R. C. Bald has kindly supplied us with this information. The letter is among the Powis MSS at the Public Record Office, London (Ref. no. 30/53/7/11), and the reference to Donne was noted by Mr. J. P. Feil, of Cornell University. "Prythergh" appears to be a form of "Pritchard."

[36] Chamberlain, *Letters,* I, 597–598.

April 30 (Vol. I of our edition, pp. 151–167) for the year 1615. But in
any case the sermon is likely to have been a comparatively early one,
preached before Donne became Dean of St. Paul's in 1621. It deals
with a case of conscience—Esther's refusal to obey the King's command that no man or woman should, on pain of death, approach him
without a royal summons. Esther was a Jewess, although she had
become the queen of Ahasuerus. Having learnt from her uncle Mordecai of Haman's plot to destroy all the Jews in Persia, for which
he had obtained the King's authority, Esther determined that her
duty to God and her own nation must overrule her submission to the
royal order, and that she must approach the King to implore him to
save her nation. She besought Mordecai and the other Jews to fast for
her three days and nights, and announced her determination in the
words of Donne's text, "If I perish, I perish." If Donne's sermon, in
which he applauds Esther's decision, had been preached after the
question of the Spanish marriage had become a burning issue between
King James and his subjects, it would almost certainly have been
interpreted as an encouragement to those preachers and pamphleteers
who were opposing the King's policy as an outrage against the Protestant faith. But in the first few years of Donne's ministry the sermon
could have been preached without offense. In it Donne shows his
interest in casuistry in its proper sense as "that part of Ethics which
resolves cases of conscience, applying the general rules of religion
and morality to particular instances in which 'circumstances alter
cases,' or in which there appears to be a conflict of duties" (*N.E.D.*)
His *Biathanatos* and *Pseudo-Martyr* had both of them been prolonged
exercises of this sort, and Walton tells us that he kept "the copies of
divers Letters and cases of Conscience that had concerned his friends,
with his observations and solutions of them;..."[37]

The sermon on *Luke* 23.34 (No. 12) is particularly interesting. It
appears in *Fifty Sermons,* and in the Ellesmere and Merton manuscripts, but in all of these it has no title, though in *Fifty Sermons* it is
included with five other sermons[38] under a general heading, "Preached

[37] Walton, *Lives* (1670), Life of Donne, pp. 62–63.
[38] These other sermons are all dated in the Folio, and four out of five
have a title which describes the place and occasion of the sermon. The one
which has no place mentioned in the Folio is given a location by the
Merton MS (see Vol. II, pp. 23–25).

to the Nobility." In its tone and character it differs from most of Donne's sermons. The sentences are shorter and simpler than usual, as in the following passages:

> Of all the conduits and conveyances of Gods graces to us, none hath been so little subject to cavillations, as this of prayer. The Sacraments have fallen into the hands of flatterers and robbers. Some have attributed too much to them, some detracted. Some have painted them, some have withdrawn their naturall complexion. It hath been disputed, whether they be, how many they be, what they be, and what they do. The preaching of the word hath been made a servant of ambitions, and a shop of many mens new-fangled wares. Almost every meanes between God and man, suffers some adulteratings and disguises: But prayer least: And it hath most wayes and addresses. It may be mentall, for we may thinke prayers. It may be vocall, for we may speake prayers. It may be actuall, for we do prayers. For deeds have voyce; the vices of *Sodome* did cry, and the Almes of *Toby.* And if it were proper for St. *John,* in the first of the *Revelations* to turne back to see a voyce, it is more likely God will looke down, to heare a worke. So then to do the office of your vocation sincerely, is to pray. . . .
> Since then every rectified man, is the temple of the Holy Ghost, when he prays; it is the Holy Ghost it selfe that prays; and what can be denyed, where the Asker gives? He plays with us, as children, shewes us pleasing things, that we may cry for them, and have them. Before we call, he answers, and when we speake, he heares: . . .[39]

> And in this contemplation, O my unworthy soule, thou art presently in the presence. No passing of guards, nor ushers. No examination of thy degree or habit. The Prince is not asleep, nor private, nor weary of giving, nor refers to others. He puts thee not to prevaile by Angels nor Archangels. But lest any thing might hinder thee, from coming into his presence, his presence comes into thee. And lest Majesty should dazell thee, thou art to speake but to thy Father.[40]

All the marginal headings of this sermon are in English: "Of Prayer," "Of this Prayer," "Forgive them," "Ignorance," and so on, instead of in Latin, as in the majority of Donne's sermons.[41] Also all

---

[39] Pp. 232–233.

[40] P. 234.

[41] The sermon on *Amos* 5.18 (Vol. II, pp. 348–363) has no Latin headings, and that on *Matthew* 19.17 (Vol. VI, pp. 223–240) has only one, *"Divisio,"* but these have no English headings to correspond to the usual Latin ones, but merely "1 Part. Context" or "Conclusion." The sermon on *Psalms* 32.10 and 11 (Vol. IX, pp. 391–411) has two Latin headings, *"Divisio"* and *"Iubilate,"* and a number of English ones such as "Sorrow," "The Wicked," "Plurality," etc.

the Scriptural references, which are usually placed in the margin, are here printed in the body of the text. Thirdly, most of the sermon is quite free from the usual quotations from and references to the Fathers. It is only in the last few pages that St. Augustine, St. Jerome, Chrysostom, and the rest, make their appearance.

Though the style of this sermon is simpler than that of most of its companions, and the sermon itself is shorter than the average, Donne certainly took pains in its preparation. In the passage on prayer quoted above, each short sentence has a wealth of thought and experience behind it, and the whole paragraph is lighted up by the final simile in which Donne, the affectionate father of many "gamesome children," as he had once called them, compares God's reception of prayer to a father's play with his children.

In determining to place this sermon in the earlier block of undated sermons we have been influenced by two considerations. The first is that it is found in the two manuscripts *E* and *M*, in company with a number of dated sermons all of which belong to the earlier part of Donne's career as a preacher, ranging, as they do, from December, 1617, to April, 1622. In all the seven MSS of Donne's sermons which we possess, there is no sermon dated later than April, 1622. It seems that when in the autumn of 1622 Donne published, at the King's order, his sermon at Paul's Cross, and followed it up by publishing his sermon to the Virginia Company at the Company's request, he discontinued his former practice of distributing handwritten copies of those sermons for which friends had made special request. He found that printing was more effective and probably more economical than sending his own manuscript to be copied by a scrivener. It seems reasonable therefore to assume that any undated sermon found in our MSS is earlier than the end of 1622.

This conclusion can be reinforced by the argument that the style of part of this sermon has some similarity with that of parts of the *Essays in Divinity,* a work written before Donne's ordination. The sermon contains a number of meditative or ejaculatory passages addressed not to the congregation but to God or to Donne himself. Compare the passage already quoted beginning "And in this contemplation, O my unworthy soule . . ." with the passages in the *Essays in Divinity* beginning "Thou shalt not then, O my faithfull soul, despise any of these erroneous pictures ... ," "Dig a little deeper, O my poor lazy soul, and thou shalt see that thou, and all mankind are delivered from an Egypt ... ," "Go one step lower, that is higher, and nearer to God, O my soul, in this Meditation ... ," "Lastly, descend, O my Soul, to the very Center ... ."[42] For passages addressed to God compare in the present sermon the passages beginning "Hast thou, O God, filled all thy Scriptures, ... hast thou filled these with prayses and perswasions of wisedome and knowledge, and must these persecutors be pardoned for their ignorance?" ... "But thy Mercy is as the Sea: ... ,"[43] and the prayer at the end of the sermon, *"O eternall God, look down from thy Throne to thy footstoole ... ,"* with the numerous prayers in the *Essays,* such as *"O Eternall and Almighty power ... ,"* "Thou hast delivered me, O God, from the Egypt of confidence and presumption ... ," *"O Eternall God ... ,"* *"O Eternall God, ... Behold us, O God, here gathered together in thy fear, according to thine ordinance ... ."*[44]

The general style of the sermon is therefore early, not late, but we cannot offer any plausible conjecture as to the year in which it was preached.

The differences which we have noted earlier between this sermon and others in the Folios may perhaps suggest that it was intended for a different type of audience from that which listened to Donne at Lincoln's Inn, St. Paul's, St. Dunstan's, or Whitehall. Is it possible that here we have a solitary example of the sermons which Donne preached every summer during the vacation at his country livings of Sevenoaks or Blunham? When he visited these, we know that he generally stayed with the Earl of Dorset at Knole, or the Earl of Kent at the great house at Blunham. On these occasions the Earl with his wife, family, and part of the retinue of servants would be present at the Sunday morning service.[45] A sermon preached on such an occasion could therefore be included by John Donne junior under the general heading "Preached to the Nobility." The fact that this ser-

---

[42] *Essays in Divinity,* ed. E. M. Simpson, 1952, pp. 22, 74, 75, 76.
[43] Pp. 237-238.
[44] *Essays in Divinity,* pp. 36-38, 75-76, 96-97, 97-98.
[45] When Donne visited Knole in 1617, the Earl of Dorset was away, but the Countess heard him preach both morning and afternoon (Vol. I, pp. 129-130).

mon has no title of its own in the manuscripts as well as in the Folio might perhaps indicate that Donne preached it more than once at two separate places. For example, he might have preached it both at Sevenoaks and at Blunham, for the one parish is in Kent, and the other in Bedfordshire, many miles away.[46]

The title of the next sermon (No. 13) tells us that it was preached "to the Earle of Carlile, and his Company, at Sion." Since James Hay is here called Earl of Carlisle we presume that it was preached after he had been raised to that dignity on September 13, 1622,[47] for in the titles of earlier sermons he is described as Viscount Doncaster. This sermon is found not only in the Folio but also in the Merton manuscript, where it has no title. We have already argued[48] that as the fourteen dated sermons found in this manuscript were all preached before the end of 1622, it is likely that the two undated ones also belong to this period, as it was late in 1622 that two of Donne's sermons were published, and after this date he does not seem to have circulated any sermons in manuscript. Since Carlisle had been ambassador in France from July, 1621, to the summer of 1622, and since in February, 1623, he went first to France and then to Spain on the business of the Spanish marriage, it is probable that Donne preached this sermon before him at some date in the autumn of 1622. The title tells us that it was preached at Sion, which was the mansion of the Earl of Northumberland, Carlisle's father-in-law, who was released in July, 1621, from the Tower, where he had been imprisoned for more than fifteen years.

Donne's friendship with Carlisle continued till his death, for in his will he bequeathed to the Earl "the picture of the blessed Virgin which hangs in the little dining-chamber." Gosse believed that the three *Holy Sonnets* found only in the Westmoreland MSS proved that "even after the death of his wife, and his subsequent conversion," Donne "hankered after some tenets of the Roman faith," or at least

---

[46] For an account of Blunham see the Appendix to the present volume.

[47] We should note that in the title of the sermon which Donne preached before Hay, Northumberland, and Buckingham on August 25, 1622, Hay is called "Earl of Carlile," but it was common talk for some months earlier (see Chamberlain, *Letters,* II, 441–442) that he was to be made Earl of Carlisle. See Vol. IV, p. 33.

[48] P. 18 above.

PULPIT IN BLUNHAM CHURCH FROM WHICH DONNE PREACHED

"still doubted as to his attitude with regard to them." Gosse discovered in this bequest to Carlisle an indication that Donne "found a sympathiser in secret" in his friend. He continued: "In the early seventeenth century, in England, such pictures were appreciated for their subject more and for their artistic merit less than has since become the fashion. Donne would not have kept for ever before his eyes in privacy, and have passed on to Lord Doncaster (then Earl of Carlisle), as a peculiar treasure, a painting of the Virgin Mary, unless they had both preserved a tender interest in her cult, and were equally out of sympathy with the iconoclastic puritanism of the age in England."[49] In Volume X we hope to rebut in full the argument from the *Holy Sonnets,* but here we wish to dispose of the theory that "it is probable" that Carlisle was "a sympathiser in secret" with Roman doctrines. Gosse does not adduce an iota of evidence apart from this bequest. We can find no historical confirmation of his conjecture. As to the picture itself, evidence has lately come to light which suggests that it was a painting of Christ with the Blessed Virgin and St. John, not one of the Virgin alone, and that it was painted by Titian. Professor W. Milgate has shown that Donne was something of an art collector, and in one of his articles, on "Dr. Donne's Art Gallery," he argues that this was the picture which, according to Vertue's *Catalogue and Description of King Charles the First's Capital Collection of Pictures* (1757), was sent to France with one other by Charles the First in return for a picture of St. John the Baptist by Leonardo da Vinci. This one is described as "done by Titian; being our Lady, and Christ, and St. John, half figures, as big as the life ... being in a carved gilded frame, and was given heretofore to his Majesty by my Lord of Carlisle, who had it of Dr Donn, painted upon the right light."[50]

In any case, whether this was or was not the painting mentioned in Donne's will, it is absurd to infer, as Gosse did, that the possession of a picture of the Virgin implied a secret hankering after Rome in either Donne or Carlisle. The Church of England celebrates the Blessed Virgin by keeping two feast days in her honour (February 2, the Feast of her Purification, and March 25, the Feast of the Annun-

---

[49] *Life and Letters of John Donne,* II, 109–110.

[50] *Notes and Queries,* CXCIV, No. 15 (July 23, 1949), pp. 318–319.

ciation, "commonly known as Lady Day"). Donne began one of the five sermons which he preached for the earlier of these two feasts by stating, "The Church, which is the Daughter of God, and Spouse of Christ, celebrates this day, the Purification of the blessed Virgin, the Mother of God."[51] This sermon was preached at St. Paul's before the Lord Mayor and the City Companies, whose custom it was to attend in their liveries on this particular day,[52] so that there was nothing secret or furtive, as Gosse suggests, about the honour paid to the Mother of Christ. Laud, Cosin, and others who belonged like Donne to the High Church wing, paid her equal honour, and were abused for it by the Puritans.

The text that Donne chose for this sermon was, "He that believeth not shall be damned," but in most of the discourse he occupied himself rather with the necessity of belief. The reader cannot help feeling that in this particular sermon Donne lays too much stress on a purely intellectual assent to Christian dogma rather than on belief in the sense usual in the Gospels, of a committal of the whole person to a following of Jesus Christ.

The close of the sermon contains a terrible and magnificent account of the horror of eternal separation from the presence of God. Here Donne lays no stress on those material torments of hell which occupied so many contemporary sermons. He sees that the essence of damnation is not in flames and brimstone, but in perpetual exclusion from the source of life and light. "What Tophet is not Paradise, what Brimstone is not Amber, ... what gnawing of the worme is not a tickling, what torment is not a marriage bed to this damnation, to be secluded eternally, eternally, eternally from the sight of God?"[53]

Sermon 14 is described in the title as "Preached at S. Pauls." We cannot ascribe any definite date to it, but it probably belongs to the period between November, 1621, and the end of 1622. There are several passages which seem to refer to the Elector's series of defeats: "I may have a full measure in my selfe, ... and yet see God abandon greater persons, and desert some whole Churches, and States, upon whom his glory and Gospel depends much more then upon me, but

---

[51] Vol. VII, p. 325.
[52] Stow, *Survey of London* (ed. Kingsford), II, 190.
[53] P. 267.

this is a prayer of charitable extension, *Satura nos,* not *me,* but *us,* all us that professe thee aright:..."[54] "God does all that he can for us; And therefore when we see others in distresse, whether nationall, or personall calamities, whether Princes be dispossest of their naturall patrimony, and inheritance, or private persons afflicted with sicknesse, or penury, or banishment, let us goe Gods way, all the way;..."[55]

There may be one reference to the rumour,[56] which moved King James to anger, that the Elector had invited the Turks into Hungary to help him in his Bohemian campaign: "But he may derive help upon us, by meanes that are not his,... he may strengthen our Armies by calling in the Turke, he may establish our peace and friendships, by remitting or departing with some parts of our Religion; at such a deare price we may be helped, but these are not his helps,..."[57]

Finally, there is a sentence which proves conclusively that the sermon was preached before the long peace of James's reign was ended by the war with Spain which broke out in 1625, and for which money was voted by Parliament in 1624: "Our Ancestors who indured many yeares Civill and forraine wars, were more affected with their first peace, then we are with our continuall enjoying thereof, And our Fathers more thankfull, for the beginning of Reformation of Religion, then we for so long enjoying the continuance thereof."[58]

The sermon itself is a good one, one of the best in this volume. Its tone is cheerful, and throughout Donne dwells on the virtue of praise. Of the Book of *Psalms* he says, "The Book is Praise, the parts are Prayer. The name changes not the nature; Prayer and Praise is the same thing." Prayer and praise "accompany one another,... they meet like two waters, and make the streame of devotion the fuller."[59] Prayer consists as much of praise for the past as of supplication for the future. "It is the counsell of the Wise man, *Prevent the Sunne to give thanks to God, and at the day-spring pray unto him.* You see still,

---

[54] P. 273.

[55] P. 279.

[56] See report of the French Ambassador, Tillières, in London, April 6/16, 1620, in Raumer, *History of the Sixteenth and Seventeenth Centuries,* English trans. [Egerton], 1835, II, 242.

[57] P. 274.

[58] P. 285.

[59] P. 270.

how these two duties are marshalled, and disposed; First Praise, and then Prayer, but both early:...Rise as early as you can, you cannot be up before God; no, nor before God raise you: Howsoever you prevent this Sunne, the Sunne of the Firmament, yet the Sonne of Heaven hath prevented you, for without his preventing Grace you could not stirre."[60] "This joy we shall see, when we see him, who is so in it, as that he is this joy it selfe. But here in this world, so far as I can enter into my Masters sight, I can enter into my Masters joy. I can see God in his Creatures, in his Church, in his Word and Sacraments, and Ordinances; Since I am not without this sight, I am not without this joy."[61]

The writing in these pages is of a different quality from that in the Christening Sermons. There Donne was trying to instruct; here his imagination is fired, and he mounts on wings. He had chosen a happy text, "O satisfie us early with thy mercy, that we may rejoyce and be glad all our dayes." This combined two of the thoughts which were dearest to him—the everlasting lovingkindness of God, and the beauty of the dawning of the day. He himself was an early riser,[62] and he loved to remember that God's mercies were new every morning, fresh and sparkling as the dewdrops in the sunlight. In the two last passages quoted above, the texture of the writing is as rich and laden with meaning as the lines of his poems. There is his favourite word-play on "the Sunne of the Firmament" and "the Sonne of Heaven," which runs through half a page, and lightens with humour his rebuke to those sluggards who have come to church without saying their morning prayers in private at home. There is his well-chosen quotation from the Book of *Wisdom,* and his glancing allusion to the parable of the talents in the antithesis—"so far as I can enter into my Masters sight, I can enter into my Masters joy." Prayer and praise make an alliterative chime throughout his sentences, and this world and the next keep each other in view. "Gods house in this world is called the house of Prayer; but in heaven it is the house of Praise: No

---

[60] P. 281.

[61] P. 287.

[62] "Nor was his age onely so industrous, but in the most unsetled dayes of his youth, his bed was not able to detain him beyond the hour of four in a morning." Walton, *Lives* (1670), Life of Donne, pp. 61–62.

surprisall with any new necessities there, but one even, incessant, and everlasting tenor of thanksgiving."[63]

The remaining five sermons (Nos. 15–19) were all preached on the Penitential Psalms, but No. 15 differs from the others in that it stands alone, and is not one of a series. It deals with a single verse of the Fifty-first Psalm, and we can find no evidence to assign it to any particular year. It is a good example of its kind, but unfortunately we have no space to discuss it here.

The four sermons on *Psalms* 6.1–5 (Nos. 16–19) contain passages which strongly resemble parts of the *Essays in Divinity,* written by Donne at some time before his ordination in 1615, but not published till after his death. The two longest of these passages are to be found in Sermon 16. We quote first a passage from *Essays in Divinity,*[64] as containing the earlier version:

So that it is truly said, there is no name given by man to God, *Ejus essentiam adæquatè representans.* And *Hermes* says humbly and reverently, *Non spero,* I cannot hope, that the maker of all Majesty, can be call'd by any one name, though compounded of many. I have therfore sometimes suspected, that there was some degree of pride, and overboldness, in the first naming of God; the rather, because I marke, that the first which ever pronounced the name, *God,* was the Divell; and presently after the woman; who in the next chapter proceeded further, and first durst pronounce that sacred and mystick name of foure letters. For when an Angell did but Ministerially represent God wrastling with *Jacob,* he reproves *Jacob,* for asking his name; *Cur quæris nomen meum?* And so also to *Manoah, Why askest thou my Name, quod est mirabile?* And God, to dignify that Angell which he promises to lead his people, says, *Fear him, provoke him not,* etc. *For my Name is in him;* but he tels them not what it is. But since, necessity hath enforced, and Gods will hath revealed some names. For in truth, we could not say this, God cannot be named, except God could be named.

---

[63] P. 271. These are only a few passages taken from a number of pages in which we find the following images—the Morning Star, the dawn, sunrise, the sun in its strength, showers of rain on the thirsty earth, associated with the thought of God's mercy and man's response in songs of praise. Compare the great passage on God's mercy in the Christmas sermon of 1624 (Vol. VI, pp. 172–174), where there is the same pun on "the Sunne of the firmament" and "his Son of glory."

[64] *Op. cit.,* pp. 23–24 (edition of 1651, pp. 44–45).

The substance of this with much of the actual wording is reproduced in an expanded form in Sermon 16:

> For though it be truly said in the Schoole, that no name can be given to God, *Ejus essentiam adæquatè repræsentans,* No one name can reach to the expressing of all that God is; And though *Trismegistus* doe humbly, and modestly, and reverently say, *Non spero,* it never fell into my thought, nor into my hope, that the maker and founder of all Majesty, could be circumscribed, or imprisoned by any one name, though a name compounded and complicated of many names, as the Rabbins have made one name of God, of all his names in the Scriptures; Though *Iacob* seeme to have been rebuked *for asking Gods name,* when he wrastled with him; And so also the Angel which was to doe a miraculous worke ... would not permit *Manoah* to enquire after his name, *Because,* as he sayes there, *that name was secret and wonderfull;* And though God himselfe, to dignifie and authorize that *Angel,* which he made his Commissioner, and the Tutelar and Nationall Guide of his people, sayes of that *Angel,* to that people, *Feare him, provoke him not, for my Name is in him,* and yet did not tell them, what that name was; Yet certainly, we could not so much as say, God cannot be named, except we could name God by some name; we could not say, God hath no name, except God had a name; for that very word, *God,* is his name.[65]

The second passage occurs soon after in the *Essays:*

> This is the Name, which the *Jews* stubbornly deny ever to have been attributed to the *Messias* in the Scriptures. ... And this is the name by which they say our Blessed Saviour did all his miracles, having learned the true use of it, by a Scedule which he found of *Solomon's,* and that any other, by that means, might do them.

[65] Pp. 322–323 of the present volume. *"Hermes"* in the first quotation and *"Trismegistus"* in the second are the two parts of the compound name (Milton's "thrice-great Hermes"), a title of the Egyptian god Thoth, which was given to the unknown author of the so-called Hermetic books. He was believed by Raleigh, Donne, and other Renaissance writers to have been an Egyptian philosopher of great antiquity. Later research has shown, however, that the books belong to the first, second, and third centuries A.D. and are probably the work of Neoplatonists. Donne's knowledge of them was not very profound. Such as it was, he probably obtained it from Patricius (Francesco Patrizzi, 1529–1597), who wrote *Nova de Universis Philosophia, libris L comprehensa ... quibus postremo sunt adjecta Zoroastris oracula ... Hermetis Trismegisti libelli et fragmenta ... Asclepii discipuli tres libelli ...* 1591.

How this name should be sounded, is now upon the anvile, and every body is beating and hammering upon it. That it is not *Jehova,* this governs me, that the *Septuagint* never called it so; Nor Christ; nor the Apostles, where they vouch the old Testament; Nor *Origen,* nor *Hierome,* curious in language. And though negatives have ever their infirmities, and must not be built on, this may, that our Fathers heard not the first sound of this word *Jehova.* For (for any thing appearing,) *Galatinus,* in their Age, was the first that offered it. For, that *Hierome* should name it in the exposition of the eighth *Psalm,* it is peremptorily averred by *Drusius,* and admitted by our learnedst Doctor, that in the old Editions it was not *Jehova.*[66]

Donne is here quite correct in stating that *Jehova* or *Jehovah* is a false transliteration of the sacred Hebrew name of four consonants, which is transliterated by modern scholars as *Yahweh.* According to the marginal note in the *Essays,* Donne was here drawing on the *Tetragrammaton* (1604) of Drusius (Jan van der Driesche, 1550–1616), of which he possessed a copy, now in the Library of the Middle Temple, London.

This passage reappears in an expanded form in Sermon 16:

This is that name which the Jews falsly, but peremptorily, (for falshood lives by peremptorinesse, and feeds and armes it selfe with peremptorinesse) deny ever to have been attributed to the *Messias,* in the Scriptures. This is that name, in the vertue and use whereof, those Calumniators of our Saviours miracles doe say, that he did his miracles, according to a direction, and schedule, for the true and right pronouncing of that name, which *Solomon* in his time had made, and Christ in his time had found, and by which, say they, any other man might have done those miracles, if he had had *Solomons* directions for the right sounding of this name, *Iehovah.* . . .

How this name which we call *Iehovah,* is truly to be sounded, because in that language it is exprest in foure Consonants onely, without Vowels, is a perplext question; we may well be content to be ignorant therein, since our Saviour Christ himselfe, in all those places which he cited out of the Old Testament, never sounded it; he never said, *Iehovah.* Nor the Apostles after him, nor *Origen,* nor *Ierome;* all persons very intelligent in the propriety of language; they never sounded this name *Iehovah.* For though in S. *Ieromes* Exposition upon the 8. Psalme, we finde that word *Iehovah,* in some Editions which we have now, yet it is a cleare case, that in the old Copies it is not so; in *Ieroms* mouth it was not so; from *Ieroms* hand it came not so. Neither doth it appeare to me, that ever the name of *Iehovah*

---

[66] *Op. cit.,* pp. 24–25.

was so pronounced, till so late, as in our Fathers time; for I think *Petrus Galatinus* was the first that ever called it so.[67]

The following sermons are not so much indebted verbally to the *Essays* as Sermon 16, but here and there some echoes can be heard. For example, the *Essays* have a remark about "such vast Names, as *Pharaoh* gave *Joseph,* which is not only *Expounder of secrets,* but *Saviour of the world."*[68] This interpretation is mentioned in order to refute it in Sermon 18: "For when it is said that *Pharaoh* called *Ioseph, Salvatorem mundi,* A Saviour of the world, [marginal reference, *Gen.* 41.45] ... there is a manifest error in that Translation, which cals *Ioseph* so, for that name which was given to *Ioseph* there, in that language in which it was given, doth truly signifie *Revelatorem Secretorum,* and no more, a Revealer, a Discoverer, a Decypherer of secret and mysterious things ..."[69] Again in Sermon 19 there is a quotation[70] from the *Heptaplus* of Pico della Mirandola, a work which is quoted several times in the *Essays in Divinity*[71] but is seldom mentioned in the Sermons. Mirandola was a pupil and friend of Ficino, the great Renaissance Italian scholar, and was an Oriental scholar who took a deep interest in the occult lore of the Cabbala.

These resemblances might be taken to suggest that this group of sermons was preached very early in Donne's ministry,[72] but in the dated sermons of 1615–1618 we find little to remind us of the *Essays in Divinity*. The link with the sermon which we print as No. 1 of Volume VI is a more definite piece of evidence. It seems likely that during the preparation of these particular sermons Donne reread the manuscript of his *Essays,* and decided that, as he did not mean to publish them, he would make use of some of the material which they

---

[67] Pp. 324–325.

[68] *Op. cit.,* p. 46.

[69] P. 378. "Salvatorem mundi" is the reading of the Vulgate. The A. V. has "Zaphnath-paaneah."

[70] P. 383.

[71] Ed. Simpson, 1952, pp. 10, 13–14, 24, 32.

[72] I made this suggestion in the second edition (1948) of my *Study of the Prose Works of John Donne,* p. 351, but I prefer to withdraw it here.

contained. Occasional echoes from the *Essays* can be found throughout the sermons, even in those of Donne's last years.[73]

In the Folio these four sermons are followed immediately by two more on the same psalm. The first of these is on verses 6 and 7, and the title describes it as "Preached to the King at White-hall upon the occasion of the Fast, April 5. 1628."[74] We can hardly suppose that when Donne was summoned to preach before King Charles on such a solemn occasion he would merely continue a series which he had already begun. In its present form it is evidently an independent sermon specially composed for the Fast, to which a number of allusions are made both at the beginning and the end. There are no references in it to the present four sermons on the same psalm. It may perhaps have replaced in the Folio an earlier sermon on verses 6 and 7, for after it there comes an undated sermon on verses 8, 9, and 10, which will be found at the beginning of Volume VI of our edition. Mr. I. A. Shapiro, who is the chief authority on the dating of Donne's letters, has pointed out to us that there is a passage in this final sermon which closely resembles part of the letter which Donne sent to Sir Robert Ker, who was in Spain during the spring and early summer of 1623, and he thinks that this sermon must be the one to which the letter refers.[75]

This particular volume does not have the unity of thought and mood which characterizes some of our other volumes. It makes a

---

[73] Compare, for example, the passage in which Donne quotes the words of St. Augustine about Moses and his account of the Creation, *Essays in Divinity,* ed. Simpson, 1952, pp. 15–16, with a very similar passage in our edition of the *Sermons,* Vol. IX, p. 94. Compare also *Essays,* pp. 7–8, on "the book of Creatures," with *Sermons,* Vol. IX, pp. 236–237. See also the reference to the antiquity of the works of Hermes Trismegistus in *Essays,* p. 12, with that in *Sermons,* Vol. VIII, p. 255.

[74] This is printed in Vol. VIII of our edition, pp. 192–218.

[75] Tobie Matthew, *Letters* (1660), pp. 306–307: "... Sir, I took up this Paper to write a Letter; but my imaginations were full of a Sermon before, for I write but a few hours before I am to Preach, and so instead of a Letter I send you a Homily." Gosse wrongly assigned this letter "to the months of Donne's convalescence, February and March, 1624" (*Life and Letters,* II, 189, 191–192). Ker had returned from Spain in the latter part of 1623, and the heading of the letter states that it was sent to him "when he was in Spain."

break in the chronological sequence; but this interruption was part
of our original editorial plan. We deemed it best to place these undated sermons close to the dated early sermons with which they are
evidently associated, and then in Volume VI to go on to the sermons
which Donne preached after the break in his work necessitated by his
severe attack of spotted fever in the early winter of 1623.[76]

[76] The necessity of splitting up the work evenly between the two editors,
and the attempt to make the volumes of approximately equal size, involved
us in the unhappy division between Vols. V and VI of this group of sermons on the sixth Psalm. The division of sermons was made very early in
the planning of the edition, as far back as 1948. We would have liked to
print in Vol. V the sermon which is now No. 1 of Vol. VI, but this would
have swollen Vol. V to a quite unmanageable size. For the fact that
Donne's "great sickness" in 1623 was an attack of spotted fever see Chamberlain, *Letters,* II, 531: "Here is a contagious spotted or purple feaver
that raigns much which together with the small pockes hath taken away
many of goode sort as well as meaner people, as Sir Henry Baker, Sir Ed:
Stafford ... and divers others, yet many scape as the Dean of Paules is like
to do though he were in great daunger." This letter was dated "From
London this 6th of December 1623." It should have been quoted in
our Introduction to Vol. VI in our account of Donne's sickness (pp. 4–6),
and our omission of it was an error which we now wish to rectify. Chamberlain's words make it clear that Donne's illness was not occasioned by a
chill caught on October 25, 1623, nor was it, as Gosse supposed, an unusually violent attack of what he called Donne's "chronic disease," of which
he wrote that "its crises were apt to be brought on by anxiety or excess of
intellectual work, as well as by cold" (*Life and Letters,* II, 181). We
should perhaps add that the Introduction to Vol. VI was written as far
back as 1948, and was published in 1953. The character of Donne's illness,
and the fact that the "spotted fever" must have been an attack of what is
now known as relapsing fever, have been made clear in an article by I. A.
Shapiro, "Walton and the Occasion of Donne's *Devotions,*" *Review of
English Studies,* n.s., IX, 18–22.

The Sermons

Number 1.

Preached upon Whitsunday.

[?*At Lincoln's Inn*]

ACTS 10.44. *WHILE PETER YET SPAKE THESE WORDS, THE HOLY GHOST FELL ON ALL THEM, WHICH HEARD THE WORD.*

Part of the second Lesson of that day.

T<small>HAT</small> which served for an argument amongst the Jews, to diminish, and under-value Christ, Have any of the Rulers be-leeved in him? had no force amongst the Gentiles, for amongst them, the first persons that are recorded to have applied themselves to the profession of the Christian Religion, were Rulers, Persons of place, and quality: Sanè propter hoc Dignitates positæ sunt, ut major pietas ostendatur, sayes S. Chrysostome, This is the true reason why men are Ennobled, why men are raised, why men are inriched, that they might glorifie God the more, by that eminency; This is truly

John 7.48

10 to be a good Student, *Scrutari Scripturas,* To search the Scriptures, in which is eternall life: This is truly to be called to the Barre, to be Crucified with Christ Jesus: And to be called to the Bench, to have part in his Resurrection, and raigne in glory with him: and to be a Judge, to judge thy selfe, that thou beest not judged to condemnation, by Christ Jesus: Offices and Titles, and Dignities, make thee, in the eye, and tongue of the world, a better man; be truly a better man, between God and thee, for them, and they are well placed. Those Pyramides and Obelisces, which were raised up on high, in the Aire, but supported nothing, were vaine testimonies of the frivolousnesse,

20 and impertinency of those men that raised them; But when we see Pil-

[Joh. 5.39]

lars stand, we presume that something is to be placed upon them. They, who by their rank and place, are pillars of the State, and pillars of the Church, if Christ and his glory be not raised higher by them, then by other men, put Gods buildings most out of frame, and most discompose Gods purposes, of any others. And therefore S. *Chrysostome* hath noted usefully, That the first of the Gentiles, which was converted to Christianity, was that Eunuch, which was Treasurer to the Queen of Æthiopia; And the second was this Centurion, in whose house S. *Peter* preached this fruitfull Sermon, at which, *While Peter* ³⁰ *yet spake these words, the Holy Ghost fell upon all them that heard the word.*

Acts 8.27

Divisio

Our Parts will be two; first some Circumstances that preceded this act, this miraculous descent and infusion of the Holy Ghost, And then the Act, the Descent it selfe. In the first, we shall consider first, the time, it was *when Peter was speaking,* when Gods Ordinance was then in executing, preaching; And secondly, what made way to this descent of the Holy Ghost, that is, what *Peter* was speaking, and preaching, *These words,* true and necessary Doctrine; And here also we shall touch a little, the place, and the Auditory, *Cornelius,* and his ⁴⁰ family. When from hence we shall descend to the second Part, The descent of the Holy Ghost, we shall looke first, (so as it may become us) upon the Person, (the third Person in the holy, blessed, and glorious Trinity) And then upon his action, as it is expressed here, *Cecidit, He fell;* As of Christ it is said, *Deliciæ ejus cum filiis hominum, His delight is to be with the sons of men,* And, (to speak humanely, a perverse delight, for it was to be with the worst men, with Publicans and sinners) so, (to speak humanely) the Holy Ghost had an extraordinary, a perverse ambition, to goe downewards, to inlarge himselfe, in his working, by falling; *He fell:* And then, he fell so, as ⁵⁰ a showre of rain falls, that does not lie in those round drops in which it falls, but diffuses, and spreads and inlarges it selfe, *He fell upon all;* But then, it was because *all heard,* They came not to see a new action, preaching, nor a new Preacher, *Peter,* nor to see one another at a Sermon, *He fell upon all that heard;* where also, I think, it will not be impertinent, to make this note, That *Peter* is said to have spoke *those words,* but they, on whom the holy Ghost fell, are said to have heard *The word;* It is not Many words, long Sermons, nor good

[Prov. 8.31]

words, witty and eloquent Sermons that induce the holy Ghost, for all these are words of men; and howsoever the whole Sermon is the
60 Ordinance of God, the whole Sermon is not the word of God: But when all the good gifts of men are modestly employ'd, and humbly received, as *vehicula Spiritus,* as S. *Augustine* calls them, The chariots of the Holy Ghost, as meanes afforded by God, to convey the word of life into us, in Those words we heare The word, and there the word and the Spirit goe together, as in our case in the Text, *While Peter yet spake those words, the holy Ghost fell upon all them that heard The word.*

When we come then to consider in the first place, the Time of this miracle, we may easily see that verified in S. *Peters* proceeding, which
70 S. *Ambrose* says, *Nescit tarda molimina Spiritus sancti gratia,* The holy Ghost cannot goe a slow pace; It is the devill in the serpent that creeps, but the holy Ghost in the Dove flyes: And then, in the proceeding with the Centurion, we may see that verified which *Leo* says, *Vbi Deus Magister, quàm citò discitur?* Where God teaches, how fast a godly man learnes? Christ did almost all his miracles in an instant, without dilatory circumstances; Christ sayes to the man sick of the palsey, *Tolle grabatum, Take up thy bed and walk,* and immediately he did so: To the deafe man he sayes, *Ephphatha, Be thine eares opened,* and instantly they were opened: He sayes to the
80 woman with the issue of bloud, *Esto sana à plaga tua,* and she was not onely well immediately upon that, but she was well before, when she had but touched the hem of his garment. Upon him who had lyen in his infirmity thirty eight yeares, at the poole, Christ makes a little stop; but it was no longer then to try his disposition with that question, *Vis sanus fieri?* Christ was sure what his answer would be; and as soone as he gives that answer, immediately he recovered. Where Christ seems to have stayed longest, which was upon the blind man, yet at his first touch, that man saw men walke, though not distinctly, but at the second touch he saw perfectly. As Christ proceeds
90 in his miracles, so doth the holy Ghost in his powerfull instructions. It is true, *Scientiæ sunt profectus,* There is a growth in knowledge, and we overcome ignorances by degrees, and by succession of more and more light: Christ himselfe grew in knowledge, as well as in stature: But this is in the way of experimentall knowledge, by study,

Marginal notes:

1 Part
Tempus

Mark 2.11
Mark 7.34

Mark 5.34

John 5.6

Mark
8.[22–25]

Chrysost.

[Luke 2.52]

by conversation, by other acquisitions. But when the holy Ghost takes a man into his schoole, he deals not with him, as a Painter, which makes an eye, and an eare, and a lip, and passes his pencill an hundred times over every muscle, and every haire, and so in many sittings makes up one man, but he deales as a Printer, that in one straine
100 delivers a whole story.

We see that in this example of S. *Peter,* S. *Peter* had conceived a doubt, whether it were lawfull for him to preach the Gospel to any of the Gentiles, because they were not within the Covenant; This was the *sanus fieri,* This very scruple was the voyce and question of God in him: to come to a doubt, and to a debatement in any religious duty, is the voyce of God in our conscience: Would you know the truth? Doubt, and then you will inquire: And *facile solutionem accipit anima, quæ prius dubitavit,* sayes S. *Chrysostome.* As no man resolves of any thing wisely, firmely, safely, of which he never
110 doubted, never debated, so neither doth God withdraw a resolution from any man, that doubts with an humble purpose to settle his owne faith, and not with a wrangling purpose to shake another mans. God rectifies *Peters* doubt immediately, and he rectifies it fully; he presents him a Book, and a Commentary, the Text, and the Exposition:

Ver. 11   He lets downe a sheet from heaven with all kinde of beasts and fowles, and tels him, that *Nothing is uncleane,* and he tells him by the same

Ver. 19   spirit, that there were three men below to aske for him, who were sent by God to apply that visible Parable, and that God meant, in saying *Nothing was uncleane,* that the Gentiles generally, and in par-
120 ticular, this Centurion *Cornelius,* were not incapable of the Gospell, nor unfit for his Ministery. And though *Peter* had beene very hungry, and would faine have eaten, as appeares in the tenth verse, yet after he received this instruction, we heare no more mention of his desire

[Joh. 4.34]   to eat; but, as his Master had said, *Cibus meus est, My meat is to doe my Fathers will that sent me,* so his meat was to doe him good that sent for him, and so he made haste to goe with those Messengers.

Cum   The time then was, when *Peter* thus prepared by the Holy Ghost,
locutus   was to prepare others for the Holy Ghost, and therefore it was, *Cum locutus, When he spoke,* that is, preached to them. For, *Si adsit pala-*
130 *tum fidei, cui sapiat mel Dei,* saies S. *Augustine,* To him who hath a spirituall taste, no hony is so sweet, as the word of God preached

according to his Ordinance. If a man taste a little of this honey at his
rods end, as *Ionathan* did, though he thinke his eyes enlightned, as
Ionathan did, he may be in *Ionathans* case, *I did but taste a little honey*
with my rod, Et ecce, morior, and behold, I dye. If a man read the
Scriptures a little, superficially, perfunctorily, his eyes seeme straight-
waies enlightned, and he thinks he sees every thing that he had pre-
conceived, and fore-imagined in himselfe, as cleare as the Sun, in the
Scriptures: He can finde flesh in the Sacrament, without bread, be-
140 cause he findes *Hoc est Corpus meum, This is my Body,* and he will
take no more of that hony, no more of those places of Scripture,
where Christ saies, *Ego vitis,* and *Ego porta,* that he is *a Vine,* and
that he is *a Gate,* as literally as he seemes to say, that *that is his Body.*
So also he can finde wormewood in this honey, because he finds in
this Scripture, *Stipendium peccati mors est,* that *The reward of sin*
is death, and he will take no more of that hony, not the *Quando-*
cunque, That at what time soever a sinner repents, he shall have
mercy. As the Essentiall word of God, the Son of God, is Light of
light, So the written Word of God is light of light too, one place of
150 Scripture takes light of another: and if thou wilt read so, and heare
so, as thine owne affections transport, and mis-lead thee; If when a
corrupt confidence in thine owne strength possesses thee, thou read
onely those passages, *Quare moriemini, domus Israel? Why will ye*
dye, O house of Israel? and conclude out of that, that thou hast such
a free will of thine owne, as that thou canst give life to thy selfe, when
thou wilt; If when a vicious dejection of spirit, and a hellish melancholy, and declination towards desperation possesses thee, thou read
only those passages, *Impossibile est, That it is impossible, that he that*
fals, after he hath beene enlightned, should be renewed againe; And
160 if thou heare Sermons so, as that thou art glad, when those sins are
declamed against, which thou art free from, but wouldst heare no
more, wouldst not have thine owne sin touched upon, though all
reading, and all hearing be honey, yet if thou take so little of this
honey, *Ionathans* case will be thy case, *Ecce, morieris,* thou wilt dye
of that hony; for the Scriptures are made to agree with one another,
but not to agree to thy particular tast and humour.

But yet, the counsell is good, on the other side too, *Hast thou found*
honey? eate so much thereof as is sufficient for thee, lest thou be filled

1 Sam.
14.27

[Joh. 15.1]
[Joh. 10.9]

[Rom. 6.23]

[Ezek.
18.31]

[Heb. 6.4, 6]

Prov. 25.16

therewith, and vomit it. Content thy selfe with reading those parts
¹⁷⁰ of Scriptures, which are cleare, and edifie, and perplex not thy selfe
with Prophesies not yet performed; and content thy selfe with hearing those Sermons, which rectifie thee *In credendis,* and *In agendis,*
in all those things, which thou art bound to beleeve, and bound to
practise, and run not after those Men, who pretend to know those
things, which God hath not revealed to his Church. Too little, or too
much of this honey, of this reading, and of this hearing, may be un-
wholesome: God hath chosen waies of mediocrity; He Redeemed us
not, by God alone, nor by man alone, but by him, who was both. He
instructs us not, by the Holy Ghost alone, without the Ministery of
¹⁸⁰ man, nor by the Minister alone, without the assistance of the Holy
Ghost. An Angel appeared to *Cornelius,* but that Angel bid him *send
for Peter:* The Holy Ghost visits us, and disposes us, but yet the Holy
Ghost sends us to the Ministery of man: *Non dedignatur docere per
hominem, qui dignatus est esse homo,* sayes S. *Augustine;* He that
came to us, as Man, is content that we go to men, for our instruction.
Preaching is the ordinary meanes; that which S. *Peter* wrought upon
them, was, *Cum locutus,* when he had, and because he had preached
unto them.

Dum 　　　　And it was also *Dum locutus est, Whilst he yet spake those words;*
locutus ¹⁹⁰ *Non permittit Spiritus absolvi Sermonem,* saies S. *Chrysostome;* The
Holy Ghost did not leave them to future meditations, to future con-
ferences, he did not stay till they told one another after the Sermon,
That it was a learned Sermon, a consciencious Sermon, a usefull Sermon, but whilst the Preacher yet spoke, the Holy Ghost spoke to their
particular consciences. And as a Gardiner takes every bough of a
young tree, or of a Vine, and leads them, and places them against a
wall, where they may have most advantage, and so produce, most,
and best fruit: So the Holy Ghost leads and places the words, and
sentences of the Preacher, one upon an Usurer, another upon an Adul-
²⁰⁰ terer, another upon an ambitious person, another upon an active or
passive Briber, when the Preacher knowes of no Usurer, no Adulterer,
no ambitious person, no Briber active or passive, in the Congregation.
Nay, it is not onely *whilst he was yet speaking,* but, as S. *Peter* him-
Ver. 15 selfe reports the same Story, in the next Chapter, *As I began to speake,
the Holy Ghost fell upon them.*

Perchance in the beginning of a Sermon, the reprehension of the Preacher fals not upon me, it is not come to me; But, when as the duties of the Preacher are expressed by the Apostle, to be these three, *To reprove,* or *convince* by argument, to settle truths, to overthrow
²¹⁰ errors; And *to exhort,* to rectifie our manners; And *to rebuke,* to denounce Gods Judgements upon the refractary; whatsoever he sayes the two first wayes, by *Convincing,* and by *Exhorting,* all that belongs to all, from the beginning; And for that which he shall say, the third way, by way of *Rebuking,* As I know at midnight, that the Sun will breake out upon me to morrow, though I know not how it works upon those places, where it shines then, So, though I know not how the rebukes of the Preacher worke upon their consciences, whose sins he rebukes at the beginning, yet I must make account that he wil meet with my sin too; and if he do not meet with my present
²²⁰ sin, that sin which is my second wife, that sin which I have married now, (not after a divorce from my former sin, so, as that I have put away that sin, but after the death of that sin, which sickness or poverty hath made me unable to continue in) yet if he bend himselfe upon that sin, which hath been my sin, or may be my sin, I must be sensible that the Holy Ghost hath offered himselfe to me, whilst he yet speaks, and ever since he began to speake; And, *Cum locutus,* Because Preaching is the ordinary meanes, and, *Dum locutus,* Because the Holy Ghost intends all for my edification, I must embrace and entertaine the Holy Ghost, who exhibits himselfe to me, from
²³⁰ the beginning, and not say, This concernes not me; for whatsoever the Preacher can say of Gods mercy in Christ Jesus to any man, all that belongs to me, for no man hath received more of that, then I may doe; And whatsoever the Preacher can say of sinne, all the way, all that belongs to me, for no man hath ever done any sin, which I should not have done, if God had left me to my selfe, and to mine own perversnesse towards sin, and to mine own insatiablenesse in sin.

It was then, when he preached, and whilst he preached, and as soone as he preached, but when, and whilst, and as soon as he preached Thus, thus as is expressed here, *Whilest hee spake these words:* In
²⁴⁰ which, we shall onely touch, but not much insist upon, his manner first, and then his matter; And for his manner, we consider onely here, his preparation, and no other circumstance. Though S. *Peter*

2 Tim. 4.2

Hæc verba

say to them, when he came, *I aske therefore, for what intent you have sent for me,* yet God had intimated to him before, That it was to Preach the Gospell to the Gentiles; And therefore some time of meditation he had; Though in such a person as S. *Peter,* so filled with all gifts necessary for his function, and to such persons as *Cornelius* was, who needed but Catechizing in the rudiments of the Gospell, much preparation needed not. The case was often of the same sort, after, 350 in the Primitive Church; The persons were very able, and the people very ignorant; and therefore it is easie to observe a far greater frequency of Preaching amongst the Ancient Fathers, then ordinarily, men that love ease, will apprehend. We see evidently in S. *Augustines* hundred forty fourth Sermon *De Tempore,* And in S. *Ambroses* forty fourth Sermon *De sancto Latrone,* And in S. *Bernards* twelve Sermons upon one Psalme, that all these blessed and Reverend Fathers, preached more then one day, divers dayes together, without intermission: And we may see in S. *Basils* second Homilie upon the six dayes worke, that he preached in the after-noone; And so, by 260 occasion of his often preaching, it seemes by his second Homilie *De Baptismo,* that he preached sometimes extemporally. But of all this, the reason is as evident as the fact, The Preachers were able to say much, The people were capable but of little: And where it was not so, the Clergy often assisted themselves with one anothers labours; as S. *Cyrils* Sermons were studied without book, and preached over againe to their severall Congregations, by almost all the Bishops of the Easterne Church. Sometimes we may see Texts extended to very many Sermons, and sometimes Texts taken of that extent and largenesse, as onely a paraphrase upon the Text would make the Sermon; 270 for we may see by S. *Augustines* tenth Sermon *De verbis Apostoli,* that they tooke sometimes the Epistle and Gospell of the day, and the Psalme before the Sermon for their text.

But in these our times, when the curiosity, (allow it a better name, for truly, God be blessed for it, it deserves a better name) when the capacity of the people requires matter of more labour, as there is not the same necessity, so there is not the same possibility of that assiduous, and that sudden preaching. No man will think that we have abler Preachers then the Primitive Church had; no man will doubt, but that we have learneder, and more capable auditories, and congrega-

²⁸⁰ tions then theirs were. The Apostles were not negligent, when they
mended their nets: A preacher is not negligent, if he prepare for
another Sermon, after he hath made one; nor a hearer is not negligent, if he meditate upon one Sermon, though he heare not another
within three houres after. S. *Peters* Sermon was not extemporall;
neither if it had (his person, and the quality of the hearers, being
compared with our times) had that been any precedent, or patterne
for our times, to do the like. But yet, Beloved, since our times are
such, as are overtaken with another necessity, that our adversaries
dare come, *Cum locutus est,* As soon as the Preacher hath done, and
²⁹⁰ meet the people comming out of the Church, and deride the Preacher,
and offer an answer to any thing that hath been said; since they are
come to come to Church with us, and *Dum locutus est,* Then when
the Preacher is speaking, to say to him, that sits next him, That is
false, that is heretical; since they are come to joyn with us at the Communion, so that it is hard to finde out the *Iudas,* and if you do finde
him, he dares answer, Your Minister is no Priest, and so your Bread
and Wine no Sacrament, and therefore I care not how much of it I
take; since they are come to boast, that with all our assiduity of
preaching, we cannot keep men from them; since it is thus, as we
³⁰⁰ were alwayes bound by Christs example, *To gather you as a hen*   [Mat. 23.37]
gathers her chickens, (to call you often to this assembling of your
selves) so are we now much more bound to hide and cover you, as
a hen doth her chickens, and because there is a Kite hovering in every
corner, (a seducer lurking in every company) to defend and arme
you, with more and more instructions against their insinuations. And
if they deride us, for often preaching, and call us fooles for that, as   [2 Sam.
David said, *He would be more vile,* he would Dance more, So let   6.22]
us be more fooles, in this foolishnesse of preaching, and preach more.   [1 Cor. 1.21]
If they think us mad, since we are mad for your soules, (as the Apostle
³¹⁰ speakes) let us be more mad; Let him that hath preached once, do it
twice, and him that hath preached twice, do it thrice. But yet, not
this, by comming to a negligent, and extemporall manner of preaching, but we will bee content to take so many hours from our rest, that
we, with you, may rest the safelyer in *Abrahams* bosome, and so many
more houres from our meat, that we, with you, may the more surely
eat, and drink with the Lamb, in the kingdome of heaven. Christ

[Mat. 24.35]
hath undertaken, that his word shall not passe away, but he hath not undertaken that it shall not passe from us: There is a *Ne exeas mundum* served upon the world, The Gospell cannot goe, nor be 320 driven out of the world, till the end of the world; but there is not a *Ne exeas regnum,* The Gospell may go out of this, or any Kingdome, if they slacken in the doing of those things which God hath ordained for the meanes of keeping it, that is, a zealous, and yet a discreet, a sober, and yet a learned assiduity in preaching.

Res
    Thus far then we have been justly carried, in consideration of this circumstance in the manner of his preaching, his preparation; In descending to the next, which is the matter of his Sermon, we see much of that in his Text. S. *Peter* tooke his Text here, *ver.* 34. out of
Deut. 10.17
Deuteronomy, Of a truth I perceive, that God is no respecter of per- 330 *sons.* Where, because the words are not precisely the same in *Deuteronomy,* as they are in this Text, we finde just occasion to note, That neither Christ in his preaching, nor the holy Ghost in penning the Scriptures of the new Testament, were so curious as our times, in citing Chapters and Verses, or such distinctions, no nor in citing the very, very words of the places. *Heb.* 4. 4. There is a sentence cited thus indefinitely, *It is written in a certaine place,* without more particular note: And, to passe over many conducing to that purpose, if
Esay 6.10
we consider that one place in the Prophet *Esay,* (*Make the heart of this people fat, make their eyes heavy, and shut them, lest they see* 340 *with their eyes, and heare with their eares, and understand with their hearts, and convert, and be healed*) and consider the same place, as it is cited six severall times in the new Testament, we shall see, that they stood not upon such exact quotations, and citing of the very words. But to that purpose, for which S. *Peter* had taken that text, he follows his text. Now, Beloved, I doe not goe about to include S. *Peters* whole Sermon into one branch, of one part, of one of mine: Only I refresh to your memories, that which I presume you have often
Ver. 34, 35
read in this Story, and this Chapter, that though S. *Peter* say, *That God is no such accepter of persons, but that in every Nation, he that* 350 *feareth him, and worketh righteousnesse, is accepted with him,* yet it is upon this ground, Christ Jesus is Lord of all; And, (as it is, *ver.* 42) *He hath commanded us to preach;* that is, he hath established a Church, and therein, visible meanes of salvation; And then, this is

Ver. 43

our generall text, the subject of all our Sermons, *That through his name, whosoever beleeveth in him shall have remission of sins.* So that this is all that we dare avow concerning salvation, that howsoever God may afford salvation to some in all nations, yet he hath manifested to us no way of conveying salvation to them, but by the manifestation of Christ Jesus in his Ordinance of preaching.

360 And such a manifestation of Christ, had God here ordained for this Centurion *Cornelius.* But why for him? I doe not ask reasons of Gods mercy to particular men; for if I would do so, when should I finde a reason, why he hath shewed mercy to me? But yet, *Audite omnes, qui in Militia estis, & Regibus assistitis,* All that serve in Wars, or Courts, may finde something to imitate in this Centurion: *He was a devout man;* A Souldier, and yet devout; God forbid they were so incompatible, as that courage, and devotion might not consist: *A man that feared God;* A Souldiers profession is fearlesnesse; And only he that feares God, feares nothing else: *He and all his house;* A Souldier,
370 yet kept a house, and did not alwayes wander; He kept his house in good order, and with good meanes: *He gave much almes;* Though Armes be an expensive profession for outward splendor, yet he reserved for almes, much almes: *And he prayed to God alwayes;* Though Armes require much time for the duties thereof, yet he could pray at those times; In his Trenches, at the Assault, or at the defence of a Breach, he could pray: All this the holy Ghost testifies of him together, *ver.* 2. And this was his generall disposition; and then, those who came from him to *Peter,* adde this, *That he had a good report amongst all the Nation of the Iews, ver.* 22. And this to a
380 stranger, (for the Jews loved not strangers) and one that served the State, in such a place, as that he could not choose but be heavy to the Jews, was hard to have. And then, himself, when *Peter* comes to him, addes thus much more, That this first mercy of God in having sent his Angel, and that farther mercy, that that Angel named a man, and then that man came, was exhibited to him, then, when he was fasting. And then, this man, thus humbled and macerated by fasting, thus soupled and entendered with the feare of God, thus burnt up and calcined with zeal and devotion, thus united to God by continuall prayer, thus tributary to God by giving almes, thus exemplar in him-
390 self at home, to lead all his house, and thus diffusive of himselfe to

Chrysost.

Ver. 30

others abroad, to gain the love of good men, this man prostrates himselfe to *Peter* at his comming, in such an over-reverentiall manner,
as *Peter* durst not accept, but took him up, and said, *I my selfe am*
also a man; Sudden devotion comes quickly neare superstition.

Ver. 26

This is a misery, which our time hath been well acquainted with,
and had much experience of, and which grows upon us still, That
when men have been mellowed with the feare of God, and by heavy
corrections, and calamities, brought to a greater tendernesse of conscience then before, in that distemper of melancholy, and inordinate
⁴⁰⁰ sadnesse, they have been easiliest seduced and withdrawne to a superstitious and Idolatrous religion. I speak this, because from the highest
to the lowest place, there are Sentinels planted in every corner, to
watch all advantages, and if a man lose his preferment at Court, or
lose his childe at home, or lose any such thing as affects him much,
and imprints a deep sadnesse for the losse thereof, they work upon
that sadnesse, to make him a Papist. When men have lived long from
God, they never think they come neare enough to him, except they
go beyond him; because they have never offered to come to him before, now when they would come, they imagine God to be so hard
⁴¹⁰ of accesse, that there is no comming to him, but by the intervention,
and intercession of Saints; and they thinke that that Church, in
which they have lived ill, cannot be a good Church; whereas, if they
would accustome themselves in a daily performing of Christian duties, to an ordinary presence of God, Religion would not be such a
stranger, nor devotion such an Ague unto them. But when *Peter* had
rectified *Cornelius,* in this mistaking, in this over-valuing of any
person, and then saw *Cornelius* his disposition, who had brought
materials to erect a Church in his house, by calling his kinsmen, and
his friends together to heare *Peter, Peter* spoke those words, *Which*
⁴²⁰ *whilest he yet spake, the holy Ghost fell upon all them that heard the*
word. And so we are fallen into our second part.

2 Part

In this, the first Consideration falls upon the person that fell: And
as the Trinity is the most mysterious piece of our Religion, and hardest to be comprehended, So in the Trinity, the Holy Ghost is the
most mysterious person, and hardest to be expressed. We are called

[Eph. 2.19]
[Gal. 6.10]

the houshold of God, and the family of the faithfull; and therefore
out of a contemplation, and ordinary acquaintance with the parts

of families, we are apter to conceive any such thing in God himself,
as we see in a family. We seeme not to goe so farre out of our way
430 of reason, to beleeve a father, and a son, because father and son are
pieces of families: nor in beleeving Christ and his Church, because
husband and wife are pieces of families. We goe not so farre in beleeving Gods working upon us, either by ministring spirits from
above, or by his spirituall ministers here upon earth, for master and
servants are pieces of families. But does there arise any such thing,
out of any of these couples, Father and Son, Husband and Wife,
Master and Servant, as should come from them, and they be no whit
before neither? Is there any thing in naturall or civill families, that
should assist our understanding to apprehend this, That in heaven
440 there should be a Holy Spirit, so, as that the Father, and the Son,
being all Spirit, and all Holy, and all Holinesse, there should be another Holy Spirit, which had all their Essentiall holiness in him, and
another holinesse too, *Sanctitatem Sanctificantem,* a holinesse, that
should make us holy?

It was a hard work for the Apostles, and their successors, at first,
to draw the Godhead, into one, into an unity: when the Gentiles had
been long accustomed to make every power and attribute of God,
and to make every remarkable creature of God a severall God, and
so to worship God in a multiplicity of Gods, it was a great work to
450 limit, and determine their superstitious, and superfluous devotion in
one God. But when all these lines were brought into one center, not
to let that center rest, but to draw lines out of that againe, and bring
more persons into that one centricall God-head, this was hard for
reason to digest: But yet to have extended that from that unity, to a
duality, was not so much, as to a triplicity. And thereupon, though
the Arians would never be brought to confesse an equality between
the Son and the Father, they were much farther from confessing it
in the Holy Ghost: They made, sayes S. *Augustine, Filium creaturam,*   Hæres. 49
The Son, they accounted to be but a creature; but they made the Holy
460 Ghost *Creaturam Creaturæ,* not onely a Creature, and no God, but
not a Creature of Gods, but a Creature, a Messenger of the Son, who
was himselfe (with them) but a Creature. But these mysteries are
not to be chawed by reason, but to be swallowed by faith; we professed three persons in one God, in the simplicity of our infancy, at

our baptisme, and we have sealed that contract, in the other Sacrament often since; and this is eternall life, to die in that beliefe. *There
are three that beare witnesse in heaven, The Father, the Word, and
the Holy Ghost, and these three are one;* And in that testimony we
rest, that there is a Holy Ghost, and in the testimony of this text, that
⁴⁷⁰ this Holy Ghost falls down upon all that heare the word of God.

Now, it is as wonderfull that this Holy Ghost should fall down
from heaven, as that he should be in heaven. *Quomodo cecidisti?
How art thou fallen from heaven, O Lucifer, thou son of the morning?* was a question asked by the Prophet, of him, who was so fallen,
as that he shall never returne againe. But the Holy Ghost, (as mysterious in his actions, as in his Essentiall, or in his Personall beeing)
fell so from heaven, as that he remained in heaven, even then when
he was fallen. This Dove sent from heaven, did more then that Dove,
which was sent out of the Arke; That went and came, but was not in
⁴⁸⁰ both places at once; *Noah* could not have shewed that Dove to his
sons and daughters, in the Arke, then, when the Dove was flowne
out: But now, when this Dove, the Holy Ghost, fell upon these men,
at *Peters* Sermon, *Stephen,* who was then come up to heaven, saw
the same Dove, the same Holy Ghost, whom they, whom he had left
upon the earth, felt upon the earth then: As if the Holy Ghost fall
upon any in this Congregation now, now the Saints of God see that
Holy Ghost in heaven, whom they that are here, feele falling upon
them here. In all his workings, the Holy Ghost descends, for there
is nothing above him. There is a third heaven; but no such third
⁴⁹⁰ heaven, as is above the heaven of heavens, above the seat and residence
of the Holy Ghost: so that whatsoever he doth, is a descent, a diminution, a humiliation, and an act of mercy, because it is a Communication of himselfe, to a person inferiour to himselfe.

But there is more in this Text, then a descent. When the Holy
Ghost came upon Christ himselfe, after his Baptisme, there it is said,
He descended: Though Christ as the Son of God, were equall to him,
and so it was no descent for the Holy Ghost to come to him, yet because Christ had a nature upon him, in which he was not equall to
the Holy Ghost, here was a double descent in the Holy Ghost, That
⁵⁰⁰ he who dwells with the Father and the Son, *In luce inaccessibili,*
In light inaccessible, and too bright to be seene, would descend in a

1 John 5.7

Cecidit

Esay 14.12

Gen. 8.8

[Mat. 3.16]

[1 Tim.
6.16]

visible form, to be seene by men, And that he descended and wrought
upon a mortall man, though that man were Christ. Christ also had a
double descending too; He descended to be a man, and he descended
to be no man; He descended to live amongst us, and he descended
to die amongst us; He descended to the earth, and he descended to
hell: Every operation of every person of the holy, and blessed, and
glorious Trinity, is a Descending; But here the Holy Ghost is said
to have fallen, which denotes a more earnest communicating of him-
510 selfe, a throwing, a pouring out of himselfe, upon those, upon whom
he falls: He falls as a fall of waters, that covers that it falls upon; as
a Hawk upon a prey, it desires and it will possesse that it falls upon;
as an Army into a Countrey, it Conquers, and it Governes where it
fals. The Holy Ghost fals, but farre otherwise, upon the ungodly. *Who-*
soever shall fall upon this stone, shall be broken, but upon whomsoever   Mat. 21.44
this stone shall fall, it will grinde him to powder. Indeed, he fals upon
him so, as haile fals upon him; he fals upon him so, as he fals from him,
and leaves him in an obduration, and impenitiblenesse, and in an irrecoverable ruine of him, that hath formerly despised, and despighted the
520 Holy Ghost. But when the Holy Ghost fals not thus in the nature of a
stone, but puts on the nature of a Dove, and a Dove with an Olive-
branch, and that in the Ark, that is, testimonies of our peace, and reconciliation to God, in his Church, he fals as that kinde of lightning, which
melts swords, and hurts not scabbards; the Holy Ghost shall melt thy
soule, and not hurt thy body; he shall give thee spirituall blessings,
and saving graces, under the temporall seales of bodily health, and
prosperity in this world: He shall let thee see, that thou art the childe
of God, in the obedience of thy children to thee, And that thou art the
servant of God, in the faithfulnesse of thy servants to thee, And that
530 thou standest in the favour of God, by the favor of thy superiours to
thee; he shall fall upon thy soul, and not wound thy body, give thee
spirituall prosperity, and yet not by worldly adversity, and evermore
over-shadow and refresh thy soul, and yet evermore keep thee in his
Sunshine, and the light of his countenance.

But there is more then this, in this falling of the Holy Ghost, in this
Text. For, it was not such a particular insinuation of the Holy Ghost,
as that he convaied himselfe into those particular men, for their particular good, and salvation, and determined there; but such a power-

full, and diffusive falling, as made his presence, and his power in
540 them, to work upon others also. So when he came upon Christ, it was
not to adde any thing to Christ, but to informe others, that that was
Christ: So when Christ breathed his spirit into the Apostles, it was not
meerly to infuse salvation into them, but it was especially to seale to
[Joh. 20.23]   them that Patent, that Commission, *Quorum remiseritis,* That others
might receive remission of sins, by their power. So the Holy Ghost
fell upon these men here, for the benefit of others, that thereby a
great doubt might be removed, a great scruple devested, a great disputation extinguished, whether it were lawfull to preach the Gospel
to the Gentiles, or no; for, as we see in the next Chapter, *Peter* him
Ver. 2   550 selfe was reproved of the Jews, for this that he had done: and therefore, God ratified, and gave testimony to this service of his, by this
miraculous falling of the Holy Ghost, as S. *Augustine* makes the
reason of this falling, very justly to have been; so then, this falling
of the Holy Ghost, was not properly, or not meerly an infusing of
justifying grace, but an infusing of such gifts, as might edifie others:
for, S. *Peter* speaking of this very action, in the next Chapter, sayes,
Ver. 15   *The Holy Ghost fell on them, as on us, in the beginning;* Which was,
when he fell upon them, as this day. This doth not imply *Graduum*
æqualitatem, an equall measure of the same gifts, as the Apostles had,
560 who were to passe over the whole world, and work upon all men, But
it implies *Doni identitatem,* it was the same miraculous expressing of
the presence, and working of the Holy Ghost, for the confirmation of
Peter, that the Gentiles might be preached unto, and for the consolation of the Gentiles, that they might be enabled to preach to one
Ver. 46   another: for so it is expresly said in this Chapter, *That they heard these*
men speake with divers tongues; they that heard the Preacher, were
made partakers of the same gifts that the Preacher had; A good hearer
becomes a good Preacher, that is, able to edifie others.

It is true, that these men were not to be literally Preachers, as the
570 Apostles (upon whom the Holy Ghost fell, as upon them) were, and
therefore the gift of tongues may seeme not to have beene so necessary
to them. But it is not onely the Preacher, that hath use of the tongue,
for the edification of Gods people, but in all our discourses, and con-
ferences with one another, we should preach his glory, his goodnesse,

his power, that every man might speake one anothers language, and
preach to one anothers conscience; that when I accuse my selfe, and
confesse mine infirmities to another man, that man may understand,
that there is, in that confession of mine, a Sermon, and a rebuke, and
a reprehension to him, if he be guilty of the same sin; Nay, if he be
580 guilty of a sin contrary to mine. For, as in that language in which
God spoke, the Hebrew, the same roote will take in words of a contrary signification, (as the word of *Iobs* wife signifies blessing and
cursing too) so the covetous man that heares me confesse my prodigality, should argue to himself, If prodigality, which howsoever it
hurt a particular person, yet spreads mony abroad, which is the right
and naturall use of money, be so heavy a sin, how heavy is my
covetousnesse, which, besides that it keepes me all the way in as
much penuriousnesse, as the prodigall man brings himselfe to at last,
is also a publique sin, because it emprisons that money which should
590 be at liberty, and employed in a free course abroad? And so also when
I declare to another, the spirituall and temporall blessings which God
hath bestowed upon me, he may be raised to a thankfull remembrance,
that he hath received all that from God also. This is not the use of
having learnt divers tongues, to be able to talk of the wars with
Dutch Captains, or of trade with a French Merchant, or of State with
a Spanish Agent, or of pleasure with an Italian Epicure; It is not to
entertaine discourse with strangers, but to bring strangers to a better
knowledge of God, in that way, wherein we, by his Ordinance, do
worship and serve him.

600 Now this place is ill detorted by the Roman Church, for the confirmation of their Sacrament of Confirmation: That because the Holy
Ghost fell upon men, at another time then at Baptisme, therefore
there is a lesse perfect giving of the Holy Ghost, in Baptisme. It is too
forward a triumph in him, who sayes of this place, *Locus insignis ad
assertionem Sacramenti manus impositionis:* That is an evident place
for Confirmation of the Sacrament of Confirmation: It is true, that
S. *Cyprian* sayes there, That a man is not truly sanctified, *Nisi utroque
Sacramento nascatur,* Except he be regenerate by both Sacraments:
And he tels us what those two Sacraments are, *Aqua & Spiritus,*
610 Water and the Spirit, That except a man have both these seales,

[Job 2.9]

Pamelius
Annot. in
Cypr.
Epist. 72

inward and outward, he is not safe: And S. *Cyprian* requires (and usefully truly) an outward declaration of this inward seale, of this giving of the Holy Ghost: For, he instances expresly in this, which was done in this Text, That there was both Baptisme, and a giving of the Holy Ghost. Neither would S. *Cyprian* forbeare the use of Confirmation, because it was also in use amongst some Heretiques,

Cypr.
Epist. 72

Quia Novatianus facere audet, non putabimus nos esse faciendum? Shall we give over a good custome, because the Novatians doe the like? *Quia Novatianus extra Ecclesiam, vendicat sibi veritatis im-* ⁶²⁰ *aginem, relinquemus Ecclesiæ veritatem?* Shall the Church forebeare any of those customes, which were induced to good purposes, because some Heretiques, in a false Church, have counterfaited them, or corrupted them? And therefore, sayes that Father, It was so in the Apostles time, *Et nunc quoque apud nos geritur,* We continue it so in our time, That they who are Baptized, *Signaculo Dominico consummentur,* That they may have a ratification, a consummation in this seale of the Holy Ghost: Which was not in the Primitive Church (as in the later Roman Church) a confirmation of Baptisme, so, as that that Sacrament should be but a halfe-Sacrament, but it was a ⁶³⁰ Confirmation of Christians, with an encrease of grace, when they came to such yeares, as they were naturally exposed to some tentations.

Our Church acknowledges the true use of this Confirmation; for, in the first Collect in the office of Confirmation, it confesses, that that child is already regenerated by water and the holy Ghost; and prayes onely for farther strength: And having like a good mother, taught us the right use of it, then our Church, like a supreme Commander too, enjoyns expresly, that none be admitted to the Communion, till they have received their Confirmation. And though this injunction be not in rigour and exactnesse pursued and executed, yet it is very ⁶⁴⁰ necessary that the purpose thereof should be maintained; That is, that none should be received to the Communion, till they had given an account of their faith and proficiencie. For, he is but an interpretative, but a presumptive Christian, who, because he is so old, ventures upon the Sacrament. A beard does not make a man fit for the Sacrament, nor a Husband, a woman: a man may be a great officer in the State, and a woman may be a grandmother in the family, and yet not be fit for that Sacrament, if they have never considered more in it, but onely to doe as others doe. The Church enjoynes a precedent Confirmation; where that is not, wee require yet a precedent Examination, before any bee admitted, at first, to the Sacrament.

    This was then the effectuall working of the Holy Ghost, *Non spiravit,* He did not only breathe upon them, and try whether they would receive the savour of life unto life, or no: *Non sibilavit,* He did not onely whisper unto them, and try whether they had a disposition to heare, and answer; *Non incubabat,* He did not onely hover over them, and sit upon them, to try what he could hatch, and produce out of them; *Non descendit,* He did not onely descend towards them, and try whether they would reach out their hand to receive him; But *Cecidit,* He fell, so, as that he possessed them, enwrapped them, invested them with a penetrating, with a powerfull force; And so, he fell upon them All. As we have read of some Generals, in secular story, that in great Services have knighted their whole Army, So the Holy Ghost Sanctifies, and Canonizes whole Congregations.

    They are too good husbands, and too thrifty of Gods grace, too sparing of the Holy Ghost; that restraine Gods generall propositions, *Venite omnes,* Let all come, and *Vult omnes salvos,* God would have all men saved, so particularly, as to say, that when God sayes *All,* he meanes some of all sorts, some Men, some Women, some Jews, some Gentiles, some rich, some poore, but he does not meane, as he seemes to say, simply All. Yes; God does meane, simply All, so as that no man can say to another, God meanes not thee, no man can say to himselfe, God meanes not me. *Nefas est dicere, Deum aliquid, nisi bonum prædestinare;* It is modestly said by S. *Augustine,* and more were immodesty; There is no predestination in God, but to good. And therefore it is *Durus sermo,* They are hard words, to say, That God predestinated some, not onely *Ad damnationem,* but *Ad causas damnationis,* Not onely to damnation because they sinned, but to a necessity of sinning, that they might the more justly be damned; And to say, That God rejected some *Odio libero,* Out of a hate, that arose primarily in himselfe, against those persons, before those persons were created, (so much as in Gods intention) and not out of any hate of their sins, which he foresaw.

    Beloved, we are to take in no other knowledge of Gods Decrees, but

Marginal notes:

Super omnes
[Gen. 2.7]
[2 Cor. 2.16]
[Isa. 5.26]
[Gen. 1.2]

[Mat. 11.28]
[1 Tim. 2.4]

Line numbers: 650, 660, 670, 680

by the execution thereof; How should we know any Decree in God, of the creation of Man, according to his Image, but by the execution? Because I see that Man is created so, as I conceive to be intended in this phrase, *After his Image,* I beleeve that he Decreed to Create him so: because God does nothing extemporally, but according to his 690 owne most holy, and eternall preconceptions, and Ideas, and Decrees. So, we know his Decree of Election, and Reprobation, by the execution; And how is that? Does God ever say, that any shall be saved or damned, without relation, without condition, without doing, (in the Old Testament) and, in the New Testament, without beleeving in Christ Jesus? If faith in Christ Jesus be in the Execution of the Decree, faith in Christ Jesus was in the Decree it selfe too. Christ wept for the imminent calamities, temporall, and spirituall, which hung over Jerusalem; And *Lacrymæ Legati doloris,* saies S. *Cyprian,* Teares are the Ambassadours of sorrow; And they are *Sanguis animi vul-*700 *nerati,* saies S. *Augustine,* Teares are the bloud of a wounded soule; And would Christ bleed out of a wounded soule, and weepe out of a sad heart, for that, which himselfe, and onely himselfe, by an absolute Decree, had made necessary and inevitable? *The Scribes and Pharisees rejected the Counsell of God,* sayes S. *Luke:* In this new language we must say, They fulfilled the Counsell of God, if positively, and primarily, and absolutely, Gods determinate Counsell were, that they should do so. But this is not Gods Counsaile upon any, to be so far the Author of sin, as to impose such a necessity of sinning, as arises not out of his owne will. *Perditio nostra ex nobis,*710 Our destruction is from our owne sin, and the Devill that infuses it; not from God, or any ill purpose in him that enforces us. The blood of Christ was shed for all that will apply it, And the Holy Ghost is willing to fall, with the sprinkling of that blood, upon all that do not resist him; And that is, as follows in our text, *Qui audiunt,* The Holy Ghost fell upon all that heard.

Faith in Christ is in the Execution of Gods Decree, and Hearing is the meanes of this faith: And the proposition is not the lesse generall, if it except them, who will not be included in it, if the Holy Ghost fall not on them, who will not come to heare. Let no man 720 thinke that he hath heard enough, and needs no more; why did the

[Gen. 1.27]

Luke 7.30

Qui audiunt

Holy Ghost furnish his Church with foure Euangelists, if it were enough to reade one? And yet every one of the foure, hath enough for salvation, if Gods abundant care had not enriched the Church with more: Those Nations which never heard of Christ, or of Euangelist, shall rise up in judgement against us, and though they perish themselves, thus far aggravate our condemnation, as to say, you had foure Euangelists, and have not beleeved, if we had had any one of them, we would have been saved. It is the glory of Gods Word, not that it is come, but that it shall remain for ever: It is the glory of a
730 Christian, not that he hath heard, but that he desires to heare still. Are the Angels weary of looking upon that face of God, which they looked upon yesterday? Or are the Saints weary of singing that song, which they sung to Gods glory yesterday? And is not that *Alleluiah,* that song which is their morning and evening sacrifice, and which shall be their song, world without end, called still *A new song?*   [Rev. 5.9]

Be not you weary of hearing those things which you have heard from others before: Do not say, if I had knowne this, I would not have come, for I have heard all this before; since thou never thoughtest of it since that former hearing, till thou heardst it again now,
740 thou didst not know that thou hadst heard it before. *Gideons* Fleece,   Iud. 6.37 that had all the dew of heaven in it self alone, and all about it dry, one day, next day was all dry in it self, though all about it had received the dew: He that hath heard, and beleeved, may lose his knowledge, and his faith too, if he will heare no more. They say there is a way of castration, in cutting off the eares: There are certain veines behinde the eares, which, if they be cut, disable a man from generation. The Eares are the Aqueducts of the water of life; and if we cut off those, that is, intermit our ordinary course of hearing, this is a castration of the soul, the soul becomes an Eunuch, and we grow to a rust, to
750 a mosse, to a barrennesse, without fruit, without propagation. If then God have placed thee under such a Pastor, as presents thee variety, blesse God, who enlarges himselfe, to afford thee that spirituall delight, in that variety; even for the satisfaction of that holy curiosity of thine. If he have placed thee under one, who often repeats, and often remembers thee of the same things, blesse God even for that, that in that he hath let thee see, that the Christian religion is *Verbum*

abbreviatum, A contracted doctrine, and that they are but a few things which are necessary to salvation, and therefore be not loath to heare them often.

Verbum   760   Our errand hither then, is not to see; but much lesse not to be able to see, to sleep: It is not to talk, but much lesse to snort: It is to heare, and to heare all the words of the Preacher, but, to heare in those words, the Word, that Word which is the soule of all that is said, and is the true Physick of all their soules that heare. *The Word was made flesh;* that is, assumed flesh; but yet the Godhead was not that flesh. The Word of God is made a Sermon, that is, a Text is dilated, diffused into a Sermon; but that whole Sermon is not the word of God. But yet all the Sermon is the Ordinance of God. *De-*

[Psa. 37.4]   *light thy self in the Lord, and he will give thee thy hearts desire;*
770   Take a delight in Gods Ordinance, in mans preaching, and thou wilt finde Gods Word in that. To end all in that Metaphor which we mentioned at beginning, As the word of God is as hony, so sayes

Prov. 16.24   *Solomon, Pleasant words are as the hony combe:* And when the pleasant words of Gods servants have conveyed the saving word of God himselfe into thy soule, then maist thou say with Christ to the

Cant. 5.1   Spouse, *I have eaten my hony combe with my hony,* mine understanding is enlightned with the words of the Preacher, and my faith is strengthned with the word of God; I glorifie God much in the gifts of the man, but I glorifie God much more in the gifts of his grace;
780   I am glad I have heard him, but I am gladder I have heard God in him; I am happy that I have heard those words, but thrice happy, that in those words, I have heard the Word; Blessed be thou that

[Psa. 118.26]   camest in the name of the Lord, but blessed be the Lord, that is come to me in thee; Let me remember how the Preacher said it, but let me remember rather what he said. And beloved, all the best of us all, all that all together, all the dayes of our life shall be able to say unto you, is but this, That if ye will heare the same Jesus, in the same Gospell, by the same Ordinance, and not seeke an imaginary Jesus, in an illusory sacrifice, in another Church, If you will heare so, as
790   you have contracted with God in your Baptisme, The holy Ghost shall fall upon you, whilest you heare, here in the house of God, and the holy Ghost shall accompany you home to your own houses, and make your domestique peace there, a type of your union with God

in heaven; and make your eating and drinking there, a type of the
abundance, and fulnesse of heaven; and make every dayes rising to
you there, a type of your joyfull Resurrection to heaven; and every
nights rest, a type of your eternall Sabbath; and your very dreames,
prayers, and meditations, and sacrifices to Almighty God.

Number 2.

Preached upon Whitsunday.

[? At St. Paul's, 1622]

ROM. 8.16. *THE SPIRIT IT SELFE BEARETH WITNESSE WITH OUR SPIRIT, THAT WE ARE THE CHILDREN OF GOD,*

I TAKE these words, to take occasion by them, to say something of the holy Ghost: Our order proposed at first, requires it, and our Text affords it. Since we speak by Him, let us love to speak of Him, and to speak for Him: but in both, to speak with Him, that is, so, as he hath spoken of himselfe to us in the Scriptures. God will be visited, but he will not be importuned; He will be looked upon, but he will not be pryed into. A man may flatter the best man; If he do not beleeve himself, when he speaks well of another, and when he praises him, though that which he sayes of him be true, yet he flat-
¹⁰ ters; So an Atheist, that temporises, and serves the company, and seemes to assent, flatters. A man may flatter the Saints in heaven, if he attribute to them that which is not theirs; and so a Papist flatters. A man may flatter God himself; If upon pretence of magnifying Gods mercy, he will say with *Origen,* That God at last will have mercy upon the devill, he flatters. So, though God be our businesse, we may be too busie with God; and though God be infinite, we may go beyond God, when we conceive, or speak otherwise of God, then God hath revealed unto us. By his own light therefore we shall look upon him; and with that reverence, and modesty, that *That Spirit*
²⁰ *may beare witnesse to our spirit, that we are the children of God.*

Divisio   That which we shall say of these words, will best be conceived, and retained best, if we handle them thus; That whereas Christ hath

58

bidden us to judge our selves, that we be not judged, to admit a triall [Mat. 7.1]
here, lest we incurre a condemnation hereafter, This text is a good
part of that triall, of that judiciall proceeding. For, here are first, two
persons that are able to say much, *The Spirit it self,* and *Our spirit;*
And secondly, their office, their service, *They beare witnesse;* And
thirdly, their testimony, *That we are the children of God;* And these
will be our three parts. The first will have two branches, because there
³⁰ are two persons, *The Spirit,* and *Our spirit;* And the second, two
branches, *They witnesse,* and *They witnesse together,* for so the
word is; And the third also two branches, They testifie of us, their
testimony concernes us, and they testifie well of us, *That we are the*
children of God. The persons are without exception, the Spirit of
God cannot be deceived, and the spirit of man will not deceive himself: Their proceeding is Legall, and faire, they do not libell, they
do not whisper, they do not calumniate; They testifie, and they agree
in their testimony: And lastly, the case is not argued so, as amongst
practisers at the Law, that thereby, by the light of that they may after
⁴⁰ give Counsell to another in the like, but the testimony concernes our
selves, it is our own case. The verdict upon the testimony of the Spirit,
and our spirit, is upon our selves, whatsoever it bee; And, blessed be
the Father, in the Son, by the Holy Ghost, The verdict is, *That we*
are the children of God. The Spirit beareth, &c.

First then, a slacknesse, a supinenesse, in consideration of the divers   1 Part
significations of this word *Spirit,* hath occasioned divers errours, when
the word hath been intended in one sense, and taken in another. All
the significations will fall into these foure, for these foure are very
large; It is spoken of God, or of Angels, or of men, or of inferiour
⁵⁰ creatures. And first, of God, it is spoken sometimes Essentially, sometimes Personally. *God is a Spirit, and they that worship him, must*   Iohn 4.24
worship him in spirit and truth. So also, *The Ægyptians are men,*   Esay 31.3
and not God, and their horses flesh, and not spirit; For, if they were
God, they were Spirit. So, God altogether, and considered in his
Essence, is a Spirit: but when the word *Spirit* is spoken, not essentially of all, but personally of one, then that word designeth *Spiritum*
sanctum, The holy Ghost: *Goe and baptize, In the name of the Father,*   Mat. 28.19
and Sonne, & Spiritus sancti, and the holy Ghost. And as of God, so
of Angels also it is spoken in two respects; of good Angels, *Sent forth*   Heb. 1.14

⁶⁰ *to minister for them, that shall be heires of salvation,* And evill An-
gels, *The lying Spirit,* that would deceive the King by the Prophet;
The Spirit of Whoredome, spirituall whoredome, when the people
ask counsell of their stocks, And *Spiritus vertiginis, The spirit of giddinesse, of perversities,* (as we translate it) which the Lord doth
mingle amongst the people, in his judgement. Of man also, is this
word Spirit, spoken two wayes; The Spirit is sometimes the soule,
Into thy hands I commend my Spirit, sometimes it signifies those
animall spirits, which conserve us in strength, and vigour, *The poyson of Gods arrowes drinketh up my spirit;* And also, the superiour
⁷⁰ faculties of the soule in a regenerate man, as there, *My soule doth
magnifie the Lord, and my spirit rejoyceth in God my Saviour.* And
then lastly, of inferiour creatures it is taken two wayes too, of living
creatures, *The God of the spirits of all flesh;* and of creatures without
life, (other then a metaphoricall life) as of the winde often, and of
Ezekiels wheeles, *The Spirit of life was in the wheeles.* Now in this
first Branch of this first Part of our Text, it is not of Angels, nor of
men, nor of other creatures, but of God, and not of God Essentially,
but Personally, that is, of the Holy Ghost.

    Origen sayes, *Antecessores nostri,* The Ancients before him had
⁸⁰ made this note, That where we finde the word *Spirit* without any
addition, it is alwayes intended of the *Holy Ghost.* Before him, and
after him, they stuck much to that note; for S. *Hierome* makes it too,
and produces many examples thereof; but yet it will not hold in all.
Didymus of *Alexandria,* though borne blinde, in this light saw light,
and writ so of the Holy Ghost, as S. *Hierome* thought that work
worthy of his Translation; And hee gives this note, That wheresoever
the Apostles intend the *Holy Ghost,* they adde to the word *Spirit,
Sanctus, Holy Spirit,* or at least the Article *The, The Spirit.* And this
note hath good use too, but yet it is not universally true. If we supply
⁹⁰ these notes with this, That whensoever any such thing is said of the
Spirit, as cannot consist with the Divine nature, there it is not meant
of the Holy Ghost, but of his gifts, or of his working; (as, when it is
said, *The Holy Ghost was not yet,* (for his person was alwayes) And
where it is said, *Quench not the Holy Ghost* (for the Holy Ghost
himselfe cannot be quenched) we have enough for our present purpose. Here, it is *Spirit* without any addition, and therefore fittest to

1 King.
22.22
Hosea 4.12
Esay 19.14

Psal. 31.5

Job 6.4

Luke
1.[46,] 47

Numb.
16.22
Ezek. 1.21

Iohn 7.39
1 Thess.
5.19

bee taken for the *Holy Ghost;* And it is *Spirit,* with that emphaticall article, *The, The Spirit,* and in that respect also fittest to be so taken. And though it be fittest to understand the Holy Ghost here, not of his person, but his operation, yet it gives just occasion to looke piously, and to consider modestly, who, and what this person is, that doth thus worke upon us. And to that purpose, we shall touch upon foure things: First, His Universality, He is All, He is God; Secondly, His Singularity, He is One, One Person; Thirdly, His roote from whence he proceeded, Father and Son; And fourthly, His growth, his emanation, his manner of proceeding: for our order proposed at first, leading us now to speak of this third person of the Trinity, it will be almost necessary, to stop a little upon each of these.

First then, the Spirit mentioned here, the Holy Ghost is God, and if so, equall to Father and Son, and all that is God. He is God, because the Essentiall name of God is attributed to him; He is called Jehovah; *Iehovah sayes to Esay, Goe and tell this people, &c.* And S. *Paul* making use of these words, in the *Acts,* he sayes, *Well spake the Holy Ghost, by the Prophet Esay.* The Essentiall name of God is attributed to him, and the Essentiall Attributes of God. He is Eternall; so is none but God; where we heare of the making of every thing else, in the generall Creation, we heare that *the Spirit of God moved,* but never that the Spirit was made. He is every where; so is none but God; *whither shall I goe from thy Spirit?* He knowes all things; so doth none but God; *The Spirit searcheth all things, yea the deep things of God.* He hath the name of God, the Attributes of God, and he does the works of God. Is our Creator, our Maker, God? *The Spirit of God hath made me.* Is he that can change the whole Creation, and frame of nature, in doing miracles, God? *The Spirit lead the Israelites miraculously through the wildernesse.* Will the calling and the sending of the Prophets, shew him to be God? *The Lord God, and his Spirit hath sent me.* Is it argument enough for his God-head, that he sent Christ himselfe? Christ himselfe applies to himselfe that, *The Spirit of the Lord is upon me, and hath anointed me to preach.* He foretold future things, *The Holy Ghost by the mouth of David spoke before,* sayes S. *Peter.* He establishes present things, *The Spirit of truth guides into all truth.* And he does this, by wayes proper onely to God; for, our illumination is his, *He shall re-*

Deus

Esay 6.9

Acts 28.25

Gen. 1.2

Psal. 139.7
1 Cor. 2.10

Iob 33.4

Esay 63.14

Esay 48.16

Esay 61.1
Luke 4.18
Acts 1.16
Iohn 16.13
Ver. 14

ceive of me, (sayes Christ) *and shew it you.* Our Justification is his;

1 Cor. 6.11

Iohn 3.5

Iohn 16.8

Acts 9.31

Rom. 8.11

2 Cor. 1.22

Eph. 1.13
Iohn 4.14

Mat. 3.11
Zach. 12.10
Heb. 1.9

Rom. 8.26

Iohn 16.7

August.

1 Cor. 12.4

1 Cor. 6.17

Persona

Ye are justified, in the name of the Lord Iesus, by the Spirit of God. Our regeneration is his; There is a necessity of being *borne againe of Water, and the Spirit.* The holy sense of our naturall wretchednesse is his; For, *It is he, that reproves the world of Sin, of Righteousnesse, of Iudgement.* The sense of true comfort is his; *The Churches were*
140 *multiplied in the comforts of the Holy Ghost.* All from the Creation to the Resurrection, and the Resurrection it selfe, is his; *The Spirit of him that raised Iesus from the dead, shall quicken your mortall bodies, by the same Spirit.* He is *Arrha,* The earnest that God gives to them now, to whom he will give all hereafter. He is *Sigillum,* that seale of our evidence, *You are sealed with that holy Spirit of promise.* He is *the water, which whosoever drinks, shall never thirst,* when Christ hath given it; And he is that fire, with which Christ baptizes, *who baptizes with fire, and with the Holy Ghost.* He is *Spiritus precum,* The Spirit of grace, and supplication; And he is *Oleum*
150 *lætitiæ,* The oyle of gladnesse, that anoints us, when we have prayed. He is our Advocate, *He maketh intercession for us, with groanings which cannot be uttered;* And when our groanings under the calamities of this world, are uttered without remedy, he is that *Paracletus,* The Comforter, who when Christ himselfe seemes to be gone from us, comes to us; who is, (as *Tertullian* expresses it, elegantly enough, but not largely enough) *Dei Villicus, & Vicaria vis Christi,* The Vicegerent of Christ, and the Steward of God; but he is more, much more, infinitely more, for he is God himselfe. All that which S. *Iohn* intends, in the *seaven Spirits,* which are about the Throne, is in this
160 *One,* in this onely Spirit, who is *Vnicus & septiformis, solus & multiplex;* One and yet seaven, that is infinite; for, *Though there be diversity of gifts, yet there is but one Spirit.* He is God, because the essentiall name of God is his; Therefore let us call upon his name: And because the Attributes of God are his; Therefore let us attribute to him, All Might, Majesty, Dominion, Power, and Glory: And he is God, because the Works of God are his; Therefore let us co-operate, and work with this Spirit, and we shall be the same Spirit with him.

He is God, That was our first step, and our second is, that he is a
170 distinct Person in the God-head. He is not *Virtus à Deo in homine*

exaltata, Not the highest and powerfullest working of God in man; Not *Afflatus Divinus,* The breathing of God into the soule of man; These are low expressions; for they are all but *Dona, Charismata,* The gifts of the Holy Ghost, not the Holy Ghost himselfe: But he is a distinct person, as the taking of the shape of a Dove, and the shape of fiery tongues doe declare, which are acts of a distinct person. It is not the Power of the King, that signes a pardon, but his Person. When the power of the Government was in two Persons, in the two Consuls at *Rome,* yet the severall acts were done by their severall
180 Persons. Wilt thou ask me, What needs these three Persons? Is there any thing in the three Persons, that is not in the one God? Yes, The Father, the Son, the Holy Ghost, fals not in the bare consideration of that one God. Wilt thou say, What if they doe not? What lack we if we have one Almighty God? Though that God had no Son, nor they two, no Holy Ghost? We lacked our redemption; we lacked all our direction; wee lacked the revealed will of God, the Scriptures; we have not God, if we have him not, as he hath delivered himselfe; and he hath done that in the Scriptures; and we imbrace him, as we finde him there; and we finde him there, to be one God
190 in three Persons, and the Holy Ghost to bee one of those three; and in them we rest.

He is one; but one that proceeds from two, from the Father, and from the Son. Some in the Greek Church, in later times, denied the proceeding of the Holy Ghost from the Son; but this was especially a jealousie in termes; They thought that to make him proceed from two, were to make *duo principia,* two roots, two beginnings from whence the Holy Ghost should proceed, and that might not be admitted, for the Father, and the Son are but one cause of the Holy Ghost, (if we may use that word, Cause, in this mystery.) And there-
200 fore it is as suspiciously, and as dangerously said by the Master of the Sentences, and by the later Schoole, That the Holy Ghost proceeds *Minùs Principaliter,* Not so radically from the Son, as from the Father; for, in this action, The Father and the Son are but one roote, and the Holy Ghost equally from both: In the generation of the Son, the Father is in order before the Son, but in the procession of the holy Ghost, he is not so. He is from both; for where he is first named, he is called *Spiritus Elohim, The Spirit of Gods,* in the plurall. In

Ex filio

Gen. 1.2

this Chapter, in the ninth verse, he is the Spirit of the Son, *If any man have not the Spirit of Christ, he is none of his;* And so in the

Gal. 4.6 [210] Apostle, *God hath sent the Spirit of his Son into your hearts.* God
Iohn 16.7 sent him, and Christ sent him, *If I depart, I will send the Comforter unto you.* He sent him after he went, and he gave him when he was
20.22 here, *He breathed upon his Apostles, and said, Receive ye the holy Ghost.* So he is of both.

Processio   But by what manner comes he from them? By proceeding. That is a very generall word; for, Creation is proceeding, and so is Generation too: Creatures proceed from God, and so doth God the Son proceed from God the Father; what is this proceeding of the holy Ghost, that is not Creation, nor Generation? *Exponant cur & quo-*
Nazianz. [220] *modo Spiritus pulsat in arteriis, & tum in processionem Spiritus sancti inquirant:* When they are able clearly, and with full satisfaction to tell themselves how and from whence that spirit proceeds, which beats in their pulse, let them inquire how this Spirit proceeds from the Father and the Sonne. And let them think till they be mad, and speak till they be hoarse, and reade till they be blind, and write till they be lame, they must end with S. *Augustine, Distinguere inter Processionem, & Generationem, nescio, non valeo, non sufficio,* I cannot distinguish, I cannot assigne a difference between this Generation, and this Proceeding. We use to say, they differ *principio,*
[230] That the Son is from the Father alone, the holy Ghost from both: but when this is said, that must be said too, That both Father and Son are but one beginning. We use to say, They differ *ordine,* because the Son is the second, and the holy Ghost the third person; but the second was not before the third in time, nor is above him in dignity.

There is *processio corporalis,* such a bodily proceeding, as that that which proceeds is utterly another thing then that from which it proceeds: frogs proceed (perchance) of ayre, and mise of dust, and worms of carkasses; and they resemble not that ayre, that dust, those carkasses that produced them. There is also *processio Metaphysica,*
[240] when thoughts proceed out of the minde; but those thoughts remaine still in the mind within, and have no separate subsistence in themselves: And then there is *processio Hyperphysica,* which is this which we seek and finde in our soules, but not in our tongues, a proceeding of the holy Ghost so from Father and Son, as that he re-

maines a subsistence alone, a distinct person of himselfe. This is as far as the Schoole can reach, *Ortu, qui relationis est, non est à se; Actu, qui personæ est, per se subsistit:* Consider him in his proceeding, so he must necessarily have a relation to another, Consider him actually in his person, so he subsists of himselfe. And *De modo,* for
250 the manner of his proceeding, we need, we can say but this, As the Son proceeds *per modum intellectus,* (so as the mind of man conceives a thought) so the holy Ghost proceeds *per modum voluntatis;* when the mind hath produced a thought, that mind, and that discourse and ratiocination produce a will; first our understanding is setled, and that understanding leads our will. And nearer then this (though God knows this be far off) we cannot goe, to the proceeding of the holy Ghost.

    This then is *The Spirit,* The third person in the Trinity, but the first person in our Text, The other is our spirit, *The Spirit beareth*
260 *witnesse with our spirit.* I told you before, that amongst the manifold acceptations of the word *spirit,* as it hath relation particularly to man, it is either the soul it self, or the vitall spirits, (the thin and active parts of the bloud) or the superiour faculties of the soul, in a regenerate man; and that is *our spirit* in this place. So S. *Paul* distinguishes soul and spirit, *The word of God pierces to the dividing asunder soule and spirit;* where The soule is that which inanimates the body, and enables the organs of the senses to see and heare; The spirit is that which enables the soule to see God, and to heare his Gospel. The same phrase hath the same use in another place, *I pray God your*
270 *spirit, and soule, and body may be preserved blamelesse:* Where it is not so absurdly said, (though a very great man call it an absurd exposition) That the soule, *Anima,* is that, *qua animales homines,* (as the Apostle calls them) that by which men are men, naturall men, carnall men, And the spirit is the spirit of Regeneration, by which man is a new creature, a spirituall man, But that, that Expositor himselfe hath said enough to our present purpose, The soule is the seat of Affections, The spirit is rectified Reason. It is true, this Reason is the Soveraigne, these Affections are the Officers, this Body is the Executioner: Reason authorizes, Affections command, the Body exe-
280 cutes: And when we conceive in our mind, desire in our heart, performe in our body nothing that displeases God, then have we had

*Spiritus
noster*

Heb. 4.12

1 Thes. 5.23

Calvin

benefit of S. *Pauls* prayer, *That in body, and soule, and spirit we may be blamelesse.* In summe, we need seek no farther for a word to expresse this *spirit,* but that which is familiar to us, *The Conscience:* A rectified conscience is this spirit; *My conscience bearing me witnesse,* says the Apostle: And so we have both the persons in this judiciall proceeding; *The Spirit* is the holy Ghost; *Our spirit* is our Conscience: And now their office is to testifie, to beare witnesse, which is our second generall part, *The Spirit bears witnesse, &c.*

²⁹⁰ To be a witnesse, is not an unworthy office for the holy Ghost himselfe: Heretiques in their pestilent doctrines, Tyrans in their bloody persecutions, call God himselfe so often, so far into question, as that he needs strong and pregnant testimony to acquit him. First, against Heretiques, we see the whole Scripture is but a Testament; and *Testamentum* is *Testatio mentis,* it is but an attestation, a proofe what the will of God is: And therefore when *Tertullian* deprehended himselfe to have slipped into another word, and to have called the Bible *Instrumentum,* he retracts and corrects himselfe thus, *Magìs usui est dicere Testamentum quàm Instrumentum,* It is more proper ³⁰⁰ to call the Scripture a Testament, then a Conveyance or Covenant: All the Bible is Testament, Attestation, Declaration, Proofe, Evidence of the will of God to man. And those *two witnesses* spoken of in the Revelation, are very conveniently, very probably interpreted to be the two Testaments; And to the Scriptures Christ himselfe refers the Jews, *Search them, for they beare witnesse of me.* The word of God written by the holy Ghost is a witnesse, and so the holy Ghost is a witnesse against Heretiques. Against Tyrans and Persecuters, the office of a witnesse is an honourable office too; for that which we call more passionately, and more gloriously Martyrdome, is but Tes- ³¹⁰ timony; A Martyr is nothing but a Witnesse. He that pledges Christ in his own wine, in his own cup, in bloud; He that washes away his sins in a second Baptisme, and hath found a lawfull way of Re-baptizing, even in bloud; He that waters the Prophets ploughing, and the Apostles sowing with bloud; He that can be content to bleed as long as a Tyran can foame, or an Executioner sweat; He that is pickled, nay embalmed in bloud, salted with fire, and preserved in his owne ashes; He that (to contract all, nay to enlarge beyond all) suffers in the Inquisition, when his body is upon the rack, when the

Rom. 9.1

2 Part

Apoc. 11.3

Iohn 5.39

rags are in his throat, when the boots are upon his legs, when the
320 splinters are under his nailes, if in those agonies he have the vigour
to say, I suffer this to shew what my Saviour suffered, must yet make
this difference, He suffered as a Saviour, I suffer but as a witnesse.
But yet to him that suffers as a Martyr, as a witnesse, a crowne is
reserved; It is a happy and a harmonious meeting in *Stephens* martyrdome; *Proto-martyr,* and *Stephanus;* that the first Martyr for
Christ should have a Crown in his name. Such a blessed meeting
there is in *Ioash* his Coronation, *Posuit super eum Diadema & Testi-*   2 King.
monium, They put the Crowne upon his head, and the Testimony;   11.12
that is, The Law, which testified, That as he had the Crowne from
330 God, so he had it with a witnesse, with an obligation, that his Government, his life, and (if need were) his death should testifie his
zeale to him that gave him that Crowne.

Thus the holy Ghost himselfe is a witnesse against Heretiques in
the word; and those men who are full of the holy Ghost, (as *Stephen*   [Acts 7.55]
was) are witnesses against persecution, in action, in passion. At this
time, and by occasion of these words, we consider principally the
first, The testification of the holy Ghost himselfe; and therein we
consider thus much more, That a witnesse ever testifies of some matter of fact, of something done before; The holy Ghost, the Spirit
340 here, (as we shall see anon) witnesses that we are the children of
God. Now if a Witnesse prove that I am a Tenant to such Land, or
Lord of it, I doe not become Lord nor Tenant by this Witnesse, but
his testimony proves that I was so before. I have therefore a former
right to be the child of God, that is, The eternall Election of God in
Christ Jesus. Christ Jesus could as well have disobeyed his Father,
and said, I will not goe, or disappointed his Father, and said, I will
not goe yet, as he could have dis-furnished his Father, and said, He
would not redeem me. The holy Ghost bears witnesse, that is, he
pleads, he produces that eternall Decree for my Election. And upon
350 such Evidence shall I give sentence against my selfe? *Si testaretur*   Chrysost.
Angelus, vel Archangelus, posset quisquam addubitare? I should
not doubt the testimony of an Angel, or Archangel, and yet Angels
and Archangels, all sorts of Angels were deceivers in the Serpent.
And therefore the Apostle presents it (though impossible in it selfe)
as a thing that might fall into our mis-apprehension: *If we,* (that is,

Gal. 1.8

the Apostles) *or if an Angel from heaven preach any other Gospel,*
Anathema sit, let him be accursed. But *Quando Deus testatur, quis*
locus relinquitur dubitationi? when God testifies to me, it is a rebellious sin to doubt: And therefore how hyperbolically soever S.
360 *Paul* argue there, If Apostles, If Angels teach the contrary, teach
false Doctrine, it never entred into his argument (though an argument *ab Impossibili*) to say, If God should teach, or testifie false
doctrine. Though then there be a former evidence for my being the
child of God, a Decree in heaven, yet it is not enough that there is
such a Record, but it must be produced, it must be pleaded, it must
be testified to be that, it must have the witnesse of the Spirit, and by
that, *Innotescit,* though it doe not become my Election then, it makes
my election appeare then, and though it be not Introductory, it is
Declaratory. The Root is in the Decree, the first fruits are in the
370 testimony of the Spirit; but even that spirit will not be *testis singu-*
laris, he will not be heard alone, and single, but it is *Cum spiritu*
nostro, The Spirit testifies with our spirit, &c.

Cum spiritu
nostro
[Deut. 17.6]

    The holy Ghost will fulfill his owne law, *In ore duorum, In the*
mouth of two witnesses. Sometimes our spirit bears witnesse of some
things appertaining to the next world, without the testimony of the
holy Ghost. *Tertullian* in that excellent Book of his, *De testimonio*
Animæ, Of the testimony which the soule of man gives of it selfe to
it selfe, where he speaks of the soule of a naturall, an unregenerate
man, gives us just occasion to stop a little upon that consideration.
380 If, sayes he, we for our Religion produce your own Authors against
you, (he speaks to naturall men, secular Philosophers) and shew you
out of them, what Passions, what Vices even they impute to those
whom you have made your Gods, then you say, they were but *Poetæ*
vani, Those Authors were but vaine, and frivolous Poets; But when
those Authors speake any thing which sound against our Religion,
then they are Philosophers, and reverend and classique Authors. And
therefore, sayes he, I will draw no witnesse from them, *Perversæ*
fœlicitatis, quibus in falso potiùs creditur, quàm in vero, Because they
have this perverse, this left-handed happinesse, to be beleeved when
390 they lye, better then when they say true. *Novum testimonium adduco,*
saies he; I wayve all them, and I call upon a new witnesse: A witnesse,
Omni literaturi notius, More legible then any Character, then any

text hand, for it is the intimation of mine owne soule, and conscience; and *Omni Editione vulgatius,* More publique, more conspicuous then any Edition, any impression of any Author, for Editions may be called in, but who can call in the testimony of his owne soule? He proceeds, *Te simplicem, & Idioticum compello,* I require but a simple, an unlearned soule, *Qualem te habent, qui te solam habent,* Such a soule, as that man hath, who hath nothing but a soule, no learning;
400 *Imperitia tua mihi opus est, quoniam aliquantulæ peritiæ tuæ nemo credit;* I shall have the more use of thy testimony, the more ignorant thou art, for, in such cases, Art is suspicious, and from them who are able to prove any thing, we beleeve nothing; And therefore, saies he, *Nolo Academiis, bibliothecis instructam,* I call not a soule made in an University, or nursed in a Library, but let this soule come now, as it came to me in my Mothers wombe, an inartificiall, an unexperienced soule; And then, (to contract *Tertullians* Contemplation) he proceeds to shew the notions of the Christian Religion, which are in such a soule naturally, and which his spirit, that is, his rectified reason,
410 rectified but by nature, is able to infuse into him. And certainly, some of that, which is proved by the testimony mentioned in this text, is proved by the testimony of our owne naturall soule, in that Poet whom the Apostle cites, that said, *Genus ejus, We are the off-spring of God.* Acts 17.28

So then our spirit beares witnesse sometimes when the Spirit does not; that is, Nature testifies some things, without addition of particular grace: And then the Spirit, the Holy Ghost oftentimes testifies, when ours does not: How often stands he at the doore, and knocks? How often spreads he his wings, to gather us, as a Hen her chickens?
420 How often presents he to us the power of God in the mouth of the Preacher, and we beare witnesse to one another of the wit and of the eloquence of the Preacher, and no more? How often he bears witnesse, that such an action is odious in the sight of God, and our spirit beares witnesse, that it is acceptable, profitable, honourable in the sight of man? How often he beares witnesse, for Gods Judgements, and our spirit deposes for mercy, by presumption, and how often he testifies for mercy, and our spirit sweares for Judgement, in desperation? But when the Spirit, and our spirit agree in their testimony, That he hath spoke comfortably to my soule, and my soule hath

[Mat. 11.17]
[Luke 1.47]

⁴³⁰ apprehended comfort by that speech, That, (to use Christs similitude) *He hath piped, and we have danced,* He hath shewed me my Saviour, and my Spirit hath rejoyced in God my Saviour, He deposes for the Decree of my Election, and I depose for the seales and marks of that Decree, These two witnesses, *The Spirit,* and *My spirit,* induce a third witnesse, the world it selfe, to testifie that which is the testimony of this text, *That I am the child of God.* And so we passe from the two former parts, The persons, The Spirit, and our spirit, And their office, to witnesse, and to agree in their witnesse, and we are fallen into our third part, The Testimony it selfe, *That we are the Children* ⁴⁴⁰ *of God.*

3 Part   This part hath also two branches; First, That the Testimony concernes our selves, *We are;* And then, That that which we are is this, *We are the Children of God.* And in the first branch, there will be two twiggs, two sub-considerations; ¹*Wee,* A personall appropriation of the grace of God to our selves, ²*We are,* we are now, a present possession of those Graces. First, consider we the Consolation in the particle of appropriation, *Wee.* In the great Ant-hill of the whole world, I am an Ant; I have my part in the Creation, I am a Creature; But there are ignoble Creatures. God comes nearer; In the great field ⁴⁵⁰ of clay, of red earth, that man was made of, and mankind, I am a clod; I am a man, I have my part in the Humanity; But Man was worse then annihilated again. When Satan in that serpent was come, as *Hercules* with his club into a potters shop, and had broke all the vessels, destroyed all mankind, And the gracious promise of a Messias to redeeme all mankind, was shed and spread upon all, I had my drop of that dew of Heaven, my sparke of that fire of heaven, in the universall promise, in which I was involved; But this promise was appropriated after, in a particular Covenant, to one people, to the Jewes, to the seed of *Abraham.* But for all that I have my portion ⁴⁶⁰ there; for all that professe Christ Jesus are by a spirituall engrafting, and transmigration, and transplantation, in and of that stock, and that seed of *Abraham;* and I am one of those. But then, of those who doe professe Christ Jesus, some grovell still in the superstitions they were fallen into, and some are raised, by Gods good grace, out of them; and I am one of those; God hath afforded me my station, in that Church, which is departed from Babylon.

Now, all this while, my soule is in a cheerefull progresse; when I
consider what God did for Goshen in Egypt, for a little parke in the
midst of a forest; what he did for Jury, in the midst of enemies, as a
470 shire that should stand out against a Kingdome round about it: How
many Sancerraes he hath delivered from famins, how many Genevaes
from plots, and machinations against her; all this while my soule is
in a progresse: But I am at home, when I consider Buls of excom-
munications, and solicitations of Rebellions, and pistols, and poysons,
and the discoveries of those; There is our *Nos, We,* testimonies that
we are in the favour, and care of God; We, our Nation, we, our
Church; There I am at home; but I am in my Cabinet at home, when
I consider, what God hath done for me, and my soule; There is the
Ego, the particular, the individuall, I. This appropriation is the con-
480 solation, *We are;* But who are they? or how are we of them? *Testi-*
monium est clamor ipse, sayes S. *Chrysostome* to our great advantage,
Even this, that we are able *to cry Abba, Father, by the Spirit of*   Ver. 15
Adoption, is this testimony, *that we are his Children;* if we can truly
do that, that testifies for us. The Spirit testifies two wayes; Directly,
expresly, personally, as in that, *Man, thy sins are forgiven thee,* And   Luke 5.20
so to *David* by *Nathan, Transtulit, The Lord hath taken away thy*   [2 Sam.
sin; And then he testifies, *Per indicia,* by constant marks, and in-   12.13]
fallible evidences. We are not to looke for the first, for it is a kind of
Revelation; nor are we to doubt of the second, for the marks are
490 infallible. And therefore, as S. *Augustine* said of the Maniches, concerning the Scriptures, *Insani sunt adversus Antidotum, quo sani esse*
possunt, They are enraged against that, which onely can cure them
of their rage, that was, the Scriptures; so there are men, which will
still be in ignorance of that which might cure them of their ignorance,
because they will not labour to finde in themselves, the marks and
seales of those who are ordained to salvation, they will needs thinke,
that no man can have any such testimony.

They say, It is true, there is a blessed comfort, in this appropriation,   *Sumus*
if we could be sure of it; They may; we are; we are already in posses-
500 sion of it. The marks of our spirituall filiation, are lesse subject to
error, then of temporall. Shall the Mothers honesty be the Evidence?
Alas, we have some such examples of their falshood, as will discredit
any argument, built meerely upon their truth. He is like the Father;

Is that the evidence? Imagination may imprint those Characters: He
hath his land; A supposititious child may have that. Spirituall marks
are not so fallible as these: They have so much in them, as creates

1 Iohn 3.2
5.19

even a knowledge, *Now we are the Sons of God, and we know that
we shall be like him; And we know, that we are of God.* Is all this
but a conjecturall knowledge, but a morall certitude? No tincture of
510 faith in it? Can I acquire, and must I bring *Certitudinem fidei,* an
assurance out of faith, That a Councell cannot erre; And then, such
another faithfull assurance, That the Councell of Trent was a true
councell; And then another, That the Councell of Trent did truly and
duly proceed in all wayes essentiall to the truth of a Councell, in
constituting their Decree against this doctrine? And may I not bring
this assurance of faith to S. *Paul,* and S. *Iohn* when they say the contrary? Is not S. *Pauls sumus,* and S. *Iohns scimus,* as good a ground
for our faith, as the servile and mercenary voices of a herd of new
pensionary Bishops, shovelled together at Trent for that purpose, are
520 for the contrary?

Cat[h]arinus

A particular Bishop in the Romane Church, cites an universall
Bishop, a Pope himselfe in this point, and he sayes well, *Legem
credendi statuit lex supplicandi,* Whatsoever we may pray for, we
may, we must beleeve *Certitudine fidei,* With an assurance of faith;
If I may pray, and say *Pater noster,* if I may call God Father, I may
beleeve with a faithfull assurance, that I am the childe of God. *Stet
invicta Pauli sententia,* Let the Apostles doctrine, sayes that Bishop,
remain unshaked; *Et velut sagitta,* sayes he, This doctrine, as an
arrow shot at them, will put out their eyes that think to see beyond
530 S. *Paul.* It is true, sayes that Bishop, there are differences, *Inter
Catholicos,* Amongst Catholiques themselves in this point; And then,
why do they charge us, whom they defame, by the name of Heretiques, with beginning this doctrine, which was amongst themselves
before we were at all, if they did date us aright? *Attestatur spiritus, &
ei damus fidem, & inde certi sumus,* sayes that Bishop: The holy
Ghost beares witnesse, and our spirit with him, and thereby we are
sure: but, sayes he, they will needs make a doubt whether this be a
knowledge out of faith; which doubt, sayes he, *Secum fert absurdi-
tatem,* There is an absurdity, a contradiction in the very doubt: *Ex
540 Spiritu sancto, & humana?* Is it a knowledge from the holy Ghost,

Idem

and is it not a divine knowledge then? But, say they, (as that Bishop
presses their objections) The holy Ghost doth not make them know,
that it is the holy Ghost that assures them; This is, sayes he, as absurd
as the other; For, *Nisi se testantem insinuet, non testatur,* Except he
make them discern, that he is a witnesse, he is no witnesse to them:
He ends it thus, *Sustinere coguntur quod excidit;* and that is indeed
their case, in very many things controverted; That when it conduced
to their advantage in argument, or to their profit in purse, such and
such things fell from them, and now that opposition is made against
550 such sayings of theirs, their profit lyes at stake, and their reputation
too, to make good, and to maintain that which they have once, how
undiscreetly soever, said. Some of their severest later men, even of
their Jesuits, acknowledge that we may know our selves to be the
children of God, with as good a knowledge, as that there is a Rome,
or a Constantinople, And such an assurance as delivers them from all
feare that they shall fall away; and is not this more then that assurance which we take to our selves? We give no such assurance as may
occasion security, or slacknesse in the service of God, and they give
such an assurance as may remove all feare and suspition of falling
560 from God.

    It was truly good counsell in S. *Gregory,* when, writing to one of
the Empresses bedchamber, a religious Lady of his own name, who
had written to him, that she should never leave importuning him,
till he sent her word, that he had received a revelation from God that
she was saved: for, sayes he, *Rem difficilem postulas, & inutilem,* It
is a hard matter you require, and an impertinent, and uselesse matter:
for I am not a man worthy to receive revelations, and besides, such a
revelation as you require, might make you too secure: And *Mater
negligentiæ solet esse securitas,* (sayes he) Such a security might make
570 you negligent in those duties which should make sure your salvation.
S. *Augustine* felt the witnesse of *The Spirit,* but not of *his spirit,* when
he stood out so many solicitations of the holy Ghost, and deferred, and
put off the outward meanes, his Baptisme. In that state, when he had
a disposition to Baptisme, he sayes of himselfe, *Inferbui exultando, sed
inhorrui timendo;* Still I had a fervent joy in me, because I saw the
way to thee, and intended to put my selfe into that way, but yet, because I was not yet in it, I had a trembling, a jealousie, a suspition of

Vegas

Pererius

my self. *Insinuati sunt mihi in profundo nutus tui,* In that halfe darknesse, in that twi-light I discerned thine eye to be upon me; *Et*
⁵⁸⁰ *gaudens in fide, laudavi nomen tuum,* And this, sayes he, created a
kinde of faith, a confidence in me, and this induced an inward joy,
and that produced a praising of thy goodnesse, *Sed ea fides securum
me non esse sinebat,* But all this did not imprint, and establish that
security, that assurance which I found as soon as I came to the outward seales, and marks, and testimonies of thine inseparable presence
with me, in thy Baptisme, and other Ordinances. S. *Bernard* puts the
marks of as much assurance, as we teach, in these words of our
Saviour, *Surge, tolle grabatum, & ambula, Arise, Take up thy bed,
and walk. Surge ad divina,* Raise thy thoughts upon the next world;
⁵⁹⁰ *Tolle corpus, ut non te ferat, sed tu illud,* Take up thy body, bring thy
body into thy power, that thou govern it, and not it thee; And then,
Ambula, non retrospicias, Walk on, proceed forward, and looke not
backe with a delight upon thy former sins; And a great deale an elder

Remigius

man then *Bernard,* expresses it well, *Bene viventibus perhibet testimonium, quòd jam sumus filii Dei,* To him that lives according to a
right faith, the Spirit testifies that he is now the childe of God, *Et
quòd talia faciendo, perseverabimus in ea filiatione,* He carries this
testimony thus much farther, That if we endeavour to continue in
that course, we shall continue in that state, of being the children of
⁶⁰⁰ God, and never be cast off, never disinherited. Herein is our assurance,
an election there is; The Spirit beares witnesse to our spirit, that it is
ours; We testifie this in a holy life; and the Church of God, and the
whole world joynes in this testimony, *That we are the children of
God;* which is our last branch, and conclusion of all.

    The holy Ghost could not expresse more danger to a man, then

Luk. 16.8

Ephes. 5.6

Acts 13.10

John 17.[12]

Mat. 23.15

when he calls him *Filium sæculi, The childe of this world;* Nor a
worse disposition, then when he cals him, *Filium diffidentiæ, The
childe of diffidence, and distrust in God;* Nor a worse pursuer of that
ill disposition, then when he calls him *Filium diaboli,* (as S. *Peter*
⁶¹⁰ calls *Elymas*) *The childe of the devill;* Nor a worse possessing of the
devill, then when he calls him *Filium perditionis, The childe of
perdition;* Nor a worse execution of all this, then when he calls him
Filium gehennæ, The childe of hell: The childe of this world, The
childe of desperation, The childe of the devill, The childe of perdition,

The childe of hell, is a high expressing, a deep aggravating of his
damnation; That his damnation is not only his purchase, as he hath
acquired it, but it is his inheritance, he is the childe of damnation.
So is it also a high exaltation, when the holy Ghost draws our Pedegree from any good thing, and calls us the childen of that: As, when
he cals us *Filios lucis, The children of light,* that we have seen the day-
star arise, when he cals us *Filios sponsi, The children of the bride-
chamber,* begot in lawfull marriage upon the true Church, these are
faire approaches to the highest title of all, to be *Filii Dei, The children
of God;* And not children of God, *Per filiationem vestigii,* (so every
creature is a childe of God) by having an Image, and impression of
God, in the very Beeing thereof, but *children* so, as that we are *heires,*
and *heires* so, as that we are *Co-heires with Christ,* as it follows in the
next verse, and is implyed in this name, *Children of God.*

Heires of heaven, which is not a Gavel-kinde, every son, every man
alike; but it is an universall primogeniture, every man full, so full,
as that every man hath all, in such measure, as that there is nothing in
heaven, which any man in heaven wants. Heires of the joyes of
heaven; Joy in a continuall dilatation of thy heart, to receive aug-
mentation of that which is infinite, in the accumulation of essentiall
and accidentall joy. Joy in a continuall melting of indissoluble bowels,
in joyfull, and yet compassionate beholding thy Saviour; Rejoycing
at thy being there, and almost lamenting (in a kinde of affection,
which we can call by no name) that thou couldst not come thither,
but by those wounds, which are still wounds, though wounds
glorified. Heires of the joy, and heires of the glory of heaven; where
if thou look down, and see Kings fighting for Crownes, thou canst
look off as easily, as from boyes at stool-ball for points here; And
from Kings triumphing after victories, as easily, as a Philosopher from
a Pageant of children here. Where thou shalt not be subject to any
other title of Dominion in others, but *Iesus of Nazareth King of the
Iews,* nor ambitious of any other title in thy selfe, but that which
thou possessest, *To be the childe of God.* Heires of joy, heires of glory,
and heires of the eternity of heaven; Where, in the possession of this
joy, and this glory, The Angels which were there almost 6000. yeares
before thee, and so prescribe, and those soules which shall come at
Christs last comming, and so enter but then, shall not survive thee,

Iohn 12.36
Mat. 9.15

but they, and thou, and all, shall live as long as he that gives you all that life, as God himselfe.

Heires to heaven, and co-heires with Christ: There is much to be said of that circumstance; but who shall say it? I that should say it, have said ill of it already, in calling it a Circumstance. To be co-heires with Christ, is that Essentiall salvation it selfe; and to that he intitled us, when after his Resurrection he said of us, *Goe tell my brethren that I am gone.* When he was but borne of a woman, and submitted to the law, when in his minority, he was but a Carpenter, and at full age, but a Preacher, when they accused him in generall, that he was a Malefactor, or else they would not have delivered him, but they knew not the name of his fault, when a fault of secular cognizance was objected to him, that he moved sedition, that he denied tribute, And then a fault of Ecclesiasticall cognizance, that he spoke against the Law, and against the Temple, when *Barrabas* a seditious murderer was preferred before him, and saved, and yet two theeves left to accompany him, in his torment and death, in these diminutions of Christ, there was no great honour, no great cause why any man should have any great desire to be of his kindred; to be brother, or co-heire to his Crosse. But if to be his brethren, when he had begun his triumph in his Resurrection, were a high dignity, what is it to be co-heires with him in heaven, after his Ascension? But these are inexpressible, unconceivable things; bring it backe to that which is nearest us; to those seales and marks which wee have in this life; That by a holy, a sanctified passage through this life, and out of this life, from our first seale in Baptisme, to our last seale upon our death-bed, *The Spirit may beare witnesse to our spirit, that we are the children of God. Amen.*

John 20.17

John 18.30

Number 3.

Preached upon Whitsunday.

[? At St. Paul's, 1623]

MAT. 12.31. *WHEREFORE I SAY UNTO YOU, ALL MANNER OF SIN AND BLASPHEMY SHALL BE FORGIVEN UNTO MEN; BUT THE BLASPHEMY AGAINST THE HOLY GHOST SHALL NOT BE FORGIVEN UNTO MEN.*

As WHEN a Merchant hath a faire and large, a deep and open Sea, into that Harbour to which hee is bound with his Merchandize, it were an impertinent thing for him, to sound, and search for lands, and rocks, and clifts, which threaten irreparable shipwrack; so we being bound to the heavenly City, the new Jerusalem, by the spacious and bottomelesse Sea, the blood of Christ Jesus, having that large Sea opened unto us, in the beginning of this Text, *All manner of sin, and blasphemy shall be forgiven unto men,* It may seeme an impertinent diversion, to turne into that little Creek, nay upon that desperate, and irrecoverable rock, *The blasphemy against the Holy Ghost shall not be forgiven to men.* But there must be Discoverers, as well as Merchants; for the security of Merchants, who by storme and tempest, or other accidents, may be cast upon those sands, and rocks, if they be not knowne, they must be knowne. So though we saile on, with a merry gale and full sailes, with the breath of the holy Ghost in the first Part, *All manner of sin, and blasphemy shall be forgiven unto men,* yet we shall not leave out the discovery of that fearfull and ruinating rock too, *But the blasphemy against the holy Ghost shall not be forgiven unto men.*

77

20   I would divide the Text, and fewer Parts then two, we cannot make, and this Text hath scarce two Parts: The whole Text is a conveiance; it is true; but there is a little Proviso at the end: The whole Text is a rule; it is true; but there is an exception at the end; The whole text is a Royall Palace; it is true; but there is a Sewar, a Vault behinde it; Christ had said all, that of himselfe he would have said, when he said the first part, *All manner of sin and blasphemy shall be forgiven to men,* But the iniquity of the Pharisees extorted thus much more, *But the blasphemy against the holy Ghost shall not be forgiven unto men:* The first part is the sentence, the proposition, and the sense is

30 perfect in that, *All manner of sin, &c.* The last part is but a *Parenthesis,* which Christ had rather might have been left out, but the Pharisees, and their perversenesse inserted, *But the blasphemy, &c.* But since it deserves, and requires our consideration, as well, that the mercy of God can have any stop, any rub, determine any where, as that it can extend, and spread it selfe so farre, as it doth in this text, let us make them two parts: And in the first consider with comfort, the largenesse, the expansion of Gods mercy, that there is but one sin, that it reacheth not to; And in the second let us consider with feare,

40 and trembling, that there is one sin, so swelling, so high, as that even the mercy of God does not reach to it. And in the first we shall proceed thus, in the magnifying Gods mercy, first, in the first terme, *Sin,* we shall see that sin is even a wound, a violence upon God; and then *Omne peccatum,* Every sin is so; and nothing is so various, so divers as sin; and even that sin, that amounts to *Blasphemy,* a sin not onely conceived in the thought, but expressed in contumelious words; and those contumelious and blasphemous words uttered against *the Son,* (for so it is expressed in the very next verse) All this *shall be forgiven:* But yet it is *in futuro, They shall be:* No mans sins are for-

50 given him, then when he sins them; but by repentance they shall be forgiven; *forgiven unto men;* that is, first, unto any man, and then, unto none but men; for the sin of the Angels shall never be forgiven: And these will be the Branches of the first Part. And in the second Part, we shall looke as farre as this text occasions it, upon that debated sin, *the sin against the holy Ghost,* and *the irremissiblenesse of that;* of which Part, we shall derive and raise the particular Branches anon, when we come to handle them.

First then, for the first terme, *Sin,* we use to ask in the Schoole,
whether any action of mans can have *rationem demeriti,* whether it
60 can be said to offend God, or to deserve ill of God: for whatsoever
does so, must have some proportion with God. With things which
are inanimate, things that have no will, and so no good nor bad purpose, as dust, or the winde, or such, a man cannot properly be so
offended, as to say that they deserve ill of him. With those things
which have no use, no command of their will, as children, and fooles,
and mad men, it is so too; And then, there is no creature so poore, so
childish, so impotent in respect of man, as the best man is in respect
of God: How then can he sin, that is, offend, that is, deserve ill of
him? The question begun not in the Schoole; It was asked before of
70 *Iob: If thou sinnest, what doest thou against him? or if thy trans-*
gressions be multiplied, what doest thou unto him? Thy wickednesse
may hurt a man as thou art; but what is it to God? for, as *Gregory*
sayes upon that place, *Humana impietas ei nocet, quem pervertendo*
inquinat, Our sins hurt them, whom our example leads into tentation;
but our sins cannot draw God to be accessory to our sins, or to make
him sin with us. Our sin cannot hurt him so; nor hurt him directly
any way; not his person: But his Subjects, whom he hath taken into his
protection, it may; His Law, which he hath given for direction, it may;
His Honour, of which he is jealous, which Honour consists much in
80 our honouring of him, it may. Wherein is a Kings Person violated, by
coyning a false peny, or counterfaiting a seale? and yet this is Treason.
God cannot be robbed, he cannot be damnified; whatsoever is taken
from him (and there is a sacriledge in all unjust takings) wheresoever it
be laid, he sees it, and it is still in his possession, and in his house, and in
his hands. God cannot be robbed, nor God cannot be violated, he cannot be wounded, for he hath no limmes. But God is *Vltimus finis,* The
end to which we all goe, and his Law is the way to that end; And *tran-*
silire lineam, to transgresse that Law, to leave that way, is a neglecting
of him: and even negligences, and pretermissions, and slightings, are
90 as great offences, as actuall injuries. So God is *communis Pater,* the
Father of all creatures; and so the abuse of the creature reflects upon
God, as the injuries done to the children, doe upon the Parents.

If then we can sin so against God, as we can against the King, and
against the Law, and against Propriety, and against Parents; wee have

wayes enow of sinning against God. Sin is not therefore so absolutely
nothing, as that it is (in no consideration) other then a privation,
onely *Absentia recti,* and nothing at all in it selfe: but, not to enter
farther into that inextricable point, we rest in this, that sin is *Actus*
inordinatus, It is not only an obliquity, a privation, but it is an action
100 deprived of that rectitude, which it should have; It does not onely
want that rectitude, but it should have that rectitude, and therefore
hath a sinfull want. We shall not dare to call sin meerly, absolutely
nothing, if we consider either the punishment due to sin, or the
pardon of that punishment, or the price of that pardon. The punishment is everlasting; why should I beleeve it to be so? *Os domini*
locutum, The mouth of the Lord hath said it. But why should it be
so? *Iustum est ut qui in suo æterno peccavit contra Deum, in Dei*
æterno puniatur, It is but justice, that he that sins in his eternity,
should be punished in Gods eternity: Now to sin in our eternity, is to
110 sin as long as we live, and if we could live eternally, to desire to sin
eternally. God can cut off our eternity, he can shorten our life; If wee
could cut off his eternity, and quench hell, our punishment were not
eternall. We consider sin to be *Quoddam infinitum;* as it is an aver-
sion from God, who is infinite goodnesse, it is an infinite thing: and
as it is a turning upon the Creature, it is finite, and determined; for
all pleasure taken in the creature, is so: and accordingly sin hath a
finite, and an infinite punishment: That which we call *Pœnam*
sensus, The torment which we feele, is not infinite; (otherwise, then
by duration) for that torment is not equall in all the damned, and
120 that which is infinite must necessarily be equall; but that which we
call *Pœnam damni,* The everlasting losse of the sight of the everliving
God, that is infinite, and alike, and equall in all the damned. Sin is
something then, if we consider the punishment, and so it is, if we
consider our deliverance from this punishment: That which God
could not pardon in the way of justice without satisfaction, that for
which nothing could be a satisfaction, but the life of all men, or of
one man worth all, the Sonne of God, that that tore the Son out of the
armes of his Father, in the *Quid dereliquisti,* when he cryed out,
Why hast thou forsaken me? That which imprinted in him, who was
130 anointed with the Oyle of gladnesse above his fellowes, a deadly
heavinesse, in his *Tristis anima,* when his soule was heavy unto

[Isa. 58.14]

Gregor.

[Mat. 27.46]

[Heb. 1.9]
[Mat. 26.38]

death, That which had power to open Heaven in his descent hither, and to open hell, in his descent thither, to open the wombe of the Virgin in his Incarnation, and the wombe of the Earth in his Resurrection, that which could change the frame of Nature in Miracles, and the God of Nature in becomming Man, that that deserved that punishment, that that needed that ransome (say the Schoole men what they will of privations) cannot be meerely, absolutely nothing, but the greatest thing that can be conceived; and yet that shall be
140 forgiven.

That, and all that; *Sin,* and *all sin:* And there is not so much of any thing in the world, as of sin. Every vertue hath two extreames, two vices opposed to it; there is two to one; But *Abrahams* taske was an easie taske to tell the stars of Heaven; so it were to tell the sands, or haires, or atomes, in respect of telling but our owne sins. And will God say to me, *Confide Fili, My Son, be of good cheere, thy sins are forgiven thee?* Does he meane all my sins? He knowes what originall sin is, and I doe not; and will he forgive me sin in that roote, and sin in the branches, originall sin, and actuall sin too? He knowes my
150 secret sins, and I doe not; will he forgive my manifest sins, and those sins too? He knowes my relapses into sins repented; and will he forgive my faint repentances, and my rebellious relapses after them? will his mercy dive into my heart, and forgive my sinfull thoughts there, and shed upon my lips, and forgive my blasphemous words there, and bathe the members of this body, and forgive mine uncleane actions there? will he contract himselfe into himselfe, and meet me there, and forgive my sins against himselfe, And scatter himselfe upon the world, and forgive my sins against my neighbour, and emprison himselfe in me, and forgive my sins against my selfe? Will
160 he forgive those sins, wherein my practise hath exceeded my Parents, and those wherein my example hath mis-led my children? Will he forgive that dim sight which I have of sin now, when sins scarce appeare to be sins unto me, and will he forgive that over-quick sight, when I shall see my sins through Satans multiplying glasse of desperation, when I shall thinke them greater then his mercy, upon my death-bed? *In that he said all, he left out nothing,* is the Apostles argument: and, he is not almighty, if he cannot; his mercy endures not for ever, if he doe not forgive all.

Omne

[Gen. 15.5]

Mat. 9.2

Heb. 2.8

Blasphemia

1 Tim. 6.1

Iude 8, 10

1 Cor. 4.13
Tit. 3.2

Aquin. 2. 2.
q. 13. ar. 4

Luke 16.24

Sin, and *all sin,* even *blasphemy:* now blasphemy is not restrained to
170 God alone; other persons besides God, other things, besides persons,
may be blasphemed. The word of God, the Doctrine, Religion may
be blasphemed. Magistracy and Dignities may be blasphemed. Nay,
Omnia quæ ignorant, saies that Apostle, *They blaspheme all things
which they know not.* And for persons, the Apostle takes it to his
owne person, *Being blasphemed, yet we intreat;* and he communicates
it to all men, *Neminem blasphemate, Blaspheme no man.* Blasphemy,
as it is a contumelious speech, derogating from any man, that good
that is in him, or attributing to any man, that ill that is not in him,
may be fastned upon any man. For the most part it is understood a
180 sin against God, and that directly; and here, by the manner of Christ
expressing himselfe, it is made the greatest sin; *All sin,* even *blasphemy.* And yet, a drunkard that cannot name God, will spue out a
blasphemy against God: A child that cannot spell God, will stammer
out a blasphemy against God: If we smart, we blaspheme God, and
we blaspheme him if we be tickled; If I lose at play, I blaspheme, and
if my fellow lose, he blasphemes, so that God is always sure to be a
loser. An Usurer can shew me his bags, and an Extortioner his houses,
the fruits, the revenues of his sinne; but where will the blasphemer
shew mee his blasphemy, or what hee hath got by it? The licentious
190 man hath had his love in his armes, and the envious man hath had
his enemy in the dust, but wherein hath the blasphemer hurt God?

In the Schoole we put it for the consummation of the torment of
the damned, that at the Resurrection, they shall have bodies, and so
be able, even verbally, to blaspheme God; herein we exceed the Devill
already, that we can speake blasphemously. There is a rebellious part
of the body, that *Adam* covered with figge leaves, that hath damned
many a wretched soule; but yet, I thinke, not more then the tongue;
And therefore the whole torment that *Dives* suffered in hell, is expressed in that part, *Father Abraham, have mercy upon me, and send*
200 *Lazarus, that he may dip the tip of his finger in water, and coole my
tongue.* The Jews that crucified God, will not sound the name of God,
and we for whom he was Crucified, belch him out in our surfets, and
foame him out in our fury: An Impertinent sin, without occasion
before, and an unprofitable sin, without recompence after, and an
incorrigible sin too; for, almost what Father dares chide his son for

blasphemy, that may not tell him, Sir I learnt it of you? or what Master his servant, that cannot lay the same recrimination upon him? How much then do we need this extent of Gods mercy, that he will forgive *sin,* and *all sin,* and even this sin of *blasphemy,* and (which is
210 also another addition) *blasphemy against the Son.*

This emphaticall addition arises out of the connexion in the next verse, *A word,* (that is, a blasphemous word) *against the Son, shall be forgiven.* And here wee carry not the word *Son* so high, as that the Son should be the eternall Son of God, Though words spoken against the eternall Son of God by many bitter and blasphemous Heretiques have beene forgiven: God forbid that all the Photinians who thought that Christ was not at all, till he was borne of the Virgin *Mary,* That all the Nativitarians, that thought he was from all eternity with God, but yet was not the Son of God, That all the Arians, that thought him
220 the Son of God, but yet not essentially, not by nature, but by grace and adoption, God forbid that all these should be damned, and because they once spoke against the Son, therefore they never repented, or were not received upon repentance. We carry not the word, Son, so high, as to be the eternall Son of God, for it is in the text, *Filius hominis, The Son of Man;* And, in that acceptation, we doe not meane it, of all blasphemies that have beene spoken of Christ, as *the Son of man,* that is, of Christ invested in the humane nature; though blasphemies in that kind have beene forgiven too: God forbid that all the Arians, that thought Christ so much the Son of Man as that
230 he tooke a humane body, but not so much, as that he tooke a humane soule, but that the Godhead it selfe (such a Godhead as they allowed him) was his soule; God forbid that all the Anabaptists that confesse he tooke a body, but not a body of the substance of the Virgin; That all the Carpocratians, that thought onely his soule, and not his body ascended into Heaven, God forbid all these should be damned, and never called to repentance, or not admitted upon it: There were fearfull blasphemies against the Son, as the Son of God, and as the Son of Man, against his Divine, and against his Humane Nature, and those, in some of them, by Gods grace forgiven too. But here we con-
240 sider him onely as the Son of Man, meerely as Man; but as such a Man, so good a Man, as to calumniate him, to blaspheme him, was an inexcusable sin. To say of him, who had fasted forty dayes and forty nights,

In filium

Mat. 11.19

Mar. 12.14

[Isa. 9.6]
Heb. 12.3

[Psa. 22.6]

In futuro

Ecce homo vorax, Behold a man gluttonous, and a wine-bibber, To say of him, of whom themselves had said elsewhere, *Master, we know that thou art true, and carest for no man,* that he was *a friend of Publicans and sinners,* That this man who was *The Prince of Peace,* should *indure such contradiction,* This was an inexcusable sin. If any man therefore have had his good intentions mis-construed, his zeale to assist Gods bleeding and fainting cause, called Innovation, his pro-
250 ceeding by wayes good in themselves, to ends good in themselves, called Indiscretion, let him be content to forgive them, any Calumniator, against himselfe, who is but *a worme and no man,* since God himselfe forgave them against Christ, who was so *Filius hominis, The Son of Man,* as that he was *the Son of God* too.

There is then forgivenesse for *sin,* for *all sin,* even for *blasphemy,* for *blasphemy against the Son,* but it is *In futuro remittetur, It shall be forgiven.* It is not *Remittebatur,* It was forgiven; Let no man anti-date his pardon, and say, His sins were forgiven in an Eternall Decree, and that no man that hath his name in the book of life, hath the addi-
260 tion, sinner; that if he were there from the beginning, from the beginning he was no sinner. It is not, in such a sense, *Remittebatur,* It was forgiven; nor it is not *Remittitur,* that even then, when the sin is committed, it is forgiven, whether the sinner think of it or no, That God sees not the sins of his Children, That God was no more affected with *Davids* adultery, or his murder, then an indulgent Father is to see his child do some witty waggish thing, or some sportfull shrewd turne. It is but *Remittetur,* Any sin *shall be,* that is, may be *forgiven,* if the meanes required by God, and ordained by him, be entertained. If I take into my contemplation, the Majesty of God, and the uglinesse of
270 sin, If I devest my selfe of all that was sinfully got, and invest my self in the righteousnesse of Christ Jesus, (for else I am ill suted, and if I clothe my self in Mammon, the righteousnesse of Christ is no Cloke for that doublet) If I come to Gods Church for my absolution, and the seale of that reconciliation, the blessed Sacrament, *Remittetur,* by those meanes ordained by God any sin shall be forgiven me. But if I relie upon the *Remittebatur,* That I had my *Quietus est* before hand, in the eternall Decree, or in the *Remittuntur,* and so shut mine eyes, in an opinion that God hath shut his, and sees not the sins of his children, I change Gods Grammer, and I induce a dangerous sole-

²⁸⁰ cisme, for, it is not They were forgiven before they were committed, nor They are forgiven in the committing, but, They shall be, by using the meanes ordained by God, they may be; And so, *They shall be forgiven unto men,* saies the Text, and that is, first, unto every man.

The Kings of the earth are faire and glorious resemblances of the King of heaven; they are beames of that Sun, Tapers of that Torch, they are like gods, they are gods: *The Lord killeth and maketh alive, He bringeth down to the grave, and bringeth up:* This is the Lord of heaven; The Lords anointed, Kings of the earth do so too; They have the dispensation of judgement, and of mercy, they execute, and ²⁹⁰ they pardon: But yet, with this difference amongst many other, that Kings of the earth (for the most part, and the best, most) binde themselves with an oath, not to pardon some offences; The King of heaven sweares, and sweares by himselfe, That there is no sinner but he can, and would pardon. At first, *Illuminat omnem hominem, He is the true light, which lightneth every man that commeth into the world;* Let that light (because many do interpret that place so) let that be but that naturall light, which only man, and every man hath; yet that light makes him capable of the super-naturall light of grace; for if he had not that reasonable soule, he could not have grace; and even by ³⁰⁰ this naturall light, he is able to see the invisible God, in the visible creature, and is inexcusable if he do not so. But because this light is (though not put out) brought to a dimnesse, by mans first fall, Therefore *Iohn Baptist* came to *beare witnesse of that light, that all men, through him, might beleeve:* God raises up a *Iohn Baptist* in every man; every man findes a testimony in himselfe, that he draws curtaines between the light and him; that he runs into corners from that light; that he doth not make that use of those helpes which God hath afforded him, as he might.

Thus God hath mercy upon all before, by way of prevention; thus ³¹⁰ he enlightneth every man that commeth into the world: but, because for all this men do stumble, even at noon, God hath given *Collyrium,* an *Eye-salve* to all, by which they may mend their eye-sight; He hath opened a poole of Bethesda to all, where not only he that comes at first, but he that comes even at last, he that comes washed with the water of Baptisme in his infancy, and he that comes washed with the teares of Repentance in his age, may receive health and cleannesse;

Omni homini 1 Sam. 2.6

John 1.9

[Rom. 1.20]

Ver. 7

Apoc. 3.18

For, the Font at first, and the death-bed at last, are Cisterns from this poole, and all men, and at all times, may wash therein: And from this power, and this love of God, is derived both that Catholique
320 promise, *Quandocunque, At what time soever a sinner repents,* And that Catholique and extensive Commission, *Quorum remiseritis, Whose sins soever you remit, shall be remitted.* All men were in *Adam;* because the whole nature, mankinde, was in him; and then, can any be without sin? All men were in Christ too, because the whole nature, mankinde, was in him; and then, can any man be excluded from a possibility of mercy? There were whole Sects, whole bodies of Heretiques, that denied the communication of Gods grace to others; The Cathari denied that any man had it but themselves: The Novatians denied that any man could have it again, after he had once
330 lost it, by any deadly sin committed after Baptisme, But there was never any Sect that denied it to themselves, no Sect of despairing men. We have some somewhere sprinkled; One in the old Testament, *Cain,* and one in the new, *Iudas,* and one in the Ecclesiastique Story, *Iulian;* but no body, no Sect of despairing men. And therefore he that abandons himself to this sin of desperation, sins with the least reason of any, for he prefers his sin above Gods mercy, and he sins with the fewest examples of any, for God hath diffused this light, with an evidence to all, That all sins may be forgiven unto men, that is, unto all men; and then, herein also is Gods mercy to man magnified, that
340 it is to man, that is, only to man.

Non Angelis   Nothing can fall into this comparison, but Angels; and Angels shall not be forgiven: We shall be like the Angels, we shall participate of their glory which stand; But the Angels shall never be like us; never return to mercy, after they are fallen. They were *Primogeniti Dei,* Gods first born, and yet disinherited; and disinherited without any power, at least, without purpose of revocation, without annuities, without pensions, without any present supply, without any future hope. When the Angels were made, and when they fell, we dispute; but when they shall return, falls not into question. Howsoever *Origen*
350 vary in himselfe, or howsoever he fell under that jealousie, or misinterpretation, that he thought the devill should be saved at last, I am sure his books that are extant, have pregnant and abundant testimony of their everlasting, and irreparable condemnation. To judge by our

[Joh. 20.23]

evidence, the evidence of Scriptures, for their sin, and the evidence of our conscience, for ours, there is none of us that hath not sinned more then any of them at first; and yet Christ hath not taken the nature of Angels, but of man, and redeemed us, having *reserved them in ever-*   Iude 6
lasting chaines, under darknesse: How long? *Vnto the judgement of the great day,* sayes that Apostle; And is it but till then, then to have
360 an end? Alas no; It is not *untill* that day, but *unto* that day; not that that day shall end or ease their torments which they have, but inflict accidentall torments, which they have not yet; That is, an utter evacuation of that power of seducing, which, till that day come, they shall have leave to exercise upon the sons of men: To that are they reserved, and we to that glory, which they have lost, and lost for ever; and upon us, is that prayer of the Apostle fallen effectually, *Mercy, and*   Ver. 2
peace, and love is multiplied unto us; for, *sin,* and *all sin, blasphemy,* and *blasphemy against the Son, shall be,* that is, is not, nor was not, but may be *forgiven to men,* to all men, to none but men; And so we
370 passe to our second part.

In this second part, which seemes to present a banke even to this   2 Part
Sea, this infinite Sea of the blood of Christ Jesus; And an Horizon   *Divisio*
even to this heaven of heavens, to the mercy of God, we shall proceed thus: First, we shall inquire, but modestly, what that *blasphemy,* which is commonly called *The sin against the holy Ghost,* is: And secondly, how, and wherein it is irremissible, that it shall never be forgiven: And then thirdly, upon what places of Scripture it is grounded; amongst which, if this text do not constitute and establish that sin, *The sin against the holy Ghost,* yet we shall finde, that that
380 sin which is directly intended in this text, is a branch of that sin, *The sin against the holy Ghost:* And therefore we shall take just occasion from thence, to arme you with some instructions against those wayes which leade into that irrecoverable destruction, into that irremissible sin: for though the sin it self be not so evident, yet the limmes of the sin, and the wayes to the sin, are plain enough.

S. *Augustine* says, There is no question in the Scripture harder   *Quid*
then this, what this sin is: And S. *Ambrose* gives some reason of the difficulty in this, *Sicut una divinitas, una offensa:* As there is but one Godhead, so there is no sin against God (and all sin is so) but it is
390 against the whole Trinity: and that is true; but as there are certain

attributes proper to every severall person of the Trinity, so there are certaine sins, more directly against the severall attributes and properties of those persons, and in such a consideration, against the persons themselves. Of which there are divers sins against *power,* and they are principally against the *Father;* for to the *Father* we attribute *power;* and divers sins against *wisdome,* and *wisdome* we attribute to the *Son;* and divers against *goodnesse,* and *love,* and these we attribute to the *holy Ghost.* Of those against the holy Ghost, considered in that attribute of goodnesse, and of love, the place to speak, will be in our
400 conclusion. But for this particular sin, *The sin against the holy Ghost,* as hard as S. *Augustine* makes it, and justly, yet he sayes too, *Exercere nos voluit difficultate quæstionis, non decipere falsitate sententiæ,* God would exercise us with a hard question, but he would not deceive us with a false opinion: *Quid sit quæri voluit, non negari;* God would have us modestly inquire what it is, not peremptorily deny that there is any such sin.

"It is (for the most part) agreed, that it is a totall falling away from the Gospell of Christ Jesus formerly acknowledged and professed, into a verball calumniating, and a reall persecuting of that Gospel, with
410 a deliberate purpose to continue so to the end, and actually to do so, to persevere till then, and then to passe away in that disposition." It fals only upon the professors of the Gospell, and it is totall, and it is practicall, and it is deliberate, and it is finall. Here we have that sin, but, by Gods grace, that sinner no where.

It is therefore somewhat early, somewhat forwardly pronounced,
Calvin   though by a reverend man, *Certum reprobationis signum, in spiritum blasphemia,* That it is an infallible assurance, that that man is a Reprobate that blasphemes the holy Ghost. For, whatsover is an infallible signe, must be notorious to us; If we must know another thing
420 by that, as a signe, we must know that thing which is our signe, in it selfe: And can we know what this blaspheming of the holy Ghost is? Did we ever heare any man say, or see any man doe any thing against the holy Ghost, of whom we might say upon that word, or upon that action, This man can never repent, never be received to mercy? And yet, sayes he, *Tenendum est, quod qui exciderint, nunquam resurgent;* We are bound to hold, that they who fall so, shall never rise again. I presume, he grounded himselfe in that severe

judgement of his, upon such places, as that to the Romanes, *When*   Rom. 1.28
they did not like to retaine God in their knowledge, God gave them
³⁰ *over to a reprobate minde:* That that is the ordinary way of Gods
justice, to withdraw his Spirit from that man that blasphemes his
Spirit; but S. *Paul* blasphemed, and S. *Peter* blasphemed, and yet were
not divorced from God.

    S. *Augustines* rule is good; not to judge of this sin, and this sinner
especially, but *à posteriori,* from his end, from his departing out of
this world. Neither though I doe see an ill life, sealed with an ill
death, dare I be too forward in this judgement. He was not a Christian
in profession, but worse then he are called Christians, that said, *Qui*   Trismeg.
pius est, summè Philosophatur; The charitable man is the great
⁴⁰ Philosopher; and it is charity not to suspect the state of a dead man.
Consider in how sudden a minute the holy Ghost hath sometimes
wrought upon thee; and hope that he hath done so upon another.
It is a moderation to be imbraced, that *Peter Martyr* leads us to: The
Primitive Church had the spirit of discerning spirits; we have not;
And therefore, though by way of definition, we may say, This is that
sin, yet by way of demonstration, let us say of no man, This is that
sinner: I may say of no man, This sin in thee is irremissible.

    Now, in considering this word, Irremissible, That it cannot be for-   *Irremis-*
given, wee finde it to be a word, rather usurped by the Schoole, then   *sibilitas*
⁵⁰ expressed in the Scriptures: for in all those three Euangelists, where
this fearfull denunciation is interminated, still it is in a phrase, of
somewhat more mildnesse, then so; It is, *It shall not be forgiven,* It
is not, it cannot be forgiven: It is an irremission, it is not an irremissiblenesse. Absolutely there is not an impossibility, and irremissiblenesse on Gods part: but yet some kinde of impossibility there is on his
part, and on ours too. For, if he could forgive this sin, he would; or
else, his power were above his mercy; and his mercy is above all his
works. But God can doe nothing that implies contradiction; and God
having declared, by what meanes onely his mercy and forgivenesse
⁵⁰ shall be conveyed to man, God should contradict himselfe, if he
should give forgivenesse to them, who will fully exclude those meanes
of mercy. And therefore it were not boldly, nor irreverently said, That
God could not give grace to a beast, nor mercy to the Devill, because
either they are naturally destitute, or have wilfully despoiled them-

selves of the capacity of grace, and mercy. When we consider, that God the Father, whom, as the roote of all, we consider principally in the Creation, created man in a possibility, and ability, to persist in that goodnesse, in which he created him, And consider that God the Son came, and wrought a reconciliation for man to God, and so brought
470 in a treasure, in the nature thereof, a sufficient ransome for all the world, but then a man knowes not this, or beleeves not this, otherwise then Historically, Morally, Civilly, and so evacuates, and shakes off God the Son, And then consider that the holy Ghost comes, and presents meanes of applying all this, and making the generall satisfaction of Christ, reach and spread it selfe upon my soule, in particular, in the preaching of the Word, in the seales of the Sacraments, in the absolution of the Church, and I preclude the wayes, and shut up my selfe against the holy Ghost, and so evacuate him, and shake him off, when I have resisted Father, Son, and holy Ghost, is there a fourth
480 person in the God-head to work upon me? If I blaspheme, that is, deliberately pronounce against the Holy Ghost, my sin is irremissible therefore, because there is no body left to forgive it, nor way left, wherein forgivenesse should work upon me; So farre it is irremissible on Gods part, and on mine too.

And then, take it there, in that state of irremissiblenesse, and consider seriously the fearefulnesse of it. I have been *angry;* and then, (as Christ tells me) I have been *in danger of a judgement;* but in judgement, I may have counsell, I may be heard; I have said *Racha,* expressed my anger and so been *in danger of a Councell;* but a Coun-
490 cell does but consult, what punishment is fit to be inflicted; and so long there is hope of mitigation, and commutation of penance; But I have said *fatue,* I have called my brother *foole,* and so am *in danger of hell fire.* In the first, there is *Ira,* an inward commotion, an irregular distemper; In the second, there is *Ira & vox;* In the first it is but *Ira carnis, non animi,* It is but my passion, it is not I that am angry, but in the second I have suffered my passion to vent and utter it selfe; but in the third, there is *Ira, vox & vituperatio,* A distemper within, a declaration to evill example without, and an injury and defamation to a third person, and this exalts the offence to the height: But then
500 when this third Person comes to be the third Person in the Trinity, the Holy Ghost, in all the other cases, there is danger, danger of

Mat. 5.22

August.

Chrysost.

judgement, danger of a Councell, danger of hell, but here is irremissiblenesse, hell it selfe, and no avoiding of hell, no cooling in hell, no deliverance from hell; Irremissible; Those hands that reached to the ends of the world, in creating it, and span the world in preserving it, and stretched over all in redeeming it, those hands have I manacled, that they cannot open unto me: That tendernesse that is affected to all, have I damped, retarded that pronenesse, stupified that alacrity, confounded that voyce, diverted those eyes, that are naturally disposed to all: And all this, Irremissibly, for ever; not, though he would, but because he will not shew mercy; not, though I would, but because I cannot ask mercy: And therefore beware all approaches towards that sin, from which there is no returning, no redemption.

We are come now, in our order, to our third and last Branch of this last Part, That this Doctrine of a *sin against the Holy Ghost,* is not a dreame of the Schoole-men, though they have spoken many things frivolously of it, but grounded in evident places of Scriptures: Amongst which, we looke especially, how farre this Text conduces to that Doctrine. There are two places ordinarily cited, which seeme directly to concerne this sin; and two others, which to me seeme not to doe so. Those of the first kinde, are both in the Epistle to the *Hebrewes:* There the Apostle says, *For those who were once inlightned, and have tasted of the heavenly gift, and were made partakers of the Holy Ghost, If they fall away, it is impossible to renew them by repentance.* Now, if finall impenitence had been added, there could have been no question, but that this must be The sin against the Holy Ghost; And because the Apostle speaks of such a totall falling away, as precludes all way of repentance, it includes finall impenitence, and so makes up that sin. The other place from which it rises most pregnantly, is, *Of how sore a punishment shall they be thought worthy, who have trodden under foot the Son of God, and have done despite unto the Spirit of grace?* As he had said before, *If we sin wilfully, after we have received the knowledge of truth, there remaineth no more sacrifice for sins, but a certain fearfull looking for of judgement, and fiery indignation.* But yet, though from these places, there arises evidence, that such a sin there is, as naturally shuts out repentance, and so is thereby irremissible, yet there arise no markes, by which I can say, This man is such a sinner; not though hee himselfe

In quibus Script.

Heb. 6.4

Heb. 10.29

Ver. 26

would sweare to me, that he were so now, and that he would con-
⁵⁴⁰ tinue so, till death.

The other places that doe not so directly concerne this sin, and yet
are sometimes used in this affaire, are, one in S. *Iohn,* and this text

1 Iohn 5.16   another. That in S. *Iohn* is, *There is a sin unto death, I doe not say,*
that he shall pray for it. It is true, that the Master of the Sentences,
and from him, many of the Schoole, and many of our later Interpreters too, doe understand this, of the sin against the Holy Ghost,
because we are (almost) forbidden to pray for it; but yet we are not
absolutely forbidden, in that we are not bidden. And if we were for-

Ier. 7.16   bidden, when God sayes to *Ieremy, Pray not thou for this people,*
⁵⁵⁰ *neither lift up cry, nor prayer for them, neither make intercession to*
11.14   *me, for I will not heare thee,* And againe, *Pray not for them, for I*
will not heare them, Not them, though they should come to pray
for themselves, God forbid that we should therefore say, that all that
people had committed the sin against the Holy Ghost. And for this
particular place of S. *Iohn,* that answer may suffice, which very good
Divines have given, Pray not for them, is indeed pray not with them,
admit them to no part in the publique prayers of the Congregation,
but if they sin a sin unto death, a notorious, an inexcusable sin, let
them be persons excommunicated to thee.

⁵⁶⁰   For the words in this text, which seeme to many appliable to that
great sin, it is not cleare, it is not much probable, that they can be
so applied. Take the words invested in their circumstance, in the
context and coherence, and it will appeare evident. Christ speaks this
to the Pharisees, upon occasion of that which they had said to him,
and of him before, and he carries it, intends it no farther. That appeares by the first word of our text, *Propterea, Therefore I say unto*
you; Therefore, that is, Because you have used such words unto me.

Marke 3.30   And S. *Marke* makes it more cleare, *He said this to them, because*
they said, He had an uncleane spirit; because they said he did his
⁵⁷⁰ Miracles by the power of the Devill. Now, this was certainly a sin
against the Holy Ghost, so far, as that it was distinguished from the
sins against the Son of Man; But it was not the sin against the Holy
Ghost; for, Christ being a mixt person, God and Man, did some
things, in which his Divinity had nothing to doe, but were onely
actions of a meere naturall man, and when they slandered him in

these, they blasphemed the Son of Man. Some things he did in the power of his Godhead, in which his humanity contributed nothing; as all his Miracles; and when they attributed these works to the Devill, they blasphemed the Holy Ghost. And therefore S. *Augustine*
580 sayes, That Christ in this place, did not so much accuse the Pharisees, that they had already incurred the sin of the Holy Ghost, as admonish them, that by adventuring upon such sins as were sins against the Holy Ghost, they might at last fall into The sin, that impenitible, and therfore irremissible sin. But that sin, this could not be, because the Pharisees had not embraced the Gospel before, and so this could not be a falling from the Gospel, in them: Neither does it appeare to have continued to a finall impenitence; so far from it, as that S. *Chrysostom* makes no doubt, but that some of these Pharisees did repent upon Christs admonition.

590 Now, beloved, since we see by this collation of places, that it is not safe to say of any man, he is this sinner, nor very constantly agreed upon, what is this sin, but yet we are sure, that such a sin there is, that captivates even God himself, and takes from him the exercise of his mercy, and casts a dumnesse, a speechlesnesse upon the Church it selfe, that she may not pray for such a sinner; and since we see, that Christ, with so much earnestnesse, rebukes the Pharisees for this sin in the text, because it was a limbe of that sin, and conduced to it, let us use all religious diligence, to keep our selves in a safe distance from it. To which purpose, be pleased to cast a particular,
600 but short and transitory glaunce, upon some such sins, as therefore, because they conduce to that, are sometimes called sins against the holy Ghost. Sins against *Power,* (that is the *Fathers* Attribute) sins of infirmity are easily forgiven; sins against *Wisdome,* (that is the *Sons* Attribute) sins of Ignorance are easily forgiven; but sins against *Goodnesse,* (that is the *Holy Ghosts* Attribute,) sins of an hard and ill nature are hardly forgiven: Not at all, when it comes to be The sin; not easily, when they are Those sins, those that conduce to it, and are branches of it.

For branches, the Schoolemen have named three couples, which
610 they have called *sins against the Holy Ghost,* because naturally they shut out those meanes by which the Holy Ghost might work upon us. The first couple is, *presumption* and *desperation;* for presump-

tion takes away the feare of God, and desperation the love of God. And then, they name *Impenitence,* and *hardnesse of heart;* for Impenitence removes all sorrow for sins past, and hardnesse of heart all tendernesse towards future tentations. And lastly, they name *The resisting of a truth acknowledged before,* and *the envying of other men, who have made better use of Gods grace then we have done;* for this resisting of a Truth, is a shutting up of our selves against it,
620 and this envying of others, is a sorrow, that that Truth should prevaile upon them. And truly (to reflect a very little upon these three couples again) To presume upon God, that God cannot damne me eternally in the next world, for a few half-houres in this; what is a fornication, or what is an Idolatry to God? what is a jest, or a ballad, or a libel to a King? Or to despaire, that God will not save me, how well soever I live, after a sin? what is a teare, what is a sigh, what is a prayer to God? what is a petition to a King? To be impenitent, senslesse of sins past; I past yesterday in riot, and yesternight in wantonnesse, and yet I heare of some place, some office, some good fortune
630 fallen to me to day; To be hardned against future sins; shall I forbeare some company, because that company leads me into tentation? Why, that very tentation wil lead me to preferment; To forsake the truth formerly professed, because the times are changed, and wiser men then I change with them; To envy and hate another, another State, another Church, another man, because they stand out in defence of the truth, ·(for, if they would change, I might have the better colour, the better excuse of changing too) al these are shrewd and slippery approaches towards the sin against the Holy Ghost, and therefore the Schoolemen have called all these six, (not without just
640 reason, and good use) by that heavy name.

And some of the Fathers have extended it farther, then to these six. S. *Bernard,* in particular, sayes, *Nolle obedire,* To resist lawfull Authority; And another, *Simulata pœnitentia,* To delude God with relapses, and counterfait repentances; and another also, *Omne schisma,* All schismaticall renting of the peace of the Church, All these they call in that sense, *Sins against the Holy Ghost.* Now, all sins against the Holy Ghost, are not irremissible. *Stephen* told his persecutors, *They resisted the Holy Ghost,* and yet he prayed for them. But because these sins may, and ordinarily doe come to that

Acts 7.51, 60

[2 Sam.
11.2]

⁵⁵⁰ sin, stop betimes. *David* was far from the murder of *Vriah,* when
he did but looke upon his Wife, as she was bathing. A man is far
from defying the holy Ghost, when he does but neglect him; and
yet *David* did come, and he will come to the bottome quickly. It may
make some impression in you, to tell, and to apply a short story. In a
great Schisme at Rome, *Ladislaus* tooke that occasion to debauch and
corrupt some of the Nobility; It was discerned; and then, to those
seven Governors, whom they had before, whom they called *Sapientes,*
Wise men, they added seven more, and called them *Bonos,* Good
men, honest men, and relied, and confided in them. Goodnesse is the
⁶⁶⁰ Attribute of the Holy Ghost; If you have Greatness, you may seeme
to have some of the Father, for Power is his: If you have Wisdome,
you may seeme to have some of the Son, for that is his: If you have
Goodnesse, you have the Holy Ghost, who shall lead you into all
truth. And Goodnesse is, To be good and easie in receiving his impressions, and good and constant in retaining them, and good and
diffusive in deriving them upon others: To embrace the Gospel, to
hold fast the Gospel, to propagate the Gospel, this is the goodnesse
of the Holy Ghost. And to resist the entrance of the Gospel, to abandon it after we have professed it, to forsake them, whom we should
⁶⁷⁰ assist and succour in the maintenance of it, This is to depart from
the goodnesse of the Holy Ghost: and by these sins against him, to
come too neare the sin, the irremissible sin, in which the calamities
of this world shall enwrap us, and deliver us over to the everlasting
condemnation of the next. This is as much as these words do justly
occasion us to say of that sin; and into a more curious search thereof,
it is not holy sobriety to pierce.

Number 4.

Preached at a Christning.

REVEL 7.17. *FOR THE LAMB WHICH IS IN THE MIDST OF THE THRONE, SHALL GOVERN THEM, AND SHALL LEADE THEM UNTO THE LIVELY FOUNTAINS OF WATERS, AND GOD SHALL WIPE AWAY ALL TEARES FROM THEIR EYES.*

Phil. 3.20

[Psa. 84.10]

Iob 39.27
Greg.
Moral.
31, 34

1 Iohn 1.3

IF *our conversation be in heaven,* as the Apostle says his was, and if that conversation be, (as *Tertullian* reads that place) *Municipatus noster,* our City, our dwelling, the place from whence onely we receive our *Laws,* to which onely we direct our *services,* in which onely we are capable of *honours,* and *offices,* where even the office of *a doore-keeper* was the subject of a great *Kings* ambition; if our conversation be there, even *there,* there cannot be better company met, then we may see and converse withall in this Chapter. Upon those words, *doth the Eagle mount up at thy Commandement,* or *make* [10] *his nest on high?* S. Gregory says, *Videamus aquilam, nidum sibi in arduis construentem; Then we saw an Eagle make his nest on high, when we heard S.* Paul *say so, Our conversation is in heaven;* and then doth an *Eagle* mount up *at our commandement,* when our *soul,* our *devotion,* by such a conversation in heaven, associates it self with all this blessed company that are met in this Chapter, that *our fellowship may be with the Father, and with his Son Jesus Christ,* and with all the *Court* and *Quire* of the Triumphant Church. If you go to *feasts,* if you goe to *Comedies,* sometimes onely to meet company, nay if you come to *Church* sometimes onely upon that errand, to meet [20] company, (as though the House of God, were but as the presence of

96

an earthly Prince, which upon solemne Festivall days must be fill'd
and furnished, though they that come, come to doe no service there)
command your Eagle to mount up, and to build his nest on high,
command your *souls* to have their conversation in heaven by meditation of this Scripture, and you shall meet company, which no stranger
shall interrupt, for they are all of a knot, and such a knot as nothing
shall unty, as inseparably united to one another, as that God, with
whom they are made one Spirit, is inseparable in himself.

Here you shall see the *Angell that comes from the East,* (yea, that
30 Angel which *is the East,* from whence all beams of grace and glory
arise, for so the Prophet calls *Christ Jesus* himself, (as S. *Hierome*
reads that place) *Ecce vir, Oriens nomen ejus, Behold him, whose
name is the East*) you shall see him come with the seal of the living
God, and hold back those Angels which had power given them to
hurt the Sea, and the Earth, and you shall hear him say, *Hurt not
the earth, nor the sea, nor the trees, till we have sealed the servants
of our God in the foreheads.* And as you shall see him forward, so
you shall see him large, and bountifull in imprinting that Seal, you
shall see *an hundred and forty four thousand of the Tribes of the*
40 *Children of Israel,* and you shall see *a great multitude, which no man
can number, of all Nations, and kindreds, and people, and tongues,
stand before the Throne, and before the Lamb, and cry out, and say,
Salvation commeth of our God, that sitteth upon the Throne, and
of the Lamb:* and you shall see all the Angels stand round about the
Throne, and about the Elders, and the four Beasts, all falling upon
their faces, and worshipping God, saying, *Amen, praise, and glory,
and wisdome, and thanks, and honour, and power, and might be
unto our God, for evermore, Amen.* And this is good company, and
good Musique.
50 And lest you should lose any of the Joy of this conversation, of this
society, by ignorance what they were, one of the Elders prevents you;
and (as the Text says) *answers you,* saying, *What are these that are
araid in white?* he answers *by* a question, which is somewhat strange;
but he answers *before* any question, which is more strange: but God
sees questions in our hearts before he hears them from our lips; and
as soon as our hearts conceive a desire to be informed, he gives a full
and a present satisfaction; he answers *before* we ask; but yet he

Rev. 7.2

Zecha. 6.12

Rev. 7.3

vers. 4

verse 9 and 10

verse 11
verse 12

verse 13

answers *by* a question, that thereby he may give us occasion of farther discourse, of farther questioning with him. There, this Elder shall tell

60 thee, that those are they which are come out of the Tribulations of

this world, and *have made their Robes white in the blood of the Lamb;* that therefore they are in the presence of the Throne of God, that they serve him day and night in the Temple, that they shall hunger no more, thirst no more, nor be offended with heat, or Sun; That is, as many as are appointed to receive this Seal of the living God upon their foreheads, though they be not actually delivered from all the incommodities of this life, yet nothing in this life shall deprive them of the next. For as you see the Seal given in this Chapter, and the promise of all these blessings annexed to it, so you see in

70 this Text the reason of all this, for *the Lamb which is in the midst of the Throne shall govern them, and shall leade them unto the lively fountains of waters, and God shall wipe away all teares from their eyes.*

Divisio

In which words, we shall consider for order and distinction, first the *matter,* and then the *form:* by the *matter* we mean the purpose and *intention* of the Holy Ghost in these words; and by the *form,* the declaring, the proving, the *illustrating,* and the heightning of that

vers. 3

purpose of his. For the matter, we take this *imprinting of the Seal* of the living God in the forehead of the Elect, and this *washing in*

verse 14

80 *the blood* of the Lamb, to be intended of the *Sacrament of Baptisme:* In that which we call the *form,* which is the *illustrating* of this, we shall first look upon the great benefits and blessings which these servants of God so *sealed,* and so *washed,* are made partakers of; for those blessings which are mentioned in the verses before, are rooted and enwrapped in this particular of this Text, *Quoniam, for;* they are blessed; *for* the *Lamb* shall doe this and this for them; And then we shall consider *what* that is which this Lamb will doe for them; first, *Reget illos, He shall govern them,* take them into his care, make them heirs of the Covenant, breed them in a *visible Church:* secondly,

90 *Deducet eos, He shall lead them to the lively fountains of waters;* give them outward and visible means of Sanctification: thirdly, *Absterget omnem lachrymam, He shall wipe away all tears from their eyes;* even in *this life* he shall settle and establish a heavenly joy in the faithfull apprehension of the joyes of heaven here.

First then to speak of the *matter,* that is, of the purpose and intention of these words, it is true, they are diversly understood: They have
been understood of the state of the *Martyrs,* which are now come to
the possession of their Crown in heaven, because they are said to have
made their long Robes white in the blood of the Lamb; And so S.
¹⁰⁰ *Augustine* and S. *Gregory* (when, by occasion of the subject which
they were then in hand with, they were full of the contemplation of
Martyrdome, and encouragements to that) doe seem to understand
these words, of *Martyrs.* But since it is not said, that they washed
their robes *in their own blood,* which is proper to *Martyrs,* but *in the
blood of the Lamb,* which is communicated *to all* that participate of
the *merit* of Christ, the words seem larger then so, and not to be restrained onely to *Martyrs.* Others have enlarged them farther then
so, beyond Martyrs: but yet limit them to the *Triumphant Church;*
that because it is said, that *they are come out of great tribulation,* and
¹¹⁰ that *they are in the presence of the Throne of God,* and that *they shall
hunger no more,* they see no way of admitting these perfections, in
this life. But S. *Paul* saw a way, when he said of the *Elect,* even in
this life, God which is rich in mercy, Convivificavit, conresuscitavit,
considere fecit; *he hath quickned us, he hath raised us, he hath made
us sit together in the heavenly places, in Christ Jesus:* That is, as he
is our *Head,* and is there *himself,* and we with Christ Jesus, as we are
his *Members;* we are with him there too. In the same place where the
Apostle says, *That we look for our Saviour from heaven,* (there is
our *future,* our expectation) he says also, *our conversation is in
¹²⁰ heaven,* there is our *present,* our actuall possession. That is it which
S. *Augustine* intends, *Dilexisti me Domine plusquam te; Lord thou
hast loved me more then thou has loved thy self:* Not onely that thou
gavest thy self for me, that thou didst neglect thy self to consider me,
but whereas thou hadst a glory with the *Father,* before the world
was made, thou didst admit a *cloud,* and a slumber upon that glory,
and staiedst for thy glory till thy *death,* yet thou givest *us,* (naturally
inglorious, and miserable creatures) a reall possession of glory, and
of inseparablenesse from thee, in *this life.* This is that *Copiosa redemptio,* there is with the Lord *plentifull redemption;* though that
¹³⁰ were *Matura redemptio,* a seasonable redemption, if it should meet
me upon my *death-bed,* and that the Angels then should receive my

Materia

verse 14
Aug.
Gregor.

Ephes. 2.4

Phil. 3.20

Aug.

Psal. 130.7

soul, to lay it in *Abrahams* bosome, yet this is my Saviours *plentifull redemption,* that my soul is in *Abrahams* bosome now whilest it is in this body, and that I am already in the presence of his Throne, now when I am in your sight, and that *I serve him already day and night in his Temple,* now when I meditate, or execute his Commission, in this service, in this particular Congregation.

Those words are not then necessarily restrained to *Martyrs,* they are not restrained to the state of the *Triumphant Church,* they are
[140] spoken to all the *Children of righteousnesse,* and of godlines; and

1 Tim. 4.8   *godlinesse hath the promises of the life present, and that, that is to come.* That which involves all these promises, that which is the kernell, and seed, and marrow of all, the last clause of the text, *God shall wipe all teares from their eyes,* those words, that clause, is *thrice* repeated intirely in the Scriptures: When it is spoken *here,* when it is spoken in the one and twentieth Chapter of the *Revelation,* and at the fourth verse, in both places, it is derived from the Prophet

25.8   *Esay,* which is an *Eucharisticall chapter,* a Chapter of thanksgiving for Gods deliverance of his children, even in *this world,* from the
[150] afflictions, and tribulations thereof, and therefore this text belongs also to *this world.*

This *imprinting* then of *the seale* in *the forehead,* this *washing*
Ambr.   of *the robes* in *the bloud of the Lambe,* S. *Ambrose* places conveniently to be accomplished in the *Sacrament* of *Baptisme:* for this is *Copiosissima Redemptio,* this is the most plentiful redemption, that can be applied to us, not onely at last in *Heaven,* nor at my last step towards heaven, at my *death,* nor in all the steps that I make in the course of my life, but in my *first step* into the *Church,* nay before I can make any step, when I was carried in anothers armes thither,
[160] even in the beginning of this life; and so do divers of the later Men, and of those whom we call *ours,* understand all this, of *baptisme;* because if we consider this *washing away of teares,* as Saint *Cyprian* says, *young children* doe most of all need this mercy of God and this assistance of Man, because as soone as they come into this world *Plorantes, ac flentes, nihil aliud faciunt, quam deprecantur,* they beg with teares something at our hands, and therefore need this abstersion, this wiping. For though *they* cannot tell *us,* what they aile, though (if we will enter into curiosities) *we* cannot tell *them* what

they aile, that is, we cannot tell them what properly, and exactly
¹⁷⁰ *Originall sin is,* yet they aile something, which naturally disposes
them, to *weep,* and *beg,* that something might be done, for the *wiping
away of teares from their eyes.* And therefore though the other errors
of the *Anabaptist* be ancient, 1000. year old, yet the *denying of baptisme* to children, was never heard of till within 100. years, and lesse.
The *Arrians,* and the *Donatists* did *rebaptize* those who were baptized by the true Christians, whom they counted *Heretiques;* but yet
they refused not to baptize children: The *Pelagians* denied *originall
sin* in children; but yet they *baptized* them. All Churches, *Greek,*
and *Russian,* and *Ethiopique,* howsoever they differ in the *body* of
¹⁸⁰ the Church, yet they meet, they agree in the *porch, in Limine Ecclesiæ,*
in the *Sacrament* of *baptisme,* and acknowledge that it is communicable to *all children,* and to *all Men;* from the child new borne to the
decrepit old Man, from him that is come out of one mothers wombe,
to him that is going into another, into his grave. *Sicut nullus prohi-
bendus à baptismo, ita nullus est qui non peccato moritur in baptismo,
As baptisme is to be denied to none, so neither is it to be denied, that
all, that are rightly baptized, are washed from sin.* Let him that will
contentiously say, that there are *some* children, that take no profit
by baptisme, shew me *which* is one of them, and *qui testatur de*
¹⁹⁰ *scientia, testetur de modo scientiæ;* If he say he knowes it, let him
tell us *how* he knowes that which the Church of God doth not know.

    We come now to the second part; in which we consider first, this
first word *quoniam, for,* which is *verbum prægnans,* a word that includes all those great blessings, which God hath ordained for them,
whom in his *eternall decree,* he hath prepared for this *sealing* and
this *washing.* Those blessings, which are immediately before the text,
are, that in Gods *purpose,* they are *already come out of great tribulations,* they have *already* received a *whitenes* by the bloud of the
Lambe, they are *already in the presence of the throne of the Lambe,*
²⁰⁰ they have already *overcome all hunger, and thirst, and heat.* Those
particular blessings we cannot insist upon; that requires rather a
Comment upon the Chapter, then a *Sermon* upon the text. But in
this word of inference, *for,* we onely wil observe this: That though
all the promises of God in him, are Yea, and Amen, certain, and
infallible in *themselves,* through his *Name,* that makes them be *Amen,*

Augustin.

2 Part

2 Cor. 1.20

Revel. 3.14
(*Thus saith Amen, the faithfull and true witnesse*) and therefore
there needs no better security, then *his word*, for all those blessings,
yet God is pleased to give that abundant satisfaction to Man, as that
his *reason* shall have something to build upon, as well as his *faith*,
²¹⁰ he shall know *why* he should beleeve all these blessings to belong to
them who are to have these Seales, and this washing. For God requires no such *faith*, nay he accepts, nay he excuses no such faith, as
beleeves without reason; beleeves he knowes not why. As faith without *fruit*, without *works*, is no faith; so faith without a *root*, without
reason, is no faith, but an *opinion*. All those blessings by the *Sacrament of Baptism*, and all Gods other promises to his children, and
all the mysteries of Christian Religion, are therefore beleeved by us,
because they are grounded in the Scriptures of God; we beleeve them
for that reason; and then it is not a worke of my *faith* primarily, but
²²⁰ it is a worke of my *reason*, that assures me, that these are the Scriptures, that these Scriptures are the word of God. I can answer other
Mens reasons, that argue against it, I can convince other men by
reason, that my reasons are true: and therefore it is a worke of reason,
that I beleeve these to be Scriptures.

To prove a beginning of the world, I need not the Scriptures;
reason will evict it forcibly enough against all the world; but, when I
come beyond all Philosophy, that for *Adams* fault six thousand year
agoe, I should be condemned now, because that fault is naturally in
me, I must find *reason*, before I beleeve this, and my reason is, because

[Eph. 2.3]
²³⁰ I find it in the *Scriptures; Nascimur filii Iræ,* and therefore, *nisi
renatus, we are borne children of wrath,* and therefore must be borne
againe. That a *Messias* should come to deliver Mankind from this

[Gen. 3.15]
sinne, and all other sins, my reason is, the *Semen mulieris, the seed*

[John 1.29]
of the woman, for the promise, and the *Ecce agnus Dei*, Behold the
Lambe of God, for the performance. That he *should* come, I rest in
that, *The seed of the woman shall bruise the Serpents head;* And that
he is come, I rest in this, that *John Baptist* shewed the *Lambe of God
that taketh away the sinnes of the world.* That this merit of his should

[Gen. 17.7]
be applied to *certaine Men*, my reason is in the *Semini tuo*, Gods
²⁴⁰ Covenant, to *Abraham*, and *to his seed;* That we are of that number,

[Rom. 8.15]
included in that Covenant to *Abraham*, my reason is, *In spiritu adop-
tionis*, the spirit of adoption hath ingraffed us, inserted us into the

same Covenant. When my reason tells me that the *Seale* of that Covenant, *Circumcision* is gone, (I am not circumcised, and therefore might doubt) my reason tells me too, that in the Scriptures, there is a *new Seale, Baptisme:* when my reason tells mee, that after that *regeneration,* I have *degenerated* againe, I have fallen from those graces which I received in *Baptisme,* my reason leades mee againe to those places of Scripture, where God hath established a *Church* for 250 *the remission* and absolution of sinnes. If I have been negligent of all these helpes, and now my reason beginnes to worke to my prejudice, that I beginne to gather and heape up all those places of the *Law,* and *Prophets,* and *Gospell,* which threaten certaine condemnation unto such sinners, as I find my selfe to bee, yet if my reason can see light at the *Nolo mortem peccatoris,* at the *Quandocunque resipiscet;* That *God would not the death of any sinner,* That no time is unseasonable for repentance: That scatters the *clouds of witnesses* againe; and so till my reason can tell me (which it can never doe) that it hath found places in Scripture, of a measure, and *finitenesse* in 260 *God,* (that his *mercy* can goe no farther) and then of an *infinitenesse* in *Man* (that his sinne can goe beyond God) my reason will defend me from *desperation;* I meane the reason, that is grounded upon the Scripture; still I shall find there, that *Quia,* which *David* delighted in so much, as that he repeats it almost *thirty times,* in one Psalm, *For his mercy endureth for ever.*

    God leaves no way of satisfaction unperformed unto us; sometimes he workes upon the phantasie of Man; as in those often *Visions,* which he presented to his Prophets in *dreames;* sometimes he workes upon the *senses,* by preparing objects for them; So he filled the 270 Mountaine round about with horses, and chariots, in defence of *Elisha;* but alwayes he workes upon our *reason;* he bids us feare no judgment, he bids us hope for no mercy, except it have a *Quia, a reason,* a foundation, in the Scriptures. For God is *Logos, speech* and *reason:* He declares his will by his *Word,* and he proves it, he confirmes it; he is *Logos,* and he proceeds *Logically.* It is true, that we have a *Sophistry,* which as farre as concernes our owne destruction, frustrates his Logique; If *Peter* make a *Quia,* a reason why his fellowes could not bee drunke, *Because it was but nine a Clocke,* wee can find Men that can overthrow that reason, and rise drunke out of

[Ezek. 33.11]
[Heb. 12.1]

136

2 Reg. 6.17

Act. 2.15

²⁸⁰ their beds; If Christ make a *Quia,* a reason against *fashionall,* and
Circumstantiall christians, that doe sometimes some offices of religion,
out of custome, or company, or neighborhood, or necessity, because

no man peeceth an old garment with new cloth, nor puts new wine
into old vessells, yet since S. *Augustine* says well, *Carnalitas vetustas,*
gratia novitas, our carnall delights, are our old garments, and those
degrees and beames of grace, which are shed upon us, are the new, we
do peece this old with this new, that is, long habits of sin, with short
repentances, flames of *concupiscence,* with little sparks of *remorse;*
and into old *vessells,* (our sin-worne *bodies*) we put in once a year,
²⁹⁰ some drops, of *new wine,* of the *bloud of our Saviour Christ Iesus,* in
the *Sacrament,* (when we come to his *table,* as to a *vintage,* because
of the season, and we *receive* by the *Almanack,* because it is *Easter*)
and this new wine so taken in, *breakes the vessells,* (as Christ speakes
in that similitude) And his breaking shall be, as the *breaking of a
Potters pot, which is broken without pity, and in the breaking thereof
is not found a shard, to take fire at the hearth, nor to take water out
of the pit;* No way in the Church of God, to repaire that Man, because he hath made either a *Mockery,* or at best, but a *Civill action* of
Gods institution in the Church. To conclude this, all sin is but fallacy
³⁰⁰ and *Sophistry; Religion* is *reason* and *Logique;* The devill hides, and
deludes, Almighty God demonstrates and proves: That fashion of his
goes through all his precepts, through all his promises, which is in
Esay, Come now, and let us reason together; that which was in *Iob,* is
abundantly in God, *That he did not contemne the judgment of his
servant, nor of his maid, when they did contend with him. Nec decet*
Dei iudicium quicquid habere affine tyrannidi, we may not think that
here is any thing in God, like a *Tyran;* and it is a Tyrannicall proceeding, as to give no reason of his cruelties, so to give no assurance of his
benefits; and therefore God seales his promises with a *Quia,* a reason,
³¹⁰ an assurance.

Now much of the strength of the assurance, consists in the person,
whose seale it is; and therefore as Christ did, we ask next, *Cujus
inscriptio,* whose Image, whose inscription is upon his seale, who gives
this assurance? And it is the *Lambe that is in the midst of the throne;*
If it were the *Lion,* the Lion of the tribe of *Iuda,* is able to perform
his promises: but there are more then Christ, out of this world,

that beare the Lion; The *devill* is a *Lion* too, that *seeketh whom he*   [1 Pet. 5.8]
may devoure: but he never seales with that *Lambe,* with any impression of *humility;* to a *Lambe* he is never compared; in the likenesse
320 of a lambe, he is never noted to have appeared, in all the *Legends.*

It is the Lambe, *that is in the midst,* thereby disposed to shed, and
dispense his spirituall benefits on all sides; The Lambe is not im-
mured in *Rome,* not coffined up in the ruines, and rubbidge of old
wals, nor thrust into a corner in *Conventicles. The Lambe is in the*
midst; and he is in the midst *of the throne;* though al his great, and
glorious company be round about him, *one hundred and forty foure*
thousand Israelites, innumerable multitudes of all Nations, Angels,
and Elders, yet it is the Lambe, that is in the midst of them, and not
they that are about him, that sheds down these blessings upon us;
330 And it is the Lambe, that is there still, in the *midst of the throne;* not
kneaded into an *Agnus Dei,* of *wax,* or *wafer* here, not called down
from heaven, to an *Altar,* by every Priests charme, to be a witnesse of
secrecy in the *Sacrament,* for every bloudy, and seditious enterprise,
that they undertake; It is *Agnus qui est in medio Throni,* the Lambe
that is there, and shall be so, till he come at last, as a *Lion* also, to
devoure them, who have made false opinions of him to serve their
mischievous purposes here.

This is the *person* then, that gives the assurance, that all these blessings belong to them who are ordained to be so *sealed,* and so *washed;*
340 this is he that assures us, and approves to us, that all this shall be,
first, *Quia reget,* because he shall *govern them;* secondly, *Quia*
deducet, because he *shall lead them to the fountaines of waters;*
thirdly, *Quia absterget,* because *he shall wipe all teares from their eyes.*

First, *he shall govern them;* he shall establish a *spirituall Kingdome*   *Reget*
for them in this world; for to *govern,* which is the word, of the first
translation, and to *feed,* which is in the second, is all one in Scriptures.
Dominabitur gentium, he shall be Lord of the Gentiles; but *Rex*   [John 1.49]
Israelis, he shall governe his people Israel, *as a King,* by a certain, and
a cleare *law;* So that, as we shal have interest in the Covenant, as well
350 as the *Israelites,* so we shal have interest in that glorious acclamation
of theirs; Unto *what nation are their Gods come so neare unto them,*   [Deut. 4.7–8]
as the Lord our God, is come neare unto us; what nation hath Laws,
and ordinances so righteous as we have? for in that *Paul* and *Barnabas*

Act. 14.16

express the heaviest indignation of God upon the Gentiles, *that God suffered the Gentiles to walke in their own ways;* he shewed them not his ways, he setled no church, no kingdome, amongst them, he did not govern them. Except one of those *Eight* persons whom God pre-

[Gen. 7.13]

served in *the Arke,* were here to tell us, the unexpressible comfort, that he conceived in his safety, when he saw that flood wash away

360 Princes from their thrones, misers from their bagges, lovers from their embracements, Courtiers from their wardrobes, no man is able to expresse that true comfort, which a Christian is to take, even in this, That God hath taken him into his *Church,* and not left him in that desperate, and irremediable inundation of *Idolatry,* and *paganisme,* that overflowes all the world beside. For beloved, who can expresse,

[1 Cor.
15.51]
[1 Thes.
4.17]

who can conceive that strange confusion, which shall overtake, and oppresse those infinite multitudes of Soules, which *shall be changed* at the last day, and shall meet Christ Jesus in the clouds, and shall receive an irrevocable judgment of everlasting condemnation, out of

370 his mouth, whose name they never heard of *before;* that must be con-demned by a Judge, of whom they knew nothing *before,* and who never had *before* any apprehension of torments of *Hell,* till by that lamentable experience they began to learn it? What blessed meanes of preparation against that fearfull day doth he afford us, even in this, that he *governes us* by his law, delivered in his Church.

The first thing, that the *housholder in the parable,* is noted to have

Mat. 21.33

done for his Vineyard, was, *Sepe circumdedit, he hedged it in.* That, God hath done for us, in making us *his Church;* he hath inlaid us, he

Eccles. 10.8

hath hedged us in. *But he that breaketh the hedge, a Serpent shall bite*

380 *him;* he that breaketh this hedge, the peace of the Church, by his *Schisme,* the *old Serpent* hath bitten, and poysoned him, and shall bite worse hereafter: and if God, having thus severed us, and hedged us in, have expected *grapes,* and we bring none, though we breake no hedge here amongst our selves, that is, no *Papist* breaks in upon us, no *Separatist* breakes out from us, we enjoy security enough, yet even for

Esay 5.5

our own barrennes, *God will take away the hedge, and it shall be eaten up, he will breake the wall, and it shall be troden down.* Surely, says the Prophet there, *The Vineyard of the Lord of hosts is the house of Israel, and the Men of Iudah are his pleasant plant:* Surely we are the

390 *Church,* which God hath hedged in; but yet if we answer not his

expectation, certainly the confusion of the Gentiles, at the last day, (when they shal say to themselves of Christ, *Nescivi te, dost thou condemne us, and we knew thee not?*) shall not be so great, as our confusion shall be, when we shall hear Christ say to us, whom he bred in his Church, *Nescio vos, I know not whence you are.* Even this, that the ill use of this mercy of having been bred in his Church, shall aggravate our condemnation then, shewes the great benefit, which we may receive now by this *Quod regit nos,* that he takes care of us in his Church; for how many in the world would have lived ten times
400 more *christianly* then we do, if they had but halfe that knowledge of *Christ,* which we have?

[Luk. 13.25]

When he hath then brought us into his kingdome, that we are his *subjects,* (for all the heathen are in the condition of *slaves*) he brings us nearer, into his *service;* he gives us outward distinctions, liveries, badges, names, *visible markes in Baptisme:* yea he incorporates us more inseparably to himself, then that which they imagine to be done in the Church of *Rome,* where their *Canonists* say, that a *Cardinall* is so incorporated in the *Pope,* he is so made one flesh, and bloud with him, as that he may not let bloud without his leave, because he
410 bleeds not his own, but the *Popes* bloud: But of us it is true, that by this *Sacrament* we are so incorporated into Christ, that in all our afflictions after we fulfill the sufferings of Christ in our flesh, and in all afflictions, which we lay upon any of our Christian brethren, our consciences hear Christ crying to us, *Quid me persequeris?* why persecutest thou me? Christs body is wounded *in us,* when we suffer, Christs body is wounded *by us,* when we violate the peace of the Church, or offend the particular members thereof.

Deducet

[Col. 1.24]

[Acts 9.4]

First then *deducet,* he *shall lead them,* it is not he shall *force them,* he shall *thrust them,* he shall *compell them;* it implies a gentle, and
420 yet an effectuall way, *he shall lead them.* Those which come to *Christianity,* from *Iudaisme,* or *Gentilisme,* when they are of *years of discretion,* he shall lead them by instruction, by *Catechisme,* by *preaching* of his word, before they be baptized, for they that are of years and are baptized, *without the word,* that is, *without understanding,* or considering the institution, and vertue of baptisme, expressed in Gods word, and so receive baptisme onely for *temporall,* and *naturall* respects, they are not *led to the waters,* but they *fall* into

them: and so, as a Man may be drowned in a wholsome bath, so such
a Man, may perish eternally in *baptisme,* if he take it, for satisfaction
430 of the *State,* or any other by-respect, to which that Sacrament is not
ordained, in the word of God. He shall lead *Men of years,* by *Instruction;* and he shall *lead young children,* in good company, and with a
strong guard, he shall lead them by the *faith* of his *Church,* by the
faith of their *Parents,* by the faith of their *sureties* and undertakers.
    He shall *lead* them; and then, when he hath taken them into his
government; for first it is *Reget,* he shall govern them, and then
Deducet, that is, he shall lead them, in *his Church;* and therefore they
that are led to baptisme, *any other way then by the Church,* they are

Esay 19.14

misled; nay they are miscarried, misdriven, *Spiritu vertiginis,* with
440 the spirit of giddinesse. They that joyne any in commission with the
Trinity, though but as an assistant, (for so they say in the Church of

Aquin.

Rome; baptisme may be administred, in the name of the *Father,
Sonne,* and *holy Ghost, and the virgin Mary*) they follow not, as

[Mat. 19.8]

Christ led in his Church, *Non fuit sic ab initio, It was not so from the
beginning;* for *quod extra hos tres est, totum Conservum est;* though
much dignity belong to the memory of the *Saints* of God, yet whoso-

Basil

ever is none of the three Persons, *Conservus est,* he is our fellow-
servant: though his service lie *above staires,* and ours *below,* his in
the *triumphant,* ours in the *militant* Church, *Conservus est,* yet he, or
450 she, is in that respect, but our *fellow-servant,* and not Christs *fellow-*

Exod. 15.
[23–25]

redeemer. So also, if we be led to *Marah,* to the *waters of bitternesse,*
that we bring a bitter taste, of those institutions of the Church for the
decency, and signification in Sacramentall things, things belonging to
Baptisme, if we bring a misinterpretation of them, an indisposition to
them, an aversnesse from them, and so nourish a bitternes, and uncharitablenesse towards one another, for these *Ceremonies,* if we had
rather *crosse* one another, and *crosse* the Church, then *crosse* the
child, as God shewed *Moses, a tree,* which made those waters in the
wildernesse sweet, when it was cast in, so remember that there is the
460 *tree of life,* the *crosse of Christ Iesus,* and his Merits, in this water of
baptisme, and when we all agree in that, that all the vertue proceeds
from the *crosse of Christ,* the God of unity and peace and concord, let
us admit any representation of *Christs crosse,* rather then admit the
true *crosse of the devill,* which is a bitter and *schismaticall* crossing of

Christ in his Church: for it is there in his Church, that he leads us to these waters.

Well then, they to whom these waters belong, have Christ in his Church to lead them; and therefore they need not stay, till they can come *alone;* till they be of age and years of discretion, as the *Anabap-* ⁴⁷⁰ *tists* say: for it is *Deducet,* and *Deducet eos;* generally, universally; *all* that are of this government, *all* that are appointed for the *Seal,* all *the one hundred and forty foure thousand,* all the *Innumerable multitudes of all Nations,* Christ leads them *all. Be Baptized every one of you, in the name of Iesus Christ, for the remission of sinnes; for the promise is made unto you, and your children.* Now all promises of God, are sealed in the *holy Ghost;* To whom soever any promise of God belongs, he hath the holy Ghost; and therefore *Nunquid aquam quis prohibere potest? Can any Man forbid water, that those should not be baptized, which have received the holy Ghost, as well as we?* ⁴⁸⁰ says S. *Peter.* And therefore the *Children* of the Covenant which have the *promise,* have the *holy Ghost,* and all they are in this Regiment, *Deducet eos,* Christ shall lead *them all.*

But whither? *unto the lively,* (says our first edition) *unto the liv-* *ing,* (says our last edition) *fountaines of waters;* In the *originall, unto the fountaines of the water of life.* Now in the Scriptures nothing is more ordinary, then by the name of *waters* to designe and meane *tribulations:* so, amongst many other, God says of the City of *Tyre,* that he would make it a desolate City, and bring the deep upon it, and *great waters should cover it.* But then there is some such addition, ⁴⁹⁰ as leads to that sense; either they are called *Aquæ multæ, great waters,* or *Profunda aquarum, deep waters,* or *Absorbebit aqua, whirle-* *pooles* of waters, or *Tempestas aquæ,* tempestuous waters, or *Aqua Fellis,* bitter water, (God *hath mingled gall in our water:*) but we shall never read *fontes aquarum, fountaines of waters,* but it hath a gratious sense, and presents Gods benefits. So, *they have forsaken me* *the fountaine of living waters;* So, *the water, that I shall give, shall be in him, a well of water, springing up unto everlasting life;* and so, every where else, when we are brought *to the fountaines,* to this water, in the fountaine, in the *institution,* howsoever we puddle it with im- ⁵⁰⁰ pertinent *questions* in disputation, howsoever we foule it with our *sinnes,* and ill conversation, the fountaine is *pure; Baptisme* presents, and offers grace, and remission of sinnes to *all.*

Eos

Act. 2.38

Act. 10.47

Ad aquas

Ezek. 26.19

Ier. 8.14

Ier. 2.13

Ioh. 4.14

Basil
1 Pet. 3.21
Psal. 29.10

[Psa. 32.5–6]

Mic. 7.19

1 Reg. 7.23

[Heb. 12.6]
Luke 24.[26]

Absterget

Nay not onely, this *fountaine* of water, but the greatest water of all, the *flood* it selfe, Saint *Basil* understands, and applies to *Baptisme,* as the Apostle himselfe does, *Baptisme, was a figure,* of the *flood,* and the *Arke,* for upon that place, *The Lord sitteth upon the flood, and the Lord doth remaine King for ever,* he says, *Baptismi gratiam Diluvium nominat, nam delet & purgat; David* calls *Baptisme* the *flood,* because it destroyes all that was sinfull in us; and so also he ⁵¹⁰ referres to Baptisme, those words, (when *David* had confessed his sinnes) *I thought I would confesse against my selfe my wickednesse, unto the Lord;* and when it is added, *Surely in the flood of great waters, they shall not come near him, peccata non appropinquabunt,* says he, *originall sinne* shall not come neare him, that is truly *baptized;* nay all the *actuall sinnes* in his future life, shall be drowned in this baptisme, as often, as he doth religiously, and repentantly consider, that in *Baptisme,* when the merit of Christ was communicated to him, he received an *Antidote* against all poyson, against all sinne, if he applied them together, sinne and the merit of Christ; for so also ⁵²⁰ he says, of that place, God will subdue all our iniquities, and *cast our sinnes into the bottome of the Sea, Hoc est, in mare Baptismi,* says *Basil,* into the *Sea of Baptisme:* There was a *Brasen Sea in the Temple;* and there is a *golden Sea in the Church* of Christ, which is *Baptisterium,* the *font,* the *Sea,* into which God flings all their sinnes, who rightly, and effectually receive that Sacrament.

These fountaines of waters then in the text, are the waters of baptisme: and if we should take them also, in that sense, that waters signifie *tribulations,* and *afflictions,* it is true too, that in *baptisme,* (that is, in the profession of Christ,) we are delivered over to many ⁵³⁰ tribulations; The rule is generall, *Castigat omnes,* he *chastiseth all;* The example, the precedent is peremptory, *Oportuit pati, Christ ought to suffer,* and so *enter into glory:* but howsoever waters be afflictions, they are *waters of life* too, says the text; Though baptisme imprint a *crosse* upon us, that we should not be ashamed of *Christs crosse,* that we should not be afraid of our *owne crosses,* yet by all these waters, by all these *Crosse ways,* we goe directly to the eternall life, the kingdome of heaven, for they are *lively fountaines, fountaines of life.*

And this is intended, and promised, in the last words, *Absterget omnem Lachrymam, God shall wipe all teares from our eyes;* God

540 shall give us a joyfull apprehension of heaven, *here* in his Church *in this life.* But is this a way to wipe teares from the childes face, to sprinkle water upon it? Is this a wiping away, to powre more on? It is the powerfull, and wonderfull way of his working; for as his *red bloud,* makes our *red soules, white,* that his rednesse, gives our rednesse a candor, so his water, his baptisme, and the powerfull effect thereof, shall dry up, and wipe away *Omnem lachrymam, all teares from our Eyes,* howsoever occasioned. This water shall dry them up; Christ had many occasions of teares; we have more; some of our owne, which he had not: we must weep because we are not so good,
550 as we *should* be: we *cannot* performe the *law.* We must weepe, because we are not so good, as we *could* be; our *free will* is lost; but yet every Man findes, he might be better, if he *would:* but the sharpest, and saltest, and smartest occasion of our teares, is from this, that we *must not* be so good, as we *would* be; that the profanenesse of the *Libertine,* the reproachfull *slanders,* the contumelious *scandalls,* the *scornfull* names, that the wicked lay upon those, who in their measure desire to expresse their zeale to Gods glory, make us afraid, to professe our selves so religious as we could find in our hearts to be, and could truly be if we might. Christ wept often in contemplation of oth-
560 *ers;* foreseeing the calamities of *Ierusalem,* he wept over the City: comming to the grave of *Lazarus,* he wept with them, but in his owne Agony in the garden, it is not said that *he wept;* If we could stop the flood of teares, in our afflictions, yet there belongs an excessive griefe to this, that the ungodly disposition of *other Men,* is a slacking of our godlinesse, of our sanctification too. Christ Jesus *for the joy that was set before him endured the Crosse;* we for the joy of this promise, *that God will wipe all teares from our eyes,* must suffer all this; whether they be teares of *Compunction,* or teares of *Compassion,* teares for our selves, or teares for others; whether they be *Magdalens*
570 *teares,* or *Peters teares;* teares for sinnes of *infirmity* of the *flesh,* or teares for *weaknesse* of our *faith;* whether they be teares for thy *parents,* because they are improvident towards thee, or teares for thy *children,* because they are disobedient to thee, whether they be teares for the *Church,* because our Sermons, or our Censures pinch you, or teares for the *State,* that penall laws, pecuniary, or bloudy, lie heavy upon you, *Deus absterget omnem lachrymam,* here's your comfort,

[Luk. 19.41]
[Joh. 11.35]

Heb. 12.[2]

that as he hath promised inestimable blessings to them, that are *sealed,*
and *washed* in him, so he hath given you security, that these blessings
belong to you: for, if you find, that he hath *governed* you, (bred you in
580 his visible Church) and *led you to his fountain of the water of life* in
baptisme, you may be sure, that he will in his due time, *wipe all teares
from your eyes,* establish the kingdome of heaven upon you, *in this
life,* in a holy, and modest *infallibility.*

Number 5.

Preached at a Christning.

EPHES. 5.25, 26, 27. *HUSBANDS LOVE YOUR WIVES, EVEN AS CHRIST LOVED THE CHURCH, AND GAVE HIMSELFE FOR IT, / THAT HE MIGHT SANCTIFIE IT, AND CLEANSE IT, BY THE WASHING OF WATER, THROUGH THE WORD: / THAT HE MIGHT MAKE IT UNTO HIMSELFE A GLORIOUS CHURCH, NOT HAVING SPOT, OR WRINKLE, OR ANY SUCH THING; BUT THAT IT SHOULD BE HOLY, AND WITHOUT BLAME.*

ALMIGHTY GOD ever loved *unity*, but he never loved *singularity;* God was always *alone* in heaven, there were no *other Gods,* but he; but he was never *singular,* there was never any time, when there were not *three persons* in heaven; *Pater & ego unum sumus;* The *father and I are one,* says Christ: one in *Essence,* and one in *Consent;* our *substance* is the same, and our *will* is the same; but yet, *Tecum fui ab initio,* says Christ, in the person of *Wisdome,* I was with thee, disposing all things, at the Creation. As then God seemes to have been eternally delighted, with this eternall generation, (with persons that had ever a relation to one another, *Father,* and *Sonne*) so when he came to the Creation of this lower world, he came presently to those three relations, of which the whole frame of this world consists; of which, (because the principall foundation, and preservation of all States that are to continue, is *power*) the first relation was

[Joh. 10.30]

[Prov. 8.30]

113

between *Prince* and *Subject,* when God said to Man, *Subjicite &* *dominamini,* subdue and govern all Creatures; The second relation was between *husband* and *wife,* when *Adam* said, *This now is bone of my bone, and flesh of my flesh;* And the third relation was between *parents* and *children,* when *Eve* said, that she *had obtained a Man by* ²⁰ *the Lord,* that by the plentifull favour of God, she had conceived and borne a sonne: from that time, to the dissolution of that frame, from that beginning to the end of the world, these three relations, of *Master* and *Servant, Man* and *Wife, Father* and *Children,* have been, and ever shall be the materialls, and the elements of all society, of families, and of Cities, and of Kingdomes. And therefore it is a large, and a subtill philosophy which S. *Paul* professes in this place, to shew all the qualities, and properties of these severall *Elements,* that is, all the duties of these severall callings; but in this text, he handles onely the mutuall duties of the second couple, *Man,* and *wife,* and in that ³⁰ consideration, shall we determine this exercise, because a great part of that concernes the education of Children, (which especially occasions our meeting now.)

The generall duty, that goes through all these three relations, is expressed, *Subditi estote invicem, Submit your selves to one another, in the feare of God;* for God hath given no Master such imperiousnesse, no husband such a superiority, no father such a soverainty, but that there lies a burden upon them too, to consider with a compassionate sensiblenesse, the grievances, that oppresse the other part, which is coupled to them. For if the servant, the wife, the sonne be ⁴⁰ oppressed, worne out, annihilated, there is no such thing left as a Master, or a husband, or a father; They depend upon one another, and therefore he that hath not care of his fellow, destroys himselfe.

The wife is to submit herselfe; and so is the husband too: They have a burden both. There is a greater subjection lies upon her, then upon the *Man,* in respect of her transgression towards her husband at first: Even before there was any Man in the world, to sollicite, or tempt her *chastity,* she could finde another way to be false and treacherous to her husband: both the husband, and the wife offended against God, but the husband offended not towards his wife, but ⁵⁰ rather eate the Apple, *Ne contristaretur delicias suas,* as S. *Hierome* assignes the cause, lest by refusing to eate, when she had done so, he

Gen. 1.28

2.23

4.1

v. 21

Hier.

should deject her into a desperate sense of her sinne. And for this
fault of hers, her Subjection was so much aggravated, *Thy desire* [Gen. 3.16]
shall be subject to thy husband, and he shall rule over thee. But if
she had not committed that fault, yet there would have been a mutuall
subjection between them; as there is even in *Nature,* between both the
other couples; for if *Man* had continued in innocency, yet it is most
probably thought, that as there would certainly have been *Mariage,*
and so *children,* so also there would have been *Magistracy,* and
60 *propriety,* and *authority,* and so a mutuall submitting, a mutuall
assisting of one another, in all these three relations.

Now, that submitting, of which the Apostle speakes of here; is a
submitting to one another, *a bearing of one anothers burthens:* what [Gal. 6.2]
this submission is on the wives part, is expressed in the two former
verses; And I forbeare that, because husbands at home, are likely
enough to remember them of it; but in the duty, in the submitting
of the husband, we shall consider first, what that submitting is, and
that is *love, Husbands love your wives;* Even the love of the husband
to the wife, is a burthen, a submitting, a descent; and secondly, the
70 patterne and example of this love, *Even as Christ loved his Church.*

In which second part, as sometimes the accessory is greater then
the principall, the *Symptome,* the accident, is greater then the *disease,*
so that from which the comparison is drawn in this place, is greater
then that which is illustrated by it; the love of Christ to his Church
requires more consideration, then the love of the husband to the wife;
and therefore it will become us to spend most of our thoughts upon
that; and to consider in that, *Quod factum,* and *Quis finis;* what
Christ did for his Church; and that was, a bounty, which could not
be exceeded, *seipsum tradidit,* he gave, he delivered himselfe for it;
80 And then, secondly, what he intended that should worke; and that
was, first, that he might make it to himselfe *a glorious Church,* and
without spot and *wrinkle,* in the *Triumphant* state of the Church at
last; And then, that whilst it continues in a *Militant* state upon Earth,
it might have preparations to that glory, by being *sanctified* and
cleansed by the washing of water, through his Word; he provides the
Church meanes of sanctification here, by his *Word,* and *Sacraments.*

First then *De Amore maritali,* of this contracting a Mans love to *Amor*
the person of a wife, of one woman, as we find an often exclamation

[Isa. 22.1]
[Nah. 1.1]
[Zech. 12.1]

Gen. 38

in the Prophets, *Onus visionis,* The burden of my prophecy upon
⁹⁰ *Nineveh,* and *Onus verbi Domini,* The burden of the word of God
upon *Israel,* so there is *Onus amoris,* a burden of love, when a Man
is appointed whom he shall love. When *Onan* was appointed by his
father *Judah,* to goe in to his brothers widow, and to doe the office
of a kinsman to her, he conceived such an unwillingnesse to doe so,
when he was *bid,* as that he came to that detestable act, for which
God slew him. And therefore the Panegyrique, that raised his wit as
high as he could, to praise the Emperour *Constantine,* and would
expresse it, in praising his *continence,* and *chastity,* he expressed it
by saying that he *maried young;* that as soon as his years endangered
¹⁰⁰ him, *formavit animum maritalem, nihil de concessu ætati voluptati-
bus admittens:* he was content to be a husband, and accepted not
that freedome of pleasure, which his years might have excused. He
concludes it thus, *Novum jam tum miraculum, Juvenis uxorius;* Behold a miracle, such a young Man, limiting his affections, in a wife. At
first the heates and lusts of youth overflow all, as the waters overflowed all at the beginning; and when they did so, the *Earth* was
not onely *barren,* (there were no Creatures, no herbs produced in
that) but even the *waters* themselves, that did overflow all, were
barren too; there were no fishes, no fowls produced out of that; as
¹¹⁰ long as a Mans affections are scattered, there is nothing but accursed
barrennesse; but when God says, and is heard, and obeyed in it, *Let
the waters be gathered into one place,* let all thy affections be setled
upon one wife, then the earth and the waters became fruitfull, then
God gives us a type, and figure of the eternity of the *joyes* of heaven,
in the succession, and propagation of children here upon the earth.
It is true, this contracting of our affections is a *burden,* it is a submitting of our selves; All States that made Lawes, and proposed *rewards*
for *maried Men,* conceived it so; that naturally they would be loth
to doe it. God maried his first couple, as soone as he made them;
¹²⁰ he dignified the state of Mariage, by so many *Allegories,* and *figures,*
to which he compares the uniting of Christ to his Church, and the
uniting of our soules to Christ, and by directing the first Miracle of
Christ, to be done at a Mariage. Many things must concurre to the
dignifying of *Mariage,* because in our corrupt nature, the apprehension is generall, that it is burdenous, and a submitting, and a descend-

Gen. 1.9

ing thing, to mary. And therefore Saint *Hierome* argues truly out of these words, *Husbands love your Wives, Audiant Episcopi, audiant presbyteri, audiant doctores, subjectis suis se esse subjectos,* let Bishops, and Priests, and Doctors learne in this, that when they have maried
130 themselves to a charge, They are become subject to their Subjects. For, by being a husband, I become subject, to that sex which is naturally subject to Man, though this subjection be no more in this place, but to *love* that one woman.

Love then, when it is limited by a law, is a subjection, but it is a subjection commanded by God; *Nihil majus à te subjecti animo factum est, quam quod imperare cœpisti;* A Prince doth nothing so like a subject as when he puts himselfe to the pain to consider the profit, and the safety of his Subjects; and such a subjection is that of a Husband, who is bound to study his wife, and rectify all her infirmities;
140 Her *infirmities* he must bear; but not her sins; if he bear them they become his own. The pattern, the example goes not so far; Christ maried himself to our Nature, and he bare all our *infirmities,* hunger, and wearinesse, and sadnesse, and death, actually in his own person; but so, he contracted no *sin* in himselfe, nor encouraged us to proceed in sin. Christ was *Salvator corporis,* A Saviour of his body, of the Church, to which he maried himselfe, but it is a tyranny, and a devastation of the body, to whom we mary our selves, if we love them so much, as that we love their *Sin* too, suffer them to goe on in that, or if we love them so little, as to make their sin our way to
150 profit, or preferment, by prostituting them, and abandoning them to the solicitation of others; still we must love them so, as that this love be a subjection, not a neglecting, to let them doe, what they will; nor a *tyrannizing,* to make them doe what we will.

You must love them then, first, *Quia vestræ,* because they are yours; As we said at first, God loves *Couples;* He suffers not our body to be alone, nor our soule alone, but he maries them together; when that's done, to remedy the *væ soli,* lest this Man should be alone, he maries him to a help meet for him; and to avoid fornication, (that is, if fornication cannot be avoided otherwise) Every Man is to have his
160 wife, and every woman her own husband. When the love comes to exceed these bounds, that it departs *à vestris,* from a Mans *own* wife, and settles upon another, though he may think he discharges him-

Hier.

Plinius
Trajano

v. 23

Gen. 2.20

1 Cor. 7.2

selfe of some of his subjection which he was in before, yet he becomes
much more subject; subject to houshold and forain *Jealousies,* subject
to ill grounded *quarrels,* subject to blasphemous protestations, to
treacherous misuse of a confident friend, to ignoble and unworthy
disguises, to base *satisfactions;* subject, lastly, either to a clamorous
Conscience, or that which is worse slavery, to a sear'd and obdurate,
and stupefied Conscience, and to that *Curse,* which is the heavier
¹⁷⁰ because it hath a kind of scorn in it, *Be not deceived,* (as though we

[1 Cor. 6.9]
were cousened of our souls) *Be not deceived,* for *no adulterer shal
enter into the kingdom of heaven.* All other things, that are ours, we

[Mat. 19.21]
may be the better for leaving; *Vade & vende,* which Christ said to
the yong Man, that seemed to desire perfection, reached to all his
goods; Goe and sell them sayes Christ, and thou shalt follow me the
better. But there is no selling, nor giving, nor lending, nor borrow-
ing of wives; we must love them *Quia nostræ,* because they are ours;
and if that be not a ty, and obligation strong enough, that they are
Nostræ, ours, we must love them *Quia nos,* because they are our

v. 29 ¹⁸⁰ selves; for no man yet ever hated *his own flesh.*

Vxor
We must love them then, *Quia nostræ,* because they are ours, those
whom God hath given us, and *Quia uxores,* because they are our
wives. Saint *Paul* does not bid us love them here, *Quanquam uxores,*
but *Quia,* not *though* they be, but *because* they are our wives; Saint
Paul never thought of that indisposition, of that disaffection, of that
impotency, that a Man should come to hate her, whom he could love
well enough, *but that she is his wife.* Were it not a strange distemper,
if upon consideration of my soule, finding it to have some seeds of
good dispositions in it, some compassion of the miseries of others,
¹⁹⁰ some inclination to the glory of God, some possibility, some interest
in the kingdome of heaven, I should say of this soule, that I would
fast, and pray, and give, and suffer any thing for the salvation of this
Soule if it were not mine own soule, if it were any bodies else, and
now abandon it to eternall destruction, because it is mine own? If
no Man have felt this barbarous inhumanity towards his owne soul,
I pray God no man have felt it towards his own wife neither, That he
loves her the lesse, for being his own wife. For we must love them,
not *Quanquam,* says Saint *Paul, though* she be so; That was a Caution, which the Apostle never thought he needed, but *Quia,* because

²⁰⁰ in the sight of God, and all the Triumphant Church, we have bound
our selves, that we would do so. Here Mariages are sometimes *clan-
destine,* and witnesses dye, and in that case no Man can bind me to
love her, *Quia uxor,* because she is my wife, because it lyes not in
proofe, that she is so; Here sometimes things come to light, which
were concealed before, and a Mariage proves no Mariage, *Decepta
est Ecclesia,* The Church was deceived, and the poor woman loses
her plea, *Quia uxor,* because she is his wife, for it fals out that she is
not so; but, if thou have maried her, in the presence of God, and all
the *Court,* and *Quire* of heaven, what wilt thou doe to make away
²¹⁰ all these witnesses? who shall be of thy Councell to assign an Error
in Gods judgement? whom wilt thou bribe to embezill the Records
of heaven? It is much that thou are able to doe in heaven; Thou art
able, by thy sins, to blot thy name out of the book of life, but thou
are not able to blot thy wifes name out of the Records of heaven, but
there remains still the *Quia uxor,* because she is thy wife. And this
Quia uxor is *Quamdiu uxor;* since thou are bound to love her because she is thy wife, it must be as long as she is so. You may have
heard of that *quinquennium Neronis;* The worst tyran that ever was,
was the best Emperour that ever was for five years; the most corrupt
²²⁰ husbands may have been good at first: but that love may have been
for other respects: satisfaction of *parents,* establishing of *hopes,* and
sometimes *Ignorance* of evill; that ill company had not taught them
ill conditions; it comes not to be *Quia uxor,* because she is thy wife,
to be the love which is commanded in this text, till it bring some
subjection, some burthen. Till we love her then, when we would
not love her, except she were our wife, we are not sure, that we love
her *Quia uxor,* that is, for that, and for no other respect. How long
that is, how long she is thy wife, never ask wrangling Controverters,
that make *Gypsie-knots* of Mariages; ask thy Conscience, and that
²³⁰ will tell thee that thou wast maried *till death should depart you.*
If thy mariage were made by the *Devill* (upon dishonest Conditions)
the Devill may break it *by sin;* if it were made by God, Gods way
of breaking of Mariages, is onely *by death.*

It is then a *Subjection,* and it is such a subjection, as is a *love;* and
such a love, as is upon a *Reason,* (for love is not alwayes so.) This is;
Quia uxor, because our wife, and that implies these three uses; God

hath given Man a wife, *Ad adjutorium, ad sobolem, ad medicinam;* for a Help, for Children, and for a Remedy, and Physick. Now the first, *Society,* and *encrease,* we love naturally; we would not be
240 banish'd, we would not be robb'd, we would not be alone, we would not be poor; *Society* and *encrease,* every Man loves; but doth any Man love *Physick?* he takes it for necessity; but does he love it? Husbands therefore are to love wives *Ad Sobolem,* as the Mothers of their Children; *Ad adjutorium,* as the comforters of their lives; but

[1 Cor. 7.9]

for that, which is *Ad medicinam,* for physick, *to avoid burning,* to avoid fornication, that's not the subject of our love, our love is not to be placed upon that; for so it is a love, *Quia mulier,* because she is a woman, and not *Quia uxor,* because she is my wife. A Man may be a drunkard at home, with his *own wine,* and never goe out to
250 Taverns; A man may be an *adulterer* in his wives bosome, though he seek not strange women.

2 Part

We come now to the other part, the pattern of this love, which is Christ Jesus: we are commanded to be holy, and pure, *as our Father is holy, and pure;* but that's a proportion of which we are incapable;

[Mat. 11.29]

And therefore we have another Commandement, from Christ, *Discite à me,* learn of me; there is no more looked for, but that we should still be Scholars, and learners how to *love;* we can never love so much as he hath lov'd: It is still *Discite;* still something to be learnt, and added; and this something is, *Quia mitis,* learn of me, make me your
260 pattern, because *I am meek, and gentle;* not suspitious, not froward, not hard to be reconcil'd; not apt to discomfort my spouse, my Church; not with a sullen silence, for I speak to her alwayes in my Word; not apt to leave her unprovided of apparell, and decent ornaments, for I have allow'd her such *Ceremonies,* as conduce to edification; not apt to pinch her in her diet; she hath her two *Courses,* the first, and the second *Sacrament:* And whensoever she comes to a spirituall hunger and thirst under the heat, and weight of sin, she knowes how, and where there is plentifull refreshing and satisfaction to be had, in the *absolution* of sinne. Herein consists the substance
270 of the Comparison, *Husbands love your wives, as Christ did his Church:* that is, expresse your loves in a gentle behaviour towards them, and in a carefull providence of Conveniencies for them. The comparison goes no farther, but the love of Christ to his Church goes

farther. In which we consider first, *Quid factum,* what Christ did for his spouse, for his Church.

It were pity to make too much hast, in considering so delightfull a thing, as the expressing of the love of Christ Jesus to his Church. It were pity to ride away so fast from so pleasant, so various a prospect, where we may behold our Saviour, in the Act of his liberality,
²⁸⁰ *Giving;* in the matter of his liberality, *Giving himselfe;* and in the poor exchange that he took, a few *Contrite hearts,* a few *broken spirits,* a few lame, and blind, and leprous sinners, to make to himselfe, and his Spirit a Church, a house to dwell in; no more but these, and glad if he can get these.

First then, *Ille dedit,* He gave, it was his own act; as it was he, that gave up the ghost, he that laid down his soule, and he that took it again; for no power of Man had the power, or disposition of his life. It was an insolent, and arrogant question in *Pilate* to *Christ, Nescis, quia potestatem habeo, Knowest not thou that I have power to Cruci-*
²⁹⁰ *fie thee, and have power to loose thee?* If *Pilate* thought that his power extended to *Christ,* yet *Tua damnaris sententia; qui potestate latronem absolvis, autorem vitæ interficis.* His own words and actions condemned him, when having power to condemn and absolve, he would condemn the Innocent, and absolve the guilty. A good Judge does nothing, sayes he, *Domesticæ proposito voluntatis,* according to a resolution taken at home; *Nihil meditatum domo defert,* he brings not his judgement from his *chamber* to the *bench,* but he takes it there according to the Evidence. If *Pilate* thought he had power, his Conscience told him he misused that power; but *Christ* tels him he
³⁰⁰ could have none, *Nisi datum desuper,* Except it had been given him from above; that is, except *Christ* had given him power over himselfe: for *Christ* speaks not in that place of Pilates *generall* power and Jurisdiction, (for so, also, all power is *Desuper,* from above) but for this *particular* power that *Pilate* boasts to have over him, *Christ* tels him that he could have none over *him,* except himselfe had submitted himselfe to it. So, before this passage with *Pilat, Judas* had delivered *Christ;* and there arose a sect of Heretiques, *Judaists,* that magnified this act of *Judas,* and said we were beholden to him for the hastning of our salvation, because when he was come to the knowl-
³¹⁰ edge that God had decreed the Crucifying of *Christ* for Mankind,

Quid factum

Ille

Ioh. 19.10

Ambr. Serm. 20 in Ps. 119 v. 4

Philaster

Judas took compassion of Mankind, and hastned their Redemption, by delivering up of *Christ* to the Iewes. But *Judas* had no such good purpose in his hast; though our *Jesus* permitted *Judas* to doe it, and to doe it *quickly,* when he said *Quod facis fac citò.* For out of that ground in the Schooles, *Missio in divinis est nova operatio in Creatura,* When any person of the Trinity, is said to be sent, that onely denotes an extraordinary manner of working of that person: Saint *Augustine* sayes truly, that as Christ *Misit seipsum,* he sent himself, and *Sanctificavit seipsum,* he sanctified himselfe, so *tradidit seipsum;* ³²⁰ *Judas* could not have given him, if he had not given himselfe; *Pilate* could not give him, *Judas* could not give him; nay, if we could consider severall wils in the severall Persons of the Trinity, we might be bold to say, *That the Father could not have given him, if he had not given himselfe.* We consider the unexpressible mercy of the *Father,* in that he would accept any satisfaction at all for all our Sinnes. We consider the unexpressible working of the *Holy Ghost* that brings this satisfaction and our soules together; for without that, without the application of the Holy Ghost, we are as far from Christ's love now, as we were from the Father's before Christ suffered. But the ³³⁰ unexpressible and unconceiveable love of Christ is in this, that there was in him a willingnesse, a propensnesse, a forwardnesse to give himselfe to make this great peace and reconciliation, between God and Man; It was he himselfe that gave himselfe; Nothing enclined him, nothing wrought upon him, but his own goodnesse.

It was then his Deed; and it was his gift; it was his *Deed of gift:* and it hath all the formalities and circumstances that belong to that; for here is a *seale* in his blood; and here is a *delivering,* pregnantly implied in this word, which is not onely *Dedit,* he gave, but *Tradidit,* he delivered. First, *Dedit,* he gave himselfe for us to his Father, in ³⁴⁰ that eternall Decree, by which he was *Agnus occisus ab origine mundi,* The Lamb slain from the beginning of the world. And then *Tradidit,* he delivered possession of himselfe to *Death,* and to all humane infirmities, when he took our *Nature* upon him, and became one of us. Yea this word implies a further operativenesse, and working upon himself, then all this; for the word which the *Apostle* uses here, for Christ giving of himselfe, is the same word, which the *Evangelists* use still, for *Judas* betraying of him: so that Christ did

Marginal notes:

Ioh. 13.27
Aug.

Dedit

[Apoc. 13.8]

not onely *give* himselfe to the will of the Father, in the eternall Decree; nor onely deliver himselfe to the power of death in his Incar-
350 nation, but he *offered,* he exhibited, he *exposed,* (we may say) he
betrayed himselfe to his enemies; and all this, for worse enemies; to
the *Jewes,* that Crucified him once, for us, that make sinne our sport,
and so make the Crucifying of the Lord of life a Recreation.

It was a *gift* then, free, and absolute; Hee keeps us not in fear of
Resumption; of ever taking himselfe from the Church again; nay he
hath left himself no power of Revocation: *I am with you,* sayes he,
to the end of the world. To particular men, he comes, and he knocks,
and he enters, and he stays, and he sups, and yet for their unworthi-
nesse goes away again; but with the Church he is *usque ad consum-*
360 *mationem,* till the end; It is a permanent gift; *Dedit,* and *Dedit
seipsum;* It was he that did it; That which he did was to give; and
that which he gave, was himselfe. Now since the Holy Ghost, that is
the God of unity and peace, hath told us at once, that the satisfaction
for our sins is Christ himselfe, and hath told us no more, Christ entirely, Christ altogether, let us not divide and mangle Christ, or tear
his Church in pieces, by froward and frivolous disputations, whether
Christ gave his *divinity* for us, or his *humanity;* whether the divine
Nature, or the humane Nature redeemed us; for neither his divinity
nor his humanity, is *Ipse,* He himselfe, and *Dedit seipsum,* He gave
370 himselfe: Let us not *subdivide* him into lesse pieces, then those, *God,*
and *Man;* and enquire contentiously, whether he suffered in *soul,* as
well as in *body,* the pains of *Hell,* as well as the sting of *Death;* the
Holy Ghost hath presented him unite, and knit together. For neither
soul nor body was *Ipse,* He himselfe, and *Dedit seipsum,* He gave
himselfe; let us least of all shred Christ Iesus into lesse scruples and
atoms then these, Soul, and body; and dispute whether consisting of
both, it were his *active,* or his *passive* obedience that redeemed us;
whether it were his death and passion onely, or his innocency, and
fulfilling of the Law too; let us onely take Christ, *himselfe,* for onely
380 that is said, *he gave himselfe.* It must be an Innocent person, and this
Innocent person must die for us; seperate the *Innocency,* and the
Death, and it is not *Ipse,* it is not Christ himselfe: and *Dedit seipsum,*
it was himselfe. Let us abstain from all such curiosities, which are all
but forc'd dishes of hot brains, and not sound meat, that is, from all

Seipsum

[Mat. 28.20]

perverse wranglings, whether *God,* or *Man* redeemed us; and then, whether this God, and Man suffered in *soule,* or in *body;* and then whether this person, consisting of soule and body, redeemed us, by his *action,* or by his *passion* onely; for as there are spirituall *wicked-nesses,* so there are spirituall *wantonnesses,* and unlawfull and dan-
390 gerous dallyings with mysteries of Divinity. Money that is changed into small pieces is easily lost; gold that is beat out into leaf-gold, cannot be coyned, nor made currant money: we know the Heathens lost the true God, in a thrust; they made so many false gods, of every particular quality, and attribute of God, that they scattered him, and evacuated him, to an utter vanishing; so doth true, and sound, and nourishing Divinity vanish away, in those impertinent Questions. All that the wit of Man adds to the Word of God, is all *quicksilver,*

[2 Tim.
1.14]

and it evaporates easily. Beloved, *Custodi Depositum,* sayes the Apostle, keep that which God hath revealed to thee; for that God
400 himselfe cals thy *Talent;* it hath weight and substance in it. Depart not from thy *old gold;* leave not thy *Catechism-divinity,* for all the *School-divinity* in the world; when we have all, what would we have more? if we know that Christ hath given himselfe for us, that we are

[1 Pet.
1.18–19]

redeemed, and not redeemed with corruptible things, but with the precious blood of Christ Jesus, we care for no other knowledge but that, *Christ,* and *Christ crucified* for us; for this is another, and a more peculiar and profitable giving of himselfe *for* thee, when he gives himselfe to thee, that is, when he gives thee a sense, and appre-hension, and application of the gift, to thy self, that Christ hath
410 given himselfe, to thy selfe.

Pro
Ecclesia

We are come now to his exchange; what Christ had for himselfe when he gave himselfe; And he had *a Church.* So this Apostle, which in this place, writes to the *Ephesians,* when he preached personally

Act. 20.28

to the *Ephesians,* he told them so too, *The Church* is that *Quam acquisivit sanguine suo,* which he purchased with his bloud. Here Christ bought a Church, but I would there were no worse Simony then this. Christ received no profit from the Church, and yet he gave himselfe for it; and he stayes with it to the end of the world; Here is no such *Non-residency,* as that the Church is left unserved: other
420 men give enough for their Church, but they withdraw themselves, and necessary provision; And if we consider this Church that Christ

bought, and paid so dearly for, it was rather an *Hospitall,* then a *Church:* A place where the *blind* might recover sight; that is, Men borne in *Paganisme,* or *Superstition,* might see the true God, truly worshipped: and where the *lame* might be established; that is, those that *Halted between two Religions,* might be *rectified* in the truth: where the *Deaf* might receive so quicke a hearing, as that they might discerne *Musique* in his *Thunder,* in all his fearefull threatnings; that is, mercy in his Judgments, which are still accompanied with
430 conditions of repentance; and they might finde *Thunder,* in his *Musique,* in all his *promises;* that is, threatnings of Judgements, in our misuse of his mercies. Where the hereditary *Leper,* the new borne Child, into whose marrow, his fathers transgression cleaves in *originall sinne,* and he that hath enwrapped *Implicatos morbos,* one disease in another, in *Actuall sinnes,* might not onely come, if he would but be intreated to come, yea *compelled* to come, as it is expressed in the Gospell, when the Master of the feast sends into the streets, and to the hedges to *compell blind and lame to come in to his*   Luke 14.21 *feast.* A fountaine breaks out in the wildernesse, but that fountaine
440 cares not, whether any Man come to fetch water, or no; A fresh, and fit gale blowes upon the Sea, but it cares not whether the Mariners hoise saile or no; A rose blowes in your garden, but it calls you not to smell to it. Christ Jesus hath done all this abundantly; he hath bought an *Hospitall,* he hath stored it with the true balme of *Palestine,* with his bloud, which he shed there, and he calls upon you all to come for it, *Hoe every one that thirsteth; you that have no money, come buy*   Esay 55.1 *Wine, and Milke without money: eate that which is good, and let your soules delight in fatnesse, and I will make an everlasting Covenant with you, even the sure mercies of David.* This *Hospitall,*
450 this way, and meanes to cure spirituall diseases, was all that Christ had for himselfe: but he improved it, he makes it a *Church,* and a glorious Church: which is our last consideration, *Quis finis,* to what end, he bestowed all this cost.

His end was, that *he might make it to himselfe a glorious Church,*   *Quis finis* *not having spot, or wrinkle;* but that end, must be in the end of all;   Augustin. here it cannot be: *Cum tota dicat ecclesia, quamdiu hîc est, Dimitte*   Retrac. *debita nostra, non utique hîc est sine macula et ruga,* Since as yet the   l. 1. c. 7 whole Church says, *forgive us our Trespasses,* the Church as yet is   [Mat. 6.12]

not without spots or wrinkles. The *wrinkles* are the Testimonies of
⁴⁶⁰ our *age;* that is, our sinne derived from *Adam;* and the *spots* are the
sinnes, which we contract our selves; and of these *spots,* and *wrinkles,*
we cannot be delivered in this world. And therefore the Apostle says
here, that Christ hath bestowed all this cost on this purchase, *ut sisteret*
sibi Ecclesiam, that he might setle such a glorious, and pure Church
to himselfe: first, *ut sisteret,* that he might setle it; which can onely
be done in *heaven;* for here in Earth, the Church will always have

[1 Cor.   *earthquakes. Oportet hæreses esse;* stormes, and schismes must neces-
11.19]   sarily be; the Church is in a warfare, the Church is in a pilgrimage,
and therefore here is no setling. And then he doth it, *ut sisteret sibi,*
⁴⁷⁰ to setle it *to himselfe;* for, in the tyranny of *Rome,* the Church was in
some sort setled, things were carried quietly enough; for no Man
durst complaine; but the Church was setled all upon the *Vicar,* and
none upon the *Parson:* the glory of the *Bishop of Rome,* had eclipsed,
and extinguished the glory of *Christ Iesus.* In other places we have
seen the Church setled, so as that no man hath done or spoken any
thing against the *government* thereof; but, this may have been a
setling by strong hand, by severe *discipline,* and heavy Lawes; we see
where Princes have changed the Religion, the Church may be setled
upon the *Prince,* or setled upon the *Prelates,* that is, be serviceable to
⁴⁸⁰ them, and be ready to promote and further any purpose of theirs, and
all this while, not be setled upon *Christ:* this purpose, *ut sisteret sibi,*
to setle such a glorious Church, without spot, or wrinkle, holy to
himselfe, is reserved for the Triumphant time when she shall be in
possession of that beauty, which Christ foresaw in her, long before

Cant. 4.7   when he said, *Thou art all faire my love, and there is no spot in thee;*
and when we that shall be the Children of the Mariage Chamber,

Apoc. 19.7   shall be glad and rejoice, and give glory to him, *because the Mariage*
of the Lambe is come, and his wife hath made her selfe ready; that is,
we that are of that Church, shall be so clothed, as that our own

[Job 9.31]   ⁴⁹⁰ clothes, shall not defile us againe; as *Iob* complaines that they doe,
as long as we are in this world; for, though I make me never so cleane,
yet *mine own clothes defile me againe,* as it is in that place.

But yet, Beloved, Christ hath not made so improvident a bargaine,
as to give so great a rate, himselfe, for a Church, so farre in reversion,
as till the day of Judgement: That he should enter into bonds for this

payment, from all eternity, even in the *eternall decree* between the Father, and him, that he should really pay this price, his precious bloud, for this Church, *one thousand six hundred years* agoe, and he should receive no glory by this Church till the next world: Here was a long lease, here were many lives; the lives of all the men in the world, to be served before him; But it is not altogether so; for he gave himselfe, that he might settle such a Church *then,* a glorious, and a pure Church: but all this while, the Church is building in heaven, by continuall accesse of holy *Soules,* which come thither, and all the way he workes to that end, *He sanctifies it, and cleanses it, by the washing of water, through the word,* as we find in our Text.

He therefore stays not so long, for our *Sanctification,* but that we have meanes of being sanctified here; Christ stays not so long for his glory, but that he hath here a *glorious Gospell,* his *Word,* and *mysterious Sacraments* here. Here then is the *writing,* and the *Seale,* the *Word,* and the *Sacrament;* and he hath given power, and commandement to his Ministers to deliver both writing, and Seale, the *Word* and *Baptisme* to his children. This Sacrament of Baptisme is the first; It is the Sacrament of *inchoation,* of *Initiation;* The Sacrament of the *Supper,* is not given but to them, who are instructed and presum'd to understand all Christian duties; and therefore the *Word,* (if we understand the Word, for the *Preaching* of the Word) may seeme more necessary at the administration of this Sacrament, then at the other. Some such thing seems to be intimated in the institution of the Sacraments. In the institution of the Supper, it is onely said, *Take, and eate and drinke,* and doe that in *remembrance of me;* and it is onely said that they *sang a Psalme, and so departed.* In the institution of *Baptisme* there is more solemnity, more circumstance; for first, it was instituted after Christs *Resurrection,* and then Christ proceeds to it, with that majesticall preamble, *All power is given unto me in heaven, and in earth;* and therefore, upon that title he gives power to his Apostles, to joine heaven and earth by *preaching,* and by *baptisme:* but here is more then *singing of a Psalme;* for Christ commands them first to *teach,* and then to *baptize,* and then after the commandement of Baptisme, he refreshes that commandement againe of *teaching* them, whom they baptized, to observe all things, that he had commanded them. I speake not this, as though *Baptisme* were un-

Mat. 26.26
Luke 22.19

Mat. 28.18

effectuall without a *Sermon;* S. *Augustines* words, *Accedat verbum, & fiat Sacramentum,* when the Word is joyned to the element, or to the Action, then there is a true Sacrament, are ill understood by two sorts of Men; first by them, that say that it is not *verbum Deprecatorium,* nor *verbum Concionatorium,* not the word of *Prayer,* nor the word of *preaching,* but *verbum Consecratorium,* and *verbum Sacramentale,* that very phrase, and forme of words, by which the water is sanctified,
540 and enabled of it selfe to cleanse our Soules; and secondly, these words are ill understood by them, who had rather their children dyed unbaptized, then have them baptized without a *Sermon;* whereas the use of *preaching* at baptisme is, to raise the whole *Congregation,* to a consideration, what they promised by others, in their baptisme; and to raise the *Father* and the *Sureties* to a consideration, what they undertake for the childe, whom they present then to be baptized; for therefore says Saint *Augustine, Accedat verbum,* there is a necessity of the *word, Non quia dicitur, sed quia creditur,* not because the word is *preached,* but because it is *beleeved;* and That, *Beleefe, faith,*
550 belongs not at all to the incapacity of the child, but to the disposition of the rest; A *Sermon* is usefull for the congregation, not necessary for the *child,* and the accomplishment of the Sacrament.

From hence then arises a convenience, little lesse, then necessary, (in a kind) that this administration of the Sacrament be accompanied with *preaching;* but yet they that would evict an *absolute necessity* of it, out of these words, force them too much, for here the direct meaning of the Apostle is, That the Church is *cleansed by water, through the word,* when the promises of God expressed in his word, are sealed to us by this Sacrament of Baptisme: for so *Saint Augustine*
560 answers himselfe in that objection, which he makes to himselfe, *Cum per Baptismum fundati sint, quare sermoni tribuit radicem.* He answers, *In Sermone intelligendus Baptismus, Quia sine Sermone non perficitur.* It is rooted, it is grounded in the *word;* and therefore true Baptisme, though it be administred, without the *word,* that is, without the *word preached,* yet it is never without the word, because the whole Sacrament, and the power thereof is rooted in the word, in the *Gospell.* And therefore since this *Sacrament* belongs to the Church, as it is said here (that Christ doth *cleanse his Church by Baptisme*) as it is argued with a strong probability, That because the

⁵⁷⁰ Apostles did *baptize* whole families, therefore they did baptize some *children,* so we argue with an invincible certainty, that because this Sacrament belongs generally to the Church as the *initiatory* Sacrament, it belongs to *children,* who are a part, and for the most part, the most innocent part of the Church.

To conclude, As all those Virgins which were beautifull, were brought into *Susan, Ad domum mulierum,* to be anointed, and perfumed, and prepared there for *Assuerus* delight, and pleasure, though *Assuerus* tooke not delight, and pleasure in them *all,* so we admit *all* those children which are within the Covenant made by God, to the ⁵⁸⁰ elect, and their seed, *In domum Sanctorum,* into the *houshold* of the *faithfull,* into the communion of Saints: whom he chooseth for his *Mariage day,* that is, for that Church which he will settle upon himselfe in heaven, we know not; but we know that he hath not promised, to take any into that glory, but those upon whom he hath first shed these fainter beames of glory, and *sanctification,* exhibited in this Sacrament: Neither has he threatned to exclude any but for *sinne* after. And therefore when this blessed child derived from faithfull *parents,* and presented by *sureties* within the obedience of the Church, shall have been *so cleansed, by the washing of water, through the* ⁵⁹⁰ *word,* it is presently sealed to the possession of that part of Christs purchase, for which he gave himselfe, (which are the meanes of preparing his Church in this life) with a faithfull assurance, I may say of it and to it, *Jam mundus es, Now you are cleane,* through the word, which Christ hath spoken unto you: The *Seale* of the promises of his Gospell hath sanctified, and cleansed you; but yet, *Mundatus mundandus,* says Saint *Augustine* upon that place, It is so sanctified by the *Sacrament* here, that it may be farther sanctified by the growth of his *graces,* and be at last a member of that glorious Church, which he shall settle upon *himselfe, without spot, or wrinkle;* which was the ⁶⁰⁰ principall, and finall purpose of that great love of his, whereby *he gave himselfe for us,* and made that love, first a patterne of Mens loves to their wives here, and then a meanes to bring Man, and wife, and child, to the kingdome of heaven. Amen.

Esther 2

Iohn 15.3

Number 6.

Preached at a Christning.

---

1 JOHN 5.7, 8. *FOR THERE ARE THREE WHICH BEARE RECORD IN HEAVEN; THE FATHER, THE WORD, AND THE HOLY GHOST; AND THESE THREE ARE ONE: / AND THERE ARE THREE WHICH BEARE RECORD IN THE EARTH; THE SPIRIT, AND THE WATER, AND THE BLOUD; AND THESE THREE AGREE IN ONE.*

IN GREAT and enormous offences, we find that the law, in a well governed State, expressed the punishment upon such a delinquent, in that form, in that curse, *Igni & aqua interdicitur;* let him have no use of *fire,* and *water,* that is, no use of any thing, necessary for the sustentation of life. Beloved, such is the miserable condition of wretched Man, as that we come all into the world under the burden of that curse; *Aqua, & igni interdicimur;* we have nothing to doe, naturally, with the spirituall *water of life,* with the fiery *beames* of the holy *Ghost,* till he that hath wrought our restitution from this
10 banishment, restore us to this *water,* by powring out his owne *bloud,* and to this lively *fire,* by laying himselfe a cold, and bloudlesse carcasse in the bowels of the Earth: till he who *baptized* none with

[Joh. 4.2] *water,* direct his Church to doe that office towards us; and he without

[Mat. 3.11] whom, none was *baptized with fire,* perfect that Ministeriall worke of his Church with the effectuall seales of his grace; for this is his testimony, the witnesse of his love.

Yea, that law, in cases of such great offences, expressed it selfe in

another Malediction, upon such offenders, appliable also to us, *In-testabiles sunto,* let them be Intestable. Now, this was a sentence, a
²⁰ Condemnation so pregnant, so full of so many heavy afflictions, as that he, who by the law was made intestable, was all these ways in-testable: First, he was able to make no *Testament* of his owne, he had lost all his interest in his owne estate, and in his owne will; Secondly, he could receive no profit by any testament of any other Man, he had lost all the effects of the love, and good disposition of other Men to him: Thirdly, he was *Intestable,* so, as that he could not testifie, he should not be beleeved in the behalfe of another; and lastly the testimony of another could doe him no good, no Man could be ad-mitted to speake for him. After that first, and heavy curse of Almighty
³⁰ God upon Man, *Morte morieris,* If thou eate, thou shalt die, and die twice, thou shall die a *bodily,* thou shalt die a *spirituall* death (a pun-ishment which no sentence of any law, or law-maker could ever equall, to deterre Men from offending, by threatning to take away their lives twice, and by inflicting a spirituall death eternally upon the Soule,) after we have all incurred that malediction, *Morte morie-mur,* we shall die both deaths, we cannot thinke to scape any lesse malediction of any law, and therefore we are all *Intestabiles,* we are all intestable, in all these senses, and apprehensions, which we have touched upon.
⁴⁰ We can make no *testament* of our owne; we have no good thing in us to dispose; we have no good inclination, no good disposition, in our *Will;* we can make no use of *anothers* testament; not of the double testaments of *Almighty God;* for in the *Old* testament, he gives promises of a *Messias,* but we bring into the world no *Faith,* to apprehend those promises; and in the *New* testament, he gives a performance, the Messias is come, but he is communicable to us, no way but by *baptisme,* and we cannot baptize our selves; we can profit no body else by our testimony, we are not able to endure *persecution,* for the testimony of Christ, to the edification of others, we are not
⁵⁰ able to doe such *workes,* as may *shine before Men, to the glorifying of our God.* Neither doth the testimony of others doe us any good; for neither the *Martyrdome* of so many Millions, in the primitive Church, nor the execution of so many judgments of God, in our owne times, doe testifie any thing to our Consciences; neither at the last day, when

[Gen. 2.17]

[Mat. 5.16]

those Saints of God, whom we have accompanied in the outward
worship of God here in the visible Church, shall be called to the
right hand, and we detruded to the left, shall they dare to open their
mouthes for us, or to testifie of us, or to say, Why Lord, these Men,
when they were in the world, did as we did, appeared, and served
60 thee in thy house, as we did, they seem'd to goe the same way that we
did upon Earth, why goe they a *sinister* way now in heaven? We are
utterly *intestable;* we can give nothing; we can take nothing; nothing
will be beleeved from us, who are all falshood it selfe; nor can we be
releeved by any thing, that any other will say for us. As long, as we
are considered under the penalty of that law, this is our case; *Inter-
dicti, intestabiles,* we are accursed, and so, as that we are *intestable.*

Now as this great malediction, *Morte morieris,* involves all other
punishments, (upon whom that falls, all fall) so when our Saviour
Christ Jesus hath a purpose to take away *that,* or the most dangerous
70 part of that, the *spirituall death,* when he will reverse that judgment,
Aqua & igni interdicitur, to make us capable of his *water,* and his
fire; when he will reverse the *intestabiles,* the intestability, and make
us able to receive his graces by faith, and declare them by works;
then, as he that will reedifie a demolished house, begins not at the
top but at the bottome, so Christ Jesus, when he will make this great
preparation, this great reedification of mankind, he beginnes at the
lowest step, which is, that we may have use of the *testimony of others,*
in our behalfe: and he proceeds strongly, and effectually; he produces
three witnesses from heaven, so powerfull, that they will be heard,
80 they will be beleeved; and *three witnesses on earth,* so neare us, so
familiar, so domestique as that they will not be denied, they will not
be discredited; *There are three that beare Record in heaven, and three
that beare record in earth.*

Since then Christ Jesus makes us all our owne *Iury,* able to conceive,
and judge upon the Evidence, and testimony of these three heavenly,
and three earthly witnesses, let us draw neare, and hearken to the
Divisio   evidence, and consider three things; *Testimonium esse, Quid sit,* and
Qui testes. That God descends to meanes proportionable to Man; he
affords him witnesse; and secondly, the matter of the proofe, what all
90 these six witnesses testifie, what they establish; Thirdly, the quality,
and value of the witnesses, and whether the matter be to be beleeved,

for their sakes, and for their reasons. God requires nothing of us, but *Testimony:* for *Martyrdome* is but that; A Martyr is but a witnesse. God offers us nothing without testimony: for his *Testament,* is but a witnesse. *Teste ipso,* is shrewd evidence; when God says, *I will speake, and I will testifie against thee; I am God, even thy God:* when the voice of God testifies against me in mine owne conscience. It is more pregnant evidence then this, when his voice testifies against me in his word, in his Scriptures: *The Lord testified against Israel, by*
¹⁰⁰ *all the Prophets and by all the Seers.* When I can never be alone, but that God speakes in me, but speakes against me; when I can never open his booke, but the first sentence mine eye is upon, is a witnesse against me, this is fearfull evidence. But in this text, we are not in that storme, for he hath made us *Testabiles,* that is, ready to testifie for him, to the effusion of our bloud; and *Testabiles,* that is, fit to take benefit by the testament, that hee hath made for us, The effusion of his bloud; which is our second branch: what is testified for us, what these witnesses establish.

First then, that which a sinner must be brought to understand, and
¹¹⁰ beleeve, by the strength of these witnesses, is *Integritas Christi;* not the Integrity, as it signifies the *Innocency* of Christ: but integrity, as it signifies *Intireness,* not as it is *Integer vitæ,* but *Integra vita;* not as he kept an integrity in his life, but as he onely, is intirely our life. That Christ was a person composed of those *two Natures,* divine, and humane, whereby he was a fit, and a full satisfaction for all our sinnes, and by death could be our life: for when the Apostle writ this Epistle, it seemes there had been a *schisme,* not about the *Mysticall* body of Christ, the Church, but even about the *Naturall;* that is to say, in the person of Christ, there had been a schisme, a separation of
¹²⁰ his two natures: for, as we see certainly before the death of this Apostle, that the Heresie of *Ebion* and of *Cerinthus,* (which denied the divine nature of Christ) was set on foot, (for against them pur- posely was the Gospell of Saint *John* written) so by *Epiphanius* his ranking of the Heresies, as they arose, where he makes *Basilides* his Heresie, (which denied that Christ had any naturall body) to be the *fourth* heresie, and *Ebions,* to be the *tenth,* it seemes, that they denied his *humanity,* before they denied his *Divinity.* And therefore it is well collected, that this *Epistle* of Saint *Iohn,* being written long before his

Psal. 50.7

2 Reg. 17.13

1 Part
*Integritas
Christi*

Gospell, was written principally, and purposely against the opposers
130 of Christs humanity, but occasionally also, in defence of his divine
nature too. Because there is *Solutio Iesu,* a dissolving of Jesus, a taking
of Jesus in peeces, a dividing of his *Natures,* or of his *Offices,* which
overthrowes all the testimonies of these six great witnesses: when
[Joh. 2.19]   Christ said, *Solvite templum hoc, destroy, dissolve this temple, and in
three dayes I will raise it,* he spoke that but of his naturall body; there
was *Solutio corporis,* Christs body and soule were parted, but there
was not *Solutio Iesu;* the divine nature parted not from the humane,
no not in death, but adhered to, and accompanied the soule, even in
hell, and accompanied the body in the grave.

1 Iohn 4.3   140   And therefore, says the Apostle, *Omnis spiritus qui solvit Iesum,
ex deo non est,* (for so *Irenæus,* and Saint *Augustine,* and Saint *Cyrill*
with the Grecians, read those words) That spirit which receives not
Jesus intirely, which *dissolves* Jesus and breakes him in peeces, that
spirit is not of God. All this then is the subject of this testimony; first
4.2   that Christ Jesus is come in the flesh; (there is a Recognition of his
humane nature) And then that this Jesus is the sonne of God; (there
5.5   is a subscription to his *divine nature:*) he that separates these, and
thereby makes him not able, or not willing to satisfie for Man, he that
separates his *Nature,* or he that separates the *worke* of the Redemp-
150 tion, and says, Christ suffered for us onely *as Man,* and not *as God,*
or he that separates the manner of the worke, and says that the
passive obedience of Christ onely redeemed us, without any respect at
all, to his *active obedience,* onely as he died, and nothing as he died
innocently, or he that separates the *perfection,* and consummation of
the worke, from his worke, and findes something to be done by *Man
himselfe,* meritorious to salvation, or he that separates the Prince, and
the Subject, Christ and his members, by nourishing *Controversies in
Religion,* when they might be well reconciled, or he that separates
himselfe from the body of the Church, and from the communion of
160 Saints, for the fashion of the garments, for the variety of indifferent
Ceremonies, all these do *Solvere Iesum,* they slacken, they dissolve
[Joh. 19.36]   that Jesus, whose bones God provided for, that they should not be
[Acts 2.31]   broken, whose flesh God provided for, that it should not see Corrup-
[Joh. 19.24]   tion, and whose garments God provided, that they should not bee
divided.

There are other luxations, other dislocations, of Jesus, when we displace him for any *worldly respect,* and prefer *preferment* before him; there are other woundings of Jesus, in blasphemous *oathes,* and execrations; there are other maimings of Jesus, in pretending to serve
170 him intirely, and yet retaine one particular beloved sinne still; there are other rackings, and extendings of Jesus when we delay him and his patience to our death-bed, when we stretch the string so farre, that it cracks there, that is, appoint him to come then, and he comes not; there are other dissolutions of Jesus, when men will melt him, and powre him out, and mold him up in a wafer Cake, or a peece of bread; there are other annihilations of Jesus when Men will make him, and his Sacraments, to be nothing but bare signes; but all these will be avoided by us, if we be gained by the testimony of these six witnesses, to hold fast that integrity, that intirenesse of Jesus, which
180 is here delivered to us by this Apostle.

In which we beleeve first *Iesum,* a Saviour; which implies his love, and his will to save us; and then we beleeve *Christum,* the anointed, that is God and man, able, and willing to doe this great worke, and that he is anointed, and sealed for that purpose; and this implies the decree, the contract, and bargaine, of acceptation by the Father, that *Pactum salis,* that eternall covenant which seasons all, by which, that which he meant to doe, as he was *Iesus,* should be done, as he was *Christ.* And then as the intirenesse of Jesus is expressed, in the verse before the text, we beleeve, *Quod venit,* that as all this *might* be done,
190 if the Father and Sonne would agree, as all this *must* be done, because they had agreed it, so all this *was* done, *Quia venit,* because this Jesus is already come; and that, for the farther intirenesse, for the perfection, and consummation, and declaration of all, *venit per aquam & sanguinem,* He came by *water,* and *bloud.* [Num. 18.19]

Which words Saint *Bernard* understands to imply but a difference between the comming of *Christ,* and the comming of *Moses;* who was drawn out of the *water,* and therefore called by that name of *Moses.* But before *Moses* came to be a leader of the people, he passed through *bloud* too, through the bloud of the *Egyptian,* whom he slew;
200 and much more when he established all their *bloudy sacrifices,* so that *Moses* came not onely by water. Neither was the first Testament ordained without bloud. Others understand the words onely to put

Bernard

[Exod. 2.12]

Heb. 9.18

a difference between *Iohn Baptist,* and *Christ:* because *Iohn Baptist* is still said to *baptize with water. Because he should be declared to*

Iohn 1.31

Israel; therefore am I come, baptizing with water: but yet *Iohn Baptists* baptisme had not onely a relation to bloud, but a demonstration of it, when still he pointed to the Lambe, *Ecce Agnus,* for that

[Apoc. 13.8]

Lambe was *slaine* from the beginning of the world. So that Christ, which was this Lambe, came by water, and bloud, when he came, in

210 the *rituall types,* and *figures* of *Moses;* and when he came in the baptisme of *Iohn:* for in the Law of *Moses,* there was so frequent use of *water,* as that we reckon above *fifty* severall *Immunditias,* uncleannesses, which might receive their expiation by washing, without being put to their bloudy sacrifices for them: And then there was

Heb. 9.22

so frequent use of *bloud,* that *almost all things are by the Law purged with bloud, and without shedding of bloud, is no Remission.* But this was such water, and such bloud, as could not perfect the worke, but therefore was to be renewed every day. The water that Jesus

[Joh. 4.14]

comes by, is such a water, as he *that drinketh of it, shall thirst no*

220 *more;* nay there shall spring up in him a *well* of water; that is, his example shall worke to the *satisfaction of* others; (we doe not say to a satisfaction *for* others.) And then this is that bloud, that per-

Heb. 9.12

fected the whole worke at once, *By his own bloud entred he once into the holy place, and obtained eternall Redemption for us.* So that Christ came by water, and bloud, (according to the old ablutions, and old sacrifices) when he wept, when he sweat, when he powred out bloud; pretious, incorruptible, inestimable bloud, at so many channels, as he did, all the while that he was upon the altar, sacrificing himselfe in his passion. But after the immolation of this sacri-

[Joh. 19.30]

230 fice, after his *Consummatum est,* when Christ was come and gone for so much as belonged to the accomplishing of the types of the old law, then Christ came againe to us by water and bloud, in that wound, which he received upon his side, from which there flowed out miracu-

Augustine

lously true water, and true bloud. This wound Saint *Augustine* calls *Ianuam utriusque Sacramenti,* the doore of both sacraments; where we see he acknowledges but two, and both presented in this water, and bloud: and so certainely doe most of the fathers, make this wound if not the *foundation,* yet at least a *sacrament* of both the *sacraments.* And to this water, and bloud doth the Apostle here,

²⁴⁰ without doubt, aime principally; which he onely of all the Evangelists
hath recorded; and with so great asseveration, and assurednesse in
the recording thereof, *He that saw it bare record, and his record is*   Iohn 19.35
true, and he knoweth that he saith truth, that yee might beleeve it.
Here then is the matter which these six witnesses must be beleeved
in, here is *Integritas Iesu, quæ non solvenda,* the intirenesse of Christ
Jesus, which must not be broken, That a Saviour, which is *Iesus,*
appointed to that office, that is *Christ,* figured in the law, by *ablutions*
of *water,* and *sacrifices* of *bloud,* is come, and hath perfected all those
figures in water, and bloud too; and then, that he remaines still with
²⁵⁰ us in water, and bloud, by meanes instituted in his Church, to wash
away our uncleannesses, and to purge away our iniquities, and to
apply his worke unto our Soules; this is *Integritas Iesu,* Iesus the
sonne of God in heaven, Jesus the Redeemer of man, upon earth,
Jesus the head of a Church to apply that to the end, this is *Integritas
Iesu;* all that is to be beleeved of him.

Take thus much more, that when thou comest to hearken what
these witnesses shall say to this purpose, thou must finde something
in their testimony, to prove him to be come not onely *into the world,*
but *into thee;* He is a mighty prince, and hath a great traine; millions
²⁶⁰ of ministring spirits attend him, and the whole army of Martyrs follow the Lambe wheresoever he goes: Though the whole world be his   [Apoc. 14.4]
Court, thy soule is his *bedchamber;* there thou maist contract him,
there thou maist lodge, and entertaine *Integrum Iesum,* thy whole
Saviour. And never trouble thy selfe, how another shall have him, if
thou have him all; leave him, and his Church to that; make thou
sure thine owne salvation. When he comes to thee, he comes by *water*
and by *bloud;* If thy heart, and bowels have not yet melted in compassion of his passion for thy soule, if thine eyes have not yet melted,
in *tears of repentance* and contrition, he is not yet come by *water*
²⁷⁰ into thee; If thou have suffered nothing for sinne, nor found in thy
selfe a chearfull disposition to suffer; if thou have found no wresting
in thy selfe, no resistance of Concupiscences, he that comes not to set
peace, but to kindle this war, is not yet come into thee, by *bloud.*
Christ can come by land, by purchases, by Revenues, by *temporall
blessings,* for so he did still convey himselfe to the Jewes, by the
blessing of the land of promise, but here he comes by *water,* by his

owne passion, by his sacraments, by thy tears: Christ can come in a mariage and in Musique, for so he delivers himselfe to the *spouse* in the *Canticles;* but here he comes in bloud; which comming in 280 water, and bloud (that is, in meanes for the salvation of our soules, here in the militant Church) is the comming that he stands upon and which includes all the Christian Religion; and therefore he proves that comming to them, by these three great witnesses in heaven, and three in earth. *For there are three which beare record in heaven; The Father, the word, and the holy Ghost: and these three are one. And there are three which bear record in the earth; The spirit, and the water, and the bloud, and these three agree in one.*

2 Part
Mat. 18.16

By the mouth of two, or three witnesses every word shall be con-firmed, says Christ out of the law. That's as much as can be required, 290 in any Civill, or Criminall businesse; and yet Christ gives more testi-mony of himselfe, for here he produces not *Duos testes,* but *Duas Classes;* two rankes of witnesses; and the fullest number of each, not two, but *three in heaven,* and *three in earth.* And such witnesses upon earth, as are *omni exceptione majores,* without all exception. It is not the testimony of earthly men; for when Saint *Paul* produces them in abundance, (The *Patriarchs,* the *Judges,* the *Prophets,* the *elders* of the old times; of whom he exhibits an exact Catalogue,) yet he calls all them but *Nubes testium,* cloudes of witnesses; for though they be cloudes in Saint *Chrysostomes* sense, (that they invest us, 300 and enwrap us, and so defend us from all diffidence in God,) (we have their witnesse what God did for them, why should we doubt of the like?) though they be cloudes in *Athanasius* sense, they being in heaven, showre downe by their prayers, the dew of Gods grace upon the Church; Though they be cloudes, they are *but cloudes;* some darkenesse mingled in them, some controversies arising from them; but his witnesses here, are *Lux inaccessibilis,* that light, that no eye can attaine to, and *Pater Luminum,* the father of lights, from whom all these testimonies are derived. When God imployed a man, to be the witnesse of Christ, because men might doubt of his testi-310 mony, God was content to assigne him his *Compurgators;* when *Iohn Baptist* must preach, that the kingdome of God, was at hand, God fortifies the testimony of his witnesse, then, *Hic enim est, for this is he of whom that is spoken by the prophet Esay;* and lest one were

Heb. 11

Heb. 12.[1]

[1 Tim. 6.16]

[Jas. 1.17]

Mat. 3.3

not enough, he multiplies them, *as it is written, in the prophets. Iohn* Mar. 1.2
Baptist might be thought to testifie as a *man,* and therefore men must
testifie for him; but these witnesses are of a higher nature; these of
heaven are the *Trinity,* and those of earth, are the *sacraments* and
seales of the Church. The prophets were full of favor with God,
Abraham full of faith, *Stephen* full of the Holy Ghost, *Mary* full
320 of grace, and *Iohn Baptist* a prophet, and *more then a prophet,* yet
never any prophet, never any man, how much soever interessed in the
favor of Almighty God, was such an instrument of grace, as a *sacrament* or as Gods seales and institutions in his Church: and the least
of these six witnesses, is of that nature, and therefore might be beleeved without any more witnesses.

To speake then first of the three first, *the Father, the Word,* and 3
the Holy Ghost, it was but a poore plot of the devill, to goe about to *In Cœlis*
rob us, of their testimony; for as long as we have the three last, *the
spirit, the water,* and *bloud,* we have testimony enough of Christ,
330 because God is involved in his ordinance; and though he be not tyed
to the worke of the Sacrament, yet he is always present in it. Yet
this plot, the devill had upon the Church: And whereas this *first
Epistle* of Saint *Iohn* was never doubted to be Canonicall, (whereas
both the other have been called into some question) yet in this first
Epistle, *the first verse* of this text, was for a long time removed, or
expung'd, whether by malice of Heretiques, or negligence of tran-
scribers. The first Translation of the new testament, (which was into
Syriaque) hath not this verse; That which was first called *Vulgata
editio,* hath it not, neither hath *Luther* it in his *Germane translation:*
340 very many of the *Latine Fathers* have it not; and some very ancient
Greeke Fathers want it, though more ancient then they, have it; for
Athanasius in the Councell of Nice cites it, and makes use of it; and
Cyprian, beheaded before that Councell, hath it too. But now, he
that is one of the witnesses himselfe, the Holy Ghost, hath assured
the Church, that this verse belongs to the Scripture; and therefore
it becomes us to consider thankfully, and reverently, this first ranke
of witnesses, *the Father, the Word, and the Holy Ghost.*

The Father then hath testified *De integritate Christi,* of this intire- *Pater*
nesse, that Christ should be all this and doe all this, which we have
350 spoken of, abundantly: he begunne before Christ was borne, in giving

Mat. 1.21

his name, *Thou shalt call his name Iesus: for he shall save his people from sin.* Well; how shall this person be capable to doe this office of saving his people from sinne? Why, in him, says God the father, (in the representation of an Angell) shall be fulfilled that prophecy, *A virgin shall beare a Sonne, and they shall call his name Emanuel,* which is by interpretation *God with us:* This seemes somewhat an incertaine testimony, of a Man, with an *Aliàs dictus,* with two names. God says he shall be called *Jesus,* that the prophecy may be fulfilled which says he shall be called *Emanuel:* but therein consists, *Integritas Christi,* this intirenesse; he could not be Jesus, not a *Saviour,* except he were *Emanuel,* God with us, God in our nature. Here then is Jesus, a Saviour, a Saviour that is God, and Man, but where is the Testimony *De Christo;* that he was anointed, and prepared for this sacrifice; that this worke of his was contracted between the Father, and him, and acceptable to him? It is twice testified by the Father; both in Christs act of *humiliation,* when he would be *Baptized by John;* when he would accept an ablution, who had no uncleannesse, then God says, *This is my beloved Sonne, in whom I am well pleased,* he was well pleased in his *person,* and he was well pleased, in his *act,* in his *office.* And he testifies it againe in his first act of glory, in his *transfiguration;* where the Father repeates the same words with an addition, *Heare him:* God is pleased in him, and would have Men pleased in him too. He testified first, onely for *Josephs sake,* that had entertained, and lodged some scrupulous suspition against his *wife,* the Blessed Virgine; His second testimony at the *baptisme,* had a farther extent; for that was for the confirmation of *Iohn Baptist,* of the preacher himselfe, who was to convey his doctrine to many others; His third testimony in the *transfiguration,* was larger then the *Baptisme;* for that satisfied *three,* and *three* such as were to carry it farre, *Peter,* and *James,* and *John:* All which no doubt made the same use of his testimony, as we see *Peter* did, who preached out of the strength of his manifestation, *we followed not deceivable fables, but with our owne eyes we saw his Majesty; for he received of God the Father, honor, and glory, when there came such a voice to him, from the Excellent glory, This is my beloved Sonne, in whom I am well pleased.* But yet the Father gave a more free, a more liberall testimony of him, then this, at his *Conception,* or *Baptisme,* or *Transfiguration:* when

23

360

Mat. 3 ult.

370

Mat. 17.5

380

2 Pet. 1.16

upon Christs prayer, *Father glorifie thy Name, there came a voice* Iohn 12.28
from heaven, I have both glorified it and will glorifie it againe. For
390 this all the people apprehended; some imputed it to *Thunder,* some to
an *Angel;* but all heard it; and all heard Christs comment upon it,
That that voice came not for him, but *for their sakes;* so that when
the Father had testified of a *Jesus,* a *Saviour,* and a Christ, a Saviour
sent to that purpose, and a *Sonne* in whom he is pleased, and whom
we must heare, when it is said of him, moreover, *Gratificavit nos in* Ephes. 1.6
Dilecto, he hath made us accepted in his beloved, this is his way of
comming in *water,* and bloud, that is, in the *sacraments* of the
Church, by which we have assurance of being accepted by him; and
this is this *Integritas Christi,* the intirenesse of Christ, testified by our
400 first witnesse, that bears record in heaven, The *father.*

The second witnesse in heaven, is *verbum,* The *Word:* and that is *Verbum*
a welcome message, for it is *Christ* himselfe: It is not so when the
Lord sends a word; *The Lord sent a word unto Iacob, and it lighted* Esa. 9.8
upon Israel; there the word is a judgement, and an execution of the
Judgement: for that word, that signifies, a *word* there, in the same
letters exactly signifies, a *pestilence,* a Calamity; It is a word, and a
blow; but the word here, is *verbum caro,* that Word which for our
sakes was made our selves. The word then in this place, is the second
person in the Trinity, *Christ Iesus,* who in this Court of heaven,
410 where there is no corruption, no falsification, no passion, but fair and
just proceeding, is admitted to be a witnesse in his owne cause; It is
Iesus, that testifies for Iesus now, when he was upon earth, and said,
If I should beare witnesse of my selfe, my witnesse were not true, [Joh. 5.31]
whether we take those words to be spoken, *per Conniventiam,* by an
allowance, and concession, (It is not true, that is, I am content that
you should not beleeve my witnesse of my selfe to be true) (as *Saint*
Cyrill understands them) or whether we take them, *Humano more,*
that Christ as a man, acknowledged truely, and as he thought, that
in legall proceeding a mans owne testimony ought not to be beleeved
420 in his owne behalfe, (as *Athanasius* and Saint *Ambrose* understand
them) yet Christ might safely say as he did, *Though I beare record* Iohn 8.14
of my selfe, yet my record is true; why? *because I know whence I*
come, and whither I goe. Christ could not be *Singularis testis,* a single
witnesse; He was alwayes more then one witnesse, because he had

Iohn 3.11

alwayes more then *one nature;* God and man; and therefore Christ
instructing *Nicodemus,* speakes plurally, *we speake, that we know,
we testifie that we have seene,* and you receive not *Testimonium
nostrum,* our witnesse; he does not say *my witnesse,* but *ours,* because although a singular, yet he was a plurall person too.

⁴³⁰   His testimony then was credible; but how did he testifie *Integritatem,* this intirenesse, all that belonged to our faith? All consists in
this, that he was *Jesus,* capable in his nature, to be a Saviour; that he
was *Christus,* ordained, and sent for that office, and then *Quod venit,*
that he was come, and come, *in aqua & sanguine,* in water and bloud,
in *sacraments,* which might apply him to us. That he was Iesus a
person capable, his *miracles* testified aloud and frequently: that he
was *Christ,* anointed, and sent for that, his reference of all his actions
to his Father testified; both these were enwrapped in that, that he
was the *Sonne of God;* and that he professed himselfe upon the earth

Iohn 19.7

⁴⁴⁰ to be so; for so it appeares plainely, that he had plainely done: *We
have a law,* say the Jews to *Pilate, and by our law, he ought to die,
because he made himselfe the Sonne of God.* And for the last part,
that he came *In aqua & sanguine,* in water, and bloud, in such
meanes, as were to continue in the Church, for our spirituall reparation, and sustentation, he testified that, in preaching so piercing *Sermons,* in instituting so powerfull *Sacraments,* in assuring us, that the
love of God expressed to mankind in him, extended to all persons, and

Iohn 3.16

all times, *God so loved the world, that he gave his onely begotten
Sonne, that whosoever beleeveth in him, should not perish, but have*
⁴⁵⁰ *life everlasting.* And so the words beare record, *De Integritate,* of this
Intirenesse, of the whole worke of our Redemption: and therefore,
Christ is not onely truely called a *Martyr,* in that sense, as Martyr
signifies a *witnesse,* but he is truly called a *Martyr,* in that sense, as
we use the word ordinarily; for he testified this truth, and suffered

Apoc. 1.5

for the testimony of it: and therefore he is called Jesus Christ, *Martyr,*
a *faithfull witnesse.* And there is *Martyrium,* a Martyrdome attrib-

1 Tim. 6.13

uted to him, where it is said, Jesus Christ under *Pontius Pilate,* wit-
nessed a good confession; so he was a *speaking,* and a *doing,* and a
suffering witnesse.

*Spiritus
sanctus*

⁴⁶⁰   Now for the third witnesse in heaven, which is the holy Ghost;
we may contract our selves in that; for the whole work was his;

Before *Joseph* and *Mary* came together, *she was found with Child of* Mat. 1.18
the holy Ghost: which (if we take it, as *Saint Basil,* and divers others
of the Fathers doe) that *Joseph* found it, by the holy Ghost, that is,
the holy Ghost informed him of it, then here the holy Ghost was a
witnesse to *Joseph,* of this *Conception:* but we rather take it (as it is
most ordinarily taken) that the Angell intimated this to *Joseph,* That
that which was conceived in her, was of the holy Ghost; and then v. 20
the holy Ghost did so primarily testifie, this decree of God, to send a
470 *Iesus,* and a *Christ,* for our Redemption, that himselfe was a blessed
and bountifull actor in that Conception, he was conceived *by him,* by
his overshadowing. So that the holy Ghost did not onely testifie his
comming, but he brought him: And then, for his comming in *Aqua*
& sanguine, in water and bloud, that is, in *Sacraments,* in meanes,
by which he might be able to make his comming usefull, and appliable to us, first the holy Ghost, was a pregnant witnesse of that, at
his *Baptisme;* for the holy Ghost had told *Iohn Baptist* before-hand,
That upon whomsoever he should descend, and tarry still, that should Iohn 1.33
be he, that should baptize with the holy Ghost: and then according
480 to those Markes, he did descend, and tarry still upon *Christ Jesus,* in
his baptisme. And after this falling upon him, and tarrying upon
him, (which testified his *power*) in all his life, expressed in his doctrine, and in his Sermons, after his death, and Resurrection, and
Ascension, the holy Ghost gave a new testimony, when he fell upon
the Apostles in *Cloven tongues,* and made them spirituall channells, [Acts 2.3]
in which this water and bloud, the meanes of applying Christ to us,
should be convey'd to all Nations; and thus also the third witnesse
in heaven, testified *De integritate,* of this intirenesse of *Jesus.*

Of these three witnesses then, which are of heaven, we shall need 3 *Vnum*
490 to adde no more, but that which the text addes, that is, *That these*
three are one; that is, not onely one in *Consent,* (they all testifie of one
point, they all speake to one Intergatory; *Ad integritatem Christi,* to
prove this intirenesse of Christ;) but they are *Vnum Essentia,* The
Father, the Sonne, and the holy Ghost are all one *Godhead,* and so
meant and intended to be in this place. And therefore as *Saint*
Hierome complained, when some Copies were without this *seventh*
verse, that thereby we had lost a good argument for the *unity* of the
three Persons, because this verse said plainely that the three witnesses

were *all one,* so I am sorry, when I see any of our later expositors
⁵⁰⁰ deny, that in this place, there is any proofe, of such an unity, but
that this *Vnum sunt, (They are one)* is onely an unity of *consent,*
and not of *essence.* It is an unthrifty prodigality (howsoever we be
abundantly provided with arguments, from other places of Scriptures, to prove this *Vnity in Trinity*) to cast away so strong an argument, against *Jew,* and *Turke,* as is in these words, for that, and for
the *consubstantiality* of Christ, which was the Tempest, and the
Earthquake of the Primitive Church, raised by *Arius,* and his fol-
lowers then, and (God knowes) not extinguished yet.

Thus much I adde of these three witnesses, that though they be
⁵¹⁰ in heaven, their testimony is upon the earth; for they need not to
testifie to one another, this matter of Jesus: The Father heares of it
every day, by the continuall *intercession* of Christ Jesus: The Sonne
feeles it every day, in his new crucifying by our sinnes, and in the
persecution of his Mysticall body here: The holy Ghost hath a bitter
sense of it, in our sinnes against the holy Ghost, and he hath a loving
sense of it, in those abundant seas of *graces,* which flow continually
from him upon us; They need no witnesses in heaven; but these three
witnesses testifie all this, to our Consciences. And therefore the first
author, that is observed to have read, and made use of this seventh
⁵²⁰ verse (which was one of the first Bishops of *Rome*) he reads the

Higinus

words thus, *Tres in nobis,* there are three *in us,* which beare witnesse
in heaven; they testifie for our sakes, and to establish our assurance,
De Integritate Jesu; that Jesus is come, and come with meanes, to
save the world, and to save us. And therefore upon these words, Saint

Bernard

Bernard collects thus much more, that there are other witnesses in
heaven, which testifie this worke of our Redemption, *Angels,* and
Saints, all the Court, all the Quire of heaven testifie it; but *cætera
nobis occulta,* says he, what all they doe we know not: but (according
to the best dispositions here in this world) we acquaint our selves,
⁵³⁰ and we choose to keep company with the best, and so not onely the
poore Church upon the earth, but every poore soule in the Church,
may heare all these three witnesses testifying to him, *Integrum Jesum
suum,* that *all,* which Christ Jesus hath done, and suffered, appertaines
to him: but yet, to bring it nearer him, in visible and sensible things,
There are, tres de terra, three upon earth too.

The first of these three upon earth, is the *Spirit:* which Saint *Augustine* understands of the spirit, the *soule* of Christ: For when Christ commended his spirit, into the hands of his Father, this was a testimony, that he was *Verus homo,* that he had a soule; and in that 540 he laid downe his spirit, his soule, (for no Man could take it from him) and tooke it againe, at his pleasure, in his resurrection, this was a testimony, that he was *Verus Deus,* true God; And so says Saint *Augustine, Spiritus,* The spirit, that is *anima Christi,* the soule of Christ, did testifie *De integritate Jesu,* all that belonged to Jesus, as he was *God,* and as he was *Man.* But this makes the witnesses in heaven, and the witnesses in earth all one; for the personall testimony of Christs *preaching,* and living, and dying, the testimony which was given by these three Persons of the Trinity, was all involv'd in the first rank of witnesses: Those three which are in heaven. Other later 550 Men understand by the *Spirit* here the Spirit of every *Regenerate Man;* and that in the other heavenly witnesses, the spirit is *Spiritus sanctus,* the spirit that is holy in it selfe, the holy Ghost, and here it is *Spiritus sanctificatus,* that spirit of Man, which is made holy by the holy Ghost, according to that, *The same spirit, beareth witnesse, with our spirit, that we are the children of God.* But in this sense, it is too particular a witnesse, too singular, to be intended here; for that speakes but to one Man, at once; The spirit therefore here is, *Spiritus oris,* the word of God, the *Gospell;* and the preaching, and ministration thereof. *We are made Ministers of the New testament, of the* 560 *spirit, that giveth life: And if the ministration of death were glorious, how shall not the ministration of the spirit, be more glorious?* It is not therefore the Gospell meerly, but the *preaching* of the Gospell, that is this spirit. *Spiritus sacerdotis vehiculum Spiritus Dei;* The spirit of the Minister, is not so pure, as the spirit of God, but it is the chariot, the meanes, by which God will enter into you. The Gospell is the Gospell, at home, at your house; and there you doe well to read it, and reverence it, as the Gospell: but yet it is not *Spiritus,* it is not this Spirit, this first witnesse upon earth, but onely there, where God hath blessed it with his institution, and ordinance, that is, in the 70 *preaching* thereof. The stewardship, and the dispensation of the graces of God, the directing of his threatnings against refractary, and wilfull sinners, the directing of his promises to simple, and supple,

Spiritus

Rom. 8.16

2 Cor. 3.6
Ibid. [8]

and contrite penitents, the breaking of the bread, the applying of the Gospell according to their particular indigences, in the preaching thereof, this is the first witnesse.

Aqua   The second witnesse here is *The water,* and I know there are some Men which will not have this to be understood of the water of *Baptisme;* but onely of the naturall effect of water; that as the *ablutions* of the old law, by water did purge us, so we have an inward testi-
580 mony, that Christ doth likewise wash us cleane; so the water here, must not be so much as water; but a metaphoricall, and figurative water. These men will not allow water, in this place, to have any relation to the *sacrament;* and *Saint Ambrose* was so far from doubting that water in this place belonged to the sacrament, that he applies all these three witnesses to the Sacrament of *Baptisme: Spiritus mentem renovat,* All this is done in Baptisme, says he; The Spirit renewes and disposes the mind; *Aqua perficit ad Lavacrum;* The water is applied to cleanse the body; *Sanguis spectat ad pretium;* and the bloud intimates the price, and ransome, which gives force, and virtue
590 to this sacrament: And so also (says he in another place) *In sanguine mors,* in the bloud there is a representation of death, in the water, of our buriall, and in the spirit, of our owne life. Some will have none of these witnesses on earth to belong to *baptisme,* not the water; and *Ambrose* will have all, spirit, and water, and bloud to belong to it.

Now both Saint *Ambrose,* who applies all the three witnesses to *Baptisme,* and those later men which deny any of the witnesses to belong to baptisme, doe both depart from the generall acceptation of these words, that *water* here, and onely that, signifies the Sacrament of *baptisme.* For as in the first creation, the first thing, that the spirit
[Gen. 1.2]   600 of God, is noted to have moved upon, was the *waters,* so the first creature, that is sanctified by Christs institution, to our Salvation, is this element of water. The first thing that produced any living sensible creature was the *water; Primus liquor quod viveret edidit; ne mirum sit quod in Baptismo, aquæ animare noverunt;* water brought forth
Tertullian   the first creatures, says *Tertullian;* That we should not wonder, that water should bring forth Christians. The first of Gods afflicting
Exod. 7.[20] miracles in Egypt, was the changing of *water* into *bloud;* and the
[Joh. 2.1–10] first miracle of *grace,* in the new Testament, was the changing of water into wine at the mariage. So that *water* hath still been a subject,

⁶¹⁰ and instrument of Gods conversation with man: So then *Aqua janua ecclesiæ,* we cannot come into the Church, but by water, by *baptisme;* for though the Church have taken knowledge of other *Baptismes,* (*Baptisma sanguinis,* which is Martyrdome, and *Baptisma Flaminis,* which is a religious desire to be baptized when no meanes can be got) yet there is no other *sacrament* of Baptisme, but *Baptisma Fluminis,* the Baptisme of water: for the rest, *Conveniunt in causando, sed non in significando,* says the Schoole; that is, God doth afford a plentifull retribution to the other baptismes *Flaminis* and *sanguinis,* but God hath not ordained them to be outward *seales,* and significations of his
⁶²⁰ grace, and to be witnesses of *Jesus* his comming upon earth, as this water is. And therefore they that provide not duly to bring their children to this water of life, (not to speake of the essential necessity thereof) they take from them, one of the *witnesses,* that *Jesus* is come into them; and (as much as they can) they shut the Church dore against them, they leave them out of the *Arke,* and for want of this water, cast them into that generall water, which overflowes all the rest of the world, which are not brought within the Covenant, by this water of baptisme. For, though in the first Translation of the new Testament, into *Syriaque,* that be said in the sixth verse, that Jesus is
⁶³⁰ come *per manus aquarum,* by the power of waters, many waters, and in this verse, this witnesse is delivered in the plurall, *spirit and waters,* (and so, *waters* in that signification, (which signification they have often in the Scriptures) that is, *affliction,* and tribulation, be good testimonies that our Lord Jesus doth visit us) though the waters of *Contrition,* and repentant *teares* be another good testimony of that too, yet that water, which testifies the presence of Jesus so, as that it doth always infallibly bring Jesus with it, (for the *sacraments* are never without *Grace,* whether it be accepted or no, there it is) That water which is made equall with the *preaching* of the Word, (so farre as to be a fellow-
⁶⁴⁰ witnesse with the Spirit) that is onely the *Sacrament of baptisme,* without which (in the ordinary dispensation of God) no soule can be surer that Jesus is come to him, then if he had never heard the Word preached; he mistakes the *spirit,* the first witnesse, if he refuse the *water,* the second.

The third witnesse upon earth, is bloud: and that is briefly the *Communion of the body, and bloud of Jesus, in the Lords Supper.* But

Sanguinis

how is that bloud upon earth? I am not ashamed to confesse, that I
know not *how*, but the bloud of Christ is a *witnesse upon earth*, in
the Sacrament, and therefore, upon the earth it is. Now this witnesse
650 being made equall with the other two, with *preaching*, and with
baptisme, it is as necessary, that he that will have an assurance, that
Jesus is come into him, doe receive this *Sacrament*, as that he doe
heare *Sermons*, and that he be *baptized*. An over vehement urging of
this *necessity*, brought in an erroneous custome in the Primitive
Church: That they would give the Sacrament of the body of Christ
to *Children*, as soon as they were *baptized;* yea, and to *dead Men* too.
But because this Sacrament is accompanied with *precepts*, which can
belong onely to *Men of understanding*, (for they must doe it in
Remembrance, and they must *discerne* the Lords body) therefore the
660 necessity lies onely upon such, as are come to those *graces*, and to
that understanding. For they that take it, and doe not *discerne it*,
(not know what they do) they take it dangerously. But else, for them,
to whom this Sacrament belongs, if they take it not, their *hearing of
Sermons*, and their *baptisme* doth them no good; for what good can
they have done them, if they have not prepared themselves for it?
And therefore, as the Religion of the Church holds a stubborne
Recusant at the table, at the Communion bord, as farre from her, as a
Recusant at the Pew, that is, a Non-communicant as ill, as a not com-
mer, or a not hearer, so I doubt not but the wisdome of the *State*
670 weighs them in the same balance; *For these three agree in one*, says
the text: that is, first they meet in *one Man*, and then they testifie the
same thing, that is, *Integritatem Jesu*, that *Jesus* is come to him in
outward Meanes, to save his soule. If his conscience find not this
testimony, all these availe him nothing. If we remaine vessells of
anger, and of dishonour still, we are under the *Væ vobis Hypocritis:
woe unto you Hypocrites, that make cleane onely the outside of your
Cuppes and Platters.* That baptize, and wash your owne, and your
childrens bodies, but not their mindes with instructions. When we
shall come to say *Docuisti in plateis, we have heard thee preach in
680 our streets*, we have continued our hearing of thy Word, when we say
Manducavimus coram te, we have eate in thy presence, at thy table,
yea *Manducavimus te*, we have eaten thee thy selfe, yet for all this
outward show of these three witnesses, of *Spirit*, and *Water*, and

[1 Cor.
11.29]

Mat. 23.25

Luke 13.26

Ibid.

bloud, Preaching, and *Baptisme* and *Communion,* we shall heare that fearfull disclaiming from Christ Jesus, *Nescio vos,* I know not whence you are. But these witnesses, he will always heare, if they testifie for us, that Jesus is come unto us; for the *Gospell,* and the *preaching* thereof, is as the deed that conveys *Jesus* unto us; the *water,* the *baptisme,* is as the *Seale,* that assures it; and the *bloud,* the *Sacrament,* is the *delivery* of Christ into us; and this is *Integritas Jesu,* the entire, and full possession of him.

To this purpose therefore, as we have found a *Trinity* in heaven, and a *Trinity* in earth, so we must make it up a Trinity of Trinities, and finde a *third Trinity* in our selves. God created one *Trinity* in us; (the observation, and the enumeration is Saint *Bernards*) which are those *three faculties* of our soule, the *reason,* the *memory,* the *will;* That Trinity in us, by another Trinity too, (by *suggestion* towards sin, by *delight* in sinne, by *consent* to sinne) is fallen into a third Trinity; The *memory* into a weaknesse, that that comprehends not *God,* it glorifies him not for benefits received; The *reason* to a blindnesse, that that discernes not what is *true;* and the *will* to a perversnesse, that that wishes not what's *good;* But the goodnesse of God, by these three witnesses on earth regenerates, and reestablishes a new Trinity in us, *faith,* and *hope,* and *charity;* Thus farre that devout Man carries it; And if this new Trinity, *faith,* and *hope,* and *charity,* witnesse to us *Integritatem Christi,* all the worke of Christ, If *my faith* testifie to me, that Christ is sealed to my soule; and my *hope,* testifie, that at the Resurrection, I shall have a perfect fruition in soule, and body, of that glory which he purchased for every beleever; and my *charity* testifies to the world, that I labour to make sure that salvation, by a good life, then there's a *Trinity* of *Trinities,* and the *six* are made *nine* witnesses: There are three in heaven that testifie that this is done for all Mankinde, Three in the Church that testifie, this may be done for me, and three in my soule, that testifie, that all this is applied to me; and then the verdict, and the Judgement must necessarily goe for me. And beloved, this Judgement will be grounded upon this intirenesse of Jesus, and therefore let me dismisse you with this note, That *Integritas* is *in continuitate,* not *in contignitate;* It is not the touching upon a thing, nor the comming neare to a thing, that makes it intire; a fagot, where the sticks touch, a peece of cloth, where the threds touch, is not intire; To come as neare Christ as we can conveniently, to trie how neare we can bring *two Religions* together, this is not to preserve *Integritatem Jesu:* In a word, Intirenesse excludes deficiency, and redundancy, and discontinuance; we preserve not intirenesse, if we preserve not the dignity of Christ, in his Church, and in his *discipline,* and that excludes the defective *Separatist;* we doe not preserve that entirenesse if we admit *traditions,* and additions of Men, in an equality to the word of God, and that excludes the redundant *Papist;* neither doe we preserve the entirenesse, if we admit a discontinuance, a slumbring of our Religion for a time, and that excludes the *temporisers,* the *Statist,* the *Politician.* And so, beloved, I recommend unto you *Integritatem Jesu,* Jesus, and his truth, and his whole truth, and this whole Truth, in your whole lives.

Number 7.

Preached at a Christning.

GAL. 3.27. *FOR, ALL YEE THAT ARE BAPTIZED INTO CHRIST, HAVE PUT ON CHRIST.*

THIS TEXT is a Reason of a Reason; an Argument of an Argument; The proposition undertaken by the Apostle to prove, is, *That after faith is come, we are no longer under the Schoolmaster,* the law. The reason, by which he proves that, is: *For yee are all the Sonnes of God by faith, in Christ Jesus;* And then the reason of that, is this text, *for all yee that are baptized into Christ, have put on Christ.*

Here then is the progresse of a *sanctified Man,* and here is his standing house; here is his *journey,* and his *Lodging;* his way, and his end.
10 The house, the lodging, the end of all is *faith; for whatsoever is not of faith, is sinne.* To be sure that you are in the right way to that, you must find your selves to be the *Sonnes of God;* And you can prove that, by no other way to your selves, but because you are *baptized into Christ.*

So that our happinesse is now at that height, and so much are we preferred before the *Jews,* that whereas the chiefest happinesse of the Jews was to have *the law,* (for *without the law they could not have known sinne,* and the law was their *Schoolmaster* to find out Christ) we are admitted to that degree of perfection, that we are got above the
20 law; It was their happinesse to have had the law, but it is ours, *not to need it:* They had the benefit of a *guide,* to direct them, but we are at our journies end; They had a *schoolmaster* to lead them to Christ; but we have proceeded so farre, as that we are in possession of Christ. The law of *Moses* therefore, binds us not at all, as it is *his Law;* Whatsoever binds a Christian, in that law, would have bound him, though

v. 25

26

[Rom. 14.23]

[Rom. 7.7]

151

there had been no law given to *Moses*. The *Ceremoniall* part of that law, which was in the institution, *Mortale,* (it was mortall, It *might* die) and by Christs determination of those Typicall things, *Mortuum,* (It *did* die) is now also *Mortiferum,* (deadly) so that it is sinne to
³⁰ draw any part of that law, into a *necessity* of observation; because the necessary admission of any *Type,* or *figure,* implies a confession, that that which was signified, or figured, is not yet come; So that that law, and Christ cannot consist together. The *Judiciall* law of *Moses,* was certainly the most absolute, and perfect law of government, which could have been given *to that people,* for whom it was given; but yet to thinke, that all *States* are bound to observe those lawes, because God gave them, hath no more ground, then that all Men are bound

[Gen. 3.21]   to goe clothed in *beasts skinnes,* because God apparelled *Adam,* and *Eve* in that fashion.

⁴⁰   And for the *morall part* of that law, and the abridgement of that morall part, the *decalogue,* that begunne not to have force, and efficacy then, when God writ it in the tables, but was always, and always shall be written in the *hearts* of Men; And though God of his goodnesse, was pleased to give that *declaration* of it, and that *provocation* to it, by so writing it, yet if he had not written it, or if (which is impossible) that writing could perish, yet that morall law, those commandements, would bind us, that are *Christians,* after the expiration of that law, which was *Moses* law, as it did (*de Iure*) bind all those which lived, before any written law was. So that he that will perfectly understand,
⁵⁰ what appertaines to his duty in any of the *ten Commandements,* he must not consider that law, with any limitation, as it was given to the *Jews,* but consider what he would have done, if he had lived before the *Tables* had been written. For certainely, even in the Commandement of the *Sabbath,* which was accompanied with so many *Ceremonies amongst the Jews, that part onely is morall, which had bound us, though that Commandement had never been given;* and he that performes that part, keepes the Sabbath; the *Ceremoniall* part of it, is not onely not necessary; but when it is done with an opinion of necessity, it is erroneous, and sinfull. For neither that Commandement nor
⁶⁰ any other of the *ten,* began to bind then, when they were written, nor doth bind now, except it bound before that.

Thus far then we are directed by this Text, (which is as far, as we can goe in this life) To prove to our selves, that we have *faith,* we must prove, that wee need not the *law;* To prove that *emancipation,* and *liberty,* we must prove, that we are the *sonnes of God;* To prove that ingraffing, and that *adoption,* we must prove, that we have *put on Christ Iesus;* And to prove that apparelling of our selves, our proofe is, that *we are baptized* into him.

70 All proofes must either arrest, and determine in some things confessed, and agreed upon, or else they proceed *in infinitum.* That which the Apostle takes to be that which is granted on all sides, and which none can deny, is this, that *to be baptized is to put on Christ:* And this putting on of Christ, doth so far carry us to that *Infinitissimum,* to God himselfe, that we are thereby made *Semen Dei,* the seed of God; The *field* is the *world,* and the *good seed* are the *Children* of the *kingdome;* And we are translated even into the nature of God, By his pretious promises we are made *partakers of the Divine nature;* yea, we are discharged of all bodily, and earthly incombrances, and we are made *all spirit,* yea the spirit of God himselfe, *He that is joyned* 80 *to the Lord, is one spirit with him.* All this we have, if we doe put on Christ: and we doe put on Christ, if we be baptized into him.

Mat. 13.[38]

2 Pet. 1.[4]

1 Cor. 6.[17]

These then are the two actions which we are now to consider:

Divisio

> Baptizari,   ⎰ To be *washed.*
> Induere,   ⎱ To be *cloathed.*

Induere, is to cover so far, as that Covering can reach; A hat covers the head; a glove the hand; and other garments, more; But Christ, when he is put on, Covers us all. If we have *weake heads,* shallow brains, either a *silence,* and a reservednes, which make the foole and the wise equall, or the good interpretation of friends, which put *good* 90 *Constructions* upon all that we say, or the dignity of *autority,* and some great place, which we hold, which puts an opinion in the people, that we are wise, or else we had never been brought thither, these cover our heads, and hide any defect in them. If we have foule hands, we can cover them, with excuses; If they be foule with *usurious Extortion,* we can put on a glove, an excuse, and say, He that borrowed my money, got more by it, then I that lent it; If, with *bribery in an office,* we can cover it and say, He that knew, that I bought my office, will be content to let me be a saver by it; If our hands be foule with *shedding of innocent bloud,* as *Saint Hierome* sayes that *Adam*

¹⁰⁰ eate the Apple, *Ne contristaretur Delicias suas,* lest he should over grieve his wife, by refusing it, *Ne contristaremur Delicias nostras,* either because we would not displease another, or because our *beloved sinne,* to which we had maried our selves, did sollicite us to it. Particular excuses cover our particular defects, from the sight of men, but to put on Christ, covers us all over, even from the *sight of God* himselfe. So that how narrowly so ever he search into us, he sees nothing but the whitenesse of his Sonnes innocency, and the rednesse of his Sonnes bloud.

When the prodigall child returned to his father, his father clothed

[Luke 15.22]   ¹¹⁰ him intirely, and all at once; he put a *robe* upon him, to cover all his defects: which Robe, when God puts upon us, in clothing us with

Augustine   Christ, that robe is not onely *Dignitas quam perdidit Adam,* as
Ambrose   *Augustine* says, but it is *Amictus sapientiæ,* as *Ambrose* enlarges it, It does not onely make us aswell, as we were in *Adam,* but it enables us better, to preserve that state; It does not onely *cover us,* that is, make us excusable, for our past, and present sinnes, but it indues us with *grace,* and *wisdome* to keep that robe still, and never to returne to our former foulnesses, and deformities.

Our first parents *Adam* and *Eve* were naked all over; but they were

¹²⁰ not sensible of *all* their nakednesse, but onely of those parts whereof they were *ashamed.* Nothing but the shame of the world makes us discerne our deformities; And onely for those faults, which shame makes us take knowledge of, we goe about to provide; And we provide nothing but *short Aprons,* as that word signified; and those but of *fig-leaves;* That which comes first to hand, and that which is withered before it is made, that doe we take for an excuse, for an aversion of our owne conscience, when she begins to cast an eye, or to examine the nakednesse, and deformities of our soules.

But when God came to cloath them, their short *aprons* were ex-

Gen. 3.21   ¹³⁰ tended to *coates,* that covered them all over, and their *fig-leaves* to strong *skins;* for God saw that not onely those parts, of which they were already ashamed, needed covering, but that in all their other parts, if they continued naked, and still exposed to the Injurie, and violence of the weather, they would contract diseases, and infirmities; and therefore God covers them so throughly, as he doth not onely provide for reparation of former inconveniences, but prepare against future.

And so perfect effects doth this garment, *Christ Jesus,* work upon us, if we put him on; He doth not onely cover *Originall sinne,* (which is the effect of those disobedient Members, which derive sinne, upon
¹⁴⁰ us, in the sinfull generation of our parents) but he covers all our *actuall sinnes,* which we multiplie every day: and not onely those, which the world makes us *ashamed of,* but which we hide from the world; yea which we hide from our selfes; that is, sinnes, which by a long custome of practise, we commit so habitually, and so indifferently, as that we have forgot, that they are sinnes.

But as it was in *Adams Clothing* there, so must it be in our spirituall putting on of Christ. The word used there, *Labash,* doth not signifie that God cloathed *Adam,* nor that *Adam* cloathed himselfe; but as the *Grammarians* call it, it is in *Hiphil,* and it signified *Induere fecit eos;*
¹⁵⁰ God caused them to be cloathed, or God caused them to cloath themselves; which is also intimated, nay evidently expressed in the words of this text; we are our selves poore, and impotent creatures, we cannot make our selves ready; we are poore and beggerly creatures, we have nothing to put on; Christ is that garment; and then Christ is the very life, by which we stretch out our armes and our legs, to put on that garment; yea he puts it on upon us, he doth the whole worke: but yet he doth not thrust it on: He makes us *able* to put it on: but if we be not *willing,* then he puts *no necessity upon our will:* but we remaine naked still.

¹⁶⁰ *Induere* then, to put on, is an extension, a dilatation over all; And sometimes it signifies an abundant, and overflowing, and overwhelming measure of Gods judgements upon us, *Princeps induetur desolatione, The prince shalbe cloathed with desolation and with astonishment:* But most commonly, the rich and all-sufficient proportion of his mercies and spirituall benefits: as he expressed it to his Apostles, at his ascension, *Stay you in the Citty, quousque induamini virtute ex alto; till ye be indued* (so we translate it) that is, cloathed with *power from on high.* And this was *per fidem ei innitendo,* and *per opera eum declarando,* says Saint *Augustine,* He onely hath put on Christ, which
¹⁷⁰ hath Christ in himselfe by *faith,* and shewes him to others by his *works,* which is *Lucerna ardens,* (as Christ said of *Iohn Baptist*) *a burning lamp,* and *a shining lamp,* profitable to others, as well as to himselfe.

Ezech. 7.27

Luke 24.49

[Joh. 5.35]

There is a degree of vanity, and pride, whereby some Men delight to weare their richest clothes innermost, and most out of sight; But in this double garment of a Christian, it is necessarily so; for *faith* is the richest, and most precious part of this garment; and this, which is our *Holy-day garment,* is worne innermost; for that (our faith) is onely seen by God; but our outward garment, of *workes,* which is our
180 *worky-day garment,* that is our *sanctification,* is seen of all the world. And that also must be put on, or else we have not put on *Christ:* and it must cover us *all over;* that is, our sanctification must goe through our *whole life* in a constant, and an even perseverance; we must not onely be *Hospitales,* and feed the poore at Christmas, be sober, and abstinent, the day that we *receive,* repent, and thinke of amendment of life, in the day of visitation, and *sicknesse;* but, as the garment, which Christ wore, was *seamlesse,* and intire, so this garment, which is *Christ Jesus,* that is, our sanctification, should be intire, and uninterrupted, in the whole course of our lives; we must remember, that

Mat. 22   190 at the Mariage which figured the kingdome of heaven, the master of the feast reprehended, and punished him, that was come in, not expresly because he had not a *wedding garment,* but *Quomodo intrasti,* says he, *how camest thou in, not having on thy wedding garment?* So that (if it could be possible) though we had put on the inside of this garment, which is *Christ,* that is, if we had *faith,* yet if we have not the outside too, that is *sanctification,* we have not put on Christ, as we should; for this is *Indui virtute ex alto;* to have both inside, *faith,* and outside, *sanctification:* and to put it on so, that it may cover us all over, that is, all our life; because it is not in our power, if we put

5.3   200 it off, by *new sinnes,* to put it on againe, when we will. *I have put off my coate, how shall I put it on?* was the doubt of the spouse, in the Canticles, even when Christ had called her: So hard a thing is it, if we devest the righteousnesse of Christ, after we have put it on, to cloth our selves againe in that garment.

        As then this word, *Induere,* to put on, to be clothed, signifies a
Psal.   largenesse, and an abundance, according to that, *The pastures are*
65.[13]   *clothed with sheep, and the vallies with corne:* So is this garment, Christ Jesus, such a garment, as is alone so all sufficient, as that if we doe put on that, we need no other; *Put yee on the Lord Jesus Christ,*
Rom. 13.[14] 210 *and take no thought for the flesh;* if ye have put on that, you are clothed, and armed, and adorned sufficiently.

[Gen. 1.26]

In the first creation, in the *Faciamus hominem ad Imaginem nostrûm,* when God seems to have held a consultation about the making of Man, man put on all the Trinity, *all God;* and in the redemption God put on *all Man;* not onely all the nature of Mankind in generall, but in particular, *every Man.* But as the spirit of God, is said to have put on a particular Man, *Spiritus Domini induit Gedeon, the spirit of the Lord, clothed, or put on Gedeon,* when he selected him for his service, so must the spirit of every particular Man, put on

Iud. 6.34

220 Christ; he must not be content, to be under the *generall cover,* (either under his general providence, because he is a *Creature,* or a member of his Mysticall body, because he adheres to a visible *Church*) he must not say, I am as warm clothed, as another, I have as much of Christ in me, as a great many, that doe well enough in the world, but he must so inwrap himselfe in Christ, and in his Merits, as to make *all that* to be his owne. No man may take the frame of Christs merit in peeces; no Man may take his forty days *fasting* and put on that, and say, Christ hath fasted for me, and therefore I may surfeit; No man may take his *Agony,* and pensivenesse, and put on that, and say,
230 Christ hath *been sad* for me, and therefore I may be merry. He that puts on Christ, must put him on *all;* and not onely find, that Christ hath dyed, nor onely that he hath died for *him,* but that he also hath died *in* Christ, and that whatsoever Christ suffered, *he* suffered *in* Christ.

For, as Christs merit, and satisfaction, is not too narrow for all the world, so is it not too large for any one Man; Infinite worlds might have been saved by it, if infinite worlds had been created; And, if there were no more Names in the book of life, but thine, all the Merit of Christ were but enough to save thy one sinfull soule, which
240 could not have been redeemed, though alone, at any lesse price, then his death.

All that Christ did, and suffered, he did and suffered for *thee, as thee;* not onely *as Man,* but as that particular Man, which bears such, or such a name; and rather, then any of those, whom he loves, should appeare naked before his Father, and so discover to his confusion, those scarres, and deformities, which his sinnes have imprinted upon him, (as his love is devoutly, and piously extended by the Schooles and some contemplative Men) Christ would be content to doe, and suffer,

as much as he hath done, for any one particular Man yet: But beyond
²⁵⁰ *Infinite,* there is no degree: and his merit was infinite, both because an
infinite Majesty resided in his person, and because an infinite Majesty
accepted his sacrifice for infinite.

But this act of Christ, this redemption makes us onely *servants;*
servi à servando, we are servants to him, that preserved, and saved us,
is the derivation of the *Law.* But the *application* of this redemption
(which is the *putting on of Christ,*) makes us *sons;* for we are not to
put on Christ, onely as a *Livery,* to be distinguished by externall
marks of *Christianity;* but so, as the sonne puts on his father; that we
may be of the same nature and substance as he; and that God may

Aquin.   ²⁶⁰ be in us, *Non tanquam in denario,* not as the King is in a peece of
coine, or a medall, but *tanquam in filio,* as he is in his sonne, in whom
the same nature both humane, and Royall doth reside.

There is then a double *Induere,* a twofold clothing; we may
Induere, 1. *Vestem,* put on a garment; 2. *Personam,* put on a person.
We may put on Christ so, as we shall be *his,* and we may put him on
so, as we shall be *He.* And even to put him on as a garment is also
twofold; The first is to take onely the *outward name,* and profession
of Christians upon us; and this doth us no good; *yee cloth ye, but are*

Hag. 1.[6]   *not warme,* says the Prophet, of this kind of putting on of Christ. For
²⁷⁰ this may be done onely to delude others; which practise God dis
covered, and threatned, in the false Prophets, *The Prophets shall not*

Zach. 13.[4] *weare a rough garment to deceive;* As God himselfe cannot be deluded, so for the encouragement of his Church, he will take off this
garment of the *Hypocrite,* and discover his nakednesse, and expose
him to the open shame of the world; *He shall not weare a rough gar-*
ment to deceive.

1 Chron.   For this is such an affront and scorne to Christ, as *Hanuns* cutting
19.4   off of *Davids* servants clothes at the middle, was; we make this garment of what stuffe, and what fashion we list; As *Hanun* did, we
²⁸⁰ cut it off in the *middle;* we will be Christians till noone, (in the outward acts of Religion) and *Libertines* in the after-noone, in putting
off that garment againe; we will be Christians all day, and returne to
wantonnesse, and licentiousnesse at night; we do that which Christ

Mat. 9.[16] says, no Man doth, (that is, no Man should doe) *we put new peeces*
to an old garment; and to that habite of sinne, which covers us as a

garment, we put a few new patches of Religion, a few flashes of *re-pentance,* a few shreds of a *Sermon,* but we put not on, that intire and seamlesse garment Christ Jesus.

And can we hope, that these disguises, these halfe coates, these im-
290 perfect services will be acceptable to God, when we our selves would not admit this, at our children, or at our servants hands? It is the argument by which the Prophet convinces the Israelites, about their uncleane sacrifices; *Offer this now unto the Prince; will he be content with thee, and accept thy person?* If thou shouldest weare the princes Livery, in a scantier proportion, or in a different fashion, or in a coarser stuffe, then belongs to thy place, would he accept it at thy hands? No more will Christ if thou put *him* on, (that is, take his profession upon thee) either in a *courser stuffe,* (*Traditions* of Men, in stead of his word) or in *scantier measure,* (not to be always a
300 Christian, but then, when thou hast *use* of being one) or in a *different fashion,* (to be singular and *Schismaticall* in thy opinion) for this is one, but an ill manner of putting on of Christ as a garment.

The second, and the good way is, to put on his righteousnesse, and his innocency, by imitation, and conforming our selves to him. Now when we goe about earnestly to make our selves *Temples,* and *Altars,* and to dedicate our selves to God, we must change our clothes; As when God bad *Jacob,* to goe up to *Bethel,* to make an *Altar,* he com-manded all his family *to change their clothes;* In which work, we have two things, to doe; first, we must put off those clothes which we
310 had; and appeare *naked* before God, without presenting any thing of our owne; (for when the Spirit of God came upon *Saul,* and that he prophecyed, his first act was, *to strip himselfe naked:*) And then secondly, we come to our transfiguration, and to have those garments of Christ communicated to us which *were as white, as the light;* and we shall be admitted into that little number, of which it is said, *Thou hast a few Names in Sardis, which have not defiled their garments, and they shall walke with me in white.*

And from this (which is *Induere vestem,*) from this putting on Christ as a garment, we shall grow up to that perfection, as that we
320 shall *Induere personam,* put on *him,* his person; That is, we shall so appeare before the Father, as that he shall take us for his owne Christ; we shall beare his name and person; and we shall every one

Mal. 1.[8]

Gen. 35.[2]

1 Sam.
19.[24]
Mat. 17.[2]
Revel. 3.[4]

Personam

be so accepted, as if every one of us were *all Mankind;* yea, as if we were *he* himselfe. He shall find in all our bodies his *woundes,* in all our mindes, his *Agonies;* in all our hearts, and actions his *obedience.* And as he shall doe this by imputation, so really in all our Agonies, he shall send his Angels to minister unto us, as he did to *Elias;* In all our tentations he shall furnish us with his Scriptures to confound the Tempter, as he in person, did in his tentation, and in our heaviest
³³⁰ tribulation, which may extort from us the voice of diffidence, *My God, My God, why hast thou forsaken me?* He shall give us the assurance to say, *In manus tuas &c. Into thy hands O Lord have I commended my spirit,* and there I am safe; He shall use us in all things, as his sonne; and we shall find restored in us, the Image of the whole Trinity, imprinted at our creation; for by this Regeneration, we are adopted by the Father in the bloud of the Sonne by the sanctification of the holy Ghost.

[Mat. 27.46]

[Luke 23.46]

Baptismus

    Now this putting on of Christ, whereby we stand in his place at Gods Tribunall, implies, as I said, both our *Election,* and our *sanctifi-*
³⁴⁰ *cation;* both the eternall purpose of God upon us, and his execution of that purpose in us. And because by the first ·(by our *Election*) we are members of Christ, in Gods purpose, before *baptisme,* and the second, (which is *sanctification*) is expressed after baptisme, in our lives, and conversation, therefore *Baptisme* intervenes, and comes *between both,* as a seale of the first, (of Election) and as an instrument, and conduit of the second, Sanctification.

    Now, *Abscondita Domino, Deo nostro, quæ manifesta sunt nobis;* let no Man be too curiously busie, to search what God does in his bedchamber; we have all enough to answer, for that, which we have
³⁵⁰ done in our bedchamber. For Gods *eternall decree,* himselfe is master of those Rolls; but out of those Rolls, he doth exemplifie those decrees in the *Sacrament of baptisme;* by which Copy, and exemplification of his invisible and unsearchable decree, we plead to the Church, that we are *Gods children,* we plead to our owne consciences, that we have the *Spirit of adoption,* and we plead to God himselfe, the obligation of his own promise, that we have a right to this garment, *Christ Jesus,* and to those graces, which must sanctifie us; for from thence comes the reason of this text, for *all yee that are baptized into Christ, have put on Christ.*

[Rom. 8.15]

360 As we cannot see the *Essence* of God, but must see him in his *glasses,* in his *Images,* in his *Creatures,* so we cannot see the decrees of God, but must see them in their *duplicats,* in their *exemplification,* in the *sacraments.* As it would doe him no good, that were condemned of treason, that a Bedchamber man should come to the Judge, and swear he saw the king signe the prisoners pardon, except he had it to pleade: so what assurance soever, what *privy marke* soever, those men, which pretend to be so well acquainted, and so familiar with the decrees of God, to give thee to know, that thou are elect to eternall salvation, yea if an Angel from heaven come downe and tell thee, that

370 he saw thy name in the booke of life, if thou have not this Exemplification of the decree, this seale, this Sacrament, if thou beest not *baptized,* never delude thy selfe with those imaginary assurances.

This Baptisme then is so necessary, that first, as *Baptisme* (in a large acceptation) signifies our dying, and buriall with Christ, and all the acts of our regeneration, so in that large sense, our whole life is a baptisme: But the very *sacrament* of Baptisme, the actuall administration, and receiving thereof, was held so necessary, that even for *legall* and *Civill* uses, (as in the law, that child, that dyed without circumcision, had no interest in the family, no participation of the honor, nor

380 name thereof; So that we see in the reckning of the Genealogy, and pedegree of *David,* that *first* sonne of his, which he had by *Bathsheba,*   1 Chron. 3 which dyed without circumcision is never mentioned, nor toucht upon.) So also, since the time of *Moses* law, in the Imperiall law, by which law, a *posthume child,* borne after the fathers death, is equall with the rest in division of the state, yet if that child dye before he be *baptized,* no person, which should derive a right from him, (as the mother might, if he dyed) can have any title by him; because he is not considered to have been at all, if he dye unbaptized. And if the State will not beleeve him to be a *full Man,* shall the Church beleeve

390 him to be a *full Christian,* before baptisme? Yea, the apprehension of the necessity of this Sacrament, was so common, and so generall, even in the beginning of the Christian Church, that out of an excessive advancing of that truth, they came also to a falshood, to an error, That even they that dyed without baptisme, might have the benefit of baptisme, if another were baptized in their name, after their death; And so, out of a mistaking of those words, *Else what shall they doe,*   1 Cor. 15.29

Qui baptizantur pro mortuis (which is, that are ready to dye, when
they are baptized) the *Marcionites* induc'd a custome, to lay one
under the dead bodyes bed, that he, in the name of the dead man,
⁴⁰⁰ might answer to all the questions usually asked, in administring of
Baptisme.

But this was a corrupt effect of pure, and sincere doctrine, which
doctrine is, *That Baptisme is so necessary, as that God hath placed
no other ordinary seale, nor conveyance of his graces in his Church,
to them that have not received that, then baptisme.* And they, who doe
not provide duly, for the Baptisme of their children, if their children
die, have a heavier accompt to make to God for that child, then if they
had not provided a *Nurse,* and suffered the child to starve. God can
preserve the child without *Milke;* and he can save the child without
⁴¹⁰ a sacrament; but as that mother that throwes out, and forsakes her
child in the field, or wood, is guilty before God of the Temporall
murder of that child, though the child die not, so are those parents
of a spirituall murder, if their children, by their fault die unbaptized,
though God preserve that child out of his abundant, and miraculous
mercy, from spirituall destruction.

When the custome of the Christian Church was to baptize but
twice in the year, at *Easter,* and *Whitsontide,* for the greater solemnity
of that action, yea when that ill custome was grown (as it was even
in the Primitive Church) that upon an opinion, that all sins were
⁴²⁰ absolutely forgiven in Baptisme, Men did defer their Baptisme, till
their *death-bed,* (as we see the Ecclesiasticall histories full of such
examples, even in some of the Christian *Emperors:* and according to
this ill custome, we see *Tertullian* chides away young children for
comming so soon to Baptisme, *Quid festinat innocens ætas, ad remis-
sionem peccatorum,* why should this child, that as yet hath done no
sinne, make such hast to be washed from sinne?) which opinion had
got so much strength, that *Saint Basil* was faine to oppose it, in the
Easterne Church, and both the *Gregories, Nazianzen* and *Nissen,* and
Saint Ambrose in the Western; yet, in the height of both their cus-
⁴³⁰ tomes, of *seldome baptizing,* and of *late baptizing,* the case of *infants,*
that might be in danger of dying without baptisme, was ever ex-
cepted, So that none of those old customes, (though some of them
were extreamly ill) went ever so farre, as to an opinion, that it were
all one, whether the child was baptized or no.

I speake not this, as though the state of *children* that died without baptisme were desperate; God forbid, for who shall shorten the Arme of the Lord? God is able to raine downe *Manna* and *Quailes* into the soules of these children, though negligent parents turne them out into the wildernesse, and put God to that extraordinary work. They may have *Manna*, and *Quailes,* but they have not the *Milke,* and *Hony,* of the Land of promise; They may have salvation from God, but they have not those graces, so sealed, and so testified to them, as God hath promised they should be in his Sacraments. When God in spirituall offences, makes *Inquisition of bloud,* he proceeds not, as Man proceeds; for we, till there appear a Man to be dead, never inquire who killed him; but in the spirituall Murder, of an unbaptized child, though there be no child spiritually dead, (though Gods mercy have preserved the child from that) yet God imputes this as such a murder to them, who endangered the child, as farre as they could, by neglecting his ordinance of baptisme.

This is then the necessity of this Sacrament; not absolutely necessary, but necessary by Gods ordinary institution; and as it is always necessary, so it is always certaine; whosoever is baptized according to Christs institution, receives the Sacrament of baptisme; and the truth is always infallibly annexed with the signe; *Nec fieri potest visio hominis, ut non sit Sacramentum quod figurat;* Though the wicked may feele no working by the Sacrament, yet the Sacrament doth offer, and present grace, as well to the unworthy as to the worthy Receiver; *Nec fallaciter promittit;* The wicked may be a cause, that the Sacrament shall doe *them no good;* but that the Sacrament, become *no Sacrament,* or that God should be false in his promises, and offer no grace, where he pretends to offer it, this the wicked cannot doe; baptisme doth truly, and without collusion, offer grace *to all;* and nothing but baptisme, by an ordinary institution, and as an ordinary meanes, doth so: for when *baptisme* is called *a figure,* yet both that figure is said there *to save us,* (The *figure that now saveth us, baptisme*) and it is a figure *of the Arke;* it hath relation to it, to that Arke which did save the world, when it is called a figure; So it may be a figure; but if we speake of reall salvation by it, baptisme is more then a figure.

Now as our putting on of Christ was double, by *faith,* and by *sanctification,* so by this Sacrament also, we are baptized *in Nomen*

440

450

460

470

Calvin

1 Pet. 3.21

Christi, into the *Name* of Christ, and *in mortem Christi,* into the
death of Christ: we are not therefore baptized into his *Name,* because
names are imposed upon us in our baptisme: for that was not always
permanently accustomed, in the Christian Church, to give a name at
baptisme. To men who were of years, and well known in the world
already by their name, if they were converted to the Christian faith,
the Church did not use to give *new names* at their baptisme: neither
to Children alwayes; but sometimes as an indifferent thing, they left
480 them to the custome of that country, or of that family, from which
they were derived. When *Saint Augustine* sayes, that he came to
Milan, to *S. Ambrose,* at that time, *quo dari nomina oportuit,* when
Names were to be given, it is true, that he speaks of a time, when
Baptisme was to be administred, but that phrase of *Giving of Names,*
was not a receiving of Names at Baptisme, (for neither *Ambrose,* nor
Augustine, received any new name at their Baptisme) but it was a
giving up of their Names, a Registring, a Matriculating of their
Names in the book of the profession of the Christian Religion, and
a publique declaration of that profession.

490   To be baptized therefore *into the name* of Christ, is to be translated
into his *Family,* by this spirituall adoption, in which adoption (when
it was *legall*) as they that were adopted, had also the name of the
family into which they were adopted, as of *Octavius Octavianus,* and
the rest, so are we so baptized, into *his name,* that we are of *Christus
Christiani;* and therefore to become truly *Christians,* to live Chris-
tainly, this is truly to be baptized into *his name.*

[Acts 4.12]   *No other name is given under heaven, whereby we can be saved;*
nor must any other name accompany the name of God, in our Baptisme. When therefore they teach in the *Romane Church,* that it is a
500 good Baptisme, which is administred in this forme, *I baptize thee in
the name of the Father, and Sonne, and holy Ghost, and the virgin
Mary,* if he which baptizes so, doe not meane in his intention, that the
virgin *Mary* is *equall* to the Trinity, but onely an *assistant,* this is not
onely an impertinent, but an impious addition to that God, that needs
no assistant. And as in our baptisme, we take no other name necessarily, but the name of Christ: So in our Christian life, we accept no
other distinctions of *Iesuits,* or *Franciscans;* but onely *Christians:* for
we are baptized *into his name,* and the whole life of a regenerate man

is a Baptisme. For as in putting on Christ, *sanctification* doth accom-
510 pany *faith,* so in baptisme, the imitation of his death (that is, *mortification*) and the application of his passion, (by fulfilling the sufferings
of Christ in our flesh) is that *baptisme into his death.* Which doe so
certainly follow one another, (that he that is truly baptized into *the
name* of Christ, is also baptized into *his death*) as that Saint *Paul*
couples them together, *Was Paul crucified for you, or were you baptized into the name of Paul?* If you were not baptized into *his name,*
then you have no interest, no benefit by his death, nor by any thing
which he suffered, that his merits, or his works of *supererogation*
should be applied to you: And if he did not suffer for you, (if all that
520 any *Paul* (much lesse any *Ignatius*) could doe, were but enough, and
too little for himselfe) then you are not baptized into *his name,* nor
to be denominate by him.

[Col. 1.24]
[Rom. 6.3]

1 Cor. 1.13

This is then to be Baptized into *Christs death, Habere, & reddere
testimonium, Christum pro me mortuum,* to be sure that Christ dyed
for me; and to be ready to dye for him; so, that I may *fulfill his sufferings,* and may think that all is not done, which belongs to my Redemption, except I finde a *mortification* in my selfe. Not that any mortification of mine, works any thing, as a *cause* of my redemption, but
as *an assurance* and testimony of it; *ut sit pignus & sigillum redemp-
530 tionis;* It is a pledge, and it is a Seale, of my redemption.

Christ calls his *death a Baptisme;* So Saint *Augustine* calls our
Baptisme a death, *Quod crux Christo, & Sepulcrum, id nobis Baptisma;* Baptisme to us, says he, is our Crosse, and our passion, and our
buriall; that is, in that, we are conformed to Christ as he suffered,
dyed, and was buried. Because if we be so baptized into his *Name,*
and into his *death,* we are thereby *dead to sinne,* and have dyed the
death of the righteous.

[Mark
10.39]

[1 Pet. 2.24]

Since then Baptisme is the *death of sinne,* and there cannot be this
death, this conquest, this victory over sinne, without *faith,* there must
540 necessarily *faith,* concurre with this baptisme; for if there be not faith,
(none in the *child,* none in the *parents,* none in the *sureties,* none in
the *Church*) then there is no baptisme performed; Now, in the
Child there is none *actually;* In the *sureties,* we are not sure, there is
any; for their infidelity cannot impeach the *sacrament;* The child is
well baptized though they should be misbeleevers; for, when the

Minister shall aske them, *Doest thou beleeve in God? dost thou re-nounce the Devill?* perchance they may ly in their owne behalfes; perchance they doe not *beleeve,* they doe not *renounce,* but they speake truth in the behalfe of the child, when they speake in the
550 voyce of the Church who receives this child for her childe, and binds her selfe to exhibit, and reach out to that child, her spirituall *paps,* for her future nourishment thereof. How comes it to passe, says *Saint Augustine,* that when a man presents another mans child at the font, to be baptized, if the Minister should aske him, Shall this man child be a valiant man, or a wise man, shall this woman child, be a chast, and a continent woman? the surety would answer, I *cannot tell,* and yet, if he be ask'd, of that child, of so few dayes old, *Doth that child beleeve in God now, will he renounce the Devill hereafter?* the surety answers confidently, in his behalfe, for the beleefe, and for the re-
560 nouncing: How comes this to passe, says *Saint Augustine?* He answers to this, that as *Sacramentum Corporis Christi, est secundum modum Corpus Christi,* so *Sacramentum fidei est fides;* As the Sac-rament of the body, and bloud of Christ, is, in some sense, and in a kinde, the body, and bloud of Christ, says *Augustine,* so in the *sacra-ment of faith,* says he, (that is, Baptisme) there is *some kinde of faith.* Here is a child borne of *faithfull parents;* and there is the voyce of God, who hath sealed a Covenant *to them, and their seed;* Here are *sureties,* that live (by Gods gratious spirit) in the unity, and in the bosome of the Church: and so, the parents present it to *them,* they
570 present it to the *Church,* and the Church takes it into her care; It is still the *naturall child,* of her parents, who begot it, it is the *spirituall child* of the Sureties that present it; but it is the *Christian child* of the Church, who in the sacrament of Baptisme, gives it a new inanima-tion, and who, if either *parents, or sureties,* should neglect their parts, will have a care of it, and breed it up to a perfection, and full growth of that faith, whereof it hath this day, an inchoation and beginning.

As then we have said, that *Baptisme* is a death, a death of sinne, and as we said before, sinne dyes not without *faith,* so also can there be no death of sinne, without *sorrow,* and *contrition,* which onely washes
580 away sinne: as therefore we see the Church, and Christs institution, furnishes this child, with *faith,* which it hath not of it selfe, so let us bring to this action, that *sorrow* and that condoling, that we produce

into the world such miserable wretches, as even by *peccatum in-voluntarium,* by that sinne, to which no act, nay no will of theirs con-curred, that is, *Originall sinne,* are yet put into the state of damnation.

But let us also rejoyce, in our owne, and this childes behalfe, that as we that have been baptized, so this child, that shall be, have, and shall put on Christ Jesus in Baptisme. Both as a *garment,* for *Sacra-menta sunt vestimenta,* As Christ is a garment, so the Sacraments are   Augustine
590 Christs garment, and as such a garment, as *Ornat militem,* and *convincit desertores,* It gives him, that continues in Gods battailes, a   Idem
dignity, and discovers him that forsakes Gods tents, to be a fugitive; Baptisme is a *garland,* in which two ends are brought together, he begins aright, and perseveres, so, *Ornat militem,* It is an honour to him, that fights out in Gods battaile, but *Convincit Desertorem,* Baptisme is our prest-money, and if we forsake our colours, after we have received that, even that forfaits our lives; our very having been baptized, shall aggravate our condemnation. Yea it is such a garment, as those of the children of Israel in the wildernesse, which are (by
600 some expositors) thought to have growne all the forty yeares, with their bodies; for so by Gods blessed provision, shall *grace* grow with this infant, to the lifes end. And both we and it, shall not onely put on Christ, as a *garment,* but we shall put on his *person,* and we shall stand before his Father, with the confidence, and assurance of bearing his person, and the dignity of his innocence.

Number 8.

Preached at Essex house, at the Churching

of the Lady Doncaster.

[*? December, 1618*]

CANT. 5.3. *I HAVE WASHED MY FEET, HOW SHALL I DEFILE THEM?*

ALL THINGS desire to goe to *their owne place,* and that's but the effect of *Nature;* But if Man desires to goe the right way, that's an effect of *grace,* and of *Religion.* A *stone* will fall to the bottome naturally, and a *flame* will goe upwards naturally; but a stone cares not whether it fall through cleane water, or through Mud; a flame cares not whether it passe through pure aire, or cloudy; but a *Christian,* whose end is heaven, will put himselfe into a *faire way* towards it, and according to this measure, *be pure as his father in heaven is pure.* That which is our end, *salvation,* we use to expresse
10 in Schooles by these two termes, we call it *visionem Dei,* the sight of God, and we call it *unionem,* an union with God; we shall *see* God,
1 Iohn 3.2   and we shall be *united* to God: for our seeing, we shall see him *Sicuti*
1 Cor. 13.12 *est,* as he is; which we cannot expresse, till we see him; *Cognoscam ut cognitus, I shall know as I am known,* which is a knowledge reserved for that Schoole, and a degree for that Commencement, and not to be
Exod. 33.23   had before. *Moses* obtained a *sight* of God here, that he might see, *Posteriora,* Gods hinder parts; and if we consider God *in posterioribus,* in his *later* works, in the fulfilling of all his *Prophecies,* concerning our Redemption, how he hath accomplished *in novissimis,* in the
[Luke 1.70] 20 *later* times, all that which he spake *ab initio, by the mouth of his Prophets, which have been since the world began,* if we see God in

168

them, it is a great beame of that *visio beatifica,* that beaticall sight of
God in heaven; for herein we see the whole way of our salvation, to
be in *Christ Jesus;* all *promise,* all *performance,* all *prophecy,* all *history* concern us, in and by *him.* And then for that *union* with God,
which is also our salvation, (as this *vision* is) when we shall be so
united, as that we shall *follow the Lambe whither soever he goes,*   [Rev. 14.4]
though that union be unexpressible here, yet here, there is an union
with God, which represents *that* too. Such an union, as that the
³⁰ *Church* of which we are parts, is his *spouse,* and that's *Eadem caro,*
the same body with him; and such an union, as that the obedient
children of the Church, are *Idem spiritus cum Domino,* we are the   [1 Cor. 6.17]
same *body,* and *the same spirit:* So united, as that by being sowed in
the visible Church, we are *Semen Dei,* the seed of God, and by grow-   1 Iohn 3.9
ing up there in godlinesse, and holinesse, we are *participes Divinæ*   [2 Pet. 1.4]
naturæ, partakers of the divine Nature it selfe. Now these two unions,
which represent our eternall union with God (that is, the union of
the *Church* to him, and the union of *every good soule* in the Church
to him) is the subject of this Song of songs, this heavenly *Poeme,* of
⁴⁰ *Solomons;* and our *baptisme,* at our entrance into this world, is a
Seale of this union; our *mariage,* in the passage of this world, is a
Sacrament of this union; and that which seems to be our dissolution,
(our *death*) is the strongest *band* of this union, when we are so
united, as nothing can disunite us more. Now, for uniting things in
this world, we are always put to imploy baser, and courser stuffe, to
unite them together, then they themselves; If we lay *Marble* upon
Marble, how well soever we polish the Marble, yet we must unite
them with morter: If we unite *riches* to *riches,* we temper a morter
(for the most part) of our owne *covetousnesse,* and the losse, and
⁵⁰ oppressing of some other Men; if we unite *honours* to *honours,* titles
to titles, we temper a morter, (for the most part) of our owne *Ambition,* and the supplanting, or excluding of some other Men; But in
the uniting of a Christian soule to Christ Jesus, here is no morter, all
of one *Nature;* Nothing but *spirit,* and *spirit,* and *spirit,* the soule of
Man to the Lord Jesus, by the holy Ghost. Worldly unions have some
corrupt foulnesses in them, but for this spirituall union, *Lavi pedes,
I have washed my feet, how shall I defile them?*
    Which words, though in the rigor of the coherence, and connexion   *Divisio*

of this Scripture, they imply a delay in the spouse of Christ, and so
⁶⁰ in every soule too, that when Christ called her, the soule was not
ready to come forth to him, but made her *excuses,* that she *had put off
her coate,* and *was loath to rise to put it on,* that she had *washed her
feet,* and *was loath to rise,* and *foule them againe,* yet because the
excuse it selfe, (if it were an excuse) hath a piety, and a Religious
care in it, the Fathers for the most part, pretermit that weaknesse that
produced an excuse, and consider in their expositions, the care that
the soule had, *not to defile her selfe againe,* being once washed. Saint

Gregory   *Gregory* says, that the soule had laid off, *Omnia externa, quæ non tam
ornant quàm onerant,* all outward ornaments, which are rather en-
⁷⁰ cumbrances, then ornaments; And Saint *Ambrose* says, *Pedes lavi,
dum egrederer de corporis contubernio,* when I departed from the con-
federation of my body, and the pampering of that, *I wash'd my feet,
Quomodo in tenebrosum carcerem reverterer?* And why should I
returne into that darke, and durty prison, againe, the love of mine
owne body? Pursuing therefore their pious acceptation of these
words, we have in them, two *festivalls* of the soule, a *Resurrection,*
and an *ascension* of it; This soule hath raised it selfe, from the durt
and Mud of this world, *Lavit pedes,* she hath washed her feet, and
then she hath ascended to a resolution, of keeping herselfe in that
⁸⁰ state, *Quomodo inquinabo eos,* how shall I defile them? Call these
two parts a *Gratulation* of the soule, and an *Indignation;* first she con-
gratulates with her good, and gratious God, that she is cleansed from
worldly corruptions, *Lavi pedes, I have washed my feet;* and then
she conceives a Religious scorne and indignation, of setting her foot
in the same foule way againe. *Quomodo,* how, how is it possible that
I should descend, to so low a disposition, as to foule them againe?
This *Resurrection* then of the soule, and *gratulation,* and this *Ascension* of the soul and *Indignation,* will be our two parts. And in the
first, we shal stop a little, upon every one of these five branches; There
⁹⁰ is *ablutio necessaria;* There is a washing, that is necessary to all; for
we enter in foulenesse, and corruption into this world; and that we
have in *Baptisme* for *Originall sinne:* Secondly, there is *ablutio
pedum,* a washing *of our feet,* of our steps, and walkes in this world,
and that's by *repentance,* sealed in the other *Sacrament,* and properly,
that is for *actuall sinnes;* Thirdly, in this ablution, there is an *Ego*

lavi, there is a washing, and *I my selfe* doe something towards this cleansing of my selfe; And fourthly, it is *Lavi,* it is, I *have* washed, not *Lavabo,* it is not, I *will* wash; it is already done, it is not put off to mine *age,* nor to my *death bed,* but *Lavi,* I *have* washed; And lastly, ¹⁰⁰ it is *Pedes meos,* I have washed *mine owne feet;* for if by my teaching, I cleanse *others,* and remaine, by my bad life, in foule ways my selfe, I am not within this text, *Lavi pedes meos;* I have not washed my feet; But if we have sincerely performed the first part, we shall performe the other too, *Quomodo,* we shall come into a religious detestation, and indignation of falling into the same foulenesse againe.

To passe then through all these (for of all these that's true which Saint *Basil* says of all words in the Scriptures, *Habent minutissimæ particulæ sua mysteria,* Every word hath force and use, as in Pearle, every *seed Pearle* is as medicinall, as the greatest, so there is a *restora-* ¹¹⁰ *tive nature* in every word of the Scriptures, and in every word, the soule findes a rise, and help for her devotion,) To begin with the first, the *necessity of washing,* consider us in our first beginning, *Concepti in peccatis,* our Mothers conceived us in sin; and being wrapped up in uncleannesse there, *can any Man bring a cleane thing out of filthinesse?* There is not one; for as we were planted, in our Mothers wombe, in *conception,* so we were transplanted from thence into this world, in our *Baptisme, Nascimur filii iræ,* for we are by nature the *children of wrath,* as well as others. And as in the bringing forth, and bringing up, of the best, and most precious, and most delicate plants, ¹²⁰ Men employ most *dung,* so the greatest persons, where the spirit and grace of God, doth not allay that intemperance, which naturally arises, out of abundance, and provocation, and out of vanity, and ambitious glory, in outward ostentations; there is *more dung,* more uncleannesse, more sinne in the conception, and birth of their children, then of meaner and poorer parents; It is a degree of uncleannesse, to fixe our thoughts too earnestly upon the uncleannesse of our conception, and of our birth: when wee call that a testimony of a right comming, if we come into the world *with our head forward,* in a head-long precipitation; and when we take no other testimony ¹³⁰ of our being *alive,* but that we were heard *cry;* and for an earnest, and a Prophecy, that we shall be *viri sanguinum, et dolosi,* bloudy, and deceitfull Men, false and treacherous, to the murdering of our owne

First Part
Basil

Psal. 51.5

Iob 14.4

Eph. 2.3

[Psa. 5.6]

soules we come into this world, as the Egyptians went out of it, swallowed, and smothered in a red sea, *Pueri sanguinum, & infirmi,* weake, and bloudy infants at our birth. But to carry our thoughts from *materiall,* to *spirituall* uncleannesses, *In peccato concepti,* we were conceived in sinne, but who can tell us *how?* That flesh in our mothers wombe, which we are, having no sinne in it selfe, (for that *masse of flesh* could not be damned, if there never came a soule into ¹⁴⁰ it) and that *soule,* which comes into that flesh from God, having no sinne in it neither, (for God creates nothing infected with sinne, neither should that soule be damned, if it came not into that body) The *body,* being without sinne, and the *soule* being without sinne, yet in the first minute, that this body and soule meet, and are united, we become in that instant, guilty of *Adams* sinne, committed *six thousand years* before. Such is our sinne and uncleannesse, in *Originall sinne,* as the subtillest Man in the Schooles, is never able to tell us, *how,* or *when* we contracted that sinne, but all have it; And therefore if there be any, any any-where, of that generation, that are *pure in* ¹⁵⁰ *their owne eyes, and yet are not washed from their filthinesse,* as *Solomon* speakes, *Erubesce vas stercorum,* says good Saint *Bernard,* If it be a vessell of gold, it is but a vessell of excrements, if it be a bed of curious plants, it is but a bed of dung; as their tombes hereafter shall be but glorious covers of rotten carcasses, so their bodies are now, but pampered covers of rotten soules; *Erubescat vas stercorum,* let that vessell of uncleannesse, that barrell of dung, confesse a *necessity* of washing, and seeke that, and rejoyce in that, for thus farre, (that is, to the pollution of *Originall sinne,*) *in peccato concepti,* and *nascimur filii iræ,* wee are *conceived in sinne,* first, and then we are *borne* ¹⁶⁰ *the children of wrath.*

But where's our remedy? Why for this, for this originall uncleannesse, is the water of *Baptisme. Oportet nos renasci;* we must be *borne againe;* we *must;* There is a *necessity* of *Baptisme:* As we are the children of Christian parents, we have *Jus ad rem,* a right to the Covenant, we may claime baptisme, the Church cannot deny it us; And as we are baptized in the Christian Church, we have *Jus in re,* a right in the Covenant, and all the benefits thereof, all the promises of the Gospell: we are sure that we are *conceived in sinne,* and sure that we are *borne children of wrath,* but not sure that we are cleansed,

¹⁷⁰ or reconciled to God, by any other meanes then that, which he hath
ordained, *Baptisme.* The Spirit of God moved first *upon the water;*   [Gen. 1.2]
Tertullian
and the spirit of life grew first in the *water; Primus liquor, quod
viveret edidit:* The first living creatures in the first creation, were in
the waters; and the first breath of *spirituall life,* came to us, from the
water of *baptisme.* In the Temple there was *Mare æneum, a brasen*   1 Reg. 7.23
sea; In the Church there is *Mare aureum,* a golden sea, which is
Baptisterium, the *font,* in which we discharge our selves, of all our
first uncleannesses, of all the guiltinesse of *Originall sinne;* but because we contract new uncleannesses, by our uncleane ways here;
¹⁸⁰ therefore there must bee *Ablutio pedum,* a washing *of our feet,* of our
ways, of our actions, which is our second branch.

    Cecidimus in lutum, & super acervum lapidum, says Saint *Bernard;*   2
Pedes
Bern.

Esay 59.10
we fell by *Adams* fall, into the *durt;* but from that, we are washed in
baptisme; but we fell upon a *heape of sharpe stones* too; and we feel
those wounds, and those bruises, all our lives after; *Impingimus
meridie,* we *stumble at noone day;* In the brightest light of the
Gospell, in the brightest light of *grace,* in the best strength of *Repentance,* and our resolutions to the contrary, yet we stumble, and
fall againe. *Duo nobis pedes,* says that Father, *Natura, & Consuetudo;*
¹⁹⁰ we stand, says he, upon *two feet, Nature,* and *Custome;* and we are
lame of one foot hereditarily, we draw a corrupt *Nature* from our
parents; and we have lamed the other foot, by crooked, and perverse
customes. Now, as God provided a liquor in his Church, for *Originall
sinne,* the water of *Baptisme,* so hath he provided another for those
actuall sinnes; that is, the bloud of his owne body, in the *other Sacrament.* In which Sacrament, besides the *naturall* union, (that Christ
hath taken our *Nature,*) and the *Mysticall union,* (that Christ hath
taken us into the body of *his Church*) by a *spirituall union,* when we
apply faithfully his Merits to our soules, and by a *Sacramentall union,*
²⁰⁰ when we receive the visible seales thereof, worthily, we are so washed
in his bloud, as that we stand in the sight of his Father, as cleane,
and innocent, as himselfe, both because he and we are thereby become
one body, and because the garment of his righteousnesse covers us all.
But, for a preparation of this washing in the bloud of Christ, in that
Sacrament, Christ commended to his Apostles, and in them, to all
the world, by his *practise,* and by his *precept* too, *ablutionem pedum,*

Iohn 13

Bernard

a washing of their feet; before they came to that Sacrament he *washed their feet;* And in that exemplary action of his, his washing of their feet, he *powred water into a Bason,* says the text: *Aqua spiritus* ²¹⁰ *sanctus, pelvis Ecclesia;* These preparatory waters are the gift of the holy Ghost, the working of his grace in repentance; but *pelvis Ecclesia,* the bason is the Church; that is, these graces are distributed, and dispensed to us, in his institution, and ordinance in the Church: No Man can wash himselfe at first, by *Baptisme;* no Man can *baptize himselfe;* no Man can wash in the second liquor, no Man, (that is but a Man) can administer the *other Sacrament to himselfe: Pelvis ecclesia,* the Church is the bason, and Gods Minister in the Church, washes in both these cases. And, in this *ablutione pedum,* in the preparatory washing of our feet, by a survey of all our sinfull actions and ²²⁰ repentance of them, no Man can *absolve himselfe,* but *pelvis ecclesia,* the bason of this water of *absolution,* is in the *Church* and in the *Minister* thereof.

First then this washing of the feet, which prepares us for the great washing, in the bloud of Christ, requires a stripping of them, a laying of them naked; *covering of the feet* in the Scriptures, is a phrase, that denotes a foule, and an uncleane action; *Saul* was said *to cover his feet, in the Cave,* and *Eglon* was said to *cover his feet* in his Parler; and we know the uncleane action, that is intended here: but for this cleane action, for *washing our feet,* we must *discover* all our sinfull ²³⁰ steps, in a free and open *confession* to almighty God. This may be that which *Solomon* calls, *sound wisdome; My sonne keep sound wisdome, and discretion.* There is not a more silly folly, then to thinke to hide any sinfull action from God. Nor sounder wisdome then to discover them to him, by an humble, and penitent *confession;* This is *sound wisdome,* and then, *discretion* is, to wash, and discerne, and debate, and examine all our *future actions,* and all the circumstances, that by this spirit of discretion we may see, where the sting, and venome of every particular action lies: *My sonne keep sound wisdome, and discretion,* says he, *And then shalt thou walke in thy way* ²⁴⁰ *safely, and thy foot shall not stumble;* If thy discretion be not strong enough, (if thou canst not always *discerne,* what is, and what is not sinne) *he shall give his Angells charge over thee, that thou dash not thy foot against a stone;* and that's good security; and if all these faile,

[1 Sam.24.3]
Iudg. 3.24

Prov. 3.21

Psal. 91.11

though thou doe fall, thou shalt not be utterly cast downe, for *the Lord shall uphold thee with his hand,* says *David;* God shall give that Man, that loves this sound wisdome, (humble *confession* of sinnes past) this *spirituall discretion,* the spirit of *discerning spirits,* that is, power to discerne a *tentation,* and to overcome it; *confesse* that which is past with true *sorrow,* that's *sound wisdome,* and God shall en-
250 lighten thee for the future, and that's holy *discretion.*

The washing of our feet then, being a cleane, and pure and sincere examination of all our actions, we are to wash all the instruments of our actions, in repentance; *Lavanda facies,* we are to wash our face, as *Joseph* did, after he had wept, before he looked upon his brethren againe: If we have murmured, and mourned, for any crosse, that God hath laid upon us, we must returne to a cheerfull countenance towards him, in embracing whatsoever he found best for us; we must wash our *Intestina,* our bowels, (as it is after commanded in the law) when *our bowels,* which should melt at the relation, and
260 contemplation, and application of the passion of our Saviour, doe melt at the apprehension, or expectation, or fruition of any sinfull delight, *Lavanda intestina,* we must wash those bowells; *Lavanda vestimenta,* we must *wash our clothes;* when we apparell and palliate our sinnes with excuses, of our owne infirmity, or of the example of greater Men, these clothes must be washed, these excuses; *Lavanda currus & arma,* as *Ahabs* chariot and armour were washed; If the power of our birth or of our place, or of our favour, have armed us against the power of the law, or against the clamour of Men justly incensed, *Lavandi currus,* these chariots, and armes, this greatnesse
270 must be washed; *Lavanda retia;* what *Nets* soever we have fished with, by what meanes soever we raise, or sustaine our fortune, *Lavanda retia,* These nets must be washed. Saint *Bernard* hath drawn a great deale of this heavenly water together, for the washing of all, when he presents, (as he cals it) *Martyrium, sine sanguine, triplex,* a threefold Martyrdome, and all without bloud; and that is, *Largitas in paupertate,* a bountifull disposition, even in a low fortune; *parcitas in ubertate,* a frugall disposition in a full fortune; and *Castitas in Juventute,* a pure, and chaste disposition, in the years, and places of tentation. These are Martyrdomes, without bloud, but not without
280 the water that washes our feet; This is *sound wisdome,* and discre-

Psal. 37.24

Gen. 43.31

Exod. 29.17

Exod. 19.10

1 Reg. 22.38

Luk. 5.2

Bernard

tion, to strip, and lay open our feet, our sinfull actions, by *Confession;* To cover them, and wrap them up by *precaution,* from new uncleannesse; and then to tye and bind up all safe, by participation of the *bloud* of Christ Jesus, in the *Sacrament;* for that's the seale of all; And Christ in the washing of his disciples feet, tooke *a towell to dry them,* as well, as water to wash them; so when he hath brought us to this washing of our feet, to a serious consideration of our actions, and to repentant teares, for them, *Absterget omnem lachrymam,* he will wipe all teares from our eyes; all teares of *confusion* towards Men, or of *diffidence* towards him; *Absterget omnem lachrymam,* and deliver us over to a setled peace of conscience.

[Joh. 13.5]

[Rev. 7.17; 21.4]

290

Ego

There is a washing then, absolutely, generally necessary, the water of *Baptisme;* and a washing occasionally necessary, because we fall into actuall sinnes, the *bloud* of our Saviour in the *Sacrament;* and there is a washing between these, preparatory to the last washing, the water of *Contrite,* and *repentant teares,* in opening our selves to God, and shutting up of our selves against future tentations: of the two first, the *two Sacraments, fons in Ecclesia,* the whole *spring,* and river is in the Church, there is no *baptisme,* no *bloud* of Christ, but in the Church; And of this later, which is most properly *ablutio pedum,* the washing of the feet, that is, *teares* shed in repentance of our sinfull lives, of this water, there is *Pelvis in Ecclesia,* the *Bason* is in the Church; for our best repentance (though this repentance be at home in our owne hearts) doth yet receive a Seale, from the *absolution* of Gods Ministers in the Church. But yet though there be no cleansing, but from the spirit of God, no ordinary working of Gods spirit, but in the Church, and his ordinances there, yet *we our selves* are not so left out, in his work, but that the spouse here, and every carefull soule here, says, truly, *Ego lavi, I* my *selfe* have *washed my feet;* which is our third branch.

300

310

It is said often in Philosophy, *Nihil in intellectu, quod non prius in sensu;* till some *sense* apprehend a thing, the *Judgment* cannot debate it, nor discourse it; It may well be said in *Divinity* too, *Nihil in gratia, quod non prius in natura,* there is nothing in grace, that was not first in nature, so farre, as that grace always finds nature, and naturall faculties to work on; though that nature be not disposed to the receiving of grace, when it comes, yet that nature, and those faculties,

which may be so disposed by grace, are there, before that grace comes.
And the grace of God doth not work this cleansing, but where there
²⁰ is a sweet, and souple, and tractable, and ductile disposition wrought
in that soule. This disposition is *no cause why* God gives his grace;
for there is no cause, but his own meer, and unmeasurable goodnesse;
But yet, *without* such a disposition, God would not give that; and
therefore *let us cleanse our selves from all filthinesse,* says the Apostle;   2 Cor. 7.1
There is something, which *we ourselves* may doe. A Man that had
powred out himselfe in a vehement, and corrupt solicitation of the
chastity of any woman, if he found himselfe surprized by the presence
of a husband, or a father, he could give over in the midst of a protesta-
tion; A Man that had set one foot into a house of dangerous provoca-
³⁰ tions, if he saw a bill of the plague, upon the doore, he could goe
backe; A Man that had drawne his sword to rob a passenger, if he
saw a *hue and cry* come, could give over that; and all this is upon
the *Ego lavi,* I have washed; without use of *grace,* his owne *naturall
reason* declines him from that sinne then. How long shall we make
this bad use, of this true doctrine, that, because we cannot doe *enough,*
for our salvation, therefore we will doe *nothing?* Shall I see any Man
shut out of heaven, that did what he could upon earth? Thou that
canst mourne for any worldly losse, mourne for thy sinne; Thou
that lovest meetings of company for society, and conversation, love
⁴⁰ the meeting of the Saints of God, in the Congregation, and communion of Saints; Thou that lovest the Rhetorique, the Musique, the
wit, the sharpnesse, the eloquence, the elegancy, of *other authors,*
love even those things in the *Scriptures,* in the word of God, where
they abound more, then in other authors. Put but thy affections out
of their ordinary sinfull way, and then *Lavasti pedes,* thou hast
washed thy feet; and God will take thy work in hand, and raise a
building farre beyond the compasse, and comprehension of thy foundation; that which the soule began, but in *good nature,* shall be
perfected in *grace.*
⁵⁰   But doe it quickly; for the glory of this soule here was in the *Lavi;*   *Lavi*
It is not *Lavabo;* that she *had* already; not that she *would* wash her
feet; since thou art come to know thy naturall uncleannesse, and
baptisme for that, and thine actuall uncleannesse, and that for that,
there is a River, that brings thee into the maine Sea, (the water of

repentance leads thee to the bottomelesse Sea of the bloud of thy
Saviour, in the Sacrament) continue not in thy foulenesse, in confidence that all shall be drowned in that at last, whensoever thou wilt
come to it. It was a common, but an erroneous practise, even in the
Primitive Church, to defer their *baptisme,* till they were *old;* because
³⁶⁰ an opinion prevailed upon them, that baptisme discharged them of
all sinnes, they used to be baptized then, when they were past sinning,
that so they might passe out of this world, in that innocency, which
their baptisme imprinted in them: And out of this custome, Men
grew to be the more carelesse all their lives, because all was done at

Augustin.

once in baptisme. But, says Saint *Augustine,* in that case, (and it was
his owne case) It were uncharitably said, *Vulneretur amplius,* that if
we saw a Man welter in his bloud, and wounded in divers places, it
were uncharitably said, *Vulneretur amplius,* give him two or three
wounds more, for the Surgeon is not come yet; It is uncharitably said
³⁷⁰ to thine owne soule, *Vulneretur amplius,* take thy pleasure in sinne
yet, when I come to receive the Sacrament, I will repent altogether,
doe not thinke to put off all to the *washing weeke;* all thy sinnes, all
thy repentance, to *Easter,* and the Sacrament then; There may be a
washing then, and no *drying;* thou maist come to weep the *teares* of
desperation, to seek mercy with teares, and not find it; teares for
worldly losses, teares for sinne, teares for bodily anguish, may overflow thee then; and whereas Gods goodnesse to those, that are his, is,
ut abstergat omnem Lachrymam, to *wipe all teares from their eyes;*
absterget nullam Lachrymam, he may leave all unwiped upon thee,
³⁸⁰ he may leave thy soule to sinke, and to shipwracke, under this tempest, and inundation, and current of divers tides, teares of all kinds,
and ease of none: for those of whom it is said, *Deus absterget omnem*
lachrymam, God shall wipe all teares from their eyes, are they *Qui*
laverunt Stolas, (as we see there) who have *already washed their long*
robes, and made them white in the bloud of the Lambe: who have
already by teares of repentance, become worthy receivers of the seale
of reconciliation, in the Sacrament of his body, and bloud; To them,
God shall wipe all teares from their eyes; but to the unrepentant sinner, he shall multiply teares; from teares, for the losse, of a horse, or
³⁹⁰ of a house, to teares for the losse of a soule, and wipe no teare from
his eyes.

[Rev. 7.14]

But yet though this *Lavi,* exclude the *Lavabo,* as it is dilatory, that
is, I will wash, but not yet, yet it excludes not the *Lavabo,* I will wash,
as it is an *often washing;* I must come to that, *Lavi,* I have washed,
but yet I will wash againe: for till our feet be so washed, as that they
be wrapped up in our last linnen, and so raised from the ground, as
that they be laid upon other Mens shoulders, our feet will touch the
ground againe and need new washing. When Christ washed his disciples feet, there is a great difference amongst the Fathers, where he
beganne, *whose feet he washed first: Saint Augustine,* and Saint
Bernard thinke he beganne with *Peter;* they thinke Christ respected
the dignity of his person: *Origen* and *Chrysostome* thinke he beganne
with *Judas;* they thinke Christ respected the necessity of the Patient,
and applied the Physique soonest, where the disease was most ma-
lignant, and venemous. None of them say he beganne with *John,*
whom it is cleere he loved most. If any soule have apprehended that
Christ came *late* to her washing, not till now, let her not argue, to
her owne danger, that he loved her the lesse for that: if he have suffered *sinne to abound,* that *grace might abound,* what Patient shall
dare to appoint that Physitian his *Dosis,* or his times; whomsoever
he washed *first* of his Apostles, he washed them *all;* and to him that
was forwardest ever in his owne strength, to *Peter,* he said, *Non
habebis partem,* If I wash thee not, thou shalt have no part with me;
If we come not to this washing of our feet, this preparatory washing
by teares of *repentance,* we can have no part in him, that is, in the
participation of his body, and his bloud; but when he hath brought
us to this *Jordan,* which is *Fluvius Judicii,* the water of Judgment,
and that we have judged, and condemned our selves of this Leprosie
of sinne, *Lavemur septies,* let us often call our selves to account, implore the councell often, often accept the *absolution* of Gods Minister,
and often settle our soules, in a true peace, by a worthy receiving of
the seale thereof, in the Sacrament: And as in that we come to the
Lavi, (a peacefull testimony, that we *have* washed our consciences)
so let us pursue it with a *Lavabo,* with an humble acknowledgment,
that we fall every day, and every day need a new washing; for as
from poore tenants, Landlords are not content to receive their rent
at the years end, but *quarterly,* or in shorter termes, so from such
beggerly and bankrupt soules as ours are, God is not content with

Augustine
and Bernard
Origen and
Chrysos-
tome

[Rom. 5.20]

[Joh. 13.8]

[2 Kings
5.14]

an anniversary repentance once a yeare, at *Easter;* but we shall finde
430 our rent, our payment heavy enough, if we pay every day, and wash
our feet every night, for the uncleannesses of that one day.

Meos   To shut up this part then; This washing of the feet, is the spirit of
discerning, and censuring particular actions: but it is *pedes meos,* a
discerning, and censuring of *my actions,* not onely, or not principally
Rom. 10.[15]   the actions of *other Men; Quàm speciosi pedes Evangelizantium, how*
Isay 52.7   *beautifull are the feet of them, that preach peace,* says Saint *Paul,* out
Nah. 1.15   of the mouth of two witnesses, two Prophets, that had said so before.
If we will *preach peace,* that is, relieve the consciences of *others,* by
presenting them their sinnes, we must have *speciosos pedes,* cleane
440 ways, and a cleane life of our owne; so it is with us, and our profession; But *Gens sancta, regale Sacerdotium,* as the Apostle joines them,
1 Pet. 2.9   If you be a *holy people,* you are also a *royall preisthood;* If you be all
Gods Saints, you are all *Gods Preists;* and if you be his preists, it is
your office to preach too; as we by words, you by your holy works;
as we by contemplation, you by conversation; as we by our doctrine,
so you by your lives, are appointed by God to preach to one another:
and therefore every particular Man, must wash his owne feet, looke
that he have *speciosos pedes,* that his example may preach to others,
for this is truly *Regale Sacerdotium,* a regall preisthood, not to work
450 upon others by words, but by actions. If we love one another, as
Christ loved us, we must *wash one anothers feet,* as he commanded
his Apostles; There is a preistly duty lies upon every Man, brotherly
to reprehend a brother, whom he sees trampling in foule ways, wal-
lowing in foule sinnes; but I may *preach to others and be my selfe*
1 Cor. 9.27   *a reprobate,* (as Saint *Paul* speakes with terror to Men of our coate)
in his owne person, I may bring others to heaven, and bee shut out
my selfe; And thou maist preach that a *Man should not steale, and*
Rom. 2.21   *steale, That a Man should not commit adultery, and commit it;* And
in these cases, *Non speciosi pedes,* here are no cleane, no faire feet,
460 and therefore no edifying. Nay if, in either kind, we, or you, *abhor*
Idols, and yet commit sacriledge, that is, reprehend a sinne in another,
which we are free from our selves, but yet are guilty our selves, of
another sinne as great, here's no cleane feet, no profitable preaching;
And therefore the onely way to doe God service, is, to wash and to

censure the feet, (that is, *particular actions*) but principally, *our owne* feet, that which we doe our selves.

There remaines yet a second part: and perchance but a little time for it; and I shall proportion, and fit my selfe to it. It is, That as this soule had a *Resurrection,* she hath an *Ascension;* As she had *vocem*
70 *gratulantis,* a thanksgiving, that she hath washed her feet, so she hath *vocem indignantis,* a religious scorne and indignation, to fall into those foule ways againe. For this holy indignation, is one linke in the Apostles chaine of Repentance, where, upon Godly *sorrow,* depends *care,* and upon that, cleansing of our selves, and upon that, *indignation,* and so *feare,* and so *desire,* and so *zeale,* and so *punishments* of our selves: every linke worthy of a longer consideration; but here we consider onely this *indignation;* when that soule that is washed, and thereby sees, to what a faire conformity with her Saviour she is come, is come also to a scorne, to a disdaine to compare any
80 beauty in this world, to that face, which Angells desire to looke upon; any nearenesse to great persons in this world, to the *following of the Lambe wheresoever he goes;* any riches of this world, to that riches wherewith the poverty of Christ Jesus hath made us rich; any length of life in this world, to that union which we shall have, to the *Antient of dayes;* where even the everliving God, shall not overlive us, but carry out our days to the unmeasured measure of his owne, to eternity. This indignation, this soule expresses here, in this question, *Quomodo, how shall I defile them?* First then, this voice of indignation, hath this force; *Quomodo, how shall I defile them,* is, *how is it pos-*
90 *sible,* that *I should defile them?* I have washed my feet, repented my sinnes and taken the seale of my Reconciliation, the Sacrament, and that hath this effect, *ut sensum minuat in minimis, & tollat consensum in magnis peccatis,* That *grace,* that God gives in the Sacrament, makes us lesse sensible of small tentations, (they move us not) and it makes us resist, and not yeild to the greatest tentations; since I am in this state, *Quomodo inquinabo? How shall I defile them?* The difference will be, of whom thou askest this question: If thou aske the world, the world will tell thee, well enough. *Quomodo, How;* It will tell thee, that it is a *Melancholy* thing, to sit thinking upon
100 thy sinnes; That it is an unsociable thing, to seeke him, who cannot be seen, an invisible God; That it is poore company, to passe thy

2 Part

2 Cor. 7.11

[Dan. 7.9]

Bernard

time with a *Priest;* Thou maiest defile thy selfe againe, by forgetting
thy sinnes, and so doing them over againe: And thou maist defile thy
selfe againe, by *remembring* thy sins, and so sinne over thy sinnes
againe, in a sinfull delight of thy passed sinnes, and a desire that thou
couldst commit them againe. There are answers enough to this
Quomodo, How, how should I defile them, if thou aske the world:
but aske thy Saviour, and he shall tell thee, *That whosoever hath
this water, shall never thirst more, but that water shall be in him an*
⁵¹⁰ *everlasting spring;* that is, he shall find meanes to keep himselfe in
that cleannesse, to which he is come; and *neither things present, nor
things to come shall separate him from the love of God.*

Iohn 4.14

Rom. 8.[38]

Thus the voice of this religious indignation, *Quomodo,* is, how is it
possible, but it is also, *Quomodo, how,* that is, *why should I?* The
first is, *how should I be so base,* the other, *how should I be so bold?*
Though I have my pardon, written in the bloud of my Saviour, sealed
to me in his Sacrament, brought home to me in the testimony of the
holy Ghost, pleaded for me, at the tribunall of the Father, yet as
Princes pardons have, so Gods pardons have too, this clause, *Ita quod*
⁵²⁰ *se bene gerat;* He that is pardoned must continue of good behaviour;
for whensoever he breakes the peace, he forfeits his pardon; When
I returne to my repented sinnes againe, I am under the burden of all
my former sinnes, and my very repentance, contracts the nature of
a sinne: and therefore *Quomodo, how should I,* that is, *why should
I defile them?* To restore you to your liberty, and to send you away
with the meditation, which concernes you most, consider, what an
astonishment this would be, that when Christ Jesus shall lay open
the great volumes of all your sinnes, to *your sight,* who had forgot
them, and to *their sight,* from whom you had disguised them, at the
⁵³⁰ last judgement, when you shall heare all the wantonnesses of your
youth, all the Ambitions of your middle years, all the covetous desires of your age, published in that presence, and thinke then, this is
the worst that can be said, or laid to my charge, this is the last indict-
ment, and the last evidence, there shall follow your very *repentances*
in the list of your *sinnes,* and it shall be told you, and all the world
then, Here, and here you deluded that God, that forbore to inflict
his Judgements, upon *new vowes, new contracts, new promises,* between *you* and *him;* even your repentances shall bind up that booke,

and tye your old sinnes, and new relapses into one body. And let this meditation bring you *ad vocem gratulantis,* to rejoyce once againe 540 in this *Lavi pedes,* that you have now washed your feet, in a present sorrow, and *ad vocem indignantis,* to a stronger indignation, and faster resolution, then heretofore you have had, never to defile them againe.

Number 9.

Preached at the Churching of the
Countesse of Bridgewater.

[? 1621 or 1623]

MICAH 2.10. *ARISE AND DEPART, FOR THIS IS*
NOT YOUR REST.

[Deut. 6.5]

[2 Chron.
15.15]

Psal. 4.8

[Num.
18.19]

[Luke 12.19]
[Psa. 94.7,
P. B. version]

ALL THAT God asks of us, is, that we *love him with all our heart:*
All that he promises us, is, that he will give us *rest, round
about us;* Judah sought the Lord with a whole desire, and
he gave her rest, round about her. Now a Man might think himselfe
well disposed for *Rest,* when he *lies down, I will lay me down, and
sleep in peace,* sayes *David;* but it is otherwise here; *Arise, and depart;*
for here, (that is, in lying, and sleeping) is not your Rest, sayes this
Prophet. These words have a three-fold acceptation, and admit a
three-fold exposition; for, first, they are a *Commination,* the Prophet
10 threatens the Jewes; Secondly, they are a *Commonition,* the Prophet
instructs all future ages; Thirdly, they are a *Consolation,* which hath
reference to the Consummation of all, to the rising at the generall
Judgement. First, he foretels the Jewes of their imminent *captivity;*
Howsoever you build upon the *pactum salis,* the Covenant of salt, the
everlasting Covenant, that God will be your God, and this land your
land, yet since that confidence sears you up in your sins, *Arise and
depart, for this is not your rest,* your *Jerusalem* must be chang'd into
Babylon; there's the Commination: Secondly, he warns us, who are
bedded and bedrid in our sins; howsoever you say to your selves,
20 *Soule take thy rest,* enjoy the honors, the pleasures, the abundances
of this world, *Tush the Lord sees it not,* The Master will not come,

we may ly still safely, and rest in the fruition of this Happinesse, yet this Rest will betray you, this rest will deliver you over to eternall disquiet: And therefore *arise and depart, for this is not your Rest,* and that's the Commonition. And in the third acceptation of the words, as they may have relation to the *Resurrection,* they may well admit a little inversion; Howsoever you feel a Resurrection by *grace* from the works of death, and darknesse in this life, yet in this life, there is no assurednesse, that he that is risen, and thinks he stands,
30 shall not fall; here you *arise and depart,* that is, rise from your sins, and depart from your sinfull purposes, but you arise, and depart so too, that you fall, and depart again into your sinfull purposes, after you have risen; and therefore *Depart and arise, for here is not your rest;* till you depart altogether out of this world, and rise to Judgement, you can have no such rest, as can admit no disquiet, no perturbation; but then you shall; and that's the Consolation.

 First then, as the words concern the *Jewes;* Here is first an increpation, a rebuke, that they are fallen from their station, and their dignity, implied in the first word, *Arise,* for then they were *fallen;*
40 Secondly, here is a demonstration in the same word, That though they lik'd that state into which they were fallen, which was a security, and stubbornnesse in their sins, yet they should not enjoy even that security, and that stubbornnesse, that fall of theirs, but they should lose that; though it were but a false contentment, yet they should be rouz'd out of that, *Arise;* first *arise,* because you are *fallen,* and then, *arise,* though you think your selves at *ease,* by that fall. And then thirdly, here is a continuation of Gods anger, when they are risen; for they are not rais'd to their former state and dignity, from which they were fallen, they are not rais'd to be established, but
50 it is *arise,* and *depart;* And in all this (which is a fourth Consideration) God precludes them from any hope by solicitation, he reveales his purpose, his Decree, and consequently his inexorablenesse evidently, in that word, *for;* never murmur, never dispute, never intreat, you must depart, *for* it is determined, it is resolved, and here is not *your Rest;* In which also the Commination is yet more, and more aggravated; first, in that they lose their Rest, which God hath sold them so dearly, by so many battailes, and so many afflictions, and which God had sworn to them so solemnly by so many ratifications;

1 Part
Divisio

they must lose their Rest, they must have no Rest, *Here;* not there;
⁶⁰ not in the Land of Promise it selfe; And then lastly, as they are denied
all rest there; There, where was the wombe, and Center of their Rest,
so there is no intimation, no hope given, that they should have rest
any where else, for as they were *to rise,* onely *to depart,* so they were
to depart into Captivity.

The first is an increpation, they were *fallen;* but from whence? It
was once said, *Qui jacet in terra, non habet unde cadat,* but he that
is earth it selfe, whither can he fall? whither can Man, derived from
earth before his life, enamored of the earth, embracing it, and maried
to it in his life, destined to the earth, betrothed to it for a second
⁷⁰ mariage after this life, whither can he fall? It is true of us all, *I shall
say to corruption, Thou art my father, and to the worme, Thou art
my Mother, and my sister;* and can we fall into worse company, contract an alliance with a more base, and beggerly kindred then this?
Not if we were left there; then we could not: but when we consider
a nation, of whom God hath said, *sponsabo te mihi,* I will mary thee,
without any respect of disparagement in thy lownesse, I will not
refuse thee for it, I will not upbraid thee with it, *I will mary thee
for ever,* and without any purpose of divorce (*sponsabo in æternum,*)
of this nation thus assum'd, thus contracted, thus endowed, thus
⁸⁰ assured, why may not we wonder as vehemently, as the Prophet did,
of the fallen Angels, *Quomodo cecidisti de cœlo, Lucifer filius Orien-
tis,* how did this nation fall out of Gods armes, out of Gods bosome?
Himselfe tells us how; what he had done to exalt them, what they
had done to devest his favours: for their *naturall lownes,* he says, *In
thy nativity when thou wast born, thy Navell was not cut, thou wast
not washed, thou wast not salted, thou wast not swadled; No eye
pitied thee, but thou wast cast into the open fields in contempt, I
passed by, and saw thee in thy bloud, and said thou shalt live;* I sware
unto thee, and entred into a covenant with thee, and thou becamest
⁹⁰ mine; I washed thee, anointed thee, and adorned thee: and thou wast
perfect through my beauty, which I set upon thee; well then, in this
state, *Quomodo cecidisti de cœlo;* how fell she out of Gods armes, out
of his bosome? thus; *Thou didst trust in thine owne beauty, because
of thy renowne, and so playedst the harlot.* When that nation was *in
massa damnata,* a loafe of *Adams* dow, through all which the infec-

tious leaven of sin had passed without difference, when that nation
had no more title, nor pretence to Gods mercy, then any of their
fellow wormes, when God had heaped, and accumulated his *temporall blessings* upon them, and above all, dwelt with them, in the
100 alliance, and in the familiarity of a *particular Religion,* which contracted God and them, and left out all the world beside, when God
had imprinted this beauty in them, and that they had a renowne,
and reputation for that, *they trusted to their owne beauty,* (to worship whom they would, and how they would) they *followed their
own invention;* yea they trusted in beauty, which was not their owne,
in borrowed beauty, in painted beauty, and so tooke in, and applied
themselves to all the spirituall fornications, to all the Idolatries of
the nations about them; some that were too *absurd* to be hearkned
to; some too *obscene,* and foule to be named now by us, though the
110 Prophets, (to their farther reproach, and confusion) have named
them; some, too *ridiculous* to fall into any Mans consideration, that
could seriously thinke of a Majesty, in a God, which should be worshipped; yet all these, absurd, and obscene, and ridiculous Idolatries,
they prostituted them selves unto.

Take them in their lowness, for any disposition towards the next
world, and this was their state, *Their navell was not cut;* that is, they
were still incorporated into their mother, to earth, and to sinne; and
they were not one step higher, then all the world beside, in *Jacobs*
ladder, whose top is in heaven. Take them in their *dignity in this* [Gen. 28.12]
120 *world,* and then we finde them in *Egypt,* where they were not *Personæ,* but *Res,* they were not their *Masters Men,* but their *Masters
goods;* they were their cattell, to vex, and wear out, with their labours
spent upon the delights of others; They must goe farre *for straw;* [Exod. 5.7]
a great labour, for a little matter; and they must *burne it,* when they
had brought it; they must *make bricke,* but others must build houses,
with their materialls, and they perish in the fields; they must beget
children, but onely for the slaughter, and to be murdred as soone as
they were borne; what nation, what Man, what beast, what worme,
what weed, if it could have understood their state, would have
130 changed with them then?

This was their dejection, their exinanition in *Egypt,* if we shall
beginne there to consider, what he did for them: As after, in the

Christian Church, he made the *bloud* of the *Martyrs,* the seed of the Church, so in *Egypt,* he propagated, and multiplied his Children, in the midst of their cruell oppressions, and slaughters, as though their *bloud* had been *seed* to encrease by; under the weight of their depressions, he gave them growth, and stature, and strength, as though their *wounds* had been *playsters,* and their *vexations cordials;* when he had made Egypt as a *Hell,* by kindling all his plagues, in her bosome, yet

[Psa. 16.10]　　¹⁴⁰ *Non dereliquit in Inferno,* he left not his beloved in this Hell, he paled in a *Paradise* in this Hell, a *Goshen* in *Egypt,* and gave his servants security; briefly, those whom the sword should have lessen'd, whom labour should have creepled, whom contempt should have begger'd, he brought out, numerous, and in multitudes, strong, and in courage,

[Exod. 14]　　rich, and in abundance; and he opened the *Red-sea,* as he should have opened the *booke of life,* to shew them their Names, their security, and he shut the sea, as that book, upon the Egyptians, to shew them their irrecoverable exclusion. If we consider, what he did for them, what he suffered from them, in their way, the *battailes,* that he fought

¹⁵⁰ for them, in an out-stretched arm, the battails, that they fought against him, in the stifnesse of their necks, and their *murmurings,* we must, to their confusion, acknowledge, that at a great deale a lesse price, then he paid for them, he might have gained all the people of the earth; all the Nations of the earth, (in appearance) would have come in to his subjection, upon the thousand part of that which he did for the Israelites in their way. But for that which he did for them, at home, when he had planted them in the Land of Promise, as it were an ungratefull thing, not to remember those blessings, so it is some degree of ingratitude, to think them possible to be numbred. Con-

¹⁶⁰ sider the *narrownesse* of the Land, (*scarce equall to three of our shires*) and their innumerable armies; consider the *barrennesse* of many parts of that Countrey, and their innumerable sacrifices of Cattell; consider their little *trade,* in respect, and their innumerable treasures; but consider especially, what God had done for their soules, in promising, and ratifying so often a *Messias* unto them, and giving them Law and Prophets, in the mean time, and there you see their true height; and then consider the abominations, and Idolatries, in which they had plung'd, and buried themselves, and there you see their lownesse, how far they were fallen.

¹⁷⁰ This then was their descent; and as *Saint Paul* sayes (when he describes this descent of the Jewes, into all manner of abominations) one step of this stayre, of this descent, is, *unnaturall affection,* they were unnaturall to themselves; that is, not sensible of their own misery, but were proud of their fall, and thought themselves at ease in their ruine; and another stayre in this fall is, that *God had delivered them up to a reprobate mind,* to suffer them to think so still. And then for their farther vexation, God would take from them, even that false, that imaginary comfort of theirs. *Surgite,* sayes God; since you have made that perverse shift, to take comfort in your fall, ¹⁸⁰ Arise from that, from that security, from that stupidity, for you shall not chuse but see your misery; when all the people were descended to that basenesse, (as nothing is more base, then to court the world, and the Devill, for poore and wretched delights, when we may have plentifull, and rich abundance in our confidence in God) when the people were all of one mind, and one voice, *omnes unius labii,* their hearts, and tongues spoke all one language, and, (*populus tanto deterior, quanto in deterioribus concors,* Men are the worse, the more they are, and the more unanime, and constant they are in ill purposes) when they were all come to that *Venite comburamus,* Come, and let ¹⁹⁰ us burn brick, and trust in our own work, and *Venite, ædificemus,* Come, and let us build a tower, and provide a safety for our selves; since they would descend from their dignity, (which dignity consists in the service of God, whose service is perfect freedome) God would descend with them, *Venite descendamus,* sayes God; but what to doe? *Descendamus, ut confundamus,* let us goe down to confound their language, and to scatter them upon the earth. *Ascensio mendax, descensio crudelis,* sayes holy *Bernard,* A false ascending, is a cruell descending: when we lye weltring in our bloud, secure in our sins, and can flatter our selves, that we are well, and where we would be, ²⁰⁰ this deceitfull ascension, is a cruell descent into hell; we lye still, we feel no pain, but it is because we have broke our necks; we doe not grone, we doe not sigh, but it is, because our breath is gone, the spirit of God is departed from us. They were descended to a flatnesse of tast, Egyptian *Onions* had a better savor, then the *Manna* of heaven; They were descended to a new-fanglednesse in *Civill government,* they liked the form of government amongst their neighbours,

Non gaudebunt

Rom. 1.28

Gen. 11
Aug.

[Book of Common Prayer, Matins]
Bern.

[Num. 11.5]

better then that of *Judges,* which God had established for them then; They were descended to a newfanglednesse in matter of *Religion,* to the embracing of a foraine, and a frivolous, and an Idolatrous wor-

²¹⁰ ship of God: but then being in their descent, when they delighted in it, as *Sea-sick* men, who had rather be troden upon, then rise up, then God frustrates that false joy and false ease of theirs, he rouses them from all that, which they had proposed to themselves, *Surgite, arise,* arise from this security, because you are fallen, you *should* rise, but because you love your misery, you *shall* rise, you shall come to a sense, and knowledge of it, you shall not enjoy the ease of an ignorance.

Depart But he raised them not, to reestablish them, to restore them to their former dignity; there was no comfort in that *Surgite,* which was accompanied with an *Ite, arise and depart:* and depart into captiv-

²²⁰ ity. If we compare the captivity, which they were going into, (that of *Babylon*) with the other bondage, which they had been delivered from, (that of *Egypt*) it is true, there were many, and reall, and im-

Exod. 6.6 portant differences. That of *Egypt* was *Ergastulum,* a *prison;* and it
Deut. 4.20 was *fornax ferrea,* an Iron fornace; but in *Babylon,* they were not *slaves,* as they were in *Egypt,* but they were such a kind of *prisoners,* as onely had not liberty, to returne to their owne countrey. But yet, if we consider their state in *Egypt* in their *roote,* in *Jacob,* and in his sonnes, they came for food thither in a time of necessity; and con-sider them in that *branch* that overshadowed, and refreshed them, in

²³⁰ *Joseph,* he came thither as a bondman, in a servile condition. So that they were but few persons, and not so great, as that their pressures could be aggravated, or taste much more the bitterly, by comparing it, with any greatnesse which they had before; Though they were fallen into great misery, they were not fallen from any remarkeable great-nesse. But between the two captivities of *Egypt,* and *Babylon,* they were come to that greatnesse, and reputation, as that they had the

Deut. 4.6 testimony of all the world, *Onely this people is wise, and of under-standing, and a great nation.* Now wherein? In that which followes: *what nation is so great, as to have the Lord come so neare unto them;*

²⁴⁰ so great, as to have *Lawes,* and *Ordinances, so righteous, as they had?* Now this peculiar greatnesse, they lost in this captivity; whether they lost absolutely the *bookes of the Law,* or not, and that they were rein-spired, and redictated againe by the holy Ghost to *Esdras,* or whether

Esdras did but recollect them, and recompile them, Saint *Hierome* will not determine: He will not say whether *Moses,* or *Esdras,* be author of the first five bookes of the Bible; but it is cleare enough, that they were out of that ordinary use wherein they had been before: and though they kept their *Circumcision,* and their *Sabbaths* in *Babylon,* yet being cast thither for their sinnes, they had lost all ordinary
250 expiations of their sinnes, for they had *no sacrifices* there; (as the *Jews,* which are now *in dispersion,* are every where without their sacrifices) They were to rise, but not to stay, *Arise and depart;* And they were to depart, both from their Imaginary comforts, which they had framed, and proposed to themselves (when they were fallen from God, they should be deceived in their trust in themselves) and they were to depart even with the law, and ordinances, in which their preheminence, and prerogative above all nations consisted: when Man comes to be content with this world, God will take this world from him: when Man frames to himselfe imaginary pleasures, God
260 will inflict reall punishments; when he would lie still, he shall not sleep; but God will take him and raise him, but to a farther vexation.

And this vexation hath another heavy weight upon it, in this little word, *for;* for this drawes a Curtain between the face of God, and them: this locks a dore between the Court of mercy, and them, when God presents his judgements with such an assurednesse, such a resolution, as leaves no hope in their heart, that God will alter it, no power in themselves to solicite God to a pardon, or a reprieve; but as he was led *as a foole to the stocks,* when he hearkened to pleasant sins before, so he is led *as an oxe to the slaughter,* when he hears of Gods Judge-
270 ments now; his own Conscience prevents God, and tels him, there is a *for,* a reason, a necessity, an irrecoverablenesse in his condemnation. God had iterated, and multiplied this *Quia,* this *for,* oftentimes in their ears: This Prophet was no upstart, no sodain, no transitory Man, to passe through the streets with a *Væ, Væ, Wo, wo unto this City,* and no more; but he prophecied constantly, during the reign of *three Kings,* of *Jotham, Ahaz,* and *Hezekiah:* He was no suspitious Man out of his singularity; but he prophecied jointly with *Isaiah,* without separation, and he held the communion of his fellow-Prophets; He was no particular man, (as many Interpreters have taken it) so, as
280 that he addressed his prophecies upon *Judah* only; but he extended

Quia

Prov. [7.22]

Mic. 1.1

it to all, to all the Tribes. It is not a prophecy limited to *Idolatry,* and the sins against the first Table, but to robbery, and murder, and fornication, and oppression, and the sins between *Man,* and *Man:* It is not a timorous prophecy, directed onely to persons, whom a low fortune, and a miserable estate, or a sense of sin, and a wounded Conscience, had depress'd, and dejected, but principally bent upon rulers and Magistrates, and great persons. So that no Man hath a *Quia* against this *Quia,* a *for* against this *for,* to say, we need not heed him, for he is an upstart, a singular person, and all these his threatnings are rather ²⁹⁰ *Satyricall,* then *Propheticall,* or Theologicall; but this thunderbolt, this *Quia,* this reason, why these judgements must necessarily fall upon them, fell upon them with so much violence, as that it stupefied with the weight, and precluded all wayes of escape. These be the heaviest Texts that a Man can light upon in the Scriptures of God, and these be the heaviest Commentaries, that a Man can make upon these Texts, that when God wakens him and raises him from his dream, and bed of sin, and pleasure, and raises him with the voice of his judgements, he suffers him to read to the *Quia,* but not to come to the *Tamen;* He comes to see reason why that Judgement must fall, ³⁰⁰ but not to see any remedy. His inordinate *Melancholy,* and halfe desperate sadnesse carries his eye, and mind upon a hundred places of Commination, of threatning in the Prophets, and in them all he finds quickly that *Quia,* This curse must fall upon me, for I am faln into it; but he comes not to the *Tamen,* to that reliefe, *yet turn to the Lord, and he will turne to thee.* This was a particular step in their misery, that when they were awaked, and risen, that is, taken away from all tast, and comfort, in their own imaginations, and pleasures, when God was ready to give fire to all that artillery, which he had charged against them, in the service of all the Prophets, they could ³¹⁰ see no refuge, no sanctuary, nothing but a *quia,* an irresistiblenesse, an irremediablenesse, a necessity of perishing; a great while there was no such thing, as Judgement, (God cannot see us) Now, there is no such thing as Mercy, (God will not see us.)

        What then is this heavy Judgement, that is threatned? It is the deprivation of *Rest.* Though there be no war, no pestilence, no new positive calamity, yet *privative calamities* are heavy Judgements; to lose that *Gospell,* that *Religion,* which they had, is a heavy losse;

[Zech. 1.3]

Quies

Deprivations are heavy Calamities; and here they are deprived of
Rest; *Here is not your Rest:* Now, besides that betwixt us and heaven,
³²⁰ there is nothing that *rests,* (all the *Elements,* all the *planets,* all the
spheres are in perpetuall motion, and vicissitude) and so the Joyes of
heaven are express'd unto us, in that name of *Rest;* Certainly this
blessing of Rest was more pretious, more acceptable to the Jewes, then
to any other Nation; and so they more sensible of the losse of it, then
any other. For as Gods first promise, and the often ratification of it,
had ever accustom'd them to a longing for that promis'd rest, as their
long, and laborious peregrinations, had made them ambitious, and
hungry of that Rest, so had they (which no other Nation had but they)
a particular feast of a *Sabbath,* appointed for them, both for a *reall*
³³⁰ cessation and rest from bodily labours, and for a *figurative* expressing
of the eternall Rest, their imagination, their understanding, their
faith, was flll'd with this apprehension of *Rest.* When the contentment and satisfaction, which God took in *Noah's* sacrifice, after he
came out of the Ark, is express'd, it is express'd thus, *The Lord smelt
a savor of Rest;* our services to God, are a Rest to him; he rests in our   Gen. 8.21
devotions; And when the Idolatrous service, and forbidden sacrifices
of the people are expressed, they are expressed thus, When I had
brought them into the Land, *Posuerunt ibi odorem quietum suarum,*   Ezek. 20.28
they placed there the sweet savors of *their own Rest;* not of Gods
³⁴⁰ Rest, (his true Religion) but their own Rest, a Religion, which they,
for collaterall respects, rested in. And therefore when God threatens
here, that there shall be *no rest,* that is, none of his rest, he would take
from them their Law, their Sacrifices, their Religion, in which he
was pleas'd, and rested gratious towards them, he will change their
Religion: And when he sayes, *Here is not your Rest,* he threatens to
take from them, that Rest, that Peace, that Quiet which they had
propos'd, and imagin'd to themselves; when they say to themselves,
Why, 'tis no great matter; we may doe well enough for all that,
though our Religion be chang'd; he will impoverish them, he will
³⁵⁰ disarm them, he wil infatuate them, he wil make them a prey to their
enemies, and take away all true, and all imaginary rest too.

Briefly, it is the mark of all men, even naturall men, *Rest:* for   Tertul.
though *Tertullian* condemn that, to call *Quietis Magisterium Sapi-
entiam,* The act of being, and living at quiet, wisdome, therein seem-

ing to exclude all wisdome, that conduces not to rest, as though there were no wisdome, in action, and in businesse; Though in the person of *Epicurus* he condemn that, and that saying, *Nemo alii nascitur, moriturus sibi,* It is no reason, that any Man should think himselfe born for others, since he cannot live to himselfe, or to labour for
360 others, since himselfe cannot enjoy rest, yet *Tertullian* leaving the *Epicures,* that placed felicity in a stupid, and unsociable retiring, sayes in his own person, and in his own opinion, almost as much, *Vnicum mihi negotium, nec aliud curo, quam ne curem,* All that I care for, is that I might care for nothing; and so, even *Tertullian,* in his Christian Philosophy, places happinesse in *rest;* Now, he speaks not onely of the things of this world, they must necessarily be car'd for, in their proportion; we must not decline the businesses of this life, and the offices of society, out of an aëry, and imaginary affection of *rest:* our principall rest is, in the testimony of our *Conscience,* and in
370 doing that which we were sent to doe; And to have a Rest, and peace, in a Conscience of having done that religiously, and acceptably to God, is our true Rest: and this was the rest, which the Jewes were to lose in this place, the testimony of their consciences, that they had perform'd their part, their Conditions, so, that they might rely upon Gods promises, of a perpetuall rest in the Land of Canaan; and that rest they could not have; not that peacefull testimony of their Consciences.

Hic

They could not have that rest, no Rest, not there, not in *Canaan;* which was the highest degree of the misery, because they were con-
380 fident in their term, their state in that Land, that it should be perpetuall; and they were confident in the goodnesse of the Land, that it should evermore give them all conveniencies in abundance, conducing to all kind of rest: for, this Land, God himself cals by the
Psal. 95.11
name of *rest,* and of *his rest; I sware they should not enter into my rest;* So that, rest was proper to this Land, and this Land was proper
Aug. Ser. 105 de tempore
to them. For, (as *St. Augustine* notes well) though God recover'd this Land for them, and reestablish'd miraculously their possession, yet they came but in their *Remitter,* and *in postliminio,* the inheritance of that Land, was *theirs* before: for, *Sem* the son of *Noah,* was in
390 possession of this Land; and the sons of *Cham,* the Canaanites, expel'd his race out of it; and *Abraham* of the race of *Sem,* was restor'd

unto it again: So that, as the goodnesse of the Land promis'd *rest,* so
the goodnesse of the *title* promis'd them the Land; and yet they might
have no rest *there.*

They had a better title then that; Those often *oathes,* which God
had sworne unto them, that that land should be theirs for ever, was
their evidence; If then that land were *Requies Domini,* the rest of the
Lord, that is, the best, and the safest Rest, and that land were *their
land,* why should they not have that rest here, when the Lord had
400 sworne they should? Why, because he swore the contrary after; but
will God sweare contrary things? why, *solus securus jurat, qui falli
non potest,* says Saint *Augustine,* onely he can sweare a thing safely,
that sees all circumstances, and foresees all occurrences; onely God
can sweare safely, because nothing can be hid from him. God therefore that knew upon what *conditions* he had taken the first oath, and
knew againe how contemptuously those conditions were broken, he
takes knowledge that he had sworne, he denies not that, but he
sweares againe, and in his anger, *I sware in my wrath, that they
should not enter into my rest.* Those Men (says he) which have seen
410 my glory and my Miracles, and have tempted me *tenne* times, and
not obeyed my voyce, *certainly they shall not see the land whereof I
sware unto their fathers;* neither shall any that provoke me see it; He
pleads not *Non est factum,* but he pleads *conditions* performed; he
denies not that he swore but he justifies himselfe, that he had done
as much as he promised; for his promise was *conditionall.* The
Apostle seemes to assigne but one reason of their exclusion, from this
Land, and from this rest, and yet he expresses that one Reason so, as
that it hath two branches; He sayes, *we see that they could not enter,
because of unbeleef;* and yet he asks the question; *To whom sware he,*
420 *that they should not enter into his Rest, but unto them, that obeyed
not? Vnbeleef* is assigned for the cause, and yet they were shut out for
disobedience; now, if the Apostle make it all one, whether want of
faith, or want of *works,* exclude us from the Land of Rest, let not us
be too curious enquirers, whether *faith* or *works* bring us thither; for
neither faith, nor works bring us thither, as a full cause; but if we
consider mediate causes, so they may be both causes; *faith, instru-
mentall, works, declaratory; faith* may be as *evidence, works* as the
seale of it; but the *cause* is onely, the free *election* of God. Nor ever

Aug.

Psal. 95.11

Numb.
14.23

Heb. 3.18,
19

shall we come thither, if we leave out either; we shall meet as many
⁴³⁰ Men in heaven, that have lived without faith, as without works.

This then was the case; God had sworne to them an inheritance
permanently there, but upon condition of their *obedience;* If they had
not had a privity in the condition, if they had not had a possibility to
perform the condition, their exclusion might have seemed unjust:
and it had been so; for though God might justly have forborne the
promise, yet he could not justly breake the promise, if they had kept
the conditions; therefore he expressed the condition without any
disguise, at first, *If thy heart turne away, I pronounce unto you this*
day that you shall surely perish: you shall not prolong your dayes in
⁴⁴⁰ the land. And then, when those conditions were made, and made
knowne, and made easie, and accepted, when they so rebelliously
broke all conditions, his first oath lay not in his way, to stop him
from the second, *As I live, saith the Lord, I will surely bring mine*
oath that they have broken, and my covenant that they have despised,
upon their head; shall they breake my covenant, and be delivered?
says God there. God confesses the oath and the covenant, to be *his*
covenant and *his oath,* but the *breach* of the oath, and covenant, was
theirs, and not his.

He expresses his promise to them, and his departing from them
⁴⁵⁰ together, in another Prophet; God says to the Prophet, *Buy thee a*
girdle, bury it in the ground, and fetch it againe; And then it was
rotten, and good for nothing: *for* says he, *as the girdle cleaveth to the*
loines, so have I tyed to me the house of Israel, and Judah, that they
might be my people, that they might have a name and a praise, and
a glory, but they would not heare; Therefore, say unto them, Every
bottle shall be filled with wine; (Here was a promise of *plenty:*) *and*
they shall say unto thee, Doe not we know, that every bottle shall be
filled with wine? (that God is bound to give us this plenty?) because
he hath tyed himselfe by *oath,* and *covenant,* and promise. But *be-*
⁴⁶⁰ hold, I fill all the inhabitants with drunkennesse; (since they trust in
their plenty, that shall be an occasion of sinne to them) and *I will*
dash them against one another, even the father, and sonnes together;
I will not spare, I will not pity, I will not have compassion, but destroy
them. God could not promise more, then he did in this place at first;
he could not depart farther from that promise, then by their occasion,

Deut. 30.17

Ezek. 17.19

v. 15

Ier. 13

he came to at last. Gods promise goes no farther with *Moses* himselfe;
My presence shall goe with thee, and I will give thee rest; If we will   Exod. 33.14
steale out of Gods presence, into darke and sinfull corners, there is no
rest promised. *Receive my words,* says *Solomon,* and *the years of thy*   Prov. 4.10
⁴⁷⁰ *life shall be many; Trust in the Lord,* says *David, and doe good,* (per-   Psal. 37.3
forme both, stand upon those two leggs, *faith,* and *works;* not that
they are alike; there is a right, and a left legge: but stand upon both;
upon one in the sight of God; upon the other in the sight of Man;)
*Trust in the Lord, and doe good, and thou shalt dwell in the land,
and be fed assuredly.* That paradise, that peace of Conscience, which
God establishes in thee, by *faith,* hath a condition, of growth, and
encrease, from *faith to faith;* heaven it selfe, in which the Angells
were, had a condition; they might, they did fall from thence; The
land of *Canaan,* was their own land, and the rest of that land, their
⁴⁸⁰ Rest by Gods oath, and covenant; and yet here was not their rest: not
here; nor for any thing expressed, or intimated in the word, any where
else. Here was a *Nunc dimittis,* but not *in pace;* The Lord lets them   [Luke 2.29]
depart, and makes them depart, but not in peace, for their *eyes saw no
salvation;* they were sent away to a heavy captivity. Beloved, we may
have had a *Canaan;* an inheritance, a comfortable assurance in our
bosomes, in our consciences, and yet heare that voice after, that *here
is not our rest,* except, as Gods goodnesse at first moved him to make
one oath unto us, of a *conditionall rest,* as our sins have put God to
his second oath, that he sware we should not have his rest, so our
⁴⁹⁰ *repentance* bring him to a third oath, *as I live I would not the death*   [Ezek.
of a sinner, that so he doe not onely make a new contract with us, but   33.11]
give us withall an ability, to performe the conditions, which he requires.

Number 10.

Preached at the Churching of the Countesse of Bridgewater.

MICAH 2.10.

[SECOND SERMON]

THUS FAR we have proceeded in the first acceptation of these words, according to their principall, and literall sense, as they appertain'd to the *Jewes,* and their state; so they were a *Commination;* As they appertain to all succeeding Ages, and to us, so they are a *Commonition,* an alarm, to raise us from the sleep, and death of sin; And then in a third acceptation, they are a *Consolation,* that at last we shall have a *rising,* and a *departing* into such a state, in the *Resurrection,* as we shall no more need this voice, *Arise, and depart,* because we shall be no more in danger of falling, no more in danger
10 of departing from the presence, and contemplation; and service, and fruition of God; And in both these latter senses, the words admit a just accommodation to this present occasion, God having rais'd his honorable servant, and hand-maid here present, to a sense of the *Curse,* that lyes upon *women,* for the transgression of the first woman, which is painfull, and dangerous *Child-birth;* and given her also, a sense of the last glorious resurrection, in having rais'd her, from that Bed of weaknesse, to the ability of coming into his presence, here in his house.

Divisio   First then to consider them, in the first of these two latter senses,
20 as a *Commonition* to them, that are in the state of *sin,* first there is an increpation implied in this word *Arise;* when we are bid arise, we are told, that we are faln: sin is an unworthy descent, and an ignoble fall; Secondly, we are bid to doe something, and therefore we are able to doe something; God commands nothing impossible so, as that that

198

degree of performance, which he will accept, should be impossible, to the man, whom his grace hath affected; That which God will accept, is possible to the godly; And thirdly, that which he commands here, is deriv'd into two branches; We are bidden to *rise:* that is, to leave our bed, our habit of sin; and then not to be idle, when we are up,
30 but to *depart;* not onely to depart from the *Custome,* but from *tentations* of *Recidivation;* and not onely that, but to *depart* into *another way,* a habit of Actions, contrary to our former Sins. And then, all this is press'd, and urged upon us, by a Reason; The Holy Ghost appears not like a ghost in one sodain glance, or glimmering, but he testifies his presence, and he presses the businesse, that he comes for; And the reason that he uses here, is, *Quia non requies,* because otherwise we lose the *Pondus animæ,* the weight, the ballast of our soule, *rest,* and peace of Conscience: for howsoever there may be some rest, some such shew of Rest, as may serve a carnall man a little while, yet, sayes
40 our Text, it is not *your Rest,* it conduces not to that Rest, which God hath ordained for you, whom he would direct to a better Rest. That Rest, (*your Rest*) is not here; not in that, which is spoken of here; not in your lying still, you must rise from it; not in your standing still, you must *depart* from it; *your Rest is not here:* but yet, since God sends us away, because our Rest is not here, he does tacitly direct us thereby, where there is Rest; And that will be the third acceptation of these words; to which we shall come anone.

For that then, which rises first, the increpation of our fall implied in the words, *Arise,* there is nothing, in which, that which is the
50 mother of all vertues, *discretion,* is more tryed, then in the conveying, and imprinting profitably a rebuke, an increpation, a knowledge, and sense of sinne, in the conscience of another. The rebuke of sin, is like the fishing of *Whales;* the Marke is great enough; one can scarce misse hitting; but if there be not *sea room* and line enough, and a dexterity in letting out that line, he that hath fixed his harping Iron, in the Whale, endangers himselfe, and his boate; God hath made us *fishers of Men;* and when we have struck a *Whale,* touch'd the conscience of any person, which thought himselfe above rebuke, and increpation, it struggles, and strives, and as much as it can, en-
60 devours to draw fishers, and boate, the Man and his fortune into contempt, and danger. But if God tye a *sicknesse,* or any other ca-

Increpatio
Bernard

lamity, to the end of the line, that will winde up this Whale againe,
to the boate, bring back this rebellious sinner better advised, to the
mouth of the Minister, for more counsaile, and to a better souplenesse,
and inclinablenesse to conforme himselfe, to that which he shall after
receive from him; onely calamity makes way for a rebuke to enter.
There was such a tendernesse, amongst the orators, which were used
to speake in the presence of the people, to the Romane Emperors,
(which was a way of *Civill preaching*) that they durst not tell them
70 then their duties, nor instruct them, what they should doe, any other
way then by saying, that they had done so before; They had no way
to make the Prince wise, and just, and temperate, but by a false
praising him, for his former acts of wisdom, and justice, and tem-
perance, which he had never done; and that served to make the
people beleeve, that the Princes were so; and it served to teach the
Prince, that he ought to be so. And so, though this were an expresse,
and a direct flattery, yet it was a collaterall increpation too; And on
the other side, our later times have seen another art, another invention, another workmanship, that when a great person hath so abused
80 the favour of his Prince, that he hath growne subject to great, and
weighty increpations, his owne friends have made *Libells* against him,
thereby to lay some light aspersions upon him, that the Prince might
thinke, that this comming with the malice of a *Libell,* was the worst
that could be said of him: and so, as the first way to the Emperors,
though it were a direct flattery, yet it was a *collaterall Increpation*
too, so this way, though it were a direct increpation, yet it was a *collaterall flattery* too. If I should say of such a congregation as this, with
acclamations and showes of much joy, Blessed company, holy congregation, in which there is no pride at all, no vanity at all, no pre-
90 varication at all, I could be thought in that, but to convey an increpation, and a rebuke mannerly, in a wish that it were so altogether.
If I should say of such a congregation as this, with exclamations and
show of much bitternesse, that they were sometimes somewhat too
worldly in their owne businesse, sometimes somewhat too remisse,
in the businesses of the next world, and adde no more to it, this were
but as a plot, and a *faint libelling*, a publishing of small sinnes to
keep greater from being talk'd of: slight increpations are but as
whisperings, and work no farther, but to bring men to say, Tush,

no body hears it, no body heeds it, we are never the worse, nor never
¹⁰⁰ the worse thought of for all that he says. And loud and bitter increpations, are as a *trumpet,* and work no otherwise, but to bring them
to say, Since he hath published all to the world already, since all the
world knowes of it, the shame is past, and we may goe forward in
our ways againe. Is there then no way to convey an increpation
profitably? *David* could find no way; *Vidi prævaricatores & tabesce-*
bam, says he, *I saw the transgressors, but I languished and consumed*
away with griefe, because they would not keep the law; he could not
mend them, and so impaired himselfe with his compassion: but God
hath provided a way here, to convey, to imprint this increpation, this
¹¹⁰ rebuke, sweetly, and succesfully; that is, by way of counsaile: by
bidding them *arise,* he chides them for falling, by presenting the
exaltation and exultation of a peacefull conscience, he brings them
to a foresight, to what miserable distractions, and distortions of the
soule, a habite of sinne will bring them to. If you will take knowledge
of Gods fearfull judgements no other way, but by hearing his mercies preached, his *Mercie is new every morning,* and his dew falls
every evening; and morning, and evening we will preach his mercies
unto you. If you will beleeve a *hell* no other way, but by hearing the
joyes of heaven presented to you, you shall heare enough of that;
¹²⁰ we will receive you in the morning, and dismisse you in the evening,
in a religious assurance, in a present inchoation of the joyes of heaven.
It is Gods way, and we are willing to pursue it; to shew you that you
are Enemies to Christ, *we pray you in Christs stead, that you would*
be reconciled to him; to shew you, that you are faln, we pray you to
arise, and *si audieritis,* if you hear us so, if any way, any means, convey this rebuke, this sense into you, *Si audieritis, lucrati sumus fra-*
trem, If you hear, we have gain'd a brother; and that's the richest
gain, that we can get, if you may get salvation by us.

    Gods rebukes and increpations then are sweet, and gentle, to the
¹³⁰ binding up, not to the scattering of a Conscience; And the particular
Rebuke in this place, conveyed by way of counsail, is, That they were
faln; and worse could not be said, how mild and easie soever the
word be. The ruin of the *Angels* in heaven, the ruin of *Adam* in
Paradise, is still call'd by that word, it is but the *fall* of Angels, and
the *fall* of *Adam;* and yet this fall of *Adam* cost the bloud of Christ,

Psal.
119.158

[Lam. 3.23]

[2 Cor. 5.20]

Mat. 18.15

Dejectio

and this bloud of Christ, did not rectifie the Angels after their fall.

Inter abjectos, abjectissimus peccator; amongst them that are faln, he fals lowest, that continues in sin: for (sayes the same Father,) Man is a *king* in his Creation; he hath that Commission, *Subjicite, &*
140 *dominamini;* the world, and himselfe, (which is a lesse world, but a greater dominion) are within his Jurisdiction; and then servilly, he submits himselfe, and all, to that, *Quo nihil magis barbarum,* then which nothing is more tyrannous, more barbarous. All persons have naturally, all Nations ever had, a detestation of falling into their hands who were more barbarous, more uncivill then themselves, *Et peccato nihil magis barbarum,* (sayes that Father) sin doth not govern us by a rule, by a Law, but tyrannically, impetuously, and tempestuously; It hath been said of Rome, *Romæ regulariter malè agitur;* There a man may know the price of a sin, before he doe it; and he
150 knowes what his *dispensation* will cost; whether he be able to sin at that rate, whether he have wherewithall, that if not, he may take a cheap sin. Thou canst never say that of thy soule, *Intus regulariter malè agitur;* Thou canst never promise thy selfe to sin safely, and so to elude the Law, for the Law is in thy heart; nor to sin wisely, and so to escape witnesses, for the testimony is in thy Conscience; nor to sin providently, and thriftily, and cheaply, and compound for the penalty, and stall the fine, for thy soule, that is the price, is indivisible, and perishes entirely, and eternally at one payment, and yet ten thousand thousand times over and over. Thou canst not say: Thou
160 wilt sin, that sin, and no more; or so far in that sin, and no farther; If thou fall from an high place, thou maist fall through thick clouds, and through moist clouds, but yet through nothing that can sustain thee, but thou fall'st to the earth; If thou fall from the grace of God, thou maist passe through *dark Clouds,* oppression of heart, and through *moist Clouds,* some compunction, some remorsefull tears; but yet, (of thy selfe) thou hast nothing to take hold of, till thou come to that bottome, which will embrace thee cruelly, to the bottomlesse bottome of Hell it selfe. Our dignity, and our greatest height, is in our interest in God, and in the world, and in our selves; and we
170 fall from all, either *non utendo,* or *abutendo;* either by neglecting God, or by over-valuing the world; our greatest fall of all is, into

Idolatry; and yet Idolatry is an ordinary fall; for *tot habemus Deos*

recentes, quot habemus vitia, As many habituall sins as we embrace, so many Idols we worship; If all sins could not be call'd so, Idols, yet for those sins, which possesse us most ordinarily, and most strongly, we have good warrant to call them so; which sins are *Licentiousnesse* in our youth, and *Covetousnesse* in our age, and *voluptuousnesse* in our middle time. For, for *Licentiousnesse, Idolatry,* and that, are so often call'd by one anothers names in the Scriptures, as many times
180 we cannot tell, when the Prophets mean *spirituall Adultery,* and when *Carnall;* when they mean *Idolatry,* and when *Fornication.* For *Covetousnesse,* that is expresly called *Idolatry* by the Apostle: and so is *voluptuousnesse* too, in those men, *whose belly is their God.* We fall then into that desperate precipitation of Idolatry by *lust,* when by fornication, we profane the temple of the Holy Ghost, and make even his temple, our bodies, a Stewes: And we fall into Idolatry by *Covetousnesse,* when we come to be, *tam putidi minutíque animi,* of so narrow, and contracted a soule, and of so sick, and dead, and buried, and putrefied a soule, as to lock up our soule, in a Cabinet
190 where we lock up our money, to ty our soul in the corner of a hand-kerchiefe, where we ty our money, to imprison our soule, in the imprisonment of those things, *Quæ te ad gloriam subvecturæ,* the dispensation, and distribution whereof, would carry thy soul to eternall glory. And when, by our *voluptuousnesse,* we raise the prices of necessary things, *Et eorum vulnera, qui à Deo flagris cæduntur, adaugemus;* and thereby scourge them with deeper lashes of famine, whom God hath scourged with poverty before, we fall into Idolatry by voluptuousnesse; *Numismatis inscriptiones inspicitis, & non Christi in fratre,* thou takest a pleasure, to look upon the figures, and
200 Images of Kings in their severall coyns, and thou despisest thine own Image in thy poore brother, and Gods Image in thy ruinous, and defaced soule, and in his Temple, thy body, demolished by thy Licentiousnesse, and by all these Idolatries. This is the fall, when we fall so farre into those sins, which have naturally a tyranny in them, and that that sinne becomes an Idoll to us; which fall of ours, God intimates unto us, and rebukes us for, by so mild a way, as to bid us rise from it.

Now when God bids us rise, as the Apostle sayes, *Be not deceived, Non irridetur Deus, God cannot be mocked* by any man, so we may

[Col. 3.5]
[Phil. 3.19]

Basil

Idem

Idem

Gal. 6.7

²¹⁰ boldly say, Be not afraid, *Non irridet Deus;* God mocks no man; God comes not to a miserable bedrid man, as a man would come in scorn to a prisoner, and bid him shake off his fetters, or to a man in a Consumption, and bid him grow strong; when God bids us arise, he tels us, we are able to rise; God bad *Moses* goe to *Pharaoh;* Moses said

Exod. 4.10

he was *Incircumcisus labiis,* heavy, and slow of tongue; but he did not deny, but he had a tongue: God bade him goe, and *I will be with thy mouth,* sayes he; He does not say, I will be thy mouth; but, thou hast a mouth, and I will be *with* thy Mouth. It was Gods presence, that made that mouth servicable, and usefull, but it was *Moses* ²²⁰ mouth; *Moses* had a mouth of his own; we have *faculties,* and *powers* of our own, to be employed in Gods service. So when God employed

Ier. 1.6

Jeremy, the Prophet sayes, *O Lord God, behold, I cannot speak, for I am a child;* but God replies, *say not thou, I am a child; for whatsoever I command thee, thou shalt speake:* When God bids thee rise from thy sin, say not thou it is *too late,* or that thou art bedrid in the custome of thy sin, and so canst not rise; when he bids thee rise, he enables thee to rise; and thou maist rise, by the power of that *will* which onely his mercy, and his grace, hath created in thee; for as God conveyes a rebuke in that counsaile, *Surgite,* arise, so he con- ²³⁰ veyes a power in it too; when he bids thee rise, he enables thee to rise.

That which we are to doe then, is *to rise;* to leave our bed, our sleep

Surgite

Aug.

of Sin. Saint *Augustine* takes knowledge of three wayes, by which he escaped sins; first, *occasionis subtractione;* and that's the safest way, not to come within distance of a tentation; secondly, *resistendi data virtute,* That the love, and the fear of God, imprinted in him, made him strong enough for the sin; Can I love God, and love this person thus? thus, that my love to it, should draw away my love from God? Can I feare God, and fear any Man, (who can have power but over my body) so, as for feare of him, to renounce my God, or the ²⁴⁰ truth, or my Religion? Or *affectionis sanitate,* that his affections, had, by a good diet, by a continuall feeding upon the Contemplation of God; such a degree of health, and good temper, as that some sins he did naturally detest, and, though he had not wanted opportunity, and had wanted particular grace, yet he had been safe enough from them. But, for this help, this detestation, of *some* particular *sins,* that will not hold out; We have seen men infinitely *prodigall* grow in-

finitely *Covetous* at last. For the other way, (the assistance of *particular grace*) that we must not presume upon; for, he that opens himselfe to a tentation, upon presumption of grace to preserve him,
250 forfaits by that, even that grace, which he had. And therefore there is no safe way, but *occasionis subtractio,* the forbearing of those places, and that Conversation, which ministers occasion of tentation to us. First therefore, let us find, that we are in our bed, that we are naturally unable to rise; We are not born *Noble:* Saint *Paul* considers himselfe, and his birth, and his Title to grace, at best; *That he was a Jew,* and *of the tribe of Benjamin, and of holy* parents, and within the Covenant; yet all this rais'd him not out of his bed, for, sayes he, *we were by nature the Children of wrath, as well as others.* But where then was the *rising?* that is, in the true receiving of Christ. *To as*
260 *many as received him, he gave, Potestatem prærogativæ, to be the sons of God;* yea, *power to become the sons of God,* as it is in our last Translation. *Christianus non de Christiano nascitur, nec facit generatio, sed regeneratio Christianum;* A Christian Mother does not conceive a Christian; onely the Christian Church conceives Christian Children. *Judæus circumcisus generat filium incircumcisum,* A Jew is circumcised, but his child is born uncircumcised: The Parents may be up, and ready, but their issue abed, and in their bloud, till *Baptisme* have wash'd them, and till the spirit of Regeneration have rais'd them, from that bed, which the sins of their first Parents have
270 laid them in, and their own continuing sins continued them in. This rising is first, from *Originall sin,* by baptism, and then from *actuall sin,* best, by withdrawing from the occasions of tentation to future sins, after repentance of former.

But it is not, *Arise,* and stand still: But *Surgite, & ite,* arise, and depart; But whither? Into actions, contrary to those sinfull actions, and habits contrary to those habits. *Let him that is righteous, be righteous still, and him that is holy, be holy still;* and that cannot be, without this; for it is but a small degree of *Convalescence,* and reparation of health, to be able to rise out of our bed, to be able to forbear
280 sin: *Qui febri laborat, post morbum infirmior est;* though the fever be off, we are weake after it; though we have left a sinne, there is a weaknesse upon us, that makes us reel, and leane towards that bed, at every turne; decline towards that sinne, upon every occasion. And

2 Tim. 1.3

[Rom. 11.1]

Ephes. 2.3

Ioh. 1.12

Tertullian

Aug.

Ite

Apoc. 22.11, 12

therefore according to that example, and pattern, of Gods proceeding
at the creation, who first made all, and then digested, and then per-

Ambros.   fected them; *Primò faciamus, deinde venustemus,* says Saint *Ambrose;* first let us make us up a good body, a good habitude, a good
constitution, by leaving our beds, our occasions of tentations; and
then *venustemus,* let us dresse our selves, adorne our selves, yea, arme

[Eph. 6.11]   ²⁹⁰ our selves, with the *whole armour of God,* which is faith in Christ
Jesus, and a holy and sanctified conversation. *Memento peregisse te*

Augusti.   *aliquid, restare aliquid:* Remember, (and do not deceive thy selfe, to
remember that, which was never done) but remember truely, that
thou hast done something, towards making sure thy salvation already, and that thou hast much more to doe; *Divertisse te ad Refec-
tionem, non ad defectionem,* that God hath given thee a bayting
place, a resting place; peace in conscience, for all thy past sinnes,
in thy present repentance; but it is, to refresh thy selfe with that
peace; it is not to take new courage, and strength to sinne againe.
³⁰⁰ Let not the ease which thou hast found in the remission of sinnes
now embolden thee to commit them againe; nor to trust to that
strength which thou hast already recovered; but *arise and depart;*
avoid old tentations, and apply thy selfe to a new course in the world,
and in a calling; for there may be as much sinne, to leave the world,
as to cleave to the world: and he may be as inexcusable at the last day,
that hath done *Nothing* in the world, as hee that hath done *some ill.*

Quia   Now, we noted it to be a particular degree of Gods mercy, that he
insisted upon it, that he pressed it, that he urged it with a reason;
doe thus, says God, *for,* it stands thus with you. It is always a bold-

³¹⁰ nesse, to aske a reason of those decrees of God, which were founded,
and established onely in his owne gratious will, and pleasure; In

Luther   those cases, *Exitiales voculæ, cur & quomodo;* to aske, *why* God
elected some, and *how* it can consist with his goodnesse, to leave out
others, there the *how,* and *why* are dangerous, and deadly Monosyllables. But of Gods particular purposes upon us, and revealed to
us, which are so to be wrought and executed upon us, as that we
our selves have a fellow-working, and co-operation with God, of
those, it becomes us to aske, and to know the reason. When the Angell
Gabriel promised such unexpected blessings to *Zachary, Zachary*

Luke 1.18   ³²⁰ askes, *whereby shall I know this?* and the Angel does not leave him

unsatisfied. When that Angel promises a greater miracle to the blessed
Virgin *Mary,* she says also, *Quomodo, how shall this be?* and the
Angel settles, and establishes the assurance in her: Whatsoever we are
bid to beleeve, whatsoever we are bid to doe, God affords us a reason
for it, and we may try it by reason, but because that sinner, whom in
this text, he speakes to, *to arise and depart,* is likely to stand upon
false reasons, against his rising, to murmur, and ask *Cur* or *quomodo,*
why should I arise, since me thinkes I lye at my ease, *how* shall I
arise, that am already at the top of my wishes? God who is loath to
³³⁰ lose any soule, that he undertakes, followes him with this reason,
Quia non requies, Arise, and depart, for here is not your rest.

    Now this rest, is in it selfe, so gratefull, so acceptable a thing, as
all the service, which *David,* and *Solomon,* could expresse towards
God, in the dedication of the Temple, (which was then in intention,
and project) is described in that phrase, *Arise O Lord, and come into*
thy rest, thou and the Arke of thy strength; God himselfe hath a
Sabbath, in our Sabbaths; It is welcome to God, and it is so welcome
to Man, as that Saint *Augustine* preaching upon those words, *Qui*
posuit fines tuos pacem, He maketh peace in thy borders, (as we
³⁴⁰ translate it) he observed such a passion, such an alteration in his
auditory, as that he tooke knowledge of it in his Sermon; *Nihil*
dixeram, nihil exposueram, verbum pronunciavi & exclamastis, says
he; I have entred into no part of my text; I have scarce read my text;
I did but name the word, *Rest,* and *Peace* of conscience, and you are
all transported, affected, with an exultation, with an acclamation, in
the hunger, and ambition of it; That, that the naturall, that, that the
supernaturall Man affects, is *Rest; Inquire pacem, & persequere eam;*
it is not onely *sequere,* but *persequere; seek peace & ensue it;* follow
this rest, this peace so, as if it fly from you, if any interruption, any
³⁵⁰ heavinesse of heart, any warfare of this world, come between you,
and it, yet you never give over the pursuite of it, till you overtake it.
Persequere, follow it; but first *Inquire,* says *David,* seek after it, find
where it is, for *here is not your rest.*

    Vnaquæque res in sua patria fortior; If a Starre were upon the
Earth, it would give no light; If a tree were in the Sea, it would give
no fruit; every tree is fastest rooted, and produces the best fruit, in
the soile, that is proper for it. Now, *here we have no continuing City,*

[v. 34]

Requies

Psal. 132.8

Augusti.
Psal. 147.14

Psal. 34.14
[Prayer
Book
version]

Non Hic
Chrys.

Heb. 13.14

but we seek one; when we finde that, we shall finde rest. Here how

2 Cor. 7.5

shall we hope for it? for our selves, *Intus pugnæ, foris timores;* we
360 feel a warre of *concupiscencies* within, and we feare a battery of *tentations* without: *Si dissentiunt in domo uxor & maritus: periculosa

Augusti.

molestia,* says Saint *Augustine;* If the Husband, and wife agree not
at home, it is a troublesome danger; and that's every mans case; for
Caro conjux, our flesh is the wife, and the spirit is the husband, and
they two will never agree. But *si dominetur uxor, perversa pax,* says
he, and that's a more ordinary case, then we are aware of, that the
wife hath got the Mastery, that the weaker vessell, the flesh, hath got
the victory; and then, there is a show of peace, but it is a stupidity, a
security, it is not peace. Let us depart out of our selves, and looke
370 upon that, in which most ordinarily we place an opinion of rest, upon

1 Tim. 6.9

*worldly riches; They that will be rich, fall into tentations, and snares,
and into many foolish, and noysome lusts, which drowne Men in
perdition, and in destruction, for the desire of money is the root of

Theophyl.

evill;* Not the having of Money, but the *desire* of it; for it is *The-
ophylacts* observation, that the Apostle does not say this, of them that
are rich, but of them, that *will be made* rich; that set their heart upon

Ier. 17.11

the desire of riches, and will be rich, what way soever. *As the Par-
tridge gathereth the young, which she hath not brought forth, so he
that gathereth riches, and not by right, shall leave them in the midst
380 of his dayes, and at his end shall be a foole;* (he shall not make a *wise
will*) But shall his folly end, at his end, or the punishment of his
folly? We see what a restlesse fool he is, all the way; first, because

Luke 12.18

he wants roome, he says, he will *pull downe his barnes, and build
new;* (thus farre there's no rest; in the *Diruit,* and *ædificat,* in pulling
downe, and building up;) Then he says to his soule, *live at ease;* he
says it, but he gives no ease; he says it as he shall say to the Hills, *fall
downe, and cover us;* but they shall stand still; and his soule shall
heare God say, whilest he promises himselfe this ease, *O foole, this
night, they shall fetch away thy soule;* God does not onely not tell
390 him, *who* shall have his riches, but he does not tell him, *who* shall
have his soule. He leaves him no assurance, no ease, no peace, no rest,
Here.

Vestra

This rest is not then in these things; not in their *use;* for they are
got with labor, and held with feare; and these, labour and feare,

admit no rest; not in their *nature;* for they are fluid, and transitory, and moveable, and these are not attributes of rest. If that word doe not reach to *Land,* (the land is not movable,) yet it reaches to *thee;* when thou makest *thine* Inventory, put *thy selfe* amongst the *moveables,* for thou must remove from it, though it remove not from thee. 400 So that, what rest soever may be imagined in these things, it is not *your rest,* for howsoever the things may seem to rest, yet you doe not. It is not here at all: not in that *Here,* which is intimated in this Text; not in the falling, that is *Here;* for sinne is a stupidity, it is not a rest; not in the rising that is *Here,* for this remorse, this *repentance,* is but as a surveying of a convenient ground, or an emptying of an inconvenient ground, to erect a building upon; not in the *departing* that is here, for in that, is intimated a building of new habits, upon the ground so prepared, and so a continuall, and laborious travaile, no rest; falling, and rising, and departing, and surveying, and building, 410 are no words of rest, for give these words their spirituall sense, that this sense of our fall, (which is *remorse* after sinne) this rising from it, (which is *repentance* after sinne) this *departing* into a safer station, (which is the building of habits contrary to the former) doe bring an ease to the conscience, (as it doth that powerfully, and plentifully) yet, as when we journey by Coach, we have an ease in the way, but yet our rest is at home, so in the ways of a regenerate Man, there is an unexpressible ease, and consolation here, but yet even this is not *your rest;* for, as the Apostle says, *If I be not an Apostle unto* [1 Cor. 9.2] *others, yet doubtlesse I am unto you,* so what rest soever others may 420 propose unto themselves, for you, *whose conversation is in heaven,* [Phil. 3.20] (for this world to the righteous is *Atrium templi,* and heaven is that Temple it selfe, the Militant Church, is the porch, the Triumphant, is the *Sanctum Sanctorum,* this Church and that Church are all under one roofe, Christ Jesus) for you, who appertaine to this Church, your rest is in heaven; And that consideration brings us to the last of the three interpretations of these words.

The first was a *Commination,* a departing without any Rest, pro- 3 Part pos'd to the Jewes; The second was a *Commonition,* a departing into the way towards Rest, proposed to repentant sinners; And this third 430 is a *Consolation,* a departing into Rest it selfe, propos'd to us, that beleeve a Resurrection. It is a consolation, and yet it is a funerall; for

to present this eternall Rest, we must a little invert the words, to the
departing out of this world, by death, and so to arise to Judgement;
Depart, and *arise; for, &c.*

Depart This departing then, is our last *Exodus,* our last passeover, our last
transmigration, our departing out of this life. And then, the Consolation is placed in this, that we are willing and ready for this departing;

Chrysost. *Qua gratia breve nobis tempus præscripsit Deus?* How mercifully
hath God proceeded with Man, in making his life short? for by that
440 means he murmurs the lesse at the miseries of this life, and he is the
lesse transported upon the pleasures of this life, because the end of
both is short. It is a weaknesse, sayes *Saint Ambrose,* to complain,

Ambr. *De immaturitate mortis,* of dying before our time; for we were ripe
Idem for death at our birth; we were born mellow: *Secundum aliquem
modum, immortalis dici posset homo, si esset tempus intra quod mori
non posset,* is excellently said by the same Father; If there were any
one minute in a mans life, in which he were safe from death, a man
might in some sort be said to be immortall, for that minute; but Man

Idem is never so; *Nunquam ei vicinius est, posse vivere, quàm posse mori:*
450 That proposition is never truer, This man may live to morrow, then
this proposition is, This man may dy this minute. Though then shortnesse of life be a malediction to the wicked, (*The bloudy and deceit-*

Psal. 55.23 *full men shall not live halfe their dayes*) there's the sentence, the
Iob 22.16 Judgement, the Rule, (*And they were cut down before their time*)
there's the execution, the example, God hath threatned, God hath
inflicted, shortnesse of dayes to the wicked, yet the Curse consists
in their indisposition, in their over-loving of this world, in their
terrors concerning the next world, and not meerly in the shortnesse
of life; for this *Ite,* depart out of this world, is part of the Consola-
460 tion. I have a Reversion upon my friend, and (though I wish it not)
yet I am glad, if he die; Men that have inheritances after their
fathers, are glad when they dye; though not glad that they die, yet
glad when they die: I have a greater, after the death of this body, and
shall I be loath to come to that? Yet, it is not so a Consolation, as that
we should by any means, be occasions to hasten our own death; *Multi*

Aug. *Innocentes ab aliis occiduntur, à seipso nemo;* Many men get by the
malice of others, if thereby, they dy the sooner; for they are the
sooner at home, and dy innocently: but no man dies innocently, that

dies by his own hand, or by his own hast. We may not doe it, never; we may not wish it, always, nor easily. Before a perfect Reconciliation with God, it is dangerous to wish death. *David* apprehended it so, *I said, O my God, take me not away in the midst of my dayes.* In an over tender sense, and impatience of our own Calamities, it is dangerous to desire death too. Very holy men have transgressed on that hand: *Elias* in his persecution came inconsiderately to desire that he might die; *It is enough, ô Lord, take away my soule;* He would tell God how much was enough. And so sayes *Job, My soule chuseth rather to be strangled and to die, then to be in my bones;* He must have that that his soule chuses. But to omit many cases wherein it is not good, nor safe to wish Death, certainly, when it is done primarily in respect of God, for his glory, and then, for the respect which is of our selves, it is onely to enjoy the sight, and union of God, and that also with a Conditionall submission to his will, and a tacite, and humble reservation of all his purposes, we may think *David's* thought, and speak *David's* words, *My soule thirsteth for God, even for the living God, when shall I come, and appeare before the presence of* my Living *God?* Saint *Paul* had *David's* example for it, when he comes to his *Cupio dissolvi,* to desire to be dissolved; And Saint *Augustine* had both their examples, when he sayes so affectionately, *Eia Domine videam, ut hîc moriar,* O my God, let me see thee in this life, that I may *die the death of the Righteous,* dy to sin; *Et moriar ut te videam,* let me dy absolutely, that I may see thee essentially. Here we may be in his Presence, we see his *state;* there we are in his Bedchamber, and see his eternall and glorious *Rest.* The Rule is good, given by the same Father, *Non injustum est justo optare mortem,* A righteous man, may righteously desire death; *Si Deus non dederit, injustum erit, non tolerare vitam amarissimam,* but if God affords not that ease, he must not refuse a laborious life; So that, this departing, is not a going before we be call'd: Christ himselfe stay'd for his ascension, till he was *taken up.* But when there comes a *Lazare veni foras,* that God calls us, from this putrefaction, which we think life, let us be not onely obedient, but glad to depart.

For without such an *Ite,* there is no such *Surgite,* as is intended here; without this departing there is no good rising, without a joyfull Transmigration, no joyfull Resurrection; He that is loth to depart,

Psal. 102.24

1 Reg. 19.4

Iob 7.15

Psal. 42.2

Phil. 1.[23]

Aug.
[Num.
23.10]
Idem

[Joh. 11.43]

Surgite

is afraid to rise againe; and he that is afraid of the Resurrection, had rather there were none; and he that had rather there were none, *aut cæcitate, aut animositate,* says S. *Augustine,* either he will make him-selfe beleeve, that there is none, or if he cannot overcome his Con-science so absolutely, he will make the world beleeve, that he beleeves there is none: and truly to lose our sense of the Resurrection, is as heavy a losse, as of any one point of Religion; It is the knot of all, and hath this priviledge, above all, that though those Joyes of heaven, which we shall possesse immediately after our death, be infinite, yet even to these infinite Joyes, the Resurrection gives an addition, and enlarges even that which was infinite. And therefore is *Job* so pas-sionately desirous, that this doctrine of the Resurrection, might be imparted to all, imprinted in all; *Oh that my words were now written, Oh that they were written in a book; and graven with an Iron pen in lead, and stone, for ever:* what is all this, that *Job* recommends with so much devotion to all? *I am sure that my Redeemer liveth, and he shall stand the last on Earth, and though after my skin, wormes destroy this body, yet I shall see God in my flesh; whom I my selfe shall see; and mine eyes shall behold, and none other for me.* This doctrine of the Resurrection, had *Job,* so vehement, and so early a care of. Neither could the malicious, and pestilent inventions of man, no nor of Satan himselfe, abolish this doctrine of the Resurrection: for, as Saint *Hierome* observes, from *Adrian*'s time, to *Constantin*'s, for 180 yeares, in the place of *Christs birth,* they had set up an Idoll, a statue of *Adonis;* In the place of his *Crucifying,* they had set up an Idoll of *Venus;* and in the place of his *Resurrection,* they had erected a *Jupiter:* in opinion, that these Idolatrous provisions of theirs, would have abolish'd the Mysteries of our Religion; but they have outliv'd all them, and shall outlive all the world, eternally beyond all Genera-tions. And therefore doth Saint *Ambrose* apply well, and usefully to our Death, and Resurrection, to our departing, and rising, these words, *Come my people, enter thou into thy Chambers, and shut thy dores after thee; Hide thy selfe for a very little while, untill the Indignation passe over thee;* that is, Goe quietly, to your graves, attend your Resurrection, till God have executed his purpose upon the wicked of this world; Murmur not to admit the dissolution of body, and soul, upon your death-beds, nor the resolution, and putre-

faction of the body alone in your graves, till God be pleased to repaire all, in a full consummation, and reuniting of body and soule,
in a blessed Resurrection. *Ite & Surgite,* depart so, as you may desire
to rise; Depart with an *In manus tuas,* and with a *Veni Domine Jesu;* [Luk. 23.46]
with a willing surrendring of your soules, and a cheerfull meeting [Rev. 22.20]
of the Lord Jesus.

For else, all hope of profit, and permanent Rest is lost: for, as Saint *Requies*
50 *Hierome* interprets these very words; *Here* we are taught that there
is no rest, in this life, *Sed quasi à mortuis resurgentes, ad sublime* Hier.
tendere, & ambulare post Dominum Jesum; we depart, when we
depart from sin, and we rise, when we raise our selves to a conformity
with Christ: And not onely after his *example,* but after his *person,*
that is, to hasten thither, whither he is gone to prepare us a Room.
For, this *Rest,* in the Text, though it may be understood of the *Land
of Promise;* and of the *Church,* and of the *Arke,* and of the *Sabbath,*
(for, if we had time to pursue them, we might make good use of all
these acceptations) yet we accept *Chrysostome*'s acceptation best,
60 *Requies est ipse Christus,* our rest is Christ himselfe. Not onely that Chrys.
rest that is *in Christ,* (peace of conscience in him) but that Rest, that
Christ is in; eternall rest in his kingdome, *There remaineth a Rest,*
to the people of God; besides that inchoation of Rest, which the godly Heb. 4.9
have here, there remains a fuller Rest. *Jesus is entred into his Rest,* 10
sayes the Apostle there; his Rest was not here, in this world; and,
Let us study to enter into that Rest, sayes he; for no other can accom- 11
plish our peace. *It is righteousnesse with God, to recompence tribu-*
lation to them, that trouble you, and to you, which are troubled, Rest; 2 Thes. 1.6
but, when? in this world? no: *when the Lord Jesus shall shew him-*
70 *selfe from heaven, with his mighty Angels;* then comes your Rest;
for, for the grave, the body lies still, but it is not a Rest, because it is
not sensible of that lying still; in heaven the body shall rest, rest in
the sense of that glory.

This Rest then is *not here,* Not onely not *Here,* as this *Here,* was *Non hîc*
taken in the first interpretation, *Here in the Earth;* but not *Here* in
the second interpretation, not in *Repentance* it selfe; for all the Rest
of this life, even the *spirituall Rest,* is rather a *Truce,* then a *peace,*
rather a *Cessation,* then an *end* of the war. For when these words,
(I will set the Egyptians against the Egyptians, Every one shall fight Esa. 19.2

⁵⁸⁰ *against his brother, and every one against his neighbour, City against City, and Kingdome against Kingdome*) may be interpreted, and are so interpreted of the time of the Gospell of Christ Jesus, when

Mat. 10.34

Christ himselfe says, *Nolite putare quod venerim mittere pacem in terrâ,* Never think that I came to settle peace, or Rest in this world;

Luke 14.24

Nay, when Christ sayes, *None of them that were bidden shall come to his supper,* and that may be verified of any Congregation, none of us that are call'd now, shall come to that Rest, a Man may be at a security in an opinion of Rest, and be far from it; A man may be neerer Rest in a troubled Conscience, then in a secure.

⁵⁹⁰   Here we have often *Resurrections,* that is, purposes to depart from sin: but they are such Resurrections, as were at the time of Christs Resurrection: when (as the strongest opinion is) *Resurrexerunt iterum morituri,* Many of the dead rose, but they died again; we rise from our sins here, but here we fall again; *Monumenta aperta sunt;*

Hier.

(it is Saint *Hierome*'s note,) The graves were opened, presently upon

Mat. 27.[52]

Christs death; but yet the bodies did not arise, till Christs Resurrection: The godly have an opening of their graves, they see some light, some of their weight, some of their Earth is taken from them, but a Resurrection to enter into the City, to follow the Lamb, to come into

⁶⁰⁰ an established security, that they have not, till they be united to Christ in heaven. Here we are still subject to *relapses,* and to looking back;

Aug.

Memento uxoris Lot, Ipsa in loco manet, transeuntes monet, Shee is fixed to a place, that she might settle those, that are not fix'd; *Vt quid in statuam salis conversa, si non homines, ut sapiant, condiat?* to teach us the danger of looking back, till we be fix'd, she is fix'd. When the

1 Reg. 19.5

Prophet *Eliah* was at the dore of *Desperation,* an Angell touch'd him, and said, *Vp,* and *eat:* and there was bread, and water provided, and he did eat; but he slept again; and we have some of these excitations, and we come, and eat, and drink, even the *body, and bloud of Christ,*

⁶¹⁰ but we sleep again, we doe not perfect the work. Our Rest Here then,

Hebr. 4.1

is never without a fear of losing it: This is our best state, *To fear lest at any time, by forsaking the promise of entring into his rest, we should seem to be depriv'd.* The Apostle disputes not, (neither doe I) whether we can be depriv'd or no; but he assures us, that *we may fall back* so far, as that to the Church, and to our own Consciences we

Alicubi

may *seem* to be depriv'd; and that's argument enough, that here is no *Rest*. To end all, though there be no Rest in all this world, no not in our *sanctification* here, yet this being a Consolation, there must be rest some where; And it is, *In superna Civitate, unde amicus non exit,* qûa *inimicus non intrat,* In that City, in that Hierusalem, where there shall never enter any man, whom we doe not love, nor any goe from us, whom we doe love. Which, though we have not yet, yet we shall have: for upon those words, (*because I live, ye shall live also*) Saint *Augustine* sayes, that because his Resurrection was to follow so soon, Christ takes the present word, *because I doe live.* But because their life was not to be had here, he says, *Vivetis, you shall live,* in heaven; not *Vivitis;* for here, we doe not live. So, *as in Adam we all die, even so in Christ shall all be made alive,* says the Apostle: All our deaths are here, present now; now we dy; our quickning is re-serv'd for heaven, that's future. And therefore let us attend that Rest, as patiently as we doe the things of this world, and not doubt of it therefore, because we see it not yet: even in this world we consider invisible things, more then visible; *Vidimus pelagus, non autem mercedem,* The Merchant sees the tempestuous Sea, when he does not see the commodities, which he goes for: *Videmus terram, non autem messem,* The Husbandman sees the Earth, and his labour, when he sees no harvest; and for these hopes, that there will be a gain to the Merchant, and a harvest to the Labourer, *Naturæ fidimus,* we rely upon Creatures; for our Resurrection, *fidejussorem habemus Coronatum;* Not Nature, not Sea, nor Land, is our surety, but our surety is one, who is already crown'd, with that Resurrection. *Num in hominibus terra degenerat, quæ omnia regenerat,* sayes Saint *Ambrose,* will the earth, that gives a new life to all Creatures, faile in us, and hold us in an everlasting winter, without a spring, and a Resurrection? Certainly no; but if we be content so to depart into the wombe of the Earth, our grave, as that we know that, to be but the Entry into glory, as we depart contentedly, so we shall arise glori-ously, to that place, where our eternall Rest shall be, though here there be not our Rest; for he that shoots an arrow at a mark, yet means to put that arrow into his Quiver again; and God that glori-fies himselfe, in laying down our bodies in the grave, means also to glorifie them, in reassuming them to himselfe, at the last day.

Aug.

Iohn 14.19
Aug.

1 Cor. 15.22

Chrysost.

Ambr.

Number 11.

Preached at the Temple.

ESTHER 4.16. *GO AND ASSEMBLE ALL THE JEWS THAT ARE FOUND IN SHUSHAN, AND FAST YE FOR ME, AND EAT NOT, NOR DRINK IN THREE DAYS, DAY NOR NIGHT: I ALSO, AND MY MAIDS WILL FAST LIKEWISE; AND SO I WILL GO IN TO THE KING, WHICH IS NOT ACCORDING TO THE LAW: AND IF I PERISH, I PERISH.*

NEXT TO the eternal and coessential Word of God, *Christ Jesus,* the written Word of God, the Scriptures concern us most; and therefore next to the person of Christ, and his Offices, the Devil hath troubled the Church, with most questions about the certainty of Scriptures, and the Canon thereof. It was late, before the Spirit of God setled and established an unanime, and general consent in his Church, for the accepting of this Book of *Esther:* For, not onely the holy Bishop *Melito* (who defended the Christians by an Apology to the Emperor) removed this Book from the Canon of
10 the Scripture, One hundred and fifty years after Christ; but *Athanasius* also, Three hundred and forty years after Christ, refused it too: Yea, *Gregory Nazianzen* (though he deserved, and had the stile and title of *Theologus, The Divine;* and though he came to clearer times, living almost Four hundred years after Christ) did not yet submit himself to an acceptation of this Book. But a long time there hath been no doubt of it; and it is certainly part of that Scripture

2 Tim. 3.16   which is profitable to teach, to reprove, to correct, and to instruct in

216

righteousness. To which purpose, we shall see what is afforded us
in this History of this Heroical Woman, *Esther;* what she did in a
²⁰ perplexed and scrupulous case, when an evident danger appeared, and
an evident Law was against her action; and from thence consider,
what every Christian Soul ought to do, when it is surprised and overtaken with any such scruples or difficulties to the Conscience.

For *Esther* in particular, this was her case. She being Wife to the
King, *Haman,* who had great power with the King, had got from
him an Edict, for the destruction of all her people the *Jews.* When
this was intimated to her by *Mordecai,* who presented to her Conscience, not onely an irreligious forsaking of God, if she forbore to
mediate and use her interest in the King for the saving of hers, and
³⁰ Gods people; but an unnatural and unprovident forsaking of her self,
because her danger was involved in theirs; and that she her self being
of that Nation, could not be safe in her person, though in the Kings
house, if that Edict were executed, though she had not then so ordinary access to the King, as formerly she had had: yea, though there
were a Law in her way, that she might not come till she was called,
yet she takes the resolution to go, she puts off all Passion, and all particular respects, she consecrates the whole action to God; and having
in a rectified and well informed Conscience found it acceptable to
him, she neglects both that particular Law, That none might have
⁴⁰ access to the King uncalled, and that general Law, That every Man
is bound to preserve himself; and she exposes her self to an imminent,
and (for any thing she knew) an unescapable danger of death: *If I
perish, I perish.*

For the ease of all our memories, we shall provide best, by contracting all, which we are to handle, to these two parts; *Esthers* preparation, and *Esthers* resolution: How she disposed her self, how she
resolved: What her consultation was, what her execution was to be.
Her preparation is an humiliation; and there, first she prepares, that
that glory which God should receive, by that humiliation, should be
⁵⁰ general; All the people should be taught, and provoked to glorifie
God; *vade, congrega, Go, and assemble all.* Secondly, The act which
they were to do, was to fast, *Jejunate:* And thirdly, It was a limited
fast, *Tribus diebus, Eat not, nor drink in three days, and three nights:*
And then, this fast of theirs, was with relation, and respect to her,

Divisio

Jejunate super me, Fast ye for me. But yet so, as she would not receive
an ease by their affliction; put them to do it for her, and she do nothing
for her self; *Ego cum Ancillis; I and my Maids will fast too;* and
similiter, likewise, that is, As exactly as they shall. And so far extends
her preparation: Her resolution derives it self into two branches. First,
60 That she will break an Humane and Positive Law, *Ingrediar contra
legem, I will go in, though it be not according to the Law;* and secondly, She neglects even the Law of Nature, the Law of Self-preserva-
tion, *Si peream, peream.*

1 Part
Assemblies

To enter into the first part, *The assembling of the people;* though
the occasion and purpose here were religious, yet the assembling of
them was a civil act, an act of Jurisdiction and Authority. Almost all
States have multiplied Laws against Assemblies of People, by private
Authority, though upon pretences of Religious occasions. All Conventicles, all Assemblies, must have this character, this impression
70 upon them, That they be *Legitima,* lawful: And, *Legitima sola sunt,
quæ habent authoritatem principis,* onely those are lawful which are
made by the Authority of the State. *Aspergebatur infamia Alcibiades,
quòd in domo suo facere Mysteria dicebatur.* There went an ill report
of him, because he had sacrifices, and other worships of the gods at
home in his own house: And this was not imputed to him, as a Schis-
matical thing, or an act of a different Religion from the State, but an
act of disaffection to the State, and of Sedition. In times of persecution,
when no exercise of true Religion is admitted, these private Meetings
may not be denied to be lawful: As for bodily sustenance, if a man
80 could no otherwise avoid starving, the Schoolmen, and the Casuists,
resolve truly, That it were no sin to steal so much meat as would
preserve life; so, those souls, which without that, must necessarily
starve, may steal their Spiritual food in corners, and private meetings:
But if we will steal either of these foods, Temporal or Spiritual, because that meat which we may have, is not so dressed, so dished, so
sauced, so served in, as we would have it; but accompanied with some
other ceremonies then are agreeable to our taste; This is an inexcusable
Theft, and these are pernicious Conventicles.

Dan. 6

When that Law was made by *Darius,* That no man for thirty days
90 should ask any thing of God or man, but onely of the King; though
it were a Law that had all circumstances to make it no Law, yet *Daniel*

took no occasion by this, to induce any new manner of worshipping
of God; he took no more company with him to affront the Law, or
exasperate the Magistrate; onely he did as he had used to do before;
and he did not disguise, nor conceal that which he did, but he set open
his windows, and prayed in his Chamber. But in these private Conventicles, where they will not live *voto aperto,* that is, pray so, as that
they would be content to be heard what they pray for; As the *Jews* in
those Christian Countreys, where they are allowed their Synagogues,
100 pray against *Edom,* and *Edomites* by name, but they mean (as appears in their private Catechisms) by *Edom,* and *Edomites,* the Christian Church, and Christian Magistracy; so when these men pray in
their Conventicles, for the confusion, and rooting out of Idolatry and
Antichrist, they intend by their Idolatry, a Cross in Baptism; and by
their Antichrist, a man in a Surpless; and not onely the persons, but
the Authority that admits this Idolatry, and this Antichristianism.
As vapors and winds shut up in Vaults, engender Earth-quakes; so
these particular spirits in their Vault-Prayers, and Cellar-Service,
shake the Pillars of State and Church. *Domus mea, Domus orationis;*   [Isa. 56.7]
110 and *Domus orationis, Domus mea: My house is the house of Prayer,*
says God; and so the house of Prayer must be his house. The Cen-
turion, of whom Christ testified, *That he had not found so great Faith*   Matth. 8.10
even in Israel, thought not himself worthy, that Christ should come
under his Roof; and these men think no Roof, but theirs, fit for Christ;
no, not the Roof of his own House, the Church: For, I speak not of
those Meetings, where the blessed Children of God joyn in the House,
to worship God in the same manner, as is ordained in the Church, or
in a manner agreeable to that: Such Religious Meetings as these, God
will give a blessing to; but when such Meetings are in opposition, and
120 detestation of Church Service, though their purpose, which come
thither, do not always intend sedition, yet they may easily think, that
none of those Disciples is so ill a Natural Logician, but that he comes
quickly to this conclusion, That if those exercises be necessary to their
Salvation, that State that denies them those exercises deals injustly
with them: And when people are brought to that disaffection, it is not
always in their power that brought them together so far, to settle them
or hold them from going farther. In this case which we have in hand,
of *Esther* and *Mordecai's* assembling all the *Jews* in *Shusan,* which

was the principal City of *Persia,* where the Residence of the Princes
130 was, (*Persepolis* was a Metropolitan City too; but onely for the treasure, and for the Sepulchres of their Kings, but the Court was at
Shusan.) If when they had been assembled, and their desperate case
presented to them, That an Edict of a general Massacre was going out
against them, was it not more likely (judging humanely, and by comparison of like cases) that they would have turned to take arms, rather
then to fast and pray for their deliverance? How good soever their
pretence (and perchance purpose) be, that assemble people, and dis-
content them, the bridle, the stern, is no longer in their hands; but
there arise unexpected storms, of which, if they were not authors in
140 their purpose, yet they are the occasioners. In *Esthers* case, the proceeding was safe enough; for they were called to see, that the Queen
her self had undertaken their deliverance, their deliverance was very
likely to be effected; and therefore it became them to assist her purpose with their devotion, expressed first in Fasting.

Jejunate   Fasting is not a meer humane Imposition, as some have calumniated
it to be: The Commandments of it are frequent from God to his
people, and the practise of it even amongst the *Ninevites,* upon *Jona's*
Jon. 3.7   Preaching, is expressed to be rigid and severe, *Let neither man nor*
beast taste any thing, nor feed, nor drink water, but let man and beast
150 *put on sackcloth, and cry mightily unto God.* It is true, that they found
often that their Fasts did no good; but when they expostulate it with
Esai 58.3   God, *Wherefore have we fasted, and thou seest it not? we have pun-*
ished our selves, and thou regardest it not; They received a direct
answer from God, *Behold, in the days of your fast you seek your own*
Zech. 7.5   *will, and require all your debts; when ye fasted and mourned, did ye*
fast unto me? To place therefore any part of our righteousness, or to
dignifie the act of Fasting, with the name of Merit or Satisfaction, did
then, and will always corrupt and alter the nature of a true and acceptable fast: And therefore we detest the definition of a fast in the *Roman*
160 Church, *Et Abstinentia secundum formam ecclesiæ, intuitu Satisfaci-*
endi, pro peccatis, & acquirendi vitam æternam; That fasting is a
satisfaction for sins, and an acquisition of life everlasting. But since
the reason of fasting remains, the practise must remain still: For when
Christ excused his Apostles for not fasting, as the Disciples of *John*
Baptist, and as the Pharisees did, he did not say that fasting is taken

away; but he said, *The Bridegroom* was *not taken away; but he* should
be taken away and they should *fast.* When occasions press us, fasting
is required at our hands: *Caro mea jumentum,* My flesh is my beast;
via Christus, and Christ is the way I am to go; *Nonne cibaria feroci-*
170 *enti detraham?* If it be too wanton, shall not I withdraw some of the
provender? *Et fame Domem, quem ferre non possum,* If I cannot
govern him, shall I not endeavour to tame him? And therefore, though
by reason of former abuses, it be a slippery Doctrine, the practise of
Fasting, (for scarce any man puts himself to much fasting, but he is
ready to tell God of it, with the Pharisee, *I fast twice a week*: And from
Hieroms praise of it, *Jejunium non est virtus, sed gradus ad virtutem,*
That though fasting be not a vertue, yet it is the way to vertue; we
come a step farther with *Chrysostom, In choro virtutum, extremum
sortitur Jejunium,* That though fasting be the last of vertues (except
180 *Chrysostom* mean by *extremum,* the first) yet it is one; yet *Sanctificate
vobis Jejunium,* Fast with a holy purpose; and it is a holy action. As
you are bid to *cast your bread upon the waters, for many days after
you shall finde it again;* so also cast your fasting upon the waters, look
for no particular reward of it, and God shall give you a benefit by it
in the whole course of your lives.

    But the *Jejunate,* Fasting it self, hath not so much opposition as the
Tribus diebus, that it must be Three days; the certain days, and the
limiting of the time, that is it that offends. All men will say that fasting is necessary to all men; but not this proportion, and this measure
190 to all men alike. They are content with that of *Augustine, Ego in
Evangelicis & Apostolicis literis totoque instrumento novo revolvens,
video præceptum esse jejunium,* As often as I consider the Gospel,
every where I finde Commandments for fasting; but they will have
the rest too: *Quibus diebus oportet, aut non oportet jejunare, præceptum Domini & Apostolorum non video definitum,* Upon what days
we should fast, says he, I see no Commandment of Christ or the Apostles: And it is true, there is no express Commandment for it; but
there is an express Commandment to hear the Church. In the Old
Testament God gave express Commandment, *De Jejuniis stativis;*
200 certain fix'd and Anniversary Fasts: *The tenth of the same moneth
shall be a holy Convocation unto you,* et affligetis animas vestras, *Ye
shall humble your souls;* and every person that doth not that, that

Luc. 5.35

Aug.

[Luk. 18.12]
S. Hier.

Chrys.

Joel 1.14
Eccles. 11.[1]

*Tribus
Diebus*

[Mat. 18.17]

Levit. 23.27

same day, *shall even be cut off from his people.* The disease which
they had is hereditary to us; Concupiscencies in the flesh, and cold-
ness in the service of God: And though it may be true, that the Church
cannot know my particular infirmities, nor the time when they press
me; yet as no Physician for the body can prescribe me a Receipt against
a Fever, and bid me take it such a day, because perchance at that day
I shall have no Fever; yet he can prescribe me certain Rules and Re-
210 ceipts, which if I take at his times, I shall be the safer all the year: So
our Spiritual Physician, the Church, though she cannot know when
my body needs this particular Physick of fasting, yet she knows, that
by observing the time which she prescribes, I shall always be in the
better spiritual health. As soon as the Church was setled, Fasts were
setled too: When in the Primitive Church they fix'd certain times for
giving Orders, and making Ministers, they appointed Fasts at those
times; when they fix'd certain times for solemn Baptism, (as they
did *Easter* and *Whitsontide*) they appointed Fasts then too; and so
they did in their solemn and publick Penances. So also when Chris-
220 tians encreased in number, and that therefore, besides the Sabbath-day,
they us'd to call them to Church, and to give the Sacrament upon other
days too; as soon as Wednesday and Friday were appointed for that
purpose, for the Sacrament, they were appointed to be fasted too. And
Cyril   therefore when St. *Cyril* says, *Vis tibi ostendam, quale jejunare debes
jejunium? Jejuna ab omni peccato.* Shall I tell you what Fast God
looks for at your hands, *Fast from sin;* yet this is not all the Fasting
that he exacts, (though it be indeed the effect and accomplishment
of all) but he adds, *Non ideo hoc dicimus,* We say not this, says he,
because we would give liberty, *Habemus enim quadragesimum, &
230 quartum, & sextum Hebdomadæ diem quibus solemniter jejunamus,*
We have a fixed Lent to fast in, and we have Wednesdays and Fridays
fixt to fast in. In all times, Gods people had fixed and limited Fasts,
besides these Fasts which were enjoyned upon emergent dangers, as
this of *Esther.* In which there is a harder circumstance then this, That
it was a Fast limited to certain days; for it is, *Jejunate pro me,* Fast
you for me. And these words may seem to give some colour, some
countenance to the Doctrine of the *Roman* Church, That the merits
of one man may be applyed to another; which Doctrine is the foundation of Indulgences, and the fuel of Purgatory: In which they go so

²⁴⁰ far, as to say, That one may fee an Attorney to satisfie God for him; he may procure another man to Fast, or do other works of mortification for him: And he that does so for his Client, *Sanguinem pro sanguine Christo reddit,* He pays Christ his blood again, and gives him as much as he receiv'd from him; and more, *Deum sibi debitorem efficit,* he brings God into his debt, and may turn that debt upon whom he will; and God must wipe off so much of the other mans score, to whom he intends it. They go beyond this too; That satisfaction may be made to God, even by our selves after our death: As they say, when they had brought *Maximilian* the Emperor to that mortification, that ²⁵⁰ he commanded upon his death-bed, that his body should be whipped after he was dead; that purpose of his, though it were not executed, was a satisfaction of the Justice of God. And (as error can finde no place to stop at) they go yet farther, when they extend this power of satisfaction even to Hell it self, by authorizing those fables, That a dead man which appeared, and said he was damned, was by this flagellation, by his friends whipping of himself in his behalf, brought to repentance in hell, and so to faith in hell, and so to salvation in hell.

But in the words of *Esther* here is no intimation of this Heresie; when Queen *Esther* appoints others to fast for her, she knew she could ²⁶⁰ no more be the better for their fasting, then she could be the leaner, or in the better health for it; but because she was to have benefit by the subsequent act, by their prayers, she provokes them to that, by which their prayers might be the more acceptable and effectual, that is, to fasting. And so because the whole action was for her, and her good success in that enterprize, they are in that sense properly said to have fasted for her: So that this *Jejunate super me,* as the word is, *Gnalai, super me,* in my behalf, is no more but *Orate pro me,* Pray for me; and so Saint *Hierom* translates these words, *Orate pro me,* Pray for me. And therefore, since Prayer is the way which God hath ²⁷⁰ given us to batter Heaven, whether *facta manu Deum oramus, & vim gratam ei facimus,* whether we besiege God with our prayers, in these publick Congregations, or whether we wrastle with him hand to hand in our Chambers, in the battel of a troubled Conscience, let us live soberly and moderately; and *in Bello,* and *in Duello,* here in the Congregation, and at home in our private Colluctations, we shall be the likelier to prevail with God; for though we receive assistance from

Gretzer

Hier.

Tertul.

the prayer of others, that must not make us lazie in our own behalfs; which is *Esthers* last preparation, she bids all the people fast for her, that is, for the good success of her good purposes; but not the people
²⁸⁰ alone, she and her own maids will fast likewise.

Ego &
Ancill.

Qui fecit te sine te, non salvabit te sine te, is a saying of Saint *Augustine,* never too often repeated; and God and his Church are of one minde; for the Church that did Baptize thee without thy asking, will not fast for thee, nor pray for thee, without thou fast and pray for thy self. As in spiritual things, charity begins with our selves, and I am bound to wish my own salvation, rather then any other mans; so I am bound to trust to my making sure of my salvation, by that which I do my self, rather then by that which I procure others to do for me. *Domus Dei, Domus orationis;* we have inestimable profit by the pub-
²⁹⁰ lick Prayers of the Church, the House of God; but as there is *Deus,*

Jos. ult. 15

& Domus ejus, so there must be *Ego, & Domus mea, I and my House will serve the Lord. I also and my Maids will fast likewise,* says *Esther,* in her great enterprise; for, that which the Original expresses here, by *Gnalai,* for me, the *Chalde* Paraphrase expresses by *Gnimmi,* with me: She was as well to fast as they. It was a great confidence in that Priest that comforted Saint *Augustines* Mother, *Fieri non potest, ut filius istarum lachrymarum pereat,* It is impossible that the son, for whom so good a mother hath poured out so devout tears, should perish at last; it was a confidence which no man may take to himself, to go
³⁰⁰ to Heaven by that water, the tears of other men; but *tu & domus tua,*

[Col. 1.24]

Do thou and thy house serve the Lord; teach thine own eyes to weep, thine own body to fulfil the sufferings of Christ; thine own appetite to fast, thine own heart, and thine own tongue to pray. Come and participate of the devotions of the Church; but yet also in thy Chappel of ease, in thine own Bed-chamber, provide that thy self and thy servants, all thy senses, and all thy faculties, may also fast and pray; and so go with a religious confidence as *Esther* did, about all thy other worldly businesses and undertakings.

2 Part

This was her Preparation. Her Devotion hath two branches; she
³¹⁰ was to transgress a positive Law, a Law of the State; and she neglected the Law of Nature it self, in exposing her self to that danger. How far Humane Laws do binde the conscience, how far they lay such an obligation upon us, as that, if we transgress them, we do not only incur

the penalty, but sin towards God, hath been a perplexed question in
all times, and in all places. But how divers soever their opinions be,
in that, they all agree in this, That no Law, which hath all the essential parts of a Law, (for Laws against God, Laws beyond the power
of him that pretends to make them, are no Laws) no Law can be
so meerly a Humane Law, but that there is in it a Divine part. There
320 is in every Humane Law, part of the Law of God, which is obedience
to the Superior. That Man cannot binde the conscience, because he
cannot judge the conscience, nor he cannot absolve the conscience,
may be a good argument; but in Laws made by that power which is   [Rom. 13.1,
ordained by God, man bindes not, but God himself: And then you   5]
must be subject, not because of wrath, but because of conscience.
Though then the matter and subject of the Law, that which the Law
commands, or prohibits, may be an indifferent action, yet in all these,
God hath his part; and there is a certain Divine soul, and spark
of Gods power, which goes through all Laws, and inanimates them.
330 In all the Canons of the Church, God hath his voice, *Ut omnia*   [1 Cor.
ordine fiant; that all things be done decently, and in order; so the   14.40]
Canon that ordains that, is from God; in all the other Laws he hath
his voice too, *Ut piè & tranquillè vivatur,* That we may live peace-   [1 Tim. 2.2]
ably, and religiously, and so those Laws are from God: And in all,
of all sorts, this voice of his sounds evidently, *qui resistit ordinationi,*
he that resists his Commission, his Lieutenancy, his Authority, in Law-
makers appointed by him, resists himself. There is no Law that is
meerly humane, but only *Lex in membris, The Law in our flesh,*   [Rom. 7.23]
which rebels against the Law in our minde; and this is a Rebellion,
340 a Tyranny, no lawful Government. In all true Laws God hath his
interest; and the observing of them in that respect, as made by his
authority, is an act of worship and obedience to him; and the trans-
gressing of them, with that relation, that is, a resisting or undervaluing of that authority, is certainly sinne. How then was *Esthers*
act exempt from this? for she went directly against a direct Law,
That none should come to the King uncalled.

Whensoever divers Laws concur and meet together, that Law
which comes from the superior Magistrate, and is in the nature of the
thing commanded, highest too, that Law must prevail. If two Laws
350 lie upon me, and it be impossible to obey both, I must obey that which

comes immediately from the greatest power, and imposes the greatest
duty. Here met in her, the fix'd and permanent Law, of promoting
Gods glory, and a new Law of the King, to augment his greatness and
Majesty, by this retiredness, and denying of ordinary access to his
person. Gods Law, for his glory, which is infinite and unsearchable,
and the Kings Law, for his ease, (of which she knows the reason,
and the scope) were in the ballance together; if this Law of the King
had been of any thing naturally and essentially evil in it self, no circumstance could have delivered her from sin, if she had done against
360 it. Though the Law were but concerning an indifferent action, and
of no great importance, yet because Gods Authority is in every just
Law, if she could not have been satisfied in her conscience, that that
Law might admit an exception, and a dispensation in her case, she
had sinn'd in breaking it. But when she proceeded not upon any
precipitation, upon any singular or seditious spirit, when she debated
the matter temperately with a dispassioned man, *Mordecai;* when
she found a reservation even in the body of the Law, That if the King
held up his Scepter, the Law became no Law to that party, when she
might justly think her self out of the Law, which was (as *Josephus*
370 delivers it) *Ut nemo ex domesticis accederet,* That none of his servants should come into his presence uncalled; she was then come to
that, which onely can excuse and justifie the breaking of any Law,
that is, a probable, if not a certain assurance, contracted *Bona fide,*
in a rectified conscience, That if this present case, which makes us
break this Law, had been known and considered when the Law was
made, he that made the Law would have made provision for this case.
No presuming of a pardon, when the Law is broken; no dispensation
given before hand to break it, can settle the Conscience; nor any
other way, then a Declaration well grounded, that that particular
380 case was never intended to have been composed in that Law, nor the
reason and purpose thereof.

   So, when the Conscience of *Esther* was, and so when the Conscience
of any particular Christian, is, after due consideration of the matter,
come to a religious and temperate assurance, That he may break any
Law; his assurance must be grounded upon this, That if that Law
were now to be made, that case which he hath presently in hand,

would not be included by him that made that Law, in that Law;
otherwise to violate a Law, either because, being but a Humane Law,
I think I am discharged, paying the penalty; or, because I have good
390 means to the King, I may presume of a pardon in all cases, where my
priviledge works any other way, then as we have said, (that is, that
our case is not intended in that Law) it had been in *Esther,* it should
be in us a sin to transgress any Law, though of a low nature, and of
an indifferent action. But upon those circumstances which we mentioned before, *Esther* might see, that that Law admitted some exceptions, and that no exception was likelier then this, That the King for
all his majestical reservedness, would be content to receive information of such a dishonor done to his Queen, and to her god; she might
justly think that that Law, intended onely for the Kings ease, or his
400 state, reached not to her person, who was his wife, nor to her case,
which was the destruction of all that professed her Religion.

It was then no sin in her to go in to the King, though not according   *Si peream*
to the Law; but she may seem to have sinned, in exposing her self to
so certain a danger as that Law inflicted; with such a resolution, *Si
peream, peream, If I perish, I perish.* How far a man may lawfully,
and with a good conscience, forsake himself, and expose himself to
danger, is a point of too much largeness, and intricacy, and perplexity
to handle now: The general stream of Casuists runs thus, That a
private man may lawfully expose himself to certain danger, for the
410 preserving of the Magistrate, or of a superior person; and that reason
might have justified *Esthers* enterprise, if her ruine might have saved
her Country; but in her case, if she had perished, they were likely to
perish too. But she is safer then in that; for first, she had hope out of
the words of the Law, out of the dignity of her place, out of the Justice
of the King, out of the preparation which she had made by Prayer;
which Prayer, *Josephus* (either out of tradition, or out of conjecture
and likelihood) Records to have been, That God would make both
her Language and her Beauty acceptable to the King that day: Out
of all these, she had hope of good success; and howsoever if she failed
420 of her purpose, she was under two Laws, of which it was necessary to
obey that which concerned the glory of God. And therefore *Daniels*
confidence, and *Daniels* words became her well, *Behold, our God is*   [Dan. 3.17]

*able to deliver me, and he will deliver me; but if he will not, I must
not forsake his honor, nor abandon his service: And therefore,* Si
peream, peream, *If I perish, I perish.*

It is not always a Christian resolution, *Si peream, peream,* to say,
If I perish, I perish: I care not whether I perish, or no: To admit, to
invite, to tempt tentations, and occasions of sin, and so to put our
selves to the hazard of a spiritual perishing; to give fire to concupis-
430 cencies with licentious Meditations, either of sinful pleasures past, or
of that which we have then in our purpose and pursuit; to fewel this
fire with meats of curiosity and provocation; to blow this fire with
lascivious discourses and Letters, and Protestations, this admits no
such condition, *Si pereas,* If thou perish; but *periisti,* thou art perished
already; thou didst then perish, when thou didst so desperately cast
thy self into the danger of perishing. And as he that casts himself
from a steeple, doth not break his neck till he touch the ground; but
yet he is truly said to have killed himself, when he threw himself
towards the ground; So in those preparations, and invitations to sin,
440 we perish, before we perish, before we commit the act, the sin it self:
We perished then, when we opened our selves to the danger of the
sin; so also, if a man will wring out, not the Club out of *Hercules*
hands, but the sword out of Gods hands; if a man will usurpe upon
Gods jurisdiction, and become a Magistrate to himself, and revenge
his own quarrels, and in an inordinate defence of imaginary honor,
expose himself to danger in duel, with a *si peream, peream, If I perish,
I perish,* that is not onely true, if he perish, he perishes; if he perish
temporally, he perishes spiritually too, and goes out of the world
loaded with that, and with all his other sins; but it is also true, that if
450 he perish not, he perishes; he comes back loaded both with the temporal, and with the spiritual death, both with the blood, and with the
damnation of that man, who perished suddenly, and without repentance by his sword.

To contract this, and conclude all, If a man have nothing in his
contemplation, but dignity, and high place; if he have not Vertue, and
Religion, and a Conscience of having deserved well of his Countrey,
and the love of God and godly men, for his sustentation and assurance, but onely to tower up after dignity, as a Hawk after a prey, and
think that he may boldly say, as an impossible supposition, *Si peream,*

⁴⁶⁰ *peream, If I perish, I perish;* as though it were impossible he should
perish; he shall be subject to that derision of the King of *Babylon,*
Quomodo Cecidisti, How art thou faln from Heaven, O Lucifer, thou
son of the morning! How art thou cast down to the ground, that didst
cast lots upon the Nations!

Esa. 14.12

But that provident and religious Soul, which proceeds in all her
enterprises as *Esther* did in her preparations, which first calls an as-
sembly of all her Country-men, that is, them of the houshold of the
Faithful, the Congregation of Christs Church, and the Communion
of Saints, and comes to participate the benefit of publick Prayers in
⁴⁷⁰ his house, in convenient times; and then doth the same in her own
house, within doors, she, and her maids, that is, she and all her senses
and faculties, This soul may also come to *Esthers* resolution, to go
in to the King, though it be not according to the Law; though that
Law be, That neither fornicator, nor adulterer, nor wanton, nor thief,
nor drunkard, nor covetous, nor extortioner, nor railer, shall have
access into the Kingdom of Heaven; yet this soul thus prepared shall
feel a comfortable assurance, that this Law was made for servants, and
not for sons, nor for the Spouse of Christ, his Church, and the living
Members thereof; and she may boldly say, *Si peream, peream;* It is
⁴⁸⁰ all one though I perish; or as it is in the Original, *Vecasher, quomodo-*
cunque peream; whether I perish in my estimation and opinion
with men, whether I perish in my fortunes, honor, or health, *quo-*
modocunque, it is all one; *Heaven and earth shall pass away, but Gods*
word shall not pass; and we have both that word of God, which shall
never have end, and that word of God which never had beginning.
His Word, as it is his Promise, his Scriptures, and his Word, as it is
himself: Christ Jesus for our assurance and security, that that Law
of denying sinners access, and turning his face from them, is not a
perpetual, not an irrevocable Law; but that that himself says, belongs
⁴⁹⁰ to us: *For a little while have I forsaken thee, but with great compassion*
will I gather thee; for a moment in mine anger I hid my face from
thee for a little season, but with everlasting mercy have I had com-
passion on thee, saith the Lord Christ thy Redeemer. How riotously
and voluptuously soever I have surfeited upon sin heretofore, yet if
I fast that fast now; how disobedient soever I have been to my Supe-
riors heretofore, yet if I apply my self to a conscionable humility to

[1 Cor.
6.9–10]

[Mat. 24.35]

[Isa. 54.7]

them now; howsoever, if I have neglected necessary duties in my self,
or neglected them in my Family, that either I have not been careful
to give good example, or not careful that they should do according to
my example, (and by the way, it is not only the Master of a house
that hath the charge of a Family, but every person, every servant in
the house, that hath a body and a soul, hath a house, and a family
to look to, and to answer for) yet if I become careful now, that both
I, I my self will, and my whole house, all my family shall serve the
Lord; If I be thus prepar'd, thus dispos'd, thus matur'd, thus mellow'd,
thus suppled, thus entendred, to the admitting of any impressions
from the hand of my God; though there seem to be a general Law
spread over all, an universal War, an universal Famine, an universal
Pestilence over the whole Nation, yet I shall come either to an assurance, that though there fall so many thousands on this and on that
hand, it shall not reach me; *Etsi pereant,* Though others perish, I
shall not perish; or to this assurance, *Si peream, peream,* If I perish by
the good pleasure of God, I shall be well content to perish so; and to
this also, *Etsi peream, non pereo,* Though I perish, I do not perish;
though I die, I do not die; but as that piece of money which was but
the money of a poor man, being given in Subsidy, becomes a part of
the Royal Exchequer: So this body, which is but the body of a sinful
man, being given in Subsidy, as a Contribution to the Glory of my
God, in the grave, becomes a part of Gods Exchequer; and when he
opens it, he shall issue out this money, that is, manifest it again cloth'd
in his Glory: that body which in me was but a piece of Copper money,
he shall make a Talent of Gold; and which in me was but a grain of
Wheat buried in the earth, he shall multiply into many ears, not of
the same Wheat, but of Angels food; The Angels shall feed and rejoyce at my resurrection, when they shall see me in my soul, to have all
that they have, and in my body, to have that that they have not.

Number 12.

Preached to the Nobility.

LUKE 23.24. *FATHER FORGIVE THEM, FOR THEY KNOW NOT WHAT THEY DO.*

THE WORD of God is either the co-eternall and co-essentiall Sonne, our Saviour, which tooke flesh (*Verbum Caro factum est*) or it is the spirit of his mouth, by which we live, and *not by bread onely*. And so, in a large acceptation, every truth is the word of God; for truth is uniforme, and irrepugnant, and indivisible, as God. *Omne verum est omni vero consentiens*. More strictly the word of God, is that which God hath uttered, either in writing, as twice in the Tables to *Moses;* or by ministery of Angels, or Prophets, in words; or by the unborne, in action, as in *John Baptists* exultation within his mother; or by new-borne, from the mouths of babes and sucklings; or by things unreasonable, as in *Balaams* Asse; or insensible, as in the whole booke of such creatures, *The heavens declare the glory of God, &c.* But nothing is more properly the word of God to us, then that which God himself speakes in those Organs and Instruments, which himself hath assumed for his chiefest worke, our redemption. For in creation God spoke, but in redemption he did; and more, he suffered. And of that kinde are these words. God in his chosen man-hood saith, *Father, forgive them, for they know not what they do.*

These words shall be fitliest considered, like a goodly palace, if we rest a little, as in an outward Court, upon consideration of prayer in generall; and then draw neare the view of the Palace, in a second Court, considering this speciall prayer in generall, as the face of the whole palace. Thirdly, we will passe thorow the chiefest rooms of the palace it self; and then insist upon foure steps: 1. Of whom he

[Joh. 1.14]
[Deut. 8.3;
Mat. 4.4]

[Psal. 19.1]

begs, (*Father.*) 2. What he asks, (*forgive them.*) 3. That he prays upon reason, (*for.*) 4. What the reason is, (*they know not.*) And lastly, going into the backside of all, we will cast the objections: as why onely *Luke* remembers this prayer: and why this prayer, (as it
30 seemes by the punishment continuing upon the Jews to this day) was not obtained at Gods hands.

Of Prayer
[Mat. 7.7]

[Luk. 19.46]

So therefore prayer is our first entry, for when it is said, *Ask and it shall be given,* it is also said, *Knock and it shall be opened,* showing that by prayer our entrance is. And not the entry onely, but the whole house: *My house is the house of prayer.* Of all the conduits and conveyances of Gods graces to us, none hath been so little subject to cavillations, as this of prayer. The Sacraments have fallen into the hands of flatterers and robbers. Some have attributed too much to them, some detracted. Some have painted them, some have with-
40 drawn their naturall complexion. It hath been disputed, whether they be, how many they be, what they be, and what they do. The preaching of the word hath been made a servant of ambitions, and a shop of many mens new-fangled wares. Almost every meanes between God and man, suffers some adulteratings and disguises: But prayer least: And it hath most wayes and addresses. It may be mentall, for we may thinke prayers. It may be vocall, for we may speake prayers. It may

[Gen. 18.20]
[Tobit 12.9]
[1.12]

be actuall, for we do prayers. For deeds have voyce; the vices of *Sodome* did cry, and the Almes of *Toby.* And if it were proper for St. *John,* in the first of the *Revelations* to turne back to see a voyce, it is
50 more likely God will looke down, to heare a worke. So then to do the office of your vocation sincerely, is to pray. How much the favourites of Princes, and great personages labour, that they may be thought to have been in private conference with the Prince. And though they be forced to wait upon his purposes, and talk of what he will, how fain they would be thought to have solicited their own, or their Dependants businesse. With the Prince of Princes, this every man may doe truly; and the sooner, the more begger he is: for no man is heard here, but *in formâ pauperis.*

Here we may talk long, welcomely, of our own affaires, and be
60 sure to speed. You cannot whisper so low alone in your Chamber, but he heares you, nor sing so lowd in the Congregation, but he distinguishes you. He grudges not to be chidden and disputed with, by

Job. The Arrows of the Almighty are in me, and the venim thereof [6.4, 12]
hath drunk up my spirit. Is my strength, the strength of stones, or is
my flesh of brasse, &c. Not to be directed and counselled by *Jonas:*
who was angry and sayd; Did not I say, when I was in my Country, [4.2, 9]
thou wouldest deale thus? And when the Lord sayd, *Doest thou well*
to be angry? He replyed, *I doe well to be angry to the death.* Nor
almost to be threatned and neglected by *Moses: Doe this, or blot my* [Exod.
70 *name out of thy book.* It is an Honour to be able to say to servants, 32.32]
Doe this: But to say to God, *Domine fac hoc,* and prevail, is more;
And yet more easie. God is replenishingly every where; but most
contractedly, and workingly in the Temple. Since then every rectified
man, is the temple of the Holy Ghost, when he prays; it is the Holy
Ghost it selfe that prays; and what can be denyed, where the Asker
gives? He plays with us, as children, shewes us pleasing things, that
we may cry for them, and have them. Before we call, he answers, and
when we speak, he heares: so *Esay* 65.24. Physicians observe some
symptomes so violent, that they must neglect the disease for a time,
80 and labour to cure the accident; as burning fevers, in Dysenteries. So
in the sinfull consumption of the soule, a stupidity and indisposition
to prayer, must first be cured. For, *Ye lust, and have not, because ye*
aske not, Jam. 4.2. The adulterous Mother of the three great brothers,
Gratian, Lombard, and *Comestor,* being warned by her Confessour,
to be sorry for her fact, sayd, she could not, because her fault had so
much profited the Church. At least, sayd he, be sorry that thou canst
not be sorry. So whosoever thou be, that canst not readily pray, at
least pray, that thou mayst pray. For, as in bodily, so in spirituall
diseases, it is a desperate state, to be speechlesse.
90 It were unmannerlinesse to hold you longer in the Entry. One turne Of this
in the inner Court, of this speciall prayer in generall, and so enter the Prayer
Palace. This is not a prayer for his own ease, as that in his Agony
seemes. It hath none of those infirmities, which curious schismatikes
finde in that. No suspicion of ignorance, as there, (*If it be possible.*) [Mat. 26.39]
No tergiversation nor abandoning the noble worke which he had
begunne, as there, (*Let this cup passe.*) It is not an exemplar, or
forme, for us to imitate precisely, (otherwise then in the Doctrine) as
that Prayer, *Mat.* 6. which we call the Lords Prayer, not because he
sayd it, for he could never say, *forgive us our trespasses,* but because

[11.2]

¹⁰⁰ he commanded us to say it. For though by *Matthew,* which saith, *After this manner pray,* we seem not bound to the words, yet *Luke* sayth, *When you pray,* say, *Our Father which art, &c.* But this is a prayer of God, to God. Not as the Talmudist Jews faine God to pray to himselfe, *Sit voluntas mea, ut misericordia mea superet iram meam;* But as when forain merchandise is mis-ported, the Prince may permit, or inhibit his Subjects to buy it, or not to buy it. Our blessed Saviour arriving in this world fraited with salvation, a thing which this world never had power to have without him, except in that short time, between mans Creation and fall, he by this prayer begs, that ¹¹⁰ even to these despisers of it, it may be communicable, and that their ignorance of the value of it, may not deprive them of it. Teaching that by example here, which he gave in precept before, *Mat.* 5.44. *Pray for them which persecute you, that you may be the children of*

Father   *your Father which is in heaven.* Therefore, doing so now, he might well say, *Father, forgive them,* which is the first room in this glorious Palace. And in this contemplation, O my unworthy soule, thou art presently in the presence. No passing of guards, nor ushers. No examination of thy degree or habit. The Prince is not asleep, nor private, nor weary of giving, nor refers to others. He puts thee not to prevaile ¹²⁰ by Angels nor Archangels. But lest any thing might hinder thee, from coming into his presence, his presence comes into thee. And lest Majesty should dazell thee, thou art to speake but to thy Father. Of which word, *Abba,* the root is, *To will;* from which root, the fruit also must be willingnesse, and propensenesse to grant. God is the Father of Christ, by that mysticall and eternall unexpressible generation, which never began nor ended. Of which incomprehensible mystery, *Moses* and the ancient Prophets spake so little, and so indirectly, that till the dawning of the day of Christ, after *Esdras* time, those places seem not to be intended of the Trinity. Nay, a good while ¹³⁰ after Christ, they were but tenderly applyed to that sense. And at this day, the most of the writers in the reformed Churches, considering that we need not such farre fetcht, and such forced helps, and withall, weighing how well the Jews of these times are provided with other expositions of those places, are very sparing in using them, but content themselves modestly herein, with the testimonies of the New Testament. Truly, this mystery is rather the object of faith then rea-

son; and it is enough that we believe Christ to have ever been the Son
of God, by such generation, and our selves his sonnes by adoption. So
that God is Father to all; but yet so, that though Christ say, *Iohn* 10. [29, 30]
¹⁴⁰ *My Father is greater then all,* he addes, *I and my Father are all one,*
to shew his eternall interest: and *Iohn* 20. Hee seemes to put a difference, *I goe to my Father, and your Father, my God, and your God.* [17]
The Roman stories have, that when *Claudius* saw it conduce to his
ends, to get the tribuneship, of which he was incapable, because a
Patrician, he suffered himself to be adopted. But against this Adoption, two exceptions were found; one, that he was adopted by a man
of lower ranke, a Plebeian; which was unnaturall; and by a younger
man then himselfe, which took away the presentation of a Father.
But our Adoption is regular. For first, we are made the sonnes of the
¹⁵⁰ Most High, and thus alsoe by the ancient of daies. There was no one
word, by which he could so nobly have maintained his Dignity, kept
his station, justified his cause, and withall expressed his humility and
charity, as this, Father. They crucifyed him, for saying himself to be
the Sonne of God. And in the midst of torment, he both professes the
same still, and lets them see, that they have no other way of forgivenesse, but that he is the Sonne of that Father. For no man cometh to [Joh. 14.6]
the Father but by the Son.

   And at this voice (Father) O most blessed Saviour, thy Father, Forgive
which is so fully thine, that for thy sake, he is ours too, which is so them
¹⁶⁰ wholly thine, that he is thy selfe, which is all mercy, yet will not
spare thee, all justice, yet will not destroy us. And that glorious Army
of Angels, which hitherto by their own integrity maintained their
first and pure condition, and by this worke of thine, now neare the
Consummatum est, attend a confirmation, and infallibility of ever [Joh. 19.30]
remaining so; And that faithfull company of departed Saints, to
whom thy merit must open a more inward and familiar room in thy
Fathers Kingdome, stand all attentive, to heare what thou wilt aske
of this Father. And what shall they hear? what doest thou aske?
Forgive them, forgive them? Must murderers be forgiven? Must the
¹⁷⁰ offended aske it? And must a Father grant it? And must he be
solicited, and remembred by the name of Father to doe it? Was not
thy passion enough, but thou must have compassion? And is thy
mercy so violent, that thou wilt have a fellow-feeling of their im-

minent afflictions, before they have any feeling? The Angels might expect a present employment for their destruction: the Saints might be out of feare, that they should be assumed or mingled in their fellowship. But thou wilt have them pardoned. And yet doest not out of thine own fulnesse pardon them, as thou didst the theef upon the Crosse, because he did already confesse thee; but thou tellest them, 180 that they may be forgiven, but at thy request, and if they acknowledge their Advocate to be the Son of God. *Father, forgive them.* I that cannot revenge thy quarrell, cannot forgive them. I that could not be saved, but by their offence, cannot forgive them. And must a Father, Almighty, and well pleased in thee, forgive them? Thou art more charitable towards them, then by thy direction wee may be to our selvs. We must pray for our selvs limitedly, forgive us, as we forgive. But thou wilt have their forgivenes illimited and unconditioned. Thou seemest not so much as to presume a repentance; which is so essentiall, and necessary in all transgressions, as where by mans fault 190 the actions of God are diverted from his appointed ends, God himself is content to repent the doing of them. As he repented first the making of man, and then the making of a King. But God will have them within the armes of his generall pardon. And we are all delivered from our Debts; for God hath given his word, his co-essentiall word, for us all. And though, (as in other prodigall debts, the Interest exceed the Principall) our Actuall sinnes exceede our Originall, yet God by giving his word for us, hath acquitted all.

But the Affections of our Saviour are not inordinate, nor irregular. He hath a *For,* for his Prayer: *Forgive them, for, &c.* And where he 200 hath not this *For,* as in his Praier in his agony, he quickly interrupts the violence of his request, with a But, *Father, let this cup passe;* but *not my will:* In that form of Prayer which himself taught us, he hath appointed a *for,* on Gods part, which is ever the same unchangeable: *For thine is the Kingdome;* Therefore supplications belong to thee: *The power, Thou openest thy hand and fillest every living thing: The Glory,* for thy Name is glorified in thy grants. But because on our part, the occasions are variable, he hath left our *for,* to our religious discretion. For, when it is said, James 4. *You lust and have not, because you aske not;* it followeth presently, *You aske and misse,* 210 *because you aske amisse.* It is not a fit *for,* for every private man, to

[Gen. 6.6]
[1 Sam. 15.11]

For

[Psa. 145.16]

[ver. 2]
[ver. 3]

aske much means, for he would doe much good. I must not pray,
Lord put into my hands the strength of Christian Kings, for out of
my zeale, I will imploy thy benefits to thine advantage, thy Souldiers
against thine enemies, and be a bank against that Deluge, wherewith
thine enemy the Turk threatens to overflow thy people. I must not
pray, Lord fill my heart with knowledge and understanding, for I
would compose the Schismes in thy Church, and reduce thy garment
to the first continuall and seemlesse integrity; and redresse the deafnesses and oppressions of Judges, and Officers. But he gave us a con-
220 venient scantling for our *fors,* who prayed, Give me enough, for I
may else despair, give me not too much, for so I may presume. Of
Schoolmen, some affirm Prayer to be an act of our will; for we would
have that which we aske. Others, of our understanding; for by it we
ascend to God, and better our knowledge, which is the proper aliment
and food of our understanding; so, that is a perplexed case. But all
agree, that it is an act of our Reason, and therefore must be reasonable. For onely reasonable things can pray; for the beasts and Ravens,
Psalme 147.9. are not said to pray for food, but *to cry.* Two things are
required to make a Prayer. 1. *Pius affectus,* which was not in the
230 Devills request, Matth. 8.31. *Let us goe into the Swine;* nor Job 1.11.
Stretch out thy hand, and touch all he hath; and, *stretch out thy hand,
and touch his bones;* and therefore these were not Prayers. And it
must be *Rerum decentium:* for our government in that point, this
may inform us. Things absolutely good, as Remission of sinnes, we
may absolutely beg: and, to escape things absolutely ill, as sinne. But
mean and indifferent things, qualified by the circumstances, we must
aske conditionally and referringly to the givers will. For 2 Cor. 12.8.
when *Paul* begged *stimulum Carnis* to be taken from him, it was not
granted, but he had this answer, *My grace is sufficient for thee.*
240 Let us now (not in curiosity, but for instruction) consider the
reason: *They know not what they doe.* First, if Ignorance excuse:
And then, if they were ignorant.
Hast thou, O God, filled all thy Scriptures, both of thy *Recorders*
and *Notaries,* which have penned the *History of thy love, to thy
People;* and of thy *Secretaries* the Prophets, admitted to the fore-
knowledge of thy purposes, and instructed in thy Cabinet; hast thou
filled these with prayses and perswasions of wisedome and knowl-

[Prov. 30.8, 9]

[Job 2.5]

They know
not
Ignorance

edge, and must these persecutors be pardoned for their ignorance?
Hast thou bid *Esay* to say, 27.11. *It is a people of no understanding,*
²⁵⁰ *therefore he that made them, shall not have compassion of them.* And
Hosea 4.6. *My people are destroyed for lack of knowledge;* and now
dost thou say, Forgive them because they know not? Shall ignorance,
which is often the cause of sinne, often a sinne it self, often the punishment of sinne, and ever an infirmity and disease contracted by the
first great sinne, advantage them? *Who can understand his faults?*
saith the man according to thy heart, *Psalme* 19.12. *Lord cleanse me
from my secret faults:* He durst not make his ignorance the reason
of his prayer, but prayed against ignorance. But thy Mercy is as the
Sea: both before it was the Sea, for it overspreads the whole world;
²⁶⁰ and since it was called into limits: for it is not the lesse infinite for
that. And as by the Sea, the most remote and distant Nations enjoy
one another, by traffique and commerce, East and West becoming
neighbours: so by mercy, the most different things are united and
reconciled; Sinners have Heaven; Traytors are in the Princes bosome;
and ignorant persons are in the spring of wisdome, being forgiven,
not onely though they be ignorant, but because they are ignorant. But
all ignorance is not excusable; nor any lesse excusable, then not to
know, what ignorance is not to be excused. Therefore, there is an
ignorance which they call *Nescientiam,* a not knowing of things not
²⁷⁰ appertaining to us. This we had had, though *Adam* had stood; and
the Angels have it, for they know not the latter day, and therefore
for this, we are not chargeable. They call the other privation, which if
it proceed meerly from our owne sluggishnesse, in not searching the
meanes made for our instruction, is ever inexcusable. If from God,
who for his owne just ends hath cast clouds over those lights which
should guide us, it is often excusable. For 1 *Tim.* 1.13. *Paul* saith, *I
was a blasphemer, and a persecutor, and an oppressor, but I was received to mercy, for I did it ignorantly, through unbelief.* So, though
we are all bound to believe, and therefore faults done by unbeliefe
²⁸⁰ cannot escape the name and nature of sinne, yet since beliefe is the
immediate gift of God, faults done by unbeliefe, without malicious
concurrences and circumstances, obtaine mercy and pardon from that
abundant fountaine of grace, Christ Jesus. And therefore it was a just
reason, *Forgive them, for they know not.* If they knew not, which is

evident, both by this speech from truth it self, and by 1 *Cor.* 2.8. *Had they known it, they would not have crucified the Lord of glory;* and *Acts* 3.17. *I know that through ignorance ye did it.* And though after so many powerfull miracles, this ignorance were vincible, God having revealed enough to convert them, yet there seemes to be enough on their parts, to make it a perplexed case, and to excuse, though not a malitious persecuting, yet a not consenting to his Doctrine. For they had a Law, *Whosoever shall make himself the sonne of God, let him dye:* And they spoke out of their Lawes, when they said, *We have no other King but Cæsar.* There were therefore some among them reasonably, and zealously ignorant. And for those, the Sonne ever-welcome, and well-heard, begged of his Father, ever accessible, and exorable, a pardon ever ready and naturall.

We have now passed through all those roomes which we unlockt and opened at first. And now may that point, Why this prayer is remembred onely by one Evangelist, and why by *Luke,* be modestly inquired: For we are all admitted and welcommed into the acquaintance of the Scriptures, upon such conditions as travellers are into other Countries: if we come as praisers and admirers of their Commodities and Government, not as spies into the mysteries of their State, nor searchers, nor calumniators of their weaknesses. For though the Scriptures, like a strong rectified State, be not endangered by such a curious malice of any, yet he which brings that, deserves no admittance. When those great Commissioners which are called the Septuagint, sent from *Hierusalem,* to translate the Hebrew Scriptures into Greeke, had perfected their work, it was, and is an argument of Divine assistance, that writing severally, they differed not. The same may prove even to weake and faithlesse men, that the holy Ghost super-intended the foure Evangelists, because they differ not; as they which have written their harmonies, make it evident: But to us, faith teacheth the other way. And we conclude not, because they agree, the holy Ghost directed; for heathen Writers and Malefactors in examinations do so; but because the holy Ghost directed, we know they agree, and differ not. For as an honest man, ever of the same thoughts, differs not from himself, though he do not ever say the same things, if he say not contraries; so the foure Evangelists observe the uniformity and samenesse of their guide, though all did not say all the

[Joh. 19.7]

[Joh. 19.15]

same things, since none contradicts any. And as, when my soule, which enables all my limbs to their functions, disposes my legs to go, my whole body is truly said to go, because none stayes behinde; so when the holy Spirit, which had made himself as a common soule to their foure soules, directed one of them to say any thing, all are well understood to have said it. And therefore when to that place in *Matth.* 27.9. where that Evangelist cites the Prophet *Jeremy,* for words spoken by *Zachary,* many medicines are applyed by the Fathers; as,
330 That many copies have no name, That *Jeremy* might be binominous, and have both names, a thing frequent in the Bible, That it might be the error of a transcriber, That there was extant an *Apocryph* booke of *Jeremy,* in which these words were, and sometimes things of such

[2 Tim. 3.8]

books were vouched, as *Jannes* and *Jambres* by *Paul;* St. *Augustine* insists upon, and teaches rather this, That it is more wonderfull, that all the Prophets spake by one Spirit, and so agreed, then if any one of them had spoken all those things; And therefore he adds, *Singula sunt omnium, & omnia sunt singulorum,* All say what any of them say; And in this sense most congruously is that of St. *Hierome* apply-
340 able, that the foure Evangelists are *Quadriga Divina,* That as the foure Chariot wheeles, though they looke to the foure corners of the world, yet they move to one end and one way, so the Evangelists have both one scope, and one way.

Yet not so precisely, but that they differ in words: For as their generall intention, common to them all begat that consent, so a private reason peculiar to each of them, for the writing of their Histories at that time, made those diversities which seem to be. For *Matthew,* after he had preached to the Jewes, and was to be transplanted into another vineyard, the Gentiles, left them written in their owne tongue,
350 for permanency, which he had before preached unto them transitorily by word. *Mark,* when the Gospell fructified in the West, and the Church enlarged her self, and grew a great body, and therefore required more food, out of *Peters* Dictates, and by his approbation published his Evangile. Not an Epitome of *Matthewes,* as Saint *Jerome* (I know not why) imagines, but a just and intire History of our blessed Saviour. And as *Matthewes* reason was to supply a want in the Eastern Church, *Markes* in the Western; so on the other side *Lukes* was to cut off an excesse and superfluitie: for then many had

undertaken this Story, and dangerously inserted and mingled uncer-
360 tainties and obnoxious improbabilities: and he was more curious and
more particular then the rest, both because he was more learned, and
because he was so individuall a companion of the most learned Saint
Paul, and did so much write *Pauls* words, that *Eusebius* thereupon
mistaketh the words 2 *Tim.* 2.8. *Christ is raised according to my
Gospell,* to prove that *Paul* was author of this Gospell attributed to
Luke. John the Minion of *Christ* upon earth, and survivor of the
Apostles, (whose books rather seem fallen from Heaven, and writ
with the hand which ingraved the stone Tables, then a mans work)
because the heresies of *Ebion* and *Cerinthus* were rooted, who upon
370 this true ground, then evident and fresh, that Christ had spoke many
things which none of the other three Evangelists had Recorded,
uttered many things as his, which he never spoke: *John* I say, more
diligently then the rest handleth his Divinity, and his Sermons, things
specially brought into question by them. So therefore all writ one
thing, yet all have some things particular. And *Luke* most, for he
writ last of three, and largeliest for himselfe, *Act.* 1.1 saith, *I have
made the former Treatise of all that Jesus began to doe and teach,
untill the Day that he was taken up;* which speech, lest the words in
the last of *John, If all were written which Jesus did, the world could*
380 *not contain the Bookes,* should condemne, *Ambrose* and *Chrysostome*
interpret well out of the words themselves, *Scripsit de omnibus, non
omnia,* He writ of all, but not all: for it must have the same limitation, which *Paul* giveth his words, who saith, *Acts* 20. in one verse,
*I have kept nothing back, but have shewed you all the counsell of
God;* and in another, *I kept back nothing that was profitable.* It is   [27]
another peculiar singularity of *Lukes,* that he addresseth his History   [20]
to one man, *Theophilus.* For it is but weakely surmised, that he chose
that name, for all *lovers of God,* because the interpretation of the
word suffereth it, since he addeth *most noble Theophilus.* But the
390 work doth not the lesse belong to the whole Church, for that, no more
then his Masters Epistles doe though they be directed to particulars.

It is also a singularitie in him to write upon that reason, because
divers have written. In humane knowledge, to abridge or suck, and
then suppresse other Authors, is not ever honest nor profitable: We
see after that vast enterprise of *Justinian,* who distilled all the Law

into one vessell, and made one Booke of 2000, suppressing all the rest, *Alciate* wisheth he had let them alone, and thinketh the Doctors of our times, would better have drawn usefull things from those volumes, then his *Trebonian* and *Dorothee* did. And *Aristotle* after, by
400 the immense liberality of *Alexander,* he had ingrossed all Authors, is said to have defaced all, that he might be in stead of all: And therefore, since they cannot rise against him, he imputes to them errours which they held not: vouches onely such objections from them, as he is able to answer; and propounds all good things in his own name, which he ought to them. But in this History of *Lukes,* it is otherwise: He had no authority to suppresse them, nor doth he reprehend or calumniate them, but writes the truth simply, and leaves it to out-
[Exod. 7.12] weare falshood: and so it hath: *Moses* rod hath devoured the Conjurers rods, and *Lukes* Story still retains the majestie of the maker,
410 and theirs are not.

Other singularities in *Luke,* of form or matter, I omit, and end with one like this in our Text. As in the apprehending of our blessed
[Mat. 26.51; Saviour, all the Evangelists record, that *Peter* cut off *Malchus* eare,
Mark 14.47; but onely *Luke* remembers the healing of it again: (I think) because
Luke 22.50– that act of curing, was most present and obvious to his consideration,
51; who was a Physician: so he was therefore most apt, to remember this
Joh. 18.10] Prayer of Christ, which is the Physick and *Balsamum* of our Soule, and must be applied to us all, (for we doe all Crucifie him, and we know not what we do.) And therefore Saint *Hierome* gave a right
420 Character of him, in his Epistle to *Paulinus, Fuit Medicus, & pariter omnia verba illius, Animæ languentis sunt Medicinæ,* As he was a Physitian, so all his words are Physick for a languishing soule.

Now let us dispatch the last consideration, of the effect of this Prayer. Did Christ intend the forgivenesse of the Jewes, whose utter ruine God (that is, himselfe) had fore-decreed? And which he foresaw, and bewaild even then hanging upon the Crosse? For those
[Mat. 27.46] Divines which reverently forbeare to interpret the words *Lord, Lord, why hast thou forsaken me?* of a suffering hell in his soule, or of a
[v. 32] departing of the Father from him; (for *Joh.* 16. it is, *I am not alone,*
430 *for the Father is with me*) offer no exposition of those words more convenient, then that the foresight of the Jewes imminent calamities, expressed and drew those words from him: *In their Afflictions, were*

all kindes, and all degrees of Miserie. So that as one writer of the
Roman story saith elegantly, *He that considereth the Acts of Rome,
considereth not the Acts of one People, but of Mankinde:* I may truly
say of the Jewes Afflictions, he that knoweth them, is ignorant of
nothing that this world can threaten. For to that which the present
authority of the Romanes inflicted upon them, our Schools have
added upon their posterities; that they are as slaves to Christians,
440 and their goods subject to spoile, if the Lawes of the Princes where
they live, did not out of indulgency defend them. Did he then aske,
and was not heard? God forbid. A man is heard, when that is given
which his will desired; and our will is ever understood to be a will
rectified, and concurrent with God. This is *Voluntas,* a discoursed
and examined will. That which is upon the first sight of the object,
is *Velleitas,* a willingnesse, which we resist not, onely because we
thought not of it. And such a willingnesse had Christ, when suddenly
he wished that the cup might passe: but quickly conformed his will
to his Fathers. But in this Prayer his will was present, therefore
450 fulfilled. Briefly then, in this Prayer he commended not all the Jewes,
for he knew the chief to sin knowingly, and so out of the reach of
his reason, (*for they know not.*) Nor any, except they repented after:
for it is not ignorance, but repentance, which deriveth to us the
benefit of Gods pardon. For he that sinnes of Ignorance, may be
pardoned if he repent; but he that sinnes against his Conscience, and
is thereby impenitible, cannot be pardoned. And this is all, which I
will say of these words, *Father forgive them, for they know not what
they do.*

460 *O eternall God, look down from thy Throne to thy footstoole:
from thy blessed Company of Angels and Saints, to us, by our own
faults made more wretched and contemptible, then the wormes which
shall eat us, or the dust which we were, and shall be. O Lord, under
the weight of thy Justice we cannot stand. Nor had any other title to
thy mercie, but the Name of Father, and that we have forfeited. That
name of Sonnes of God, thou gavest to us, all at once in* Adam; *and
he gave it away from us all by his sinne. And thou hast given it again
to every one of us, in our regeneration by Baptisme, and we have lost
it again by our transgressions. And yet thou wert not weary of being*

⁴⁷⁰ *mercifull, but diddest choose one of us, to be a fit and worthy ransome*
for us all; and by the death of thy Christ, our Jesus, gavest us again
the title and priviledge of thy Sonnes; but with conditions, which
though easie, we have broke, and with a yoke, which though light,
and sweet, we have cast off. How shall we then dare to call thee
Father? Or to beg that thou wilt make one triall more of us? These
hearts are accustomed to rebellions, and hopelesse. But, O God, create
in us new hearts, hearts capable of the love and feare, due to a Father.
And then we shall dare to say, Father, *and to say,* Father forgive us.
Forgive us O Father, and all which are engaged, and accountable to
⁴⁸⁰ *thee for us: forgive our Parents, and those which undertooke for us*
in Baptisme. Forgive the civill Magistrate, and the Minister. Forgive
them their negligences, and us our stubbornnesses. And give us the
grace that we may ever sincerely say, both this Prayer of Example
and Counsell, Forgive our enemies, *and that other of Precept,* Our
Father which art in Heaven, *&c.*

Number 13.

Preached to the Earle of Carlile, and his Company, at Sion. [? 1622]

MARK 16.16. *HE THAT BELEEVETH NOT, SHALL BE DAMNED.*

THE FIRST words that are recorded in the Scriptures, to have been spoken by our Saviour, are those which he spoke to his father and mother, then when they had lost him at Jerusalem, *How is it that you sought me? knew yee not that I must be about my Fathers businesse?* And the last words, which are in this Euangelist recorded to have been spoken by him, to his Apostles, are then also, when they were to lose him in Jerusalem, when he was to depart out of their presence, and set himselfe in the heavenly Jerusalem, at the right hand of his Father: of which last words of his, this Text is a part. In his first words, those to his father and mother, he doth not rebuke their care in seeking him, nor their tendernesse in seeking him, (as they told him they did) *with heavy hearts:* But he lets them know, that, if not the band of nature, nor the reverentiall respect due to parents, then no respect in the world should hold him from a diligent proceeding in that worke which he came for, the advancing the kingdome of God in the salvation of mankinde. In his last words to his Apostles, he doth not discomfort them by his absence, for he sayes, *I am with you alwayes, even unto the end of the world:* But he incourageth them to a chearfull undertaking of their great worke, *the preaching of the Gospel to all Nations,* by many arguments, many inducements, of which, one of the waightiest is, That their preaching of the Gospel was not like to be uneffectuall, because he had given them the sharpest spur, and the strongest bridle upon man-

Mat. 28.20

kinde; *Præmium & pœnam,* Authority to reward the obedient, and authority to punish the rebellious and refractary man; he put into their hands the double key of Heaven, and of Hell; power to convey to the beleever Salvation, and upon him that beleeved not, to inflict eternall condemnation; *He that beleeveth not, shall be damned.*

Divisio

That then which man was to beleeve upon paine of damnation, if
30 he did not, being this Commission which Christ gave to his Apostles, we shall make it our first part of this Exercise, to consider the Commission it selfe, the subject of every mans necessary beliefe; And our second part shall be, The penalty, the inevitable, the irreparable, the intolerable, the inexpressible penalty, everlasting condemnation, *He that beleeveth not, shall be damned.* In the first of these parts, we shall first consider some circumstantiall, and then the substantiall parts of the Commission; (for though they be essentiall things, yet because they are not of the body of the Commission, we call them branches circumstantiall) First, *An sit,* whether there be such a Commission
40 or no; secondly, the *Vbi,* where this Commission is; and then the *Vnde,* from whence this Commission proceeds; And lastly the *Quò,* how farre it extends, and reaches; And having passed thorow these, wee must looke back for the substance of the Commission; for in the Text, *He that beleeveth not,* is implied this particle, *this,* this word *this, Hee that beleeveth not this,* that is, that which Christ hath said to his Apostles immediatly before the Text, which is indeed the substance of the Commission, consisting of three parts, *Ite prædicate,* goe and preach the Gospel, *Ite Baptizate,* goe and baptize them, *Ite docete,* goe and teach them to doe, and to practise all that I have
50 commanded; And after all these which doe but make up the first part, we shall descend to the second, which is the penalty; and as farre as the narrownesse of the time, and the narrownesse of your patience, and the narrownesse of my comprehension can reach, wee shall shew you the horror, the terror of that fearefull intermination, *Damnabitur, He that beleeveth not, shall be damned.*

1 Part
An sit

First then, it is within this *Crediderit,* that is, It is matter of faith to beleeve, that such a Commission there is, that God hath established meanes of salvation, and propagation of his Gospel here. If then this be matter of faith, where is the root of this faith? from
60 whence springs it? Is there any such thing writ in the heart of man,

that God hath proceeded so? Certainly as it is *in Agendis,* in those things which we are bound to do, which are all comprehended in the Decalogue, in the Ten Commandements, that there is nothing written there, in those stone Tables, which was not written before in the heart of man, (exemplifie it in that Commandement which seemes most removed from naturall reason, which is the observing of the Sabbath, yet even for that, for a Sabbath, man naturally finds this holy impression, and religious instinct in his heart, That there must bee an outward worship of that God, that hath made, and preserved
⁷⁰ him, and that is the substance, and morall part of that Commandement of the Sabbath) And it is *in Agendis,* that all things, that all men are bound to doe, all men have means to know; And as it is *in Sperandis, in Petendis,* of those things which man may hope for at Gods hand, or pray for, from him, there is a knowledge imprinted in mans heart too; (for the Lords Prayer is an abridgement of all those, and ex-emplifies also this in that Petition of the Lords Prayer, which may seeme most removed from naturall reason, That we must forgive those who have trespassed against us, yet even in that, every naturall man may see, That there is no reason for him, to looke for forgive-
⁸⁰ nesse from God, who can, and may justly come to an immediate execution of us, as soone as we have offended him, if we will not forgive another man, whom we cannot execute our selves, but must implore the Law, and the Magistrate to revenge our quarrell) As it is *in Agendis,* in all things which wee are bound to doe; As it is *in Petendis,* in all things which we may pray for, so it is *in Credendis,* all things that all men are bound to beleeve, all men have meanes to know.

This then, that God hath established meanes of salvation, being *Inter credenda,* one of those things which he is bound to beleeve,
⁹⁰ (for *hee that beleeveth not this, shall be damned*) Man hath thus much evidence of this in nature, that by naturall reason we know, that that God which must be worshipped, hath surely declared how he will be worshipped, and so we are led to seeke his revealed and manifested will, and that is no where to bee found but in his Scrip-tures. So that when all is done, the Ten Commandements, which is the sum of all that we are to doe; The Lords Prayer, which is the summe of all that we are to ask; and the Apostles Creed, which is

the summe of all that wee are to beleeve, are but declaratory, not introductory things; The same things are first written in mans heart,
100 though dimly and sub-obscurely, and then the same things are extended, shed in a brighter beame, in every leafe of the Scripture; And
the same things are recollected againe, into the Ten Commandements, into the Lords Prayer, and into the Apostles Creed, that we
might see them al together, and so take better view and hold of them.
The knowledge which wee have in nature, is the substance of all, as
[Gen.   all matter, Heaven and earth were created at once, in the beginning;
1.1–16]   and then the further knowledge which we have in Scripture, is
that light which God created after; for as by that light, men distinguished particular creatures, so by this light of the Scripture, wee
110 discerne our particular duties. And after this, as in the Creation, all
the light was gathered into the body of the Sunne, when that was
made; so all that is written in our hearts radically, and diffused in the
Scriptures more extensively, is reamassed, and reduced to the Ten
Commandements, the Lords Prayer, and to the Creed.

Cant. 4.12   The heart of man is *hortus,* it is a garden, a Paradise, where all
that is wholsome, and all that is delightfull growes, but it is *hortus
conclusus,* a garden that we our selves have walled in; It is *fons,* a
fountaine, where all knowledge springs, but *fons signatus,* a fountaine that our corruption hath sealed up. The heart is a booke,
120 legible enough, and intelligible in it selfe; but we have so interlined
that booke with impertinent knowledge, and so clasped up that
booke, for feare of reading our owne history, our owne sins, as that
we are greatest strangers, and the least conversant with the examination of our owne hearts. There is then *Myrrhe* in this garden,
but wee cannot smell it; and therefore, *All thy garments smell of*
Psal. 45.8   *Myrrhe,* saith *David,* that is, Gods garments; those Scriptures in
which God hath apparelled, and exhibited his will, they breathe the
Balme of the East, the savour of life, more discernably unto us. But
Cant. 1.13   after that too, there is *fasciculus Myrrhæ,* a bundle of *Myrrhe* to-
130 gether, *fasciculus Agendorum,* a whole bundle of those things which
we are bound to doe, in the Ten Commandements; *fasciculus Peten-
dorum,* a whole bundle of those things, which wee are bound to pray
for, in the Lords Prayer; and *fasciculus Credendorum,* a whole bundle
of those things, which we are bound to beleeve, in the Apostles

Creed; And in that last bundle of *Myrrhe,* in that Creed, is this
particular, *Vt credamus hoc,* That wee beleeve this, this, that God
hath established meanes of salvation here, and *He that beleeveth not
this,* that such a Commission there is, *shall be damned.*

In that bundle of *Myrrhe* then, where lies this that must neces-   *Vbi*
10 sarily bee beleeved, This Commission? In that Article of that Creed,
Credo Ecclesiam Catholicam, I beleeve the holy Catholique Church;
For till I come to that graine of *Myrrhe,* to beleeve the Catholique
Church, I have not the savour of life; Let me take in the first graine
of this bundle of *Myrrhe,* the first Article, *Credo in Deum Patrem,
I beleeve in God the Father,* by that I have a being, I am a creature,
but so is a contemptible worme, and so is a venemous spider as well
as I, so is a stinking weed, and so is a stinging nettle, as well as I;
so is the earth it selfe, that we tread under our feet, and so is that
ambitious spirit, which would have been as high as God, and is lower
50 then the lowest, the devill himself is a creature as well as I; I am but
that, by the first Article, but a creature; and I were better, if I were
not that, if I were no creature, (considering how I have used my
creation) if there were no more *Myrrhe* in this bundle then that first
graine, no more to be got by beleeving, but that I were a creature:
But take a great deale of this *Myrrhe* together, consider more
Articles, That *Christ is conceived,* and *borne,* and *crucified,* and *dead,*
and *buried,* and *risen,* and *ascended,* there is some savour in this;
But yet, if when we shall come to *Iudgement,* I must carry into his
presence, a menstruous conscience, and an ugly face, in which his
50 Image, by which he should know me, is utterly defaced, all this
Myrrhe of his Merits, and his Mercies, is but a savour of death unto
death unto me, since I, that knew the horror of my owne guiltinesse,
must know too, that whatsoever he be to others, he is a just Judge,
and therefore a condemning Judge to me; If I get farther then this
in the Creed, to the *Credo in Spiritum Sanctum, I beleeve in the
Holy Ghost,* where shall I finde the Holy Ghost? I lock my doore to
my selfe, and I throw my selfe downe in the presence of my God,
I devest my selfe of all worldly thoughts, and I bend all my powers,
and faculties upon God, as I think, and suddenly I finde my selfe
70 scattered, melted, fallen into vaine thoughts, into no thoughts; I am
upon my knees, and I talke, and think nothing; I deprehend my selfe

in it, and I goe about to mend it, I gather new forces, new purposes
to try againe, and doe better, and I doe the same thing againe. *I beleeve
in the Holy Ghost,* but doe not finde him, if I seeke him onely in
private prayer; But *in Ecclesia,* when I goe to meet him in the
Church, when I seeke him where hee hath promised to bee found,
when I seeke him in the execution of that Commission, which is
proposed to our faith in this Text, in his Ordinances, and meanes
of salvation in his Church, instantly the savour of this *Myrrhe* is
180 exalted, and multiplied to me; not a dew, but a shower is powred
out upon me, and presently followes *Communio Sanctorum, The
Communion of Saints,* the assistance of the Militant and Triumphant
Church in my behalfe; And presently followes *Remissio peccatorum,
The remission of sins,* the purifying of my conscience, in that water,
which is his blood, Baptisme, and in that wine, which is his blood,
the other Sacrament; and presently followes *Carnis resurrectio, A
resurrection of my body;* My body becomes no burthen to me; my
body is better now, then my soule was before; and even here I have
Goshen in my *Egypt,* incorruption in the midst of my dunghill,
190 spirit in the midst of my flesh, heaven upon earth; and presently followes *Vita æterna, Life everlasting;* this life of my body shall not last
ever, perchance not to put the last word to this sentence, nay the life
of my soul in heaven is not such as it is at the first. For that soule
there, even in heaven, shall receive an addition, and accesse of Joy,
and Glory in the resurrection of our bodies in the consummation.

When a winde brings the River to any low part of the banke, instantly it overflowes the whole Meadow; when that winde which
blowes where he will, *The Holy Ghost,* leads an humble soule to the
Article of the Church, to lay hold upon God, as God hath exhibited
200 himselfe in his Ordinances, instantly he is surrounded under the
blood of Christ Jesus, and all the benefits thereof; *The communion
of Saints, the remission of sins, the resurrection of the body, and the
life everlasting,* are poured out upon him. And therefore of this great
worke, which God hath done for man, in applying himselfe to man,
in the Ordinances of his Church, S. *Augustine* says, *Obscuriùs
dixerunt Prophetæ de Christo, quàm de Ecclesia,* The Prophets have
not spoken so clearly of the person of Christ, as they have of the
Church of Christ; for though S. *Hierom* interpret aright those words

August.

Hieron.

of *Adam* and *Eve, Erunt duo in carnem unam, They two shall be one*   [Gen. 2.24]
²¹⁰ *flesh,* to be applyable to the union which is betweene Christ and his
Church, (for so S. *Paul* himselfe applies them) that Christ and his   Ephes.5.[31]
Church are all one, as man and wife are all one, yet the wife is (or at
least, it had wont to be so) easilier found at home, then the husband;
wee can come to Christs Church, but we cannot come to him; The
Church is a Hill, and that is conspicuous naturally; but the Church
is such a Hill, as may be seene every where. S. *Augustine* askes his   August.
Auditory in one of his Sermons, doe any of you know the Hill Olympus? and himselfe sayes in their behalfe, none of you know it; no
more sayes he, do those that dwell at *Olympus* know *Giddabam*
²²⁰ *vestram,* some Hill which was about them; trouble not thy selfe to
know the formes and fashions of forraine particular Churches;
neither of a Church in the lake, nor a Church upon seven hils; but
since God hath planted thee in a Church, where all things necessary
for salvation are administred to thee, and where no erronious doctrine (even in the confession of our Adversaries) is affirmed and held,
that is the Hill, and that is the Catholique Church, and there is this
Commission in this text, meanes of salvation sincerely executed; So
then, such a Commission there is, and it is in the Article of the Creed,
that is the *ubi.*
²³⁰   We are now come in our order, to the third circumstantiall branch,   *Vnde*
the *Vnde,* from whence, and when this Commission issued, in which
we consider, that since we justly receive a deepe impression from the
words, which our friends spake at the time of their death, much more
would it worke upon us, if they could come and speake to us after
their death; You know what *Dives* said, *Si quis ex mortuis,* If one   Luke 16.[30]
from the dead might goe to my Brethren, he might bring them to any
thing. Now, *Primitiæ mortuorum,* The Lord of life, and yet the first
borne of the dead, Christ Jesus, returnes againe after his death, to
establish this Commission upon his Apostles; It hath therefore all
²⁴⁰ the formalities of a strong and valid Commission; Christ gives it,
Ex mero motu, meerely out of his owne goodnesse; He foresaw no
merit in us that moved him; neither was he moved by any mans
solicitations; for could it ever have fallen into any mans heart, to
have prayed to the Father, that his Son might take our Nature and
dye, and rise again, and settle a course upon earth, for our salvation,

if this had not first risen in the purpose of God himself? Would any
man ever have solicited or prayed him to proceed thus? It was *Ex
mero motu,* out of his owne goodnesse, and it was *Ex certa scientia,*
He was not deceived in his grant, he knew what he did, he knew
²⁵⁰ this Commission should be executed, in despight of all Heretiques,
and Tyrans that should oppose it; And as it was out of his owne Will,
and with his owne knowledge, so it was *Ex plenitudine potestatis,*
He exceeded not his Power; for Christ made this Commission then,
when (as it is expressed in the other Euangelist) he produced that

Mat. 28.18   evidence, *Data est mihi, All power is given to me in Heaven and in
earth;* where Christ speakes not of that Power, which he had by his
eternall generation, (though even that power were given him, for he
was *Deus de Deo,* God of God) nor he speakes not of that Power
which was given him as Man, which was great, but all that, he had
²⁶⁰ in the first minute of his conception, in the first union of the two
Natures, Divine and Humane together; but that Power, from which
he derives this Commission, is that, which he had purchased by his

[Joh. 16.33]   blood, and came to by conquest; *Ego vici mundum,* sayes Christ,
I have conquered the world, and comming in by conquest, I may
establish what forme of Government I will; and my will is, to governe my Kingdome by this Commission; and by these Commissioners, to the Worlds end; to establish these meanes upon earth, for the
salvation of the world.

       And as it hath all these formalities of a due Commission, made
²⁷⁰ without suite, made without error, made without defect of power:
so had it this also, that it was duely and authentically testified; for,
though this Euangelist name but the eleven Apostles to have beene
present, and they in this case might be thought *Testes domestici,*
Witnesses that witnesse to their owne, or to their Masters advantage;
Yet, the opinion which is most imbraced is, That this appearing of
Christ, which is intended here, is that appearing, which is spoken

1 Cor. 15.6   of by S. *Paul,* when he appeared to more then five hundred at once;
Christ rests not in his *Teste meipso,* That himselfe was his witnesse,
as Princes use to doe, (and as he might have done best of any, because
²⁸⁰ there were alwaies two more that testified with him, the Father, and
the Holy Ghost) he rests not in calling some of his Councell, and
principall Officers, to witnesse, as Princes have used too; but in a

Parliament of all States, Upper and Common house, Spirituall and
Temporall Apostles, Disciples and five hundred Brethren, he testifies this Commission.

Who then can measure the infinite mercy of Christ Jesus to us?
which mercy begun not when he began, by comming into this world;
for we were elected in him before the foundation of the world; nor
ended it when he ended, by going out of this world, for he returned
290 to this world againe, where he had suffered so much contempt and
torment, that he might establish this object of our faith, this that
wee are therefore bound to beleeve, a Commission, a Church, an
outward meanes of Salvation here; such a Commission there is, it
is grounded in the Creed, and it was given after his Resurrection.

In which Commission (being now come to the last of the circumstantiall Branches, the extent and reach of this Commission) we
finde, that it is *Omni Creaturæ*, before the Text, *Preach to every
Creature,* that is, Meanes of Salvation offered to every Creature; and
that is large enough, without that wilde extent that their S. *Francis*
300 gives it, in the Roman Church, whom they magnifie so much for
that religious simplicity, as they call it, who thought himselfe bound
literally by this Commission, *To preach to all Creatures,* and so did,
as we see in his brutish Homilies, *Frater Asine,* and *Frater Bos,*
Brother Oxe, and brother Asse, and the rest of his spirituall kindred;
But in this Commission, *Omnis Creatura, Every Creature,* is every
man; and to every man this Commission extends; Man is called
Omnis Creatura, Every creature, as *Eve* is called *Mater omnium
viventium,* though she were but the Mother of men, she is called the
Mother of all living, and yet all other creatures live, as well as Man;
10 Man is called Every creature, as it is said, *Omnis caro, All flesh had
corrupted his wayes upon earth,* though this corruption were but in
man, and other creatures were flesh as well as man; Man is every
creature, sayes *Origen,* because in him, *Tanquam in officina, omnes
Creaturæ conflantur,* Because all creatures were as it were melted in
one forge, and poured into one mold, when man was made. For,
these being all the distinctions which are in all creatures, first, a meere
being which stones and other inanimate creatures have; and then life
and growth, which trees and plants have; and after that, sense and
feeling, which beasts have; and lastly, reason and understanding,

Quo

Gen. 3.20

Gen. 6.12

Origen

Gregor.

August.

Esay 49.6

320 which Angels have, Man hath them all, and so in that respect is every creature, sayes *Origen:* He is so too, sayes *Gregory, Quia omnis creaturæ differentia in homine,* Because all the qualities and properties of all other creatures, how remote and distant, how contrary soever in themselves, yet they all meet in man; In man, if he be a flatterer, you shall finde the groveling and crawling of a Snake; and in a man, if he be ambitious, you shall finde the high flight and piercing of the Eagle; in a voluptuous sensual man, you shall finde [the] earthlinesse of the Hog; and in a licentious man, the intemperance, and distemper of the Goate; ever lustfull, and ever in a fever; ever in sicknesses con-
330 tracted by that sin, and yet ever in a desire to proceed in that sin; and so man is every creature in that respect, sayes *Gregory.* But he is especially so, sayes S. *Augustine, Quia omnis creatura propter hominem,* All creatures were made for man, man is the end of all, and therefore man is all, sayes *Augustine.* So that the two Euangelists have expressed one another well; for those whom this Euangelist S. *Marke* cals *all creatures,* S. *Matthew* cals *Omnes Gentes, All Nations;* And so, that which is attributed to Christ by way of Prophecy, *It is a small matter, that thou shouldest be my servant, to raise up the tribes of Iacob, and to restore the preserved of Israel, I will also give thee for*
340 *a light to the Gentiles, that thou maiest be my salvation unto the end of the earth;* That which is attributed to Christ there, is fulfilled in this Commission, given by Christ here; That he should be preached to all men; In which, wee rather admire then goe about to expresse his unexpressible mercy, who had that tendernesse in his care, that he would provide man meanes proportionable to man, visible, and audible meanes of salvation in a Church, and then that largenesse in his care, as that he would in his time impart it to all men; for els, how had it ever come to us? And so we passe from the Circumstances of the Commission, That it is, And where it is, And whence
350 it comes, And whither it goes, to the Substance it selfe.

This is expressed in three actions; first, *Ite prædicate, Goe and preach the Gospel;* And then *Baptizate, Baptize in the Name of the Father, Sonne, and Holy Ghost;* And *Docete servare, Teach them to observe all those things which I have commanded you;* for that *Hoc, Qui non crediderit hoc,* He that beleeves not this, (which is implied in this Text) reaches to all that; as well, *Qui non fecerit hoc,* He that

does not doe all this, as *Qui non crediderit hoc,* He that beleeves
not this, is within the penalty of this Text, *Damnabitur:* The first of
these three, is the ordinance and institution of preaching the Gospel;
The second is the administration of both Sacraments (as we shall
see anone;) And the third is the provocation to a good life, which is
in example as well as in preaching; first preach the Gospel, that is,
plant the roote, faith; then administer the Sacraments, that is, water
it, cherish it, fasten and settle it with that seale; and then procure
good works, that is, produce the blessed fruit of this faith, and these
Sacraments: *Qui non crediderit hoc, He that does not beleeve* all this,
shall be damned.

First then, *Qui non crediderit,* He that hath this Apostleship, this *Prædicate*
ministery of reconciliation, he that is a Commissioner for these new
buildings, to erect the kingdome of God by the Gospel, and does not
beleeve, and shew by his practise that he does beleeve himselfe to be
bound to preach, he is under the penalty of this Text. When there-
fore the Jesuit *Maldonat* pleases himselfe so well, that, as he sayes, he *In Matth. 28*
cannot chuse but laugh, when the Calvinists satisfie themselves in
doing that duty, that they doe preach; for, sayes he, *Docetis, sed
nemo misit,* You doe preach, but you have no calling; if it were not
too serious a thing to laugh at, would he not allow us to be as merry,
and to say too, *Missi estis, sed non docetis,* Perchance you may have a
calling, but I am sure you do not preach? for if we consider their
practise, their secular Clergy, those which have the care of soules in
Parishes, they doe not preach; and if we consider their Lawes, and
Canons, their Regular Clergy, their Monks and Fryers should not
preach abroad, out of their own Cloysters. And preaching was so far
out of use amongst them, as that in these later ages, under *Innocentius* *Cheppinus*
the third, they instituted *Ordinem prædicantium,* An order of Preach- *de Jure*
ers; as though there had been no order for preaching in the Church *Monast.*
of God, till within these foure hundred yeares. And we see by their
Patent for preaching, what the cause of their institution was; It was
because those who onely preached then, that is, the *Humiliati,* (which
was another Order) were unlearned, and therefore they thought it
not amisse, to appoint some learned men to preach: The Bishops
tooke this ill at that time, that any should have leave to preach within
their Diocesses; and therefore they had new Patents, to exempt them

from the Jurisdiction of the Bishops; and they had liberty to preach every where; *Modò non vellicent Pápam,* As long as they said nothing against the Pope, they might preach. It is therefore but of late yeares, and indeed, especially since the Reformation began, that the example of others hath brought them in the Roman Church to a more ordinary preaching; whereas the penalty of this Text lies upon all
400 them who have that calling, and doe it not; and so it does upon them too, who doe not beleeve, that they are bound to seeke their salvation from preaching, from that ordinance and institution.

I cannot remember that in any History, for matter of fact, nor in the framing or institution of any State, for matter of Law, there hath ever been such a Law, or such a practise, as that of Preaching. Every where amongst the Gentils, (particularly amongst the Romans, where there was a publique Office, to be *Conditor Precum,* according to emergent occasions, to make Collects and Prayers for the publique use) we finde some resemblance, some representation of our common
410 Prayer, our Liturgie; and in their ablutions, and expiations, we finde some resemblance of our Sacraments; but no where any resemblance of our Preaching. Certaine anniversary Panegyriques they had in Rome, which were Coronation Sermons, or Adoption Sermons, or Triumph Sermons, but all those, upon the matter, were but civill Commemorations. But this Institution, of keeping the people in a continuall knowledge of their religious duty, by continuall preaching, was onely an ordinance of God himselfe, for Gods own people; For, after that in the wisedome of God, the world by wisedome knew

1 Cor. 1.21   not God, *It pleased God* (sayes the Apostle) *by the foolishnesse of*
420 *Preaching to save them that beleeve.*

What was this former wisedome of God, that that could not save man? it was two-fold; First, God in his wisedome manifests a way to man, to know the Creator by the creature, *That the invisible things*

Rom. 1.20   *of him might be seene by the visible.* And this gracious and wise purpose of God tooke not effect, because man being brought to the contemplation of the creature, rested and dwelt upon the beauty and dignity of that, and did not passe by the creature to the Creator; and then, Gods wisedome was farther expressed, in a second way, when God manifested himselfe to man by his Word, in the Law, and in
430 the Prophets; and then, man resting in the letter of the Law, and

going no farther, and resting in the outside of the Prophets, and going no farther, not discerning the Sacrifices of the Law to be Types of the death of Christ Jesus, nor the purpose of the Prophets to be, to direct us upon that Messias, that Redeemer, *Ipsa, quæ per Prophetas locuta est, sapientia,* sayes *Clement,* the wisedome of God, in the mouth of the Prophets, could not save man; and then, when the wisedome of Nature, and the wisedome of the Law, the wisedome of the Philosophers, and the wisedome of the Scribes, became defective and insufficient, by mans perversenesse, God repayred, and supplyed 440 it by a new way, but a strange way, by the foolishnesse of preaching; for it is not onely to the subject, to the matter, to the doctrine, which they were to preach, that this foolishnesse is referred. To preach glory, by adhering to an inglorious person, lately executed for sedition and blasphemy; to preach salvation from a person, whom they saw unable to save himselfe from the Gallowes; to preach joy from a person whose soule was heavy unto death, this was *Scandalum Iudæis,* sayes the Apostle, even to the Jewes, who were formerly acquainted by their Prophets, that some such things as these should befall their Messias, yet for all this preparation, it was *Scandalum,* 50 the Jewes themselves were scandalized at it; it was *a stumbling blocke to the Iewes;* but *Græcis stultitia,* sayes the Apostle there, the Gentils thought this doctrine meere *foolishnesse.* But not onely the matter, but the manner, not onely the Gospel, but even preaching was a foolishnesse in the eyes of man; For if such persons as the Apostles were, heires to no reputation in the State, by being derived from great families, bred in no Universities, nor sought to for learning, persons not of the civilest education, Sea-men, Fishermen, not of the honestest professions, (*Matthew* but a Publican) if such persons should come into our streets, and porches, and preach, (I doe not say, such doctrine 50 as theirs seemed then) but if they should preach at all, should not we thinke this a meere foolishnesse; did they not mock the Apostles, and say they were drunke, as early as it was in the morning? Did not those two sects of Philosophers, who were as farre distant in opinions, as any two could be, the Stoiques, and the Epicureans, concurre in defaming S. *Paul* for preaching, when they called him *Seminiverbium,* a babling and prating fellow? But the foolishnesse of God is wiser then men, said that Apostle; and out of that wisedome, God

Clem. Alex.

1 Cor. 1.23

Act. 2.13

Acts 17.18

1 Cor. 1.25

hath shut us all, under the penalty of this Text, If we that are preachers doe not beleeve that it is our duty to preach, if you that heare doe
⁴⁷⁰ not beleeve, that this preaching is the ordinance of God, for the
salvation of soules.

Euangelium

    This then is matter of faith, That preaching is the way, and this
is matter of faith too, that that which is preached, must be matter of
faith; for the Commission is, *Prædicate Euangelium,* Preach, but
preach the Gospel; And that is, first, *Euangelium solum,* Preach the
Gospel onely, adde nothing to the Gospel, and then *Euangelium
totum,* Preach the Gospel intirely, defalke nothing, forbeare nothing of that; First then, we are to preach, you are to heare nothing but
the Gospel; And we may neither postdate our Commission, nor inter-
⁴⁸⁰ line it; nothing is Gospel now, which was not Gospel then, when

[Mat. 6.24]

Christ gave his Apostles their Commission; And *no man can serve
God and Mammon;* no man can preach those things, which belong
to the filling of Angels roomes in heaven, and those things which
belong to the filling of the Popes Coffers at Rome, with Angels upon
earth: For that was not Gospel, when Christ gave this commission.
And did Christ create his Apostles, as the Bishop of Rome creates
his Cardinals, *Cum clausura oris?* He makes them Cardinalls, and
shuts their mouths; they have mouths, but no tongues; tongues, but
no voice; they are Judges, but must give no Judgement; Cardinalls,
⁴⁹⁰ but have no interest in the passages of businesses, till by a new favour
he open their mouths againe: Did Christ make his Apostles his
Ambassadors, and promise to send their instructions after them?
Did he give them a Commission, and presently a *Supersedeas* upon
it, that they should not execute it? Did he make a Testament, a will,
and referre all to future Schedules and Codicills? Did he send them
to preach the Gospel, and tell them, You shall know the Gospel in
the Epistles of the Popes and their Decretals hereafter? You shall
know the Gospel of deposing Princes, in the Councell of Lateran
hereafter; and the Gospel in deluding Heretiques, by safe conducts,
⁵⁰⁰ in the Councell of Constance hereafter; and the Gospel of creating
new Articles of the Creed, in the Councell of Trent hereafter? If so,
then was some reason for Christs Disciples to thinke, when Christ

Mat. 16
ultim.

said, *Verily, I say unto you, there are some here, who shall not taste
death, till they see the Sonne of man come in glory;* that he spake

and meant to be understood literally, that neither *Iohn* nor the rest
of the Apostles should ever die, if they must live to preach the
Gospel, and the Gospel could not be knowne by them, till the end of
the world: And therefore it was wisely done in the Romane Church,
to give over preaching, since the preaching of the Gospel, that is,
510 nothing but the Gospel, would have done them no good to their ends:
When all their preaching was come to be nothing, but declamations
of the vertue of such an Indulgence, and then a better Indulgence
then that, to morrow, and every day a new market of fuller Indulgences, when all was but an extolling of the tendernesse, and the
bowells of compassion in that mother Church, who was content to
set a price, and a small price upon every sinne; So that if *David* were
upon the earth againe, and then when the persecuting Angel had   [1 Chron.
drawne his sword, would but send an appeale to Rome, at that price,   21.16]
he might have an inhibition against that Angel, and have leave to
520 number his people, let God take it as he list; Nay, if Sodome were
upon the earth againe, and the Angel ready to set fire to that Towne,
if they could send to Rome, they might purchase a Charter even for
that sinne (though perchance they would be loath to let that sinne
passe over their hills:) But not to speake any thing, which may savour
of jeast, or levity, in so serious a matter, and so deplorable a state, as
their preaching was come to, with humble thankes to God that we
are delivered from it, and humble prayers to God, that we never returne to it, nor towards it, let us chearfully and constantly continue
this duty of preaching and hearing the Gospel; that is, first the Gospel
530 onely, and not Traditions of men; And the next is, of all the Gospel,
nothing but it, and yet all it, add nothing, defalke nothing; for as
the Law is, so the Gospel is, *Res integra,* a whole piece; and as S.
Iames sayes of the integrity of the Law, *Whosoever keeps the whole*   James 2.10
Law, and offends in one point, he is guilty of all; So he that is afraid
to preach all, and he that is loath to heare all the Gospel, he preaches
none, he heares none. And therefore, if that imputation, which the
Romane Church layes upon us, were true, That we preach no falshood, but doe not teach all the truth, we did lacke one of the true
marks of the true Church, that is, the preaching of the Gospel; for
540 it is not that, if it be not all that; take therefore the Gospel, as we
take it from the Schoole, that it is *historia,* and *usus,* (the Gospel is

the history of the Gospel, the proposing to your understanding all that Christ did, and it is the appropriation of the Gospel, the proposing to your faith, that all that he did he did for you) and then, if you hearken to them who will tell you, that Christ did that which he never did (that he came in, when the doores were shut, so that his body passed thorough the very body of the Tymber, thereby to advance their doctrine of Transubstantiation) or that Christ did that which he did, to another end then he did it, (that when he whipt the
550 buyers and sellers out of the Temple, he exercised a secular power and soveraignty over the world, and thereby established a soveraignty over Princes, in his Vicar the Pope) These men doe not preach the Gospel, because the Gospel is *Historia & usus,* The truth of the History, and of the application; and this is not the truth of the History; So also if you hearken to them, who tell you, that though the blood of Christ be sufficient in value for you, and for all, yet you have no meanes to be sure, that he meant his blood to you, but you must passe in this world, and passe out of this world in doubt, and that it is well if you come to Purgatory, and be sure there of getting to heaven at
560 last; these men preach not the Gospel, because the Gospel is the history, and the use; and this is not the true use.

And thus it is, if wee take the Gospell from the Schoole; but if we take it from the Schoolemaster, from Christ himselfe, the Gospell is repentance, and remission of sinnes; For he came, *That repentance and remission of sinnes should be preached in his Name;* If then they will tell you, that you need no such repentance for a sinne, as amounts to a contrition, to a sorrow for having offended God, to a detestation of the sinne, to a resolution to commit it no more, but that it is enough to have an attrition, (as they will needs call it) a servill feare,
570 and sorrow, that you have incurred the torments of hell; or if they will tell you, that when you have had this attrition, that the clouds of sadnesse, and of dejection of spirit have met, and beat in your conscience, and that the allision of those clouds have brought forth a thunder, a fearefull apprehension of Gods Judgements upon you; And when you have had your contrition too, that you have purged your soule in an humble confession, and have let your soule blood with a true and sharpe remorse, and compunction, for all sinnes past, and put that bleeding soule into a bath of repentant teares, and

Luk. 24.47

into a bath of blood, the blood of Christ Jesus in the Sacrament, and
580 feele it faint and languish there, and receive no assurance of remission of sinnes, so as that it can levy no fine that can conclude God,
but still are afraid that God will still incumber you with yesterdayes
sinnes againe to morrow; If this be their way, they doe not preach
the Gospell, because they doe not preach all the Gospell; for the
Gospell is repentance and remission of sinnes; that is, the necessity
of repentance, and then the assurednesse of remission, goe together.

Thus farre then the *Crediderit* is carried, wee must beleeve that
there is a way upon earth to salvation, and that Preaching is that way,
that is, the manner, and the matter is the Gospell, onely the Gospell,
590 and all the Gospell, and then the seale is the administration of the
Sacraments, as we said at first, of both Sacraments; of the Sacrament
of Baptisme there can be no question, for that is literally and directly
within the Commission, *Goe and Baptize,* and then *Qui non crediderit, Hee that beleeves not,* not onely he that beleeves not, when
it is done, but he that beleeves not that this ought to be done, *shall
bee damned;* wee doe not joyne Baptisme to faith, *tanquam dimidiam
solatii causam,* as though Baptisme were equall to faith, in the matter of salvation, for salvation may bee had in divers cases by faith
without Baptisme, but in no case by Baptisme without faith; neither
600 doe wee say, that in this Commission to the Apostles, the administration of Baptisme is of equall obligation upon the Minister as preaching, that he may be as well excusable if hee never preach, as if hee
never Baptize; Wee know S. *Peter* commanded *Cornelius* and his
family to be Baptized, wee doe not know if hee Baptized any of them
with his owne hand; So S. *Paul* sayes of himselfe, that Baptizing was
not his principall function; *Christ sent not me to Baptize, but to
preach the Gospell,* saith he; In such a sense as God said by *Ieremy,
I spake not unto your fathers, nor commanded them concerning
burnt offerings, but I said, obey my voyce,* so S. *Paul* saith, hee was
610 not sent to Baptize; God commanded our fathers obedience rather
then sacrifice, but yet sacrifice too; and hee commands us preaching
rather then Baptizing, but yet Baptizing too; For as that is true,
In adultis, in persons which are come to yeares of discretion, which
S. *Hierome* sayes, *Fieri non potest,* It is impossible to receive the
Sacrament of Baptisme, except the soule have received *Sacramentum*

Baptizate

Acts 10 ult.

1 Cor. 1.17

Jer. 7.22

Hiero.

fidei, the Sacrament of faith, that is the Word preached, except he have been instructed and catechized before, so there is a necessity of Baptisme after, for any other ordinary meanes of salvation, that God hath manifested to his Church; and therefore *Quos Deus conjunxit,* 620 those things which God hath joyned in this Commission, let no man separate; *Except a man bee borne againe of water and the Spirit, he cannot enter into the Kingdome of heaven;* Let no man reade that place disjunctively, *Of Water or the Spirit,* for there must bee both; S. *Peter* himselfe knew not how to separate them, *Repent and bee baptized every one of you,* saith he; for, for any one that might have beene, and was not Baptized, S. *Peter* had not that seale to plead for his salvation.

Ioh. 3.5

Acts 2.[38]

The Sacrament of Baptisme then, is within this *Crediderit,* it must necessarily be beleeved to be necessary for salvation: But is the other 630 Sacrament of the Lords Supper so too? Is that within this Commission? Certainly it is, or at least within the equity, if not within the letter, pregnantly implyed, if not literally expressed: For thus it stands, they are commanded, *To teach all things that Christ had commanded them;* And then S. *Paul* sayes, *I have received of the Lord, that which also I delivered unto you, That the Lord Iesus tooke bread, &c.* (and so hee proceeds with the Institution of the Sacrament) and then he addes, that Christ said, *Doe this in remembrance of mee;* which is, not onely remember me when you doe it, but doe it that you may remember me; As well the receiving of the Sacra- 640 ment, as the worthy receiving of it, is upon commandment.

Eucharistia

Matt. 28 ult.
1 Cor. 11.23

In the Primitive Church, there was an erronious opinion of such an absolute necessity in taking this Sacrament, as that they gave it to persons when they were dead; a custome which was growne so common, as that it needed a Canon of a Councell, to restraine it. But the giving of this Sacrament to children newly baptized was so generall, even in pure times, as that we see so great men as *Cyprian* and *Augustine,* scarce lesse then vehement for the use of it; and some learned men in the Reformed Church have not so far declined it, but that they call it, *Catholicam consuetudinem,* a Catholique, an 650 universall custome of the Church. But there is a farre greater strength both of naturall and spirituall faculties required for the receiving of this Sacrament of the Lords Supper, then the other of Baptisme. But

Carthag.
3. c. 6

Musculus

for those who have those faculties, that they are now, or now should be able, to discerne the Lords body, and their owne soules, besides that inestimable and inexpressible comfort, which a worthy receiver receives, as often as he receives that seale of his reconciliation to God, since as Baptisme is *Tessera Christianorum,* (I know a Christian from a Turke by that Sacrament) so this Sacrament is *Tessera orthodoxorum* (I know a Protestant from a Papist by this Sacrament) it 660 is a service to God, and to his Church to come frequently to this Communion; for truly (not to shake or afright any tender conscience) I scarce see, how any man can satisfie himselfe, that he hath said the Lords Prayer with a good conscience, if at the same time he were not in such a disposition as that he might have received the Sacrament too; for, if he be in charity, he might receive, and if he be not, he mocked Almighty God, and deluded the Congregation, in saying the Lords Prayer.

There remaines one branch of that part, *Docete servare,* Preach the Gospell, administer the Sacraments, and teach them to practise and 670 doe all this: how comes matter of fact to be matter of faith? Thus; *Qui non crediderit,* he that does not beleeve, that he is bound to live well, as well as to beleeve aright, is within the penalty of this text. It is so with us, and it is so with you too; Amongst us, he that sayes well, presents a good text, but he that lives well, presents a good Comment upon that text. As the best texts that we can take, to make Sermons upon, are as this text is, some of the words of Christs owne Sermons: so the best arguments we can prove our Sermons by, is our owne life. The whole weekes conversation, is a good paraphrase upon the Sundayes Sermon; It is too soone to aske when the clocke stroke 680 eleven, Is it a good Preacher? for I have but halfe his Sermon then, his owne life is the other halfe; and it is time enough to aske the Saterday after, whether the Sundayes Preacher preach well or no; for he preaches poorely that makes an end of his Sermon upon Sunday; He preaches on all the weeke, if he live well, to the edifying of others; If we say well, and doe ill, we are so far from the example of Gods children, which built with one hand, and fought with the other, as that, if we doe build with one hand, in our preaching, we pull down with the other in our example, and not only our own, but

*Docete
servare*

[Neh. 4.17]

other mens buildings too; for the ill life of particular men reflects
⁶⁹⁰ upon the function and ministery in generall.

And as it is with us, if we divorce our words and our works, so
it is with you, if you doe divorce your faith and your workes. God
hath given his Commission under seale, *Preach and Baptize;* God

[Luk. 3.8]

lookes for a returne of this Commission, under seale too; *Believe,
and bring forth fruits worthy of beliefe.* The way that *Iacob* saw to

[Gen. 28.12]

Heaven, was a ladder; It was not a faire and an easie staire case, that
a man might walke up without any holding. But *manibus inniten-*

August.

dum, sayes S. *Augustine,* in the way to salvation there is use of
hands, of actions, of good works, of a holy life; *Servate omnia,* doe
⁷⁰⁰ then all that is commanded, all that is within the Commission: If
that seeme impossible, doe what you can, and you have done all;

August.

for then is all this done, *Cum quod non sit ignoscitur,* When God
forgives that which is left undone; But God forgives none of that
which is left undone, out of a wilfull and vincible ignorance. And
therefore search thy conscience, and then Christs commandement

[Joh. 5.39]

enters, *Scrutamini Scripturas,* then search the Scriptures; for till then,
as long as thy conscience is foule, it is but an illusion to apprehend
any peace, or any comfort in any sentence of the Scripture, in any
promise of the Gospell: search thy conscience, empty that, and then
⁷¹⁰ search the Scriptures, and thou shalt finde abundantly enough to fill
it with peace and consolation; for this is the summe of all the Scriptures, *Qui non crediderit hoc, He that believes not this,* that he must
be saved by hearing the word preached, by receiving the Sacraments,
and by working according to both, is within the penalty of this text,
Damnabitur, He shall be damned.

2 Part

How know we that? many persons have power to condemne,
which have not power to pardon; but Gods word is evidence enough
for our pardon and absolution, whensoever we repent we are pardoned, much more then for our condemnation; and here we have
⁷²⁰ Gods word for that; if that were not enough we have his oath; for
it is in another place, God hath *sworne,* that there are some, which

Heb. 4.3

shall not enter into his rest, and to whom did he sweare that, sayes
S. *Paul,* but to them *that beleeved not?* God cannot lye, much lesse
be forsworne, and God hath said and sworne, *Damnabitur, he that
beleeveth not, shall be damned.* He shall be; but when? does any

man make hast? though that be enough that S. *Chrysostome* sayes, Chrysost.
It is all one, when that begins, which shall never end, yet the tense
is easily changed in this case, from *damnabitur* to *damnatur;* for
he that beleeveth not, is condemned already. But why should he be Iohn 3.18
730 so? condemned for a negative? for a privative? here is no opposition,
no affirming the contrary, no seducing or disswading other men that
have a mind to beleeve, that is not enough; for, *He that beleeveth* 1 Iohn 5.10
not God, hath made God a lyar, because he beleeveth not the record
that God gave of his Son. Here is the condemnation we speake of,
as S. *Iohn* sayes, *Light was presented, and they loved darknesse;* so Iohn 3.19
that howsoever God proceed in his unsearchable judgements with
the Heathen, to whom the light and name of Christ Jesus was never
presented, certainely we, to whom the Gospell hath beene so freely,
and so fully preached, fall under the penalty of this text, if we be-
740 leeve not, for we have made God a lyar in not beleeving the record
he gives of his Son.

That then there is damnation, and why it is, and when it is, is
cleare enough; but what this damnation is, neither the tongue of
good Angels that know damnation by the contrary, by fruition of
salvation, nor the tongue of bad Angels who know damnation by a
lamentable experience, is able to expresse it; A man may saile so at
sea, as that he shall have laid the North Pole flat, that shall be fallen
out of sight, and yet he shall not have raised the South Pole, he shall
not see that; So there are things, in which a man may goe beyond
750 his reason, and yet not meet with faith neither: of such a kinde are
those things which concerne the locality of hell, and the materiality
of the torments thereof; for that hell is a certaine and limited place,
beginning here and ending there, and extending no farther, or that
the torments of hell be materiall, or elementary torments, which in
naturall consideration can have no proportion, no affection, nor
appliablenesse to the tormenting of a spirit, these things neither settle
my reason, nor binde my faith; neither opinion, that it is, or is not
so, doth command our reason so, but that probable reasons may be
brought on the other side; neither opinion doth so command our
760 faith, but that a man may be saved, though hee thinke the contrary;
for in such points, it is alwaies lawfull to thinke so, as we finde does
most advance and exalt our owne devotion, and Gods glory in our
estimation; but when we shall have given to those words, by which

hell is expressed in the Scriptures, the heaviest significations, that either the nature of those words can admit, or as they are types and representations of hell, as *fire,* and *brimstone,* and *weeping,* and *gnashing,* and *darknesse,* and *the worme,* and as they are laid to-

gether in the Prophet, *Tophet,* (that is, hell) *is deepe and large,* (there is the capacity and content, roome enough) *It is a pile of fire* ⁷⁷⁰ *and much wood,* (there is the durablenesse of it) *and the breath of the Lord to kindle it, like a streame of Brimstone,* (there is the vehemence of it:) when all is done, the hell of hels, the torment of torments is the everlasting absence of God, and the everlasting impossibility of returning to his presence; *Horrendum est,* sayes the

Apostle, *It is a fearefull thing to fall into the hands of the living God.*

Yet there was a case, in which *David* found an ease, to fall into the

hands of God, to scape the hands of men: *Horrendum est,* when Gods hand is bent to strike, *it is a fearefull thing, to fall into the hands of the living God;* but to fall out of the hands of the living God, is ⁷⁸⁰ a horror beyond our expression, beyond our imagination.

That God should let my soule fall out of his hand, into a bottomlesse pit, and roll an unremoveable stone upon it, and leave it to that which it finds there, (and it shall finde that there, which it never imagined, till it came thither) and never thinke more of that soule, never have more to doe with it. That of that providence of God, that studies the life and preservation of every weed, and worme, and ant, and spider, and toad, and viper, there should never, never any beame flow out upon me; that that God, who looked upon me, when I was nothing, and called me when I was not, as though I had been, out ⁷⁹⁰ of the womb and depth of darknesse, will not looke upon me now, when, though a miserable, and a banished, and a damned creature, yet I am his creature still, and contribute something to his glory, even in my damnation; that that God, who hath often looked upon me in my foulest uncleannesse, and when I had shut out the eye of the day, the Sunne, and the eye of the night, the Taper, and the eyes of all the world, with curtaines and windowes and doores, did yet see me, and see me in mercy, by making me see that he saw me, and sometimes brought me to a present remorse, and (for that time) to a forbearing of that sinne, should so turne himselfe from me, to his ⁸⁰⁰ glorious Saints and Angels, as that no Saint nor Angel, nor Christ Jesus himselfe, should ever pray him to looke towards me, never remember him, that such a soule there is; that that God, who hath so often said to my soule, *Quare morieris?* Why wilt thou die? and so often sworne to my soule, *Vivit Dominus,* As the Lord liveth, I would not have thee dye, but live, will neither let me dye, nor let me live, but dye an everlasting life, and live an everlasting death; that that God, who, when he could not get into me, by standing, and knocking, by his ordinary meanes of entring, by his Word, his mercies, hath applied his judgements, and hath shaked the house, this

⁸¹⁰ body, with agues and palsies, and set this house on fire, with fevers and calentures, and frighted the Master of the house, my soule, with horrors, and heavy apprehensions, and so made an entrance into me; That that God should loose and frustrate all his owne purposes and practises upon me, and leave me, and cast me away, as though I had cost him nothing, that this God at last, should let this soule goe away, as a smoake, as a vapour, as a bubble, and that then this soule cannot be a smoake, nor a vapour, nor a bubble, but must lie in darknesse, as long as the Lord of light is light it selfe, and never a sparke of that light reach to my soule; What Tophet is not Paradise, what

⁸²⁰ Brimstone is not Amber, what gnashing is not a comfort, what gnawing of the worme is not a tickling, what torment is not a marriage bed to this damnation, to be secluded eternally, eternally, eternally from the sight of God? Especially to us, for as the perpetuall losse of that is most heavy, with which we have been best acquainted, and to which wee have been most accustomed; so shall this damnation, which consists in the losse of the sight and presence of God, be heavier to us then others, because God hath so graciously, and so evidently, and so diversly appeared to us, in his pillar of fire, in the light of prosperity, and in the pillar of the Cloud, in hiding himselfe

⁸³⁰ for a while from us; we that have seene him in the Execution of all the parts of this Commission, in his Word, in his Sacraments, and in good example, and not beleeved, shall be further removed from his sight, in the next world, then they to whom he never appeared in this. But *Vincenti & credenti,* to him that beleeves aright, and overcomes all tentations to a wrong beliefe, God shall give the accomplishment of fulnesse, and fulnesse of joy, and joy rooted in glory, and glory established in eternity, and this eternity is God; To him that beleeves and overcomes, God shall give himselfe in an everlasting presence and fruition, *Amen.*

[Ezek. 18.31]

[Exod. 13.21]

Number 14.

Preached at S. Pauls.

PSAL. 90.14. *O SATISFIE US EARLY WITH THY MERCY, THAT WE MAY REJOYCE AND BE GLAD ALL OUR DAYES.*

THEY have made a Rule in the Councel of Trent, that no Scripture shall be expounded, but according to the unanime consent of the Fathers: But in this Book of the Psalms, it would trouble them to give many examples of that Rule, that is, of an unanime consent of the Fathers, in the interpretation thereof. In this Psalme, *Bellarmine* in his Exposition of the Psalms, finds himselfe perplexed; He sayes (and sayes truly) *Hieronymus constanter affirmat, Augustinus constanter negat,* S. *Hierome* doth confidently and constantly affirme, and S. *Augustine* with as much confidence, and constancy deny, that this Psalme, and all that follow to the hundredth Psalme, are *Moses* Psalms, and written by him. And this diverse constancy in these two Fathers, S. *Hierome* and S. *Augustine,* shake the constancy of that Canon, which binds to a following of an unanime consent, for that cannot be found. *Bellarmine* expedites himselfe herein, that way, which is indeed their most ordinary way amongst their Expositors, which is, where the Fathers differ, to adhere to S. *Augustine.* So he doth in this point; though most of the Ancients of the Christian Church, most of the Rabbins of the Jews, most of the Writers in the Reformation, take it to be *Moses* Psalme, and that way runs the greatest streame, and nearest to a concurrence. And thus far I have stopped upon this consideration, Whether this be *Moses* Psalme or no, That when it appears to be his Psalme, and that we see, that in the tenth verse of this Psalm, mans life is limited to seventy years, or at most to eighty, and then remem-

ber, that *Moses* himselfe, then when he said so, was above eighty, and
in a good habitude long after that, we might hereby take occasion to
consider, that God does not so limit, and measure himselfe in his
blessings to his servants, but that for their good and his glory he
enlarges those measures. God hath determined a day, from Sun to
³⁰ Sun, yet when God hath use of a longer day, for his glory, he commands the Sun to stand still, till *Ioshua* have pursued his victory. So
God hath given the life of man, into the hand of sicknesse; and yet
for all that deadly sicknesse, God enlarges *Hezekiah's* years: *Moses*
was more then fourescore, when he told us, that our longest terme
was fourescore.

If we require exactly an unanime consent, that all agree in the
Author of this Psalme, we can get no farther, then that the holy
Ghost is the Author. All agree the words to be Canonicall Scripture,
and so from the holy Ghost; and we seek no farther. The words are
⁴⁰ his, and they offer us these considerations; First, That the whole
Psalme being in the Title thereof called a Prayer, *A Prayer of Moses
the man of God,* it puts us justly, and pertinently upon the consideration of the many dignities and prerogatives of that part of our worship
of God, Prayer; for there we shall see, That though the whole Psalme
be not a Prayer, yet because there is a Prayer in the Psalme, that
denominates the whole Psalme, the whole Psalme is a Prayer. When
the Psalm grows formally to be a Prayer, our Text enters, *O satisfie
us early with thy mercy, that we may rejoyce and be glad all our
dayes:* And in that there will be two Parts more, The Prayer it selfe,
⁵⁰ *O satisfie us early with thy mercy,* And the effect thereof, *That we
may rejoyce and be glad all our dayes.* So that our Parts are three;
First Prayer, Then this Prayer, And lastly the benefit of all Prayer.

For the first, which is Prayer in generall, I will thrust no farther
then the Text leads me in, that is, That Prayer is so essentiall a part
of Gods worship, as that all is called Prayer. S. *Hierome* upon this
Psalme sayes, *Difficillimum Psalmum aggredior,* I undertake the
exposition of a very hard Psalme, and yet, sayes he, I would proceed
so in the exposition thereof, *ut interpretatio nostra aliena non egeat
interpretatione,* That there should not need another Comment upon
⁶⁰ my Comment, that when I pretend to interpret the Psalme, they that
heare me, should not need another to interpret me: which is a fre-

1 Part
Prayer

quent infirmity amongst Expositors of Scriptures, by writing, or preaching, either when men will raise doubts in places of Scripture, which are plaine enough in themselves, (for this creates a jealousie, that if the Scriptures be every where so difficult, they cannot be our evidences, and guides to salvation) Or when men will insist too vehemently, and curiously, and tediously in proving of such things as no man denies; for this also induces a suspition, that that is not so absolutely, so undeniably true, that needs so much art, and curiosity, 70 and vehemence to prove it. I shall therefore avoid these errors; and because I presume you are full of an acknowledgment of the duties, and dignities of Prayer, onely remember you of thus much of the method, or elements of Prayer, That whereas the whole Book of Psalms is called *Sepher Tehillim,* that is, *Liber Laudationum,* The Book of Praise, yet this Psalme, and all that follow to the hundredth Psalme, and divers others besides these, (which make up a faire limme of this body, and a considerable part of the Book) are called Prayers; The Book is Praise, the parts are Prayer. The name changes not the nature; Prayer and Praise is the same thing: The name scarce changes 80 the name; Prayer and Praise is almost the same word; As the duties agree in the heart and mouth of a man, so the names agree in our eares; and not onely in the language of our Translation, but in the language of the holy Ghost himselfe, for that which with us differs but so, Prayer, and Praise, in the Originall differs no more then so, *Tehillim,* and *Tephilloth.*

And this concurrence of these two parts of our devotion, Prayer and Praise, that they accompany one another, nay this co-incidence, that they meet like two waters, and make the streame of devotion the fuller; nay more then that, this identity, that they doe not onely 90 consist together, but constitute one another, is happily expressed in this part of the Prayer, which is our Text; for that which in the Originall language is expressed in the voice of Prayer, *O satisfie us, &c.* in the first Translation, that of the Septuagint, is expressed in the voice of praise, *Saturasti, Thou hast satisfied us;* The Original makes it a Prayer, the Translation a Praise. And not to compare Original with Translation, but Translation with Translation, and both from one man, we have in S. *Hieroms* works two Translations of the Psalmes; one, in which he gives us the Psalmes alone; another,

in which he gives them illustrated with his notes and Commentaries.
100 And in one of these Translations he reads this as a Prayer, *Reple nos,*
O fill us early with thy mercie, and in the other he reads it as a Praise,
Repleti sumus, Thou hast filled us, &c. Nay, not to compare Originall
with Translation, nor Translation with Translation, but Originall
with Originall, the holy Ghost with himselfe, In the Title of this
Psalme, (and the Titles of the Psalms are Canonicall Scripture) the
holy Ghost calls this Psalme a *Prayer,* and yet enters the Psalme, in
the very first verse thereof, with praise and thanksgiving, *Lord, thou*
hast been our dwelling place in all generations. And such is the constitution and frame of that Prayer of Prayers, That which is the
110 extraction of all prayers, and draws into a summe all that is in all
others, That which is the infusion into all others, sheds and showres
whatsoever is acceptable to God, in any other prayer, That Prayer
which our Saviour gave us, (for as he meant to give us all for asking,
so he meant to give us the words by which we should ask) As that
Prayer consists of seven petitions, and seven is infinite, so by being at
first begun with glory and acknowledgement of his raigning in
heaven, and then shut up in the same manner, with acclamations of
power and glory, it is made a circle of praise, and a circle is infinite
too, The Prayer, and the Praise is equally infinite. Infinitely poore
120 and needy man, that ever needst infinite things to pray for; Infinitely
rich and abundant man, that ever hast infinite blessings to praise
God for.

Gods house in this world is called the house of Prayer; but in [Isa. 56.7]
heaven it is the house of Praise: No surprisall with any new necessities there, but one even, incessant, and everlasting tenor of thanksgiving; And it is a blessed inchoation of that state here, here to be
continually exercised in the commemoration of Gods former goodnesse towards us. *My voyce shalt thou heare in the morning, O Lord,* Psal. 5.3
sayes *David.* What voice? the voice of his prayer; it is true; *In the*
130 *morning will I direct my prayer unto thee,* saies *David* there. And not
only then, but at noone and at night he vowes that Sacrifice; *Evening*
and morning, and at noone will I pray, and cry unto thee. But *Davids* Psal. 55.17
devotion began not, when his prayers began; one part of his devotion
was before morning; *At midnight will I rise, to give thanks unto thee* Psal. 119.62
O Lord, says he. Doubtlesse when he lay downe and closed his eyes,

he had made up his account with God, and had received his *Quietus est* then: And then the first thing that he does when he wakes againe, is not to importune God for more, but to blesse God for his former blessings. And as this part of his devotion, Praise, began all, so it

Psal. 34.1

¹⁴⁰ passes through all, *I will blesse the Lord at all times, and his praise shall be continually in my mouth.* He extends it through all times, and all places, and would faine do so through all persons too, as we see

[Psal. 107.8]

by that adprecation which is so frequent with him, *O that men would therefore praise the Lord, and declare the wondrous workes that he doth for the children of men!*

If we compare these two incomparable duties, Prayer, and Praise, it will stand thus, Our Prayers besiege God, (as *Tertullian* speakes, especially of publique Prayer in the Congregation, *Agmine facto obsidemus Deum*) but our praises prescribe in God, we urge him,
¹⁵⁰ and presse him with his ancient mercies, his mercies of old; By Prayer we incline him, we bend him, but by praise we bind him; our thanks for former benefits, is a producing of a specialty, by which he hath contracted with us for more. In Prayer we sue to him, but in our Praise we sue him himselfe; Prayer is as our petition, but Praise is as our Evidence; In that we beg, in this we plead. God hath no law upon himselfe, but yet God himselfe proceeds by precedent: And whensoever we present to him with thanksgiving, what he hath done, he does the same, and more againe. Neither certainly can the Church institute any prayers, more effectuall for the preservation of Religion,
¹⁶⁰ or of the State, then the Collects for our deliverances, in the like cases before: And when he heares them, though they have the nature of Praise onely, yet he translates them into Prayers, and when we our selves know not, how much we stand in need of new deliverances, he delivers us from dangers which we never suspected, from Armies and Navies which we never knew were prepared, and from plots and machinations which we never knew were brought into Consultation, and diverts their forces, and dissipates their counsels with an untimely abortion. And farther I extend not this first part of Prayer in generall, in which, to that which you may have heard often, and usefully of
¹⁷⁰ the duty and dignity of Prayer, I have only added this, of the method and elements thereof, that prayer consists as much of praise for the past, as of supplication for the future.

We passe now to our second Part, To this particular Prayer, and those limmes that make up this body, those pieces that constitute this Part. They are many; as many as words in it: *Satisfie,* and *satisfie Vs,* and doe that *early,* and doe that with that which is *thine,* and let that be *mercy.* So that first it is a prayer for fulnesse and satisfaction, *Satura, satisfie;* And then it is a prayer not onely of appropriation to our selves, *Satisfie me,* But of a charitable dilatation and extension to 180 others, *Satisfie us,* all us, all thy servants, all thy Church; And then thirdly, it is a prayer of dispatch and expedition, *Satura nos mane, Satisfie us early;* and after that, it is a prayer of evidence and manifestation, Satisfie us with that which is, and which we may discerne to be *thine;* And then lastly, it is a prayer of limitation even upon God himselfe, that God will take no other way herein, but the way of *mercy, Satisfie us early with thy mercy.*

And because these are the land-markes that must guide you in this voyage, and the places to which you must resort to assist your memory, be pleased to take another survay and impression of them. 190 I may have an apprehension of a conditionall promise of God, and I may have some faire credulity and testimony of conscience, of an endevour to performe those conditions, and so some inchoations of those promises, but yet this is not a fulnesse, a satisfaction, and this is a prayer for that, *Satura, satisfie:* I may have a full measure in my selfe, finde no want of temporall conveniencies, or spirituall consolation even in inconveniencies, and so hold up a holy alacrity and cheerefulnesse for all concerning my selfe, and yet see God abandon greater persons, and desert some whole Churches, and States, upon whom his glory and Gospel depends much more then upon me, but 200 this is a prayer of charitable extension, *Satura nos,* not *me,* but *us,* all us that professe thee aright: This also I may be sure that God will doe at last, he will rescue his owne honour in rescuing or establishing his Servants, he will bring Israel out of Egypt, and out of Babylon, but yet his Israel may lye long under the scourge and scorne of his and their enemies, 300. yeares before they get out of Egypt, seventy yeares before they get out of Babylon, and so fall into tentations of conceiving a jealousie, and suspition of Gods good purpose towards them, and this is a Prayer of Dispatch and Expedition, *Satura nos mane, Satisfie us early,* O God make speed to save us, O Lord make

2 Part

[Book of Common Prayer, Morning Prayer]

²¹⁰ hast to help us: But he may derive help upon us, by meanes that are
not his, not avowed by him, He may quicken our Counsels by bringing in an *Achitophell,* he may strengthen our Armies by calling in the
Turke, he may establish our peace and friendships, by remitting or
departing with some parts of our Religion; at such a deare price we
may be helped, but these are not his helps, and this is a prayer of
manifestation, that all the way to our end hee will bee pleased to let
us see, that the meanes are from him, *Satura nos tua, Satisfie us* with
that, which is *thine,* and comes from *thee,* and so directs us to *thee:*
All this may be done too, and yet not that done which we pray for
²²⁰ here; God may send that which is his, and yet without present comfort therein; God may multiply corrections, and judgements, and
tribulations upon us, and intend to helpe us that way, by whipping
and beating us into the way, and this is his way; but this is a Prayer
of limitation even upon God himselfe, That our way may be his, and
that his way may be the way of *mercy, Satisfie us early with thy mercy.*

Satura   First then, the first word *Satura,* implies a fulnesse, and it implies
a satisfaction, A quietnesse, a contentednesse, an acquiescence in that
fulnesse; *Satisfie* is, let us bee full, and let us feele it, and rest in that
fulnesse. These two make up all Heaven, all the joy, and all the
²³⁰ glory of Heaven, fulnesse and satisfaction in it. And therefore S.
Hierom refers this Prayer of our Text, to the Resurrection, and to that
fulnesse, and that satisfaction which we shall have then, and not till
then. For though we shall have a fulnesse in Heaven, as soone as we
come thither, yet that is not fully a satisfaction, because we shall desire,
and expect a fuller satisfaction in the reunion of body and soule. And
when Heaven it selfe cannot give us this full satisfaction till then, in
what can wee looke for it in this world, where there is no true fulnesse, nor any satisfaction, in that kind of fulnesse which wee seeme
to have? Pleasure and sensuality, and the giving to our selves all that
Ezek.   ²⁴⁰ we desire, cannot give this; you heare God reproaches Israel so, *You*
16.[29]   *have multiplied your fornications, & yet are not satisfied.* Labor for
profit, or for preferment, cannot doe it; you see God reproaches
Hagg. 1.[6]   Israel for that too, *Ye have sowne much, and bring in little, ye eat,*
but have not enough, ye drinke, but are not filled, ye cloath you, but
are not warme, and he that earneth wages, putteth it into a broken

bag; that is, it runs out as fast as it comes in, he finds nothing at the yeares end, his Midsommer will scarce fetch up Michaelmas, and if he have brought about his yeare, and made up his Circle, yet he hath raised up nothing, nothing appears in his circle. If these things could
²⁵⁰ fill us, yet they could not satisfie us, because they cannot stay with us, or not we with them: *He hath devoured substance, and he shall vomit* Iob. 20.[15] *it.* He devoured it by bribery, and he shall vomit it by a fine; He devoured it by extortion, and he shall vomit it by confiscation; He devoured it in other Courts, and shall vomit it in a Star-chamber. If it stay some time, it shall be with an anguish and vexation; *When he shall be filled with abundance, it shall be a paine to him,* as it is in the same place. Still his riches shall have the nature of a vomit, hard to get downe, and hard to keep in the stomach when it is there; hardly got, hardly kept when they are got. If all these could be over-
²⁶⁰ come, yet it is clogged with a heavy curse, *Wo be unto you that are* *full, for ye shall be hungry:* Where, if the curse were onely from Luke 6.[25] them, who are poore by their owne sloth, or wastfulnesse, who for the most part delight to curse and maligne the rich, the curse might be contemned by us, and would be throwne back by God into their owne bosomes; but *Os Domini locutum,* The mouth of the Lord hath spoken it, Christ himselfe hath denounced this curse upon worldly men, That they shall be hungry, not onely suffer impaire-ment and diminution, but be reduced to hunger.

There is a spirituall fulnesse in this life, of which S. *Hierom*
²⁷⁰ speakes, *Ebrietas fœlix, satietas salutaris,* A happy excesse, and a wholesome surfet; *quæ quanto copiosiùs sumitur, majorem donat sobrietatem,* In which the more we eate, the more temperate we are, and the more we drinke, the more sober. In which, (as S. *Bernard* also expresses it, in his mellifluence) *Mutuâ, interminabili, inex-plicabili generatione,* By a mutuall and reciprocall, by an undetermin-able and unexpressible generation of one another, *Desiderium generat satietatem, & satietas parit desiderium,* The desire of spirituall graces begets a satiety, if I would be, I am full of them, And then this satiety begets a farther desire, still we have a new appetite to those spirituall
²⁸⁰ graces: This is a holy ambition, a sacred covetousnesse, and a whol-some Dropsie. *Napthalies* blessing, *O Napthali satisfied with favour,* Deut. 33.23

Act. 6.5
[Luke 1.28]
Act. 9.36

ªLuk. 2.40
ᵇLuk. 4.1
ᶜJoh. 1.14

[1 Cor. 2.2]

[Exod.
16.16]

and full with the blessing of the Lord; S. *Stephens* blessing, *Full of faith and of the Holy Ghost;* The blessed Virgins blessing, *Full of Grace;* Dorcas blessing, *Full of good works, and of Almes-deeds;* The blessing of him, who is blessed above all, and who blesseth all, Christ Jesus, ªFull of wisedome, ᵇFull of the Holy Ghost, ᶜFull of grace and truth. But so far are all temporall things from giving this fullnesse or satisfaction, as that even in spirituall things, there may be, there is often an error, or mistaking.

290   Even in spirituall things, there may be a fulnesse, and no satisfaction, And there may be a satisfaction, and no fulnesse; I may have as much knowledge, as is presently necessary for my salvation, and yet have a restlesse and unsatisfied desire, to search into unprofitable curiosities, unrevealed mysteries, and inextricable perplexities: And, on the other side, a man may be satisfied, and thinke he knowes all, when, God knowes, he knowes nothing at all; for, I know nothing, if I know not Christ crucified, And I know not that, if I know not how to apply him to my selfe, Nor doe I know that, if I embrace him not in those meanes, which he hath afforded me in his Church, in his Word, and

300 Sacraments; If I neglect this meanes, this place, these exercises, howsoever I may satisfie my selfe, with an over-valuing mine own knowledge at home, I am so far from fulnesse, as that vanity it selfe is not more empty. In the Wildernesse, every man had one and the same measure of Manna; The same Gomer went through all; for Manna was a Meat, that would melt in their mouths, and of easie digestion. But then for their Quailes, birds of a higher flight, meat of a stronger digestion, it is not said, that every man had an equall number: some might have more, some lesse, and yet all their fulnesse. Catechisticall divinity, and instructions in fundamentall things, is our Manna;

310 Every man is bound to take in his Gomer, his explicite knowledge of Articles absolutely necessary to salvation; The simplest man, as well as the greatest Doctor, is bound to know, that there is one God in three persons, That the second of those, the Sonne of God, tooke our nature, and dyed for mankinde; And that there is a Holy Ghost, which in the Communion of Saints, the Church established by Christ, applies to every particular soule the benefit of Christs universall redemption. But then for our Quails, birds of higher pitch, meat of a stronger digestion, which is the knowledge how to rectifie every stray-

ing conscience, how to extricate every entangled, and scrupulous, and
320 perplexed soule, in all emergent doubts, how to defend our Church,
and our Religion, from all the mines, and all the batteries of our Adversaries, and to deliver her from all imputations of Heresie, and
Schisme, which they impute to us, this knowledge is not equally
necessary in all; In many cases a Master of servants, and a Father of
children is bound to know more, then those children and servants,
and the Pastor of the parish more then parishioners: They may have
their fulnesse, though he have more, but he hath not his, except he
be able to give them satisfaction.

This fulnesse then is not an equality in the measure; our fulnesse
330 in heaven shall not be so; *Abraham dyed,* sayes the text, *Plenus*
dierum, full of yeares; It is not said so in the text of *Methusalem,*
that he dyed full of yeares, and yet he had another manner of Gomer,
another measure of life then *Abraham,* for he lived almost eight
hundred yeares more then he; But he that is best disposed to die, is
fullest of yeares; One man may be fuller at twenty, then another at
seaventy. *David* lived not the tithe of *Methusalems* yeares, not ten to
his hundred, he lived lesse then *Abraham,* and yet *David* is said to
have dyed *Plenus dierum, full of yeares;* he had made himselfe agreeable to God, and so was ripe for him. So *David* is said there to have
340 dyed *full of honor;* God knowes *David* had cast shrowd aspersions
upon his own, and others honor; but, as God sayes of Israel, *Because*
I loved thee, thou wast honorable in my sight; so because God loved
David, and he persevered in that love to the end, he dyed full of
honor. So also it is said of *David,* that he dyed *full of Riches;* for,
though they were very great additions, which *Solomon* made, yet
because *David* intended that which he left, for Gods service, and for
pious uses, he dyed full of Riches; fulnesse of riches is in the good
purpose, and the good employment, not in the possession. In a word,
the fulnesse that is inquired after, and required by this prayer, carry
350 it upon temporall, carry it upon spirituall things, is such a proportion
of either, as is fit for that calling, in which God hath put us; And
then, the satisfaction in this fulnesse is not to hunt and pant after
more worldly possessions, by undue meanes, or by macerating labour,
as though we could not be good, or could doe no good in the world,
except all the goods of the world passed our hands, nor to hunt and

Gen. 25.8
[Gen. 5.27]

1 Chro.
29.28

[Isa. 43.4]

pant after the knowledge of such things, as God by his Scriptures
hath not revealed to his Church, nor to wrangle contentiously and
uncharitably about such points, as doe rather shake others consciences,
then establish our own, as though we could not possibly come to
360 heaven, except we knew what God meant to doe with us, before he
meant to make us. S. *Paul* expresses fully what this fulnesse is, and

Colos. 4.12

satisfies us in this satisfaction, *Vt sitis pleni in omni voluntate Dei,
That yee may be filled according to the will of God:* What is the will
of God? How shall I know the will of God upon me? God hath
manifested his will in my Calling; and a proportion, competent to this
Calling, is my fulnesse, and should be my satisfaction, that so God
may have *Odorem quietis,* (as it is said in *Noahs* sacrifice, after he

Gen. 8.21

came out of the Arke, *that God smelt a savour of rest*) a sacrifice, in
which he might rest himselfe; for God hath a Sabbath in the Sabbaths
370 of his servants, a fulnesse in their fulnesse, a satisfaction when they
are satisfied, and is well pleased when they are so.

Nos

So then this Prayer is for fulnesse, and fulnesse is a competency in
our calling, And a prayer for satisfaction, and satisfaction is a contentment in that competency; And then this prayer is not onely a
prayer of appropriation to our selves, but of a charitable extention to
others too, *Satura nos, Satisfie us,* All us, all thy Church. Charity
begins in our selves, but it does not end there, but dilates it selfe to
others; The Saints in heaven are full, as full as they can hold, and yet
they pray; Though they want nothing, they pray that God would
380 powre down upon us graces necessary for our peregrination here,
as he hath done upon them, in their station there. We are full; full
of the Gospel; present peace and plenty in the preaching thereof, and
faire apparances of a perpetuall succession; we are full, and yet we
pray; we pray that God would continue the Gospel where it is, restore
the Gospel where it was, and transfer the Gospel where it hath not

[1 Cor. 13.5]

yet been preached. Charity desires not her own, sayes the Apostle;
but much lesse doth charity desire no more then her own, so as not
to desire the good of others too. True love and charity is to doe the
most that we can, all that we can for the good of others; So God him-

[Isa. 5.4]

390 selfe proceeds, when he sayes, *What could I doe, that I have not done?*
And so he seems to have begun at first; when God bestowed upon
man, his first and greatest benefit, his making, it is expressed so,

Faciamus hominem, Let us, All us, *make man;* God seems to sum-   [Gen. 1.26]
mon himselfe, to assemble himselfe, to muster himselfe, all himselfe,
all the persons of the Trinity, to doe what he could in the favour of
man. So also when he is drawne to a necessity of executing judgement, and for his own honor, and consolidation of his servants, puts
himselfe upon a revenge, he proceeds so too; when man had rebelled,
and began to fortifie in Babel, then God sayes, *Venite, Let us,* All   Gen. 11.7
400 us come together, And *Descendamus, & confundamus, Let us,* all us,
goe down, and confound their language, and their machinations, and
fortifications. God does not give patterns, God does not accept from
us acts of half-devotion, and half-charities; God does all that he can
for us; And therefore when we see others in distresse, whether nationall, or personall calamities, whether Princes be dispossest of their
naturall patrimony, and inheritance, or private persons afflicted with
sicknesse, or penury, or banishment, let us goe Gods way, all the way;
First, *Faciamus hominem ad imaginem nostram,* Let us make that
Man according unto our image, let us consider our selves in him, and
410 make our case his, and remember how lately he was as well as we,
and how soone we may be as ill as he, and then *Descendamus &
confundamus,* Let us, us, with all the power we have, remove or
slacken those calamities that lie upon them.

This onely is charity, to doe all, all that we can. And something
there is which every man may doe; There are Armies, in the levying
whereof, every man is an absolute Prince, and needs no Commission,
there are Forces, in which every man is his owne Muster-master, The
force which we spoke of before, out of *Tertullian,* the force of prayer;
In publique actions, we obey God, when we obey them to whom
420 God hath committed the publique; In those things which are in our
own power, the subsidies and contributions of prayer, God looks
that we should second his *Faciamus,* with our *Dicamus,* That since
he must doe all, we would pray him that he would doe it, And his
Descendamus, with our *Ascendamus,* That if we would have him
come down, and fight our battayls, or remove our calamities, we
should first goe up to him, in humble and fervent prayer, That he
would continue the Gospel where it is, and restore it where it was,
and transfer it where it was never as yet heard; Charity is to doe all
to all; and the poorest of us all can doe this to any.

Mane   430   I may then, I must pray for this fulnesse, (and fulnesse is suffi-
ciency) And for this satisfaction, (and satisfaction is contentment)
And that God would extend this, and other his blessings, upon others
too, And if God doe leave us in an Egypt, in a Babylon, without
reliefe, for some time I may proceed to this holy importunity, which
David intimates here, *Satura nos mane,* O Lord, make haste to helpe
us, *Satisfie us early with thy mercy,* and God will doe so. *Weeping*
Psal. 30.5   *may endure for a night,* sayes *David. David* does not say, It must
indure for a night, that God will by no meanes shorten the time;
perchance God will wipe all teares from thine eyes, at midnight, if
440   thou pray; Try him that way then. If he doe not, *If weeping doe
indure for a night,* all night, *yet joy commeth in the morning,* saith
David; And then he doth not say, Joy may come in the morning, but
it commeth certainly, infallibly it comes, and comes in the morning.
God is an early riser; *In the Morning-watch, God looked upon the*
Exod. 14.24   *host of the Egyptians.* Hee looked upon their counsels to see what
they would doe, and upon their forces to see what they could doe. He
is not early up, and never the nearer; *His going forth is prepared as*
Hos. 6.3   *the Morning,* (there is his generall Providence, in which he visits
every creature) *And hee shall come to us, in the former, and later*
450   *raine upon the earth;* Hee makes haste to us in the former, and
seconds his former mercies to us, in more mercies. And as he makes
hast to refresh his servants, so goes he the same pace, to the ruine of
his enemies, *In matutino interficiam, I will early destroy all the*
Psal. 101.8   *wicked of the land:* It is not a weakning of them, It is a destruction;
It is not of a squadron or regiment, It is all; It is not onely upon the
Land, but the wicked of any Land, he will destroy upon the Sea too.
This is his promise, this is his practise, this is his pace. Thus he did in
2 King.   *Sennacheribs* Army, *When they arose early in the Morning, behold*
19.35   *they were all dead carcasses;* They rose early that saw it, but God had
460   been up earlier, that had done it. And that story, God seemes to have
had care to have recorded almost in all the divisions of the Bible, for
it is in the Historicall part, and it is in the Propheticall part too; and
because God foresaw, that mens curiosities would carry them upon
Apocryphal Books also, it is repeated almost in every Book of that
kinde, in *Ecclesiasticus,* in *Tobit,* in the *Maccabees* in both Books,
That every where our eye might light upon that, and every soule

might make that Syllogisme, and produce that conclusion to it selfe,
If God bee thus forward, thus early in the wayes of Judgement, much
more is he so in the wayes of mercy; with that he will satisfie us
⁴⁷⁰ *Mane,* early, and as *Tremellius* reads this very Text, *unoquoque
mane,* betimes in the morning, and every morning.

Now if we looke for this early mercy from God, we must rise
betimes too, and meet God early. God hath promised to give *Matu-
tinam stellam,* the Morning-star; but they must be up betimes in the   Revel. 2.28
morning, that will take the Morning-star. He himselfe who is it, hath
told us who is this Morning star; *I Iesus am the bright and Morning*   Revel. 22.16
starre. God will give us Jesus; Him, and all his, all his teares, all his
blood, all his merits; But to whom, and upon what conditions? That
is expressed there, *Vincenti dabo, To him that overcommeth I will*
⁴⁸⁰ *give the Morning-star.* Our life is a warfare, our whole life; It is not
onely with lusts in our youth, and ambitions in our middle yeares,
and indevotions in our age, but with agonies in our body, and tentations in our spirit upon our death-bed, that we are to fight; and he
cannot be said to overcome, that fights not out the whole battell. If
he enter not the field in the morning, that is, apply not himselfe to
Gods service in his youth, If hee continue not to the Evening, If hee
faint in the way, and grow remisse in Gods service, for collaterall
respects, God will overcome his cause, and his glory shall stand fast,
but that man can scarce be said to have overcome.

⁴⁹⁰   It is the counsell of the Wise man, *Prevent the Sunne to give thanks*   Wisd. 16.28
to God, and at the day-spring pray unto him. You see still, how these
two duties are marshalled, and disposed; First Praise, and then
Prayer, but both early: And it is placed in the Lamentations, as
though it were a lamentable negligence to have omitted it, *It is good*   Lament.
for a man, that he beare his yoake in his youth. Rise as early as you   3.27
can, you cannot be up before God; no, nor before God raise you:
Howsoever you prevent this Sunne, the Sunne of the Firmament,
yet the Sonne of Heaven hath prevented you, for without his preventing Grace you could not stirre. Have any of you slept out their
⁵⁰⁰ Morning, resisted his private motions to private Prayer at home,
neglected his callings so? Though a man doe sleepe out his fore-
noone, the Sunne goes on his course, and comes to his Meridionall
splendor, though that man have not looked towards it. That Sonne

which hath risen to you at home, in those private motions, hath
gone on his course, and hath shined out here, in this house of God,
upon Wednesday, and upon Friday, and upon every day of holy
Convocation; All this, at home, and here, yee have slept out and
neglected. Now, upon the Sabbath, and in these holy Exercises, this
Sonne shines out as at noone, the Grace of God is in the Exaltation,
510 exhibited in the powerfullest and effectuallest way of his Ordinance,
and if you will but awake now, rise now, meet God now, now at
noone, God will call even this early. Have any of you slept out the
whole day, and are come in that drowsinesse to your evening, to the
closing of your eyes, to the end of your dayes? Yet rise now, and God
shall call even this an early rising; If you can make shift to deceive
your owne soules and say, We never heard God call us; If you neglected your former callings so, as that you have forgot that you have
been called; yet, is there one amongst you, that denies that God calls
him now? If he neglect this calling now, to morrow he may forget that
520 he was called to day, or remember it with such a terror, as shall blow
a dampe, and a consternation upon his soule, and a lethargy worse
then his former sleepe; but if he will wake now, and rise now, though
this be late in his evening, in his age, yet God shall call this early.
Bee but able to say with *Esay* this night, *My soule hath desired thee*
in the night, and thou maist be bold to say with *David* to morrow
morning, *Satura nos mane, Satisfie us early with thy mercy,* and he
shall doe it.

But yet no prayer of ours, howsoever made in the best disposition,
in the best testimony of a rectified conscience, must limit God his
530 time, or appoint him, in what morning, or what houre in the morning, God shall come to our deliverance. The Sonne of man was not
the lesse the Sonne of God, nor the lesse a beloved Sonne, though
God hid from him the knowledge of the day of the generall Judgement. Thou art not the lesse the servant of God, nor the lesse rewarded by him, though he keepe from thee the knowledge of thy
deliverance from any particular calamity. All Gods deliverances are
in the morning, because there is a perpetuall night, and an invincible
darknesse upon us, till he deliver us. God is the God of that Climate,
where the night is six Moneths long, as well as of this, where it is but
540 halfe so many houres. The highest Hill hinders not the roundnesse

Isai. 26.9

[Mar. 13.32]

of the earth, the earth is round for all that hill; The lowest vaults, and mines hinder not the solidnesse of the earth, the earth is solid for all that; Much lesse hath a yeare, or ten yeares, or all our three-score and ten, any proportion at all to eternity; And therefore God comes early in a sort to me, though I lose abundance of my reward by so long lingring, if he come not till hee open me the gate of heaven, by the key of death. There are Indies at my right hand, in the East; but there are Indies at my left hand too, in the West. There are testimonies of Gods love to us, in our East, in our beginnings;
50 but if God continue tribulation upon us to our West, to our ends, and give us the light of his presence then, if he appeare to us at our transmigration, certainly he was favourable to us all our peregrina-tion, and though he shew himselfe late, hee was our friend early. The Prayer is, that he would come early, but it is, if it be rightly formed, upon both these conditions; first, that I rise early to meet him, and then that I magnifie his houre as early, whensoever he shall be pleased to come.

All this I shall doe the better, if I limit my prayer, and my   *Tuâ*
practise, with the next circumstance in *Davids* prayer, *Tuâ, Satisfie*
60 *us early with* that which is thine, *Thy mercy:* For there are mercies, (in a faire extent and accommodation of the word, that is Refresh-ings, Eases, Deliverances) that are not his mercies, nor his satisfac-tions. How many men are satisfied with Riches (I correct my selfe, few are satisfied; but how many have enough to satisfie many?) and yet have never a peny of his mony? Nothing is his, that comes not from him, that comes not by good meanes. How many are there, that are easie to admit scruples, and jealousies, and suspitions in matter of Religion: Easie to think, that that Religion, and that Church, in which they have lived ill, cannot bee a good Religion, nor
70 a true Church; In a troubled, and distempered conscience, they grow easie to admit scruples, and then as over-easie to admit false satisfac-tions, with a word whispered on one side in a Conventicle, or a word whispered on the other side in a Confession, and yet have never a dram of satisfaction from his word, whose word is preached upon the house top, and avowed, and not in corners? How many men   [Luke 12.3]
are anguished with torturing Diseases, racked with the conscience of ill-spent estates, oppressed with inordinate melancholies, and

irreligious dejections of spirit, and then repaire, and satisfie themselves with wine, with women, with fooles, with comedies, with
[Job 16.2]   ⁵⁸⁰ mirth, and musique, and with all *Iobs* miserable comforters, and all
this while have no beames of his satisfaction, it is not *Misericordia
ejus,* his mercy, his satisfaction? In losses of worldly goods, in sicknesses of children, or servants, or cattell, to receive light or ease from
Witches, this is not his mercy. It is not his mercy, except we goe by
good wayes to good ends; except our safety be established by allyance
with his friends, except our peace may bee had with the perfect
continuance of our Religion, there is no safety, there is no peace. But
let mee feele the effect of this Prayer, as it is a Prayer of manifestation,
Let mee discerne that, that that is done upon mee, is done by the
⁵⁹⁰ hand of God, and I care not what it be: I had rather have Gods
Vinegar, then mans Oyle, Gods Wormewood, then mans Manna,
Gods Justice, then any mans Mercy; for, therefore did *Gregory
Nyssen* call S. *Basil* in a holy sense, *Ambidextrum,* because he tooke
every thing that came, by the right handle, and with the right hand,
because he saw it to come from God. Even afflictions are welcome,
when we see them to be his: Though the way that he would chuse,
and the way that this Prayer intreats, be only mercy, *Satisfie us early
with thy mercy.*

Misericordia   That rod and that staffe with which we are at any time corrected,
⁶⁰⁰ is his. So God cals the Assyrians, *The rod of his anger,* and he sayes,
Esay 10.5   *That the staffe that is in their hand, is his Indignation.* He comes to
a sharper execution, from the rod, and the staffe to the sword, and
Ezek. 30.24   that also is his, *It is my sword, that is put into the hands of the King
of Babylon, and he shall stretch out my sword upon the whole land;*
God will beat downe, and cut off, and blow up, and blow out at his
pleasure; which is expressed in a phrase very remarkeable by *David,*
Psal. 135.7   *He bringeth the winde out of his Treasuries;* And then follow in
that place, all the Plagues of Egypt: stormes and tempests, ruines and
devastations, are not onely in Gods Armories, but they are in his
⁶¹⁰ Treasuries; as hee is the Lord of Hosts, hee fetches his judgements
from his Armories, and casts confusion upon his enemies, but as he
is the God of mercy, and of plentifull redemption, he fetches these
judgements, these corrections out of his treasuries, and they are the
Money, the Jewels, by which he redeemes and buyes us againe; God

does nothing, God can doe nothing, no not in the way of ruine and destruction, but there is mercy in it; he cannot open a doore in his Armory, but a window into his Treasury opens too, and he must looke into that.

But then Gods corrections are his Acts, as the Physitian is his ⁶²⁰ Creature, God created him for necessity. When God made man, his first intention was not that man should fall, and so need a Messias, nor that man should fall sick, and so need a Physitian, nor that man should fall into rebellion by sin, and so need his rod, his staffe, his scourge of afflictions, to whip him into the way againe. But yet sayes the Wiseman, *Honour the Physitian for the use you may have of him; slight him not, because thou hast no need of him yet.* So though Gods corrections were not from a primary, but a secondary intention, yet, when you see those corrections fall upon another, give a good interpretation of them, and beleeve Gods purpose to be not to de- ⁶³⁰ stroy, but to recover that man: Do not thou make Gods Rheubarbe thy Ratsbane, and poyson thine owne soule with an uncharitable misinterpretation of that correction, which God hath sent to cure his. And then, in thine owne afflictions, flie evermore to this Prayer, *Satisfie us with thy mercy;* first, Satisfie us, make it appeare to us that thine intention is mercy, though thou enwrap it in temporall afflictions, in this darke cloud let us discerne thy Son, and though in an act of displeasure, see that thou art well pleased with us; Satisfie us, that there is mercy in thy judgements, and then satisfie us, that thy mercy is mercy; for such is the stupidity of sinfull man, That ⁶⁴⁰ as in temporall blessings, we discerne them best by wanting them, so do we the mercies of God too; we call it not a mercy, to have the same blessings still: but, as every man conceives a greater degree of joy, in recovering from a sicknesse, then in his former established health; so without doubt, our Ancestors who indured many yeares Civill and forraine wars, were more affected with their first peace, then we are with our continuall enjoying thereof, And our Fathers more thankfull, for the beginning of Reformation of Religion, then we for so long enjoying the continuance thereof. *Satisfie us with thy mercie,* Let us still be able to see mercy in thy judgements, lest ⁶⁵⁰ they deject us, and confound us; *Satisfie us with thy mercie,* let us be able to see, that our deliverance is a mercy, and not a naturall thing

Ecclus. 38.1

that might have hapned so, or a necessary thing that must have hapned so, though there had beene no God in Heaven, nor providence upon earth. But especially since the way that thou choosest, is to goe all by mercy, and not to be put to this way of correction, so dispose, so compose our minds, and so transpose all our affections, that we may live upon thy food, and not put thee to thy physick, that we may embrace thee in the light, and not be put to seeke thee in the darke, that wee come to thee in thy Mercy, and not be whipped
660 to thee by thy Corrections. And so we have done also with our second Part, The pieces and petitions that constitute this Prayer, as it is a Prayer for Fulnesse and Satisfaction, a Prayer of Extent and Dilatation, a Prayer of Dispatch and Expedition, and then a Prayer of Evidence and Declaration, and lastly, a Prayer of Limitation even upon God himselfe, *Satisfie,* and *satisfie us,* and *us early,* with that which we may discerne to be *thine,* and let that way be *mercy.*

3 Part   There remaines yet a third Part, what this Prayer produces, and
Gaudium   it is joy, and continual joy, *That we may rejoyce and be glad all our dayes.* The words are the Parts, and we invert not, we trouble not
670 the Order; the Holy Ghost hath laid them fitliest for our use, in the Text it selfe, and so we take them. First then, the gaine is joy. Joy is Gods owne Seale, and his keeper is the Holy Ghost; wee have many sudden ejaculations in the forme of Prayer, sometimes inconsiderately made, and they vanish so; but if I can reflect upon my prayer, ruminate, and returne againe with joy to the same prayer, I have Gods Seale upon it. And therefore it is not so very an idle thing, as some have mis-imagined it, to repeat often the same prayer
[Mat. 26.44]   in the same words; Our Saviour did so; he prayed a third time, and in the same words; This reflecting upon a former prayer, is that that
680 sets to this Seale, this joy, and if I have joy in my prayer, it is granted so far as concernes my good, and Gods glory. It hath beene disputed by many, both of the Gentiles, with whom the Fathers disputed, and of the Schoolemen, who dispute with one another, *An sit gaudium in Deo, de semet,* Whether God rejoyce in himselfe, in contemplation of himselfe, whether God be glad that he is God: But it is disputed by them, onely to establish it, and to illustrate it, for I doe not remember that any one of them denyes it. It is true, that *Plato* dislikes, and justly, that salutation of *Dionysius* the Tyran to God,

Gaude, & servato vitam Tyranni jucundam; that he should say to
690 God, Live merrily, as merrily as a King, as merrily as I doe, and then
you are God enough; to imagine such a joy in God, as is onely a
transitory delight in deceivable things, is an impious conceit. But
when, as another Platonique sayes, *Deus est quod ipse semper voluit,*   Plotinus
God is that which hee would be, If there be something that God
would be, and he be that, If *Plato* should deny, that God joyed in
himselfe, we must say of *Plato* as *Lactantius* does, *Deum potius
somniaverat, quàm cognoverat, Plato* had rather dreamed that there
was a God, then understood what that God was. *Bonum simplex,*
sayes S. *Augustine,* To be sincere Goodnesse, Goodnesse it selfe, *Ipsa*
700 *est delectatio Dei,* This is the joy that God hath in himselfe, of himselfe; And therefore sayes *Philo Iudæus, Hoc necessarium Philo-
sophiæ sodalibus,* This is the tenent of all Philosophers, (And by that
title of Philosophers, *Philo* alwaies meanes them that know and
study God) *Solum Deum verè festum agere,* That only God can be
truly said to keepe holy day, and to rejoyce.

This joy we shall see, when we see him, who is so in it, as that he
is this joy it selfe. But here in this world, so far as I can enter into
my Masters sight, I can enter into my Masters joy. I can see God in
his Creatures, in his Church, in his Word and Sacraments, and Ordi-
710 nances; Since I am not without this sight, I am not without this joy.
Here a man may *Transilire mortalitatem,* sayes that Divine Morall   Seneca
man; I cannot put off mortality, but I can looke upon immortality;
I cannot depart from this earth, but I can looke into Heaven. So I
cannot possesse that finall and accomplished joy here, but as my
body can lay downe a burden or a heavy garment, and joy in that
ease, so my soule can put off my body so far, as that the concupiscencies thereof, and the manifold and miserable encumbrances of
this world, cannot extinguish this holy joy. And this inchoative joy,
David derives into two branches, *To rejoyce,* and *to be glad.*
720 The Holy Ghost is an eloquent Author, a vehement, and an abun-   *Exultatio*
dant Author, but yet not luxuriant; he is far from a penurious, but
as far from a superfluous style too. And therefore we doe not take
these two words in the Text, *To rejoyce,* and *to be glad,* to signifie
meerely one and the same thing, but to be two beames, two branches,
two effects, two expressings of this joy. We take them therefore, as

they offer themselves in their roots, and first naturall propriety of the words. The first, which we translate *To rejoyce,* is *Ranan;* and *Ranan* denotes the externall declaration of internall joy; for the word signifies *Cantare,* To sing, and that with an extended and loud voyce, 730 for it is the word, which is oftnest used for the musique of the Church, and the singing of Psalmes; which was such a declaration of their zealous alacrity in the primitive Church, as that, when to avoyd discovery in the times of persecution, they were forced to make their meetings in the night, they were also forced to put out their Candles, because by that light in the windowes they were discovered; After that this meeting in the darke occasioned a scandall and ill report upon those Christians, that their meetings were not upon so holy purposes, as they pretended, they discontinued their vigils, and night-meetings, yet their singing of Psalmes, when they 740 did meet, they never discontinued, though that, many times, exposed them to dangers, and to death it selfe, as some of the Authors of the secular story of the Romans have observed and testified unto us. And some ancient Decrees and Constitutions we have, in which such are forbidden to be made Priests, as were not perfect in the Psalmes. And though S. *Hierome* tell us this, with some admiration, and note of singularity, That *Paula* could say the whole book of Psalmes without booke, in Hebrew; yet he presents it as a thing well known to be their ordinary practise; *In villula Christi Bethlem, extra psalmos silentium est,* In the village where I dwell, sayes he, where Christ was 750 borne, in Bethlem, if you cannot sing Psalmes, you must be silent, here you shall heare nothing but Psalmes; for, (as he pursues it) *Arator stivam tenens,* The husbandman that follows the plough, he that sowes, that reapes, that carries home, all begin and proceed in all their labours with singing of Psalmes. Therefore he calls them there, *Cantiones amatorias,* Those that make or entertaine love, that seeke in the holy and honorable way of marriage, to make themselves acceptable and agreeable to one another, by no other good parts, nor conversation, but by singing of Psalmes. So he calls them, *Pastorum sibilum,* and *Arma culturæ,* Our shepheards, sayes S. 760 *Hierome,* here, have no other Eclogues, no other Pastoralls; Our labourers, our children, our servants no other songs, nor Ballads, to recreate themselves withall, then the Psalmes.

And this universall use of the Psalmes, that they served all for all, gives occasion to one Author, in the title of the Booke of Psalmes, to depart from the ordinary reading, which is, *Sepher Tehillim,* The booke of Praise, and to read it, *Sepher Telim,* which is *Acervorum,* The booke of Heapes, where all assistances to our salvation are heaped and treasured up. And our Countryman *Bede* found another Title, in some Copies of this booke, *Liber Soliloquiorum de* 770 *Christo,* The Booke of Meditations upon Christ; Because this booke is (as *Gregory Nyssen* calls it) *Clavis David,* that key of *David,* which lets us in to all the mysteries of our Religion; which gave the ground to that which S. *Basil* sayes, that if all the other Books of Scripture could be lost, he would aske no more then the Booke of Psalmes, to catechize children, to edifie Congregations, to convert Gentils, and to convince Heretiques.

But we are launched into too large a Sea, the consideration of this Booke of Psalmes. I meane but this, in this, That if we take that way with God, The way of prayer, prayer so elemented and constituted, 780 as we have said, that consists rather of praise and thankesgiving, then supplication for future benefits, God shall infuse into us, a zeale of expressing our consolation in him, by outward actions, to the establishing of others; we shall not disavow, nor grow slacke in our Religion, nor in any parts thereof; God shall neither take from us, The Candle and the Candlestick, The truth of the Gospel, which is the light, And the cheerfull, and authorized, and countenanced, and rewarded Preaching of the Gospel, which is the Candlestick that exalts the light; nor take from us our zeale to this outward service of God, that we come to an indifferency, whether the service of God 790 be private or publique, sordid or glorious, allowed and suffered, by way of connivency, or commanded and enjoyned by way of authority. God shall give us this *Ranan,* this rejoycing, this externall joy, we shall have the publique preaching of the Gospel continued to us, and we shall shew that we rejoyce in it, by frequenting it, and by instituting our lives according unto it.

But yet this *Ranan,* this *Rejoycing,* this outward expressing of our inward zeale, may admit interruptions, receive interceptions, intermissions, and discontinuances; for, without doubt, in many places there live many persons, well affected to the truth of Religion, that

Delectabimur

⁸⁰⁰ dare not avow it, expresse it, declare it, especially where that fearfull
Vulture, the Inquisition, hovers over them. And therefore the Holy
Ghost hath added here another degree of joy, which no law, no
severe execution of law, can take from us, in another word of lesse
extent, *Shamach,* which is an inward joy, onely in the heart, which
we translate here, to be *Glad*. How far we are bound to proceed in
outward declarations of Religion, requires a serious and various con-

Dan. 6.10   sideration of Circumstances. You know how far *Daniel* proceeded;
The Lords had extorted a Proclamation from the King, That no
man should pray to any other God, then the King, for certaine dayes;
⁸¹⁰ *Daniel* would not onely not be bound by this Proclamation, and so
continue his set and stationary houres of private prayer in his chamber, but he would declare it to all the world; He would set open
his chamber windows, that he might be seen to pray; for, though
some determine that act of *Daniel,* in setting open his windows at
prayer, in this, That because the Jewes were bound by their law,
wheresoever they were, in war, in captivity, upon the way, or in their
sick beds, to turne towards Jerusalem, and so towards the Temple,
whensoever they prayed, according to that stipulation, which had

[1 Kings   passed between God and *Solomon,* at the Dedication of the Temple,
8.30]   ⁸²⁰ When thy servants pray towards this house, heare them in it; There-
[Isa. 38.2]   fore as *Hezekias,* in his sicke bed, when he turned towards the wall
to pray, is justly thought, to have done so, therefore that he might
pray towards the Temple, which stood that way; so *Daniel* is thought
to have opened his windows to that purpose too, that he might have
the more free prospect towards Jerusalem from Babylon; though
some, I say, determine *Daniels* act in that, yet it is by more, and more
usefully extended, to an expressing of such a zeale, as, in so apparant
a dishonor to his God, could not be suffocated nor extinguished with
a Proclamation.

⁸³⁰   In which act of his, which was a direct and evident opposing and
affronting of the State, though I dare not joyne with them, who
absolutely and peremptorily condemne this act of *Daniel,* because
Gods subsequent act in a miraculous deliverance of *Daniel* seems to
imply some former particular revelation from God to *Daniel,* that
he should proceed in that confident manner, yet dare I much lesse
draw this act of *Daniels* into consequence, and propose it for an

Example and precedent to private men, least of all, to animate seditious men, who upon pretence of a necessity, that God must be served
in this, and this, and no other manner, provoke and exasperate the
840 Magistrate with their schismaticall conventicles and separations. But
howsoever that may stand, and howsoever there may be Circumstances which may prevaile either upon humane infirmity, or upon
a rectified Conscience, or howsoever God in his Judgements, may
cast a cloud upon his own Sunne, and darken the glory of the Gospel,
in some place, for some time, yet, though we lose our *Ranan,* our
publique Rejoycing, we shall never lose our *Shamach,* our inward
gladnesse, that God is our God, and we his servants for all this. God
will never leave his servants without this internall joy, which shall
preserve them from suspicions of Gods power, that he cannot main-
850 taine, or not restore his cause, and from jealousies, that he hath aban-
doned or deserted them in particular. God shall never give them
over to an indifferency, nor to a stupidity, nor to an absence of tendernesse, and holy affections, that it shall become all one to them, how
Gods cause prospers, or suffers. But if I continue that way, prayer,
and prayer so qualified, if I lose my *Ranan,* my outward declarations
of Rejoycing; If I be tyed to a death-bed in a Consumption, and cannot rejoyce in comming to these publique Congregations, to participate of their prayers, and to impart to them my Meditations; If I be
ruined in my fortune, and cannot rejoyce in an open distribution to
860 the reliefe of the poore, and a preaching to others, in that way, by
example of doing good works; If at my last minute, I be not able
to edifie my friends, nor Catechize my children, with any thing that
I can doe or say; if I be not able so much, as with hand or eye to make
a signe, though I have lost my *Ranan,* all the Eloquence of outward
declaration, yet God shall never take from me, my *Shamach,* my internall gladnesse and consolation, in his undeceivable and undeceiv-
ing Spirit, that he is mine, and I am his; And this joy, this gladnesse,
in my way, and in my end, shall establish me; for that is that which
is intended in the next, and last word, *Omnibus diebus,* we shall
870 *Rejoyce and be Glad all our dayes.*

Nothing but this testimony, *That the Spirit beares witnesse with
my spirit,* that upon my prayer, so conditioned, of praise, and prayer,
I shall still prevaile with God, could imprint in me, this *joy, all my*

*Omnibus
diebus*
[Rom. 8.16]

dayes. The seales of his favour, in outward blessings, fayle me in the dayes of shipwracke, in the dayes of fire, in the dayes of displacing my potent friends, or raysing mine adversaries; In such dayes I cannot rejoyce, and be glad. The seales of his favour, in inward blessings, and holy cheerfulnesse, fayle me in a present remorse after a sinne newly committed. But yet in the strength of a Christian hope,
880 as I can pronounce out of the grounds of Nature, in an Eclipse of the Sunne, that the Sunne shall returne to his splendor againe, I can pronounce out of the grounds of Gods Word, (and Gods Word is much better assurance, then the grounds of Nature, for God can and does shake the grounds of Nature by Miracles, but no Jod of his Word shall ever perish) that I shall returne againe on my hearty penitence, if I delay it not, and rejoyce and be glad all my dayes, that is, what kinde of day soever overtake me. In the dayes of our youth, when the joyes of this world take up all the roome, there shall be roome for this holy Joy, that my recreations were harmelesse, and my
890 conversation innocent; and certainly to be able to say, that in my recreations, in my conversation, I neither ministred occasion of tentation to another, nor exposed my selfe to tentations from another, is a faire beame of this rejoycing in the dayes of my youth. In the dayes of our Age, when we become incapable, insensible of the joyes of this world, yet this holy joy shall season us, not with a sinfull delight in the memory of our former sinnes, but with a re-juveniscence, a new and a fresh youth, in being come so neere to another, to an immortall life. In the dayes of our mirth, and of laughter, this holy joy shall enter; And as the Sunne may say to the starres at
900 Noone, How frivoulous and impertinent a thing is your light now?
So this joy shall say *unto laughter, Thou art mad, and unto mirth, what dost thou?* And in the mid-night of sadnesse, and dejection of spirit, this joy shall shine out, and chide away that sadnesse, with *Davids* holy charme, *My soule, why art thou cast downe, why art thou disquieted within me?* In those dayes, which *Iob* speaks of, *Prævenerunt me dies afflictionis meæ, Miseries are come upon me before their time;* My intemperances have hastned age, my riotousnesse hath hastned poverty, my neglecting of due officiousnesse and respect towards great persons hath hastned contempt upon me, Afflic-
910 tions which I suspected not, thought not of, have prevented my

Eccles. 2.2

Iob 30.27

Verse 16

[Gen. 19.22]

[Gen. 45.10]

feares; and then in those dayes, which *Iob* speaks of againe, *Possident me dies afflictionis,* Studied and premeditated plots and practises swallowe mee, possesse me intirely, In all these dayes, I shall not onely have a *Zoar* to flie to, if I can get out of *Sodom,* joy, if I can overcome my sorrow; There shall not be a *Goshen* bordering upon my *Egypt,* joy, if I can passe beyond, or besides my sorrow, but I shall have a *Goshen* in my *Egypt,* nay my very *Egypt* shall be my *Goshen,* I shall not onely have joy, though I have sorrow, but therefore; my very sorrow shall be the occasion of joy; I shall not onely
920 have a Sabbath after my six dayes labor, but *Omnibus diebus,* a Sabbath shall enlighten every day, and inanimate every minute of every day: And as my soule is as well in my foot, as in my hand, though all the waight and oppression lie upon the foot, and all action upon the hand, so these beames of joy shall appeare as well in my pillar of cloud, as in theirs of fire; in my adversity, as well as in their prosperity; And when their Sun shall set at Noone, mine shall rise at midnight; they shall have damps in their glory, and I joyfull exaltations in my dejections.

And to end with the end of all, *In die mortis,* In the day of my
930 death, and that which is beyond the end of all, and without end in it selfe, The day of Judgement, If I have the testimony of a rectified conscience, that I have accustomed my selfe to that accesse to God, by prayer, and such prayer, as though it have had a body of supplication, and desire of future things, yet the soule and spirit of that prayer, that is, my principall intention in that prayer, hath been praise and thanksgiving, If I be involved in S. *Chrysostoms* Patent, *Orantes, non natura, sed dispensatione Angeli fiunt,* That those who pray so, that is, pray by way of praise, (which is the most proper office of Angels) as they shall be better then Angels in the next world, (for they shall
940 be glorifying spirits, as the Angels are, but they shall also be glorified bodies, which the Angels shall never bee) so in this world they shall be as Angels, because they are employed in the office of Angels, to pray by way of praise, If, as S. *Basil* reads those words of that Psalme, not *spiritus meus,* but *respiratio mea laudet Dominum,* Not onely my spirit, but my very breath, not my heart onely, but my tongue, and my hands bee accustomed to glorifie God, *In die mortis,* in the day of my death, when a mist of sorrow, and of sighes shall fill my

chamber, and a cloude exhaled and condensed from teares, shall bee
the curtaines of my bed, when those that love me, shall be sorry to
⁹⁵⁰ see mee die, and the devill himselfe that hates me, sorry to see me
die so, in the favour of God; And *In die Iudicii,* In the day of Judgement, when as all Time shall cease, so all measures shall cease; The
joy, and the sorrow that shall be then, shall be eternall, no end, and
infinite, no measure, no limitation, when every circumstance of sinne
shall aggravate the condemnation of the unrepentant sinner, and the
very substance of my sinne shall bee washed away, in the blood of my
Saviour, when I shall see them, who sinned for my sake, perish eternally, because they proceeded in that sinne, and I my selfe, who occasioned their sin received into glory, because God upon my prayer, and
⁹⁶⁰ repentance had satisfied me early with his mercy, early, that is, before
my transmigration, *In omnibus diebus,* In all these dayes, the dayes
of youth, and the wantonnesses of that, the dayes of age, and the
tastlesnesse of that, the dayes of mirth, and the sportfulnesse of that,
and of inordinate melancholy, and the disconsolatenesse of that, the
days of such miseries, as astonish us with their suddennesse, and of
such as aggravate their owne waight with a heavy expectation; In
the day of Death, which pieces up that circle, and in that day which
enters another circle that hath no pieces, but is one equall everlast-
ingnesse, the day of Judgement, Either I shall rejoyce, be able to
⁹⁷⁰ declare my faith, and zeale to the assistance of others, or at least be
glad in mine owne heart, in a firme hope of mine owne salvation.

    And therefore, beloved, as they, whom lighter affections carry to
Shewes, and Masks, and Comedies; As you your selves, whom better
dispositions bring to these Exercises, conceive some contentment,
and some kinde of Joy, in that you are well and commodiously placed,
they to see the Shew, you to heare the Sermon, when the time comes,
though your greater Joy bee reserved to the comming of that time;
So though the fulnesse of Joy be reserved to the last times in heaven,
yet rejoyce and be glad that you are well and commodiously placed
⁹⁸⁰ in the meane time, and that you sit but in expectation of the fulnesse
of those future Joyes: Returne to God, with a joyfull thankfulnesse
that he hath placed you in a Church, which withholds nothing from
you, that is necessary to salvation, whereas in another Church they
lack a great part of the Word, and halfe the Sacrament; And which

obtrudes nothing to you, that is not necessary to salvation, whereas in another Church, the Additionall things exceed the Fundamentall; the Occasionall, the Originall; the Collaterall, the Direct; And the Traditions of men, the Commandements of God. Maintaine and hold up this holy alacrity, this religious cheerfulnesse; For inordinate sad-
990 nesse is a great degree and evidence of unthankfulnesse, and the departing from Joy in this world, is a departing with one piece of our Evidence, for the Joyes of the world to come.

Number 15.

Preached upon the Penitentiall Psalmes.

PSAL. 51.7. *PURGE ME WITH HYSSOPE, AND I SHALL BE CLEANE; WASH ME, AND I SHALL BE WHITER THEN SNOW.*

IN THE Records of the growth, and propagation of the Christian Church, The Ecclesiasticall Story, we have a relation of one *Pambo,* an unlearned, but devout, and humble Ermit, who being informed of another man, more learned then himselfe, that professed the understanding, and teaching of the Book of Psalmes, sought him out, and applied himselfe to him, to be his Disciple. And taking his first lesson casually, at the first verse of the thirty ninth Psalme, *I will take heed to my wayes, that I sin not with my tongue,* He went away with that lesson, with a promise to returne againe
10 when he was perfect in that. And when he discontinued so long, that his Master, sometimes occasionally lighting upon him, accused him of this slacknesse, for almost twenty yeares together he made severall excuses, but at last professed, that at the end of those twenty yeares, he was not yet perfect in his first lesson, in that one verse, *I will take heed to my wayes, that I sinne not with my tongue.* Now, that which made this lesson hard unto him, was, that it employed all his diligence, and his watchfulnesse upon future things; to examine and debate all his actions, and all his words; for, else he did not take heed to his wayes; at least, not so, as that hee would not sin
20 with his tongue. But if he had begun with this lesson, with this Psalme, which is but a calling to our memory that which is past, The sinfull employment of that time, which is gone, and shall not returne, The sinfull heats of our youth, which, since we wanted remorsefull teares to quench them, even the sin it selfe, and the excesse thereof

296

hath overcome, and allayed in us, sinfull omissions, sinfull actions, and habits, and all those transitory passages, in which the Apostle shewes us, our prodigality, our unthriftinesse, our ill bargaine, when he askes us that question of Confusion, *What fruit had you then in those things, whereof ye are now ashamed?* If he had begun his first
30 lesson at this, with the presenting of all his passed sins, in the sight of the Father, and in the Mediation and merit of the Sonne, he would have been sooner perfect in that lesson, and would have found himselfe, even by laying open his disease, so *purged with Hyssop* as that he should have been *cleane,* and so *washed,* as that he should have been *whiter then snow.* For, Repentance of sins past is nothing but an Audit, a casting up of our accounts, a consideration, a survey, how it stands between God and our soule. And yet, as many men run out of plentifull estates, onely because they are loath to see a list of their debts, to take knowledge how much they are
40 behind hand, or to contract their expenses: so we run out of a whole and rich inheritance, the Kingdome of heaven, we profuse and poure out even our own soule, rather then we will cast our eye upon that which is past, rather then we will present a list of our spirituall debts to God, or discover our disease to that Physician, who onely can *Purge us with hyssope, that we may be cleane, and wash us, that wee may be whiter then snow.*

Rom. 6.21

In the words we shall consider the Person, and the Action, who petitions, and what he asks. Both are twofold; for, the persons are two, the Physitian and the Patient, God and *David,* Doe *thou* purge
50 *me,* doe *thou* wash *me;* and the Action is twofold, *Purgabis,* doe thou *purge* me, and *Lavabis,* doe thou *wash* me. In which last part, and in the first branch thereof, wee shall see first, the Action it selfe, *Purgabis, Thou shalt purge mee,* and what that imports; And then the meanes, *Purgabis hyssopo, Thou shalt purge me with hyssope,* what that implies; and then the effect, *Mundabor, I shall bee made cleane,* and what that comprehends. And in the other branch of that second part, *Lavabis, Thou shalt wash me,* wee shall also looke upon the Action on Gods part, *Lavabis, Thou shalt wash mee,* and the Effect on our part, *Dealbabor, I shall be white,* and the Degree, the
60 Extent, the Exaltation of that Emundation, that Dealbation, that Cleansing, *supra nivem, I shall be whiter then snow.* And then we

Divisio

shall conclude all with that consideration, That though in the first part, we finde two persons in action; for God works, but man prayes that God would worke; yet in the other part, the worke it selfe, though the worke bee divers, a purging, and then a washing of the soule, the whole worke is Gods alone: *David* doth not say, no man can say, Doe thou purge me, and then, I will wash my selfe; nor doe thou make the Medicine, and I will bring the Hyssope; nor doe thou but wash mee, begin the worke, and I will goe forward with

70 it, and perfit it, and make my selfe whiter then snow; but the intire worke is his, who onely can infuse the desire, and onely accomplish that desire, who onely gives the will, and the ability to second, and execute that will, He, He purges me, or I am still a vessell of peccant

[2 Kings 4.40]
humors; His, His is the hyssope, or there is *Mors in olla,* Death in the cup; He, He washes me, or I am still in my blood; He, He exalts that cleannesse, which his, his washing hath indued, or I returne againe to that red earth, which I brought out of *Adams* bowels; Therefore *Doe thou purge mee with Hyssope, and I shall be cleane; Do thou wash me, and I shalbe whiter then snow.*

1 Part
Deus
Rom. 10.20
80   First then, for our first part, wee consider the persons. Of these God is the first; *Esay spoke boldly,* saith the Apostle, *when hee said, God is found by them that seeke him not;* But still we continue in that humble boldnesse, to say, God is best found, when we seeke him, and observe him in his operation upon us. God gives audiences, and admits accesses in his solemne and publike and out-roomes, in his Ordinances: In his Cabinet, in his Bed-chamber, in his unrevealed purposes, wee must not presse upon him. It was ill taken in the Roman State, when men enquired in *Arcana Imperii,* the secrets of State, by what wayes, and meanes, publike businesses were carried:

90 Private men were to rest in the generall effects, peace, and protection, and Justice, and the like, and to enquire no more; But to enquire in *Arcana Domus,* what was done in the Bed-chamber, was criminall, capitall, inexcusable. We must abstaine from enquiring *De modo,* how such or such things are done in many points, in which it is necessary to us to know that such things are done: As the maner of Christs presence in the Sacrament, and the maner of Christs descent into Hell, for these are *Arcana Imperii,* secrets of State, for the maner is secret, though the thing bee evident in the Scriptures. But

the entring into Gods unrevealed, and bosome-purposes, are *Arcana*
domus, a man is as farre from a possibility of attaining the knowledge, as from an excuse for offering at it. That curiosity will bring a
man to that blasphemy of *Alfonsus* King of Castile, the great Astron-
omer, who said, That if hee had beene of Gods Counsell in the creation
of the world, hee could have directed him to have done many things
better then he did. They that looke too farre into Gods unrevealed
purposes, are seldome content with that that they thinke God hath
done; but stray either into an uncharitable condemning of other men,
or into a jealous, a suspitious, a desperate condemning of themselves.
Here, in this first branch of this first part, wee seeke God, and because
we seeke him, where he hath promised to be, we are sure to find him;
Because we joyne with *David,* in an humble confession of our sins,
the Lord joyns us with *David,* in a fruition of himselfe. And more of
that first Person, God himselfe, we say not, but passe to the other, to
the petitioner, to the penitent, to the patient, to *David* himselfe.

His example is so comprehensive, so generall, that as a well made,   *David*
and well placed Picture in a Gallery looks upon all that stand in
severall places of the Gallery, in severall lines, in severall angles, so
doth *Davids* history concerne and embrace all. For his Person includes all states, betweene a shepherd and a King, and his sinne includes all sinne, between first Omissions, and complications of Habits
of sin upon sin: So that as S. *Basil* said, hee needed no other Booke,
for all spirituall uses, but the Psalmes, so wee need no other Example
to discover to us the slippery wayes into sin, or the penitentiall wayes
out of sin, then the Author of that Booke, *David.* From his Example
then, we first deduce this, That in the war-fare of this life, there are
no *Emeriti milites;* none of that discipline, that after certaine yeares
spent in the warres, a man should returne to ease, and honour, and
security, at home. A man is not delivered from the tentation of
Ambition, by having overcome the heats and concupiscences of his
youth; nor from the tentation of Covetousnesse in his age, by having
escaped ambition, and contented himselfe with a meane station in
his middle yeares. *David,* whom neither a sudden growth into such
degrees of greatnesse, as could not have fallen into his thought, or
wish before, nor the persecution of *Saul,* which might have enraged
him to a personall revenge, considering how many advantages, and

occasions hee might have made shift to thinke that God had put into
his hands, to execute that revenge; *David,* whom neither the con-
course and application of the people, who tooke knowledge of him,
as of a rising Sun, nor the interest and nearenesse in the love and
¹⁴⁰ heart of *Ionathan* the Kings Son, which fals seldome upon a new, and
a popular man; *David,* whom not that highest place, to which God
had brought him, in making him King, nor that addition even to that
highest place, that he made him Successor to a King of whom the
State was weary; (for, as the Panegyrique sayes, *Onerosum est succedere bono principi,* It is a heavy thing, and binds a Prince to a
great diligence, to come immediately after one, whom his subjects
loved, So had *David* an ease, in comming after one, with whom the
Kingdome was discontented) David, whom this sudden preferment,
and persecutions, and popularity, did not so shake, but that wee may
[Job. 1.22] ¹⁵⁰ say of him, as it is said of *Iob,* That in all this height, *David did not
sin,* nor in all these afflictions, *He did not charge God foolishly;*
Though he had many victories, he came not to a Triumph; but him,
whom an Army, and an armed Giant, *Goliah,* neare hand, could not
hurt, a weaker person, and naked, and farre off, overthrowes and
ruines.

It is therefore but an imperfect comfort for any man to say, I have
overcome tentations to great sins, and my sins have beene but of
infirmity, not of malice. For herein, more then in any other contemplation appeares the greatnesse, both of thy danger, and of thy
¹⁶⁰ transgression. For, consider what a dangerous, and slippery station
thou art in, if after a victory over Giants, thou mayest be overcome
by Pigmees; If after thy soule hath beene Canon proofe against strong
tentations, she be slaine at last by a Pistoll; And, after she hath swom
over a tempestuous Sea, shee drowne at last, in a shallow and standing ditch. And as it showes the greatnesse of thy danger, so it aggra-
vates the greatnesse of thy fault; That after thou hast had the
experience, that by a good husbanding of those degrees of grace,
which God hath afforded thee, thou hast beene able to stand out the
great batteries of strong tentations, and seest by that, that thou art
¹⁷⁰ much more able to withstand tentations to lesser sins, if thou wilt,
yet by disarming thy selfe, by devesting thy garisons, by discontinuing
thy watches, meerely by inconsideration, thou sellest thy soule for

nothing, for little pleasure, little profit, thou frustratest thy Saviour of that purchase, which he bought with his precious blood, and thou enrichest the Devils treasure as much, with thy single money, thy frequent small sins, as another hath done with his talent; for, as God was well pleased with the widowes two farthings, so is the Devill well pleased, with the negligent mans lesser sins. O who can be so confident in his footing, or in his hold, when *David,* that held
180 out so long, fell, and if we consider but himselfe, irrecoverably, where the tempter was weake, and afar off?

De longè vidit illam in qua captus est. Berseba was far off; *Mulier longè, libido prope,* but *Davids* disposition was in his owne bosome. Yet *David* came not up into the Teras, with any purpose or inclination to that sin. Here was no such plotting as in his son *Hammons* case, to get his sister *Tamar,* by dissembling himselfe to be sick, to his lodging. That man post-dates his sin, and begins his reckning too late, that dates his sin at that houre, when he commits that sin. You must not reckon in sin, from the Nativity, but the Conception;
190 when you conceived that sin in your purpose, then you sinned that sin, and in every letter, in every discourse, in every present, in every wish, in every dreame, that conduces to that sin, or rises from that sin, you sin it over, and over againe, before you come to the committing of it, and so your sin is an old, an inveterate sin, before it bee borne, and that which you call the first, is not the hundredth time, that you have sinned that sinne.

It is not much that *David* contributed to this sin on his part: He is onely noted in the Text, to have beene negligent in the publique businesse, and to have given himselfe too much ease in this particular,
200 that he lay in bed all day; *When it was evening, David arose out of his bed, and walked upon the Teras.* And it is true, that the justice of God is subtile, as searching, as unsearchable; and oftentimes punishes sins of Omission, with other sins, Actuall sins, and makes their lazinesse, who are slack in doing that they should, an occasion of doing that they should not.

It was not much that *Bathsheba* contributed to this tentation, on her part. The Vulgat Edition of the Roman Church, hath made her case somewhat the worse, by a mistranslation, *Ex adverso super solarium suum,* as though she had beene washing her selfe, upon her

August.

[2 Sam. 13]

2 Sam.
11.[2]

²¹⁰ owne Teras, and in the eye of the Court; whereas indeed, it is no more, but that *David* saw her, he upon his Teras, not her upon hers. For her washing, it may well be collected out of the fourth verse, that it was a Legall washing, to which shee was bound by the Leviticall Law, being a purification after her naturall infirmity, and which it had beene a sin in her, to have omitted. But had it beene a washing

[Sus. 1.17]

of Refreshing, or of Delicacy, even that was never imputed to *Susanna* for a fault, that she washed in a Garden, and in the day, and employed not onely sope, but other ingredients and materials, of more delicacy, in that washing.

²²⁰ Certainly the limits of adorning and beautifying the body are not so narrow, so strict, as by some sowre men they are sometimes conceived to be. Differences of Ranks, of Ages, of Nations, of Customes, make great differences in the enlarging, or contracting of these limits, in adorning the body; and that may come neare sin at some time, and in some places, which is not so alwaies, nor every where. Amongst the women there, the Jewish women, it was so generall a thing to helpe themselves with aromaticall Oyles, and liniments, as that that which is said by the Prophets poore Widow, to the Prophet

2 King. [4.2]

Elisha, That she had nothing in the house but a pot of Oyle, is very ²³⁰ properly by some collected from the Originall word, that it was not Oyle for meate, but Oyle for unction, aromaticall Oyle, Oyle to make her looke better; she was but poore, but a Widow, but a Prophets Widow, (and likely to be the poorer for that) yet she left not that. We see that even those women, whom the Kings were to take for their Wives, and not for Mistresses, (which is but a later name for Concubines) had a certaine, and a long time assigned to be prepared by those aromaticall unctions, and liniments for beauty. Neither do

[Gen. 12]

those that consider, that when *Abraham* was afraid to lose his wife *Sara* in Egypt, and that every man that saw her, would fall in love

[Gen. 20.2]

²⁴⁰ with her, *Sara* was then above threescore; And when the King *Abimelech* did fall in love with her, and take her from *Abraham,* she was fourscore and ten, they doe not assigne this preservation of her complexion, and habitude to any other thing, then the use of those unctions, and liniments, which were ordinary to that Nation. But yet though the extent and limit of this adorning the body, may be larger then some austere persons will allow, yet it is not so large, as that it

should be limited onely, by the intention and purpose of them that doe it; So that if they that beautifie themselves, meane no harme in it, therefore there should be no harme in it; for, except they could as
50 well provide, that others should take no harme, as that they should meane no harme, they may participate of the fault. And since we finde such an impossibility in rectifying and governing our owne senses, (we cannot take our owne eye, nor stop our owne eare, when we would) it is an unnecessary, and insupportable burden, to put upon our score, all the lascivious glances, and the licentious wishes of other persons, occasioned by us, in over-adorning our selves.

And this may well have beene *Bathshebaes* fault, That though she did not bathe with a purpose to be seene, yet she did not enough to provide against the infirmity of others. It had therefore been well if
260 *David* had risen earlier, to attend the affaires of the State; And it had been well, if *Bathsheba* had bathed within doores, and with more caution; but yet these errors alone, we should not be apt to condemne in such persons, except by Gods permitting greater sins to follow upon these, we were taught, that even such things, as seeme to us in their nature to be indifferent, have degrees of naturall and essentiall ill in them, which must be avoyded, even in the probability, nay even in the possibility that they may produce sin.

And as from this Example, we draw that Conclusion, That sins, which are but the Children of indifferent actions, become the Parents
270 of great sins; which is the industry of sin, to exalt it selfe, and (as it were) ennoble it selfe, above the stocke, from which it was derived, The next sin will needs be a better sin then the last: So have we also from *David* this Conclusion, that this generation of sin is infinite; infinite in number, infinite in duration; So infinite both waies, as that *Luther* (who seldome checks himselfe in any vehement expression) could not forbeare to say, *Si Nathan non venisset,* If *Nathan* had not come to *David, David* had proceeded to the sin against the Holy Ghost. O how impossible a thing is it then, for us to condition and capitulate with God, or with our owne Nature, and say to him,
280 or to our selves, We will sin thus long and no longer, Thus far, and no farther, this sin, and no more; when not onely the frailty of man, but even the justice of God provokes us (though not as Author, or cause of sin) to commit more and more sins, after wee have entangled and

enwrapped our selves in former! Who can doubt, but that in this yeares space, in which *David* continued in his sin, but that he did ordinarily all the externall acts of the religious Worship of God? who can doubt but that he performed all the Legall Sacrifices, and all the Ceremoniall Rites? Yea, we see, that when *Nathan* put *Davids* case in another name, of a rich man that had taken away a poore

²⁹⁰ mans onely sheepe, *David* was not onely just, but he was vehement in the execution of Justice; *Hee was,* saies the text, *exceeding wroth, and said, As the Lord liveth, that man shall dye;* But yet, for all this externall Religion, for all this Civill justice in matter of government, no mention of any repentance in all this time. How little a thing then is it, nay how great a thing, that is, how great an aggravating of thy sin, if thou thinke to bribe God with a Sabboth, or with an almes; And, as a criminall person would faine come to Sanctuary, not because it is a consecrated place, but because it rescues him from the Magistrate, So thou comest to Church, not because God is here, but

³⁰⁰ that thy being here may redeeme thee from the imputation of pro-phanenesse. At last *Nathan* came; *David* did not send for him, but God sent him; But yet *David* laid hold upon Gods purpose in him. And he confesses to God, he confesses to the Prophet, he confesses to the whole Church; for, before he pleads for mercy in the body of the Psalme, in the title of the Psalme, which is as Canonicall Scripture, as the Psalme it selfe, hee confesses himselfe plainly, *A Psalme of David, when the Prophet Nathan came to him, after he had gone in to Bathsheba.*

August.   *Audiunt male viventes, & quærunt sibi patrocinia peccandi;* Wee

³¹⁰ heare of *Davids* sin, and wee justifie our sins by him; *Si David, cur non & ego?* If *David* went in to a *Bathsheba,* why may not I? That Father tels you why, *Qui facit, quia David fecit, id facit, quod David non fecit,* He that does that, because *David* did it, does not doe that

August.   which *David* did; *Quia nullum exemplum proposuit,* For *David* did not justifie his sin, by any precedent example; So that he that sins as *David* did, yet sins worse then *David* did; and hee that continues as unsensible of his sin, as *David* was, is more unsensible then *David* was; *Quia ad te mittitur ipse David,* For God sends *Nathan* to thee, with *David* in his hand; He sends you the Receit, his invitations to

³²⁰ Repentance, in his Scriptures, and he sends you a *Probatum est,* a

[2 Sam. 12.5]

personall testimony how this Physicke hath wrought upon another, upon *David.*

And so having in this first Part, which is the Consideration of the persons in our Text, God and *David,* brought them by *Nathans* mediation, together, consider wee also, for a conclusion of this Part, the personall applications, that *David* scatters himselfe upon none but God, *Tu me,* and hee repeats it, doe *Thou* purge mee, doe *Thou* wash mee.

Tu

Damascen hath a Sermon of the Assumption of the blessed Virgin,
330 which whole Sermon is but a Dialogue, in which *Eve* acts the first part, and the blessed Virgin another; It is but a Dialogue, yet it is a Sermon. If I should insist upon this Dialogue, between God and *David, Tu me, Tu me,* Doe thou worke upon me, it would not be the lesse a profitable part of a Sermon for that. For first, when we heare *David* in an anhelation and panting after the mercy of God, cry out, *Domine Tu,* Lord doe thou that that is to be done, doe Thou purge, doe Thou wash, and may have heard God, (thereby to excite us to the use of his meanes) say, *Purget natura, purget lex,* I have infused into thee a light and a law of nature, and exalted that light and that
340 law, by a more particular law and a clearer light then that, by which thou knowest what is sin, and knowest that in a sinfull state thou canst not be acceptable to me, *Purget natura, purget lex,* let the light of nature, or of the law purge thee, and rectifie thy selfe by that; Doe but as much for thy selfe, as some naturall men, some *Socrates,* some *Plato* hath done, we may heare *David* reply, *Domine Tu,* Lord put me not over to the catechizing of Nature, nor to the Pedagogie of the Law, but take me into thine owne hands, do Thou, Thou, that is to be done upon me. When we heare God say, *Purget Ecclesia,* I have established a Church, settled constant Ordinances, for the purging
350 and washing of souls there; *Purget Ecclesia,* Let the Church purge thee, we may hear *David* reply, *Domine Tu,* Alas Lord, how many come to that Bath, and goe foule out of it? how many heare Sermons, and receive Sacraments, and when they returne, returne to their vomit? *Domine Tu,* Lord, except the power of thy Spirit make thine Ordinance effectuall upon me, even this thy Jordan will leave me in my leprosie, and exalt my leprosie, even this Sermon, this Sacrament will aggravate my sin. If we heare God say, Shall I purge thee? Doest

thou know what thou askest, what my method in purging is, That if
I purge, I shall purge thee with fire, with seaven fires, with tribula-
360 tions, nay, with tentations, with temporall, nay, with spirituall calamities, with wounds in thy fortune, wounds in thine honor, wounds in
thy conscience, yet we may heare *David* reply, *Tu Domine;* As the

Josh. 24.16

people said to *Ioshuah, God forbid we should forsake the Lord, we
will serve the Lord;* And when *Ioshuah* said, *You cannot serve the
Lord, for he is a jealous God; and if yee turne from him, he will turne
and doe you hurt, and consume you after he hath done you good;* The
people replyed, *Nay, but we will serve the Lord;* so whatsoever God
threatens *David* of afflictions and tribulations, and purgings in fire,
we may heare *David* reply, Nay but Lord, doe Thou doe it, do it how
370 Thou wilt, but doe Thou doe it: Thy corrosives are better then others
fomentations; Thy bitternesses sweeter then others honey; Thy fires
are but lukewarme fires, nay, they have nothing of fire in them, but
light to direct me in my way; And thy very frowns are but as trenches
cut out, as lanes that leade me to thy grave, or Rivers or Channels,
that lead me to the sea of thy bloud. Let me go upon Crouches, so I go
to Heaven; Lay what waight thou wilt even upon my soule, that that
be heavy, and heavy unto death, so I may have a cheerfull transmigration then. *Domine Tu,* Lord doe thou doe it, and I shall not wish it
mended.
380 And then when we heare *David* say, *Domine Me,* Lord purge
Me, wash *Me,* and returne foure times in this short Text, to that
personall appropriation of Gods worke upon himselfe, Purge *Me,*
that I may be cleane, wash *Me,* that I may be whiter then snow, if we
heare God say (as the language of his mercy is, for the most part,
generall) As the Sea is above the Earth, so is the blood of my Son
above all sin; Congregations of three thousand, and of five thousand
were purged and washed, converted and baptized at particular Sermons of S. *Peter,* whole legions of Souldiers, that consisted of thousands, were purged in their owne blood, and became Martyrs in one
390 day. There is enough done to worke upon all; Examples enow given
to guide all; we may heare *David* reply, *Domine Me;* Nay but Lord,
I doe not heare *Peter* preach, I live not in a time, or in a place, where
Crownes of Martyrdome are distributed, nor am I sure my Constancy
would make me capable of it if I did, Lord I know, that a thousand

of these worlds were not worth one drop of thy blood, and yet I know, that if there had been but one soule distressed, and that soule distressed but with one sin, thou wouldest have spent the last drop of that blood for that soule; Blessed be thy Name, for having wrapped me up in thy generall Covenants, and made me partaker of thy generall Ordinances, but yet Lord, looke more particularly upon me, and appropriate thy selfe to me, to me, not onely as thy Creature, as a man, as a Christian, but as I am I, as I am this sinner that confesses now, and as I am this penitent that begs thy mercy now. And now, Beloved, we have said so much towards enough of the persons, God and *David;* The accesse of *David* to God, and the appropriation of God to *David,* as that we may well passe to our other generall part, the petitions which *David* in his own and our behalfe makes to God, *Purge me with Hyssop, and I shall be cleane, wash me, and I shall be whiter then snow.*

In this, the first is a great worke, That which we translate, *Purge me.* And yet how soone *David* is come to it? It is his first period. The passage of a Spirit is very quick, but it is not immediate; Not from extreame to extreame, but by passing the way between. The Evill spirit passes not so; no good soule was ever made very ill in an instant, no, nor so soone as some ill have been made good: No man can give me Examples of men so soone perverted, as I can of men converted. It is not in the power of the Devill to doe so much harme, as God can doe good; Nay, we may be bold to say, it is not in the will, not in the desire of the Devill to doe so much harme, as God would doe good; for illnesse is not in the nature of the Devill; The Devill was naturally good, made, created good. His first illnesse was but a defection from that goodnesse; and his present illnesse is but a punishment for that defection; but God is good, goodnesse in his nature, essentially, eternally good; and therefore the good motions of the Spirit of God worke otherwise upon us, then the tentations of the evill Spirit doe. How soone, and to what a height came *David* here? He makes his Petition, his first Petition with that confidence, as that it hath scarce the nature of a Petition: for it is in the Originall, *Thou wilt purge me, Thou wilt wash me,* Thou hadst a gracious will, and purpose to doe it, before thou didst infuse the will and the desire in me to petition it. Nay, this word may well be translated not onely

2 Part

Purgabis

Thou wilt, but by the other denotation of the future, *Thou shalt, Thou shalt purge me, Thou shalt wash me,* Lord I doe but remember thee of thy debt, of that which thy gracious promise hath made thy debt, to shew mercy to every penitent sinner. And then, as the word implies confidence, and acceleration, infallibility, and expedition too, That as soone as I can aske, I am sure to be heard; so does it imply a totality, an intirenesse, a fulnesse in the worke; for the roote of the word is *Peccare,* to sin, for purging is a purging of peccant humors;
⁴⁴⁰ but in this Conjugation in that language, it hath a privative signification, and literally signifies *Expeccabis;* and if in our language, that were a word in use, it might be translated, Thou shalt un-sin me; that is, look upon me as a man that had never sinned, as a man invested in the innocency of thy Sonne, who knew no sin. *David* gives no man rule nor example of other assurance in God, then in the remission of sins: Not that any precontract or Election makes our sins no sins, or makes our sins no hindrances in our way to salvation, or that we are in Gods favour at that time when we sin, nor returned to his favour before we repent our sin; It is onely this expeccation,
⁴⁵⁰ this unsinning, this taking away of sins formerly committed, that restores me; And that is not done with nothing; *David* assignes, proposes a meanes, by which he looks for it, Hyssop, *Thou shalt purge me with Hyssop.*

Hyssopo

The Fathers taking the words as they found them, and fastning with a spirituall delight, as their devout custome was, their Meditations upon the figurative and Metaphoricall phrase of purging by Hyssop, have found purgative vertues in that plant, and made usefull and spirituall applications thereof, for the purging of our soules from sin. In this doe S. *Ambrose,* and *Augustine,* and *Hierome* agree, that
⁴⁶⁰ Hyssop hath vertue in it proper for the lungs, in which part, as it is the furnace of breath, they place the seat of pride and opposition against the Truth, making their use of that which was said of *Saul,*

Acts 9.[1]

That he breathed out threatnings and slaughter against the Disciples of the Lord. And by this interpretation, *Davids* disease that he must be purged of, should be pride. But except, as the Schoolemen, when they have tyred themselves in seeking out the name of the sin of the Angels, are content at last for their ease to call it Pride, both because they thought they need goe no farther, for, where pride is, other sins

will certainly accompany it; and because they extended the name of
Pride to all refusals and resistances of the will of God, and so pride,
in effect, includes all sin; Except, I say, the Fathers take Pride in so
large a sense as that they would not prescribe Hyssop to purge *Davids*
lungs, for his disease lay not properly there; They must have purged
his liver, the seate of blood, the seat of concupiscence; They must have
purged his whole substance, for the distemper was gone over all. And
to this rectifying of his blood, by the application of better blood, had
David relation in this place.

All the sacrifices of Expiation of sin, in the old Law, were done
by blood, and that blood was sprinckled upon the people, by an
instrument made of a certain plant, which because the word in
Hebrew is *Ezob,* for the nearnesse of the sound, and for the indifferency of the matter, (for it imports us nothing to know, of what plant
that *Aspergillum,* that Blood-sprinckler was made) the Interpreters
have ever used in all languages to call this word Hyssop. And though
we know no proper word for Hyssop in Hebrew, (for when they
finde not a word in the Bible, the Hebrew Rabbins will acknowledge
no Hebrew word for any thing) yet the other languages deduced
from the Hebrew, Syriaque, and Arabique, have clearly another word
for Hyssop, *Zuf;* And the Hebrew Rabbins think this word of our
text, *Ezob,* to signifie any of three or foure plants, rather then our
Hyssop. But be the plant what it will, the forme and the use of that
Blood-sprinkler is manifest. In the institution of the Passeover, *Take*   Exod.
a bunch of Hyssop, and dip it in blood. In the cleansing of the Leper,   12.[22]
there was to be the blood of a sparrow, and then Cedar wood, and   Levit. 14.[4]
scarlet lace, and Hyssop: And about that Cedar stick, they bound
this Hyssop with this lace, and so made this instrument to sprinkle
blood. And so the name of the *Hyssop,* because it did the principall
office, was after given to the whole Instrument; all the sprinkler was
called an *Hyssop;* As we see when they reached up a sponge of
vinegar to Christ upon the Crosse, *They put it,* sayes the text, *upon*   Ioh. 19.29
Hyssop, that is, upon an Hyssop; not upon an Hyssop stalke, (as the
old translation had it) for no Hyssop hath such a stalke, but they
called such sticks of Cedar, as ordinarily served for the sprinkling of
blood, Hyssops. And whether this were such a Cedar stick, or some
other thing, fit to reach up that spunge to Christ, we cannot say. For
S. *Matthew* calls that, that S. *Iohn* calls an *Hyssop,* a *Reed.*   Mat. 27.48

This then was *Davids* petition here; first, That hee might have the blood of Christ Jesus applied and sprinkled upon him; *David* thought of no election, hee looked for no sanctification, but in the blood of ⁵¹⁰ Christ Jesus. And then he desired this blood to be applied to him, by that Hyssope, by that Blood-sprinkler, which was ordained by God, for the use of the Church. Home-infusions, and inward inspirations of grace, are powerfull seales of Gods love; but all this is but the Privy seale, *David* desired to bring it to the Great seale, the publike

[Exod. 16.12–15]

Ordinance of the Church. In a case of necessity God gave his children Manna and Quailes; In cases of necessity God allowes Sermons, and Sacraments at home; But as soone as ever they came to the Land of

Iosh. 5.[12]

promise, the same day both Manna and Quailes ceased: God hath given us a free and publike passage of his Word, and Sacraments, the ⁵²⁰ diet and the ordinary food of our souls, and he purges us with that Hyssope, with the application of his promises, with the absolution of our sins, with a redintegration into his mysticall body, by the seales of reconciliation. And this reconciliation to God, by the blood of Christ, applied in the Ordinances of the Church, is that which *David* begs for his cleansing, and is the last circumstance of this branch, *Purge me with Hyssope, and I shall be cleane.*

Cleansing

This *Cleansing* then implies that, which wee commonly call the enwrapping in the Covenant, the breeding in the visible Church, when God takes a Nation out of the Common, and encloses it, em-⁵³⁰ pailes it for his more peculiar use, when God withdrawes us from the impossibility, under which the Gentiles sterve, who heare not Christ preached, to live within the sound of his voyce, and within the reach of our spirituall food, the Word and Sacraments. It is that state, which the holy Ghost so elegantly expresses and enlarges, That God found

Ezek. 16

Jerusalem, *Her father an Amorite, and her mother an Hittite,* none of the seed of the faithfull in her; that he found her *in Canaan,* not so much as in a place of true profession; that he found her *in her blood, and her navell uncut,* still incorporated in her former stock; And, *The time was a time of love,* says God, *and I covered thy naked-*⁵⁴⁰*nesse, and sware unto thee, and entred into a covenant with thee, and thou becamest mine.* Will you say, this could not be the subject of *Davids* petition, this could not bee the cleansing that he begged at Gods hand, to bee brought into that Covenant, to bee a member of

that Church? for hee was in possession of that before. Beloved, how
many are borne in this Covenant, and baptized, and catechized in it,
and yet fall away? How many have taught, and wrought, and
thought in their owne conscience that they did well, in defence of
the Covenant, and yet fell away? And from how many places, which
gave light to others, hath God removed the Candlestick, and left
550 themselves in darknesse? Though *David* say, *A day in thy Courts is*
better then a thousand, (then a thousand any where else) yet he
expresses his desire, *That hee might continue in that happinesse all*
the dayes of his life; It is as fearefull a thing to be removed from the
meanes of salvation, as never to have had them.

This then is *Cleansing,* To be continued in the disposition, and
working of the meanes of cleansing, that he may alwayes grow under
the dew, and breath in the ayre of Gods grace exhibited in his Ordinance. Amongst the Jewes there were many uncleannesses, which did
not amount to sin: They reckon in the Ceremoniall law, at least fifty
560 kinds of uncleannesses, from which if they neglected to cleanse
themselves, by those ceremonies which were appropriated to them,
then those uncleannesses became sins, and they were put to their
sacrifices, before they could be discharged of them. Many levities,
many omissions, many acts of infirmity might be prevented by consideration before, or cleansed by consideration now, if we did truly
value the present grace, that is alwayes offered us in these Ordinances
of God. What sin can I be guilty of, that is without example of
mercy, in that Gospel which is preached to me here? But if you will
not accept it, when God offers it, you can never have it so good
570 cheape, because hereafter you shall have this present sin, of refusing
that offer of grace, added to your burthen. *Because I have purged*
thee, & thou wast not purged, thou shalt not be purged any more,
til I have caused my fury to light upon thee. But shall we be purged
then? Then, when his fury in any calamity hath lighted upon us?
Is not this *donec,* this *untill,* such a *donec,* as *donec faciam, Till I*
make thine enemies thy footstoole: Such a *donec* as the *donec peperit,*
shee was a Virgin, *Till shee brought forth her first sonne?* Is it not an
everlasting *donec?* That we shall not be purged till Gods Judgements
fall upon us, nor then neither: Physicke may be ministred too late to
580 worke, and Judgements may fall too late, to souple or entender the

Psal. 84.10

[Psal. 27.4]

Ezek. 24.13

[Psal. 110.1]

[Mat. 1.25]

soule: For as wee may die with that Physick in our stomach, so may we be carried to the last Judgement, with that former Judgement upon our shoulders. And therefore our later Translation hath expressed it more fully, Not that that fury shall *light,* but shall *rest* upon us.

This cleansing therefore, is that disposition, which God by his grace, infuses into us, That we stand in the congregation, and Communion of Saints, capable of those mercies, which God hath by his Ordinance, annexed to these meetings; That we may so feele at all ⁵⁹⁰ times when we come hither, such a working of his Hyssop, such a benefit of his Ordinance, as that we beleeve all our former sins to be so forgiven, as that if God should translate us now, this minute, to another life, this *Dosis* of this purging Hyssop, received now, had so wrought, as that we should be assuredly translated into the Kingdome of heaven. This cleansing applies to us those words of our Saviour,

[Mat. 9.2]   *My sonne, be of good cheare, thy sinnes are forgiven thee;* But yet there is a farther degree of cleanenesse expressed in Christs following
[John 8.11] words, *Goe, and sin no more;* And that grace against relapses, the gift of sanctification, and perseverance, is that that *David* askes in his ⁶⁰⁰ other Petition, *Lava me, Wash me, and I shall be whiter then snow.*

Lava   Here we proposed first the action, *Lava, Wash me.* This is more then a sprinkling, A totall, and intire washing; More then being an ordinary partaker of the outward meanes, The Word, and Sacraments; more then a temporary feeling of the benefit thereof in a present sense; for it is a building up of habits of religious actions, visible to others, and it is a holy and firme confidence created in us by the Spirit of God, that we shall keepe that building in reparation,

[2 King.   and goe forward with it to our lives end. It is a washing like *Naamans*
5.14]   in Jordan, to be iterated seaven times, seaventy seaven times, daily, ⁶¹⁰ hourly, all our life; A washing begun in Baptisme, pursued in sweat, in the industry of a lawfull calling, continued in teares, for our deficiencies in the workes of our calling, and perchance to bee consummated in blood, at our deaths. Not such a washing, as the Washes have, which are those sands that are overflowed with the Sea at every Tide, and then lie dry, but such a washing as the bottome of the Sea hath, that is alwayes equally wet. It is not a *stillicidium,* a spout, a showre, a bucket powred out upon us, when we come to Church, a

Sabbath-sanctification, and no more, but a water that enters into every office of our house, and washes every action proceeding from every faculty of the soule. And this is the washing, A continuall succession of Grace, working effectually to present Habits of religious acts, and constituting a holy purpose of persevering in them, that induces the Whitenesse, the Candor, the Dealbation that *David* begs here, *Lava & Dealbabor.*

The purging with Hyssope, which we spoke of before, which is the benefit which we have by being bred in a true Church, delivers us from that rednesse, which is in the earth of which wee are made, from that guiltinesse, which is by our naturall derivation from our Parents imprinted in us; Baptisme doth much upon that; but that that is not Red, is not therefore White. But this is our case: Our first colour was white; God made man righteous. Our rednesse is from *Adam,* and the more that rednesse is washed off, the more we returne to our first whitenesse; And this which is petitioned here, is a washing of such perfection, as cleanses us *Ab omni inquinamento,* from all filthinesse of flesh and spirit. Those *inquinamenta,* which are ordinary, are first in the flesh, Concupiscence and Carnality, and those other, of which the Apostle sayes, *The works of the flesh are manifest;* And in the spirit, they are Murmuring, Diffidence in God, and such others. But besides these, as an over-diligent cleansing of the Body, and additionall beauty of the Body, is *inquinamentum carnis,* one of S. *Pauls* filthinesses upon the flesh, so an over purifying of the spirit, in an uncharitable undervaluing of other men, and in a schismaticall departing from the unity of the Church, is *Inquinamentum spiritus:* False beauties are a foulnesse of the body, false purity is a foulnesse of the spirit. But the washing, that wee seeke, cleanses us *Ab omni inquinamento,* from all foulnesse of flesh and spirit. All waters will not cleanse us, nor all fires dry us, so as wee may be cleane, smoaky fires will not doe that. *I will poure cleane water upon you, and you shall be cleane.* The Sunne produces sweat upon us, and it dries us too: Zeale cleanses us; but it must be zeale impermixt as the Sun, not mingled with our smoaky, sooty, factious affections. Some Grammarians have noted, the word *Washing* here, to be derived from a word, that signifies a Lambe; we must be washed in the blood of the Lambe, and we must be brought to the whitenesse, the candor, the

Dealbabor

2 Cor. 7.1

Gal. 5.19

Ezek. 36.25

simplicity of the Lambe; no man is pure, that thinks no man pure but himselfe. And this whitenesse, which is Sanctification in our selves, and charitable interpretation of other men, is exalted here to that Superlative, *Super Nivem, Wash me, and I shall be whiter then Snow.*

Super nivem
Esay 1.18

Marke 9.3

[Psal. 12.6]

Though your sins be as Scarlet, they shall be as white as snow. ⁶⁶⁰ *Esay* was an Euangelicall Prophet, a propheticall Euangelist, and speaks still of the state of the Christian Church. There, by the ordinary meanes exhibited there, our Scarlet sins are made as white as Snow; And the whitenesse of Snow, is a whitenesse that no art of man can reach to; So Christs garments in his Transfiguration are expressed to have beene *as white as Snow, so, as no Fuller on earth could white them.* Nothing in this world can send me home in such a whitenesse, no morall counsaile, no morall comfort, no morall constancy; as Gods Absolution by his Minister, as the profitable hearing of a Sermon, the worthy receiving of the Sacrament do. This is to be as white as ⁶⁷⁰ snow; In a good state for the present. But *David* begs a whitenesse above Snow; for Snow melts, and then it is not white; our present Sanctification withers, and we lose that cheerefull verdure, the testimony of an upright conscience; And Snow melted, Snow water, is the coldest water of all; Devout men departed from their former fervor are the coldest and the most irreducible to true zeale, true holinesse. Therefore *David* who was metall tried seven times in the fire, and desired to be such gold as might be laid up in Gods Treasury, might consider, that in transmutation of metals, it is not enough to come to a calcination, or a liquefaction of the metall, (that must ⁶⁸⁰ be done) nor to an Ablution, to sever drosse from pure, nor to a Transmutation, to make it a better metall, but there must be a Fixion, a settling thereof, so that it shall not evaporate into nothing, nor returne to his former nature. Therefore he saw that he needed not only a liquefaction, a melting into teares, nor only an Ablution, and a Transmutation, those he had by this purging and this washing, this station in the Church of God, and this present Sanctification there, but he needed *Fixionem,* an establishment, which the comparison of Snow afforded not; That as he had purged him with Hyssop, and so cleansed him, that is, enwrapped him in the Covenant, and made ⁶⁹⁰ him a member of the true Church; and there washed him so, as that he was restored to a whitenesse, that is, made his Ordinances so

effectuall upon him, as that then he durst deliver his soule into his
hands at that time: So he would exalt that whitenesse, above the
whitenesse of Snow, so as nothing might melt it, nothing discolour it,
but that under the seale of his blessed Spirit, he might ever dwell in
that calme, in that assurance, in that acquiescence, that as he is in a
good state this minute, he shall be in no worse, whensoever God
shall be pleased to translate him.

We end all the Psalmes in our service, those of Praise, and those of   *Conclusio*
Prayer too, with a *Gloria Patri, Glory be to the Father, &c*. For our
conclusion of this Prayer in this Psalme, we have reserved a *Gloria
Patri* too, This consideration for the glory of God, that though in the
first Part, The Persons, the persons were varied, God and man, yet
in our second Part, where we consider the worke, the whole worke is
put into Gods hand, and received from Gods hand. Let God be true,   [Rom. 3.4]
and every man a liar; Let God be strong and every man infirme;
Let God give, and man but receive. What man that hath no propriety
therein, can take a penny out of another mans house, or a roote out
of his Garden, but the Law will take hold of him? Hath any man a
propriety in Grace? what had he to give for it? Nature? Is Nature
equivalent to Grace? No man does refine, and exalt Nature to the
height it would beare, but if naturall faculties were exalted to their
highest, is Nature a fit exchange for Grace? and if it were, is Nature
our owne? Why should we be loath to acknowledge to have all our
ability of doing good freely from God, and immediately by his grace,
when as, even those faculties of Nature, by which we pretend to do
the offices of Grace, we have from God himselfe too? For that ques-
tion of the Apostle involves all, *What hast thou that thou hast not*   [1 Cor. 4.7]
received? Thy naturall faculties are no more thine owne, then the
Grace of God is thine owne; I would not be beholden to God for Grace,
and I must be as much beholden to him for Nature, if Nature do supply Grace; Because he hath made thee to be a man, he hath given thee
naturall faculties; because he hath vouchsafed thee to be a Christian,
he hath given thee meanes of Grace. But, as thy body, conceived in
thy Mothers wombe, could not claime a soule at Gods hand, nor wish
a soule, no nor know that there was a soule to be had: So neither by
being a man indued with naturall faculties canst thou claime grace,
or wish grace; nay those naturall faculties, if they be not pre-tincted

with some infusion of Grace before, cannot make thee know what
730 Grace is, or that Grace is. To a child rightly disposed in the wombe,
God does give a soule; To a naturall man rightly disposed in his
naturall faculties, God does give Grace; But that soule was not due
to that child, nor that grace to that man.

Therefore, (as we said at first) *David* does not bring the Hyssop,
and pray God to make the potion, but, Doe thou purge me with
Hyssop, All is thine owne; There was no pre-existent matter in the
world, when God made the world; There is no pre-existent merit
in man, when God makes him his. *David* does not say, Do thou
wash me, and I will perfect thy worke; Give me my portion of Grace,
740 and I will trouble thee for no more, but deale upon that stocke; But
[Rev. 22.11] *Qui sanctificatur, sanctificetur adhuc,* Let him that is holy be more
holy, but accept his Sanctification from him, of whom he had his
Justification; and except he can think to glorifie himself because he
is sanctified, let him not think to sanctifie himself because he is justified; God does all. Yet thus argues S. *Augustin* upon *Davids* words,
Tuus sum Domine, Lord I am thine, and therefore safer then they,
that thinke themselves their owne. Every man can and must say, I
was thine, Thine by Creation; but few can say, I am thine, few that
have not changed their Master. But how was *David* his so especially?
750 sayes S. *Augustine: Quia quæsivi justificationes tuas,* as it followes
there; Because I sought thy Righteousnesse, thy Justification. But
where did he seeke it? Hee sought it, and he found it in himselfe.
In himselfe, as himselfe, there was no good thing to be found, how
far soever he had sought: But yet he found a Justification, though
of Gods whole making, yet in himselfe.

So then, this is our Act of Recognition, we acknowledge God, and
God onely to doe all; But we doe not make him Soveraigne alone,
as that we leave his presence naked, and empty; Nor so make him
King alone, as that we depopulate his Country, and leave him with-
760 out Subjects; Nor so leave all to Grace, as that the naturall faculties
of man do not become the servants, and instruments of that Grace. Let
all, that we all seeke, be, who may glorifie God most; and we shall
agree in this, That as the Pelagian wounds the glory of God deepely,
in making Naturall faculties joynt-Commissioners with Grace, so
do they diminish the glory of God too, if any deny naturall faculties

to be the subordinate servants and instruments of Grace; for as Grace could not worke upon man to Salvation, if man had not a faculty of will to worke upon, because without that will man were not man; so is this Salvation wrought in the will, by conforming this will of man to the will of God, not by extinguishing the will it selfe, by any force or constraint that God imprints in it by his Grace: God saves no man without, or against his will. *Glory be to God on high, and on earth Peace, and Good will towards men;* And to this God of Glory, the Father, and this God of Peace and reconciliation, the Son, and this God of Good will and love amongst men, the Holy Ghost, be ascribed all praise, etc.

[Luk. 2.14]

Number 16.

Preached upon the Penitentiall Psalmes.

PSAL. 6.1. *O LORD, REBUKE ME NOT IN THINE ANGER, NEITHER CHASTEN ME IN THY HOT DISPLEASURE.*

---

1 King. 15.5

G OD imputes but one thing to *David,* but one sin; *The matter of Vriah the Hittite:* nor that neither, but by way of exception, not till he had first established an assurance, that *David* stood well with him. First he had said, *David did that which was right in the eyes of the Lord, and turned not aside from any thing, that he had commanded him all the dayes of his life:* Here was rectitude, *He did that which was right in the eyes of the Lord;* no obliquity, no departing into by-wayes, upon collaterall respects; Here was integrity to Gods service, no serving of God and Mammon, *Hee turned*
10 *not from any thing that God commanded him;* And here was perpetuity, perseverance, constancy, *All the dayes of his life:* And then, and not till then, God makes that one, and but that one exception, *Except the matter of Vriah the Hittite.* When God was reconciled to him, he would not so much as name that sin, that had offended him.

And herein is the mercy of God, in the merits of Christ, a sea of mercie, that as the Sea retaines no impression of the Ships that passe in it, (for Navies make no path in the Sea) so when we put out into the boundlesse Sea of the blood of Christ Jesus, by which onely wee have reconciliation to God, there remaines no record against us; for
20 God hath cancelled that record which he kept, and that which Satan kept God hath nailed to the Crosse of his Son. That man which hath seene me at the sealing of my Pardon, and the seale of my Reconciliation, at the Sacrament, many times since, will yet in his passion, or in his ill nature, or in his uncharitablenesse, object to me the sins of

my youth; whereas God himselfe, if I have repented to day, knowes
not the sins that I did yesterday. God hath rased the Record of my
sin, in Heaven; it offends not him, it grieves not his Saints nor Angels there; and he hath rased the Record in hell; it advances not
their interest in me there, nor their triumph over me. And yet here,
30 the uncharitable man will know more, and see more, and remember
more, then my God, or his devill remembers, or knowes, or sees: He
will see a path in the Sea; he will see my sin, when it is drowned in
the blood of my Saviour. After the Kings pardon, perchance it will
beare an action, to call a man by that infamous name, which that
crime, which is pardoned, did justly cast upon him before the pardon: After Gods reconciliation to *David,* he would not name *Davids*
sin in the particular.

But yet for all this, though God will be no example, of upbraiding
or reproaching repented sinnes, when God hath so far exprest his
40 love, as to bring that sinner to that repentance, and so to mercy, yet,
that he may perfect his owne care, he exercises that repentant sinner
with such medicinall corrections, as may inable him to stand upright
for the future. And to that purpose, was no man ever more exercised
then *David. David* broke into anothers family; he built upon anothers ground; he planted in anothers Seminary; and God broke into
his family, his ground, his Seminary. In no story, can wee finde so
much Domestick affliction, such rapes, and incests, and murders, and
rebellions, from their owne children, as in *Davids* storie. Under the
heavy waight and oppression of some of those, is *David,* by all Ex-
50 positors, conceived to have conceived, and uttered this Psalme. Some
take it to have beene occasioned by some of his temporall afflictions;
either his persecution from *Saul,* or bodily sicknesse in himselfe, of
which traditionally the Rabbins speake much, or *Absoloms* unnaturall rebellion. Some others, with whom wee finde more reason to
joyne, finde more reason to interpret it, of a spirituall affliction; that
David, in the apprehension, and under the sense of the wrath and
indignation of God, came to this vehement exclamation, or deprecation, *O Lord rebuke me not in thine anger, neither chasten me in thy
hot displeasure.*

60 In which words we shall consider, first the person, upon whom   *Divisio*
David turned for his succour, and then what succour he seeks at his

hands. First his word, and then his end; first to whom, and then for what he supplicates. And in the first of these, the Person, we shall make these three steps; first that he makes his first accesse to God onely, *O Lord rebuke me not;* doe not thou, and though I will not say, I care not, yet I care the lesse who doe. And secondly, that it is to God by Name, not to any universall God, in generall notions; so naturall men come to God; but to God whom he considers in a par-ticular name, in particular notions, and attributes, and manifestations
⁷⁰ of himselfe; a God whom he knowes, by his former workes done upon him. And then, that name in which hee comes to him here, is the name of *Iehovah;* his radicall, his fundamentall, his primarie, his essentiall name, the name of *being, Iehovah.* For, he that deliberately, and considerately beleeves himselfe to have his very being from God, beleeves certainely that he hath his well being from him too; He that acknowledges, that it is by Gods providence that he breathes, beleeves that it is by his providence that he eates too. So his accesse is to God, and to God by name, that is by particular considerations, and then, to God in the name of *Iehovah,* to that God that hath done all, from his
⁸⁰ first beginning, from his Being. And in these three we shall determine our first part.

1 Part
To God

First, in this first branch of this part, *David* comes to God, but with-out any confidence in himselfe. Here is *Reus ad rostra sine patrono,* here is the prisoner at the Barre, and no Counsell allowed him. He confesses Indictments, faster then they can be read: If he heare him-selfe indicted, that he looked upon *Bathsheba,* that he lusted after *Bathsheba,* he cryes, Alas, I have done that, and more; dishonored her, and my selfe, and our God; and more then that, I have continued the act into a habit; and more then that, I have drowned that sinne in
⁹⁰ bloud, lest it should rise up to my sight; and more then all that, I have caused the Name of God to be blasphemed; and lest his Majesty, and his greatnesse should be a terrour to me, I have occasioned the enemy to undervalue him, and speake despightfully of God himselfe. And when he hath confest all, all that he remembers, he must come to his

[Psa. 19.12]

Ab occultis meis, Lord cleanse me from my secret sinnes; for there are sins, which we have laboured so long to hide from the world, that at last, they are hidden from our selves, from our own memories, our own consciences. As much as *David* stands in feare of this Judge, he must intreat this Judge, to remember his sinnes; Remember them, O Lord, for els they will not fall into my pardon; but remember them in mercy, and not in anger; for so they will not fall into my pardon neither.

Whatsoever the affliction then was, temporall, or spirituall, (we take it rather to be spirituall) *Davids* recourse is presently to God. He doth not, as his predecessour *Saul* did, when he was afflicted, send for one that was cunning upon the Harp, to divert sorrow so. If his Subjects rebell, he doth not say, Let them alone, let them goe on, I shall have the juster cause, by their rebellion, of confiscations upon their Estates, of executions upon their persons, of revocations of their lawes, and customes, and priviledges, which they carry themselves so high upon. If his sonne lift up his hand against him, he doth not place his hope in that, that that occasion will cut off his sonne, and that then the peoples hearts which were bent upon his sonne, will returne to him againe. *David* knew he could not retyre himselfe from God in his bedchamber; Guards and Ushers could not keepe him out. He knew he could not defend himselfe from God in his Army; for *the Lord of Hosts is Lord of his Hosts.* If he *fled to Sea, to Heaven, to Hell,* he was sure to meet *God there;* and there thou shalt meet him too, if thou fly from God, to the reliefe of outward comforts, of musicke, of mirth, of drinke, of cordialls, of Comedies, of conversation. Not that such recreations are unlawfull; the minde hath her physick as well as the body; but when thy sadnesse proceeds from a sense of thy sinnes, (which is Gods key to the doore of his mercy, put into thy hand) it is a new, and a greater sin, to goe about to overcome that holy sadnesse, with these prophane diversions; to fly *Ad consolatiunculas creaturulæ* (as that elegant man *Luther* expresses it, according to his naturall delight in that elegancy of Diminutives, with which he abounds above all Authors) to the little and contemptible comforts of little and contemptible creatures. And as *Luther* uses the physick, *Iob* useth the Physitian; *Luther* calls the comforts, Miserable comforts; and *Iob* calls them that minister them, *Onerosos consolatores, Miserable comforters are you all. David* could not drowne his adultery in blood; never thinke thou to drowne thine in wine. The Ministers of God are Sonnes of Thunder, they are falls of waters, trampling of horses, and runnings of Chariots; and if these

1 Sam. 16.14

[Psal. 139.8–9]

[Job 16.2]

voyces of these Ministers, cannot overcome thy musick, thy security, yet the Angels trumpet will; That *Surgite qui dormitis, Arise yee that*

[Eph. 5.14]

sleepe in the dust, in the dust of the grave, is a Treble that over-reaches

[Mat. 25.41]

all; That *Ite maledicti, Goe yee accursed into Hell fire,* is a Base that
140 drowns all. There is no recourse but to God, no reliefe but in God; and therefore *David* applied himselfe to the right method, to make his first accesse to God.

To God
by Name

    It is to God onely, and to God by name, and not in generall notions; for it implies a nearer, a more familiar, and more presentiall knowledge of God, a more cheerfull acquaintance, and a more assiduous conversation with God, when we know how to call God by a Name, a Creator, a Redeemer, a Comforter, then when we consider him onely as a diffused power, that spreads itselfe over all creatures; when we come to him in Affirmatives, and Confessions, This thou hast
150 done for me, then when we come to him onely in Negatives, and say, That that is God, which is nothing els. God is come nearer to us then to others, when we know his Name. For though it be truly said in the Schoole, that no name can be given to God, *Ejus essentiam adæquatè repræsentans,* No one name can reach to the expressing of all that God is; And though *Trismegistus* doe humbly, and modestly, and reverently say, *Non spero,* it never fell into my thought, nor into my hope, that the maker and founder of all Majesty, could be circumscribed, or imprisoned by any one name, though a name compounded and complicated of many names, as the Rabbins have made

Gen. 32.29

160 one name of God, of all his names in the Scriptures; Though *Iacob* seeme to have been rebuked *for asking Gods name,* when he wrastled with him; And so also the Angel which was to doe a miraculous

Judg. 13.18

worke, a worke appertaining onely to God, to give a Childe to the barren, because he represented God, and had the person of God upon him, would not permit *Manoah* to enquire after his name, *Because,* as he sayes there, *that name was secret and wonderfull;* And though

Exod. 23.20

God himselfe, to dignifie and authorize that *Angel,* which he made his Commissioner, and the Tutelar and Nationall Guide of his people, sayes of that *Angel,* to that people, *Feare him, provoke him not, for*
170 *my Name is in him,* and yet did not tell them, what that name was; Yet certainly, we could not so much as say, God cannot be named, except we could name God by some name; we could not say, God

hath no name, except God had a name; for that very word, *God,* is his name. God calls upon us often in the Scriptures, *To call upon his Name;* and in the Scriptures, he hath manifested to us divers names, by which we may call upon him. Doest thou know what name to call him by, when thou callest him to beare false witnesse, to averre a falshood? Hath God a name to sweare by? Doest thou know what name to call him by, when thou wouldest make him thy servant, thy 180 instrument, thy executioner, to plague others, upon thy bitter curses and imprecations? Hath God a name to curse by? Canst thou wound his body, exhaust his bloud, teare off his flesh, breake his bones, excruciate his soule; and all this by his right name? Hath God a name to blaspheme by? and hath God no name to pray by? is he such a stranger to thee? Dost thou know every faire house in thy way, as thou travellest, whose that is; and dost thou not know, in whose house thou standest now?

Beloved, to know God by name, and to come to him by name, is to consider his particular blessings to thee; to consider him in his 190 power, and how he hath protected thee there; and in his wisedome, and how he hath directed thee there; and in his love, and how he hath affected thee there; and exprest all, in particular mercies. He is but a darke, but a narrow, a shallow, a lazy man in nature, that knows no more, but that there is a heaven, and an earth, and a sea; He that will be of use in this world, comes to know the influences of the heavens, the vertue of the plants, and mines of the earth, the course and divisions of the Sea. To the naturall man, God gives generall notions of himselfe; a God that spreads over all as the heavens; a God that sustaines all as the earth; a God that transports, and communicates all 200 to all as the sea: But to the Christian Church, God applies himselfe in more particular notions; as a Father, as a Son, as a holy Ghost; And to every Christian soule, as a Creator, a Redeemer, a Benefactor; that I may say, This I was not born to, and yet this I have from my God; this a potent adversary sought to evict from me, but this I have recovered by my God; sicknesse had enfeebled my body, but I have a convalescence; calumnie had defamed my reputation, but I have a reparation; malice in other men, or improvidence in my selfe, had ruined my fortune, but I have a redintegration from my God. And then by these, which are indeed but *Cognomina Dei,* his sir-names,

²¹⁰ names of distinction, names of the exercise of some particular proper-
ties, and attributes of his, to come to the root of all, to my very Being,
that my present Being in this world, and my eternall Being in the
next, is made knowne to me by his name of *Iehovah,* which is his
Essentiall name, to which *David* had recourse in this exinanition;
when his affliction had even annihilated, and brought him to nothing,
he fled to *Iehovah,* the God of all Being, which is the foundation of
all his other Attributes, and includes all his other names, and is our
next and last branch in this first Part.

Iehovah   This name then of *Iehovah* that is here translated *Lord,* is agreed
²²⁰ by all to be the greatest name by which God hath declared and mani-
fested himselfe to man. This is that name which the Jews falsly, but
peremptorily, (for falshood lives by peremptorinesse, and feeds and
armes it selfe with peremptorinesse) deny ever to have been attributed to the *Messias,* in the Scriptures. This is that name, in the
vertue and use whereof, those Calumniators of our Saviours miracles
doe say, that he did his miracles, according to a direction, and
schedule, for the true and right pronouncing of that name, which
Solomon in his time had made, and Christ in his time had found, and
by which, say they, any other man might have done those miracles,
²³⁰ if he had had *Solomons* directions for the right sounding of this name,
Iehovah. This is that name, which out of a superstitious reverence
the Jews alwayes forbore to sound, or utter, but ever pronounced some
other name, either *Adonai,* or *Elohim,* in the place thereof, wheresoever they found *Iehovah.* But now their Rabbins will not so much as
write that name, but still expresse it in foure other letters. So that
they dare not, not onely not sound it, not say it, but not see it.

How this name which we call *Iehovah,* is truly to be sounded,
because in that language it is exprest in foure Consonants onely,
without Vowels, is a perplext question; we may well be content to be
²⁴⁰ ignorant therein, since our Saviour Christ himselfe, in all those places
which he cited out of the Old Testament, never sounded it; he never
said, *Iehovah.* Nor the Apostles after him, nor *Origen,* nor *Ierome;*
all persons very intelligent in the propriety of language; they never
sounded this name *Iehovah.* For though in S. *Ieromes* Exposition
upon the 8. Psalme, we finde that word *Iehovah,* in some Editions
which we have now, yet it is a cleare case, that in the old Copies it is

not so; in *Ieroms* mouth it was not so; from *Ieroms* hand it came not
so. Neither doth it appeare to me, that ever the name of *Iehovah* was
so pronounced, till so late, as in our Fathers time; for I think *Petrus*
250 *Galatinus* was the first that ever called it so. But howsoever this name
be to be sounded, that which falls in our consideration at this time,
is, That *David* in his distresses fled presently to God, and to God by
name, that is, in consideration and commemoration of his particular
blessings; and to a God that had that name, the name of *Iehovah,*
the name of Essence, and Being, which name carried a confession,
that all our wel-being, and the very first being it selfe, was, and was
to be derived from him.

    David therefore comes to God *In nomine totali; in nomine in-*
tegrali; He considers God totally, entirely, altogether; Not altogether,
260 that is, confusedly; but altogether, that is, in such a Name as comprehends all his Attributes, all his Power upon the world, and all his
benefits upon him. The Gentiles were not able to consider God so;
not so entirely, not altogether; but broke God in pieces, and changed
God into single money, and made a fragmentarie God of every
Power, and Attribute in God, of every blessing from God, nay of
every malediction, and judgement of God. A clap of thunder made
a *Iupiter,* a tempest at sea made a *Neptune,* an earthquake made a
Pluto; Feare came to be a God, and a *Fever* came to be a God; Every
thing that they were in love with, or afraid of, came to be canonized,
270 and made a God amongst them. *David* considered God as a center,
into which and from which all lines flowed. Neither as the Gentiles
did, nor as some ignorants of the Roman Church do, that there must
be a stormie god, S. *Nicholas,* and a plaguie god, S. *Rook,* and a sheep-
shearing god, and a swineherd god, a god for every Parish, a god for
every occupation, God forbid. Acknowledg God to be the Author of
thy Being; find him so at the spring-head, and then thou shalt easily
trace him, by the branches, to all that belongs to thy well-being. The
Lord of Hosts, and the God of peace, the God of the mountaines,
and the God of the valleyes, the God of noone, and of midnight, of
280 all times, the God of East and West, of all places, the God of Princes,
and of Subjects, of all persons, is all one and the same God; and that
which we intend, when we say *Iehovah,* is all Hee.

    And therefore hath S. *Bernard* a patheticall and usefull meditation

to this purpose: Every thing in the world, sayes he, can say, *Creator meus es tu,* Lord thou hast made me; All things that have life, and growth, can say, *Pastor meus es tu,* Lord thou hast fed me, increast me; All men can say, *Redemptor meus es tu,* Lord I was sold to death through originall sin, by one *Adam,* and thou hast redeemed me by another; All that have falne by infirmity, and risen againe by grace,
290 can say, *Susceptor meus es tu,* Lord I was falne, but thou hast undertaken me, and dost sustaine me; But he that comes to God in the name of *Iehovah,* he meanes all this, and all other things, in this one Petition, Let me have a Being, and then I am safe, for *In him we live, and move, and have our Being.* If we solicite God as the Lord of Hosts, that he would deliver us from our enemies, perchance he may see it fitter for us to be delivered to our enemies: If we solicite him as Proprietarie of all the world, as the beasts upon a thousand mountaines are his, as all the gold and silver in the earth is his, perchance he sees that poverty is fitter for us: If we solicite him for health, or
300 long life, he gives life, but he kills too, he heales, but he wounds too; and we may be ignorant which of these, life or death, sicknesse or health, is for our advantage. But solicite him as *Iehovah,* for a Being, that Being which flowes from his purpose, that Being which he knowes fittest for us, and then we follow his owne Instructions, *Fiat voluntas tua,* thy will be done upon us, and we are safe.

Now that which *Iehovah* was to *David, Iesus* is to us. Man in generall hath relation to God, as he is *Iehovah,* Being; We have relation to Christ, as he is *Iesus,* our Salvation; Salvation is our Being, *Iesus* is our *Iehovah.* And therfore as *David* delights himself with that
310 name *Iehovah,* for he repeats it eight or nine times in this one short Psalm, and though he ask things of a diverse nature at Gods hands, though he suffer afflictions, of a diverse nature, from Gods hands, yet still he retains that one name, he speaks to God in no other name in all this Psalm but in the name of *Iehovah:* So in the New Testament, he which may be compared with *David,* because he was under great sins, and yet in great favour with God, S. *Paul,* he delights himself with that name of *Iesus* so much, as that S. *Ierome* says, *Quem superfluè diligebat, extraordinariè nominavit,* As he loved him excessively, so he named him superabundantly. It is the name that cost God most,
320 and therefore he loves it best; it cost him his life to be a *Iesus,* a

[Acts 17.28]

[Psal. 50.10]

[1 Sam. 2.6]

[Mat. 6.10]

Iesus

Saviour. The name of Christ, which is Anointed, he had by office; he was anointed as King, as Priest, as Prophet. All those names which he had in *Isaiah, The Counsellor, The Wonderfull, The Prince of Peace,* and the name of *Iehovah* it self, which the Jews deny ever to be given to him, and is evidently given to him in that place, Christ had by nature; But his name of *Iesus,* a Saviour, he had by purchase, and that purchase cost him his bloud. And therefore, as *Iacob* preferred his name of *Israel,* before his former name of *Iacob,* because he had that name upon his wrastling with God, and it cost him a lame-
330 nesse; so is the name of *Iesus* so precious to him who bought it so dearly, that not only every knee bows at the name of *Iesus* here, but Jesus himself, and the whole Trinity, bow down towards us, to give us all those things which we ask in that name. For even of a devout use of that very name, do some of the Fathers interpret that, *Oleum effusum Nomen tuum,* That the name of *Iesus* should be spread as an ointment, breathed as perfume, diffused as a soul over all the petitions of our prayers; As the Church concludes for the most part, all her Collects so, *Grant this O Lord, for our Lord and Saviour Christ Iesus sake.* And so much does S. *Paul* abound in the use of this name,
340 as that he repeats it thrice, in the superscription of one of his Letters, the title of one of his Epistles, his first to *Timothy.* And with the same devotion, S. *Augustine* sayes, even of the name, *Melius est mihi non esse, quam sine Iesu esse,* I were better have no being, then be without Jesus; *Melius est non vivere, quam vivere sine vita,* I were better have no life, then any life without him. For as *David* could finde no beeing without *Iehovah,* a Christian findes no life without *Iesus.* Both these names imply that which is in this Text, in our Translation, *The Lord, Dominus;* to whom only, and intirely we appertaine; his we are. And therefore whether we take *Dominus,* to be *Do minas,* to threaten, to
350 afflict us, or to be *Do manus,* to succour, and relieve us, (as some have pleased themselves with those obvious derivations) as *David* did still, we must make our recourse to him, from whom, as he is *Iehovah,* Beeing, our being, our wel-beeing, our eternall beeing, our Creation, Preservation, and Salvation is derived; all is from him.

Now when he hath his accesse to the Lord, to this Lord, the Lord that hath all, and gives all, and is all, the first part of *Davids* prayer, and all his prayer which falls into our Text, is but Deprecatory; he

Esay 9.[6]

Gen. 32.28

[Phil. 2.10]

[Cant. 1.3]

2 Part

does but pray that God would forbeare him. He pretends no error, he
enterprises no Reversing of Judgement; no at first, he dares not sue
³⁶⁰ for pardon; he onely desires a Reprieve, a respit of execution, and that

[Psa. 6.1;
6.2. Vulg.]
Deprecation

not absolutely neither; but he would not be executed in hot blood;
Ne in ira, ne in furore, not in Gods anger, not in his hot displeasure.

   First then, *Deprecari,* is not *Refragari,* to Deprecate, is not to Contend against a Judge, nor to defend ones selfe against an Officer, but
it is onely in the quality, and in the humility of a Petitioner, and Sup-
pliant, to begge a forbearance. The Martyrs in the Primitive Church
would not doe that. *Nihil de causa sua deprecatur, qui nihil de conditione sua miratur,* sayes *Tertullian;* and in that he describes a
patience of Steele, and an invincible temper. He meanes that the
³⁷⁰ Christians in those times of Persecution, did never intreat the Judge
for favour, because it was not strange to them, to see themselves,

[Phil. 3.20]

whose conversation was in heaven, despised, and contemned, and
condemned upon earth: *Nihil mirantur de conditione,* They wondred
not at their misery, they thought it a part of their Profession, a part of
the Christian Religion, to suffer, and therefore, *Nihil deprecati de
causa,* They never solicited the Judge for favour. They had learnt by
experience of daily tribulation, the Apostles Lesson, *Think it not
strange, when tentations and tribulations fall;* That is, make that your
daily bread, and you shall never sterve, use your selves to suffering, at

[1 Pet. 4.12]

³⁸⁰ least to the expectation, the contemplation of suffering, acquaint your
selves with that, accustome your selves to that before it come, and it
will not be a stranger to you when it comes. *Tertullians* Method may
be right, and it may work that effect in very great afflictions; a man
may be so used to them, as that he will not descend to any low
deprecation, or sute to be delivered of them. But *Davids* affliction
was spirituall; and howsoever, as a naturall man, nay, as a devout and
religious man, (for even in rectified men there are affections of a
middle nature, that participate of nature, and of grace too, and in
which the Spirit of God moves, and naturall affections move too;
³⁹⁰ for nature and grace doe not so destroy one another, as that we should
conclude, Hee hath strong naturall affections, therefore he hath no
grace) *David* I say, that might justly wonder at his own condition,
and think it strange, that he that put his trust so intirely in God,
should so intirely be delivered over to such afflictions, might also justly

deprecate, and boldly say, *Ne facias,* O Lord deale not thus with thy
servant.

Our Saviour Christs *Transeat calix, Let this cup passe from me,* was
a deprecation in his owne behalfe; And his *Pater dimitte illis, Father,
forgive them, they know not what they doe,* was a deprecation in the
400 behalfe of his enemies; And so was *Stephens, Ne statuas illis, O Lord,
lay not this sin to their charge,* A deprecation in the behalfe of his
Executioners. And these Deprecations for others, for our selves, are
proposed for our imitation. But for *Moses* his *Dele me,* Pardon this
people, or blot my name out of thy Booke, and for S. *Pauls Anathema,*
rather then his brethren should not be saved, let himselfe be condemned, for such Deprecations for others, as were upon the matter,
Imprecations upon themselves, those may not well be drawne into
consequence, or practise; for in *Moses* and S. *Paul* themselves, there
was, if not an irregularity, and an inordinatenesse, at least an incon-
410 sideration, not to be imitated by us now, not to be excused in them
then; but for the Prayer that is meerly deprecatory, though some have
thought it lesse lawfull then the postulatory prayer, because when
God is come to the act of afflicting us, he hath then revealed, and
declared, and manifested his will to be such, and against the revealed
and manifested will of God we may not pray, yet because his afflictions are not peremptory, but we have every day to shew cause, why
that affliction should be taken off, and because all his judgements
are conditionall, and the condition of every particular judgement is
not alwaies revealed to us, and this is alwaies revealed to us, *Misera-*
420 *tiones ejus super omnia opera ejus,* That his mercy is above all his
judgements, therefore we may come to that Deprecation, that God
will make his hand lighter upon us, and his corrections easier unto
us.

As the Saints in heaven have their *Vsquequo,* How long Lord, holy
and true, before thou begin to execute judgement? So the Saints on
earth have their *Vsquequo,* How long Lord, before thou take off the
execution of this judgement upon us? For, our Deprecatory prayers,
are not Mandatory, they are not Directory, they appoint not God his
waies, nor his times; but as our Postulatory prayers are, they also are
430 submitted to the will of God, and have all in them, that ingredient,
that herb of grace, which Christ put into his owne prayer, that

[Mat. 26.39]
[Luk. 23.34]

[Act. 7.60]

[Exod.
32.32]
[Rom. 9.3]

[Psa. 145.9;
144.9 Vulg.]

[Apoc. 6.10]

[Mat. 26.39]
[Mat. 6.10]

Veruntamen, Yet not my will, but thy will be fulfilled; And they have that ingredient, which Christ put into our prayer, *Fiat voluntas, Thy will be done in earth as it is in heaven;* In heaven there is no resisting of his will; yet in heaven there is a soliciting, a hastning, an accelerating of the judgement, and the glory of the Resurrection; So though we resist not his corrections here upon earth, we may humbly present to God, the sense which we have of his displeasure; for this sense, and apprehension of his corrections, is one of the principall
⁴⁴⁰ reasons, why he sends them; he corrects us therefore, that we might be sensible of his corrections; that when we, being humbled under his hand, have said with his Prophet, *I will beare the wrath of the Lord, because I have sinned against him,* He may be pleased to say to his Correcting Angell, as he did to his Destroying Angell, *This is enough,* and so burne his rod now, as he put up his sword then.

Micah 7.9

[2 Sam.
24.16]

For though *David* doe, well for himselfe, and well for our example, deprecate the anger of God, exprest in those Judgements, yet we see he spends but one verse of the Psalme in that Deprecation. In all the rest he leaves God wholly to his pleasure, how farre he will extend,
⁴⁵⁰ or aggravate that Judgement; and he turns wholly upon the Postula-tory part, *That God would have mercy upon him, and save him, and deliver his soule.* And in that one verse, hee does not deprecate all afflictions, all corrections. *David* knowes what moves God to correct us; It is not onely our ilnesse that moves him; for he corrects us when we are not ill in his sight, but made good by his pardon: But his goodnesse, as well as our ilnesse, moves him to correct us; If he were not good, not only good in himselfe, but good to us, he would let us alone, and never correct us. But, *Ideo eos qui errant corripis, quia*

Wisd. 12.1

bonus & suavis es Domine, as the Vulgate reades that place, The Lord
⁴⁶⁰ corrects us, not onely as he is good, but as he is gentle; he were more cruell, more unmercifull, if he did alwayes shew mercy; That *David*

[Psal. 99.8]

intends, when he sayes, *Propitius fuisti,* Thou wast a Mercifull God, because thou didst punish all their inventions.

Ier. 30.11

So then, our first worke is to consider, that that in the Prophet, is a promise, and hath the nature of a mercy, *I will correct thee in meas-ure;* where the promise does not fall only upon the measure, but upon the correction it selfe; and then, since this is a promise, a mercy, a part of our daily bread, we may pray as the same Prophet directs us,

O Lord correct me, but with judgement, not in thine anger; Where Ier. 10.24
470 also the petition seems to fall, not onely upon the measure, but upon
the correction it selfe; and then, when I have found some correction
fit to be prayed for and afforded me by God upon my praier, if that
correction at any time grow heavy, or wearisome unto me, I must
relieve my selfe upon that consideration, *Whether God have smitten
me, as he smote them that smote me,* Whether it be not another manner of execution, which God hath laid upon mine enemies then that
which he hath laid upon me, in having suffered them to be smitten
with the spirit of sinfull glory, and triumph in their sin, and my
misery, and with excecation, and obduratenesse, with impenitence,
480 and insensiblenesse of their owne case. Or at least, let me consider,
as it is in the same place, *Whether I be slain according to the slaughter*
of them that were slaine by me; That is, whether my oppression, my Esay 27.7
extortion, my prevarication have not brought other men to more
misery, then God hath yet brought me unto. And if we consider this,
as no doubt *David* did, and finde that correction is one loafe of our
daily bread, and finde in our heaviest corrections, that God hath
been heavier upon our enemies, then upon us, and we heavier upon
others, then God upon us too, we shall be content with any *Rebuke,*
and any *Chastisement,* so it be not *in anger,* and *in hot displeasure,*
490 which are the words that remaine to be considered.

Now these two phrases, *Argui in furore,* and *Corripi in ira,* which
we translate, *To rebuke in anger,* and *to chasten in hot displeasure,* are
by some thought, to signifie one and the same thing, that *David* intends the same thing, and though in divers words, yet words of one
and the same signification. But with reverence to those men, (for
some of them are men to whom much reverence is due) they doe not
well agree with one another, nor very constantly with themselves.
S. *Ierome* sayes, *Furor & ira maxime unum sunt,* That this *anger,* and
hot displeasure, are meerly, absolutely, intirely, one and the same
500 thing, and yet he sayes, that this Anger is executed in this world, and
this hot Displeasure reserved for the world to come. And this makes a
great difference; no waight of Gods whole hand here, can be so heavy,
as any finger of his in hell; the highest exaltation of Gods anger in
this world, can have no proportion to the least spark of that in hell;
nor a furnace seaven times heat here, to the embers there. So also S.

Augustine thinks, that these two words, to *Rebuke,* and to *Chasten,* doe not differ at all; or if they doe, that the latter is the lesser. But this is not likely to be *Davids* method, first to make a praier for the greater, and that being granted, to make a second praier for the lesser,
⁵¹⁰ included in that which was askt, and granted before. A later man in the Roman Church, allowes the words to differ, and the later to be the heavier, but then he refers both to the next life; that to *Rebuke in anger,* should be intended of Purgatorie, and of a short continuance there, and to be *Chastened in hot displeasure,* should be intended of hell, and of everlasting condemnation there. And so *David* must make his first petition, *Rebuke me not in thine anger,* to this purpose, Let me passe at my death immediately to Heaven, without touching at any fire, and his second petition, *Chasten me not in thy hot displeasure* to this purpose, If I must touch at any fire, let it be but Purgatory, and
⁵²⁰ not Hell.

But by the nature, and propriety, and the use of all these words in the Scriptures, it appeares, that the words are of a different significa-tion, which S. *Ierome* it seemes did not thinke; and that the last is the heaviest, which S. *Augustine* it seemes did not thinke; and then, that they are to be referred to this life, which *Ayguanus* did not think. For the words themselves, all our three Translations retaine the two first words, to *Rebuke* and to *Chasten;* neither that which we call the *Bishops Bible,* nor that which we call the *Geneva Bible,* and that which wee may call the *Kings,* depart from those two first words.
⁵³⁰ But then for the other two, *Anger* and *Hot displeasure,* in them all three Translations differ. The first cals them *Indignation* and *Dis-pleasure,* the second *Anger* and *Wrath,* and the last *Anger* and *Hot displeasure.*

To begin with the first, to be *Rebuked* was but to be chidden, but to be *Chastened,* was to be beaten; and yet *David* was heartily afraid of the first, of the least of them, when it was to be done in anger: This word that is here to Rebuke, *Iacach,* is for the most part, to Reprove, to Convince by way of argument, and disputation. So it is in *Esay, Come now, and let us reason together,* saies God. The
⁵⁴⁰ naturall man is confident in his Reason, in his Philosophy; and yet God is content to joyne in that issue, If he doe not make it appeare, even to your reason, that he is God, *Chuse whom ye will serve,* as

Ayguanus

Rebuke

Esay 1.18

[Jos. 24.15]

Ioshuah speakes; If he doe not make it appeare, that he is a good
God, change him for any other God that your reason can present to
be better. In *Micah,* the word hath somewhat more vehemence; *The*
Lord hath a quarrell against his people, and he will plead with   Micah 6.2
Israel. This is more then a Disputation; it is a Suite. God can maintaine his possession other waies; without Suite; but he will recover
us, by matter of Record, openly, and in the face of the County; he
550 will put us to a shame, and to an acknowledgement, of having dis-
loially devested our Allegeance. Yea, the word hath sometimes somewhat more sharpnesse then this, for in the book of Proverbs, it comes
to Correction, *The Lord correcteth him whom he loveth, even as the*   [Prov. 3.12]
father doth the child, in whom he delighteth. Though it be a fatherly
correction, yet it is a correction; and that is more then the Reasoning
or Disputing, more then the Suing or Impleading.

Now though all this, Disputing, Impleading, Correcting, in S.
Augustines interpretation, amount but to an Instruction, and an
Amendment, yet saies he of *David, In ira emendari non vult, erudiri*
560 *non vult,* He is loath to fall into Gods hands, loath to come into Gods
fingers at all, when God is angry; he would not be disputed withall,
not Impleaded, not Corrected, no, not Instructed, not Amended by
God in his Anger. The Anger of God is such a Pedagogie, such a
Catechisme, such a way of teaching, as the Law was. *Lex pædagogus;*   [Gal. 3.24]
the Law is a Schoolmaster, saies the Apostle; but *Litera occidit,* the   [2 Cor. 3.6]
Law is such a Schoolemaster, as brings not a rod, but a sword. Gods
Anger should instruct us, but if we use it not aright, it hardens us.
And therefore, *Kisse the Son lest he be angry,* sayes *David,* And what   [Psa. 2.12]
is the danger if he be? that which followes, *Lest yee perish in the*
570 *way;* Though his Anger be one of his wayes, yet it is such a way, as
you may easily stumble in; and, as you would certainely perish without that way, so you may easily perish in that way. For when a sinner
considers himself to be under the Anger of God, naturally he con-
ceives such a horror, as puts him farther off. As soonè as *Adam*   [Gen. 3.8]
heard the voice of God, and in an accent of Anger, or as he tuned it
in his guilty conscience, to an accent of Anger, (for as a malicious
man will turne a Sermon to a Satyre, and a Panegyricke to a Libel,
so a despairing soule will set Gods comfortablest words, to a sad tune,
and force a *Væ* even in Gods *Euge,* and find Anger, and everlasting

⁵⁸⁰ Anger in every Accesse, in every Action of God) when *Adam* heard God but walking in the Garden, but the noise of his going, and approaching towards him, (for God had then said nothing to him, not so much as called him) *Adam* fled from his presence and hid him-selfe amongst the trees. When the guilty man was but spoken to, and spoken to mildly, by the Master of the Marriage feast, *Amice quo-modo intrasti? Friend how came you in?* we see he was presently *speechlesse,* and being so, not able to speake, to come to any confes-sion, any excuse, he fell farther and farther into displeasure, till he was bound hand and foote, and cast irrecoverably away. For *Si* ⁵⁹⁰ *repente interroget, quis respondebit ei?* If God surprize a Conscience with a sudden question, if God deprehend a man in the Act of his sin, and while he accomplishes and consummates that sin, say to his soul, Why dost thou this, upon which mine anger hangs? there God speaks to that sinner, but he confounds him with the question; It is not a leading Intergatorie, it gives him no light to answer, till Gods anger be out of his contemplation, he cannot so much as say *Domine vim patior, responde pro me,* O Lord I am oppressed, doe thou answer for me; do thou say to thy selfe for me, *My Spirit shall not alwaies strive with man, because he is but flesh.* If the Lord come in anger, ⁶⁰⁰ if he speake in Anger, if he doe but looke in Anger, a sinner perishes; *Aspexit & dissolvit Gentes;* He did but looke, and he dissolved, he melted the Nations; he powred them out as water upon the dust, and he blew them away as dust into the Sea, *The everlasting mountaines were broken, and the ancient hils did bow.*

It is not then the disputing, not the impleading, not the correcting, which this word *Iacach* imports, that *David* declines, or deprecates here, but that Anger, which might change the nature of all, and make all the Physick poison, all that was intended for our mollifying, to advance our obduration. For when there was no anger in the case, ⁶¹⁰ *David* is a forward Scholar, to hearken to Gods Reasoning, and Dis-puting, and a tractable Client, and easie Defendant, to answer to Gods Suite, and Impleading, and an obsequious Patient, to take any Physick at his hands, if there were no Anger in the cup. *Vre renes & cor meum,* saies *David,* he provokes God with all those emphaticall words, *Iudge me, Prove me, Trie me, Examine me,* and more, *Vre renes,* bring not onely a candle to search, but even fire, to melt me;

[Mat. 22.12]

Iob 9.12

Esay 38.14

Gen. 6.3

Hab. 3.6

Psal. 26.2

But upon what confidence all this? *For thy loving kindnesse is ever before mine eyes.* If Gods Anger, and not his loving kindnesse had beene before his eyes, it had beene a fearfull apparition, and a danger-
620 ous issue to have gone upon. So also he surrenders himselfe entirely to God in another Psalme, *Trie me O God, and know my heart; prove me, and know my thoughts, and consider, if there be any way of wickednesse in me.* But how concludes he? *And lead me in the right way for ever.* As long as I have God by the hand, and feele his loving care of me, I can admit any waight of his hand; any fornace of his heating. Let God mould me, and then melt me againe, let God make mee, and then breake me againe, as long as he establishes and main- taines a rectified assurance in my soule, that at last he meanes to make me a Vessell of honour, to his Glory, howsoever he Rebuke or
630 Chastise me, yet he will not *Rebuke me in Anger,* much lesse *Chasten me in hot Displeasure,* which is the last, and the heaviest thing, that *David* deprecates in this Prayer.

Both these words, which we translate to *Chasten,* and *Hot dis- pleasure,* are words of a heavie, and of a vehement signification. They extend both, to expresse the eternity of Gods indignation, even to the binding of the soule and bodie in eternall chaines of darknesse. For the first, *Iasar,* signifies oftentimes in the Scriptures, *Vincire,* to binde, often with ropes, often with chaines; to fetter, or manacle, or pinion men, that are to be executed; so that it imports a slaverie, a
640 bondage all the way, and a destruction at last. And so the word is used by *Rehoboam, My Father chastised you with whips, but I will chastise you with Scorpions.* And then, the other word, *Camath,* doth not onely signifie *Hot displeasure,* but that effect of *Gods hot dis- pleasure,* which is intended by the Prophet *Esay, Therefore hath he powred forth his fierce wrath, and the strength of battel, and that set him on fire round about, and he knew it not, and it burnt him up, and he considered it not;* These be the fearful conditions of Gods hot displeasure, to be in a fornace, and not to feele it; to be in a habit of sin, and not know what leads us into temptation; to be burnt to
650 ashes, and so not onely without all moisture, all holy teares, but, as ashes, without any possibility, that any good thing can grow in us. And yet this word, *Camath,* hath a heavier signification then this; for it signifies Poison it selfe, Destruction it selfe, for so is it twice taken

Psal. 139.23

1 Reg. 12.11

Esay 42 ult.

Psal. 58.4

in one verse, *Their poison is like the poison of a Serpent;* so that this *Hot displeasure,* is that poison of the soule, obduration here, and that extention of this obduration, a finall impenitence in this life, and an infinite impenitiblenesse in the next, to dye without any actuall penitence here, and live without all possibility of future penitence for ever hereafter.

⁶⁶⁰ *David* therefore foresees, that if God *Rebuke in anger,* it will come to a *Chastening in hot displeasure.* For what should stop him? For, *If a man sinne against the Lord, who will plead for him?* sayes *Eli; Plead thou my cause,* sayes *David;* It is onely the Lord, that can be of counsell with him, and plead for him; and that Lord, is both the Judge, and angry too. So *Davids* prayer hath this force, *Rebuke me not in anger,* for though I were able to stand under that, yet thou wilt also *Chasten mee in thine hot displeasure,* and that no soule can beare; for as long as Gods anger lasts, so long he is going on towards our utter destruction. In that State, (it is not a State) in that Exinanition, ⁶⁷⁰ in that annihilation of the soule, (it is not an annihilation, the soule is not so happy as to come to nothing) but in that misery, which can no more receive a name, then an end, all Gods corrections are borne with grudging, with murmuring, with comparing our righteousnesse with others righteousnesse; In *Iobs* impatience, *Quare posuisti me contrarium tibi? Why hast thou set me up as a marke against thee, O Thou preserver of men?* Thou that preservest other men, *hast bent thy bow, and made me a mark for thine arrowes,* sayes the Lamentation: In that state we cannot cry to him, that he might answer us; If we doe cry, and he answer, we cannot heare; if we doe heare, we ⁶⁸⁰ cannot beleeve that it is he. *Cum invocantem exaudierit,* sayes *Iob, If I cry, and he answer, yet I doe not beleeve that he heard my voyce.* We had rather perish utterly, then stay his leisure in recovering us. *Si flagellat, occidat semel,* sayes *Iob* in the Vulgat, *If God have a minde to destroy me, let him doe it at one blow; Et non de pœnis rideat, Let him not sport himselfe with my misery.* Whatsoever come after, we would be content to be out of this world, so we might but change our torment, whether it be a temporall calamity that oppresses our state or body, or a spirituall burthen, a perplexity that sinks our understanding, or a guiltinesse that depresses our conscience. *Vt in* ⁶⁹⁰ *inferno protegas,* as *Iob* also speaks, *O that thou wouldest hide me,*

1 Sam. 2.25

[Psa. 43.1]

Job 7.20

Lam. 3.12

Job 9.16

Ver. 23

Job 14.13

In inferno, In the grave, sayes the afflicted soule, but *in Inferno, In hell* it selfe, sayes the dispairing soule, rather then keepe me in this torment, in this world!

This is the miserable condition, or danger, that *David* abhors, and deprecates in this Text, *To be rebuked in anger,* without any purpose in God to amend him; and *to be chastned in his hot displeasure;* so, as that we can finde no interest in the gracious promises of the Gospel, no conditions, no power of revocation in the severe threatnings of the Law; no difference between those torments which have attached us
700 here, and the everlasting torments of Hell it selfe. That we have lost all our joy in this life, and all our hope of the next; That we would faine die, though it were by our own hands, and though that death doe but unlock us a doore, to passe from one Hell into another. This is *Ira tua Domine, & furor tuus, Thy anger, O Lord,* and, *Thy hot displeasure.* For as long as it is but *Ira patris,* the anger of my Father, which hath dis-inherited me, Gold is thine, and silver is thine, and thou canst provide me. As long as it is but *Ira Regis,* some mis-information to the King, some mis-apprehension in the King, *Cor Regis in manu tua, The Kings heart is in thy hand,* and thou canst rectifie
710 it againe. As long as it is but *Furor febris,* The rage and distemper of a pestilent Fever, or *Furor furoris,* The rage of madnesse it selfe, thou wilt consider me, and accept me, and reckon with me according to those better times, before those distempers overtooke me, and overthrew me. But when it comes to be *Ira tua, furor tuus, Thy anger,* and, *Thy displeasure,* as *David* did, so let every Christian finde comfort, if he be able to say faithfully this Verse, this Text, *O Lord, rebuke me not in thine anger, neither chasten me in thy hot displeasure;* for as long as he can pray against it, he is not yet so fallen under it, but that he hath yet his part in all Gods blessings, which
720 we shed upon the Congregation in our Sermons, and which we seale to every soule in the Sacrament of Reconciliation.

[Hag. 2.8]

[Prov. 21.1]

Number 17.

Preached upon the Penitentiall Psalmes.

PSAL. 6.2, 3. *HAVE MERCY UPON ME, O LORD, FOR I AM WEAKE; O LORD, HEALE ME, FOR MY BONES ARE VEXED: MY SOULE IS ALSO SORE VEXED; BUT THOU, O LORD, HOW LONG?*

THIS whole Psalme is prayer; And the whole prayer is either Deprecatory, as in the first verse, or Postulatory. Something *David* would have forborne, and something done. And in that Postulatory part of *Davids* prayer, which goes through six verses of this Psalme, we consider the Petitions, and the Inducements; What *David* asks, And why: of both which, there are some mingled, in these two verses, which constitute our Text. And therefore, in them, we shall necessarily take knowledge of some of the Petitions, and some of the Reasons. For, in the Prayer, there are five petitions; First,
10 *Miserere, Have mercy upon me,* Thinke of me, looke graciously towards me, prevent me with thy mercy; And then *Sana me, O Lord, heale me,* Thou didst create me in health, but my parents begot me in sicknesse, and I have complicated other sicknesses with that, Actuall with Originall sin, O Lord, heale me, give me physick for them; And thirdly, *Convertere, Returne, O Lord,* Thou didst visit me in nature, returne in grace, Thou didst visit me in Baptisme, returne in the other Sacrament, Thou doest visit me now, returne at the houre of my death; And, in a fourth petition, *Eripe, O Lord, deliver my soule,* Every blessing of thine becomes a snare unto me, and thy bene-
20 fits I make occasions of sinne, In all conversation, and even in my solitude, I admit such tentations from others, or I produce such ten-

338

tations in my selfe, as that, whensoever thou art pleased to returne
to me, thou findest me at the brinke of some sinne, and therefore
Eripe me, O Lord, take hold of me, and deliver me; And lastly,
Salvum me fac, O Lord, save me, Manifest thy good purpose upon
me so, that I may never be shaken, or never overthrown in the faithfull hope of that salvation, which thou hast preordained for me. These
are the five petitions of the Prayer, and two of the five, The *Miserere,*
Have mercy upon me, and the *Sana, O Lord, heale me,* are in these
30 two verses. And then, the Reasons of the prayer, arising partly out
of himselfe, and partly out of God; and some being mixt, and growing out of both roots together, some of the Reasons of the first nature,
that is, of those that arise out of himselfe, are also in this Text.

Therefore in this Text, we shall consider, first the extent of those
two petitions that are in it, *Quid miserere,* what *David* intends by this
prayer, *Have mercy upon me,* And then *Quid sana me,* what he intends by that, *O Lord, heale me.* And secondly, we shall consider the
strength of those Reasons, which are in our text, *Quia infirmus,* why
God should be moved to mercy with that, Because *David* was weake,
40 And then *Quia turbata ossa,* why, Because his bones were vexed;
And againe, *Quia turbata anima valde,* Because his soule was sore
vexed. And in a third Consideration, we shall also see, that for all
our petitions, for mercy, and for spirituall health, and for all our
Reasons, weaknesse, vexation of bones, And sore vexation of the
soule it selfe, God doth not alwayes come to a speedy remedy, but
puts us to our *Vsquequò, But thou, O Lord, how long? How long*
wilt thou delay? And then lastly, That how long soever that be,
yet we are still to attend his time, still to rely upon him; which is
intimated in this, That *David* changes not his Master, but still ap-
50 plies himselfe to the Lord; with that Name, that he begun with in
the first verse, he proceeds; and thrice in these few words he calls
upon him by this name of Essence, *Iehova, O Lord have mercy upon*
me, O Lord heale me, O Lord how long wilt thou delay? He is not
weary of attending the Lord, he is not inclinable to turn upon any
other then the Lord; *Have mercy upon me O Lord, &c.*

First then in our first part, that part of *Davids* postulatory prayer
in this Text, *Have mercy upon me,* This mercy that *David* begs here,
is not that mercy of God which is above all his works; for those

1 Part
Quid
misereri

works which follow it, are above it; *To heale him,* in this Text, *To*
⁶⁰ *returne to him, To deliver his soule, To save him,* in the next verses,
are greater works then this, which he calls here in that generall name
of Mercy. For this word *Chanan* used in this place, is not *Dele iniqui-*
tates, Have mercy upon me so, as to blot out all mine iniquities; It
is not *Dimitte debita,* Have mercy upon me so, as to forgive all my
sins; but it is onely *Des mihi gratiam,* Lord shed some drops of grace
upon me, or as *Tremellius* hath it, *Gratiosus sis mihi,* Be a gracious
Lord unto me. For this word is used, where *Noah* is said *to have*
found grace in the eyes of the Lord; which grace was, that God had
provided for his bodily preservation in the Arke. And this word is
⁷⁰ used, not onely of God towards men, but also of men towards God;
when they expresse their zeale towards Gods house, and the compassion, and holy indignation which they had of the ruines thereof,
they expresse it in this word, *Thy servants delight in the stones of*
Sion, & miserti sunt pulveris ejus, They had mercy, they had com-
passion upon the dust and rubbish thereof. So that here this *Miserere*
mei, which is the first grone of a sick soule, the first glance of the
soule directed towards God, imports onely this, Lord turne thy countenance towards me, Lord bring me to a sense that thou art turned
towards me, Lord bring me within such a distance, as my soule may
⁸⁰ feele warmth and comfort in the rising of that Sunne; *Miserere mei,*
Look graciously upon me.

At the first meeting of *Isaac* and *Rebecca,* he was gone out to meditate in the fields, and she came riding that way, with his fathers man,
who was imployed in making that mariage; and when upon asking
she knew that it was he who was to be her husband, *she tooke a vaile*
and covered her face, sayes that story. What freedome, and nearnesse
soever they were to come to after, yet there was a modesty, and a
bashfulnesse, and a reservednesse required before; and her first kindnesse should be but to be seen. A man would be glad of a good coun-
⁹⁰ tenance from her that shall be his, before he aske her whether shee
will be his or no; A man would be glad of a good countenance from
his Prince, before he intend to presse him with any particular suit:
And a sinner may be come to this *Miserere mei Domine,* to desire
that the Lord would think upon him, that the Lord would look
graciously towards him, that the Lord would refresh him with the

Marginal notes: [Psa. 51.1; 50.3 Vulg.] [Mat. 6.12] Gen. 6.8 Psal. 102.14 Gen. 24.63

beams of his favour, before he have digested his devotion into a formall prayer, or entred into a particular consideration, what his necessities are.

Upon those words of the Apostle, *I exhort you that supplications,* *and prayers, and Intercessions, and giving of thanks be made for all men,* S. *Bernard* makes certaine gradations, and steps, and ascensions of the soule in prayer, and intimates thus much, That by the grace of Gods Spirit inanimating and quickning him, (without which grace he can have no motion at all) a sinner may come *Ad supplicationes,* which is S. *Pauls* first step, To supplications, which are *à suppliciis,* That out of a sense of some Judgement, some punishment, he may make his recourse to God; And then, by a farther growth in that grace, he may come *Ad orationes,* which are *Oris rationes,* The particular expressing of his necessities, with his mouth; and a faithfull assurance of obtaining them, in his prayer; And after, he may come farther; *Ad Intercessiones,* to an Intercession, to such an interest in Gods favour, as that he durst put himselfe betwixt God and other men, as *Abraham* in the behalfe of Sodome, to intercede for them, with a holy confidence that God would doe good to them, for his sake; And to a farther step then these, which the Apostle may intend in that last, *Ad gratiarum actiones,* to a continuall Thanksgiving, That by reason of Gods benefits multiplyed upon him, he finde nothing to aske, but his Thanksgivings, and his acknowledgements, for former blessings, possesse and fill all his prayers; Though he be growne up to this strength of devotion, To Supplications, to Prayers, to Intercessions, to Thanksgivings, yet, sayes S. *Bernard,* at first, when he comes first to deprehend himselfe in a particular sin, or in a course of sin, he comes *Verecundo affectu,* Bashfully, shamefastly, tremblingly; he knows not what to aske, he dares ask no particular thing at Gods hand; But though he be not come yet, to particular requests, for pardon of past sins, not for strength against future, not to a particular consideration of the waight of his sins, nor to a comparison betwixt his sin, and the mercy of God, yet he comes to a *Miserere mei Domine,* To a sudden ejaculation, O Lord be mercifull unto me, how dare I doe this in the sight of my God?

It is much such an affection as is sometimes in a Felon taken in the manner, or in a condemned person brought to execution: One

1 Tim. 2.1

Bern. De 4. modis orandi

desires the Justice to be good to him, and yet he sees not how he can Baile him; the other desires the Sherife to be good to him, and yet he knowes he must doe his Office. A sinner desires God to have mercy upon him, and yet he hath not descended to particular considerations requisite in that businesse. But yet this spirituall Malefactor is in better case, then the temporall are; They desire them to be good to them, who can doe them no good; but God is still able, and still
140 ready to reprieve them, and to put off the execution of his Judgements, which execution were to take them out of this world under the guiltinesse, and condemnation of unrepented sins. And therefore,

Basil as S. *Basil* sayes, *In scala, prima ascensio est ab humo,* He that makes but one step up a staire, though he be not got much nearer to the top of the house, yet he is got from the ground, and delivered from the foulnesse, and dampnesse of that; so in this first step of prayer, *Miserere mei,* O Lord be mercifull unto me, though a man be not established in heaven, yet he is stept from the world, and the miser-

1 John 3.8 able comforters thereof; *He that committeth sin, is of the Devill:*
150 Yea, he is of him, in a direct line, and in the nearest degree; he is the

Iohn 8.44 Off-spring, the son of the Devill; *Ex patre vestro estis,* sayes Christ, *You are of your father the Devill.*

Basil Now, *Qui se à maligni patris affinitate submoverit,* He that withdraws himself from such a Fathers house, though he be not presently come to meanes to live of himself, *Quam feliciter patre suo orbatus!* How blessed, how happy an Orphan is he become! How much better shall he finde it, to be fatherlesse in respect of such a father, then masterlesse in respect of such a Lord, as he turnes towards in this first ejaculation, and generall application of the soule, *Miserere mei,*
160 *Have mercy upon me, O Lord,* so much mercy, as to looke graciously towards me! And therefore, as it was, by infinite degrees, a greater work, to make earth of nothing, then to make the best creatures of earth; So in the regeneration of a sinner, when he is to be made up a new creature, his first beginning, his first application of himselfe to God, is the hardest matter. But though he come not presently to looke God fully in the face, nor conceive not presently an assurance of an established reconciliation, a fulnesse of pardon, a cancelling of all former debts, in an instant, Though hee dare not come to touch God, and lay hold of himselfe, by receiving his Body and Blood in the

¹⁷⁰ Sacrament, yet the Euangelist calls thee to a contemplation of much comfort to thy soule, in certaine preparatory accesses, and approaches. *Behold,* sayes he; that is, Look up, and consider thy patterne: *Behold, a woman diseased came behinde Christ, and touched the hem of his garment; for she said in her self, If I may but touch the hem of his garment onely, I shall be whole.* She knew there was vertue to come out of his Body, and she came as neare that, as she durst: she had a desire to speake; but she went no farther, but to speak to her selfe; *she said to her selfe,* sayes that Gospel, *if I may but touch, &c.* But Christ Jesus supplied all, performed all on his part, abundantly. ¹⁸⁰ *Presently he turned about,* sayes the Text: And this was not a transitory glance, but a full sight, and exhibiting of himselfe to the fruition of her eye, that she might see him. *He saw her,* sayes S. *Matthew:* Her; he did not direct himselfe upon others, and leave out her; And then, hee spake to her, to overcome her bashfulnesse; he called her *Daughter,* to overcome her diffidence; He bids her *be of comfort,* for she had met a more powerfull Physitian, then those, upon whom she had spent her time, and her estate; one that could cure her; one that would; one that had already; for so he sayes presently, *Thy faith hath made thee whole.* From how little a spark, how great a fire? ¹⁹⁰ From how little a beginning, how great a proceeding? She desired but the hem of his garment, and had all him.

    Beloved in him, his power, and his goodnesse ended not in her; *All that were sick were brought, that they might but touch the hem of his garment, and as many as touched it, were made whole.* It was farre from a perfect faith, that made them whole; To have a desire to touch his garment, seemes not, was not much: Neither was that desire that was, always in themselves, but in them that brought them. But yet, come thou so farre: Come, or be content to be brought, to be brought by example, to be brought by a statute, to be brought by ²⁰⁰ curiosity, come any way to touch the hem of his garment, yea the hem of his servant, of *Aarons* garment, and thou shalt participate of the sweet ointment, which flowes from the head to the hem of the garment. Come to the house of God, his Church; Joyne with the Congregation of the Saints; Love the body, and love the garments too, that is, The Order, the Discipline, the Decency, the Unity of the Church; Love even the hem of the garment, that that almost touches

Mat. 9.20

Mat. 14.[35,] 36

[Psal. 133.2]

the ground; that is, Such Ceremonies, as had a good use in their first
institution, for raising devotion, and are freed and purged from that
superstition, which, as a rust, was growne upon them, though they
²¹⁰ may seeme to touch the earth, that is, to have been induced by earthly
men, and not immediate institutions from God, yet love that hem
of that garment, those outward assistances of devotion in the Church.

Bring with thee a disposition to incorporate thy selfe with Gods
people here; and though thou beest not yet come to a particular consideration of thy sins, and of the remedies, Though that spirit that
possesses thee, that sin that governes thee, lie still a while, and sleepe
under all the thunders, which wee denounce from this place, so that
for a while thou beest not moved nor affected with all that is said,
yet *Appropinquas, & nescis,* (as S. *Augustine* said, when he came
²²⁰ onely out of curiosity to heare S. *Ambrose* preach at Milan) Thou
doest come nearer and nearer to God, though thou discerne it not,
and at one time or other, this blessed exorcisme, this holy Charme,
this Ordinance of God, the word of God in the mouth of his servant,
shall provoke and awaken that spirit of security in thee, and thou
shalt feele him begin to storme, and at first that spirit, thy spirit, will

1 Kings
say to the spirit of the Preacher, *Tune qui conturbas? Art thou he*

18.[17]
that troublest Israel? (as *Ahab* said to *Eliah*) Art thou he that
troublest the peace of my conscience, and the security of my wayes?
And, when the Spirit of God shall search farther and farther, even
²³⁰ *ad occulta,* to thy secretest sins, and touch upon them, and that that
spirit of disobedience, when he feeles this powerfull Exorcisme, shall

1 King.
say in thee, and cry as *Ahab* also did, *Invenisti me? Hast thou found*

21.20
me, O mine enemy? God shall answer, *Inveni te, I have found thee,*
and found that thou hadst *sold thy selfe to worke wickednesse in the*
sight of the Lord, And so shall bring thee to a more particular consideration of thine estate, and from thy having joyned with the

Psal. 102.13
Church, in a *Dominus miserebitur Sion,* In an assurance, and acknowledgement, *that the Lord will arise, and have mercy upon Sion,*

Psal. 67.1
that is, on his whole Catholique Church, And then come to a *Dominus*
²⁴⁰ *misereatur nostri, God be mercifull unto us, and blesse us, and cause his*
face to shine upon us, upon us that are met here, according to his Ordinance, and in confidence of his promise, upon this Congregation, of
which thou makest thy selfe a part, thou wilt also come to this of *David*

here, *Domine miserere mei, Have mercy upon me,* me in particular, and thou shalt heare God answer thee, *Miserans miserebor tibi,* With great mercy will I have mercy upon thee; upon thee; *For, with him is plentifull Redemption;* Mercy for his whole Church, mercy for this whole Congregation, mercy for every particular soule, that makes her selfe a part of the Congregation. Accustome thy selfe therefore to a
²⁵⁰ generall devotion, to a generall application, to generall ejaculations towards God, upon every occasion, and then, as a wedge of gold, that comes to be coyned into particular pieces of currant money, the Lord shall stamp his Image upon all thy devotions, and bring thee to particular confessions of thy sins, and to particular prayers, for thy particular necessities. And this we may well conceive and admit, to be the nature of *Davids* first prayer, *Miserere mei, Have mercy upon me;* And then, the reason, upon which this first petition is grounded, (for so it will be fittest to handle the parts, first the prayer, and then the reason) is, *Quia infirmus, Have mercy upon me, for I am weak.*

²⁶⁰ First then, how imperfect, how weak soever our prayers be, yet still if it be a prayer, it hath a *Quia,* a Reason, upon which it is grounded. It hath in it, some implied, some interpretative consideration of our selves, how it becomes us to aske that, which wee doe ask at Gods hand, and it hath some implied, and interpretative consideration of God, how it conduces to Gods glory to grant it: for, that prayer is very farre from faith, which is not made so much as with reason; with a consideration of some possibility, and some conveniency in it. *Every man that sayes Lord, Lord, enters not into heaven;* Every *Lord, Lord,* that is said, enters not into heaven, but vanishes
²⁷⁰ in the ayre. A prayer must be with a serious purpose to pray; for else, those fashionall and customary prayers, are but false fires without shot, they batter not heaven; It is but an Interjection, that slips in; It is but a Parenthesis, that might be left out, whatsoever is uttered in the manner of a prayer, if it have not a *Quia,* a Reason, a ground for it. And therefore, when our Saviour Christ gave us that forme of prayer, which includes all, he gave us in it a forme of the reason too, *Quia tuum, For thine is the Kingdome, &c.* It were not a prayer, to say, *Adveniat Regnum, Thy Kingdome come,* if it were not grounded upon that faithfull assurance, that God hath a Kingdome here; Nor to say *Sanctificetur*
²⁸⁰ *nomen, Hallowed be thy name,* If he desired not to be glorified by us;

[Psa. 130.7]

Quia

[Mat. 7.21]

[Mat. 6.13]

Nor to aske *daily bread,* nor *forgivenesse of sins,* but for the *Quia po-
testas,* Because he hath all these in his power. We consider this first accesse to God, *Miserere mei, Have mercy upon me,* to be but a kind of
imperfect prayer, but the first step; but it were none at all, if it had no
reason, and therefore it hath this, *Quia infirmus, Because I am weake.*

*Quia
infirmus
Iohn 11.3*

This reason of our own weaknesse is a good motive for mercy, if
in a desire of farther strength we come to that of *Lazarus* sisters, to
Christ, *Ecce, quam amas, infirmatur,* Behold Lord, that soule that
thou lovest, and hast dyed for, is weak, and languishes. Christ an-
²⁹⁰ swered then, *Non est infirmitas ad mortem, This weaknesse is not unto
death, but that the Son of God might be glorified.* He will say so to thee

[Ezek.
18.31]
[2 Cor. 12.9]

too; if thou present thy weaknesse with a desire of strength from him,
he will say, *Quare moriemini, domus Israel?* why will ye die of this disease? *Gratia mea sufficit;* you may recover for all this; you may repent,
you may abstaine from this sin, you may take this spirituall physick,

[Josh. 1.7]

the Word, the Sacraments, if you will; *Tantummodo robustus esto,* (as
God sayes to *Ioshuah*) Only be valiant, and fight against it, and thou
shalt finde strength grow in the use thereof. But for the most part, *De*

*De gradibus
humilitatis*

infirmitate blandimur, sayes S. *Bernard,* we flatter our selves with an
³⁰⁰ opinion of weaknesse; *& ut liberiùs peccemus, libenter infirmamur,* we
are glad of this naturall and corrupt weaknesse, that we may impute
all our licentiousnesse to our weaknesse, and naturall infirmity. But did
that excuse *Adam,* (sayes that Father) *Quòd per uxorem tanquam per
carnis infirmitatem peccavit,* That he took his occasion of sinning from
his weaker part, from his wife? *Quia infirmus,* That thou art weak of

Esay 53.4

thy selfe, is a just motive to induce God to bring thee to himselfe; *Qui
verè portavit languores tuos,* who hath surely borne all thine infirmities; But to leave him againe when he hath brought thee, to refuse so

[Mat. 11.30]

light and easie yoake as his is, not to make use of that strength which he
³¹⁰ by his grace offers thee, this is not the affection of the Spouse, *Languor*

[Cant. 2.5]

amantis, when the person languishes for the love of Christ, but it is
Languor amoris, when the love of Christ languishes in that person.
And therefore if you be come so far with *David,* as to this *Miserere
quia infirmus,* that an apprehension of your owne weaknesse have
brought you to him, in a prayer for mercy, and more strength, goe
forward with him still, to his next Petition, *Sana me, O Lord heale
me,* for God is always ready to build upon his owne foundations,
and accomplish his owne beginnings.

Acceptus in gratiam, hilariter veni ad postulationes: When thou
³²⁰ art established in favour, thou maist make any suit; when thou art
possest of God by one prayer, thou mayst offer more. This is an encouragement which that Father S. *Bernard* gives, in observing the
diverse degrees of praying, That though *servandæ humilitatis gratia,
divina pietas ordinavit,* To make his humility the more profitable
to him, God imprints in an humble and penitent sinner, this apprehension, *Vt quanto plus profecit, eo minus se reputet profecisse,* That
the more he is in Gods favour, the more he feares he is not so, or the
more he fears to lose that favour, because it is a part, and a symptome
of the working of the grace of God, to make him see his owne unworth-
³³⁰ inesse, the more manifestly, the more sensibly, yet, it is a religious insinuation, and a circumvention that God loves, when a sinner husbands
his graces so well, as to grow rich under him, and to make his thanks
for one blessing, a reason, and an occasion of another; so to gather
upon God by a rolling Trench, and by a winding staire, as *Abraham*   [Gen. 18.23–
gained upon God, in the behalfe of Sodome; for this is an act of the   33]
wisedome of the Serpent, which our Saviour recommends unto us, in
such a Serpentine line, (as the Artists call it) to get up to God, and
get into God by such degrees, as *David* does here, from his *Miserere,*
to a *Sana,* from a gracious looke, to a perfect recovery; from the act
³⁴⁰ of the Levite that looked upon the wounded man, to the act of the   Luke
Samaritane that undertooke his cure; from desiring God to visit him   10.[32–35]
as a friend, (as *Abraham was called the friend of God*) to study   Iames 2.23
him as a Physitian. Because the Prophet *Esay* makes a Proclamation
in Christs name, *Ho, every one that thirsteth, &c.* And because the   Esay 55.1
same Prophet sayes of him, *Verè portavit, He hath truly born upon*   Esay 53.4
himselfe (and therefore taken away from us) *all our diseases, Ter-*
tullian sayes elegantly, that *Esay* presents Christ, *Prædicatorem, &*
Medicatorem, as a Preacher, and as a Physitian; Indeed he is a Physitian both wayes; in his Word, and in his Power, and therefore in that
³⁵⁰ notion onely, as a Physitian, *David* presents him here.
　　Now Physitians say, That man hath in his Constitution, in his
Complexion, a naturall vertue, which they call *Balsamum suum,* his
owne Balsamum, by which, any wound which a man could receive
in his body, would cure it selfe, if it could be kept cleane from the

anoiances of the aire, and all extrinsique encumbrances. Something
that hath some proportion and analogy to this Balsamum of the body,
there is in the soule of man too: The soule hath *Nardum suam,* her
Spikenard, as the Spouse sayes, *Nardus mea dedit odorem suum,*
she had a spikenard, a perfume, a fragrancy, a sweet savour in her
360 selfe. For, *Virtutes germaniùs attingunt animam, quàm corpus sanitas,*
Vertuous inclinations, and a disposition to morall goodnesse, is more
naturall to the soule of man, and nearer of kin to the soule of man,
then health is to the body. And then, if we consider bodily health,
Nulla oratio, nulla doctrinæ formula nos docet morbum odiisse, sayes
that Father: There needs no Art, there needs no outward Eloquence,
to perswade a man, to be loath to be sick: *Ita in anima inest naturalis,*
& citra doctrinam mali evitatio, sayes he; So the soule hath a naturall
and untaught hatred, and detestation of that which is evill. The
Church at thy Baptisme doth not require Sureties at thy hands, for
370 this: Thy Sureties undertake to the Church in thy behalfe, That
thou shalt forsake the flesh, the world, and the devill, That thou
shalt beleeve all the Articles of our Religion, That thou shalt keepe
all the Commandements of God; But for this knowledge and detestation of evill, they are not put to undertake them then, neither doth
the Church Catechize thee, in that after: for, the summe of all those
duties which concerne the detestation of evill, consists in that un-
written law of thy conscience which thou knowest naturally. *Scis*
quod boni proximo faciendum, sayes that Father, Naturally thou
knowest what good thou art bound to doe to another man; *Idem*
380 *enim est, quod ab aliis tute tibi fieri velis;* for, it is but asking thy
selfe, What thou wouldest that that other man should do unto thee:
Non ignoras quid sit ipsum malum, Thou canst not be ignorant, what
evill thou shouldest abstaine from offering to another, *Est enim quod*
ab alio fieri nolis, It is but the same, which thou thinkest another
should not put upon thee. So that the soule of man hath in it *Bal-*
samum suum, Nardum suam, A medicinall Balsamum, a fragrant
Spikenard in her selfe, a naturall disposition to Morall goodnesse, as
the body hath to health. But therein lyes the souls disadvantage, that
whereas the causes that hinder the cure of a bodily wound, are ex-
390 trinsique offences of the Ayre, and putrefaction from thence, the
causes in the wounds of the soule, are intrinsique, so as no other man

Cant. 1.12

Basil

[Book of
Common
Prayer,
Baptismal
Office]

can apply physick to them; Nay, they are hereditary, and there was no time early inough for our selves to apply any thing by way of prevention, for the wounds were as soone as we were, and sooner; Here was a new soule, but an old sore; a yong childe, but an inveterate disease. As S. *Augustin* cannot conceive any interim, any distance, between the creating of the soule, and the infusing of the soule into the body, but eases himselfe upon that, *Creando infundit,* and *infundendo creat,* The Creation is the Infusion, and the Infusion is
400 the Creation, so we cannot conceive any Interim, any distance, betweene the infusing and the sickning, betweene the comming and the sinning of the soule. So that there was no meanes of prevention; I could not so much as wish, that I might be no sinner, for I could not wish that I might be no Child. Neither is there any meanes of separation now; our concupiscencies dwell in us, and prescribe in us, and will gnaw upon us, as wormes, till they deliver our bodies to the wormes of the grave, and our consciences to the worme that never dyes.

From the dangerous effects then of this sicknesse, *David* desires to
410 be healed, and by God himselfe, *Sana me Domine, O Lord heale me;* for that physick that Man gives, is all but drugs of the earth; Morall and Civill counsailes, rather to cover then recover, rather to disguise then to avoid: They put a clove in the mouth, but they do not mend the lungs. To cover his nakednesse *Adam* tooke but *fig-leaves;* but to recover *Ezechias,* God tooke *figs themselves.* Man deales upon   Esay 38.21 leaves, that cover, and shadow, God upon fruitfull and effectuall meanes, that cure, and nourish. And then, God tooke *a lumpe of figs;*   2 King. 20.7 God is liberall of his graces, and gives not over a cure, at one dressing: And they were *dry figs too,* sayes that story; you must not looke for
420 figs from the Tree, for immediate Revelations, for private inspirations from God; but the medicinall preaching of the Word, medicinall Sacraments, medicinall Absolution, are such dry figs as God hath preserved in his Church for all our diseases. S. *Paul* had a strong desire, and he expressed it in often prayer to God, to have this peccant humour, this malignity cleane purged out, to have that *Stimulus*   [2 Cor. *carnis,* that concupiscence absolutely taken away. God would not do   12.7–9] so; but yet he applied his effectuall physick, *sufficient Grace.*

This then is the soules *Panacæa,* The *Pharmacum Catholicum,* the

Medicina omnimorbia, The physick that cures all, the sufficient Grace,
⁴³⁰ the seasonable mercy of God, in the merits of Christ Jesus, and in the
love of the Holy Ghost. This is the physick; but then, there are ever
Vehicula medicinæ, certaine syrups, and liquors, to convey the
physick; water, and wine in the Sacraments; And certaine Physitians to ordaine and prescribe, The Ministers of the Word and Sacraments; The Father sends, The Son makes, The Holy Ghost brings,
Basil   The Minister laies on the plaister. For, *Medicinæ ars à Deo data, ut
inde rationem animæ curandæ disceremus,* Gods purpose in giving
us the science of bodily health, was not determined in the body: but
his large and gracious purpose was, by that restitution of the body,
⁴⁴⁰ to raise us to the consideration of spirituall health. When Christ had
said to him, who was brought sick of the palsie, *Thy sins are for-
Marke 2   given thee,* and that the Scribes and Pharisees were scandalized with
that, as though he, being but man, had usurped upon the power of
God, Christ proves to them, by an actuall restoring of his bodily
health, that he could restore his soule too, in the forgivenesse of sins:
He asks them there, *Whether is it easier to say, Thy sins are forgiven
thee, or to say, Arise, take up thy bed, and walke. Christus facit
Bernar.   sanitatem corporalem argumentum spiritualis;* Christ did not determine his doctrine in the declaration of a miraculous power exercised
⁴⁵⁰ upon his body, but by that, established their beliefe of his spirituall
power, in doing that, which in their opinion was the greater worke.
Pursue therefore his method of Curing; And if God have restored
thee in any sicknesse, by such meanes, as he of his goodnesse hath
imprinted in naturall herbs, and Simples, thinke not that that was
done onely or simply for thy bodies sake, but that, as it is as easie for
God to say, Thy sins are forgiven thee, as Take up thy bed and
walke, so it is as easie for thee, to have spirituall physick, as bodily;
because, as God hath planted all those medicinall Simples in the open
fields, for all, though some do tread them under their feet, so hath
⁴⁶⁰ God deposited and prepared spirituall helps for all, though all do not
make benefit of those helps which are offered. It is true, that God
Cant. 4.12   sayes of his Church, *Hortus conclusus soror mea, My sister, my
Spouse is a Garden enclosed, as a spring shut in, and a fountaine
sealed up;* But therein is our advantage, who, by being enwrapped in
the Covenant, as the seed of the faithfull, as the children of Christian

Parents, are borne if not within this walled Garden, yet with a key in our hand to open the doore, that is, with a right and title, to the Sacrament of Baptisme. The Church is a Garden walled in, for their better defence and security that are in it; but not walled in to keepe
470 any out, who, either by being borne within the Covenant, inherit a right to it, or by accepting the grace which is offered them, acquire, and professe a desire to enter thereinto. For, as it is a Garden, full of *Spikenard,* and of *Incense,* and of *all spices,* (as the Text sayes there) so that they who are in this Garden, in the Church, are in possession of all these blessed meanes of spirituall health; So are these spices, and Incense, and Spikenard, of a diffusive and spreading nature, and breath even over the wals of the Garden: *Oleum effusum nomen ejus;* The name of Christ is unction, Oyntment; but it is an Oyntment powred out, an Oyntment that communicates the
480 fragrancy thereof, to persons at a good distance; And, as it is said there, Christ cals up the *North* and the *South* to *blow upon his Garden,* he raises up men to transport and propagate these meanes of salvation to all Nations, so that, in every Nation, they that feare him are acceptable to him; not that that feare of God in generall, as one universall power, is sufficient in it selfe, to bring any man to God immediately, but that God directs the Spikenard, and Incense of this Garden upon that man, and seconds his former feare of God, with a love of God, and brings him to a knowledg, and to a desire, and to a possession, and fruition of our more assured meanes of salvation.
490 When he does so, this is his method, as in restoring bodily health, he said, *Surge, Tolle, Ambula,* Arise, Take up thy bed, and Walke: So to every sick soule, whose cure he undertakes, he sayes so too, *Surge, Tolle, Ambula.* Our beds are our naturall affections; These he does not bid us cast away, nor burne, nor destroy; since Christ vouchsafed *Induere hominem,* wee must not *Exuere hominem;* Since Christ invested the nature of man, and became man, we must not pretend to devest it, and become Angels, or flatter our selves in the merit of Mortifications, not enjoyned, or of a retirednesse, and departing out of the world, in the world, by the withdrawing of our selves from the
500 offices of mutuall society, or an extinguishing of naturall affections. But, *Surge,* sayes our Saviour, Arise from this bed, sleepe not lazily in an over-indulgency to these affections; but, *Ambula,* walke sincerely

Cant. 1.3

4.16

[Act. 10.35]

[John 11.4]
in thy Calling, and thou shalt heare thy Saviour say, *Non est infirmitas hæc ad mortem,* These affections, nay, these concupiscencies shall not destroy thee.

David then doth not pray for such an exact and exquisite state of health, as that he should have no infirmity; Physitians for our bodies tell us, that there is no such state; The best degree of health is but *Neutralitas;* He is well (that is, as well as Man can be) that is not ⁵¹⁰ dangerously sick; for, absolutely well no man can be. Spirituall Physitians will tell you so too; He that sayes you have no sinne, or that God sees not your sinne, if you be of the Elect, deceives you. It is not for an Innocency that *David* prayes; but it is against deadly diseases, and against violent accidents of those diseases. He doth not beg, he cannot hope for an absolute peace: Nature hath put a warre upon us; True happinesse, and apparant happinesse fight against one another: sin hath put a war upon us; The flesh and the Spirit fight

[Gal. 5.17]
against one another: Christ Jesus himselfe came to put a war upon us; The zeale of his glory, and the course of this world, fight against one ⁵²⁰ another. It is not against all warre; nay, it is not against all victory that *David* prayes, He cannot hope that he should be overcome by no Tentations; but against such a war, and such a victory, as should bring him to servility, and bondage to sinne, That sin entring by Conquest upon him, should governe as a tyran over him, against such a sicknesse as should induce a consumption, it is that he directs this prayer, *Sana me Domine,* Not, Lord make me impeccable, but Lord make me penitent, and then heale me. And he comes not to take physick upon wantonnesse; but because the disease is violent, because the accidents are vehement; so vehement, so violent, as that it hath ⁵³⁰ pierced *Ad ossa,* and *Ad animam, My bones are vexed, and my soule is sore troubled,* Therefore *heale me;* which is the Reason upon which he grounds this second petition, *Heale me, because my bones are vexed &c.*

Ossa
We must necessarily insist a little upon these termes, *The Bones, The Soule, The Trouble,* or *Vexation.* First, *Ossa, Bones,* We know in the naturall and ordinary acceptation, what they are; They are these Beames, and Timbers, and Rafters of these Tabernacles, these

[1 Cor. 6.19]
Temples of the Holy Ghost, these bodies of ours. But *Immanebimus nativæ significationi?* sayes S. *Basil,* Shall we dwell upon the native

[540] and naturall signification of these *Bones? Et intelligentia passim obvia contenti erimus?* Shall we who have our conversation in heaven, finde no more in these *Bones,* then an earthly, a worldly, a naturall man would doe? By S. *Basils* example, we may boldly proceed farther: *Membra etiam animæ sunt,* sayes he: The soule hath her limbs as well as the body. *Surdi audite, cæci aspicite,* sayes God in *Esay;* If their soules had not eares and eyes, the blinde could not see, the deafe could not heare, and yet God cals upon the deafe and blinde, to heare and see. As S. *Paul* sayes to the Ephesians, *The eyes of your understanding being enlightned;* so *David* sayes, *Dentes peccatorum* [550] *contrivisti, Thou hast broken the teeth;* That is, the pride and the power, the venom and malignity of the wicked: *Membra etiam animæ sunt,* The soule hath her Bones too; and here *Davids Bones* were the strongest powers and faculties of his soule, and the best actions and operations of those faculties, and yet they were shaken. For this hereditary sicknesse, Originall sinne, prevayles so far upon us, that upon our good dayes we have some grudgings of that Fever; Even in our best actions, we have some of the leaven of that sinne. So that if we goe about to comfort our selves, with some dispositions to Gods glory, which we finde in our selves, with some sparks of [560] love to his precepts, and his commandements, with some good strength of faith, with some measure of good works, yea, with having something for the Name, and glory of Christ Jesus: yet if we consider what humane and corrupt affections have been mingled in all these, *Conturbabuntur ossa,* our Bones will be troubled, even those that appeared to be strong works, and likely to hold out, will need a reparation, an exclamation, *Sana me Domine,* O Lord heale these too, or els these are as weake as the worst. *Ossa non dolent;* The Bones themselves have no sense, they feele no paine. We need not say, That those good works themselves, which we doe, have in their [570] nature, the nature of sinne; That every good worke considered alone, and in the substance of the act it selfe is sinne; But *membranæ dolent;* Those little membrans, those filmes, those thin skins, that cover, and that line some bones, are very sensible of paine, and of any vexation. Though in the nature of the worke it selfe, the worke be not sinne, yet in those circumstances that invest, and involve the worke, in those things which we mingle with the worke, whether

Esay 42.[18]

[Eph. 1.18]
Psal. 3.7

desire of glory towards men, or opinion of merit towards God; Whensoever those bones, those best actions come to the examination of a tender and a diligent Conscience, *Si ossa non dolent, membranæ*
⁵⁸⁰ *dolent,* If the worke be not sinfull, the circumstances are, and howsoever they may be conceived to be strong, as they are *Ossa,* Bones, works, in a morall consideration, good, yet, as they are *Ossa mea,* sayes *David,* as they are *My bones,* such good works as taste of my ill corruptions, so long they are vexed, and troubled, and cannot stand upright, nor appeare with any confidence in the sight of God.

Anima

Thus far then first *David* needed this sanation, this health that he prayes for, that his best actions were corrupt; But the corruption went farther, to the very roote and fountaine of those actions, *Ad ipsam animam,* His very *soule* was *sore vexed.* It is true, that as this
⁵⁹⁰ word *Anima, the soule,* is sometimes taken in the Scriptures, this may seeme to goe no farther then the former, no more that his soule was vexed, then that his bones were so: for, *Anima,* in many places, is but *Animalis Homo,* The soule signifies but the naturall man: And so *opponitur spiritui,* The *soule* is not onely said to be a diverse thing, but a contrary thing to the *Spirit.* When the Apostle sayes to the

1 Thes.
ult. 23

Thessalonians, *Now the very God of peace sanctifie you throughout, that your whole spirit, and soule, and body, may be kept blamelesse unto the comming of our Lord Iesus Christ;* And where the same

Heb. 4.12

Apostle sayes to the Hebrews, *The word of God divideth asunder*
⁶⁰⁰ *the soule and the spirit;* here is a difference put between corrupt nature, and the working of the Spirit of God, the Holy Ghost in man: for here, the *soule* is taken for *Animalis homo,* The naturall man, and the *Spirit* is taken for the Spirit of God. But besides this, these two words, *Soule* and *Spirit,* are sometimes used by the Fathers, in a sense diverse from one another, and as different things, and yet still as parts of one and the same man; Man is said by them, not onely to have a body, and a soule, but to have a soule, and a spirit; not as Spirit is the Spirit of God, and so an extrinsecall thing, but as Spirit is a constitutive part of the naturall man. So, in particular, amongst
⁶¹⁰ many, *Gregory Nyssen* takes the Body to be spoken *De nutribili,* The flesh and bloud of man, And the soule *De sensibili,* The operation of the senses, And the Spirit *De Intellectuali,* The Intellectuall, the reasonable faculties of man; That in the body, Man is conformed

to Plants that have no sense, In the soule, to Beasts, that have no reason, In the spirit, to Angels. But so, The Spirit is but the same thing with that, which now we doe ordinarily account the soule to be; for we make account, that the Image of God is imprinted in the soule, and that gives him his conformity to Angels: But divers others of the Ancients have taken *Soule* and *Spirit,* for different things, 620 even in the Intellectuall part of man, somewhat obscurely, I confesse, and, as some venture to say, unnecessarily, if not dangerously. It troubled S. *Hierome* sometimes, how to understand the word *Spirit* in man: but he takes the easiest way, he dispatches himselfe of it, as fast as he could, that is, to speake of it onely as it was used in the Scriptures: *Famosa quæstio,* sayes he, *sed brevi sermone tractanda;* It is a question often disputed, but may be shortly determined, *Idem spiritus hic, ac in iis verbis, Nolite extinguere spiritum;* When we heare of the Spirit in a Man, in Scriptures, we must understand it of the gifts of the Spirit; for so, fully to the same purpose, sayes S. *Chrys-* 630 *ostome, Spiritus est charisma spiritus,* The Spirit is the working of the Spirit, The gifts of the Spirit: and so when we heare, *The Spirit was vexed, The Spirit was quenched,* still it is to be understood, The gifts of the Spirit. And so, as they restraine the signification of *Spirit,* to those gifts onely, (though the word do indeed, in many places, require a larger extension) so do many restraine this word in our text, *The Soule,* onely *Ad sensum,* to the sensitive faculties of the soule, that is, onely to the paine and anguish that his body suffered; But so far, at least, *David* had gone, in that which he said before, *My bones are vexed.*

640 Now, *Ingravescit morbus,* The disease festers beyond the bone, even into the marrow it selfe. His Bones were those best actions that he had produced, and he saw in that Contemplation, that for all that he had done, he was still, at best, but an unprofitable servant, if not a rebellious enemy; But then, when he considers his whole soule, and all that ever it can do, he sees all the rest will be no better; The poyson, he sees, is in the fountaine, the Canker in the roote, the rancor, the venom in the soule it selfe. *Corpus instrumentum, anima ars ipsa,* sayes S. *Basil:* The body, and the senses are but the tooles, and instruments, that the soule works with; But the soule is the art, 650 the science that directs those Instruments. The faculties of the soule

Ad
Hedibiam
q. 12.
Epist. 150

[1 Thes.
5.19]

[Luk. 17.10]

are the boughs that produce the fruits; and the operations, and particular acts of those faculties are the fruits; but the soule is the roote
of all. And *David* sees, that this art, this science, this soule can direct
him, or establish him in no good way; That not onely the fruits, his
particular acts, nor onely the boughs, and armes, his severall faculties,
but the roote it selfe, the soule it selfe, was infected. His bones are
shaken, he dares not stand upon the good he hath done, his soule
is so too, he cannot hope for any good he shall do: He hath no merit
for the past, he hath no free-will for the future; that is his case.

Turbata ⁶⁶⁰ This *troubles* his *bones,* this *troubles* them *soule,* this *vexes* them
both; for, the word is all one, in both places, as our last Translators
have observed, and rendred it aright; not *vexed* in one place, and
troubled in the other, as our former Translators had it; But in both
places it is *Bahal,* and *Bahal* imports a vehemence, both in the in-
tensnesse of it, and in the suddennesse, and inevitablenesse of it:
And therefore it signifies often, *Præcipitantiam,* A headlong down-
fall and irrecoverablenesse; And often, *Evanescentiam,* an utter vanishing away, and annihilation. *David,* (whom we always consider
in the Psalmes, not onely to speake literally of those miseries which
⁶⁷⁰ were actually upon himselfe, but prophetically too, of such measures,
and exaltations of those miseries, as would certainly fall upon them,
as did not seeke their sanation, their recovery from the God of all
health) looking into all his actions, (they are the fruits) and into all
his faculties, (they are the boughs) and into the root of all, the soule
it selfe, considering what he had done, what he could do, he sees
that as yet he had done no good, he sees he should never be able to
doe any; *His bones are troubled,* He hath no comfort in that which
is growne up, and past, And *his soule is sore troubled,* (for to the
trouble of the soule, there is added in the Text, that particle, *Valde,*
⁶⁸⁰ It is a sore trouble that falls upon the soule, *A troubled spirit who*
[Prov. 18.14] *can beare?*) because he hath no hope in the future; He was no surer
for that which was to come, then for that which was past; But he,
(that is, all, considered in that case which he proposes) he comes
(as the word signifies) *ad præcipitantiam,* That all his strength can
scarce keepe him from precipitation into despaire, And he comes (as
the word signifies too) *ad Evanescentiam,* to an evaporating, and a
vanishing of his soule, that is, even to a renouncing, and a detestation

of his immortality, and to a willingnesse, to a desire, that he might
die the death of other Creatures, which perish altogether, and goe
690 out as a Candle. This is the trouble, the sore trouble of his soule, who
is brought to an apprehension of Gods indignation for not performing Conditions required at his hands, and of his inability to performe
them, and is not come to the contemplation of his mercy, in supply
thereof.

There is *Turbatio Timoris,* A trouble out of feare of danger in this
world, *Herods* trouble; *When the Magi brought word of another*   Mat. 2.3
King, Herod was troubled, and all Ierusalem with him. There is
Turbatio confusionis, The Mariners trouble in a tempest; *Their soule*   Psal. 107.26
melteth for trouble, sayes *David.* There is *Turbatio occupationis;*   Luk. 10.41
700 *Martha's* trouble; *Martha thou art troubled about many things,* sayes
Christ. There is *Turbatio admirationis,* The blessed Virgins trouble,   Luk. 1.29
When she saw the Angel, she was troubled at his saying. To contract
this, There is *Turbatio compassionis,* Christs own trouble, *When he*   John 11.33
saw Mary weepe for her brother Lazurus, he groaned in the spirt,
and was troubled in himselfe. But in all these troubles, *Herods* feare,
The Mariners irresolution, *Martha's* multiplicity of businesse, The
blessed Virgins sudden amazement, Our Saviours compassionate
sorrow, as they are in us, worldly troubles, so the world administers
some means to extenuate, and alleviate these troubles; for, feares are
710 overcome, and stormes are appeased, and businesses are ended, and
wonders are understood, and sorrows weare out; But in this trouble
of the bones, and the soule, in so deepe and sensible impressions of
the anger of God, looking at once upon the pravity, the obliquity, the
malignity of all that I have done, of all that I shall doe, Man hath
but one step between that state, and despaire, to stop upon, to turne
to the Author of all temporall, and all spirituall health, the Lord of
life, with *Davids* prayer, *Cor mundum crea, Create a cleane heart*   Psal. 51.10
within me; Begin with me againe, as thou begunst with *Adam,* in
innocency; and see, if I shall husband and governe that innocency
720 better then *Adam* did; for, for this heart which I have from him,
I have it in corruption; and, *who can bring a cleane thing out of*   Job [14.]4
uncleannesse? Therefore *Davids* prayer goes farther in the same
place, *Renew a constant spirit in me;* Present cleannesse cannot be
had from my selfe; but if I have that from God, *mine owne cloathes*   [Job 9.31]

will make me foule againe, and therefore doe not onely create a
cleane spirit, but renew a spirit of constancy and perseverance. There-

Psal. 51.12   fore I have also another Prayer in the same Psalme, *Spiritu principali
confirma me,* Sustaine me, uphold me with thy free spirit, thy large,
thy munificent spirit: for thy ordinary graces will not defray me, nor
730 carry me through this valley of tentations; not thy single money, but
thy Talents; not as thou art thine owne Almoner, but thine owne
Treasurer; It is not the dew, but thy former and later raine that must
water, though it be thy hand that hath planted; Not any of the Rivers,
though of Paradise, but the Ocean it selfe, that must bring me to thy
Jerusalem. Create a clean heart; Thou didst so in *Adam,* and in him
I defiled it. Renew that heart; Thou didst so in Baptisme; And thy
upholding me with thy constant spirit, is thy affording me means,
which are constant, in thy Church; But thy confirming me with thy
principall spirit, is thy making of those meanes, instituted in thy
740 Church, effectuall upon me, by the spirit of Application, the spirit of
Appropriation, by which the merits of the Son, deposited in the
Church, are delivered over unto me.

Iob 20.11   This then is the force of *Davids* reason in this Petition, *Ossa im-
plentur vitiis,* as one of *Iobs* friends speaks, *My bones are full of the
sins of my youth,* That is, my best actions, now in mine age, have
some taste, some tincture from the habit, or some sinfull memory of
the acts of sin in my youth; *Adhæret os meum carni,* as *David* also
Psal. 102.5   speaks, *My bones cleave to my flesh,* my best actions taste of my
Lam. 4.8   worst; And *My skin cleaves to my bones,* as *Ieremy* laments, That
750 is, My best actions call for a skin, for something to cover them: And
Therefore, not Therefore because I have brought my selfe into this
state, but because by thy grace I have power to bring this my state
into thy sight, by this humble confession, *Sana me Domine, O Lord
Exod. 13.19   heale me;* Thou that art my Messias, be my *Moses,* and carry these
bones of thy *Ioseph* out of Egypt; Deliver me, in this consideration
of mine actions, from the terror of a self-accusing, and a jealous, and
1 King.   suspicious conscience: *Bury my bones beside the bones of the man of
13.31   God;* Beside the bones of the Son of God: Look upon my bones as
they are coffind, and shrowded in that sheet, the righteousnesse of
Ezek. 37.7 760 Christ Jesus. *Accedant ossa ad ossa,* as in *Ezekiels* vision, Let our

bones come together, bone to bone, mine to his, and looke upon them
uno intuitu, all together, and there shall come sinews, and flesh, and
skin upon them, and breathe upon them, and in Him, in Christ Jesus,
I shall live; My bones being laid by his, though but gristles in themselves, my actions being considered in his, though imperfect in themselves, shall bear me up in the sight of God. And this may be the
purpose of this prayer, this sanation, grounded upon this reason, *O
Lord heale me, for my bones are vexed, &c.* But yet *David* must, and
doth stop upon this step, he stayes Gods leisure, and is put to his
770 *Vsquequo? But thou, O Lord, how long?*

Vsquequo

David had cryed *Miserere,* he had begged of God to look towards
him, and consider him; He had revealed to him his weak and troublesome estate, and he had entreated reliefe; but yet God gave not that
reliefe presently, nor seemed to have heard his prayer, nor to have
accepted his reasons. *David* comes to some degrees of expostulation
with God; but he dares not proceed far; it is but *usquequo Domine?*
which if we consider it in the Originall, and so also in our last Translation, requires a serious consideration. For it is not there as it is in
the first Translation, *How long wilt thou delay? David* charges God
780 with no delay: But it is onely, *Et tu Domine, usquequo? But thou
O Lord, how long?* And there he ends in a holy abruptnesse, as
though he had taken himselfe in a fault, to enterprise any expostulation with God. He doth not say, How long ere thou heare me?
If thou heare me, how long ere thou regard me? If thou regard me,
how long ere thou heale me? How long shall my bones, how long
shall my soule be troubled? He sayes not so; but leaving all to his
leisure, he corrects his passion, he breaks off his expostulation. As
long as I have that commission from God, *Dic animæ tuæ, Salus tua
sum,* Say unto thy soule, I am thy salvation, my soule shall keep si-
790 lence unto God, of whom commeth my salvation: Silence from murmuring, how long soever he be in recovering me; not silence from
prayer, that he would come; for that is our last Consideration; *David*
proposed his Desire, *Miserere,* and *Sana,* Looke towards me, and
Heale me, that was our first; And then his Reasons, *Ossa, Anima,
My bones, my soule is troubled,* that was our second; And then he
grew sensible of Gods absence, for all that, which was our third

Psal. 35.3

Proposition; for yet, for all this, he continues patient, and solicites the same God in the same name, The Lord, *But thou O Lord, how long?*

Domine   800   Need we then any other example of such a patience then God himselfe, who stayes so long in expectation of our conversion? But we have *Davids* example too, who having first made his Deprecation,

Ver. 1   That God would not reprove him in anger, having prayed God to forbeare him, he is also well content to forbeare God, for those other things which he asks, till it be his pleasure to give them. But yet he neither gives over praying, nor doth he encline to pray to any body else, but still *Domine miserere, Have mercy upon me O Lord,* and *Domine sana, O Lord heale mee:* Industry in a lawfull calling, favour of great persons, a thankfull acknowledgement of the ministery and
810   protection of Angels, and of the prayers of the Saints in heaven for us, all these concur to our assistance; But the root of all, all temporall, all spirituall blessings, is he, to whom *David* leads us here, *Dominus, The Lord;* Lord, as he is Proprietary of all creatures; He made All, and therefore is Lord of All; as he is *Iehovah,* which is the name of Essence, of Being, as all things have all their being from him, their very being, and their well-being, their Creation, and their Conservation; And in that Name of Recognition and acknowledgement, that all that can be had, is to be asked of him, and him onely, Him, as he is *Iehovah, The Lord,* does *David* solicite him

Acts 4.12   820   here; for, *as there is no other Name under heaven, given amongst men, whereby we must be saved, but the Name of Iesus Christ;* So is there no other Name above in heaven proposed to men, whereby they should receive these blessings, but the Name of *Iehovah;* for *Iehovah* is the name of the whole Trinity, and there are no more, no Queen-mother in heaven, no Counsaylors in heaven in Commission with the Trinity.

In this Name therefore *David* pursues his Prayer: for, from a River, from a Cisterne, a man may take more water at once, then he can from the first spring and fountaine head; But he cannot take the
830   water so sincerely, so purely, so intemerately from the channell as from the fountaine head. Princes and great persons may rayse their Dependants faster then God does his; But sudden riches come like a land-water, and bring much foulnesse with them. We are Gods

vineyard; *The vineyard of the Lord of Hosts, is the house of Israel,* *Esay 5.7*
and the men of Iudah are his pleasant plant, sayes the Prophet. And
God delights to see his plants prosper, and grow up seasonably. More
then once Christ makes that profession, *That he goes downe into* *Cant. 6.11*
the Garden of Nuts, to see the fruits of the valley, And to see whether *Cant. 7.12*
the Vine flourished, and whether the Pomegranet budded; And he
840 *goes up early into the vineyard, to see whether the tender grape ap-*
peared. He had a pleasure in the growth and successive encrease of
his plants, and did not looke they should come hastily to their height
and maturity. If worldly blessings, by a good industry, grow up in
us, it is naturall; But if they fall upon us, *Pluit laqueos,* God rains *Psal. 11.6*
downe springes and snares, occasions of sinne in those abundances, *Exod. 9.23*
and *Pluit grandinem,* He will raine downe Hailstones; Hailstones *Rev. 16.21*
as big as Talents, as in the Revelation; as big as Milstones; He will
make our riches occasions of raysing enemies, and make those enemies Grindstones to grinde our fortunes to powder. Make not too
850 much haste to be rich: Even in spirituall riches, in spirituall health
make not too much haste. Pray for it; for there is no other way to
get it. Pray to the Lord for it: For, Saints and Angels have but
enough for themselves. Make haste to begin to have these spirituall
graces; To desire them, is to begin to have them: But make not too
much haste in the way; Doe not thinke thy selfe purer then thou
art, because thou seest another doe some such sins, as thou hast
forborne.

Beloved, at last, when Christ Jesus comes with his scales, thou shalt
not be waighed with that man, but every man shall be waighed with
860 God: *Be pure as your Father in heaven is pure,* is the waight that *[Mat. 5.48]*
must try us all; and then, the purest of us all, that trusts to his owne
purity, must heare that fearfull *Mene Tekel Vpharsin,* Thou art *[Dan. 5.25]*
waighed, Thou art found too light, Thou art divided, separated from
the face of God, because thou hast not taken the purity of that Son
upon thee, who not onely in himselfe, but those also who are in him,
in him are pure, as his, and their Father in heaven is pure. Neither
make so much haste to this spirituall riches, and health, as to think
thy self whole before thou art: Neither murmure, nor despaire of
thy recovery, if thou beest not whole so soone as thou desiredst. If
870 thou wrastle with tentations, and canst not overcome them, If thou

purpose to pray earnestly, and finde thy minde presently strayed from
that purpose, If thou intend a good course, and meet with stops in
the way, If thou seeke peace of conscience, and scruples out of zeale
interrupt that, yet discomfort not thy selfe. God staid six daies in his
first worke, in the Creation, before he came to make thee; yet all that
while he wrought for thee. Thy Regeneration, to make thee a new
creature, is a greater worke then that, and it cannot be done in an
instant. God hath purposed a building in thee; he hath sat down,
and considered, that he hath sufficient to accomplish that building,

Luke 14.28   880 as it is in the Gospel, and therefore leave him to his leisure.

When thou hast begun with *David,* with a *Domine ne arguas,*
O Lord rebuke me not, and followed that, with a *Domine miserere,*
O Lord looke graciously towards me, and pursued that, with a
Domine sana me, O Lord heale me, If thou finde a *Domine usque-*
quo? Any degree of wearinesse of attending the Lords leisure, aris-
ing in thee, suppresse it, overcome it, with more and more petitions,
and that which God did by way of Commandement, in the first
Creation, doe thou by way of prayer, in this thy second Creation;

[Gen. 1.3]   First he said, *Fiat lux, Let there be light:* Pray thou, that he would
                890 enlighten thy darknesse. God was satisfied with that light for three

[Gen. 1.14]   daies, and then he said, *Fiant luminaria, Let there be great lights;*
                Blesse God for his present light, but yet pray that hee will inlarge
                that light which he hath given thee; And turne all those his Com-

[Gen. 1.26]   mandments into prayers, till thou come to his *Faciamus hominem,*
                Let us make man according to our own Image; Pray that he will re-

Coloss. 1.15   store his Image in thee, and conforme thee to him, who is *the Image*
                of the invisible God, our Lord and Saviour Christ Jesus. He did his
                greatest work upon thee, before time was, thine Election; And he
                hath reserved the consummation of that work, till time shall be no
                900 more, thy Glorification: And as for thy Vocation he hath taken his
                own time, (He did not call thee into the world in the time of the
                Primitive Church, nor, perchance, call thee effectually, though in the
                Church, in the dayes of thy youth) So stay his time for thy Sanctifi-

[Luk. 1.78]   cation, and, if the day-spring from on high have visited thee, but this
                morning, If thou beest come to a *fiat lux* but now, that now God
                have kindled some light in thee, hee may come this day seaven-night
                to a *fiant luminaria,* to multiply this light by a more powerfull

meanes. If not so soone, yet still remember, that it was God that made
the Sun stand still to *Ioshuah,* as well as to run his race as a Giant to
910 *David;* And God was as much glorified in the standing still of the
Sun, as in the motion thereof; And shall be so in thy Sanctification,
though it seeme to stand at a stay for a time, when his time shall be
to perfect it, in a measure acceptable to thee. Nothing is acceptable
to him, but that which is seasonable; nor seasonable, except it come
in the time proper to it: And, as S. *Augustine* sayes, *Natura rei est,
quam indidit Deus,* That is the nature of every thing, which God hath
imprinted in it, So that is the time for every thing, which God hath
appointed for it. *Pray,* and *Stay,* are two blessed Monosyllables; To
ascend to God, To attend Gods descent to us, is the Motion, and the
920 Rest of a Christian; And as all Motion is for Rest, so let all the Motions of our soule in our prayers to God be, that our wills may rest in
his, and that all that pleases him, may please us, therefore because it
pleases him; for therefore, because it pleases him, it becomes good
for us, and then, when it pleases him, it becomes seasonable unto us,
and expedient for us.

[Josh. 10.13]
[Psa. 19.5]

Number 18.

Preached upon the Penitentiall Psalmes.

PSAL. 6.4, 5. *RETURNE, O LORD; DELIVER MY SOULE; O LORD SAVE ME, FOR THY MERCIES SAKE. / FOR IN DEATH THERE IS NO REMEMBRANCE OF THEE; AND IN THE GRAVE, WHO SHALL GIVE THEE THANKS?*

T HE WHOLE Psalme is Prayer; and Prayer is our whole service to God. Earnest Prayer hath the nature of Importunity; Wee presse, wee importune God in Prayer; Yet that puts not God to a morosity, to a frowardnesse; God flings not away from that; God suffers that importunity, and more. Prayer hath the nature of Impudency; Wee threaten God in Prayer; as *Gregory Nazianzen* adventures to expresse it; He saies, his Sister, in the vehemence of her Prayer, would threaten God, *Et honesta quadam impudentia, egit impudentem;* She came, saies he, to a religious impudency with God, and to threaten him, that she would never depart from his Altar, till she had her Petition granted; And God suffers this Impudency, and more. Prayer hath the nature of Violence; In the publique Prayers of the Congregation, we besiege God, saies *Tertullian,* and we take God Prisoner, and bring God to our Conditions; and God is glad to be straitned by us in that siege. This Prophet here executes before, what the Apostle counsailes after, *Pray incessantly;* Even in his singing he prayes; And as S. *Basil* saies, *Etiam somnia justorum preces sunt,* A Good mans dreames are Prayers, he prayes, and not sleepily, in his sleepe, so *Davids* Songs are Prayers. Now in this his besieging of God, he brings up his works from a far off, closer; He begins in this Psalme, at a deprecatory Prayer; He asks nothing, but that God would doe

[1 Thess. 5.17]

nothing, that he would forbeare him; *Rebuke me not, Correct me not.*
Now, it costs the King lesse, to give a Pardon, then to give a Pension;
and lesse to give a Reprieve, then to give a Pardon; and lesse to
Connive, not to call in Question, then either Reprieve, Pardon or
Pension; To forbeare, is not much. But then, as the Mathematician
said, That he could make an Engin, a Screw, that should move the
whole frame of the World, if he could have a place assigned him, to
fix that Engin, that Screw upon, that so it might worke upon the
30 World: so Prayer, when one Petition hath taken hold upon God,
works upon God, moves God, prevailes with God, entirely for all.
David then having got this ground, this footing in God, he brings
his works closer; he comes from the Deprecatory, to a Postulatory
Prayer; not onely that God would doe nothing against him, but that
he would doe something for him. God hath suffered man to see
Arcana imperii, The secrets of his State, how he governs; He governs
by Precedent; by precedents of his Predecessors, he cannot; He hath
none; by precedents of other Gods, he cannot; There are none; And
yet he proceeds by precedents; by his owne Precedents; He does as he
40 did before; *Habenti dat,* To him that hath received, hee gives more, [Mat. 25.29]
and is willing to bee wrought, and prevailed upon, and prest with his
owne example. And, as though his doing good, were but to learne
how to do good better, still he writes after his owne copy; And *Nulla
dies sine linea,* He writes something to us, that is, hee doth something
for us, every day. And then, that which is not often seene, in other
Masters, his Copies are better then the Originals; his later mercies
larger then his former: And in this Postulatory Prayer, larger then
the Deprecatory, enters our Text, *Returne O Lord; Deliver my soule;
O save me, &c.*
50 *David,* who every where remembers God of his Covenant, as he was *Divisio*
the *God of Abraham* remembers also, how *Abraham* proceeded with
God, in the behalfe of Sodom; And he remembers, that when [Gen. 18.20–
Abraham had gained upon God, and brought him from a greater, to 33]
a lesse number of righteous men, for whose sakes God would have
spared that City, yet *Abraham* gave over asking, before God gave over
granting; And so Sodom was lost. A little more of S. *Augustines*
Importunity, of *Nazianzens* Impudence, of *Tertullians* violence in
Prayer, would have done well in *Abraham;* If *Abraham* had come

to a lesse price, to lesse then ten, God knowes what God would have
⁶⁰ done; for *God went not away,* saies the text there, *till he had left
communing with Abraham;* that is, till *Abraham* had no more to say
to him. In memory and contemplation of that, *David* gives not over
in this text, till he come to the uttermost of all, as far as man can
aske, as far as God can give; He begins at first, with a *Revertere
Domine, Returne O Lord,* and higher then that, no man can begin;
no man can begin at a *Veni Domine;* no man can pray to God, to
come, till God be come into him; *Quid peto, ut venias in me,* saies S.
Augustine, Qui non essem, si non esses in me? How should I pray,
that God would come into me, who not onely could not have the
⁷⁰ Spirit of praying, but not the Spirit of being, not life it selfe, if God
were not in me already? But then, this prayer is, that when God had
been with him, and for his sins, or his coldnesse, and slacknesse in
prayer, was departed aside from him, yet he would vouchsafe to
returne to him againe, and restore to him that light of his countenance
which he had before, *Revertere Domine, O Lord returne.* And then
he passes to his second petition, *Eripe animam, Deliver my soule;*
That when God in his returne saw those many and strong snares
which entangled him, those many and deepe tentations and tribulations which surrounded him, God, being in his mercy thus Returned,
⁸⁰ and in his Providence seeing this danger, would not now stand
neutrall, betweene them, and see him and these tentations fight it out,
but fight on his side and deliver him; *Eripe animam, Deliver my
soule.* And then, by these two petitions, hee makes way for the third
and last, which is the perfection and consummation of all, as far as
he can carry a Prayer or a Desire, *Salvum me fac, O Lord save me;*
that is, Imprint in me a strong hope of Salvation in this life, and invest
me in an irremoveable possession, in the life to come. Lord I acknowledge that thou hast visited me heretofore, and for my sins hast
absented thy selfe, *O Lord returne;* Lord, now thou art returned, and
⁹⁰ seest me unable to stand in these tentations and tribulations, *Deliver
thou my soule;* Lord thou hast delivered me againe and againe, and
againe and againe I fall back to my former danger, and therefore,
O Lord save me, place me where I may be safe; safe in a constant
hope, that the Saviour of the World intended that salvation to me;
And these three Petitions constitute our first part in *Davids* postulatory Prayer.

And then the second part, which is also within the words of this text, and consists of those reasons, by which *David* inclines God to grant his three Petitions, which are two, first, *Propter misericordiam* 100 *tuam,* Do this O Lord, *for thine own mercy sake,* And then, *Quia non in morte,* Doe it O Lord, for thine owne honours sake, *Because in death there is no remembrance of thee,* that second part will be the subject of another exercise, for, that which belongs to the three Petitions, will imploy the time allowed for this.

First then, the first step in this Prayer, *Revertere, O Lord return,* implies first a former presence, and then a present absence, and also a confidence for the future; Whosoever saies, *O Lord returne,* sayes all this, Lord thou wast here, Lord thou art departed hence, but yet, Lord thou maiest returne hither againe. God was with us all, before 110 we were any thing at all; And ever since our making, hath beene with us, in his generall providence; And so, we cannot say, *O Lord Returne,* because, so, he was never gone from us. But as God made the earth, and the fruits thereof, before he made the Sun, whose force was to work upon that earth, and upon the naturall fruits of that earth, but before he made Paradise, which was to have the Tree of Life, and the Tree of Knowledge, he made the Sun to doe those offices, of shining upon it, and returning daily to it: So God makes this earth of ours, that is our selves, by naturall wayes, and sustaines us by generall providence, before any Sun of particular grace be 120 seen to shine upon us. But before man can be a Paradise, possest of the Tree of life, and of Knowledge, this Sun is made and produced, the particular graces of God rise to him, and worke upon him, and awaken, and solicite, and exalt those naturall faculties which were in him; This Son fils him, and fits him, compasses him, and disposes him, and does all the offices of the Sun, seasonably, opportunely, maturely, for the nourishing of his soule, according to the severall necessities thereof. And this is Gods returning to us, in a generall apprehension; After he hath made us, and blest us in our nature, and by his naturall meanes, he returnes to make us againe, to make 130 us better, first by his first preventing grace, and then by a succession of his particular graces. And therefore we must returne to this Returning, in some more particular considerations.

There are beside others, three significations in the Scripture, of

Revertere

this word *Shubah*, which is here translated, to *Returne*, appliable to
our present purpose. The first is the naturall and native, the primary
and radicall signification of the word. And so, *Shubah, To Returne,*
is *Redire ad locum suum,* To returne to that place, to which a thing
is naturally affected; So heavy things returne to the Center, and light

Psal. 146.4
things returne to the Expansion; So *Mans breath departeth,* sayes
140 *David, Et redit in terram suam, He returnes into his Earth;* That
earth, which is so much his, as that it is he himselfe; Of earth he was,
and therefore to earth he returnes. But can God returne in such a
sense as this? Can we finde an *Vbi* for God? A place that is his place?

Esay 5.[7]
Yes; And an Earth which is his earth; *Surely the vineyard of the Lord
of Hosts, is the house of Israel, and the men of Iudah are his pleasant
plant.* So the Church, which is his Vineyard, is his *Vbi,* his place, his
Center, to which he is naturally affected. And when he calls us hither,
and meets us here, upon his Sabbaths, and sheds the promises of his
Gospel upon the Congregation in his Ordinance, he returnes to us
150 here, as in his *Vbi,* as in his own place. And as he hath a place of his
owne here, so he hath an Earth of his owne in this place. Our flesh is
Earth, and God hath invested our flesh, and in that flesh of ours,
which suffered death for us, he returnes to us in this place, as often
as he maketh us partakers of his flesh, and his bloud, in the blessed
Sacrament. So then, though in my dayes of sinne, God have absented
himselfe from me, (for God is absent when I doe not discerne his
presence) yet if to day I can heare his voyce, as God is returned to day
to this place, as to his *Vbi,* as to his own place; so in his entring into
me, in his flesh and bloud, he returnes to me as to his Earth, that
160 Earth which he hath made his by assuming my nature, I am become

[Prov. 8.31]
his *Vbi,* his place; *Delitiæ ejus, His delight is to be with the sonnes
of men,* and so with me; and so in the Church, in the Sermon, in the
Sacrament he returnes to us, in the first signification of this word
Shubah, as to that place to which he is naturally affected and disposed.
    In a second signification, this word is referred, not to the place of
God, not to the person of God, but (if we may so speake) to the
Passion of God, to the Anger of God; And so, the Returning of God,
that is, of Gods Anger, is the allaying, the becalming, the departing
of his Anger; and so when God returnes, God stayes; his Anger is

Esay 5.25
170 returned from us, but God is still with us. *The wrath of the Lord was*

kindled, sayes the Prophet *Esay;* and *He smote his people, so that the mountaines trembled, and their carkasses were torne in the midst of the streets.* Here is the tempest, here is the visitation, here is Gods comming to them; He comes, but in anger, and we heare of no returne; nay, we heare the contrary, *Et non redibat furor,* For all this, his wrath, his fury did not returne, that is, did not depart from them; for, as God never comes in this manner, till our multiplied sinnes call him, and importune him, so God never returnes in this sense, in withdrawing his anger and judgements from us, till both our words
180 and our works, our prayers and our amendment of life, joyne in a *Revertere Domine, O Lord Returne,* withdraw this judgement from us, for it hath effected thy purpose upon us. And so the Originall, which expresses neither signification of the word, for it is neither Returne to me, nor Returne from me, but plainely and onely Returne, leaves the sense indifferent; Lord, thou hast withdrawne thy selfe from me, therefore in mercy returne to me, or else, Lord, thy Judgements are heavy upon me, and therefore returne, withdraw these Judgements from me; which shewes the ductilenesse, the appliablenesse of Gods mercy, that yeelds almost to any forme of words, any
190 words seeme to fit it.

But then, the comfort of Gods returning to us, comes nearest us, in the third signification of this word *Shubah;* not so much in Gods returning to us, nor in his anger returning from us, as in our returning to him, *Turne us againe, O Lord,* sayes *David, Et salvi erimus, and we shall be saved;* There goes no more to salvation, but such a Turning. So that this Returning of the Lord, is an Operative, an Effectuall returning, that turnes our hearts, and eyes, and hands, and feet to the wayes of God, and produces in us Repentance, and Obedience. For these be the two legges, which our conversion to God
200 stands upon; For so *Moses* uses this very word, *Returne unto the Lord and heare his voyce;* There is no returning, without hearing, nor hearing without beleeving, nor beleeving, to be beleeved, without doing; Returning is all these. Therefore where Christ saies, *That if those works had been done in Tyre and Sidon, Tyre and Sidon would have repented in sack-cloth and ashes;* In the Syriack Translation of S. *Matthew,* we have this very word *Shubah,* They would have *Returned in sack-cloth and ashes.* So that the word which *David* receives

Psal. 80.3

Deut. 30.2

Mat. 11.21

from the Holy Ghost in this Text, being onely *Returned,* and no
more, applies it selfe to all three senses, Returne thy selfe, that is,
²¹⁰ Bring backe thy Mercy; Returne thy Wrath, that is, Call backe thy
Judgements, or Returne us to thee, that is, make thy meanes, and
offers of grace, in thine Ordinance, powerfull, and effectuall upon us.

Now when the Lord comes to us, by any way, though he come in
corrections, in chastisements, not to turne to him, is an irreverent,
and unrespective negligence. If a Pursevant, if a Serjeant come to thee
from the King, in any Court of Justice, though hee come to put thee
in trouble, to call thee to an account, yet thou receivest him, thou
entertainest him, thou paiest him fees. If any Messenger of the Lord
comes to attach thee, whether sicknesse in thy body, by thine own dis-
²²⁰ order, decay in thy estate, by the oppression of others, or terrour in
thy Conscience, by the preaching of his Ministers, turne thou to the
Lord, in the last sense of the word, and his mercy shall returne to thee,
and his anger shall returne from thee, and thou shalt have fulnesse
of Consolation in all the three significations of the word. If a Worme
be trodden upon, it turnes againe; We may thinke, that is done in
anger, and to revenge; But we know not; The Worme hath no sting,
and it may seeme as well to embrace, and licke his foote that treads
upon him. When God treads upon thee, in any calamity, spirituall or
temporall, if thou turne with murmuring, this is the turning of a
²³⁰ Serpent, to sting God, to blaspheme him; This is a turning upon
him, not a turning to him; But if thou turne like a Worme, then
thou turnest humbly to kisse the rod, to licke and embrace his foot
that treads upon thee, that is, to love his Ministers, which denounce
his judgements upon thy sinnes, yea, to love them, from whom thou
receivest defamation in thy credit, or detriment in thy state.

We see how it was imputed to *Asa,* when God trod upon him, that
is, diseased him in his feete, and exalted his disease into extremity,
Yet in his disease he sought not to the Lord, but to the Physitians.
He turned a by-way; at least, though a right way, too soone, to the
²⁴⁰ Physitian before the Lord. This is that, that exasperated God so
vehemently, *Because the people turneth not to him that smiteth them;*
neither do they seeke the Lord of Hosts; when the Lord of Hosts lies
with a heavy Army upon them. *Therefore,* sayes the Prophet there,
The Lord will cut off from Israel, head and tayle, branch and rush in

2 Chro.
16.12

Esay 9.13

one day. God is not so vehement, when they neglected him in their prosperity, as when, though he afflicted them, yet they turned not to him. Measure God by earthly Princes; (for we may measure the world by a Barly corne) If the King come to thy house, thou wilt professe to take it for an honour, and thou wilt entertaine him; and 250 yet his comming cannot be without removes, and troubles, and charges to thee. So when God comes to thee, in his word, or in his actions, in a Sermon, or in a sicknesse, though his comming dislodge thee, remove thee, put thee to some inconvenience, in leaving thy bed of sinne, where thou didst sleepe securely before, yet here is the progresse of the Holy Ghost, intended to thy soule, that first he comes thus to thee, and then if thou turne to him, he returnes to thee, and settles himselfe, and dwels in thee.

This is too lovely a Prospect, to depart so soone from; therefore looke we by S. *Augustines* glasse, upon Gods comming and returning 260 to man. God hath imprinted his Image in our soules; and God comes, says that Father, *Vt videat imaginem;* Where I have given my Picture, I would see how it is respected: God comes to see in what case his Image is in us; If we shut doores, if we draw Curtaines between him and his Image, that is, cover our soules, and disguise and palliate our sinnes, he goes away, and returnes in none of those former senses. But if we lay them open, by our free confessions, he returnes againe; that so, in how ill case soever he finde his Image, he may wash it over with our teares, and renew it with his own bloud, and, *Vt resculpat imaginem,* that he may refresh and re-engrave his 270 Image in us againe, and put it in a richer and safer Tablet. And as the Angel which came to *Abraham* at the promise and conception of *Isaac,* gave *Abraham* a farther assurance of his Returne at *Isaacs* birth, *I will certainly returne unto thee, and thy wife shall have a Sonne;* So the Lord, which was with thee in the first conception of any good purpose, Returnes to thee againe, to give thee a quickning of that blessed childe of his, and againe, and againe, to bring it forth, and to bring it up, to accomplish and perfect those good intentions, which his Spirit, by over-shadowing thy soule, hath formerly begotten in it. So then, he comes in Nature, and he returnes in Grace; He 280 comes in preventing, and returnes in subsequent graces; He comes in thine understanding, and returnes in thy will; He comes in rectifying

Gen. 18.10

thine actions, and returns in establishing habits; He comes to thee in
zeale, and returnes in discretion; He comes to thee in fervour, and
returnes in perseverance; He comes to thee in thy peregrination, all
the way, and he returns in thy transmigration, at thy last gaspe. So
God comes, and so God returnes.

Yet I am loath to depart my selfe, loath to dismisse you from this
ayre of Paradise, of Gods comming, and returning to us. Therefore
we consider againe, that as God came long agoe, six thousand years
290 agoe, in nature, when we were created in *Adam,* and then in nature
returned to us, in the generation of our Parents: so our Saviour Christ
Jesus came to us long agoe, sixteene hundred yeares agoe, in grace,
and yet in grace returnes to us, as often as he assembles us, in these
holy Convocations. He came to us then, as the Wisemen came to
him, with treasure, and gifts, and gold, and incense, and myrrhe; As
having an ambition upon the soules of men, he came with that
abundant treasure to purchase us. And as to them who live upon
the Kings Pension, it is some comfort to heare that the Exchequer
is full, that the Kings moneyes are come in: so is it to us, to know
300 that there is enough in Gods hands, paid by his Son, for the discharge
of all our debts; He gave enough for us all at that comming; But it
is his returning to us, that applyes to us, and derives upon us in
particular, the benefit of this generall satisfaction. When he returns
to us in the dispensation and distribution of his graces, in his Word
and Sacraments; When he calls upon us to come to the receipt; When
the greater the summe is, the gladder he is of our comming, that
[Rom. 5.20]   where sinne abounds, grace might abound too; When we can pursue
this Prayer, *Revertere Domine,* Returne O Lord in grace, in more
and more grace, and when we are in possession of a good measure
310 of that grace, we can pray againe, *Revertere Domine,* Returne O
[Rev. 22.20]   Lord in glory, Come Lord Jesus, come quickly; When we are so
rectified by his Ordinances here, that in a sincerity of soule, we are
not onely contented, but desirous to depart from hence, then have
we religiously followed our example, that man according to Gods
heart, *David,* in this prayer of his. If Christ have not beene thus fully
in thine heart, before, this is his comming; entertaine him now: If
he have been there, and gone againe, this is his returning; blesse him
for that: And meet him, and love him, and embrace him, as often as

he offers himselfe to thy soule, in these his Ordinances: Wish every day a Sunday, and every meale a Sacrament, and every discourse a Homily, and he shall shine upon thee in all dark wayes, and rectifie thee in all ragged wayes, and direct thee in all crosse wayes, and stop thee in all doubtfull wayes, and returne to thee in every corner, and relieve thee in every danger, and arme thee even against himselfe, by advancing thy worke, in which thou besiegest him, that is, this Prayer, and enabling thee to prevaile upon him, as in this first Petition, *Revertere Domine, O Lord returne,* so in that which followes next, *Eripe animam, Deliver my soule.*

In this Prayer, we may either consider *David* in that affection which S. *Paul* had when he desired to be delivered *ab angelo Satanæ,* from the messenger of Satan that buffeted him, that so that *Stimulus carnis* which he speaks of, that vexation, and provocation of the flesh, might have been utterly removed from him, whereby he might have past his life in Gods service in a religious calme, without any storme, or opposition, or contradiction arising in his flesh: Or we may consider it as a Prayer agreeable to that Petition in our Lords Prayer, *Libera nos à malo, Deliver us from evill;* which is not from being attempted by evill, but by being swallowed up by it. *Eripe me,* may be, Deliver me from rebellions, or Deliver me in rebellions; Either that they come not, or that they overcome not.

In that prayer of S. *Paul,* that God would remove *Angelum Satanæ,* and take away *Stimulum carnis,* first, S. *Paul* is not easily understood, and then, it may be, not safely imitated. It is hard to know what S. *Paul* means in his Prayer, and it may be dangerous to pray as he prayed. For the actions of no man, how holy soever, till we come to Christ himselfe, lay such an obligation upon us, as that we must necessarily doe as they did. Nay the actions of Christ himselfe lay not that obligation upon us, to fast as he fasted; no nor to pray as he prayed. A man is not bound in an Affliction, or Persecution, at least at all times, to that Prayer, *Si possibile,* or *Transeat calix,* If it be possible let this cup passe; But if God vouchsafe him a holy constancy, to goe through with his Martyrdome, he may proceed in it without any such Deprecation to God, or Petition to the Judge.

But first, before we consider whether he might be imitated, if we understood him, we find it hard to understand him. S. *Augustines*

*Eripe
animam*
[2 Cor. 12.7]

[Mat. 6.13]

[Mat. 26.39]

free confession, *Se nescire quid sit angelus Satanæ,* That he never
understood what S. *Paul* meant by that *Messenger of Satan,* is more
ingenuous then their interpretation, who, I know not upon what
Tradition, referre it to an extreame paine in the head, that S. *Paul*
360 should have, as *Theophylact* sayes; or refer it *Ad morbum Iliacum,*
which *Aquinas* speaks of; or to the Gout, or pains in the Stomach, as
Nazianzen, and *Basil* interpret it. *Oecumenius* understands this
Angel, this *Messenger of Satan,* to be those Heretiques, which were
his Adversaries, in his preaching of the Gospel; according to that
signification of the word *Satan,* in which *Solomon* uses it to *Hiram,*

1 King. 5.4 *Non est mihi Satan, I have no Adversary.* Others, even amongst the
Fathers, understand it particularly, and literally, of that concupiscence, and those lusts of the flesh, which even the most sanctified
men may have some sense of, and some attempts by. Others under-
370 stand it generally of all calamities, spirituall, and temporall, incident
to us in this life. But *Cajetan* goes farthest, who reads it not as we do,
Angelum Satanæ, but *Angelum Satanam;* not that Angel which
comes from Satan, but that Angel that is Satan himselfe. So that he
conceives it to be a prayer against all tentations and tribulations here,
and hereafter, which the Devill or the Devils Instruments can frame
against us.

Now, if we think we understand it aright, in understanding it so
generally, then enters our second doubt, whether we may imitate S.
Paul in so generall a prayer. We dispute in the Schoole, whether, if
380 it were in his power to doe it, man might lawfully destroy any intire
species of creatures in the world, though offensive, and venemous, as
Vipers, or Scorpions. For every species being a link of Gods great
chaine, and a limb of his great creature, the whole world, it seemes not
to be put into our power, to break his chaine, and take out a link, to
maime his great creature, and cut off a limb, by destroying any intire
species, if we could. So neither does it seeme conduceable to Gods purposes in us, (which is the rule of all our prayers) to pray utterly
against all tentations, as vehemently as against sins. God should lose
by it, and we should lose by it, if we had no tentations; for God is
390 glorified in those victories, which we, by his grace, gaine over the

August. Devill. *Nescit Diabolus, quanta bona de illo fiunt, etiam cum sævit;*
Little knowes the Devill, how much good he does us, when he tempts

us; for by that we are excited to have our present recourse to that God, whom in our former security, we neglected, who gives us the issue with the tentation. *Ego novi quid apposuerim,* I know what infirmities I have submitted thee to, and what I have laid and applied to thee. *Ego novi unde ægrotes, ego novi unde saneris;* I know thy sicknesse, and I know thy physick. *Sufficit tibi gratia mea;* Whatsoever the disease be, my grace shall be sufficient to cure it. For 400 whether we understand that, as S. *Chrysostome* does, *De gratia miraculorum,* That it is sufficient for any mans assurance, in any tentation, or tribulation, to consider Gods miraculous deliverances of other men, in the like cases; or whether we understand it according to the generall voyce of the Interpreters, that is, Be content that there remaine in thy flesh, Matter and Subject for me to produce glory from thy weaknesse, and Matter and Subject for thee to exercise thy faith and allegeance to me, still these words will carry an argument against the expedience of absolute praying against all tentations; for still, this *Gratia mea sufficit,* will import this, amount 410 to this, I have as many Antidotes, as the Devill hath poisons, I have as much mercy as the Devill hath malice; There must be Scorpions in the world; but the Scorpion shall cure the Scorpion; there must be tentations; but tentations shall adde to mine, and to thy glory, and, *Eripiam,* I will deliver thee.

This word is in the Originall, *Chalatz;* which signifies *Eripere* in such a sense, as our language does not fully reach in any one word. So there is some defectivenesse, some slacknesse in this word of our Translation, *Delivering.* For it is such a Delivering, as is a sudden catching hold, and snatching at the soule of a man, then, 420 when it is at the brink, and edge of a sin. So that if thy facility, and that which thou wilt make shift to call Good Nature, or Good Manners, have put thee into the hands of that subtile woman, that *Solomon* speaks of, *That is come forth to meet thee, and seek thy face;* If thou have followed her, *As an Oxe goeth to the slaughter, and as a foole to the correction of the stocks;* Even then, when the Axe is over thy head, then when thou hast approacht so neare to destruction, then is the season of this prayer, *Eripe me Domine,* Catch hold of me now O Lord, and *Deliver my soule.* When *Ioseph* had resisted the tentations of his Masters Wife, and resisted them

Idem
[2 Cor. 12.9]

Prov. 7.10
15
[22]

Gen. 39.10

⁴³⁰ the onely safe way, not onely not to yeeld, but as the Text sayes, not to come in her company, and yet she had found her opportunity when there was none in the house but they, he came to an inward *Eripe me Domine,* O Lord take hold of me now, and she caught, and God caught; She caught his garment, and God his soule; She delivered him, and God delivered him; She to Prison, and God from thence. If thy curiosity, or thy confidence in thine owne spirituall strength, carry thee into the house of Rimmon, to Idolatry,

2 Kings 5.[18]   to a Masse, trust not thou to *Naamans* request, *Ignoscat Dominus servo in hac re,* That God will pardon thee, as often as thou doest ⁴⁴⁰ so; but since thou hast done so now, now come to this *Eripe animam, O Lord deliver my soule* now, from taking harme now, and hereafter, from exposing my selfe to the like harme. For this is the purpose of *Davids* prayer in this signification of this word, that howsoever infirmity, or company, or curiosity, or confidence, bring us within the distance, and danger, within the Spheare, and Latitude of a tentation, that though we be not lodged in Sodome, yet we are in the Suburbs, though we be not impailed in a sin, yet we are within the purlues, ·(which is not safely done; no more then it is in a State, to trust alwaies to a Defensive Warre) yet when we are ⁴⁵⁰ ingaged, and enthralled in such a tentation, then, though God be not delighted with our danger, yet then is God most delighted to help us, when we are in danger; and then, he comes not only to deliver us from that imminent, and particular danger, according to that signification of this word, but according to that Interpretation of this word, which the Septuagint have given it, in the Prophet

Esay 58.11   *Esay, Iachalitz, Pinguefaciet;* He shall proceed in his worke, and *make fat thy soule;* That is, Deliver thee now, and preserve, and establish thee after, to the fulfilling of all, that belongs to the last Petition of this prayer, *Salvum me fac, O Lord save me;* Though ⁴⁶⁰ he have been absent, he shall *Returne;* and being *Returned,* shall not stand still, nor stand Neutrall, but *deliver* thee; and having delivered thee, shall not determine his love in that one act of mercy, but shall *Save thee,* that is, Imprint in thee a holy confidence, that

Salvum   his salvation is thine.

me fac   So then, in that manner is Gods Deliverance exprest, *They shall*

Esay 19.20   *cry unto him,* (till wee cry, he takes no knowledge at all) *and then*

he sends to them, (there is his returning upon their cry) and then,
He shall deliver them, sayes that Prophet; and so, the two former
Petitions of this prayer are answered; but the Consummation, and
470 Establishment of all, is in the third, which followes in the same
place, *He shall send them a Saviour, and a great one.* But who is
that? what Saviour? Doubtlesse he that is proclaimed by God, in
the same Prophet, *Behold, the Lord hath proclaimed unto the end*   Esay 62.11
of the world, Behold thy salvation commeth. For, that word which
that Prophet uses there, and this word, in which *David* presents this
last Petition here, is in both places, *Iashang,* and *Iashang* is the very
word, from which the name of *Iesus* is derived; so that *David* desires
here, that salvation which *Esay* proclaimed there, salvation in the
Saviour of the world, Christ Jesus, and an interest in the assurance
480 of his merits.

We finde this name of *Saviour* attributed to other men in the
Scriptures, then to *Christ.* In particular distresses, when God raised
up men, to deliver his people sometimes, those men were so called,
Saviours. And so S. *Ierome* interprets those words of the Prophet,
Ascendent salvatores, Saviours shall come up, on Mount Sion, of   Obad. 1.21
Prophets, and Preachers, and such other Instruments, as God should
raise for the salvation of soules. Those, whom in other places, he
calls *Angels of the Church,* here he calls by that higher name,   [Rev. 1.20]
Saviours. But such a Saviour as is proclaimed to the ends of the
490 world, to all the world, a Saviour in the Mountaines, in the height
of presumptuous sins, and a Saviour in the vallies, in the dejection
of inordinate melancholy too, A Saviour of the East, of rising, and
growing men, and a Saviour of the West, of withering, declining,
languishing fortunes too, A Saviour in the state of nature, by having
infused the knowledge of himselfe, into some men then, before the
light, and help of the Law was afforded to the world, A Saviour in
the state of the Law, by having made to some men then, even Types
Accomplishments, and Prophesies Histories, And, as himself *Cals*   [Rom. 4.17]
things that are not, as though they were, So he made those men
500 see things that were not, as though they were, (for so *Abraham saw*   [John 8.56]
his day and rejoyced) A Saviour in the state of the Gospel, and so,
as that he saves some there, for the fundamentall Gospels sake, that
is, for standing fast in the fundamentall Articles thereof, though

they may have been darkned with some ignorances, or may have strayed into some errors, in some Circumstantiall points, A Saviour of all the world, of all the conditions in the world, of all times through the world, of all places of the world, such a Saviour is no man called, but Christ Jesus only. For when it is said that *Pharaoh*

Gen. 41.45 called *Ioseph, Salvatorem mundi,* A Saviour of the world, (besides, 510 that if it were so, that which is called all the world, can be referred but to that part of the world which was then under *Pharaoh;* as

[Luke 2.1] when it is said, that *Augustus taxed the world,* that is intended *De orbe Romano,* so much of the world, as was under the *Romanes*) there is a manifest error in that Translation, which cals *Ioseph* so, for that name which was given to *Ioseph* there, in that language in which it was given, doth truly signifie *Revelatorem Secretorum,* and no more, a Revealer, a Discoverer, a Decypherer of secret and mysterious things; according to the occasion, upon which that name was then given, which was the Decyphering, the Interpreting of 520 *Pharaohs* Dreame.

Be this then thus establisht, that *David* for our example considers, and referres all salvation, to salvation in Christ. As he does

Psal. 98.2 also where he sayes after, *Notum fecit salutare tuum, The Lord hath made known his salvation. Quid est salutare tuum?* saies S. *Basil;* What is the Lords salvation? And he makes a safe answer

Luke 2.[30] out [of] *Simeons* mouth, *Mine eyes have seene thy salvation,* when he had seen *Christ Iesus.* This then is he, which is not only *Salvator*

[Num. *populi sui,* The Saviour of his people, the Jews, to whom he hath 18.19] betrothed himselfe, *In Pacto salis,* A Covenant of salt, an everlast-

[Eph. 5.23] 530 ing Covenant: Nor onely *Salvator corporis sui,* The Saviour of his own body, as the Apostle calls him; of that body which he hath gathered from the Gentiles, in the Christian Church: Nor only

[John 4.42; *Salvator mundi,* A Saviour of the world, so, as that which he did, 1 John 4.14] and suffered, was sufficient in it selfe, and was accepted by the Father, for the salvation of the world; but, as *Tertullian,* for the most part reads the word, he was *Salutificator;* not only a Saviour, because God made him an instrument of salvation, as though he had no interest in our salvation, till in his flesh he died for us; but he is *Salutificator,* so the Author of this salvation, as that from all 540 eternity, he was at the making of the Decree, as well as in the ful-

nesse of time he was at the executing thereof. In the work of our
salvation, if we consider the merit, Christ was sole and alone, no
Father, no Holy Ghost trod the Wine-presse with him; And if in
the work of our salvation we consider the mercy, there, though
Christ were not sole, and alone, (for that mercy in the Decree was
the joynt-act of the whole Trinity) yet even in that, Christ was
equall to the Father, and the Holy Ghost. So he is *Salutificator,*
the very Author of this salvation, as that when it came to the act,
he, and not they, died for us; and when it was in Councell, he, as
⁵⁵⁰ well as they, and as soone as they, decreed it for us.

As therefore the Church of God scarce presents any petition, any
prayer to God, but it is subscribed by Christ; the Name of Christ,
is for the most part the end, and the seale of all our Collects; all
our prayers in the Liturgy, (though they be but for temporall things,
for Plenty, or Peace, or Faire-weather) are shut up so, *Grant this
O Lord, for our Lord and Saviour Christ Iesus sake:* So *David* for
our example, drives all his petitions in this Text, to this Conclusion,
Salvum me fac, O Lord save me; that is, apply that salvation, Christ
Jesus to me. Now beloved, you may know, that your selves have a
⁵⁶⁰ part in those means, which God uses to that purpose, your selves
are instruments, though not causes of your own salvation. *Salvus
factus es pro nihilo, non de nihilo tamen;* Thou bringest nothing
for thy salvation, yet something to thy salvation; nothing worth it,
but yet somthing with it; Thy new Creation, by which thou art a
new creature, that is, thy Regeneration, is wrought as the first Creation was wrought. God made heaven and earth of nothing; but hee
produced the other creatures, out of that matter, which he had
made. Thou hadst nothing to doe in the first work of thy Regeneration; Thou couldst not so much as wish it; But in all the rest, thou
⁵⁷⁰ art a fellow-worker with God; because, before that, there are seeds
of former grace shed in thee. And therefore when thou commest
to this last Petition, *Salvum me fac, O Lord save me,* remember
still, that thou hast something to doe, as well as to say; that so thou
maist have a comfortable answer in thy soule, to the whole prayer,
Returne O Lord, Deliver my soule, and Save me. And so we have
done with our first Part, which was the Prayer it selfe; and the
second, which is the Reasons of the Prayer, we must reserve for a
second exercise.

[Isa. 63.3]

Bernard

Number 19.

Preached upon the Penitentiall Psalmes.

PSAL. 6.4, 5. *RETURNE, O LORD; DELIVER MY SOULE; O LORD SAVE ME, FOR THY MERCIE SAKE. / FOR IN DEATH THERE IS NO REMEMBRANCE OF THEE; AND IN THE GRAVE, WHO SHALL GIVE THEE THANKS?*

WEE COME now to the Reasons of these Petitions, in *Davids* Prayer; For, as every Prayer must bee made with faith, (I must beleeve that God will grant my Prayer, if it conduce to his glory, and my good to doe so, that is the limit of my faith) so I must have reason to ground a likelyhood, and a faire probability that that particular which I pray for, doth conduce to his glory and my good, and that therefore God is likely to grant it. *Davids* first Reason here is grounded on God himselfe, *Propter misericordiam,* Doe it *for thy mercy sake;* and in his second Reason,
10 though *David* himselfe, and all men with him, seeme to have a part, yet at last we shall see, the Reason it selfe to determine wholly and entirely in God too, and in his glory, *Quoniam non in morte,* Do it O Lord, *For in Death there is no remembrance of thee, &c.*

Propter misericordiam Psal. 40.11
In some other places, *David* comes to God with two reasons, and both grounded meerely in God; *Misericordia, & veritas, Let thy Mercy and thy Truth alwaies preserve me.* In this place he puts himselfe wholly upon his mercy, for mercy is all, or at least, the foundation that sustaines all, or the wall that imbraces all. That mercy, which the word of this text, *Casad* imports, is *Benignitas in*
20 *non promeritum;* Mercy is a good disposition towards him, who hath deserved nothing of himselfe; For, where there is merit, there is no

mercy. Nay, it imports more then so, For mercy, as mercy, presumes not onely no merit in man, but it takes knowledge of no promise in God, properly; For that is the difference betweene Mercy and Truth, that by Mercy at first, God would make promises to man, in generall; and then by Truth, he would performe those promises: but Mercy goeth first; and there *David* begins and grounds his Prayer, at Mercy; Mercy that can have no pre-mover, no pre-relation, but begins in it selfe. For if we consider the mercy of God to mankinde
30 subsequently, I meane, after the Death of Christ, so it cannot bee properly called mercy. Mercy thus considered, hath a ground; And God thus considered, hath received a plentifull, and an abundant satisfaction in the merits of Christ Jesus; And that which hath a ground in man, that which hath a satisfaction from man, (Christ was truly Man) fals not properly, precisely, rigidly, under the name of mercy. But consider God in his first disposition to man, after his fall, That he would vouchsafe to study our Recovery, and that he would turne upon no other way, but the shedding of the blood of his owne and innocent and glorious Son, *Quid est homo, aut filius* [Psa. 8.4;
40 *hominis?* What was man, or all mankinde, that God should be mind- 5 in Vulg.] full of him so, or so mercifull to him? When God promises that he will be mercifull and gracious to me, if I doe his Will, when in some measure I doe that Will of his, God begins not then to be mercifull; but his mercy was awake and at worke before, when he excited me, by that promise, to doe his Will. And after, in my performance of those duties, his Spirit seales to me a declaration, that his Truth is exercised upon mee now, as his mercy was before. Still, his Truth is in the effect, in the fruit, in the execution, but the Decree, and the Roote is onely Mercy.
50 God is pleased also when we come to him with other Reasons; When we remember him of his Covenant; When we remember him of his holy servants, *Abraham, Isaac,* and *Iacob;* yea when we remember him of our owne innocencie, in that particular, for which wee may be then unjustly pursued; God was glad to heare of a Righteousnesse, and of an Innocencie, and of cleane and pure hands in *David,* when hee was unjustly pursued by *Saul.* But the roote of all is in this, *Propter misericordiam,* Doe it for thy mercie sake. For when we speake of Gods Covenant, it may be mistaken, who is, and

who is not within that Covenant; What know I? Of Nations, and
⁶⁰ of Churches, which have received the outward profession of Christ,
we may be able to say, They are within the Covenant, generally
taken; But when we come to particular men in the Congregation,
there I may call a Hypocrite, a Saint, and thinke an excommunicate
soule, to be within the Covenant; I may mistake the Covenant, and
I may mistake Gods servants, who did, and who did not dye in his
favour, What know I? We see at Executions, when men pretend to
dye cheerefully for the glory of God, halfe the company will call
them Traitors, and halfe Martyrs. So if we speake of our owne innocency, we may have a pride in that, or some other vicious and defec-
⁷⁰ tive respect (as uncharitablenesse towards our malicious Persecutors,
or laying seditious aspersions upon the justice of the State) that may
make us guilty towards God, though wee be truly innocent to the
World, in that particular. But let mee make my recourse to the mercy
of God, and there can bee no errour, no mistaking.

And therefore if that, and nothing but that be my ground, God
will *Returne* to me, God will *Deliver* my soule, God will *Save* me,
For his mercy sake; that is, because his mercy is engaged in it. And
if God were to sell me this *Returning,* this *Delivering,* this *Saving,*
and all that I pray for; what could I offer God for that, so great as
⁸⁰ his owne mercy, in which I offer him the Innocencie, the Obedience,
the Blood of his onely Son. If I buy of the Kings land, I must pay
for it in the Kings money; I have no Myne, nor Mint of mine owne;
If I would have any thing from God, I must give him that which
is his owne for it, that is, his mercy; And this is to give God his
mercy, To give God thanks for his mercy, To give all to his mercy,
And to acknowledge, that if my works be acceptable to him, nay if
my very faith be acceptable to him, it is not because my works, no
nor my faith hath any proportion of equivalencie in it, or is worth
the least flash of joy, or the least spangle of glory in Heaven, in it
⁹⁰ selfe, but because God in his mercy, onely of his mercy, meerely for
the glory of his mercy, hath past such a Covenant, *Crede, & fac hoc,*
Beleeve this, and doe this, and thou shalt live, not for thy deed sake,
nor not for thy faith sake, but for my mercy sake. And farther we
carry not this first reason of the Prayer, arising onely from God.

In morte   There remaines in these words another Reason, in which *David*

himselfe, and all men seeme to have part, *Quia non in morte, For in death there is no remembrance of thee, &c.* Upon occasion of which words, because they seeme to imply a lothnesse in *David* to dye, it may well be inquired, why Death seemed so terrible to the
100 good and godly men of those times, as that evermore we see them complaine of shortnesse of life, and of the neerenesse of death. Certainely the rule is true, in naturall, and in civill, and in divine things, as long as wee are in this World, *Nolle meliorem, est corruptio primæ*   Picus
habitudinis, That man is not well, who desires not to be better; It is   Heptapl.
but our corruption here, that makes us loth to hasten to our incor-   l. 7. proem.
ruption there. And besides, many of the Ancients, and all the later Casuists of the other side, and amongst our owne men, *Peter Martyr,* and *Calvin,* assigne certaine cases, in which it hath *Rationem boni,* The nature of Good, and therefore is to be embraced, to wish our
110 dissolution and departure out of this World; and yet, many good and godly men have declared this lothnesse to dye. Beloved, waigh Life and Death one against another, and the balance will be even; Throw the glory of God into either balance, and that turnes the scale. S. *Paul* could not tell which to wish, Life, or Death; There the balance was even; Then comes in the glory of God, the addition of his soule to that Quire, that spend all their time, eternity it selfe, only in glorifying God, and that turnes the scale, and then, he comes to his *Cupio*   [Phil. 1.23]
dissolvi, To *desire to be dissolved, and to be with Christ.* But then, he puts in more of the same waight in the other scale; he sees that it
120 advances Gods glory more, for him to stay, and labour in the building of Gods Kingdome here, and so adde more soules then his owne to that state, then only to enjoy that Kingdome in himself, and that turnes the scale againe, and so he is content *to live.*

These Saints of God then when they deprecate death, and complain of the approaches of death, they are, at that time, in a charitable extasie, abstracted and withdrawne from the consideration of that particular happinesse, which they, in themselves, might have in heaven; and they are transported and swallowed up with this sorrow, that the Church here, and Gods kingdome upon earth, should lack
130 those meanes of advancement, or assistance, which God, by their service, was pleased to afford to his Church. Whether they were good Kings, good Priests, or good Prophets, the Church lost by their death;

Esay 38.18

and therefore they deprecated that death, and desired to live. *The grave cannot praise thee, death cannot celebrate thee; But the living, the living, he shall praise thee, as I doe this day,* sayes *Hezekias;* He was affected with an apprehension of a future barrennesse after his

[v. 11]

death, and a want of propagation of Gods truth; *I shall not see the Lord, even the Lord,* sayes he. He had assurance, that he should see the Lord in Heaven, when by death he was come thither; But, sayes
140 he, *I shall not see him in the land of the living;* Well, even in the land of the living, even in the land of life it selfe, he was to see him, if by death he were to see him in Heaven; But this is the losse that he laments, this is the misery that he deplores with so much holy passion, *I shall behold man no more, with the Inhabitants of the world;* Howsoever I shall enjoy God my selfe, yet I shall be no longer a meanes, an instrument of the propagation of Gods truth amongst others; And, till we come to that joy, which the heart cannot conceive, it is, I thinke, the greatest joy that the soule of man is capable of in this life, (especially where a man hath been any occasion of
150 sinne to others) to assist the salvation of others. And even that consideration, that he shall be able to doe Gods cause no more good here,

Jos. 7.9

may make a good man loath to die. *Quid facies magno nomini tuo?* sayes *Ioshuah* in his prayer to God; if the Canaanites come in, and destroy us, and blaspheme thee, *What wilt thou do unto thy mighty Name?* What wilt thou doe unto thy glorious Church, said the Saints of God in those Deprecations, if thou take those men out of the world, whom thou hadst chosen, enabled, qualified for the edification, sustentation, propagation of that Church? In a word, *David* considers not here, what men doe, or doe not in the next world; but he
160 considers onely, that in this world he was bound to propagate Gods Truth, and that that he could not doe, if God tooke him away by death.

Consider then this horrour, and detestation, and deprecation of death, in those Saints of the old Testament, with relation to their particular, and then it must be, *Quia promissiones obscuræ,* Because *Moses* had conveyed to those men, all Gods future blessings, all the joy and glory of Heaven, onely in the types of earthly things, and said little of the state of the soule after this life. And therefore the promises belonging to the godly after this life, were not so cleere

170 then, not so well manifested to them, not so well fixt in them, as that they could, in contemplation of them, step easily, or deliver themselves confidently into the jawes of death; he that is not fully satisfied of the next world, makes shift to be content with this; and he that cannot reach, or does not feele that, will be glad to keepe his hold upon this. Consider their horrour, and detestation, and deprecation of death, not with relation to themselves, but to Gods Church, and then it will be, *Quia operarii pauci,* Because God had a great harvest in hand, and few labourers in it, they were loath to be taken from the worke.

[Mat. 9.37]

180 And these Reasons might, at least, by way of excuse and extenuation, in those times of darknesse, prevaile somewhat in their behalfe; They saw not whither they went, and therefore were loath to goe; and they were loath to goe, because they saw not how Gods Church would subsist, when they were gone. But in these times of ours, when Almighty God hath given an abundant remedy to both these, their excuses will not be appliable to us. We have a full cleernesse of the state of the soule after this life, not onely above those of the old Law, but above those of the Primitive Christian Church, which, in some hundreds of yeares, came not to a cleere understanding in that point, 190 whether the soule were immortall by nature, or but by preservation, whether the soule could not die, or onely should not die. Or (because that perchance may be without any constant cleernesse yet) that was not cleere to them, (which concernes our case neerer) whether the soule came to a present fruition of the sight of God after death or no. But God having afforded us cleernesse in that, and then blest our times with an established Church, and plenty of able work-men for the present, and plenty of Schooles, and competency of endowments in Universities, for the establishing of our hopes, and assurances for the future, since we have both the promise of Heaven after, and the 200 promise that the gates of Hell shall not prevaile against the Church here; Since we can neither say, *Promissiones obscuræ,* That Heaven hangs in a Cloud, nor say, *Operarii pauci,* That dangers hang over the Church, it is much more inexcusable in us now, then it was in any of them then, to be loath to die, or to be too passionate in that reason of the deprecation, *Quia non in morte, Because in death there is no remembrance of thee &c.*

[Mat. 16.18]

Which words, being taken literally, may fill our meditation, and exalt our devotion thus; If in death there be no remembrance of God, if this remembrance perish in death, certainly it decayes in the
²¹⁰ neernesse to death; If there be a possession in death, there is an ap-

Eccles. 12.1 proach in age; And therefore, *Remember now thy Creator in the dayes of thy youth.* There are spirituall Lethargies, that make a man forget his name; forget that he was a Christian, and what belongs to that duty. God knows what forgetfulnesse may possesse thee upon thy death-bed, and freeze thee there; God knows what rage, what distemper, what madnesse may scatter thee then; And though in such cases, God reckon with his servants, according to that disposi-tion which they use to have towards him before, and not according to those declinations from him, which they shew in such distempered
²²⁰ sicknesses, yet Gods mercy towards them can worke but so, that he returnes to those times, when those men did remember him before. But if God can finde no such time, that they never remembred him, then he seales their former negligence with a present Lethargy; they neglected God all their lives, and now in death there is no remem-brance of him, nor there is no remembrance in him; God shall forget

[Jo. 19.30] him eternally; and when he thinkes he is come to his *Consummatum est,* The bell tolls, and will ring out, and there is an end of all in death, by death he comes but to his *Secula Seculorum,* to the begin-ning of that misery, which shall never end.
²³⁰ This then which we have spoken, arises out of that sense of these words, which seems the most literall; that is, of a naturall death. But as it is well noted by divers Expositors upon this Psalme, this whole Psalme is intended of a spirituall agonie, and combat of *David,* wrastling with the apprehension of hell, and of the indignation of God, even in this world, whilst he was alive here. And therefore S. *Augustine* upon the last words of this verse, in that Translation which he followed, *In inferno quis confitebitur tibi?* Not, *In the grave,* but *In hell, who shall confesse unto thee?* puts himselfe upon

[Luk. 16.23–28] this, *In Inferno Dives confessus Domino, & oravit pro fratribus,* In ²⁴⁰ hell *Dives* did confesse the name of the Lord, and prayed there for his brethren in the world. And therefore he understands not these words of a literall, and naturall, a bodily death, a departing out of this world; but he calls *Peccatum Mortem,* and then, *Cæcitatem*

animæ Infernum; He makes the easinesse of sinning to be Death, and then, blindnesse, and obduration, and remorslesnesse, and impenitence, to be this Hell. And so also doth S. *Ierome* understand all that passionate deploring of *Hezekias,* ·(which seems literally to be spoken of naturall death) of this spirituall death, of the habit of sin, and that he considered, and lamented especially his danger of
²⁵⁰ that death, of a departing from God in this world, rather then of a departing out of this world. And truely many pieces and passages of *Hezekias* his lamentation there, will fall naturally enough into that spirituall interpretation; though perchance all will not, though S. *Ierome* with a holy purpose drive them, and draw them that way. But whether that of *Hezekias* be of naturall, or of a spirituall death, we have another Author ancienter then S. *Augustine,* and S. *Ierome,* and so much esteemed by S. *Ierome,* as that he translated some of his Works, which is *Didymus* of Alexandria, who sayes, it is *Impia opinio,* not an inconvenient, or unnaturall, but an impious and
²⁶⁰ irreligious opinion, to understand this verse of naturall death; because, sayes he, The dead doe much more remember God then the living doe. And he makes use of that place, *Deus non confunditur, God is not ashamed to be called the God of the dead, for he hath prepared them a City.* And therefore reading these words of our Text, according to that Translation which prevailed in the Easterne Church, which was the Septuagint, he argues thus, he collects thus, that all that *David* sayes here, is onely this, *Non est in morte qui memor est Dei,* Not that he that is dead remembers not God, but that he that remembers God, is not dead; not in an irreparable, and
²⁷⁰ irrecoverable state of death; not under such a burthen of sin as devastates and exterminates the conscience, and evacuates the whole power and work of grace, but that if he can remember God, confesse God, though he be falne under the hand of a spirituall death, by some sin, yet he shall have his resurrection in this life; for, *Non est in morte,* sayes *Didymus,* He that remembers God, is not dead, in a perpetuall death.

And then this reason of *Davids* Prayer here, (Doe this and this, *for in death there is no remembrance of thee*) will have this force, That God would *returne* to him in his effectuall grace, That God
²⁸⁰ would *deliver* his soule in dangerous tentations, That God would

Heb. 11.16

save him in applying to him, and imprinting in him a sober, but yet confident assurance that the salvation of Christ Jesus belongs to him; Because if God did not *return* to him, but suffer him to wither in a long absence, If God did not *deliver* him, by taking hold of him when he was ready to fall into such sins as his sociablenesse, his confidence, his inconsideration, his infirmity, his curiosity brought him to the brinke of, If God did not *save* him, by a faithfull assurance of salvation after a sin committed and resented, This absence, this slipperinesse, this pretermitting, might bring him to such a deadly, 290 and such a hellish state in this world, as that *In death*, that is, In that death, he should have no remembrance of God, *In hell, In the grave*, that is, In that hell, In that grave, he should not confesse, nor praise God at all. There was his danger, he should forget God utterly, and God forget him eternally, if God suffered him to proceed so far in sin, that is, *Death*, and so far in an obduration and remorslesnesse, in sin, that is, *Hell*, The Death and the Hell of this world, to which those Fathers refer this Text.

In this lamentable state, we will onely note the force, and the emphasis of this *Tui*, and *Tibi*, in this verse; no remembrance of *Thee*, 300 no praise to *Thee*; For this is not spoken of God in generall, but of that God, to which *David* directs the last and principall part of his Prayer, which is, *To save him*; It is to God, as God is Jesus, a Saviour; and the wretchednesse of this state is, that God shall not be remembred in that notion, as he is *Iesus*, a Saviour. No man is so swallowed up in the death of sin, nor in the grave of impenitence, No man so dead, and buried in the custome or senselesnesse of sin, but that he remembers a God, he confesses a God; If an Atheist sweare the contrary, beleeve him not; His inward terrors, his midnight startlings remember him of that, and bring him to confessions of that. But here 310 is the depth, and desperatenesse of this death, and this grave, habituall sin, and impenitence in sin, that he cannot remember, he cannot confesse that God which should save him, Christ Jesus his Redeemer; he shall come, he shall not chuse but come to remember a God that shall damne him, but not a saving God, a *Iesus*.

Beloved in the bowels of that Jesus, not onely the riches, and honours, and pleasures of this world, and the favour of Princes, are, as *Iob* speaks, *Onerosi consolatores, Miserable comforters are they all*,

[Job 16.2]

all this world, but even of God himselfe (be it spoken with piety
and reverence, and far from misconstruction) we may say, *Onerosa*
320 *consolatio,* It is but a miserable comfort which we can have in God
himselfe, It is but a faint remembrance which we retaine of God
himselfe, It is but a lame confession which we make to God himselfe,
Si non Tui, Si non Tibi, If we remember not *Thee,* If we confesse
not *Thee,* our onely Lord and Saviour *Christ Iesus.* It is not halfe our
worke to be godly men, to confesse a God in generall; we must be
Christians too; to confesse God so, as God hath manifested himselfe
to us. I, to whom God hath manifested himselfe in the Christian
Church, am as much an Atheist, if I deny Christ, as if I deny God;
And I deny Christ, as much, if I deny him in the truth of his Wor-
330 ship, in my Religion, as if I denyed him in his Person. And therefore,
Si non Tui, Si non Tibi, If I doe not remember *Thee,* If I doe not
professe *Thee* in thy Truth, I am falne into this *Death,* and buried
in this *Grave* which *David* deprecates in this Text, *For in death
there is no remembrance of thee, &c.*

Textual Notes to the Sermons
in Volume V

EDITORS' NOTE

In view of the large number of words wrongly divided in the Folio texts for this volume, we have corrected these in the text without recording each instance in the Textual Notes.

Notes to Sermon No. 1

Notes to Sermon No. 2

41 case. : case, *F*
63 *mg.* Esay 19.14 : Esay 19.3 *F*
124 *mg.* Esay 63.14]
NOTE. The passage in the text is not an exact quotation, but a
paraphrase compressing together several verses.
146–147 when . . . it : *when . . . it F*
153 *mg.* Iohn 16.7 : Iohn 16.17 *F*
237 mise]
NOTE. *N.E.D.* records this as a variant form for "mice" in the
sixteenth century.
269 *mg.* 1 Thes. 5.23 : 1 Thes. 5.25 *F*
272 *animales homines*]
NOTE. "The Apostle" here seems to be St. Jude, in verse 10 of
whose epistle the Vulgate reads "quæcumque autem naturaliter,
tanquam muta animalia norunt, in his corrumpuntur." A.V.
has "but what they know naturally, as brute beasts, in these
things they corrupt themselves."
302 *mg.* Apoc. 11.3 : Apoc. 11.2 *F*
452 Satan : satan
NOTE. Though the Hebrew word in many places of the Old
Testament denotes merely an adversary, and even when used of
the devil is often prefixed by the definite article, "satan" here is
clearly a misprint.
553 acknowledge : acknowledges *F*
606 *mg.* Luk. 16.8 : Luk. 16.18 *F*
607–608 *diffidentiæ . . . diffidence*]
NOTE. This is only one of many passages in which Donne fol-

LINE

lows the Vulgate without consulting the Greek text, which has
ἀπειθίας, correctly translated in A.V. as "of disobedience."

616 his damnation : his damation *F*
629 Gavel-kinde]
NOTE. This is a legal term for a land tenure found chiefly in
Kent, by which a man's property was divided at his death
equally among his sons.

Notes to Sermon No. 3

86 *Vltimus* : *Vltimis F*
129 *Why...me?* : why...me? *F*
192 *mg.* Aquin. 2.2 : Aquin. 22*x F*
195 blasphemously : blaspemously *F*
257–258 antidate]
NOTE. *N.E.D.* admits this form as a spelling of "antedate" in
the sixteenth and seventeenth centuries.
453 irremission]
NOTE. *N.E.D.* quotes this as the only known example of the
word, which means 'the fact of not being remitted; non-remis-
sion.'
472–478 evacuates...evacuate]
NOTE. The "evacuate" is here used in the obsolete sense of 'make
void, annul, deprive of force or validity.'
521 first : fitst *F*
593 captivates even God himself]
NOTE. "Captivate" is here used in its original sense, now obsolete or archaic, of 'make captive.'
624 Idolatry : Idolatay *F*

Notes to Sermon No. 4

Text *shall govern them, and shall leade them unto the lively foun-*
tains of waters]
NOTE. Donne here quotes the Geneva version. A.V. reads "shall
feed them, and shall lead them unto living fountains of waters."
See lines 345–346 and 483–485, where Donne compares "the
first translation" (by which he apparently means the Geneva)
with "the second" or "our last edition" (the A.V.) and with
"the *originall.*" Cf. also Vol. IX, p. 294, where Donne again
uses the Geneva version of this text.

LINE

9 *mg.* Iob 39.27 : Iob 33.30 *F*

10 *on high?* : *on high; F*

12 Paul : Peter *F*

NOTE. Donne is here quoting Gregory the Great, *Moralia,* 31, 34 (*F mg.*) : "Paulus aquilæ similis. Videamus aquilam, nidum sibi in arduis construentem. Ait: Nostra conversatio in cœlis est." In line 1 of this sermon Donne had already quoted this text from St. Paul's epistle to the Philippians. Apparently in writing out the sermon he used the abbreviation "S.P." for "S. Paul," and the copyist wrongly expanded this to "S. Peter."

40 and ... see : *and ... see F*

141 *of the* : of the *F*

155–156 that can be *Al* : that that be *F*

180 *in Limine* : in *Limine F*

184 grave. : grave, *F*

205 through *Edd. conj.* : though *F*

242 ingraffed] engrafted *Al*

NOTE. "Ingraff" is a variant form of "engraff," the verb which was common in the fifteenth, sixteenth, and seventeenth centuries but has now been superseded by "engraft." For Donne's use of it elsewhere see "that ingraffing, and that *adoption*" (Sermon 7, line 66, in the present volume).

303 *mg.* Esay 1.18 : Esay 1.8 *F*

389 *and the* : and the *F*

392 Christ, : Christ *F*

393 *we knew* : *we know F*

430 by-respect : by respect *F*

473 *mg.* Act. 2.38 : Act. 2.39 *F*

473 *Nations,* : *Nations F*

473 *Be* : Be *F*

475 *and your children* : and *your children F*

478 *that those* : that *those F*

479 *which have* : which *have F*

485 *life.* Now : *life:* now *F*

489 *mg.* Ezek. 26 : Ezek. 16 *F*

491 *deep* : deep *F*

495 *they* : they *F*

496 *the water, that I shall give* : the *water,* that I shall give *F*

506 *The* : The *F*

511–512 *I thought ... the Lord* : I thought ... the Lord *F*

513 *peccata* : *peccato F*

522 *mg.* 1 Reg. 7.23 : 1 Reg. 7.24 *F*

LINE

549 owne, : owne; *F*
557 make *Al* : makes *F*
565 sanctification : sanctificationn *F*
580 *fountain of* : *fountain* of *F*

Notes to Sermon No. 5

5 *are* : are *F*
15 *Subjicite* : *Subijcite F*
19–20 *a Man by the Lord* : a Man *by the* Lord *F*
34 *mg.* v. 21 : v. 12 *F*
35 *in the* : in *the F*
54 *and* : and *F*
63 *of one* : of *one F*
70 *Christ* : Christ *F*
127 *Wives* : *Wifes F*
139 infirmities : infirmites *F*
151–152 others; ... subjection, : others. ... subjection; *F*
159 *mg.* 1 Cor. 7.2 : 1 Cor. 7.1 *F*
175 *Goe and sell them* : Goe *and sell* them *F*
230 maried *till death should depart you*]
NOTE. "Depart" is here used in the now obsolete sense of 'separate, put asunder.' Donne is here quoting from the marriage service in the Book of Common Prayer, in which the promise made by bride and bridegroom was "till death us depart" until in the revision of 1662 it was altered to "till death us do part."
253–254 *as our Father is holy, and pure*]
NOTE. This seems to be a conflation of two texts, 1 *Peter* 1.16 and *Matthew* 5.48, though the latter has "perfect" for "pure."
373 unite]
NOTE. This form of the participial adjective (from the Late Latin *unitus* meaning 'united') was common up to the eighteenth century.
380 *himselfe.* It : *himselfe,* It *F*
381 seperate]
NOTE. *N.E.D.* records this form as a variant of "separate" from the fifteenth to the eighteenth century.
420 withdraw : withraw *F*
433 transgression : transgression, *F*
447–449 *eate ... of* : eate ... of *F*
485 *mg.* Cant. 4.7 : Cant. 4.6 *F*
505 *by the* : by the *F*

LINE

520 *mg.* Luke 22.19 : Luke 11.19 *F*

571 because : becuase *F*

576–577 *Susan ... Assuerus*]
NOTE. These are the Vulgate forms which in the A.V. are replaced by "Shushan" and "Ahasuerus."

589 *by the* : by *the F*

Notes to Sermon No. 6

3 *interdicitur* : *interdicitor F*

37 *Intestabiles,* : *Intestabiles F*

67 involves : in volves *F*

96 *I am ... thy God* : I am ... thy God *F*

109 *mg.* 1 Part : 2 Part *F*

133 witnesses: : witnesses *F*

166 luxations]
NOTE. "Luxation" is a surgical term for 'dislocation,' and it is occasionally used figuratively, as in this passage.

204–205 *Because ... am I come* : Because ... am I come *F*

212 *Immunditias,* : *Immunditias F*

215–216 *almost ... and* : almost ... and *F*

222 satisfaction]
NOTE. Some copies of *F* have "satisfactio" for "satisfaction."

223 *mg.* Heb. 9.12 : Heb. 19.12 *F*

242 *mg.* Iohn 19.35 : Iohn 19.34 *F*

269 by *water* : *by water F*

271 wresting]
NOTE. *N.E.D.* gives a number of examples of this use, now obsolete, in the sixteenth and seventeenth centuries, of both the verb "wrest" and the verbal substantive "wresting" in the intransitive sense of 'struggle' or 'wrestle.'

296 *Patriarchs* : *Patriarch F, Al*
NOTE. The plural seems to be required here, for the list in *Hebrews* which Donne is quoting includes not one patriarch but several, and Donne lays stress on the "abundance" of examples.

298 *testium,* : *testium F*

312 *mg.* Mat. : Mut. *F*

312 *for* : for *F*

314 *as it is written, in* : as it is written, in *F*

319–320 *Mary* full of grace : *many* full of grace *F*
NOTE. This emendation is confirmed by Sermon 14, lines 283–

LINE

284, in this volume: "The blessed Virgins blessing, *Full of Grace . . .*"

322   God,   :   God *F*

333   *Epistle* of   :   *Epistle of F*

350   borne,   :   borne; *F*

382   *we followed*   :   we *followed F*

388 *mg.*   Iohn 12   :   Iohn 19 *F*

388–389   *there came a voice from heaven*   :   there came a voice from heaven *F*

417   understands   :   understand *F*

422   *yet*   :   yet *F*

457 *mg.*   1 Tim.   :   Tim. *F*

462   *she . . . with*   :   she . . . with *F*

478 *mg.*   Iohn 1.33   :   Iohn 1.31 *F*

559   *testament,*   :   *testament F*

560–561   *And . . . not the*   :   And . . . not the *F*

561   *be . . . glorious?*   :   be . . . glorious? *F*

607 *mg.*   Exod. 7   :   Exod. 3 *F*

638   *Grace,*   :   *Grace) F*

644   *water,*   :   *water F*

675 *mg.*   Mat. 23.25   :   Mat. 25.23 *F*

679 *mg.*   Luke 13.26   :   Luke 13.25 *F*

708   Resurrection   :   Resurection *F*

Notes to Sermon No. 7

5   *in Christ Jesus*   :   in Christ Jesus *F*

55   *amongst the*   :   *amongst* the *F*

60   then   :   them *F*

138–139   *Originall sinne,* (which is   :   *Originall sinnes,* (which is *F*

147–149   *Labash . . .* as the *Grammarians* call it, it is in *Hiphil,* and it signified *Induere fecit eos*]

NOTE. *Hiphil* is the designation of the causative form of the Hebrew verb. Donne's explanation here is therefore correct.

162 *mg.*   We have omitted "and 16.16," found in *F,* for this reference is incorrect.

162–166   *induetur . . . induamini*   :   *Induetur . . . Induamini F*

163–164   *and with astonishment*]

NOTE. These words are not part of *Ezech.* 7.27, which *F* gives as a marginal reference.

184   *Hospitales*   :   *Hospitale F*   :   hospitable *Al*

189   lives;   :   lives, *F*

LINE
193   *in, not* : *in not F*
Note. In some copies of *F* the comma has failed to print.
201   *how shall I put it on?* : how shall I put it on, *F*
295   scantier : scantler *F*
312   *naked:)* : *naked: F*
376–388 But the very *sacrament* . . . unbaptized]
Note. This sentence is obscure, since the clause beginning in line 377, "that even for *legal* and *Civill* uses," is never completed. Alford offers no emendation.
380   thereof; : thereof) *F*
590   a garment, : a garment; *F*

Notes to Sermon No. 8

8–9   *pure as his father in heaven is pure*]
Note. This misreading of *Mat.* 5.48, which has "perfect as your father . . . is perfect," is found also in Vol. VII, p. 270, and in Sermon 17, line 860, of the present volume. It must therefore be deliberate on Donne's part, but the Greek, the Vulgate, Geneva, and A.V. give no authority for it.
20   *by . . . his* : by . . . his *F*
22   beatificall : beautificall *F*
60   her *Al* : here *F*
175 *mg.* 1 Reg. 7.23 : 1 Reg. 7.24 *F*
270 *mg.* Luk. 5.2 : Luk. 1.2 *F*
365   But, . . . *Augustine,* : But . . . *Augustine F*
410   appoint : appoint, *F*
410   *Dosis*] See note in Vol. IV, p. 403, to Sermon No. 6, line 470.
435   *how* : how *F*
441   *Sacerdotium* : *Sarcerdotium F*
463   feet, : feet *F*
474   that,] In most copies the comma has failed to print, but a space is left for it.
490   *them?* : them? *F*
508 *mg.* Iohn 4.14 : Iohn 4.11 *F*
511   and *neither* : and neither *F*

Notes to Sermon No. 9

H'd'g. *Preached at the Churching of the Countesse of Bridgewater* : *Preached at a Churching F*
Note. The heading printed in our text is placed in *F* before the

LINE

second sermon on Micah 2.10 (No. 10 of our edition), but this
is evidently an error. The second sermon begins with the words,
"Thus far we have proceeded in the first acceptation of these
words, according to their principall, and literall sense." Clearly
these two sermons originally formed one, and were divided by
Donne when he revised his notes. Compare his division into two
of the one sermon preached at The Hague (Vol. II of our edition, pp. 38–39 and 269).

52	purpose,	: purpose *F*
70 *mg.*	Iob 17	: Iob 16 *F*
93–94	*because of thy renowne*	: because of thy renowne *F*
151	*murmurings*]	

NOTE. In *F* part of the final "s" has failed to print, and in line
156 the "i" of "their" is almost illegible.

212	frustrates	: frustrate *F*
269	*slaughter*	: *slaughters F*
276 *mg.*	Mic. 1.1	: v. 1 *F* (placed wrongly against line 274)
386 *mg.*	Aug. Ser. 105 de tempore]	

NOTE. The reference is correct, but the phrase *in postliminio* is
not used by Augustine, but has been supplied by Donne. It is a
legal term meaning 'by the right of return to me; old conditions
and former privileges, etc.'

417–418	as *that* it	: as *that* it *F*
444	*despised,*	: *despised F*
445	*delivered?*	: *delivered, F*
452	*for*	: for *F*
455	*Therefore, . . . them*	: Therefore, . . . them *F*
456–458	*and they . . . wine*	: and they . . . wine *F*
459	promise.	: promise.) *F*
462–464	*even . . . destroy them*	: even . . . destroy them *F*
467 *mg.*	Exod. 33	: Exod. 24 *F*
469 *mg.*	Prov. 4.10	: Prov. 4.1 *F*

Notes to Sermon No. 10

31 *Recidivation*]
NOTE. This word, now obsolete, was in common use in the
seventeenth century, and means 'relapse or falling back'
(*N.E.D.*). Donne uses it also in Vol. II, Sermon 1, line 610.

38	howsoever	: howsever *F*
78	seen	: seen, *F*

LINE

104 againe. : againe: *F*

111 them : them them *F*

146 *barbarum,* : *barbarum; F*

180 Prophets : Propehts *F*

223 *not thou* : not thou *F*

233 *subtractione* : *substractione F*

NOTE. The form *substractione* is not recorded in Souter's *Late Latin Dictionary,* which makes extensive use of St. Augustine's writings. The word is found in the *Medieval Latin Word List,* but only two fourteenth-century instances are mentioned. *N.E.D.* recognizes "substraction" as an English word derived from medieval Latin **substractio, -onem* (the asterisk implying that the form is inferred, not actually found). We have unsuccessfully tried to track down Donne's quotation here from Augustine.

245 of : *of F*

251 *subtractio* : *substractio F* (See note to line 233 above.)

347 *mg.* Psal. 34.14 : Psal. 36 *F*

360 and : aand *F*

361–363 *periculosa molestia . . .* it is a troublesome danger]

NOTE. Donne's translation inverts the order. Augustine's phrase means 'a dangerous trouble.'

372–373 *which drowne . . . for the* : which drowne . . . for the *F*

378–380 *so he . . . a foole* : so he . . . a foole *F*

383 *mg.* Luke 12.18 : Luke 12.10 *F*

434 *for, &c.* : for, &c. *F*

476 *mg.* 1 Reg. 19 : 1 Reg. 14 *F*

493–494 his Presence . . . his Bedchamber]

NOTE. Here, "Presence" is used in the now obsolete sense of 'presence-chamber' to contrast with "Bedchamber." Cp. Donne's use of the word in this sense in Satire IV, lines 171, 199 (*Poems,* ed. Grierson, I, 165, 166).

505 depart : depatt *F*

518 *mg.* 19.23 : 19.13 *F*

521–524 *I am sure . . . for me*]

NOTE. This quotation from *Job* 19.25–27 is from the Geneva Bible throughout, and has many differences from the text of A.V.

551 *resurgentes,* : *resurgentes; F*

567 *mg.* 2 Thes. : 1 Thes. *F*

568 *and to* : and, *to F*

628 *alive,* : *alive; F*

Notes to Sermon No. 11

LINE

97 they will not live *voto aperto*]
NOTE. This is from Persius, Sat. ii.7: *aperto vivere voto*. Donne uses this quotation elsewhere, e.g., Vol. VII, p. 397: "And even nature it self taught the naturall man, to make that one argument of a man truly religious, *Aperto vivere voto* ..."

113 Israel, : Israel; *F*

152 *mg.* Esai. 58.3 : Esai. 58.2 *F*

152 *not?* : *not, F*

155 *mg.* Zech. 7 : Ezech. 7 *F*
NOTE. The first part of the quotation in lines 154–155 is a continuation of the passage from *Isaiah* 58 given above, as found in the Geneva version, but the words "when ye fasted and mourned, did ye fast unto me?" come from *Zechariah*.

166 *mg.* Luc. 5.35 : Luc. 5.33 *F*

180 *mg.* Joel 1.14 : Joel 1.34 *F*

201 et affligetis animas vestras]
NOTE. It is a peculiarity of this particular Folio (*F 26*) sometimes to print the Latin part of a Scriptural quotation in roman, and the English part in italic, so reversing the usual practice.

234 *Esther* : Ester *F*

242 *mg.* Gretzer : Grether *F*
NOTE. We have been unable to identify any author known to Donne as Grether, whereas Jacob Gretzer (1561–1625) was a German Jesuit, a theologian and historian, whom Donne quotes in *Pseudo-Martyr,* and also in his Fifth Prebend Sermon (Vol. VIII, p. 116): "And it is impiously said of a Jesuit, ... *Non est Regum etiam veram doctrinam confirmare, ...*" ["Gretzer" in margin]. Donne owned a volume, now in the library of the Middle Temple, in which four of Gretzer's works are bound up together.

269 Prayer *Edd.* : Prayers *F, Al*
NOTE. The construction "Prayers is the way" seems so harsh that we have made this emendation, but when the verb "to be" is followed by a singular noun such a construction is allowed in Elizabethan English and we may be wrong in altering it.

274 *in Bello ... in Duello* : in *Bello ...* in *Duello F*

291 *mg.* Jos. ult. 15 *F corr.* : Jos. ult. 85 *F originally*

391 then as : then, as *F*

393 low nature : Law-nature *F*

421–422 *Daniels* confidence, and *Daniels* words]
         NOTE. In *Dan.* 3.17 these words belong, not to Daniel, but to
         Shadrach, Meshach, and Abed-nego.
    486 Scriptures, : Scriptures *F*

Notes to Sermon No. 12

  Text Luke 23.34 *E, M* : Luke 33.24 *F*
     3 *est*] *om. E*
     3 and : *and F*
     8 Tables to] Tables of *E*
     8 by ministery] by the ministery *E*
     9 words] word *E*
   12 such] *om. E*
18–19 *for they ... do*] *om. E*
   21 in an] in the *E*
   23 as the face] all the full *E*
25–27 1.... 2.... 3.... 4.] ffirst ... Secondly ... Thirdly ... ffourthly
         E, M
   28 lastly] last of all *E*
   28 going *E* : as *F* : *om. M*
28–29 objections; as why onely *Luke*] objection why Luke only *E*
   29 and why this prayer,] which *E, M*
   30 continuing] continued *E*
   32 when] where *E*
   33 *given*] given thee *E*
   42 ambitions] ambition *E, M*
   45 And it hath most... mentall] *om. E*
   45 most] more *M*
46–47 prayers ... prayers ... prayers] prayer ... prayer ... prayer *E, M*
   49 *Revelations*] Revelation *E*
   56 this] that *E*
   59 Here] where *E, M*
   59 our own] everie ones *E*
63–64 *The Arrows ... spirit* : The *Arrows* ... spirit *F*
64–65 *is my flesh of brasse*] my flesh the flesh of brasse *E* (as in A.V.)
   72 easie] easilie obtayned *E*
   75 it selfe] *om. E*
   76 shewes] and shewes *E*
   77 may *E, M* : might *F*

77 answers] answers us *E*
83 brothers] brethren *E, M*
85 be sorry] sorrowe *E*
87 not be sorry] not be sorrowfull *E*
87 whosoever] whatsoever *E, M*
94 (*If . . . possible.*)   :   (If . . . possible.) *F*
100 which saith] who sayes *E*
102 *you*] yee *E* (as in A.V.)
102 *which art*] *om. E, M*
103 Talmudist   :   Talmudists *F*   :   Talmuded *M*
105 mis-ported] imported *E, M*
    NOTE. *N.E.D.* gives this passage as the only example of the
    word "misport," 'to import unlawfully.' It is possible that *E, M*
    are right in reading "imported."
106 or not to buy it] *om. E, M*
113–114 *that you . . . heaven*   :   that you . . . heaven *F*
115 in] of *E, M*
116 in this] in the *E*
116 O my *E, M*   :   my *F*
    NOTE. Cp. *Essays in Divinity*, ed. Simpson, p. 22, line 34, "O my
    faithfull soul," and p. 74, line 36, "O my poor lazy soul."
129 seem] seemed *E*
131 day] tyme *E*
131 Churches] Church *E*
135 testimonies] testimonie *E*
141 *Iohn* 20] John 12 *E, M in text and margin*
142 *and your . . . your God*   :   and your . . . your God *F*
148 presentation] representation *E*
150 thus alsoe by the *M*   :   of the *F*
150 daies. There   :   daies, there *F*
150 There] where *M*
154 professes] professed *E*
173 wilt have] must have *E*
173–174 imminent] ruinous *M*
175 expect] have expected *E*
181 *Father, forgive them*   :   Father, forgive them *F*
194 his word] his word for us *E*
196 exceede our *E, M*   :   exceed *F*
197 acquitted] acquitted us of *E*
202 *will*] will etc. *E*
205 *Thou . . . thing*   :   Thou . . . thing *F*
207 our *for*] ours *E, M*

LINE

208–209   *You . . . you*] Ye . . . ye *M*

    210   a fit] fit *E*

    210   *for,* for] for *E, M*

    211   for he](for) he *E*

    212   for] (for) *E*

        NOTE. Here and in line 216 *E* uses round brackets to denote quotation, as *F* does in lines 26–27, 94, 96, and 452.

218–219   deafnesses and oppressions] deafenes and oppression *M* : easinesse and oppressions *E*

    220   scantling]

        NOTE. This means a builder's or carpenter's rod, and hence a measure (*N.E.D.*).

    225   that is a] it is a *E, M*

    230   Job 1.11   :   Job 1.2 *F*

    234   Things] That which is *E, M*

    235   and, to] and soe to *E, M*

    237   2 Cor. 12.8   :   2 Cor. 8 *F*

    244   *to thy*] to us thy *E*

245–246   fore-knowledge] knowledge *E, M*

    251   *lack*] want *E*

    255   *Who . . . faults?*   :   Who . . . faults, *F*

    258   ignorance] it *E, M*

    259   both . . . Sea, for] *om. E*

    261   And as by the Sea] but as by that Sea *E*

    277   I] *om. E, M*

    285   1 Cor. 2.8 *E, M*   :   2 Cor. 2.8 *F*

    286   *glory*] life *E*

    289   convert] content *E*

    291   his] this *E*

    294   *We*] let us *E*

    297   exorable]

        NOTE. This word, which means 'capable of being moved by entreaty,' is now rare, and survives chiefly in its negative form, "inexorable."

    311   differed] differ *E*

    325   as] *om. E, M*

    328   *Matth.* 27.9 *E, M*   :   *Matth.* 27.8 *F*

    332   *Apocryph*] *Apocriphall E*

        NOTE. *N.E.D.* records the obsolete form "apocryph" meaning 'apocryphal.'

    339   St.] *om. E, M*

340–341 as the ... though] is the ... which though *E*

347 be. For *M* : be for *F*

349 them] them that were *E*

350 for permanency] permanentlie *E*

350 had before preached unto them *M* : had to them preached before *E* : had preached *F*

353 food, : food *F*

354 Evangile]
NOTE. This is the older form (from O.F. *evangile*) of "Evangel," Gospel.

355 know not *E* : know *F, M*

358 *Lukes*] Luke *E*

359 inserted and mingled] mingled and inserted *E, M*

364 mistaketh] mistakes *M*

364 2.8 *E, M* : 2.1 *F*

370 spoke] spoken *E*

372–373 I say, more diligently] more diligent (I saye) *E*

374 writ] write *E*

376 three] the three *E*

376 largeliest] largest *E*

376 Act 1.1 *E, M* : 1 Act. 1. *F*

383 giveth] gives *M*

383 20] 10 *E, M*

397 thinketh] thinks *M*

400 the immense] meanes of the *E*

401 defaced] defeated *E*

406 or] nor *E*

408 *Moses*] Moses his *E*

410 are] doe *E*

416 therefore] *om. E*

417 our] the *E*

418–419 we know] know *E*

419 do.)] In most copies the period has failed to print.

422 are] were *E, M*

423 dispatch] come to *E*

426 the] his *E*

428 or of] or *E, M*

429 16] 18 *E*

433–434 the Roman] Roman *E, M*

434 saith] sayes *M* : writes *E*

434–435 *Acts ... Acts*] arts ... arts *E*

435 *considereth*] considers *M*

LINE

435–436   truly say *E, M*   :   truly *F*
436   knoweth] knowes *M*
439   are as *E, M*   :   are *F*
443   to be] *om. E*
448   passe] passe from him *E*
448   quickly] suddainlie *E*
458   will] can *E*
463   *and*] or *E, M*
464   *had*] add *E, M*
465   *mercie, but the*] *om. E*
466   *at*] *om. E*
469   *thou wert*   :   thou wert *E, M*   :   *thou was F*
472   *priviledge*] priviledges *M*
473   *broke*] broken *E*
474   *shall we then*] then shall wee *E*
474   *dare to*] dare *E*
475   *Or to*] Or *E*
476   *hopelesse*] helplesse *E*
479   *which*] who *E*
482   *stubbornnesses*] stubbornes *E*

Notes to Sermon No. 13

[This is the last sermon which appears in our MSS, and it is found only in *M*. In Vol. IV, p. 36, we have given our reasons for thinking that after 1622 Donne ceased to distribute written copies of his sermons among his friends, as he found printing more satisfactory. The last dated sermon in any MS known to us is that in Vol. IV, No. 3, which was preached on April 22, 1622.

The text of *M* in the present sermon is distinguished by the omission of an unusually large number of words and phrases—more than 100 separate instances. Does this indicate that it was derived from a reported text, in which the shorthand writer was unable to keep pace with Donne's delivery? The omissions are not of such a kind as to suggest revision.]

4   *knew*] knowe *M*
4   *be*] goe *M*
5   are] *om. M*
5   Euangelist]
      NOTE. See Vol. VI, p. 372, for a note on this form.
9   his, this] this *M*
10   doth] does *M* (so also line 17)

LINE

13   not] *om. M*

18   *even*] ever M

33   shall be,] of M

34   everlasting] the everlasting M

36   then] *om. M*

38   them] theis M

41   from] *om. M*

54   intermination]

Note. This obsolete word, from Latin *interminationem,* means 'a threat or menace.' It is used elsewhere by Donne, e.g., Vol. VII, No. 14, line 196.

56   *Crediderit Al*   :   *Credererit F* (see lines 355, 357, 366)

57   to beleeve] *om. M*

58   and] *om. M*

58–59   If ... faith,] *om. M*

59   is] is then M

61   *in Agendis*   :   in *Agendis F*

65   seemes] seemes to be M

67   for a Sabbath] *om. M*

71   And] as M

71–73   *in ... in ... in*   :   in ... in ... in F

73   hand] hands M

75–76   exemplifies *Edd. conj.*   :   exemplifie F

77   from naturall reason] *om. M*

82   our selves] *om. M*

84–85   *in ... in ... in*   :   in ... in ... in F

84   in all ... doe] *om. M*

85   in all ... pray for] *om. M*

89   one ... beleeve] *om. M*

92   surely] *om. M*

95,
96,   } which is] *om. M*
97

98–99   not introductory things] *om. M*

101   shed] and shed M

103   and] *om. M*

104   and so ... them] *om. M*

107   Scripture] the Scriptures M

109   Scripture] Scriptures M

113   Ten] *om. M*

114   the Lords] to the Lords M

115   where all] whereas M

126   saith] sayes M (so also lines 607, 625)

LINE

137–138 and *He ... damned*] *om. M*

139 then] *om. M*

140 of that Creed] *om. M*

142–143 to beleeve ... Church] *om. M*

148 is that *M* : is the *F*

155–156 consider ... That] *om. M*

159 menstruous] monstrous *M*

164–165 then this in] to *M*

165 to the *Credo*] *om. M*

166 the Holy Ghost] him *M*

166–167 I lock my doore to my selfe, and I throw my selfe downe in the presence of my God, ...]
Note. The whole of this passage on wandering thoughts in prayer should be compared with the more detailed and eloquent description of the same difficulties in a sermon preached on December 12, 1626 (Vol. VII, pp. 264–265).

172 and] *om. M*

173 try] rise *M*

175 *in Ecclesia* : in *Ecclesia F*

175 goe] come *M*

178 proposed] purposed *M*

179 Church,] Church, then *M*

181 and] *om. M*

182 of the Militant *M* : of Militant *F*

187 *my body;* My body] my body *M*

189 *Goshen*] a Goshen *M*

191–192 not last ever, perchance not to put the last word to this sentence, *M* : not last ever, *F*
Note. The clause beginning "perchance" has evidently been omitted in error in *F.*

192–194 nay the life of my soul in heaven is not such as it is at the first. For that soule there, even in heaven, shall receive] the liffe with my soule shall stand in heaven, shall not last ever such, as it is at first, for it shall receive *M*

194 and accesse] *om. M*

200 Ordinances] ordinance *M*

202–203 *the life*] life *M*

207–208 as they ... Christ] *om. M*

208 interpret] interprets *M*

211 that] yet *M*

212 one, as man and wife are all one, yet the wife is] one, as a wiffe is *M*

213 easilier] more easily *M*

LINE

215   that is] that a thing *M*

217   Hill] hill of *M*

221   forraine] forrain and *M*

227–229   So ... the *ubi*] *om. M*

232   justly : justlye *M* : *om. F*

235   one] any *M*

237   Now,] *om. M*

238   Christ Jesus] *om. M*

243   could] would *M*

243   any *M* : a *F*

255   *to*] *om. M*

255   *and in*] and *M*

258   *de*] *om. M*

267   these] this *M*

270   made without error, made without defect of power] *om. M*

276   here, is] was *M*

278   That ... witnesse] *om. M*

282   too] to doe *M*

282   a] *om. M*

287   begun : begone *M* : became *F*

288   foundation *M* : foundations *F*

   NOTE. "Foundation of the world," not "Foundations," is the Scriptural phrase (as in 1 *Pet.* 1.20: "foreordained before the foundation of the world," and *Ephes.* 1.4, to which Donne is alluding here).

289   it] not *M*

293–294   such ... Resurrection] *om. M*

297–298   before ... that is,] *om. M*

308–309   the *Mother*] *om. M*

309   yet all] *om. M*

312   creatures] *om. M*

314   *Creaturæ*] natura *M*

316   first,] *om. M*

320   in that respect] *om. M*

324   they all] *om. M*

325   and crawling] *om. M*

327   voluptuous : voluptous *F*

330   yet] *om. M*

338   *tribes M* : *tribe F*

   NOTE. "Tribes" is the reading of Geneva, A.V., etc. in *Isa.* 49.6, here quoted.

340   *end*] ends *M*

342–343   That ... men] *om. M*

LINE

345-346 meanes proportionable to man, visible, and audible meanes
M : meanes *F*
NOTE. We cannot suppose that the ignorant scribe of *M* invented this clause. It has evidently been omitted in *F* by homœoteleuton.

348 ever] *om. M*

349-350 That ... goes] *om. M*

355 *Qui* ... not this] *om. M*

356-357 *Qui* ... this, as] *om. M*

358 *Damnabitur*] *om. M*

360-361 Sacraments (as we . . . anone;) : Sacraments; (as we . . . anone) *F*

363 that is,] *om. M*

365 that is, produce] *om. M*

366-367 *Qui* ... *damned*] *om. M*

378 too] *om. M*

378 *estis* : *est is F*

380 those] *om. M*

381 they] *om. M*

381 and if] for if *M*

384 *Innocentius*] Innocent *M*

387 And] *om. M*

389 onely] *om. M*

389-390 (which was another Order)] *om. M*

392 at that time] *om. M*

394 they had] *om. M*

396 they might preach] *om. M*

398 in the Roman Church] *om. M*

405 that] this *M*

407 there] it *M*

410 ablutions] oblations *M*

410 we] *om. M*

413-414 or Adoption ... Triumph Sermons] *om. M*

414 upon the matter, were] *om. M*

416 duty] duties *M*

421 that that] that *M*

425 not] noe *M*

428 a second] an other *M*

429 by] in *M*

437-438 of the ... of the] of ... of *M*

452 meere] a meere *M*

456 for] for their *M*

458 but] *om. M*

LINE

467 said] sayes *M*

468–469 preachers doe not beleeve that it is our duty [dewtye, *M*] to preach, if you that heare *M* : preachers, and you that are hearers *F*

471 of soules] of our soules *M*

477 defalke] defalte *M*

NOTE. The obsolete verb "defalk" means 'to diminish by cutting off a part, to subtract' (*N.E.D.*). The scribe of *M* has substituted the more usual word "defalte," i.e., default.

478 that] it *M*

481 their] this *M*

481 And] as *M*

482 *Mammon; no*] Mammon; soe noe *M*

490 passages] passage *M*

491 make his] make the *M*

493 a Commission] Commission *M*

493 presently a] presently after a *M*

498–499 in the Councell of Lateran hereafter] hereafter in the Counsell of Lateran *M*

500 Councell of Constance *Edd.* : Council of Constance *Al* : Gospel of Constance *F*

513 fuller] better and fuller *M*

522 could] would *M*

529 that is, first] *om. M*

532 the Gospel is] is the Gospell *M*

533 *keeps*] shall keepe *M*

535 preach all] preach *M*

541 it is] is *M*

543 appropriation] application *M*

545 will] *om. M*

558 that it is] tis *M*

559–560 of getting ... last] *om. M*

560–561 the history] Historia *M*

562 And] *om. M*

564–565 For he ... *sinnes*] *om. M*

569 (as ... it)] *om. M*

573 allision] attrition and allision *M*

NOTE. "Allision" (from Lat. *allisionem*) is the action of dashing against or striking with violence upon (*N.E.D.*).

575 had] *om. M*

576 and have] and *M*

576 have let your soule blood] have let your soul bleed *Al*

NOTE. We do not consider this emendation necessary, for

"blood" is used as a transitive verb meaning 'to cause blood to flow from' (*N.E.D.*).

581	so as that it can] can yet *M*
581	can conclude] shall conclude *M*
582	still are afraid] *om. M*
583	againe] *om. M*
583	If . . . way] *om. M*
584	because] if *M*
584	doe not preach] preach not *M*
584	for] and *M*
585	that is] *om. M*
586, 587	then] *om. M*
587	wee . . . that] *om. M*
594	*Hee . . . not*] *om. M*
601	obligation] oblation *M*
605	owne] *om. M*
617	catechized : chatechized *F*
618	any other ordinary] there are not any other *M*
620	things] *om. M*
623	*Of*] or *M*
642	gave] did give *M*
646	men] ffathers *M*
649	an] and *M*
650	a] *om. M*
652	of the Lords Supper] *om. M*
652	of Baptisme] *om. M*
658–659	*orthodoxorum* (I know] : *orthodoxorum*) I know *F*
661	shake or] *om. M*
668	one] yet one *M*
672	well, as well as to beleeve aright *M* : aright *F*
674	presents] *om. M*
677	we] that we *M*
679	stroke] strikes *M*
680	it] he *M*
680	for] *om. M*
684–685	He . . . others] *om. M*
686	one] the one *M*
687	hand . . . preaching] *om. M*
688	in our example, and] *om. M*
692	doe] *om. M*
693	given] *om. M*
696	and] *om. M*

LINE

700 then] *om. M*

708 Scripture] Scriptures *M*

713 receiving the] the receiving of *M*

716 How] *M* repeats *"Damnabitur...damned"* from end of last line, before "How"

718–719 whensoever...pardoned] *om. M*

720 for that] for it *M*

721 is] *om. M*

735 *mg.* Iohn 3.19 : Iohn 1 *F*

744, 745 know] knowes *M*

754 or] and *M*

755 no affection] nor affection *M*

756 spirit] Spireitt, off a Soule, *M*

757 binde] blind *M*

757–758 that it is, or is not so, doth command our reason so] doth soe comaund our reason *M*

768 Prophet] Prophetts *M*

775 *God*] Lord *M*

779 but...God] *om. M*

783 (and it shall finde that there,] *om. M*

785 God] Gods *M*

786 life and preservation *Edd.* : life an preservation *M* : life *F*

787 never, never] never *M*

788 who] that *M*

789 me] *om. M*

793 often] soe *M*

804 soule] *om. M*

805 neither : nether *F*

805–806 let me] *om. M*

809 hath applied his judgements, and] and his Judgment in that, *M*

813 That that God] *om. M*

813 loose and frustrate *M* : frustrate *F*

815 that] and that *M*

817 nor a vapour *M* : a vapour *F*

818 never a *M* : never *F*

NOTE. We have adopted the readings of *M* in lines 813, 817, 818, because we feel that they are more in the manner of Donne, and because the usual custom of *M* is to omit words and not to supply them.

823 God] this God *M*

824 have been] are *M*

LINE

824 acquainted] acquainted with *M*
829 the pillar] his pillar *M*
830 in the Execution of *M*   :   in *F*
834 him] whom *M*

Notes to Sermon No. 14

11–13 And this diverse constancy in these two Fathers . . . shake]
NOTE. Here we have the common Elizabethan idiom by which the verb which should be singular, "shakes," is attracted into the plural by the plural nouns which intervene.

140 *mg.* Psal. 34.1 : Psal. 34.11 *F*

143 adprecation]
NOTE. This form is not recorded by *N.E.D.*, which, however, gives "Adp-, obsolete form of App-." It describes "apprecation" as 'the action of praying for or invoking a blessing on another.'

152–153 a specialty, by which he hath contracted with us for more]
NOTE. "Specialty," from O.F. (*e*)*specialté,* has a long history dating back to the fourteenth century, and in law it denotes 'a special contract, obligation, or bond, expressed in an instrument under seal' (*N.E.D.*).

193 those : thoses *F*
281 *mg.* Deut. 33 : Deut. 32 *F*
284 *mg.* Act 9.36 : Act 9.37 *F*
286 *mg.* Luk. 2.40 : Luk. 2.4 *F*

490, 497, 498– 499 *Prevent the Sunne* . . . prevent this Sunne . . . preventing grace]
NOTE. In these clauses "prevent" is used in its old sense of 'to come before,' from the Latin *prævenire.* God's "preventing grace" is the grace which anticipates human action or need. Donne was probably thinking of the Collect for the Seventeenth Sunday after Trinity: "Lord, we pray thee that thy grace may always prevent and follow us, and make us continually to be given to all good works."

538–540 God is the God of that Climate, where the night is six Moneths long, as well as of this, where it is but halfe so many houres.]
NOTE. Alford has no note on this passage, but it is very strange. The first part of the sentence apparently refers to the North Pole, which had not been reached when Donne wrote this. The second half must refer to England, and particularly to London, where Donne was preaching. "But halfe so many houres" must

mean "three hours," coming immediately after "six Moneths." Yet even in the middle of summer, when nights are at their shortest, night in the latitude of London is never less than approximately six hours long, even if we reckon that dawn begins almost an hour before sunrise, and that twilight extends for almost an hour after sunset.[1]

702   This is the tenent of all Philosophers]
NOTE. "Tenent" (meaning 'tenet') was apparently more used in the seventeenth century than "tenet," but became obsolete early in the eighteenth century (*N.E.D.*).

884   Jod]
NOTE. This is the usual spelling of the Hebrew *yōd,* the name of the smallest letter of the square Hebrew alphabet (*N.E.D.*). Compare Donne's use of this form in Vol. IX, p. 71: "No *Jod* in the Scripture shall perish; therefore no *Jod* is superfluous."

896–897   re-juveniscence]
NOTE. *N.E.D.* quotes this passage from Donne as an example of the seventeenth-century use of the form with "-iscence" instead of the more usual "rejuvenescence," a renewal of youth.

900   frivoulous]
NOTE. *N.E.D.* acknowledges this as a seventeenth-century variant of "frivolous."

927–928   exaltations : exaltions *F*
941   they : they they *F*

Notes to Sermon No. 15

41   we profuse]
NOTE. This use of "profuse" as a verb is now obsolete. It probably appeared first as a past participle "profused" from the Latin *profusus* (see *N.E.D.*). Donne uses it in *Biathanatos,* p. 58.

60   Emundation]
NOTE. This word, now obsolete, means 'the action of ceremonial cleansing' (*N.E.D.*).

60   Dealbation]
NOTE. This word is still in use, and means 'the action of whitening.'

---

[1] On and around June 21, the summer solstice, the sun rises in the latitude of London at 3.43 A.M. and sets at 8.21 P.M. if we disregard the complications which have been introduced by so-called "Summer Time."

LINE

64-65   worke;...it selfe, though   :   worke,...it selfe; Though *F*

144-145   the Panegyrique sayes, *Onerosum est succedere bono principi*]
NOTE. This is from Pliny's Panegyric to Trajan, xliv. Donne
had formerly applied it to James I succeeding Elizabeth (Vol. I
of our edition, p. 218).

182   *Berseba*] Bathsheba *Al*
NOTE. The form "Bathsheba" is used by A.V. in 2 *Sam.* 11.3
seq., but in the Septuagint the name appears as Βηρσάβεε
(Bersabee), while the Vulgate has "Bethsabee." George Peele
in his *Love of King David and Fair Bethsabe* (1599) uses
"Bethsabe" and "Bersabe" as alternative forms, one appearing
on the title page and the other in the head title, while both
forms occur in the running titles. Donne uses the form *Bathsheba* in lines 206, 261.

184
and } Teras]
201   NOTE. In 2 *Sam.* 11.2 Geneva and A.V. have "roof," but the
Vulgate has "solarium," for which "Teras [terrace]" is a suitable translation.

391   *Me;*   :   *Me, F*

412-413   The passage of a Spirit is very quick, but it is not immediate;
Not from extreame to extreame, but by passing the way be-
tween]
NOTE. Cp. *Essays in Divinity,* ed. Simpson, p. 37, lines 35-37:
*"Thou hast, O God, denyed even to Angells, the ability of arriv-
ing from one Extreme to another, without passing the mean
way between."* Also *Sermons,* Vol. VIII, p. 324: "...an Angel
it selfe cannot passe from East to West, from extreame to extreame, without touching upon the way betweene..."

441-450   *Expeccabis*...and if in our language, that were a word in use,
it might be translated, Thou shalt un-sin me; that is, look upon
me as a man that had never sinned,...this expeccation, this
unsinning]
NOTE. *N.E.D.* gives this as the only example of the meaning
'to free (a person) from being a sinner,' but it gives examples
from 1628 onwards of "unsin" in the sense 'to annul (a sin) by
subsequent action.'

449   expeccation] expectation *Al*
NOTE. *N.E.D.* describes this as a nonce-word formed by Donne
from the prefix *ex-* and the Latin *peccare,* to sin. Alford's
emendation ruins the meaning.

LINE

494-495   a sparrow ... and scarlet lace]
NOTE. Donne is here using the Geneva version. A.V. has "birds [margin: Or, *sparrows*] ... and scarlet."

550 *mg.*   Psal. 84.10   :   Psal. 84.8 F

555   disposition *Edd. conj.*   :   distance F
NOTE. "Distance" is clearly wrong. In view of lines 586-587, "This cleansing therefore, is that disposition, which God by his grace, infuses into us," we have supplied "disposition" as the most likely emendation.

613   the Washes]
NOTE. "This was a term applied specifically to the fordable portion of the estuary between Lincolnshire and Norfolk; hence used as a name for the estuary itself, now called *The Wash*" *(N.E.D.).*

622   them,   :   them F

665-666   *so, ... them*   :   so, ... them F

672   verdure]
NOTE. This word is used figuratively to denote 'fresh or flourishing condition.' Cp. Donne, *Letters* (1651), p. 222: "Whatsoever I should write now, of any passage of these days, would lose the verdure before the letter came to you ..."

681   a Fixion]
NOTE. This obsolete word, from medieval Latin *fixionem* (see line 687), is the equivalent of "fixation." See *N.E.D.*

Notes to Sermon No. 16

43   ever more   :   evermore F

250   *Galatinus*   :   *Gallatinus* F
NOTE. In the parallel passage in *Essays in Divinity* the form is *Galatinus,* and this is the correct form of the name. *N.E.D.* quotes "Galatinus, *De Arcanis Cath. Veritatis,* II. lf. xlviij," as the first passage in which the name *Iehova* is used, thereby supporting Donne's opinion expressed here.

262-268   The Gentiles were not able to consider God so; ... but broke God in pieces, ... and made a fragmentarie God of every Power, and Attribute in God, of every blessing from God, nay of every malediction, and judgement of God.... *Feare* came to be a God, and a *Fever* came to be a God]
NOTE. Donne had earlier expressed this thought in *The second Anniversary,* lines 425-428 (Grierson, I, 263):

> But as the Heathen made them severall gods,
> Of all Gods Benefits, and all his Rods,
> (For as the Wine, and Corne, and Onions are
> Gods unto them, so Agues bee, and Warre).

It also occurs in *Essays in Divinity,* ed. Simpson, p. 22: "Have they furthered, or eased thee any more, who not able to consider whole and infinit God, have made a particular God, not only of every power of God, but of every benefit? ... Out of this proceeded *Dea febris,* and *Dea fraus,* and *Tenebræ,* and *Onions,* and *Garlike.*" Cp. also Vol. VIII of our edition, p. 329.

353   our being, *Al* : or being *F*
416   every : ever *F*
469 *mg.*   Ier. 10 : Psal. 10 *F*
512   to *Rebuke* : *to Rebuke F*
595   Intergatorie]
  NOTE. This syncopated form of "interrogatory" is now obsolete *(N.E.D.)*.
613 *mg.*   Psal. 26.2 : Psal. 26.1 *F*
642, 652   *Camath*]
  NOTE. This should be *Chemah.*
647   fearful *Al* : fearfully *F*
699   attached] attacked *Al*
  NOTE. There is no need for Alford's emendation, as "attach" was used by Shakespeare and other Elizabethan writers in the now obsolete sense of 'seize, lay hold of.' See *N.E.D.*

Notes to Sermon No. 17

19   becomes *Edd. conj.* : because *F, Al*
239   on *Edd. conj.* : of *F, Al*
251–252   and then, as a wedge of gold, that comes to be coyned into particular pieces of currant money, etc.]
  NOTE. Compare Vol. II, p. 159: "Take not the grace of God, or the mercy of God as a meddall, or a wedge of gold to be layd up, but change thy meddall or thy wedge into currant money, find this grace and this mercy applyed to this end..."
351   Now Physitians say, etc.]
  NOTE. This passage has several parallels in Donne's verse and prose. See the verse letter *To the Countesse of Bedford* (Grierson, I, 190):

> In every thing there naturally growes
> A *Balsamum* to keepe it fresh, and new

If 'twere not injur'd by extrinsique blowes;
Your birth and beauty are this Balme in you.

In one of the sermons the doctrine is ascribed to Paracelsus. See Vol. VI of our edition, pp. 10–11.

415 *mg.*　Esay 38.21　:　Esay 38.11 *F*

507–509　Physitians for our bodies tell us, that there is no such state; The best degree of health is but *Neutralitas;*]
NOTE. Cp. Donne's *Anatomie of the World. The first Anniversary,* lines 91–92 (Grierson, I, 234):

There is no health; Physitians say that wee,
At best, enjoy but a neutralitie.

See also Vol. II of our edition, p. 80: "This consideration arises not onely from the Physicians Rule, that the best state of Mans body is but a *Neutrality,* neither well nor ill, but *Nulla sanitas,* a state of true and exquisit health, say they, no man hath."

567　worst.　:　worst: *F*

586,
672, } sanation]
767

NOTE. This word, now obsolete, means 'the action of healing, or the process of being healed' (*N.E.D.*).

598　*Christ;*　:　*Christ. F*

649–650　with; ... Instruments.　:　with. ... Instruments; *F*

652　fruits;　:　fruits, *F*

698 *mg.*　Psal. 107.26　:　Psal. 107.27 *F*

713　pravity]
NOTE. This word in the sense of 'depravity,' which is an analogical formation from the same root, is now almost obsolete.

830　intemerately]
NOTE. This is the only example given in *N.E.D.* of this word, which means 'purely,' from Latin *intemeratus,* inviolate.

837 *mg.*　Cant. 6.11　:　Cant. 6.10 *F*

909　the Sun ... to run his race as a Giant]
NOTE. Donne is here combining the Prayer Book version of *Psalms* 19.5, "rejoiceth as a giant to run his course," with that of A.V., "rejoiceth as a strong man to run a race."

Notes to Sermon No. 18

80　seeing　:　seing *F*

81　him　:　him, *F*

LINE

119   Sun : sun *Al* : Son *F*

Note. Here again is Donne's favourite pun on "Son" and "Sun." Cp. Sermon 14, lines 490–512, in the present volume, and Vol. VI, p. 173.

396   I have submitted   :   I / I have submitted *F*

455   the Septuagint have] the Septuagint hath *Al*

Note. Alford's emendation is unnecessary. "The Septuagint" originally meant "the 'seventy translators' of the Old Testament into Greek" (*N.E.D.*) and in the sixteenth and seventeenth centuries it was commonly used with a plural verb, but it soon acquired the present meaning of 'the Greek version of the Old Testament,' which derived its name from the story that it was made by seventy-two Palestinian Jews.

Notes to Sermon No. 19

Text
and }*thy mercie sake*]
9, 57

Note. A.V. has "thy mercy's sake." See below, lines 92-93, "thy deed sake . . . thy faith sake . . . my mercy sake."

63   excommunicate : excomunicate *F*

93   nor not : not nor *F*

145   Howsoever : Howsoever, *F*

158   Church? : Church. *F*

211–215   *Remember now thy Creator in the dayes of thy youth.* There are spirituall Lethargies, that make a man forget his name; forget that he was a Christian, . . . God knows what forgetfulnesse may possesse thee upon thy death-bed,]

Note. There is a close resemblance here to the sermon on "Remember now thy Creator in the dayes of thy youth" (Vol. II, No. 11), which contains (p. 239) the words: ". . . stay not for thy last sickness, which may be a Lethargy in which thou mayest forget thine own name, and his that gave thee the name of a Christian."

288   a sin committed and resented]

Note. "Resent" is used here in the original sense, now obsolete, 'to have a feeling of pain, to regret, repent' (*N.E.D.*), from French *ressentir*. Cp. *Ben Jonson*, ed. Herford and Simpson, VI, 198: "He . . . began, though over-late, to resent the injury he had done her."

Appendix

Appendix

Donne's Tenure of the Rectory of Blunham

SINCE we have already discussed Donne's visits to his parish church of Sevenoaks (Vol. I, pp. 129–130), this may perhaps be an appropriate place to say something about Blunham, another country parish which he was accustomed to visit in the summer vacation. Blunham is a village about six miles east of Bedford, and the presentation of the living was in the gift of Charles Grey, sixth Earl of Kent, who had promised it to Donne when it next fell vacant. On February 26, 1621/2, Donne wrote to Goodyer asking him to present his [Donne's] service to Elizabeth Lady Ruthin, daughter-in-law to the Earl, and to tell her "that this day I received a letter from my *Lord* of *Kent*, written yesterday at *Wrest:* in that his Lordship sends me word, that that favour which he hath formerly done me, in giving me *Blonham*, is now likely to fall upon me, because the Incumbent is dangerously ill: and because this is the season in which he removes from *Wrest* thither, he desires (for I give you his own word) that he may be accommodate there (if it fall now) as heretofore."[1]

Shortly afterwards the incumbent died and Donne succeeded to the living. A little over a year later, in October, 1623, Charles Grey died, and was succeeded by his eldest son, Henry Lord Ruthin, who also proved a kind friend to Donne. The Greys possessed a manor house in Blunham, while their principal seat was at Wrest, which is also in Bedfordshire.

The church in which Donne preached is a large, rather gaunt building, part of which goes back to Norman times. The earliest remaining part is the lower portion of the tower, which was built about 1100, when the church consisted of a chancel narrower and shorter than at present, a nave, and a west tower; there was evidently

---

[1] *Letters* (1651), pp. 176–177; Gosse, *Life and Letters of John Donne*, II, 157. *"Blonham"* is misprinted as *"Blouham"* in the *Letters*.

Chalice and Paten Presented by Donne to Blunham Church

PATEN, SHOWING INSCRIPTION:
"From Dr Donne Deane of Pauls, for Blunham Church"

also a north chapel. In the late thirteenth century the chancel was rebuilt and enlarged, and in the fifteenth century the present north and south chapels were erected. In the sixteenth century the tower was restored and partly rebuilt. The clerestory is late fifteenth-century work, and so is the low-pitched roof with carved bosses. In the south of the chancel near the east end is the tomb of Susan, wife of Charles, Earl of Kent, with smaller effigies of two sons. There is a Jacobean oak screen across the tower arch, and the octagonal pulpit is also Jacobean.

Donne's memory seems to have been kept alive in the parish by his gifts to the church. In 1626 he gave it a fine chalice and paten of silver-gilt bearing his name, which have been in regular use ever since. It seems possible that he may have given the Jacobean pulpit² and oak screen, but we have not found written evidence of this. In his will he left twenty pounds (equal to more than £300 of current money) to the poor of the parish of Blunham, as he did also to the poor of his two other parishes of Sevenoaks and St. Dunstan's.

It appears that Donne regularly visited Blunham during his tenure of the living. A curate was in charge, but Donne was more conscientious than most pluralists in going each year to see how the parish was faring, and in preaching there for a few weeks. In the late summer of 1628 he wrote to Mrs. Cokain telling her how after he had visited Kent and Peckham he went into Bedfordshire, and there on his third Sunday at Blunham he was seized with a fever which forced him to return to London to consult his physician, Dr. Fox. On the journey back in his coach he was afflicted with "a violent falling of the *Uvula*" complicated with a quinsy.³

It is interesting to learn from the Rev. T. C. Teape-Fugard, who was Rector of Blunham from 1948 to 1955, that he found that some of the older residents in the parish—country people who were mainly illiterate—"still talked of the days when Dr. Donne stayed at the manor, and went back to London with a load of cucumbers in his carriage."⁴

---

² See our illustration on p. 21 of the present volume.

³ See Vol. VIII, Introd., pp. 24–25, where two letters from Donne are quoted.

⁴ Extract from a letter dated February 18, 1954, from the Rev. T. C. Teape-Fugard.

Donne's holding of these country livings while he was Dean of St. Paul's may seem to us morally reprehensible, but few people in the reign of James the First saw it in that light. Pluralism was a legacy from the medieval Church, in which it had been rampant, and the Church of England, impoverished as it had been by the Elizabethan grants of church lands to favoured courtiers, found it impossible to abolish the system.[5]

In 1604 an Act was passed forbidding the alienation, even in favour of the King, by archbishops and bishops of lands belonging to their sees. This was a step in the right direction, but it did nothing to cure the mischief which had already been done. There were a multitude of vacant livings at which no candidate would look, so miserably small was their income. When Laud became Archbishop he voiced his indignation at the number of ministers who had incomes "scarce able to feed and clothe them."

On the other side of the picture there were the undoubted short-comings of many of the minor clergy. Some were almost illiterate, others had formerly been "bakers, butlers, cooks, archers, falconers, and horsekeepers" who had been appointed to their livings by un-scrupulous lay patrons. There were not enough educated ministers to fill all the benefices, and indeed there was not much financial induce-ment for any promising young man to take Holy Orders. We know from Donne's verses *To Mr Tilman after he had taken orders* that he himself was well aware of the low esteem in which the ministry was held.[6] Walton tells us that "a Court-friend" of George Herbert tried to persuade the latter to change his resolution to enter the ministry, on the ground that it was "too mean an employment, and

---

[5] See Christopher Hill, *Economic Problems of the Church* (Oxford Univ. Press, 1956), pp. 6 and 48.

[6] *Poems,* ed. Grierson, I, 351–352. Notice especially the lines:

> Thou, whose diviner soule hath caus'd thee now
> To put thy hand unto the holy Plough,
> Making Lay-scornings of the Ministry,
> Not an impediment, but victory; . . .
> Why doth the foolish world scorne that profession,
> Whose joyes passe speech? Why do they think unfit
> That Gentry should joyne families with it?

too much below his birth, and the excellent abilities and endowments of his mind."[7]

Since there were undoubtedly not enough educated men of good character to fill all the livings, the argument was sometimes put forward that it was best to give some of these livings to learned and godly men who were deans, archdeacons, or prebends of some cathedral. These would hold the living and visit it from time to time, but could appoint a curate to take the services and visit the people.

If we compare Donne's practice with that of his contemporaries, we find that his predecessor in the Deanery of St. Paul's, Valentine Cary, who was promoted to become Bishop of Exeter in 1621, held the livings of Tilbury East, Great Parndon, Epping, Orsett, and Toft, and was prebend of Chiswick, and also prebend of Stow Longa at Lincoln (*D.N.B.*) One of the most notorious pluralists was John Williams, Dean of Westminster, who in 1621 became Lord Keeper, an office generally held by a layman, and was also made Bishop of Lincoln.[8] Richard Corbett, a wit and a minor poet, a boon companion and a practical joker, obtained by his assiduous flattery of Buckingham first the Deanery of Christ Church, Oxford, and then, after fresh applications to Buckingham, the Bishopric of Oxford. He also held the vicarage of Cassington, and the prebend of Bedminster Secunda near Salisbury.[9] Finally he became Bishop of Norwich, where he died in 1635.

[7] *Lives* (1670), Life of Herbert, p. 31.

[8] On August 18, 1621, Chamberlain wrote: "The Lord Keper hath gotten the Deanrie of Westminster *in commendam,* during the time he shall continue bishop of Lincoln, besides his parsonage of Walgrave in Northamptonshire and a goode prebend of that church annexed to the bishopricke of Lincoln for ever" (*Letters,* ed. McClure, II, 397).

[9] J. A. W. Bennett and H. Trevor-Roper, *Poems of Richard Corbett,* pp. xx–xxviii.